THE GLORY OF THE GOLDEN AGE

Painting, Sculpture and Decorative Art

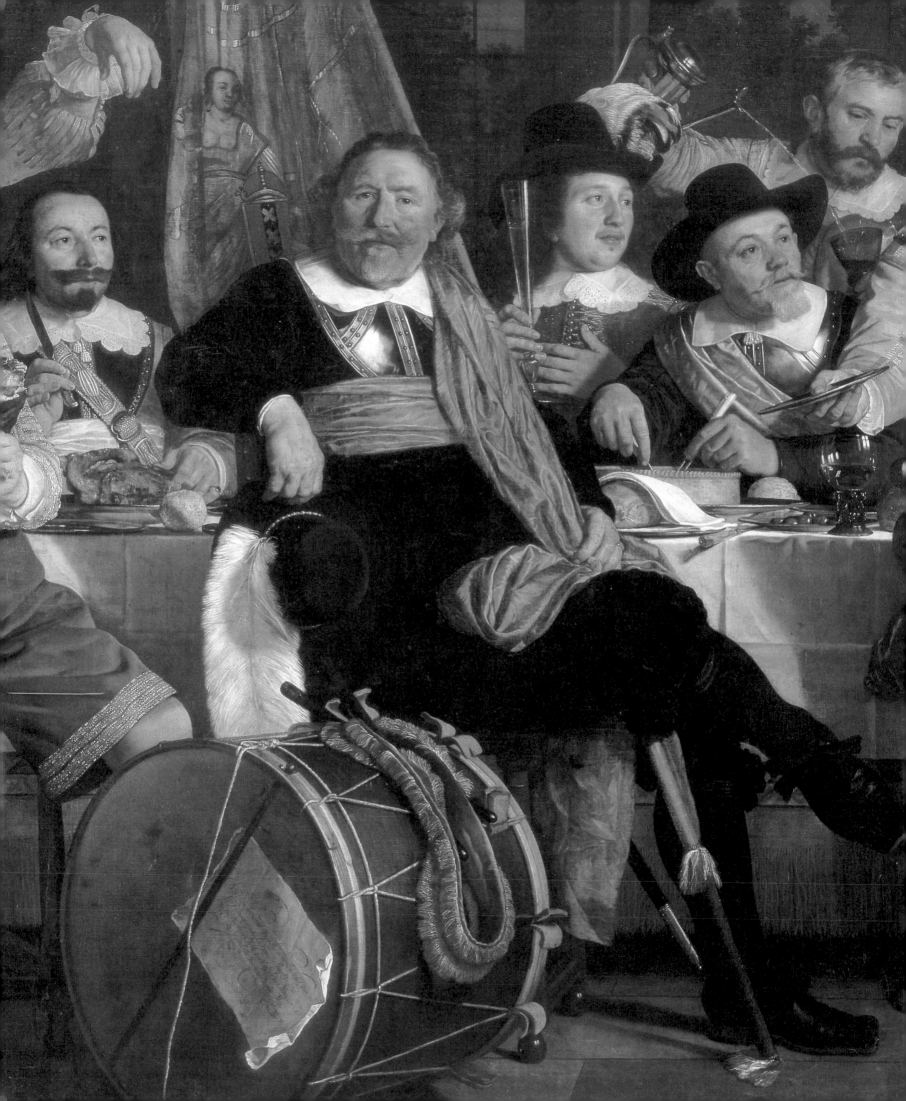

THE GLORY OF THE GOLDEN AGE

Dutch Art of the 17th Century

Painting, Sculpture and Decorative Art

WAANDERS PUBLISHERS

RIJKSMUSEUM, AMSTERDAM

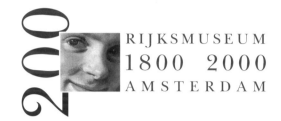

Authors:

JUDIKJE KIERS AND FIEKE TISSINK
with contributions by Jan Piet Filedt Kok and
assisted by Bart Cornelis and Henriëtte Fuhri
Snethlage.

Editors:
Bart Cornelis and Jan Piet Filedt Kok

Copy editor:
Diane Webb

Translators:
Sam Herman: pp. 1-25; 103-109
Lynne Richards: pp. 27-35; 47-57; 241-307
Diane Webb: pp. 37-45; 59-101; 111-239; 309-351

This volume accompanies the exhibition:
THE GLORY OF THE GOLDEN AGE
Dutch Art of the 17th Century
Painting, Sculpture and Decorative Art
at the Rijksmuseum in Amsterdam,
15 April-17 September 2000

Photography
Department of photography, Rijksmuseum:
Henk Bekker, Madeleine ter Kuile, Peter
Mookhoek and Margareta Svensson, with the
exception of the photographs listed in the photo
credits. Photographs of the museum buildings
(pp. 309-351) were provided by the various
institutions.

Catalogue design:
Berry Slok, BNO

Printed by:
Waanders Printers, Zwolle

Sponsors:

Achmea △

Deloitte &
Touche
△

Getronics

© 2000 Uitgeverij Waanders b.v., Zwolle
Rijksmuseum, Amsterdam

ISBN 90 400 9437 3 (hardback)
ISBN 90 400 9434 9 (paperback)
NUGI 921, 911

Cover: Gabriël Metsu, *Lady reading a letter,*
c. 1662-1665. Dublin, National Gallery of Ireland [*141b*]

Frontispiece: detail of Bartholomeus van der Helst,
*The celebration of the Treaty of Münster at the
crossbowmen's headquarters,* 1648. Amsterdam,
Rijksmuseum [66]

Contents

Lenders to the exhibition

AMSTERDAM   Amsterdams Historisch Museum

AMSTERDAM   Museum van Loon

APELDOORN   Paleis Het Loo Nationaal Museum

BALTIMORE   The Walters Art Gallery

BERLIN   Staatliche Museen zu Berlin, Gemäldegalerie

BOSTON   Museum of Fine Arts

BRAUNSCHWEIG   Herzog Anton Ulrich-Museum

BUDAPEST   Szépmüvészeti Múzeum

CARACAS   Colección Patricia Phelps de Cisneros

CARDIFF   National Museums & Galleries of Wales

CHATSWORTH   The Duke of Devonshire and the Trustees
of the Chatsworth Settlement

COPENHAGEN   Statens Museum for Kunst

DELFT   Nieuwe Kerk (Rijksgebouwendienst)

DETROIT   The Detroit Institute of Arts

DOORN   Kasteel Huis Doorn

DORDRECHT   Dordrechts Museum

DORDRECHT   Museum Mr. Simon van Gijn

DOUAI   Musée de la Chartreuse

DRESDEN   Staatliche Kunstsammlungen,
Gemäldegalerie Alte Meister

DUBLIN   National Gallery of Ireland

EDINBURGH   National Gallery of Scotland

FLORENCE   Galleria degli Uffizi

FLORENCE   Galleria Palatina, Palazzo Pitti

HAARLEM   Frans Halsmuseum

HAMBURG   Museum für Kunst und Gewerbe

HARTFORD   Wadsworth Atheneum (Private collection)

KANSAS CITY   The Nelson-Atkins Museum of Art

KASSEL   Hessisches Landesmuseum

LILLE   Musée des Beaux-Arts

LONDON   Dulwich Picture Gallery

LONDON   The National Gallery

LONDON & WINDSOR   The Royal Collection,
H.M. Queen Elizabeth II

LOS ANGELES   The J. Paul Getty Museum

LOS ANGELES   Los Angeles County Museum of Art

LUND (SWEDEN)   Museum of Cultural History, Kulturen

MADRID   Museo Thyssen-Bornemisza

MOSCOW   State Museum of the Moscow Kremlin

MUNICH   Bayerische Staatsgemäldesammlungen, Alte Pinakothek

NELAHOZEVES (CZECH REPUBLIC)   Nelahozeves Castle,
The Lobkowicz Collections

NEW YORK   The Metropolitan Museum of Art

NIKKO (JAPAN)   Nikko Toshogu Shrine

OBERLIN (OHIO)   Allen Memorial Art Museum

PARIS   Collection Frits Lugt, Institut Néerlandais

PARIS   Musée du Louvre

PRAGUE   Národní-Galerie

ROTTERDAM   Museum Boijmans Van Beuningen

SCHWERIN   Staatliches Museum Schwerin

ST PETERSBURG   The State Hermitage Museum

STOCKHOLM   Nationalmuseum

STUTTGART   Staatsgalerie Stuttgart

THE HAGUE   Gemeentemuseum

THE HAGUE   Huis ten Bosch (Rijksgebouwendienst)

THE HAGUE   Koninklijk Kabinet van Schilderijen Mauritshuis

THE HAGUE   Museum van het Boek/
Museum Meermanno-Westreenianum

TOLEDO (OHIO)   The Toledo Museum of Art

UTRECHT   Centraal Museum

VIENNA   Gemäldegalerie der Akademie der bildenden Künste

VIENNA   Kunsthistorisches Museum

WASHINGTON   National Gallery of Art

ZÜRICH   Kunsthaus Zürich (The Prof. Dr. L. Ruzicka Foundation)

Irene and Howard Stein (Atlanta)

Mrs Edward Carter (United States)

The Earl of Wemyss and March (Scotland)

and various lenders who wish to remain anonymous

FOREWORD

No story is so wondrous as that of the small republic in Northern Europe which struggled for three-quarters of a century to wrest itself from the mighty Habsburg empire and subsequently grew into a world maritime power. No spectacle is more surprising than the unique blossoming of the arts of painting, drawing and sculpture that took place in a number of Dutch cities between 1600 and 1700.

At an amazing pace, artists in Haarlem, Utrecht, Leiden, Delft, Dordrecht and Amsterdam developed their own specialisms, while their ranks swelled to unprecedented numbers. No Dutch interior was without paintings or prints hanging on its white-washed walls or glittering gold-leather wall-coverings. Fascinating indeed is the process that took place here: building on Flemish examples but without the compelling presence of a dominant court culture, new forms were created and high standards were set in the fields of genre, still life, landscape and portraiture.

The impact made by Dutch painting of the Golden Age was not confined to the Netherlands. Everywhere in Europe, Dutch paintings figured prominently in trend-setting collections, both royal and private, which often displayed a pronounced personal character. An unequivocal conception of the Golden Age has never existed: each country, each generation has drawn its own picture, creating its own canon of Dutch art produced between 1600 and 1700. This

bi-centenary exhibition at the Rijksmuseum therefore presents an overview of the art of the Golden Age that differs considerably from that displayed at the time the museum was founded. One aspect has remained the same, however: when the museum opened its doors in the Huis ten Bosch in 1800 as the Nationale Konst-Gallerij (National Art Gallery), the history and art of the Golden Age – the era of the Netherlands' political unification – was the focal point. To this day the museum considers itself the undisputed home of 17th-century Dutch art and history, especially because it also houses the Rijksprentenkabinet (Print Room), a Mecca in the field of drawing and printmaking.

The development of the Rijksmuseum's collection – subject to fits and starts in the 19th century, though gaining momentum in 1885 when it moved into the new building designed by Pierre Cuypers – broadly reflects the shifting tastes described above. It was not always possible to fill the gaps that were felt to exist in the collection. On the other hand, the Rijksmuseum has often assumed a pioneering role in calling attention to forgotten aspects of the Golden Age. After the trail-blazing exhibitions *Art before the Iconoclasm* (1986) and *Dawn of the Golden Age* (1993-1994), which plumbed the depths of art preceding the glorious 17th century, it is only fitting that in this jubilee year our attention should focus on the Golden Age itself.

Unlike most exhibitions on the Golden

Age, which usually confine themselves to presenting the arts of painting and drawing, this exhibition offers a prominent place to sculpture and superb works of decorative art. The Dutch cabinetmakers, goldsmiths and silversmiths, glass decorators, potters and tapestry-makers of the 17th century rivalled their painting confrères in every respect, and even those who did not sojourn across Europe enjoyed an international reputation, the names of Adriaen de Vries and Paulus van Vianen being exemplary in this respect. The wealth and diversity of the Rijksmuseum's collection offers ideal opportunities for exciting encounters with the various aspects of work produced by artist and artisan alike.

The Rijksmuseum has taken the occasion of its 200th anniversary to confront and complement its own top-quality pieces in the field of painting, sculpture and the decorative arts with unique loans from the world's most prominent collections. In a parallel exhibition, the Print Room presents an equally choice selection of prints and drawings from the same period. The exhibition presented to our visitors in the year 2000 may rightly be said to comprise 'the glory of the Golden Age': the finest and most exceptional examples of 17th-century Dutch artistic production.

The reactions from colleagues in the museum world and from private collectors at home and abroad were heart-warming indeed. Almost without exception, our requests for loans were honoured as a homage to this 200-year-old institution, even though we asked the lenders to part for nearly half a year with works of art that are among their greatest treasures. To name a few exceptional pieces would be doing an injustice, both to the lenders, who outdid each other in their generosity, and to the works themselves, all of which deserve to be called 'unique'. A few exceptions must be mentioned nonetheless.

A unique opportunity presented itself through the restoration being carried out at the same time on both the Oranjezaal (Orange Hall) in the Huis ten Bosch and the tomb of Willem the Silent in the New Church in Delft, making available for the first time superb works by Cesar van Everdingen and Hendrick de Keyser. We are indebted to Her Majesty Queen Beatrix for permission to exhibit these works. Her Majesty Queen Elizabeth II also made a truly regal contribution to the exhibition with her loan of two paintings and two tulip vases from the British Royal Collection.

The temporary return to Amsterdam of *The anatomy lesson of Dr Nicolaes Tulp* by Rembrandt is a magnificent gesture, for which I am very grateful to my colleague at the Mauritshuis. Another unique occurrence is the arrival in Amsterdam of a late masterpiece by Frans Hals from the Frans Halsmuseum in Haarlem, *The regents of the Old Men's Almshouse*, which can now be displayed for the first time next to Rembrandt's *Syndics*. Moreover, it has proven possible to bring to the exhibition a candelabrum made by an Amsterdam brass founder which was presented by the Dutch East India Company to the Japanese shogun in 1640. Thanks to the efforts of the Japanese ambassador to the Netherlands and Koji Miura, this candleholder has been allowed to abandon temporarily the place it has occupied for centuries in front of the temple at Nikko. This gesture underscores in a symbolic way the 400 years of Dutch-Japanese relations which are also being commemorated in the year 2000.

Indemnities received from the Ministry of Education, Culture and Science and the Ministry of Finance have made it possible to finance this costly exhibition. Important contributions have also been made by our sponsors Achmea, Deloitte & Touche and Getronics.

We are grateful to the many people, too numerous to mention by name, who have provided scientific or practical assistance in the realisation of the exhibition. Tribute must be paid individually, however, to the core of the team of organisers. The idea for the exhibition was conceived by Jan Piet Filedt Kok, director of collections, and Bart Cornelis, in close consultation with Wouter Kloek and Reinier Baarsen, who head the Departments of Painting and Sculpture & Decorative Art, respectively. The above-mentioned were also consulted in the choice of works. Peter Schatborn, Guido Jansen and many curators were involved in the project's further development. The choice of drawings and prints for the parallel exhibition in the Rijksprentenkabinet was entrusted to Peter Schatborn and Ger Luijten. A number of colleagues – including Frits Duparc, Simon Levie and Peter Hecht – made suggestions regarding the choice of works and in a few cases served as intermediaries in requesting loans.

Among those responsible for the realisation of the exhibition were Frits Scholten, head of the department of exhibitions, Wendela Brouwer and Otto de Rijk, project leaders, as well as Igor Santhagens, head of the department of museum display. The arrangement of the galleries was entrusted to Eveline Merkx (of the architects' firm Merkx + Girod) and the graphic design of the exhibition to Irma Boom.

Assistance was also provided by the interns Eddy Schavemaker, Diana Markerink-Mangir and Odilia Bonebakker in the production of both books accompanying the exhibition. The design of the exhibition catalogues was the responsibility of Berry Slok. Both books – one devoted to painting,

sculpture and the decorative arts, and the other to drawings and prints – have materialised through close collaboration between the designer, the writers and the editors, and this collaboration has also made possible the close correspondence between text and illustrations. The twenty-four chapters of the first book were written by Judikje Kiers and Fieke Tissink of the Education Department. In cooperation with the editors, they were able to draw on the rich reservoir of knowledge and insight built up by generations of specialists working at the museum. The nine chapters of the book on drawings and prints were written by Epco Runia. We hope that in taking this path we have succeeded in reaching a broad public while making no sacrifice to scholarly integrity.

On the eve of our 200th anniversary the Dutch government has demonstrated, by means of a truly generous donation, its confidence in the Rijksmuseum's status as a national institution for the visual arts and history. Premier Wim Kok expressed it in Parliament as follows: 'The Netherlands has many museums with an international allure, but there is only one Rijksmuseum.' After completion of the planned, large-scale renovations, the building – the glory of its architectonic structure restored – and its collections will form a harmonious ensemble capable of offering many new generations of visitors a fascinating confrontation with Dutch history and the visual arts.

The Glory of the Golden Age, presented at the juncture of two centuries, forms the finest possible prelude to the new Rijksmuseum, proving that this national treasurehouse has lost nothing of its vitality and allure during the 200 years of its existence.

Ronald de Leeuw
Director General

INTRODUCTION

RARELY has painting experienced such a period of achievement as in the Dutch Republic of the 17th century, the century which has become known as the Golden Age. Thousands of painters of varying talent were active during this century, producing several million paintings altogether. The production of decorative art – ceramics, glass, silver and furniture – achieved new heights too; only sculpture lagged behind at first.

The Glory of the Golden Age depicts and discusses more than 200 objects – ranging from painting and sculpture to decorative art. In the exhibition of the same name, held to celebrate the bicentenary of the Rijksmuseum, these masterpieces represent the artistic glory of the Golden Age, as do the 90 drawings and prints presented in a parallel show in the Print Room, which is the subject of the companion volume.

CLASSICAL GOLDEN AGE

The term Golden Age comes from classical antiquity, when the *aurea aetas* was held to be the first period of civilisation, in which people enjoyed a harmonious and carefree existence. In the Silver and Bronze Ages that followed, circumstances became progressively harsher for humankind, and in the final Iron Age, life became a struggle for survival. The Golden Age was a paradisiacal, idealised and therefore well-nigh unattainable state. At the end of the Middle Ages, there was a growing desire to resurrect a Golden Age in which culture would be able to flourish. It was part of the idea of *renaissance*, a 'rebirth' of classical art.

By the 18th century, people realised that the highwater mark of art in Holland had passed, but it was only in the 19th century that the world of 17th-century Dutch art began to be associated with the idea of a Golden Age: a period of exceptional achievement. These finest years of Dutch painting thus became the central focus of the country's first national museum, which opened its doors to the public on 31 May 1800 at the Huis ten Bosch in The Hague.

'NATIONALE KONST-GALLERIJ' (NATIONAL ART GALLERY)

In 1795 the rule of the House of Orange came to a temporary end with the flight of Stadholder William V to England in the face of the invading Patriots, supported by the French. The Patriots proceeded in 1798 to establish the Batavian Republic. The new regime attempted to instil a keener sense of history in the Dutch people, and the founding of a national museum fitted in well with their plans. The National Art Gallery, or Nationale Konst-Gallerij, which opened in 1800, displayed 200 objects in five rooms, presenting the nation's history and artistic heritage with the accent on the Dutch Golden Age. The selection was largely random: most of the paintings had been taken from the palaces of former stadholders and from various government buildings. The nation's history was presented mainly through portraits. In addition, the displays included historical relics, like the chair of Jacoba of Bavaria (1401-1436) and two Jacoba jugs, which the countess was said to have made herself. Among the paintings, the history pieces illustrating classical and biblical narratives received pride of place, with Dutch artists being shown alongside Italian, French and Flemish masters. The tour ended in the Orange Hall, a room decorated with allegorical art glorifying Prince Frederik Hendrik. Originally painted between 1648 and 1652 by such artists as Jacob Jordaens, Cesar van Everdingen and Jan de Bray, this hall contains fine examples of 17th-century Netherlandish history painting (see pp. 253-254).

Among the works displayed in the Gallery, paintings by late 17th-century decorative artists such as Melchior d'Hondecoeter and Gerard de Lairesse were relatively well represented. Yet there were no works by artists such as Rembrandt, Frans Hals, Jan Steen, Johannes Vermeer or Jacob van Ruisdael. Two weeks after the opening, Jan Asselijn's *Threatened swan* (fig. 1) was acquired for the Gallery. This was interpreted as an allegory of the defence of the Republic (the eggs in the nest) by the 17th-century grand pensionary Johan de

9

Witt (the swan) against the Prince of Orange and England (the dog in the water). Characteristically for the new museum, historical significance was considered alongside artistic merit.

CHANGING IMAGE

The objects displayed at the National Art Gallery were transferred to Amsterdam in 1808 and became the basis of the Rijksmuseum, which was to find a permanent home in 1885 in the present building on the Stadhouderskade.

The Rijksmuseum's 200-year history of collecting and exhibiting art (see pp. 300-307) shows the shifting perspectives from which the art of the Golden Age has been viewed over the years – the result of ever-changing aesthetic and art-historical notions.

While the objective in the late 19th century was to obtain at least one signed work by every documented master, in the 20th century the museum sought to buy – with its limited resources – key works by the great masters. In the first decades of the 20th century, for example, the museum managed to acquire a number of masterpieces by Vermeer and Rembrandt. The aim in the 19th century as regards the decorative arts had been to show the development of the various crafts by displaying complete series of examples, whereas the accent in the 20th century was placed on acquiring top-quality pieces showing clear stylistic categories.

This shift in the emphasis of acquisition policies was also reflected in the museum's presentation. In the 19th century, the walls of the museum were covered from top to bottom with paintings of varying quality (fig. 2), but in the 20th century a more discerning approach resulted in displays featuring only the finest works (fig. 3), while after the Second World War sculpture and the decorative arts were treated with equal seriousness at the Rijksmuseum, allowing the museum to exhibit, in an international context, an overview of art from the Late Middle Ages to the early 20th century. The picture galleries also underwent thorough renovation in more recent times (fig. 4).

BICENTENARY EXHIBITION

The exhibition and this accompanying publication are based on the view of 17th-century Dutch art as reflected in the Rijksmuseum's present collection. Clearly, changing insights into the art of the Golden Age have affected the Rijksmuseum's acquisition policies over the years. Purchases and bequests have on various occasions enabled underappreciated aspects of 17th-century art to find a place in the museum. The overview displayed can never be perfect, however, and there will always be room for improvement. Nonetheless, this exhibition now aims, with the help of the paintings and objects on loan, to provide an ideal picture of the art of the Golden Age.

Of the more than two hundred paintings, sculptures and decorative works of art on display, around half are from the Rijksmuseum's collections. The remainder are on loan from museums in the Netherlands and abroad, selected to augment the picture of 17th-century art presented by the Rijksmuseum's own collection. Some of these works are seminal masterpieces which are lacking in the Rijksmuseum's collection, including many that have not been shown in the Netherlands for a long time. A number of loans at the parallel exhibition of prints and drawings have been selected for the same reason.

For the compilers, the 17th century encompasses the entire period from 1600 to

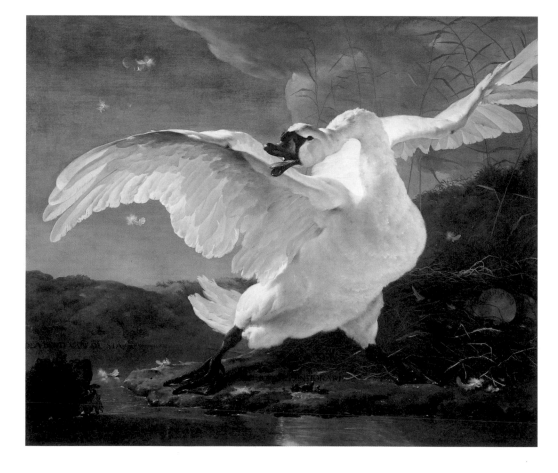

1. JAN ASSELIJN, *The threatened swan*, c. 1640-1650. Canvas 144 x 171 cm. AMSTERDAM, RIJKSMUSEUM

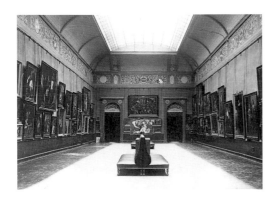

2. PICTURE GALLERY, C. 1900

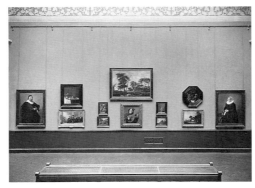

3. THE 'HAARLEM ROOM', C. 1935

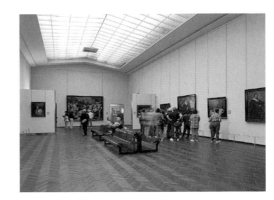

4. THE 'HAARLEM ROOM', C. 1998

1700. The tremendous variety of Northern Netherlandish art around 1600 was illustrated at the Rijksmuseum in the *Dawn of the Golden Age*, an exhibition held in the winter of 1993/94. A review of the international focus and the significance of this early period is provided in the first chapter of this book. Apart from the Italianate artists and the Caravaggisti, whose inspiration came from Italy, the development of Dutch art in the 17th century had a powerful national character, although in this period artists continued to be influenced by developments in Flanders.

Towards the end of the 17th century, a new international orientation developed. At the court of Stadholder-King William III and Queen Mary, this new focus was embodied by the Frenchman Daniel Marot, while the influence of French Classicism is visible in the work of such painters as Gerard de Lairesse. The rise of the applied arts in this period is reflected in the decorative splendour of paintings by Jan Weenix, Michiel d'Hondecoeter, Adriaen van der Werff and Gerard de Lairesse. By no means was this a period of decline.

COLLECTING ART OF THE GOLDEN AGE

The exhibition also pays homage to the great collectors of 17th-century art of the intervening centuries. Both royal patrons and private collectors in the Netherlands, England, Italy, Germany and France were already extending commissions to Dutch artists and buying their work in the 17th century. In the 18th and 19th centuries Dutch old masters were highly popular among European collectors. The collections of Dutch art in many major museums, including Braunschweig, Dresden and Vienna, were originally formed in the 18th century, whereas the foundations of others, such as those in Berlin and London, were laid in the second half of the 19th century. Most of the American collections were not formed until the 20th century. A brief history of the collections of Dutch art in museums that have lent objects for the exhibition is given in the final section of the book.

Almost all the leading museum collections of 17th-century Dutch art are represented here with one, sometimes two and in the case of the Hermitage and the Mauritshuis with even more loans. Many of these are famous works, traditional favourites among the public, which have temporarily left home to be displayed for five months at the Rijksmuseum.

The Rijksmuseum will, in future, have only incidental opportunities to augment the current survey of Dutch art in a significant way. The paintings on loan from other museums have made it possible, for the duration of the exhibition, to present a nearly ideal overview. It is our hope that this exhibition will appeal to connoisseurs and the general public alike, and will be, from beginning to end, an exciting, stimulating, and most importantly, a surprising experience.

Jan Piet Filedt Kok

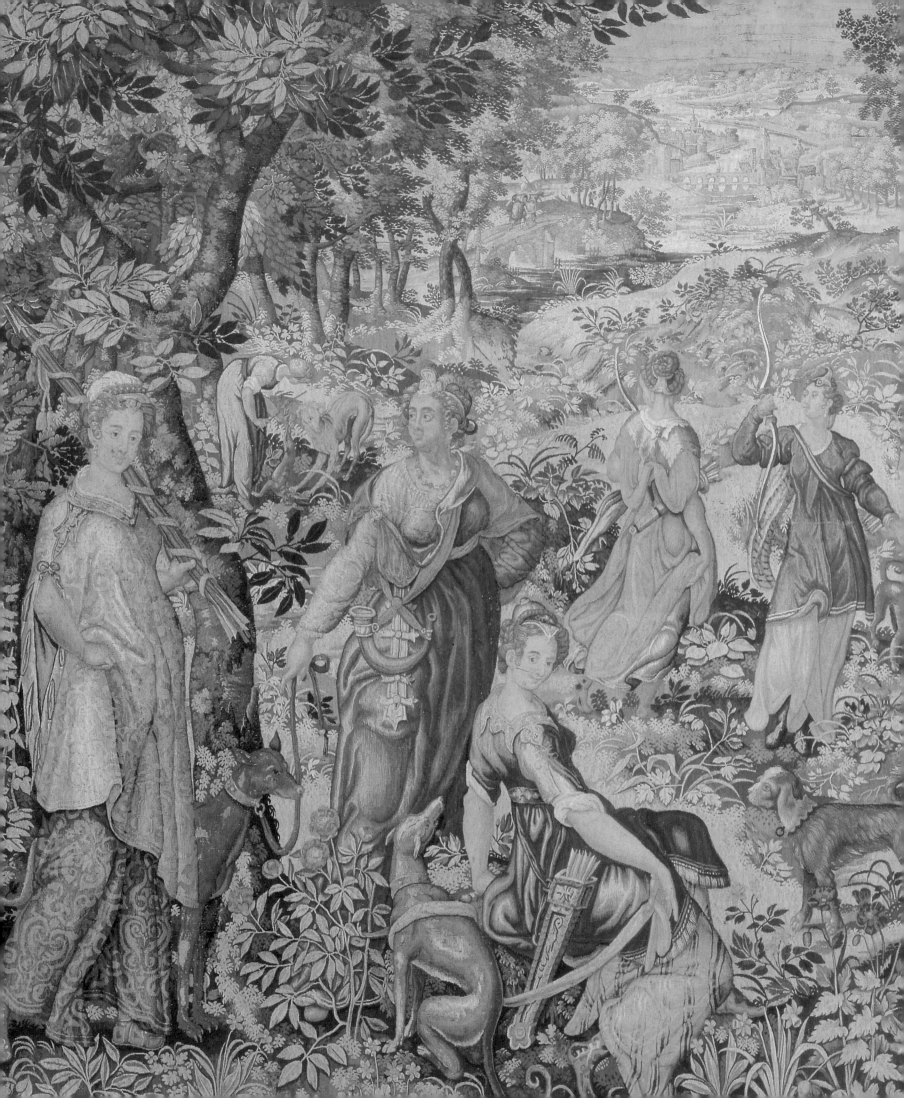

I A VARIED BEGINNING
1600-1625

PRAGUE, Haarlem, Antwerp, Delft, Utrecht, Rome: artistic ties linking these European cities influenced Dutch art in the early 17th century. Many Dutch artists tried their luck abroad and employed their talents in the service of foreign rulers. At the same time, artists were leaving the Southern Netherlands for the northern provinces, attracted by financial opportunities and the tolerant religious climate. Growing affluence in the Dutch Republic stimulated the development of various branches of the arts, with international contacts exercising an unmistakable influence on style, technique and choice of subject matter.

The court of Emperor Rudolf II in Prague was considered the cultural heart of Europe around 1600. Emperor Rudolf was a keen collector and patron of the arts and sciences. He owned an impressive collection – to which he added continually – of paintings, sculptures and decorative objects. He persuaded famous artists and scholars to come to Prague, where he followed their work closely, visiting the artists in their studios and suggesting new subjects for their work.

Several artists from the Southern and Northern Netherlands made their name in Prague, among them the Utrecht silversmith Paulus van Vianen, the Antwerp painter Bartholomeus Spranger and the Hague sculptor Adriaen de Vries. The ability of De Vries to breathe life into the dull bronze

must have pleased the emperor, since he appointed the Dutchman as his court sculptor (*Kammerbildhauer*), a prestigious position within the imperial retinue.

The artists at the Prague court were captivated by the Mannerist style that had lately arrived from Italy. In an exquisitely decorative manner they presented their stories – often tinged with eroticism – which they took from the Bible or classical mythology. The art of the Prague Mannerists was mainly populated with nude figures in unusual, sometimes highly contorted poses.

DUTCH MANNERISM

It was around 1585 that a group of artists in Haarlem saw their first Mannerist drawings by Bartholomeus Spranger. Impressed by the new style, they immediately began to adopt some of its elements. Engravers in Haarlem made prints after Spranger's work, thereby contributing to the spread of this style in Holland and abroad. Paintings by artists such as Karel van Mander, Cornelis Cornelisz van Haarlem, Joachim Wtewael and Hendrick Goltzius represent a Dutch version of Mannerism. Movement, a twisted torso and elegance are features of Wtewael's painting of St Sebastian, while the sublime style of the Diana tapestry, after a design by Karel van Mander, also demonstrates the influence of the Prague court style.

THE DUTCH REPUBLIC

In 1555 the Spanish king, Philip II, a Catholic monarch who tolerated no dissent, came into possession of the Northern and Southern Netherlands. His oppressive policies led to an armed uprising against Spanish rule. The leader of the Revolt – it was not considered a war at first – was Prince Willem of Orange (1533-1584). The uprising eventually resulted in the division of the Low Countries. The Southern Netherlands remained loyal to the Spanish crown and the Catholic Church. The Northern Netherlands set up an independent Dutch Republic: the United Provinces, with Protestantism as the dominant religion. Central authority in the Republic resided with the representatives of the seven provinces assembled in the States General. In 1648 the Dutch and Spanish agreed to end the war and the Republic was recognised as an independent state.

I

ADRIAEN DE VRIES (1556-1626)
Bacchus finding Ariadne on Naxos,
c. 1610-1612
Bronze 52.5 x 42 cm
AMSTERDAM, RIJKSMUSEUM
(acquired in 1935, see p. 315)

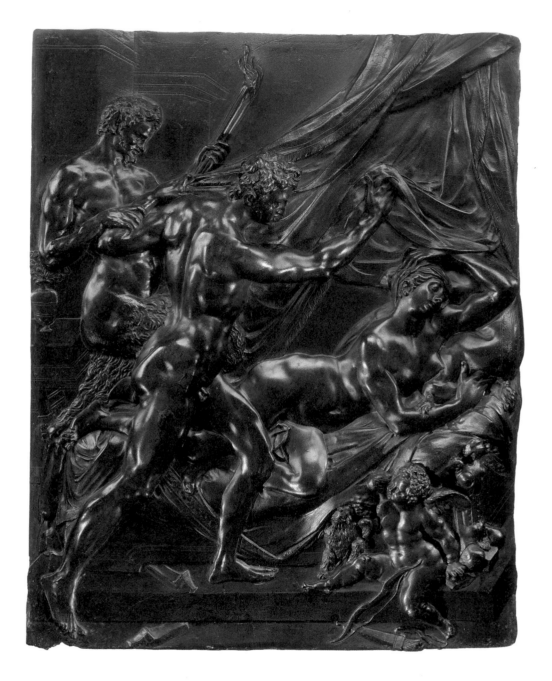

TRUE TO LIFE

Dutch Mannerism lasted only for a short time. In the years after 1600 most artists gradually moved away from this style. Compositions started to become less intense and artists began turning to new subjects. Within a relatively short period new, autonomous genres appeared in art, such as landscape, still life, figure painting, seascapes and townscapes, while existing specialisms such as history painting and portraiture were given new form. In all these subjects, scenes from everyday life now played a major role.

Yet there was one place abroad where Dutch artists continued to find inspiration. In Rome, a group of painters from Utrecht, including Hendrick ter Brugghen, became fascinated by the work of the artist Caravaggio (see chapter 4). The stark realism and powerful contrast between light and shade that they introduced into Dutch painting were decisive ingredients in the art of the Golden Age.

BACCHUS AND ARIADNE

With a single tug, Bacchus tears away the curtain of the bed. There lies Ariadne, sleeping unsuspectingly – naked, graceful, beautiful. Instantly the young god falls in love. This is the moment in the Greek myth that Adriaen de Vries depicted in bronze relief.

Ariadne, daughter of King Minos of Crete, had been left behind by her lover Theseus as she slept on a beach on the isle of Naxos. She awoke the moment Bacchus, the wine god, discovered her. Instead of a beach, however, the sculptor chose a splen-

did four-poster bed as the setting of this scene. He gave the story an erotic touch: the naked Ariadne is accompanied by an infant Cupid, leaning against the edge of the bed, ready to fan the flames of love. The scene seems to capture a moment in time. Bacchus has just come running in, and the satyr who holds up a torch for him is also in motion. The dynamism is heightened by the composition: together with the bed curtain, Bacchus forms a diagonal from lower left to upper right.

The way in which De Vries depicted Ariadne, lying somewhat uncomfortably with one leg pulled up and one hand on her head, reveals the artist's fascination for the complex poses and twists of naked bodies that typified Mannerism. He was working in this style around 1610, when he was commissioned to make this relief for Rudolf II in Prague. In his later, less polished work, Adriaen de Vries emerged as a pioneer of Baroque sculpture.

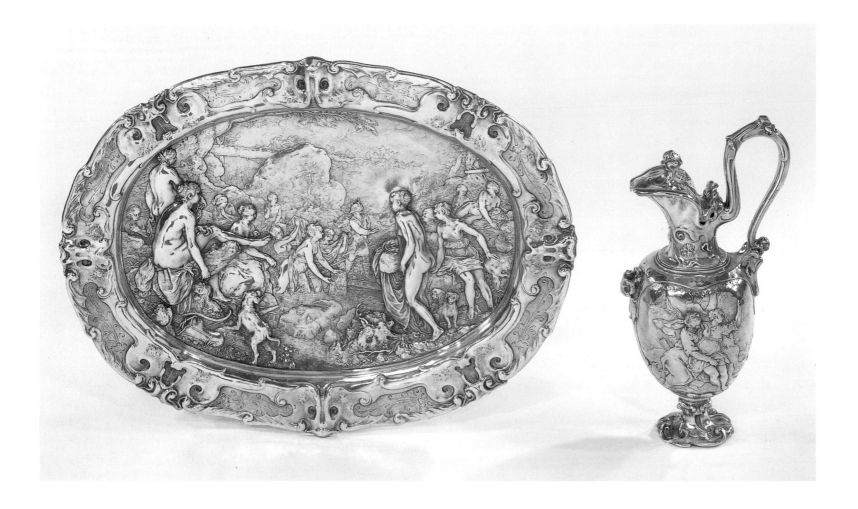

2

PAULUS VAN VIANEN (c. 1570-1613)
Ewer and basin with episodes
from the stories of Diana, 1613
Silver, ewer h. 34 cm; basin 52.3 x 40.5 cm
AMSTERDAM, RIJKSMUSEUM
(acquired in 1947, see p. 316)

DIANA AND HER NYMPHS

Like Adriaen de Vries, the Utrecht silversmith Paulus van Vianen spent many years at the imperial court of Rudolf II, living and working in Prague until his death in 1613. In that final year, Van Vianen made a silver ewer and basin with mythological scenes based on the *Metamorphoses* by the Roman poet Ovid (43 BC-c. AD 18). All the scenes chased in silver refer to the goddess Diana. In the centre of the basin she is shown semi-nude, standing in the water, as she and her nymphs bathe. No men were permitted to see them; the goddess guarded her virginity jealously and demanded the same of her entourage.

While out hunting, the young Actaeon accidentally stumbled upon the bathing nymphs and eagerly feasted his eyes on them. When Diana noticed this 'she blushed like the dawn', in the words of Ovid, and then punished Actaeon by transforming him into a stag. At the centre of the basin scene, Van Vianen portrayed the start of the metamorphosis: the appearance of antlers on Actaeon's head. The underside of the basin shows what happened next: having been changed into a stag, Actaeon is trapped by his hunting companions. Even the dogs fail to recognise him and eventually they tear their master to pieces.

The ewer that goes with the basin shows the story of Callisto, one of the nymphs in Diana's entourage. Disguised as Diana, Jupiter, the father of the gods, seduced the chaste Callisto. Jupiter can be identified on the ewer by his usual attribute, an eagle. Callisto became pregnant and when Diana discovered this she punished the nymph by changing her into a bear. Here again, the metamorphosis culminates in a hunting scene, although this time Jupiter intervenes: the bear Callisto was not killed, but transmuted by Jupiter into a constellation of stars.

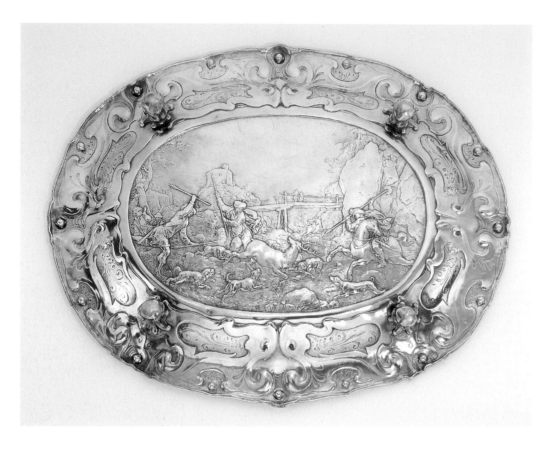

UNDERSIDE OF THE BASIN MADE BY PAULUS VAN VIANEN IN 1613 [2]

CRAFTSMANSHIP

The basin is an amazing display of crafts-manship. The scene is chased in silver, a technique that enabled Paulus van Vianen to incorporate the subtlest of nuances in the relief, particularly in the landscape in the background. The suggestion of depth is reminiscent of the artist's sketches of nature: Van Vianen chased and engraved in silver as easily as he drew on paper.

The two sheets of silver that make up the basin were chased separately before being joined with nuts and bolts, which are visible only on the underside, having been absorbed into the design of the rim. Both sides of the rim are decorated in a unique style, displaying auricular ornamentation. This fantasised decoration was inspired by lobate forms and other parts of organisms, such as folds of skin, pieces of flesh, tendons, bones, wings and monster-heads.

Neither ewer nor basin were made as utensils. They are far too richly decorated and their shape is not at all practical. The objects were clearly made for a collector who wished to display them from every possible angle.

SPIERING AND VAN MANDER

The transformations described by the Roman poet Ovid some two thousand years ago in his *Metamorphoses* have been portrayed in every art form. This large tapestry shows a series of scenes from his story of Cephalus and Procris. The painter, poet and author Karel van Mander (1548-1606) produced the design for this tapestry, made at the workshop of François Spiering for a patron whose name is no longer known.

François Spiering and Karel van Mander were both Flemish immigrants. Van Mander settled in Haarlem in 1583, whereas Spiering had moved his looms from Antwerp to Delft in 1582, building up a highly successful business. His clients included various royal courts and the States General, who presented Spiering's tapestries as diplomatic gifts. They exude the opulence that characterised international court art.

CEPHALUS AND PROCRIS

The sumptuously dressed women of Diana's entourage attract the viewer's attention and force the start of Cephalus and Procris' story into the middle distance. There, in the background under the trees, the hunter Cephalus tests the fidelity of his wife, Procris. Cephalus did this by transforming himself and attempting to seduce her in the guise of an eastern prince. Procris remained faithful, but when Cephalus offered her jewels, she wavered for a moment. Then, when he revealed his identity, the indignant and embarrassed Procris ran away. Procris remained with Diana's entourage for a while, but eventually returned to her husband. The moment of Diana's farewell to Procris is the main subject of this tapestry. The women shake hands and Procris receives a farewell gift of a dog and a hunting spear to present to Cephalus when she arrives home.

The tapestry leaves out the grizzly end of the story, in which Procris suspects her husband of infidelity and follows him out hunting: hearing a movement in the bushes, Cephalus throws his spear and unintentionally kills the woman he loves. Perhaps the absence of the final scene reflects the purpose of the tapestry. This was designed as one of a series of tapestries portraying episodes from the stories of Diana. These were often given as wedding presents, for which the dramatic conclusion of the Cephalus and Procris story was not a suitable theme.

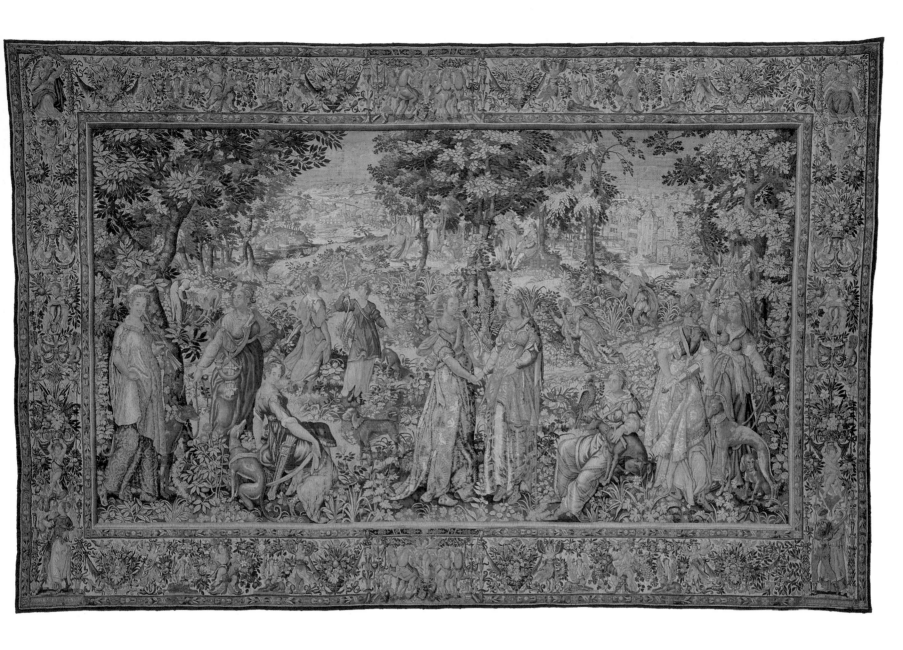

3

WORKSHOP OF FRANÇOIS SPIERING

(1549/1551-1631)

Cephalus and Procris, c. 1610

Wool and silk on woollen warp, 345 x 520 cm

AMSTERDAM, RIJKSMUSEUM

(acquired in 1954, see p. 316)

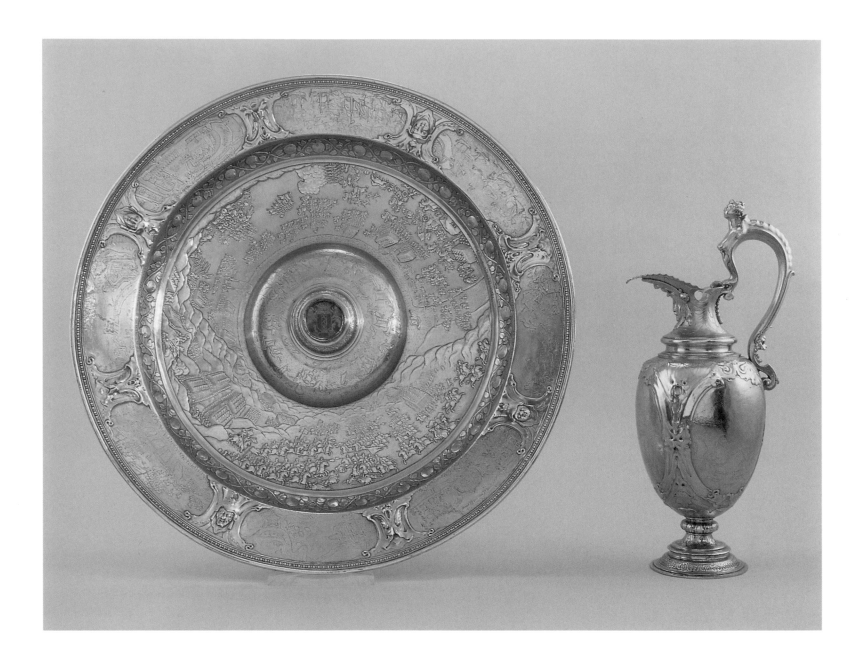

4

ADAM VAN VIANEN (1568/1569-1627)
Ewer and basin, 1614
Silver-gilt, ewer h. 38.5 cm;
basin diam. 52.5 cm
AMSTERDAM, RIJKSMUSEUM
(on loan from the City of Amsterdam
since 1885, see p. 312)

UTRECHT

While Paulus van Vianen held an important post at the court of Rudolf II in Prague, his brother Adam remained loyal to their native city of Utrecht. Like Paulus, he was a highly sought-after silversmith. The city of Amsterdam commissioned him in 1614 to make a ewer and basin. Indeed, it is a reflection of Adam's skill and fame that the city of Amsterdam chose an artist from Utrecht for this commission.

This ensemble appears to have been a gift for the stadholder Prince Maurits, as suggested by the oranges – symbols of the House of Orange – along the rim and in the centre of the basin. Moreover, the scenes on the ewer and basin portray military victories that took place under Maurits's rule during the Eighty Years' War. Maurits's greatest triumph is depicted in the centre of the basin: the battle of Nieuwpoort in 1600.

Both the ewer and basin are traditionally shaped, as are some of the decorative elements, like the rim of palmettes on the foot of the ewer. Adam van Vianen also used modern motifs, however. To separate the military scenes he applied chased auricular ornamentation, incorporating all kinds of masked heads.

THE TRIUMPH OF ORNAMENT

In the year in which Adam van Vianen made his relatively traditional ewer and basin, he also made a highly original ewer consisting entirely of auricular ornament. This silver vessel, subsequently gilt, was commissioned by the guild of Amsterdam silversmiths in memory of the maker's brother Paulus van Vianen, who had died in Prague in 1613. This unique assignment is a reflection of the regard in which their Amsterdam colleagues held the Van Vianen brothers. Paulus was hailed as the greatest silversmith of his day, and Adam was honoured with the commission for a memorial ewer.

Adam drew inspiration for this commission from his younger brother's work and undoubtedly attempted to rival him, which is why he chose his brother's trademark style of auricular ornamentation. Paulus had applied this decorative form to great acclaim on objects such as the ewer and basin of 1613. Here, however, Adam went much further. He created a ewer consisting entirely of flowing lines and lobate, oyster-like shapes. All the forms flow in and out of each other. The whole piece seems like one big ornament, even though individual figures are recognisable. The ewer is supported on the shoulders of a monkey on its haunches, while the handle consists of the hair of a woman leaning forwards, culminating in the nostrils of a monster's head with a gaping mouth.

Adam van Vianen was widely acclaimed for his masterpiece. Indeed, this ewer, which was displayed at the silversmiths' guild in Amsterdam in the 17th century, was featured in dozens of paintings.

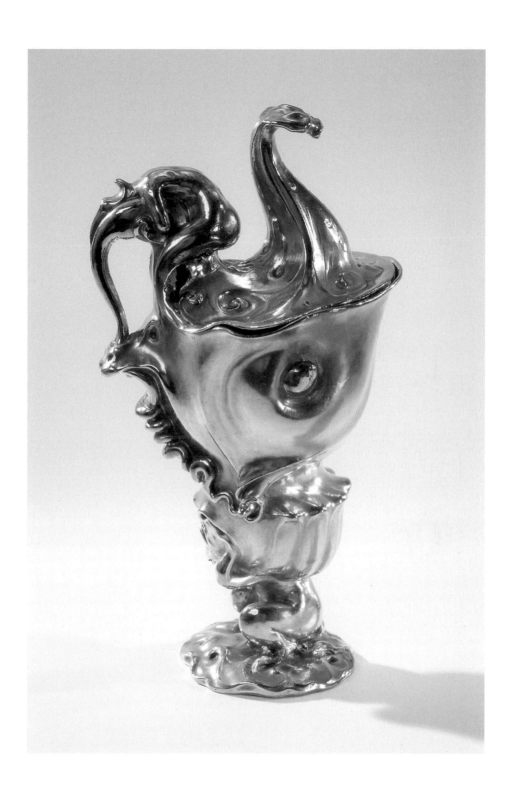

5

ADAM VAN VIANEN (1568/1569-1627)
Covered ewer, 1614
Silver-gilt h. 25.5 cm
AMSTERDAM, RIJKSMUSEUM
(acquired with the aid of the
Rembrandt Society in 1976, see p. 318)

6

JOACHIM WTEWAEL (1566-1638)
St Sebastian, 1600
Canvas 169.5 x 124.8 cm
KANSAS CITY,
THE NELSON-ATKINS MUSEUM OF ART
(acquired in 1984, see p. 335)

ST SEBASTIAN

In 1600 the painter Joachim Wtewael of
Utrecht portrayed St Sebastian, the Christian
martyr who was the patron saint of militias
and also revered as protector against the
plague. According to legend, Sebastian, an
officer in the Roman army under Emperor
Diocletian, was sentenced to death for being
a Christian and shot with arrows. He
survived the arrows, but was subsequently
cudgelled to death on the emperor's orders.

Many portrayals of St Sebastian have
been made. Traditionally shown is the
moment immediately after Sebastian has
been shot, his body pierced by a volley of
arrows. Joachim Wtewael tried a different
approach. His painting, in which two soldiers tie the saint to a tree, portrays the
moment just before the execution. The
martyr's pose is elegant and his contorted,
naked body is meticulously sculpted.
Wtewael showed Sebastian's unscathed and
seductive body according to the Mannerist
ideals of the day. The martyr looks blissfully
at the putto flying towards him holding a
laurel wreath and a palm branch, symbols of
victory over death.

It is not known for whom Wtewael
made this painting, though it seems unlikely
that a St Sebastian in this style would have
been intended for a church. Although the
size of the canvas might suggest this, the
picture itself places far too much emphasis
on the saint's physical beauty. Perhaps it
was made for the militia guild: this might
explain why Wtewael painted the various
bows and arrows so prominently in the
foreground.

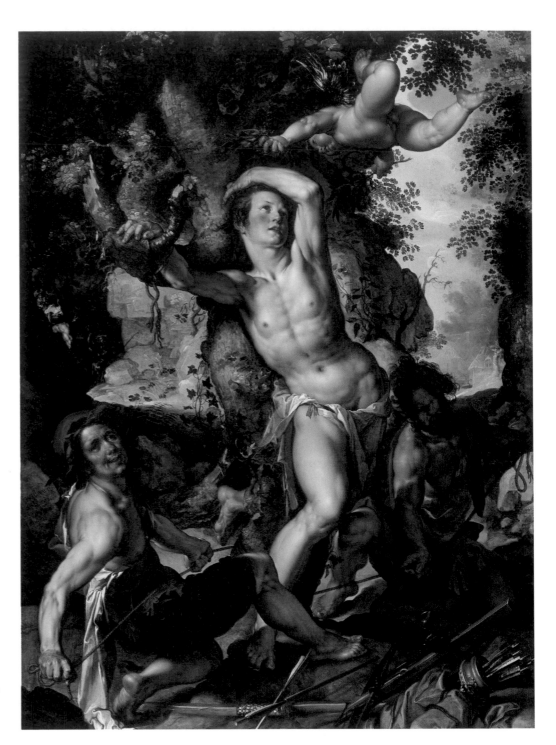

TWENTY-FIVE YEARS LATER

A quarter of a century after Wtewael painted his *St Sebastian,* Hendrick ter Brugghen
produced a large painting of the same
subject in Utrecht. Instead of a seductive,
unscathed saint, however, Ter Brugghen
portrayed Sebastian as weak and vulnerable.
A woman removes the arrows from his

7

HENDRICK TER BRUGGHEN (1588-1629)
St Sebastian, 1625
Canvas 150.2 x 120 cm
OBERLIN, ALLEN MEMORIAL ART MUSEUM
(acquired in 1953, see p. 343)

>

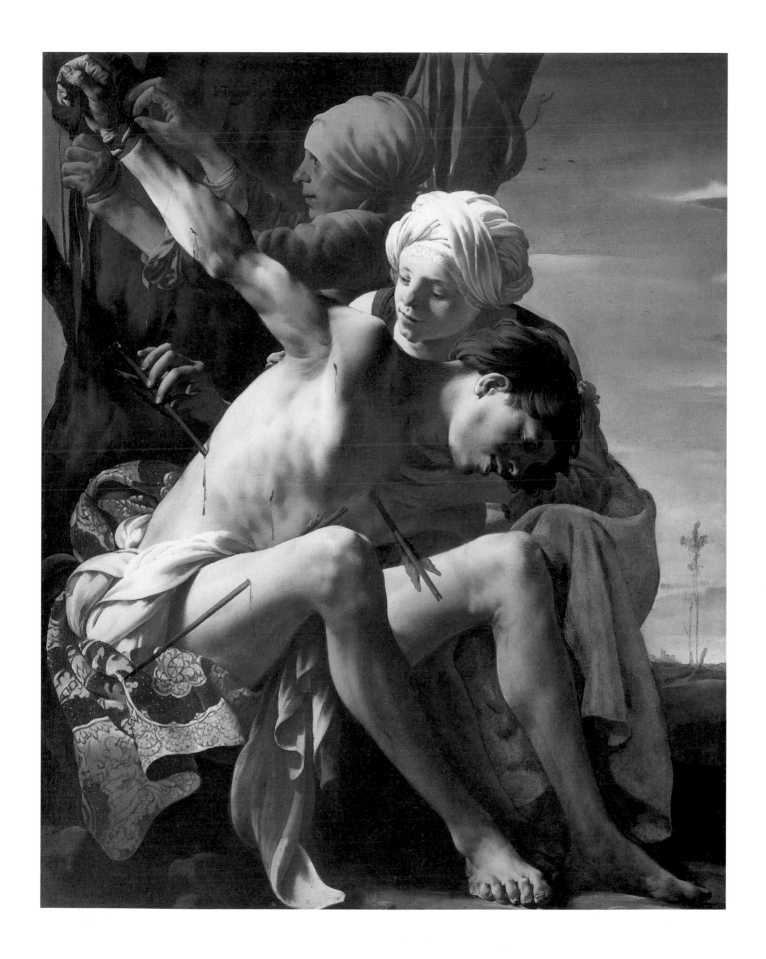

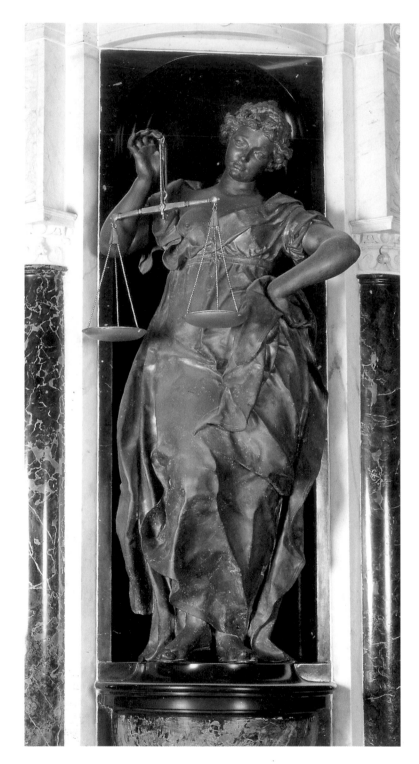

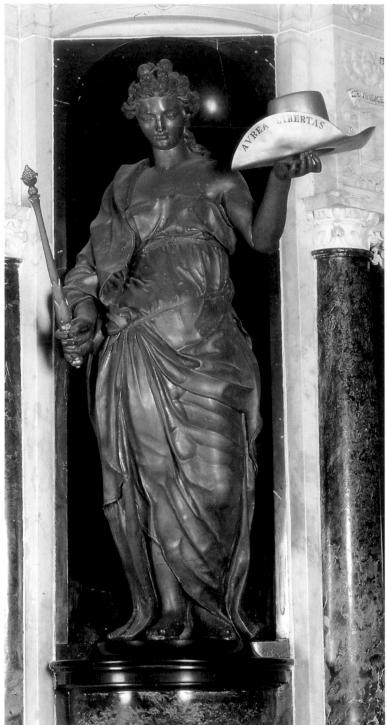

8 A

HENDRICK DE KEYSER (1565-1621)

Justice, c. 1615-1620

Bronze h. 173 cm

TOMB OF WILLEM THE SILENT

IN THE NEW CHURCH AT DELFT (see p. 326)

8 B

HENDRICK DE KEYSER (1565-1621)

Liberty, c. 1615-1620

Bronze h. 173 cm

TOMB OF WILLEM THE SILENT

IN THE NEW CHURCH AT DELFT (see p. 326)

body, while another loosens the rope with which his hand was tied to the tree. It is not known who commissioned Ter Brugghen's picture.

In the twenty-five years between Wtewael's Sebastian and that of Ter Brugghen, much had changed in art. Mannerism had faded, while Ter Brugghen and other Utrecht artists had introduced a new style. Ter Brugghen had spent ten years in Italy, mostly in Rome, where he had been fascinated by the work of the painter Caravaggio (1571-1610). The latter's work, celebrated both for its dramatic contrasts of light and dark, and for the natural depiction of the figures, left its mark on the art of Ter Brugghen and several of his fellow townsmen who became known as the Caravaggisti (see chapter 4).

In Ter Brugghen's depiction of St Sebastian, both the illumination and the composition heighten the drama of the story. The powerful light on Sebastian's upper torso, here more dead than alive, realistically reveals the martyr's wounds. Ter Brugghen's light source is located somewhere to the left, outside the painting, illuminating the saint and the face of a woman who also features in the story. According to legend, Sebastian survived the execution thanks to the generous care of a woman named Irene. By including an ordinary woman in the depiction, Ter Brugghen lent St Sebastian's martyrdom a human dimension.

HENDRICK DE KEYSER

While Adriaen de Vries was gaining fame with his Mannerist sculpture at the court in Prague, Hendrick de Keyser was the focus of attention in the Dutch Republic when it came to three-dimensional art. De Keyser was a 'master sculptor and stonemason', as well as Amsterdam's official architect. In both capacities he helped to determine the face of the fast-growing city. His buildings in Amsterdam, among them an important church – the Westerkerk – dominate the city to this day.

In 1614, Hendrick de Keyser was commissioned by the States General to design a magnificent tomb for Willem the Silent, Prince of Orange, the founder of the Dutch state and known as the father of the Dutch nation. Willem I (1533-1584) symbolised the Dutch struggle against Spain. From his base at the Prinsenhof in Delft he had led the campaign against Spanish rule. On 10 July 1584 he was assassinated on the orders of the Spanish king, Philip II. Although he received a solemn funeral, he was given only a simple grave in the New Church in Delft. By 1610 the danger of defeat had passed and the government decided to commission a monument for the prince. Hendrick de Keyser, the Republic's leading sculptor, was invited to design the tomb. For the memorial, the artist employed the full range of his skills in an impressive combination of architecture and sculpture. It surmounts the crypt which still serves as the final resting place of members of the Dutch royal house.

A HERO'S TOMB

To honour the nation's hero, De Keyser designed a freestanding monument of black and white marble specially imported from Italy and Belgium. The size of the structure is in keeping with the church's dimensions: the royal tomb is a building within a building. Beneath the canopy are two life-size figures of the prince. In the centre lies the white-marble effigy of the dead prince; in front, the prince is shown in bronze as he was in life, seated on a chair. Above him towers the winged figure of Fame, descending to blow the trumpet above the royal hero. Robust columns and niches, crowned by tall obelisks, accentuate the corners. Each niche contains the bronze figure of one of the virtues representing the political principles of Justice, Fortitude, Liberty and Faith: the foundations of the state.

To the right of the seated prince, in pride of place, stands Liberty, a strong female figure in classical garb. In her right hand she holds a sceptre, the symbol of

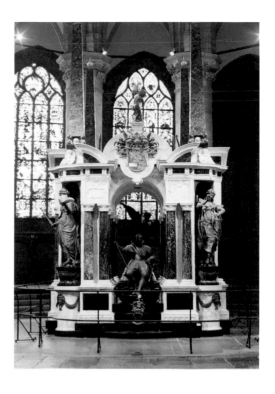

HENDRICK DE KEYSER (1565-1621)
Tomb of Willem the Silent, 1614-1621
DELFT, DE NIEUWE KERK

her dominion. This staff is one of Liberty's normal attributes. The gilt helmet, however, is an unusual departure from tradition. The text *Aurea Libertas* – 'golden liberty' – ensures that the message of this symbol of freedom is not lost. It was the first time that the concept of Liberty was depicted in this way.

The female figure on the left of the prince is Justice, recognisable by the scales with which she balances good against evil. De Keyser's portrayal of this virtue is a combination of a classical goddess and a Dutch milkmaid. The well-pleated garment, which clearly reveals the shape of her body, evokes associations with classical sculpture, yet the sturdy posture, accentuated by the hand on her hip, lends this virtue a specifically Dutch quality. The figure offers an excellent illustration of De Keyser's unique ability to render pleated material.

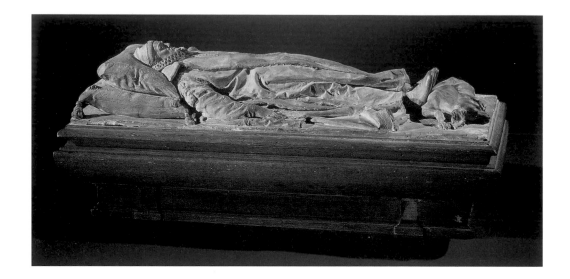

HENDRICK DE KEYSER (1565-1621)
Model for the effigy of Willem the Silent
lying in state, made for his tomb
in the New Church at Delft, c. 1614
Terracotta l. 61 cm
AMSTERDAM, RIJKSMUSEUM

The female figures in the other two corners of the monument match the style of Liberty and Justice. Faith, recognisable by her attributes – a Bible and a church – rests with her left foot on a stone on which the word *Christus* is incised. The fourth virtue, Fortitude, holds an oak twig in her hand and wears a lion's skin over her head and shoulders, a reference to the mythological strongman Hercules who killed a lion and then wore its skin as helmet and armour.

THE PRINCE OF ORANGE

Before starting on the life-size bronze and marble sculptures, the artist made a series of studies and models in clay. Such terracotta sculptures were rarely preserved. However, the model for the tomb's central effigy was saved and now forms a key exhibit in the Rijksmuseum's Dutch history section. The delicate model of the prince on his deathbed, with his dog at his feet, differs only slightly from the life-size white-marble effigy. De Keyser made a realistic rendering of the dead prince, carefully depicting the details of the face, hands and clothing.

De Keyser spent a long time working on this prestigious Delft monument. Four and a half years after receiving the commission, his patrons began to get impatient and sent him a final demand. He replied with a promise to send sections of the tomb by barge from Amsterdam to Delft as soon as possible. Moreover, he assured them that the work was now at such an advanced stage that it could easily be completed even if he were to die unexpectedly. In fact, by the time of his death on 15 May 1621, his 56th birthday, the tomb was almost finished. Hendrick's son Pieter saw to the completion of the project.

The monument has been restored on a number of occasions. During the latest thorough overhaul, begun in 1997, the tomb was taken apart piece by piece before being cleaned, restored and reconstructed. A piece of slate was discovered in the vault of the monument bearing the monograms of De Keyser and his assistants – a wonderfully modest way for the master to sign his masterpiece.

SELF-CONFIDENT BURGHER

When the wealthy Amsterdam burgher Vincent Coster (1553-1608/1610) decided to commission a portrait, instead of selecting a suitable painter, as was usual in his day, he chose a sculptor. It was a claim to an almost aristocratic status: portrait sculptures had always been the preserve of princes, kings and emperors. However rich they were, ordinary burghers were rarely portrayed in stone in the early 17th century. Coster's decision to approach 'Amsterdam's master sculptor and stonemason' Hendrick de Keyser bears witness, therefore, to great self-confidence and the growing status of the urban elite.

Vincent Jacobsz Coster was a rich man. He was nicknamed Vincent the Wine Tester, after his profession: Coster's job was to check the amount of wine in the barrels at the vintners' and taverns in order to assess the amount of tax they owed. Moreover, he owned the Oude Doolhof, a popular entertainment centre on Amsterdam's Prinsengracht.

De Keyser portrayed Coster's face with great realism. The head inclines slightly to the right, the cheeks are a little gaunt, while the forehead is wrinkled. Beneath the gently frowning eyebrows, his eyes actually appear to gaze out. De Keyser managed to portray the upright collar and the pleated cloak around Coster's shoulders with great realism in the hard marble. The artist sought an interesting way of linking the figure's upper torso to the socle: where Coster's waist would be, the folds of the cloak are gathered in a fantasy mask, a lion's head with horns against a scroll background. Such mask and scroll motifs were common ornamental elements on 16th-century buildings, furniture and jewellery.

CLASSICAL AURA

Hendrick de Keyser claimed to have introduced the use of white Italian marble to the Netherlands. The stone, which he ordered from Carrara, gave his sculptures a certain classical dignity. It is hard to say whether De Keyser really was the first Dutch artist to use marble, certainly not a common material in Dutch art. A more usual medium was softer sandstone or translucent alabaster. De Keyser's bust of Vincent Coster is the earliest known marble portrait in the Netherlands. Besides the material, the garments also give the portrait a classical feel. The decoratively draped toga recalls ancient Roman portrait busts, as does the lion's-head brooch. Coster, a rich citizen of Amsterdam, clearly wished his portrait to reflect the power and wealth of the Roman emperors. In De Keyser he found an artist capable of lending his portrait that classical splendour.

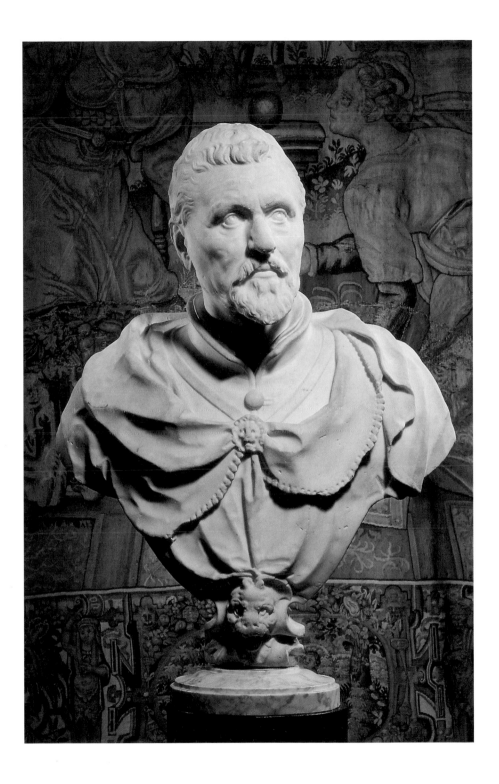

9

HENDRICK DE KEYSER (1565-1621)

Bust of Vincent Coster (1553-1608/1610), 1608

Marble h. 75 cm

AMSTERDAM, RIJKSMUSEUM

(acquired with the aid of the Rembrandt

Society in 1900, see p. 314)

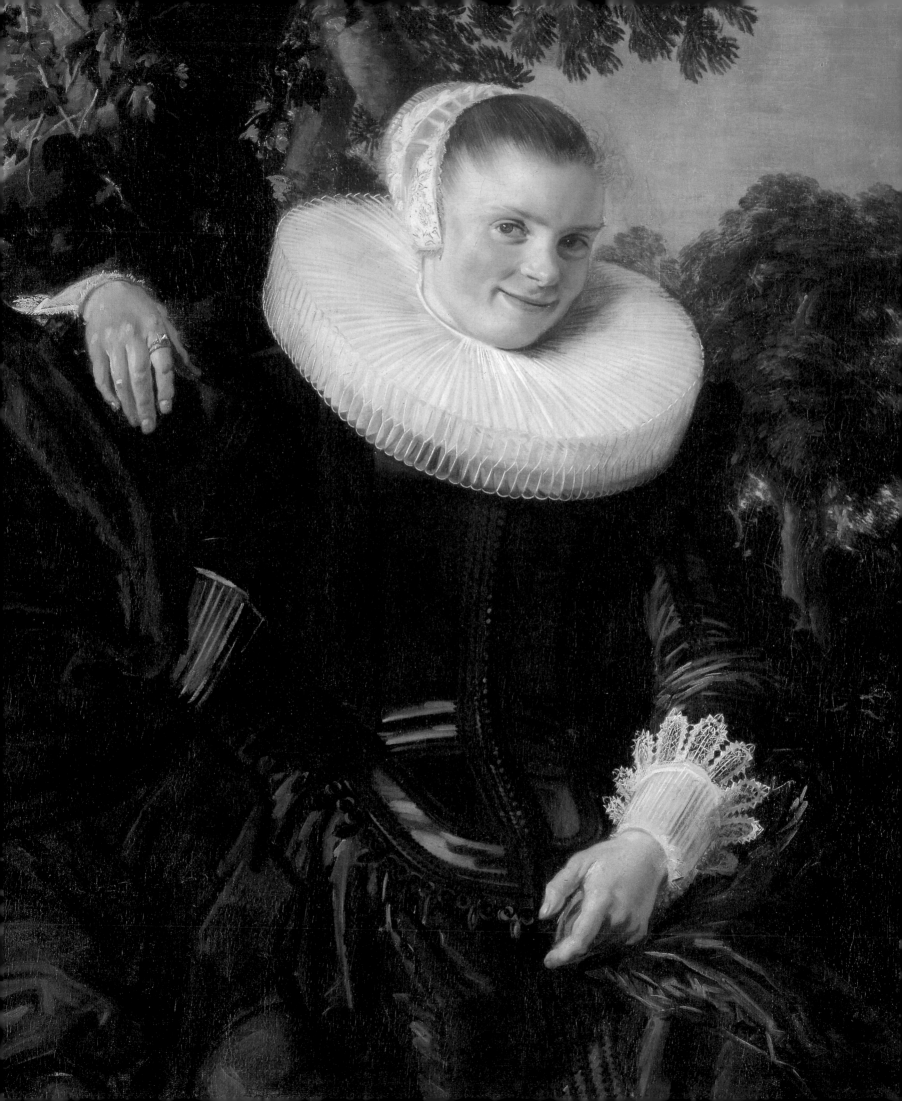

2 NEW FACES 1600-1640

Specialisation was the hallmark of Dutch painting in the Golden Age. Artists concentrated on a single genre and endeavoured to shine in that one field. There were, for example, painters who confined themselves almost exclusively to painting portraits. Their works are more than just a likeness; they also tell us something about the calling and the social status of their subjects. The sitters' dress, pose and attributes are a reflection of their wealth, profession and convictions. Although accuracy and a good likeness were paramount, portrait painters were nonetheless able to develop an individual style. Thomas de Keyser's portraits, for instance, are models of precision and refinement, while the spontaneity of the technique and the relaxed poses of their subjects make Frans Hals's paintings instantly recognisable.

UNWRITTEN RULES

Beatrix van der Laen's smile is a rare phenomenon. It was unusual for people in 17th-century Holland to allow themselves to be portrayed smiling. The smile was mistrusted, and often equated with foolishness. There was one recurring argument for this – that Christ, as far as we know, never smiled. This is why it is important, wrote a contemporary of Frans Hals, that man 'should suppress his mirth'.

Frans Hals was one of the few portrait painters who occasionally immortalised his patrons with a smile on their lips, and he frequently showed them in an informal pose. It was more usual for portrait painters to follow the unwritten rules that applied to portraiture. According to these 'rules', the sitters assumed a respectable pose and fixed their features in a solemn expression. The portrait had to present a flattering picture of the subject. There was, after all, a link between the way a person was portrayed and his conduct. This does not however mean that all Frans Hals's clients led frivolous lives. They, like virtually everyone whose portrait was painted in the 17th century, were serious, prominent citizens from the upper echelons of Dutch society. Hals probably depicted his sitters smiling because it made the work more lively.

PORTRAIT TYPES

A patron could choose from a wide variety of portraits. A great deal depended, of course, on the space and money available. For the most expensive category – a full-length, life-size portrait – the client needed not just money but a substantial wall on which to hang the work. Consequently, sitters often opted for smaller sizes or for head-and-shoulder portraits, with or without hands.

PATRONS

'Paintings hung everywhere: in the town hall, the civic-guard headquarters, orphanages and offices, in the drawing rooms of patricians' homes and in the best rooms of townspeople's houses; only not in the churches.' This was the sentence used by the historian Johan Huizinga (1872-1945) to characterise the artistic climate of the Northern Netherlands in the 17th century. During the Middle Ages many works of art had been made for churches and monasteries, but in the 17th century paintings were bought mainly by burghers seeking to decorate their own homes. Official commissions were bestowed by government institutions, guilds and other organisations, while the church practically ceased to be a patron of the arts. In Protestant churches austerity was of prime importance. The new elite, having grown rich through trade and industry, bought paintings on the free market and also extended commissions to artists. Self-assured Dutch burghers were having their portraits painted at a time when, in the rest of Europe, such activities were reserved for royalty and the nobility.

< DETAIL OF 13

There were specific portrait formulas: standard poses and standard settings. In large studios the master himself painted the face and hands, and the rest was done by his pupils. There were also set formats for group portraits, in which it was important for the artist not only to produce good individual portraits, but also to create a pleasing overall composition.

GOLDSMITH WITH RING

Bartholomeus Jansz van Assendelft (1585-1659) was a leading goldsmith in Leiden. He was also the assay-master of the guild of goldsmiths and silversmiths. Two elements in his portrait by the Amsterdam portrait painter Werner van den Valckert refer to his profession and his position in the guild. The ring illustrates Van Assendelft's profession, the stone on which his hand rests represents his post as assay-master. The stone is a 'touchstone', used by assayers to test the purity of gold or silver. To test the metal, the assayer would rub it on a hard black stone, such as jasper or basalt, and the precious metal content was then assessed from the colour of the streak left on the stone.

Van den Valckert's portrait of his client is a subtle one. He portrayed the face with meticulous care, whereas the bright white collar was painted with bravura. His rendering of the black garments captures the sheen and the weight that are the hallmark of costly fabrics. The sitter is enclosed by a stone window frame, which the artist placed at a slight angle to the picture plane. Van Assendelft bends forward slightly, his right hand extended outside the window, allowing the painter to suggest depth to great effect. Van Assendelft's left hand is brightly lit, drawing the viewer's attention to the touchstone. Here the painter was focusing attention both on the symbolic attribute of the goldsmith and on his own name. Van den Valckert signed the work: *W v Valckert fe 1617* – 'Werner van den Valckert made this in 1617' – on the black stone.

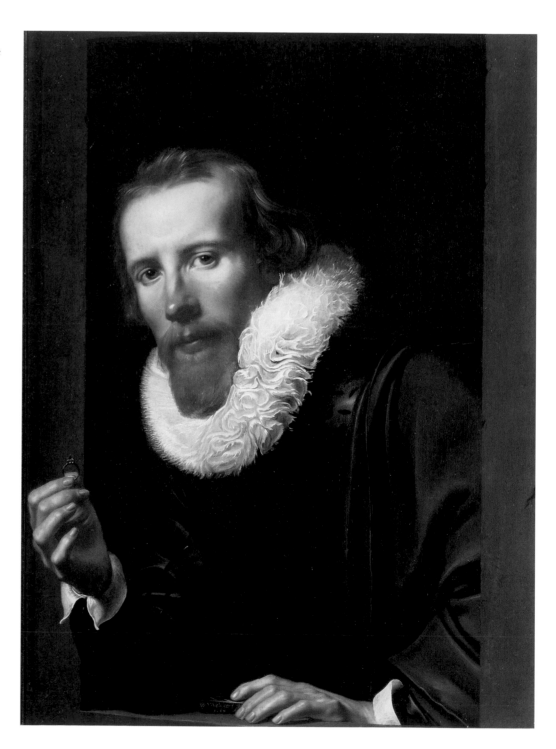

IO

WERNER VAN DEN VALCKERT

(c. 1585-1627/1628)

Portrait of a man with a ring, 1617

Panel 65 x 49.5 cm

AMSTERDAM, RIJKSMUSEUM

(acquired in 1957, see p. 316)

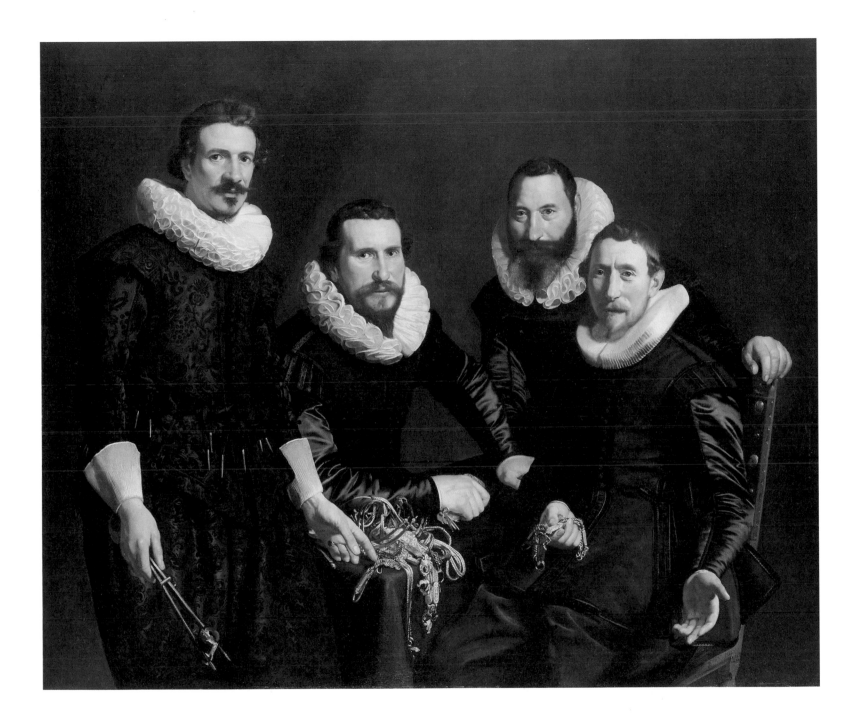

GROUP PORTRAIT

The profession of goldsmith is also central to the group portrait by the Amsterdam painter Thomas de Keyser. It portrays four senior officers – the syndics, or *hoofdmannen* – of the Amsterdam goldsmiths' guild. In 1627 these four gentlemen were responsible for overseeing the quality of the work produced by the goldsmiths. The craft was closely supervised, and the men entrusted with this responsibility pointedly display the attributes associated with their work, including ingeniously made objects and the rods of standard alloy used to determine the gold content. The man on the left, Loeff Vredericx, has assaying rods hanging from his coat and holds a pair of tongs with which he grasps two glowing coals. Held between these 'assaying coals' is a quantity of silver; after heating the sample, the silver

II

THOMAS DE KEYSER (1596/1597-1667)
The syndics of the Amsterdam goldsmiths' guild, 1627
Canvas 127.2 x 152.4 cm
TOLEDO (OHIO),
THE TOLEDO MUSEUM OF ART
(acquired in 1960, see p. 348)

content was established on the basis of the colour. Sitting next to Loeff Vredericx is Jacob le Mercier – with assaying rods in his hand – and on the right is Jacob Everts Wolff. The identity of the fourth man is not known.

De Keyser gave equal treatment to the four men portrayed here. Their faces are all lit to the same extent, and all four gentlemen are equidistant from, and look directly at, the viewer, so that each commands equal attention. The strong light, combined with De Keyser's precise technique, produces an effect that is very different from that of the portrait Van den Valckert painted of his Leiden goldsmith. De Keyser's syndics project a sternness in keeping with their position and with the place where this group portrait was to hang, probably in the goldsmiths' guildhall.

THOMAS DE KEYSER

Until Rembrandt's arrival in Amsterdam, Thomas de Keyser was the city's leading portrait painter. His elegant style and refined technique brought him numerous commissions. The painter was the son of Hendrick de Keyser, city architect and master sculptor of the city of Amsterdam (see chapter 1), and was himself skilled in these fields. He was also a stone merchant, and in 1662 he in turn was appointed city architect of Amsterdam. Thomas de Keyser nonetheless owes his fame to his painted portraits.

COMPANION PIECES

Thomas de Keyser painted these two portraits of a strikingly well-dressed lady and gentleman. It seems probable that they had these portraits painted on the occasion of their marriage – one clue is the pair of wedding gloves lying on the table beside the woman. We do not know who the couple are nor when their marriage took place. Information about their identity has been lost, and the couple are now 'separated': the painting of the man hangs in the Louvre in Paris; the portrait of the woman is in Berlin.

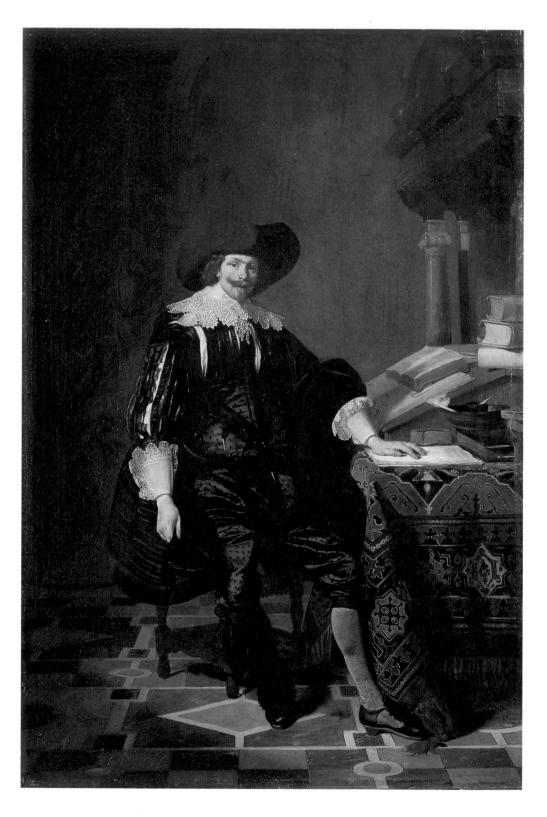

THOMAS DE KEYSER (1596/1597-1667), *Portrait of a gentleman*, c. 1632
Panel 79 x 53 cm. PARIS, MUSÉE DU LOUVRE

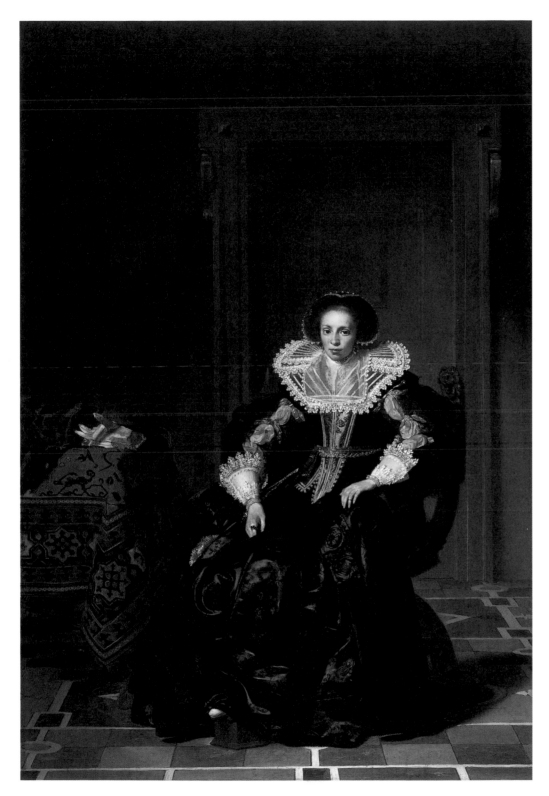

De Keyser painted these portraits according to the custom of the time, by which husband and wife were portrayed on separate canvases or panels. The paintings, known as pendants or companion pieces, hung next to each other, or perhaps on either side of a cupboard or table. The portrait of the man hung on the left, that of the woman on the right, so that they both looked towards the centre. In virtually all portraits made to this formula, the light comes from the left. The result is that the averted area of the man's face is in shadow, while the woman's face is turned to the light.

The clothes worn by the couple are remarkable for their sumptuousness. Whereas many Dutch burghers of the Golden Age dressed in plain, sober attire, these two chose to wear costly garments with a considerable degree of elegance. The sleeves of the man's satin coat are slashed, so that the light lining shows through the dark fabric. The woman wears a black silk dress. Here again, we can see the light fabric of the lining, in tufts separated by ribbons. The large, white translucent collar focuses attention on the face above it. The woman's dark hair, pinned up on her head, is set off against the dark background by the brightness of the string of pearls outlining the contours of her head. The pearls in her hair are not the woman's only jewellery. Around her waist she has a gold chain with an ostrich-feather fan suspended from it. She also wears several rings, the one on her right index finger probably being her wedding ring. In the 17th century it was customary to wear one's wedding band on this finger.

12

THOMAS DE KEYSER (1596/1597-1667)

Portrait of a lady, 1632

Panel 79 x 53 cm

BERLIN, GEMÄLDEGALERIE

(acquired in 1982, see p. 322)

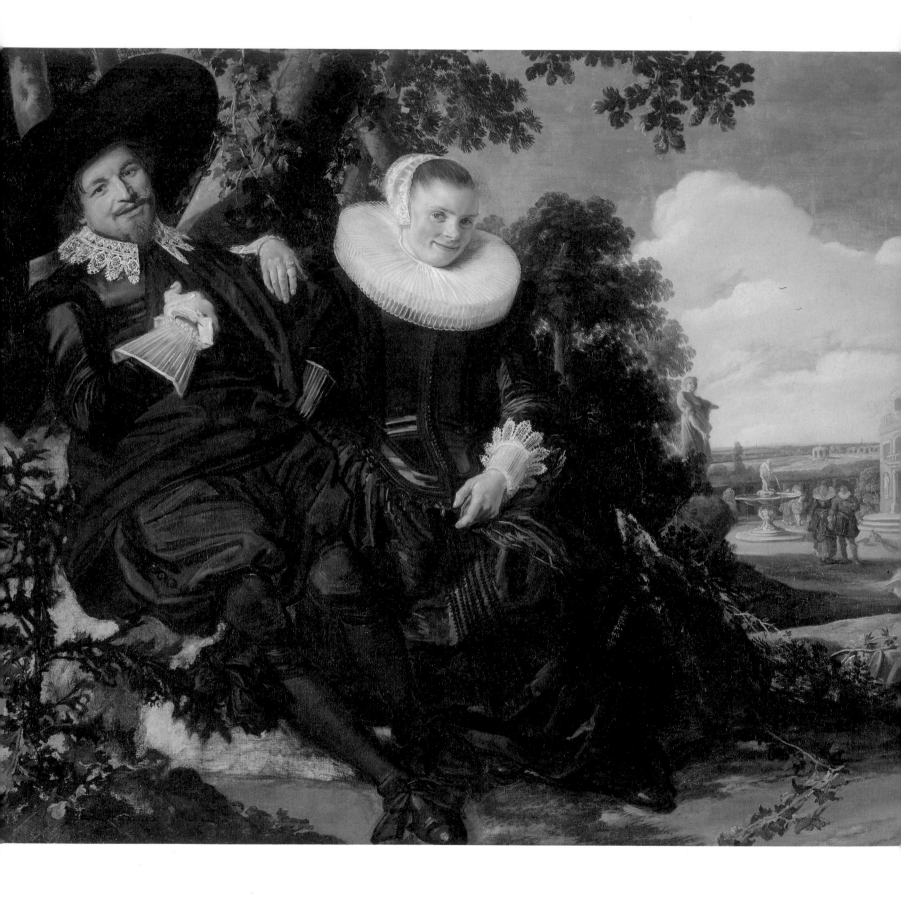

13

FRANS HALS (1582/1583-1666)
Marriage portrait of Isaac Massa and
Beatrix van der Laen, c. 1622
Canvas 140 x 166.5 cm
AMSTERDAM, RIJKSMUSEUM
(acquired in 1852, see p. 311)
<

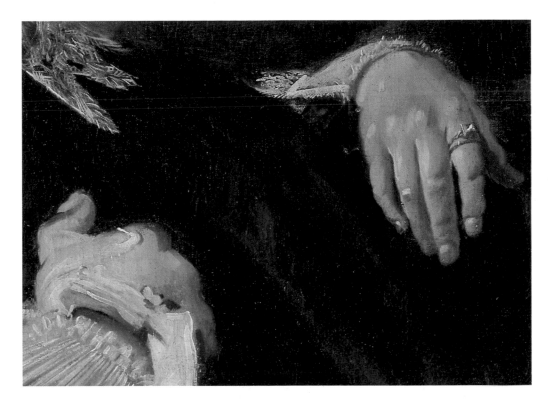

DETAIL OF 13

MASSA AND VAN DER LAEN

Two wealthy burghers of Haarlem, Isaac Massa and Beatrix van der Laen, had this portrait painted by Frans Hals on the occasion of their marriage. Isaac Abraham Massa (1586-1643) was a merchant who did a great deal of business with Russia, where he had been educated. He not only traded with Russia but also undertook diplomatic missions there for the States General. He was known as a cultured man and occupied a prominent position in the Haarlem community. On 26 April 1622, at the age of 35, he married 30-year-old Beatrix van der Laen, daughter of Gerard van der Laen, a former burgomaster. The couple belonged to the upper crust of Haarlem society.

Like no other painter of his age, Frans Hals succeeded in portraying his sitters in natural, relaxed poses. But even for Hals this portrait is exceptional. It is unusual for husband and wife to be portrayed together instead of in separate companion pieces, and also unusual for them to pose so casually, sitting by a tree in a garden. Perhaps the informality of this portrait had to do with the close ties between the artist and the sitters. Hals and Massa probably knew each other well; Isaac Massa was a witness at the baptism of one of Hals's children.

SYMBOLISM

Hals's portrait of the newly-married couple is more than two good likenesses: it also illustrates their love and the marriage vows they have exchanged, even though the symbolic language is not immediately recognisable. Comparison with 17th-century prints bearing accompanying poems or mottoes reveals that some details actually have a special significance. The bower in which Massa and Van der Laen sit looks natural enough, but in fact Frans Hals composed it of plants with hidden meanings.

The large thistle at the lower left, a spear thistle, would have been recognised by well-informed 17th-century viewers as an unmistakable symbol of fidelity. In the 17th century this plant was also known as 'man's faith' (*mannentrouw* or *Männertreu*). Here it symbolises Isaac's promise to be faithful to his wife. Beatrix has a similar symbol in the form of ivy lying near her feet: just as ivy clings to a house or a tree, so the young wife clings to her husband. The vine curling between the heads of Massa and Van der Laen, a symbol of love and friendship, again refers to the bonds between man and wife. Beneath the vine, the couple's hands are also significant. Massa lays his hand on his heart, still a gesture of fidelity today, and Van der Laen very deliberately displays the rings on her index finger, one of which is undoubtedly her wedding ring.

Next to the couple, as they sit surrounded by plants, Hals painted a view to a park-like landscape: a traditional garden of love, or pleasure-garden, which had been a recurring theme in literature and art since the Middle Ages. It contains various references to love, including peacocks – the attributes of Juno, the goddess of love – and a fountain symbolising fertility. The urns and the ruins probably refer to the transient nature of life and at the same time to the power of love, which transcends death.

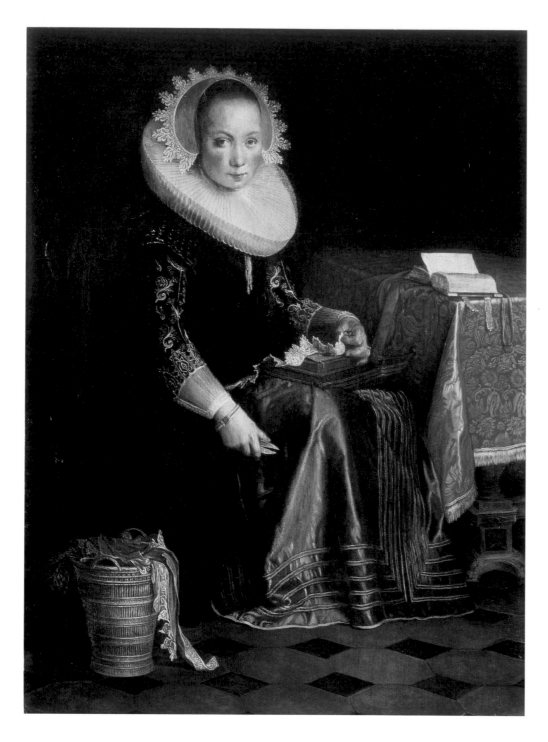

JOACHIM WTEWAEL (1566-1638), *Portrait of Eva Wtewael*, 1628
Panel 55 x 40.5 cm. UTRECHT, CENTRAAL MUSEUM

14
'Wtewael' cupboard, c. 1600-1625
Oak and ebony
255.5 x 214 x 82 cm
UTRECHT, CENTRAAL MUSEUM
(acquired in 1952, see p. 349)
>

remained in the family's possession for a long time after Wtewael's death.

In 1628 he painted his daughter Eva looking up from her lace-making. On the table before her lies an open prayer book. The girl was immortalised by her father as the model of a virtuous woman. Wtewael revealed little of the setting, but it appears that the portrait contains elements from his own home. The table, of which no more than part of a leg is visible, has survived and is now in the Centraal Museum in Utrecht, as is a cupboard that also came from the Wtewael family.

This cupboard has detailing similar to the table in the painting: both of their bases display the same ebony ornamentation. Given the impressive architectural proportions of the cupboard and the magnificently carved ebony, it would appear to be a showpiece from a town hall or the property of a royal personage. The fact that Wtewael could afford a piece of furniture of such outstanding quality was not the result of his career as an artist: he had made his fortune in the flax trade. He evidently devoted great care and attention to the furnishing of his house, which accords with his interest in the decorative arts.

JOACHIM WTEWAEL

The Utrecht painter Joachim Wtewael was a versatile artist. He painted religious and mythological scenes, genre pieces and portraits, and he also designed functional but beautiful objects. One of his designs for a salt-cellar is known, and he also designed a stained-glass window more than ten metres high for the Great Church in Gouda. For himself, he painted a series of portraits of members of his immediate family. These paintings were not intended for sale and

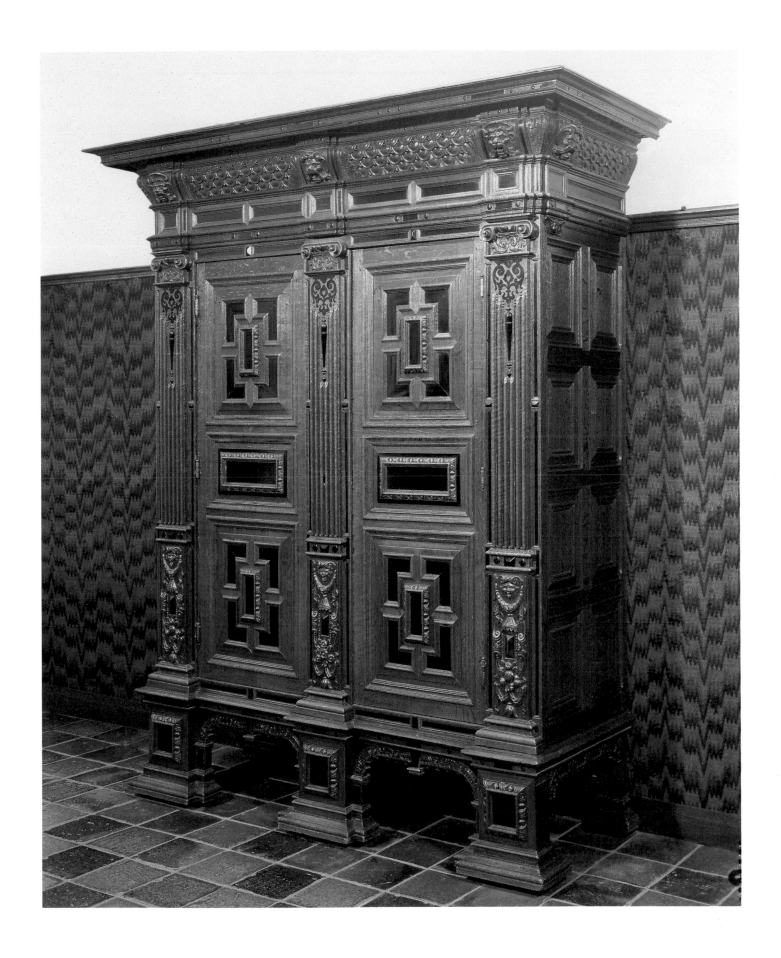

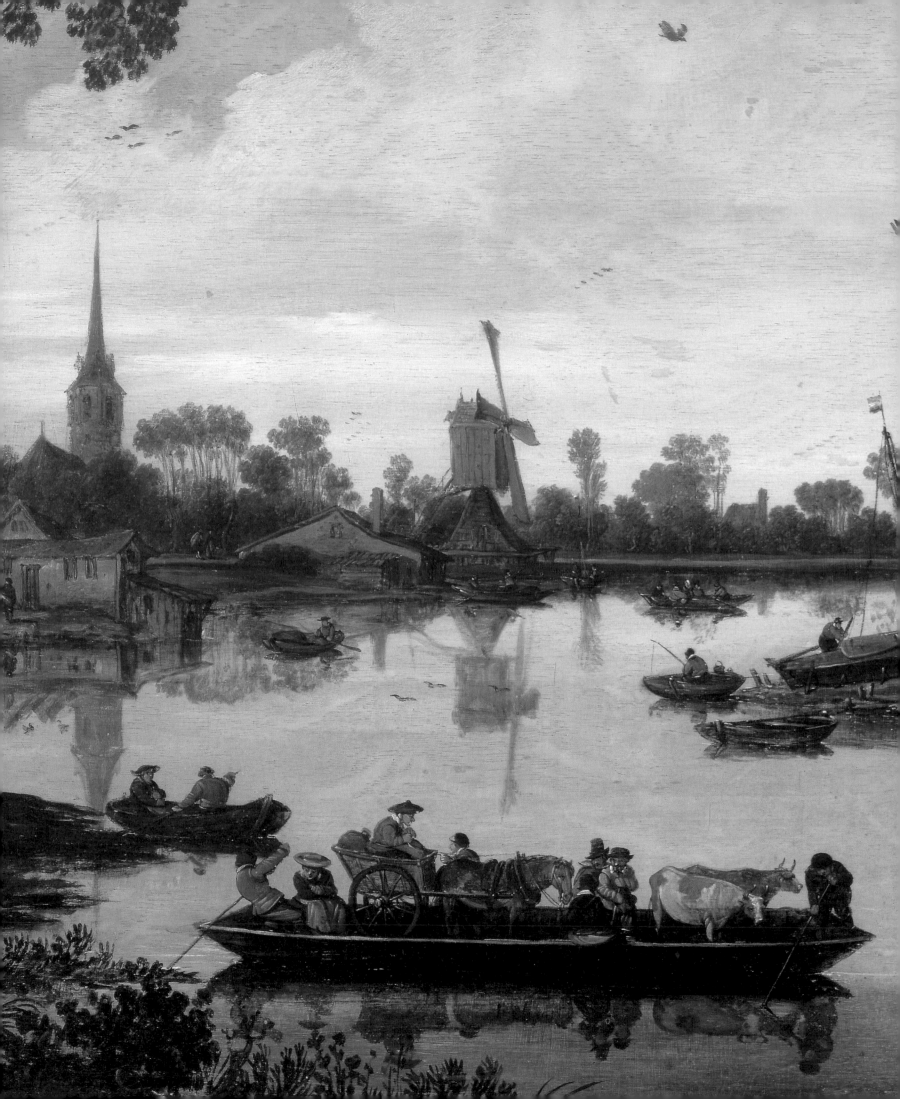

3 BLAZING A TRAIL 1610-1640

Dutch landscape painting underwent rapid development during the first three decades of the 17th century, at which time fantasised mountain landscapes made way for natural-looking Dutch landscapes. The roots of this development lay in Flanders, which had a long tradition of landscape painting, consisting mainly of fantasised landscapes which acted as a backdrop for biblical and mythological scenes. These colourful fantasy landscapes were usually rendered from a high vantage point.

In the larger Flemish workshops, backgrounds were usually executed by assistants who had specialised in the painting of landscapes. The emigration of such specialists from Flanders to the North at the end of the 16th century must have been an important stimulus to the development of landscape painting as an independent genre in Holland. Flemish prints depicting landscapes were another source of inspiration for Dutch artists. It appears that in Haarlem, which had a long tradition of printmaking and publishing, these prints found acceptance earlier than in other Dutch cities, and this perhaps led to the innovations in landscape painting which started in this city.

At the beginning of the 17th century, Dutch artists, following their Flemish colleagues, mainly painted fantasy landscapes, though they soon began to concentrate on the everyday Dutch landscape. The fact that this could become the main theme of a painting was perhaps due to an increasing awareness of nature. The landscape was admired as God's creation. Another factor in the young Dutch Republic may well have been a feeling of national pride, which led to appreciation of the beauty of one's own surroundings. The Dutch landscape painters concentrated on their immediate environment: the open fields, water, trees and woods, a village in the distance, windmills, and once in a while a person or animal.

In the 1630s the composition of the landscape changed radically: the sky now took up more space than the land, and the horizon lay beneath the middle of the painting. Painters generally started to distance themselves more and more from their Flemish example, and the Dutch landscape became more realistic in character.

No matter how true-to-life Dutch landscape paintings seem, they seldom depict an existing landscape. Although the painters based their works on observation and studies from nature, in fact they always composed the final landscape in the studio, on the basis of their sketches. There they created Dutch landscapes as they were meant to be: flat yet panoramic, with lovingly painted skies.

HAARLEM

In the early 17th century Haarlem was one of the largest cities in Holland. The Flemish immigrants who had settled there were an important stimulus, both economically and culturally. In 1634 the artists' guild had among its members 58 painters, 6 etchers, 7 glass-engravers and 6 sculptors. This flourishing of art and commerce caused Haarlem to be called the Florence of the North.

Haarlem artists were leading practitioners of the arts of painting and printmaking. They lay the foundations of the genre of landscape painting, which experienced a period of blossoming, owing in part to the influence of artists and printmakers who had flocked to the North from the Southern Netherlands. Inventories dating from that time show that many of the paintings and prints of panoramic landscapes with a profile of Haarlem on the horizon were made for local customers, whose patronage of the Haarlem painters perhaps expressed the pride they felt in their city and its surroundings.

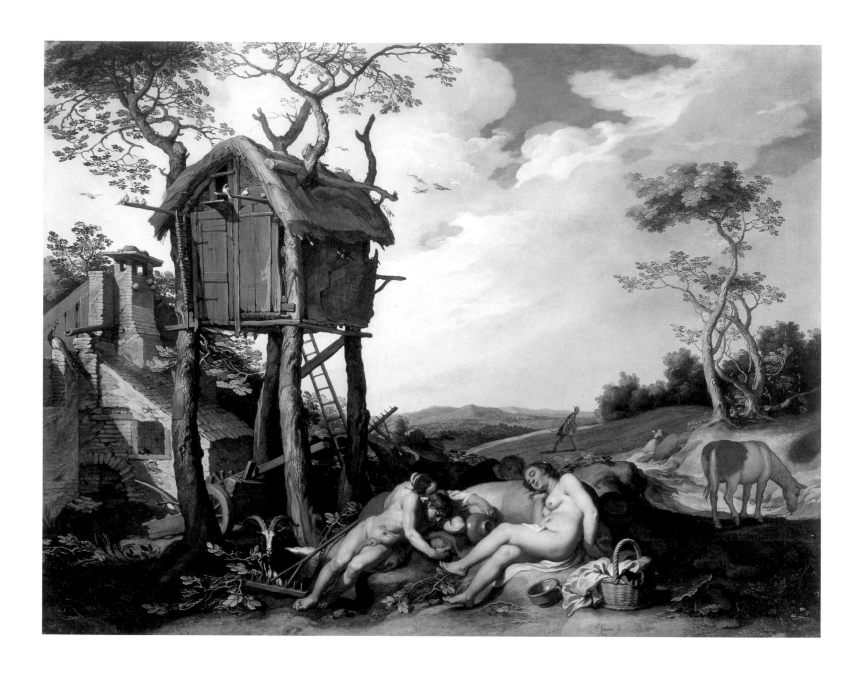

OLD-FASHIONED LANDSCAPE
In a hilly landscape a dovecote catches one's eye. Four sturdy trees – partly dead, partly green – form the supporting pillars of a hut which is inhabited by doves. Next to the dovecote is a ramshackle farmhouse and in the foreground lies a group of people fast asleep. The scene was painted by Abraham Bloemaert, an influential artist who lived and worked in Utrecht for most of his life. Bloemaert, who trained as many as a hundred apprentices over the course of his long career, painted genre pieces and mythologi-

cal and religious scenes, though he also influenced the development of landscape painting.

Nevertheless, the *Landscape with the parable of the tares among the wheat* is a rather old-fashioned painting. The landscape, which functions as a backdrop for the sleeping figures, is still reminiscent of the working method of the Flemish landscape painters who suggested depth by painting the foreground in shades of brown, the middle distance in green and the background in blue hues. The portrayal of a story in a

15

ABRAHAM BLOEMAERT (1566-1651)
Landscape with the parable of the tares among the wheat, 1624
Canvas 100.3 x 132.7 cm
BALTIMORE, THE WALTERS ART GALLERY
(acquired in 1973, see p. 322)

landscape was also somewhat antiquated at that time. Moreover, the Mannerist style in which Bloemaert rendered the nude figures was already out of fashion by 1624. Other elements of the painting, on the other hand, are completely in keeping with the artistic notions current at that time, such as the dovecote, which Bloemaert painted after a drawing made out of doors. This painting by Abraham Bloemaert typifies the transition from the mannered, narrative landscape paintings of the 16th century to the true-to-life observations of 17th-century landscape painters.

BIBLICAL STORY

Although the landscape is an important part of the depiction, it is not the main subject of the painting; it functions, rather, as the setting of a story. The key figure is the little man with horns and a tail, lurking in the background: the devil who sees his chance, now that the peasants are asleep, to sow tares among the wheat.

Portrayed here is a scene from the Bible in which Jesus tells the parable of the tares among the wheat. A farmer had sown good seed in his field, 'but while men slept, his enemy came and sowed tares among the wheat', to spoil the harvest (*Matthew* 13:25). Jesus then explained that the man who had sown the tares was the devil, and that he himself was the farmer who had sown the good seed, which was faith and trust in God.

In the continuation of the story Jesus refers explicitly to the Last Judgement. The farmer decided to let the wheat and the tares grow together, separating the tares from the wheat only after the harvest. The tares would then be burnt, and a similar fate was in store for the faithless. The wheat was carefully gathered together, just as believers would be gathered together in the kingdom of God.

The people in the foreground of Bloemaert's painting do not seem to be much bothered about this reference to the Last Judgement. Unaware of what is taking place in the field, they are sound asleep, whereas they should be working, or at least keeping an eye on things. The viewer is thus warned: an idle person is the devil's cushion. Two of the figures, moreover, are quite shamelessly naked, probably representing lust as well as indolence.

SHIPWRECK

Like Bloemaert's painting, the work of Adam Willaerts tells a story. His *Shipwreck off a rocky coast* shows an East Indiaman which has hit the rocks and three other ships doing battle with the elements. The protagonist here is overpowering nature herself.

In the 17th century quite a few outward-bound ships of the Dutch East India Company (VOC) and the Dutch West India Company (WIC) did in fact fail to return safely to their home ports. Even so, this painting does not reproduce reality. The sheer cliff with its dead fir trees, as well as the sea monster, are products of the artist's imagination. The waves, too, display a pattern which is not very natural-looking. In this respect the seascape with a shipwreck is still firmly anchored in the Flemish tradition, which is not surprising, as Adam Willaerts was born in Antwerp and fled the city when the Spanish seized power in 1585. After a stay in London he settled in Utrecht around 1602.

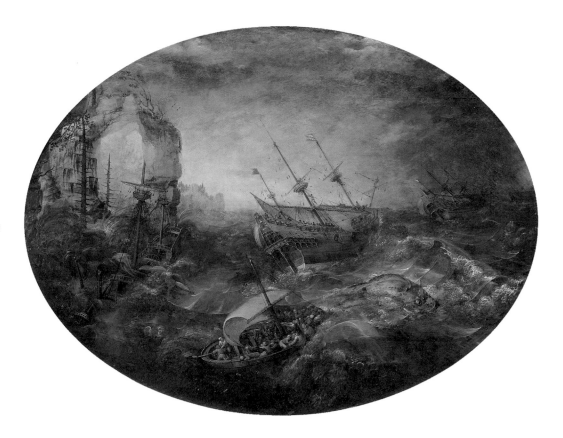

16

ADAM WILLAERTS (1577-1664)
Shipwreck off a rocky coast, 1614
Panel (oval) 65 x 86.5 cm
AMSTERDAM, RIJKSMUSEUM
(acquired in 1901, see p. 314)

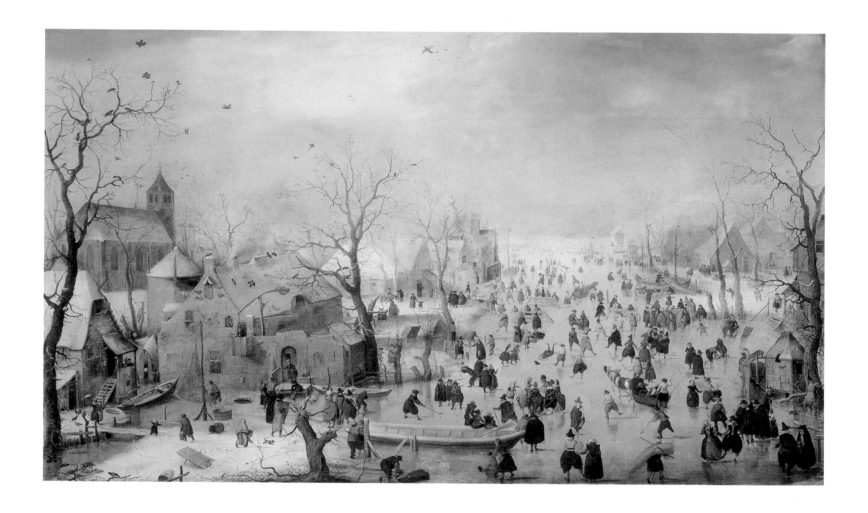

17

HENDRICK AVERCAMP (1585-1634)
Winter landscape with skaters, c. 1609
Panel 77.5 x 132 cm
AMSTERDAM, RIJKSMUSEUM
(acquired with the aid of the Rembrandt
Society in 1897, see p. 313)

WINTER LANDSCAPE

Hendrick Avercamp was one of the first
Dutch artists to specialise in faithful renderings of the landscape. He drew studies from
nature and used them as examples for his
paintings, enabling him to paint winter
landscapes 'from life', even in the summer.
These small winter landscapes, *wintertjes* as
they were called in 17th-century Holland,
were Avercamp's speciality. Like the paintings by Bloemaert and Willaerts, this work

dating from around 1609 derives from
Flemish examples.

The Flemish influence can be seen in the
composition's high horizon, in the palette
and especially in the narrative manner of
painting. By placing the horizon above the
middle of the panel, Avercamp left himself a
lot of room to show what was happening on
the ice. Most of the people are having a good
time skating and sleigh-riding. Avercamp
depicted every facet of skating: tying on the
skates, gliding over the ice, falling down and
scrambling to one's feet. Everyday activities
are also taking place. A man in the foreground carries a bundle of freshly cut reeds,
and at the left someone lugs two heavy
buckets. Near the inn – which displays the
coat of arms of Antwerp – a hole has been
cut in the ice and water is being hauled out
of it. The haystack serves as a love nest, and

a peasant answers nature's call in an old,
upturned boat. The picture is teeming with
anecdotal detail; Avercamp shows himself to
be a born storyteller.

MIDDELBURG

Attention to detail and a penchant for
anecdote is also Adriaen van de Venne's
strength. In *The departure of a dignitary
from Middelburg* [18] he cleverly combined
a townscape, a view of a canal with boats,
a crowd of people and a historical event.
Unfortunately, the identity of this dignitary
is not known. Until lately the painting was
thought to portray the English governor
Robert Sidney leaving Middelburg in 1616.
During recent cleaning of the panel, however, the date proved to be 1615, which
means that this cannot be a depiction of
Sidney's departure.

The ship in the centre of the painting is the warship *De Zeehondt* (The Seal), flying the flags of both Zeeland and Middelburg from the mast-head. Because the wind is blowing straight towards the canal, the ship must be drawn by horses to the pier, a trip of some three kilometres. Behind the horses pulling the ship ride the protagonists. At the head of the harbour the dignitary will board the ship, but in the meantime he is being seen off by a large group of people. In the foreground, in the water, we see four gentlemen on horseback, who are also part of the escort. One of these gentleman – the one on the horse third from the left – is the painter himself.

The ship on the left is Prince Maurits's yacht, recognisable by the flag with the prince's coat of arms on the bowsprit and the flag of the House of Orange flying from the stern. A salute is fired from the ship and

a flourish of trumpets rings out. Alongside all the hustle and bustle of departure, life goes on as usual. On the right the washing is laid out to bleach in the field, cows graze in the meadow and boys use poles to swing themselves over a ditch.

Depicted in the background is the profile of the city of Middelburg in the province of Zeeland. The tall tower in the middle is the *Lange Jan* of the Choir Church; the broader, shorter one to the left is the tower of the town hall. Both clocks point to two o'clock; the departure takes place in the afternoon.

In 1615 Middelburg was one of the most powerful cities in the Dutch Republic. Trade and shipping ensured it of a booming economy. It seemed to be an attractive spot for the Flemings who migrated northwards after the fall of Antwerp, but Middelburg had too little to offer painters and failed to develop into an artistic centre. Most of the artists

who tried to settle there moved on after a couple of years, and this is also what happened to Adriaen van der Venne, whose parents were of Flemish origin. He lived in Middelburg from 1614 to 1625, afterwards settling in The Hague. Van der Venne specialised in landscapes teeming with people, in which historical events are often portrayed.

18

Adriaen van de Venne (1589-1662)
The departure of a dignitary from Middelburg, 1615
Panel 64 x 134 cm
Amsterdam, Rijksmuseum
(acquired in 1898, see p. 313)

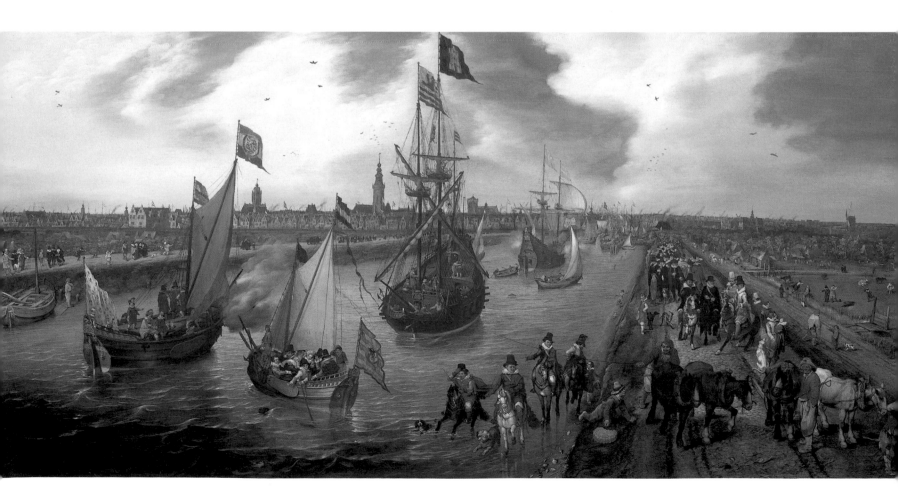

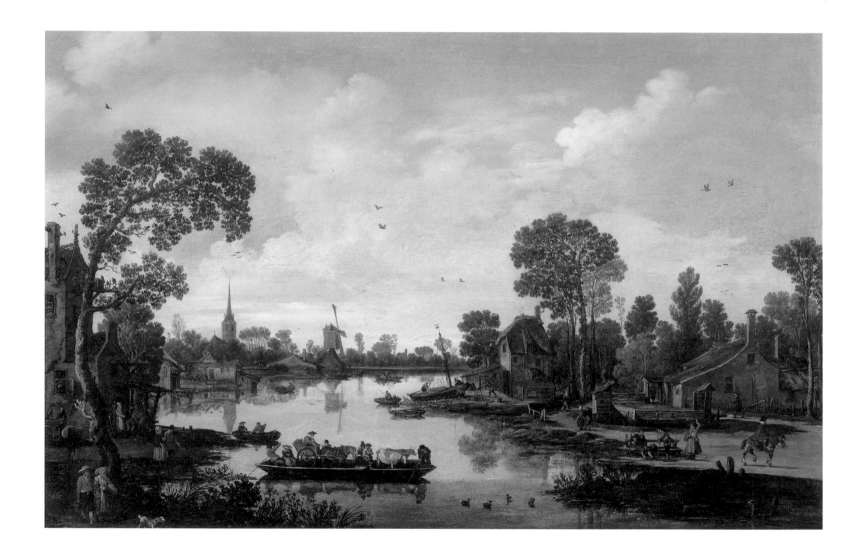

19

ESAIAS VAN DE VELDE (1587-1630)
The ferryboat, 1622
Panel 75.5 x 113 cm
AMSTERDAM, RIJKSMUSEUM
(acquired in 1885, see p. 311)

THE FERRYBOAT

An atmosphere of calm is radiated by *The ferryboat* by Esaias van de Velde. No story or historical event is portrayed. The main role has been reserved for the landscape, in which people and animals play minor roles. This is the first instance of the depiction of a typical Dutch river landscape in large format, making this painting one of the first high points in Dutch landscape painting.

A fully laden ferryboat crosses the river. The next passengers wait on the landing-stage at the right. A sailing boat is being repaired at a dock. In spite of the activity in and around the water, everything seems to happen in an atmosphere of peace and quiet. The viewer's gaze is led zigzag across the water – past a boat, ducks, a reflection in the water. In this way the painter linked the two shores, lending unity to his composition. The strip of shadow in the foreground is striking: together with the ferry and the large tree on the left, it intensifies the illusion of depth. The trees seem slightly artificial. The leaves, each of which was painted according to a fixed pattern, form decorative fans that stand out against the sky.

ESAIAS VAN DE VELDE

Esaias van de Velde played an important role in the development of Dutch landscape painting at the beginning of the 17th century. The sketches he made out of doors bespeak his original vision. He later incorporated the themes and details of these small drawings into his etchings and paintings. Van de Velde was living in The Hague when he made this painting. His parents were immigrants from Antwerp who had settled in Amsterdam, where Esaias was born in 1587. In 1609 the family moved to Haarlem. His stay in that city, which was at the forefront of developments in landscape painting, must have been important for Van de Velde's artistic growth. In 1618 Esaias van de Velde moved to The Hague, where he painted not only typical

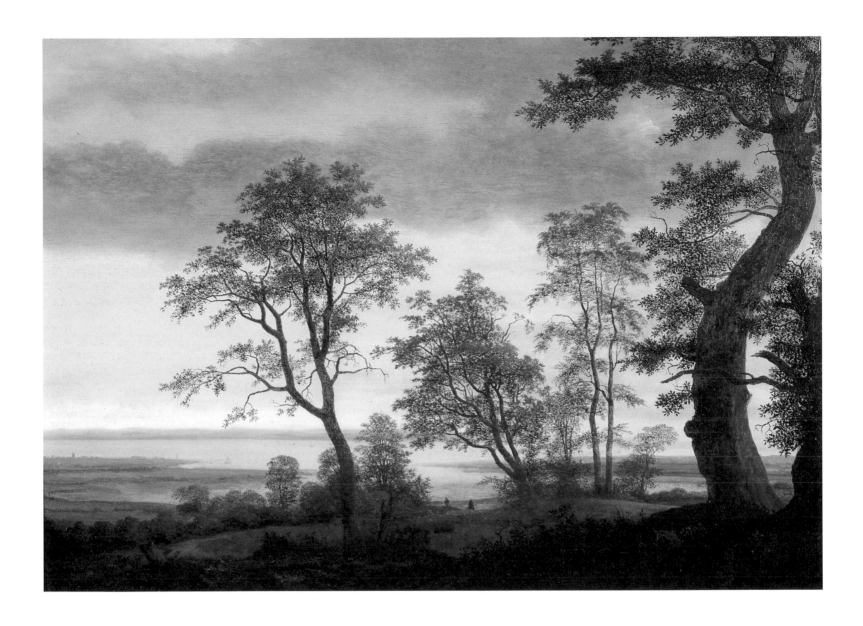

Dutch landscapes but also mountain land-scapes featuring groups of robbers and bandits. His painting of *The ferryboat* set the tone for a long tradition in the portrayal of Dutch river landscapes. His pupil Jan van Goyen, together with Salomon van Ruysdael, would develop this genre further and make repeated use of the ferryboat motif.

CORNELIS VROOM

Around 1638 Cornelis Vroom painted the *Landscape with estuary*, an atmospheric landscape whose poetic qualities ensure it a place of its own among the work of other

landscape painters. From a hill one sees a river delta that takes up the entire breadth of the panel. The depiction is dominated by gigantic trees, whose branches and leaves have the gossamer-thin quality of fine lace. Vroom's brush produced a whole range of greenery, from small, young trees to an old, bent oak on the right, part of which he left out of the picture. The foreground, the land, and the tree are dark, creating a feeling of distance between them and the lighter land and river in the background, which gradu-ally fade into the hazy sky.

Cornelis Vroom was the son of Hendrick Vroom, the Haarlem painter of seascapes,

20
CORNELIS VROOM (1591/1592-1661)
Landscape with estuary, c. 1638
Panel 50 x 67.3 cm
PRIVATE COLLECTION, ON LOAN TO
THE FRANS HALSMUSEUM, HAARLEM
(see p. 333)

who undoubtedly taught him the rudiments of painting. His first works were naval bat-tles, but around 1620 Cornelis began to con-centrate exclusively on painting landscapes.

JAN VAN GOYEN

Jan van Goyen, a pupil of Esaias van de Velde in Haarlem, was a very productive painter: 1200 landscape paintings are still known by his hand. His most important subjects were the Dutch dunes, polders and rivers. Van Goyen made a lot of drawings out of doors which served as examples for his paintings. His early works are often quite colourful, with figures that function as narrative elements. At that time he was still much influenced by his teacher, Esaias van de Velde. Around 1625 his work began to acquire a face of its own. His colours became less loud and his compositions simpler. Jan van Goyen, together with Salomon van Ruysdael, would further develop and perfect this new manner of painting, which was characterised by the use of a few shades of grey and green, as well as ochre and brown tones. These two artists thus became the masters of the so-called tonal landscape.

21

JAN VAN GOYEN (1596-1656)
Dune landscape, 1631
Panel 39.5 x 62.7 cm
BRAUNSCHWEIG,
HERZOG ANTON ULRICH-MUSEUM
(acquired in 1738, see p. 323)

DUNE LANDSCAPE

The subject is quite simple: in a dune landscape a goatherd tends his flock. A man hangs over the fence, looking at the goats. Further back four men converse and on the right, at the top of the dune, there are three people and a dog. Van Goyen demonstrated with this painting how much he had distanced himself from his teacher, Van de Velde. The latter's *Ferryboat*, with its multiplicity of small, restrained actions, displays a sampling of possibilities, but Van Goyen's *Dune landscape* presents a much more plausible picture of a Dutch landscape. More so than his teacher, Van Goyen preferred simplicity: simplicity of subject, palette and composition. His landscape is built of gradations of colour that differ little from one another. Here and there between the grey clouds a bit of blue-grey is visible, and sunny yellow accents shine through the grey-green landscape. The painting is given a feeling of depth by the diagonal composition, a method as simple as it is effective.

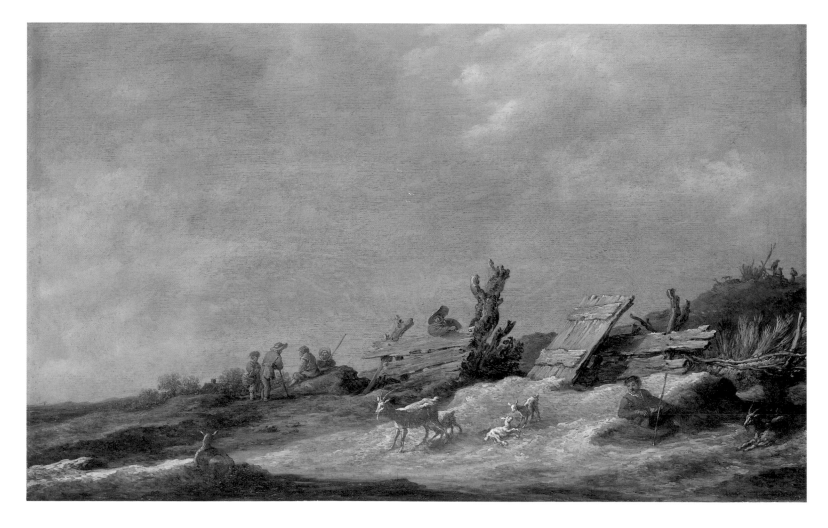

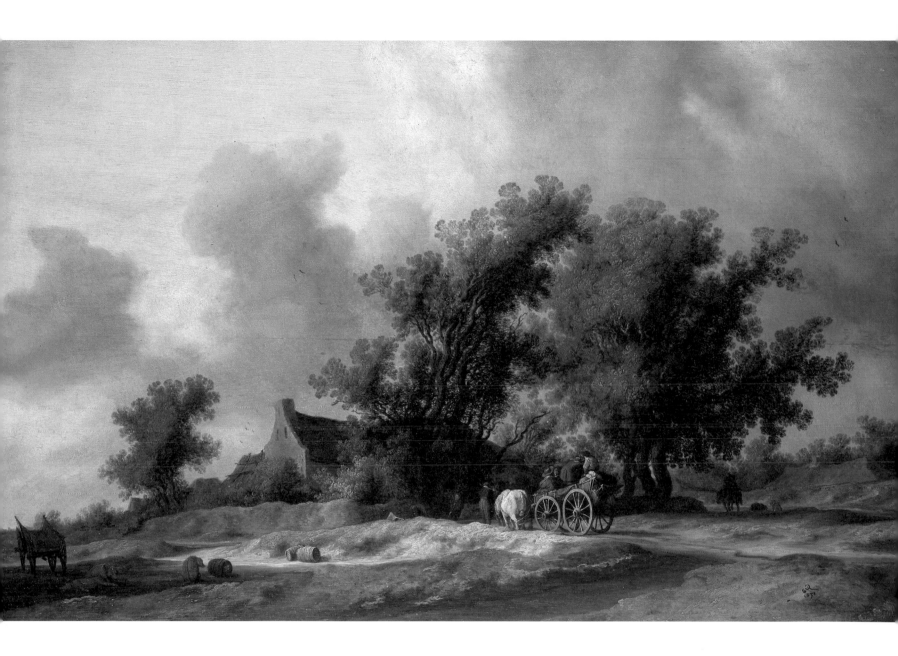

SALOMON VAN RUYSDAEL

Just as Jan van Goyen placed a goat at the left on a hill in the shade, Salomon van Ruysdael did the same with three pigs and a cart, which he placed in the shadows in the foreground, serving to create a feeling of distance between the foreground and the background. Ruysdael also adopted the formula of the diagonal composition to suggest depth. The eye naturally follows the road taken by the horse and coach, which have stopped at the farmhouse. Like Van Goyen, Ruysdael used here only a few shades of

grey-green and yellow-brown, his main concern being the atmosphere exuded by the painting. Depicted here is the moment just after a rain-shower: pigs wallow in the mud, the road looks wet and at the right the rain clouds have started to move off.

Salomon van Ruysdael, the uncle of the more famous Jacob van Ruisdael, was born in Naarden around 1600. In 1623 he became a member of the painters' guild – the Guild of St Luke – in Haarlem, the city where he would spend the rest of his life. Although it is not known who his teacher

22
SALOMON VAN RUYSDAEL
(1600/1603-1670)
Road in the dunes with a
passenger coach, 1631
Panel 56 x 86.4 cm
BUDAPEST, SZÉPMÜVÉSZETI MÚZEUM
(acquired in 1870, see p. 324)

was, his early work is strongly reminiscent of that of Esaias van de Velde.

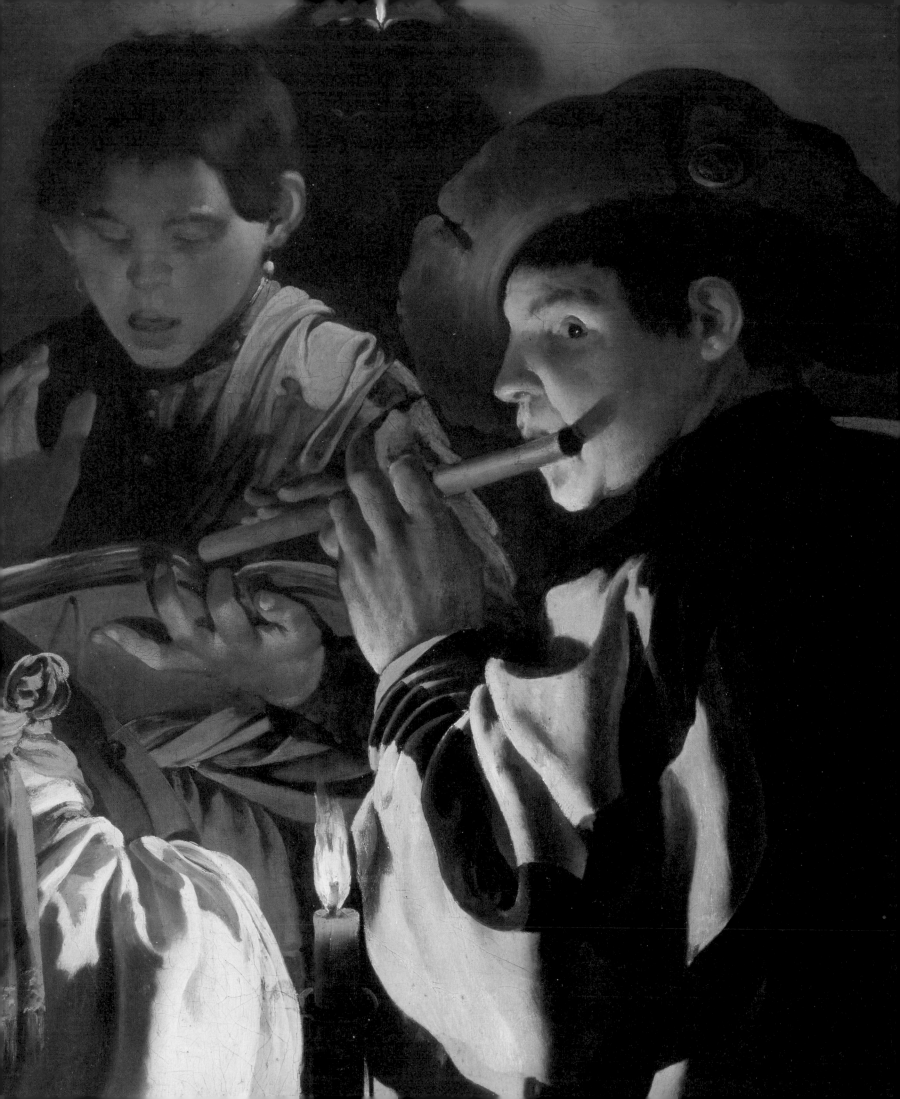

4 LIGHT AND SHADOW 1620-1640

Around 1610 a group of young painters left Utrecht and set out for Rome. They were Hendrick ter Brugghen, Gerard van Honthorst and Dirck van Baburen. At the start of their careers, artists traditionally journeyed to Rome to study classical antiquity and the art of the Renaissance. Few artists, however, were so strongly affected by their foreign travels as these three young men from Utrecht, who were not only inspired by the old art but also by the paintings of Michelangelo Merisi da Caravaggio (1573-1610). Caravaggio's idiosyncratic style must have made a tremendous impression on the travellers: they were so influenced by his work that they came to be known as the 'Caravaggisti'.

CARAVAGGIO

The contrast between light and dark – chiaroscuro – could scarcely be greater than in the detail of the flute player in Hendrick ter Brugghen's painting of *The concert*. The light of a candle illuminates the flute player's face from beneath, creating a vibrant and dramatic effect. The painting bears unmistakable witness to the influence of Caravaggio.

This Italian artist was the most talked-about painter of his day. He mainly painted religious works and his uncompromising, naturalistic style provoked fierce reactions. Contemporaries were both shocked and impressed. Caravaggio depicted saints as ordinary mortals – people who seemed to

have stepped straight out of everyday life. His compositions were daring, with figures filling the entire canvas, and his colours were rich and shimmering. His pictures had a dramatic impact, owing to his spectacular lighting effects and strong chiaroscuro.

It is these elements that the Utrecht Caravaggisti adopted in their own work, and they in their turn influenced other Dutch painters. While it is true that the work of Frans Hals, Judith Leyster and Rembrandt bears no direct relation to that of Caravaggio, their work would have been inconceivable without the influence of the Italian master.

UTRECHT

In the Middle Ages the city of Utrecht, seat of an archbishopric, was the religious centre of the Northern Netherlands. After the Reformation episcopal power admittedly waned, though Catholicism continued to play a major role in Utrecht: some 35 percent of the population remained true to the Catholic faith. The continued existence of Catholicism in Utrecht found expression in paintings with religious themes and was also reflected in the strong ties many Utrecht artists had with Italy. Various painters spent a significant part of their lives in Rome. The ideas they brought back with them to Utrecht were largely inspired by the work of the Italian artist Caravaggio. These 'Caravaggisti' transformed Utrecht into an artistic centre of international importance. The favourable cultural climate was not limited to the visual arts, but also manifested itself in the field of scholarship with the founding of the university of Utrecht in 1636.

< DETAIL OF 24

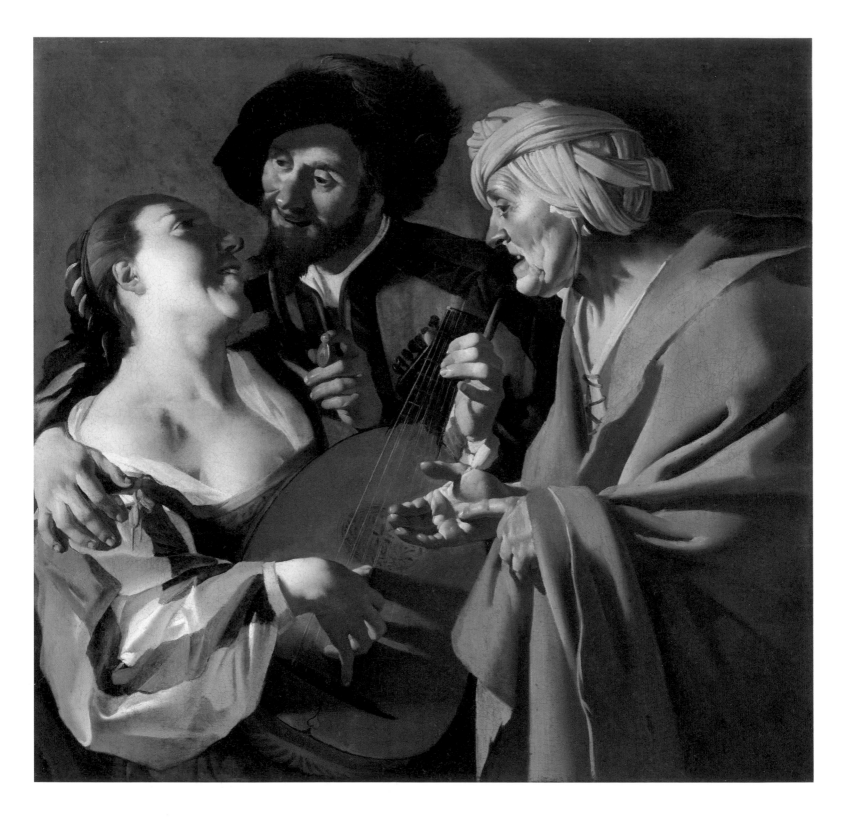

23

DIRCK VAN BABUREN (c. 1595-1624)

The procuress, 1622

Canvas 101.5 x 107.6 cm

BOSTON, MUSEUM OF FINE ARTS

(acquired in 1950, see p. 323)

THE PROCURESS

Three life-size figures fill the canvas in Dirck van Baburen's *The procuress*. In fact they do not quite fit into the picture plane and impinge on the viewer's space. Anyone looking at the picture automatically becomes a player in the scene. The striking light coming from the left creates a great contrast between light and shade and, like the Italian costumes, is unmistakable evidence of Caravaggio's influence.

The style and composition of *The procuress* are highly reminiscent of the bold work of Van Baburen's Italian colleague, but the subject chosen by Van Baburen was one that was particularly popular in Dutch art: love for sale. A young woman plays the lute, her gaze melting into that of the man who draws her to him. He holds up a coin in his left hand, showing that he is willing to pay for her favours. The third figure, an old woman wearing a turban, points emphatically at her hand and appears to conduct the negotiations. She is the procuress: with her coarse, wrinkled face and sunken mouth, she was rendered almost as a caricature by Van Baburen. Like Caravaggio, Van Baburen made a great distinction between the skin colour of the different characters, which is how he emphasised the coarseness of the procuress, whose weatherbeaten skin, like that of the man, is in stark contrast to the pallor of the young woman's exposed shoulder and breast. Caravaggio had also used this sort of exaggerated realism and had provoked a storm of adverse reactions, especially because he painted saints and martyrs in this way. This impertinent style was however ideal for a brazen subject like Van Baburen's *Procuress*.

VAN BABUREN AND VERMEER

Van Baburen's painting was probably in the possession of the much more famous 17th-century artist Johannes Vermeer, sometimes known as 'Jan' (see chapter 17). Archival records reveal that Vermeer's mother-in-law once owned the painting – or a copy of it.

Van Baburen's *Procuress* appears in two of Vermeer's paintings. The 'procuress pointing to her hand', as the painting was described at that time, forms the background for serene figures in Vermeer's works. In both of the paintings in question, the Delft master portrayed a woman playing a musical instrument in a luxurious interior. The young woman at the virginal looks directly and without doubt seductively at the viewer. The presence of Van Baburen's painting of the procuress suggests that Vermeer's painting is dedicated to love. Van Baburen's *Procuress* represents illicit lust and would thus be the negative counterpart of the virginal and the bass viol, instruments that appear as symbols of edifying love and harmony in 17th-century literature.

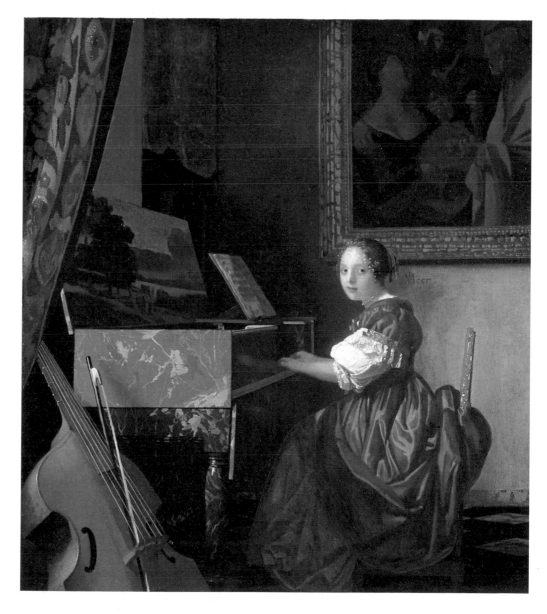

JOHANNES VERMEER (1632-1675), *Woman seated at a virginal*, c. 1674-1675
Canvas 51.5 x 45.5 cm. LONDON, NATIONAL GALLERY

49

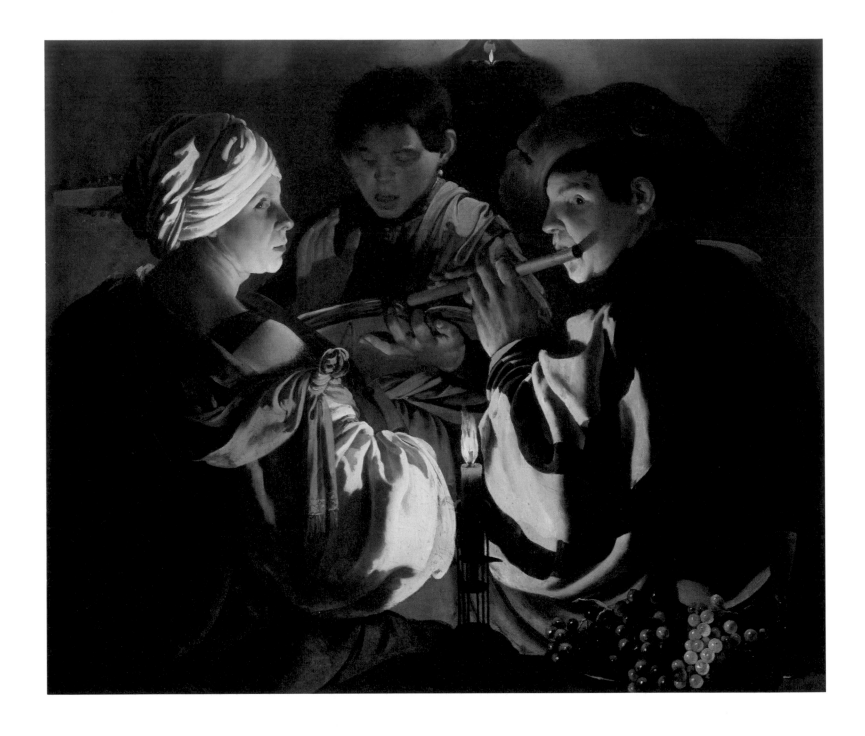

24

HENDRICK TER BRUGGHEN (1588-1629)

The concert, c. 1626-1627

Canvas 99.1 x 116.8 cm

LONDON, NATIONAL GALLERY

(acquired in 1983, see p. 337)

THE CONCERT

The composition of Hendrick ter Brugghen's *Concert* is very like that of *The procuress*: two figures in the foreground and one in the background fill the whole canvas. The clothes worn by the figures are also similar. The Utrecht Caravaggisti borrowed the theme of a company making music from their Roman source of inspiration, but they

then took it further and developed it into their own speciality.

Despite the similarities in composition, the mood generated in the two paintings by the Utrecht artists is very different, the main reason being Ter Brugghen's choice of illumination. A candle in the foreground lights up the trio from below, and another, smaller one above their heads creates a subtle glow in the background. The flame of the large candle is in the centre of the composition and lights the underside of the singer's left hand and part of his right hand, but above all, it illuminates the sleeves of the musicians in the foreground. The backs of the flautist and the lute player are unlit, reinforcing the contrast between light and dark.

THE YOUNG FLUTE PLAYER

The young flute player was one of the first works attributed to Judith Leyster; seldom has the theme been treated with such simplicity and subtlety.

Bright daylight, apparently entering through a high window, illuminates the right side of the boy's face. It falls on the flaking plaster of the wall and provides a strong contrast between the background and the boy's cap. The play of light and shadow on the young musician's left hand makes it seem as though his fingers are actually moving. We do not know whether Leyster knew the artists of the Utrecht school personally and was influenced by Caravaggism in this way. She may well have encountered the Utrecht style of painting through contacts with fellow artists in Haarlem, several of whom experimented with the effects of candlelight. The genre pieces by one of the most famous Haarlem painters, Frans Hals, also betray the influence of Utrecht in their handling of light and, above all, in their choice of subject matter.

JUDITH LEYSTER

Judith Leyster was one of the few women artists in 17th-century Holland. Most women who chose to become artists came from an artist's family, but Leyster learned the profession in the usual way, by studying under a master from the age of 11. Judith's parents lived for some time in Vreeland, a village not far from Utrecht. It is not known whether Judith herself ever lived there, since her name does not appear in the records until 1633. In that year she enrolled in the Haarlem Guild of St Luke, and this enabled her to set up as an independent painter and to take pupils. There are signed and dated works by Leyster from as early as 1629. Because she was not registered with the guild at that time, she must have sold them under the protection of a master, possibly through Frans Hals's workshop. In 1636 Leyster married the Haarlem painter Jan Miense Molenaer [*see 38*], after which she presumably stopped working as an independent artist.

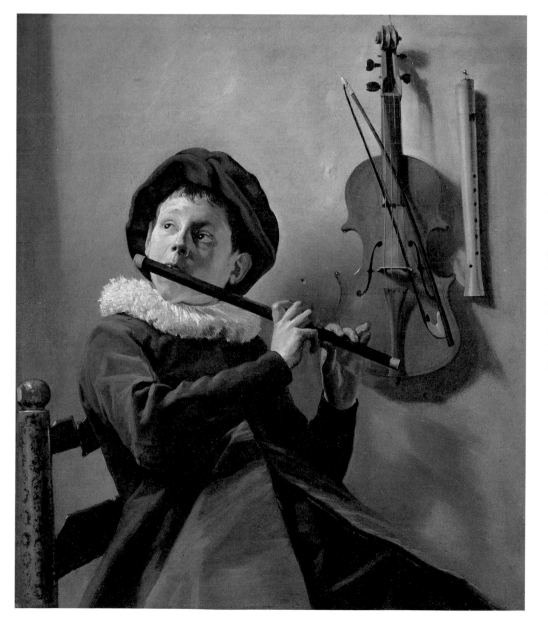

25

JUDITH LEYSTER (1609-1660)
The young flute player, c. 1635
Canvas 73 x 62 cm
STOCKHOLM, NATIONALMUSEUM
(acquired in 1871, see p. 347)

THE MERRY FIDDLER

Gerard van Honthorst worked in Rome for about ten years, between 1610 and 1620, and had a good name there. He lived for a while in the palace belonging to one of his patrons, the Marchese Giustiniani, who owned an impressive art collection that included paintings by Titian, Raphael, Carracci, Caravaggio and others. Like Ter Brugghen and Van Baburen, Honthorst was strongly influenced by Caravaggio's work during his stay in Rome. He took it to such an extreme that he elevated painting with strong chiaroscuro to a separate genre and devoted himself exclusively to painting nocturnal pieces. These scenes, lit only by a candle, earned him the nickname 'Gherardo della Notte' – Gerard of the Night. Back in Utrecht, Honthorst branched out into subjects he had not painted in Rome. Religious paintings had accounted for a significant proportion of his work in Italy, but in Utrecht he painted numerous portraits and genre pieces.

The Utrecht artists had great success with their compositions containing a single, half-length figure. In many cases the figure holds a musical instrument and sometimes, as in Honthorst's painting of the fiddler, a glass as well. Caravaggio's influence is evident in these paintings – in their realism, the handling of light and the positioning of a half-length figure at an angle in the picture plane. Honthorst and his colleagues developed the genre of the half-length figure still further, however, and created in their paintings a much stronger illusion of three-dimensionality. Honthorst's depiction of *The merry fiddler* is a good example: the man leans forward rather theatrically out of a window that is covered by an oriental hanging. By painting the hanging partly behind the musician's head, Honthorst achieved a greater sense of depth, which is further amplified by the heavy shadow on the curtain caused by the light coming from the left.

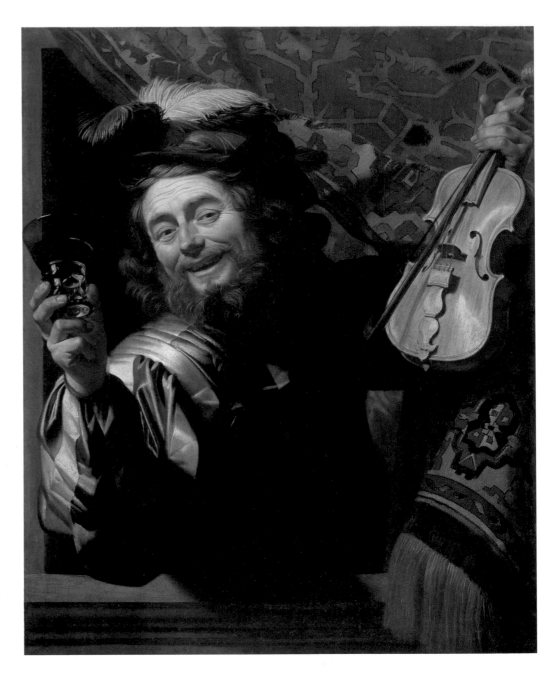

26

GERARD VAN HONTHORST (1592-1656)
The merry fiddler, 1623
Canvas 108 x 89 cm
AMSTERDAM, RIJKSMUSEUM
(acquired in 1824, see p. 310)

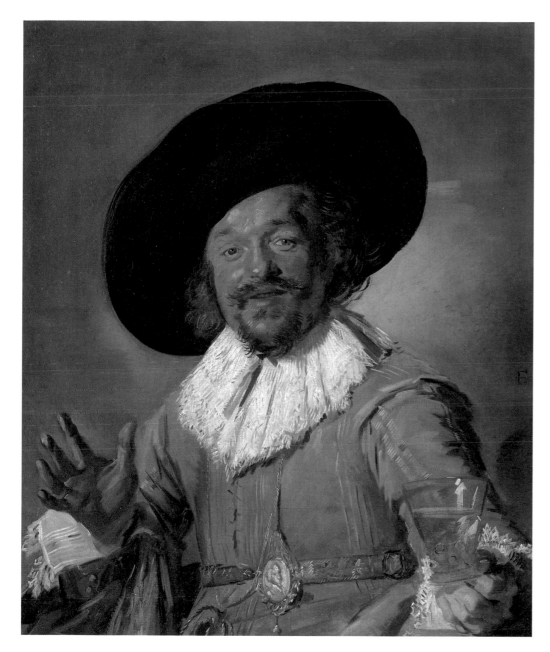

27

FRANS HALS (1582/1583-1666)
The merry drinker, c. 1628-1630
Canvas 81 x 66.5 cm
AMSTERDAM, RIJKSMUSEUM
(acquired in 1816, see p. 310)

GERARD VAN HONTHORST

Upon his return from Rome, Gerard van Honthorst established a career in Utrecht and far beyond. He had a large studio and reports have it that around 1625 some 24 pupils were working there, helping to produce portraits, genre pieces and history paintings. In 1628, at the invitation of King Charles I, Honthorst went to England, where he painted portraits of the king, the queen and others. Honthorst evidently had no difficulty adapting his style of painting and choice of subject to accommodate the wishes of royal patrons, since he produced a variety of paintings for several royal houses. In the late 1630s Honthorst settled in The Hague as court painter to the stadholder, a post he was to hold until he was 62. Honthorst painted portraits and allegorical works for the stadholder's residences at Rijswijk and Honselaersdijk, and contributed to the decoration of the Huis ten Bosch, the stadholder's summer residence near The Hague.

GRANIDA AND DAIFILO

Honthorst was commissioned by Stadholder Frederik Hendrik to paint *Granida and Daifilo* for his residence at Honselaersdijk. It illustrates a scene from *Granida*, a pastoral play written by Pieter Cornelisz Hooft (1581-1647), and was probably one of a series of paintings on pastoral themes – idyllic fantasies of the simple outdoor life.

HALS'S MERRY DRINKER

With less extreme means but at least as great an impact, Frans Hals succeeded in giving his *Merry drinker* the illusion of three-dimensionality. In this painting there is no trace of the artificiality to be found in some Utrecht works. Hals's figure is convincingly realistic. Unlike the fiddler in Honthorst's work, he is not an 'actor' exuberantly raising his glass; he neither poses in an artificial setting nor wears exotic, fantasised garb. On the contrary, he appears to be a 17th-century burgher who speaks directly to the viewer. Hals's *Merry drinker* has the realism of a snapshot. The raised right hand was painted so spontaneously and 'swiftly' that it seems to move – a slash of red, just one loose brushstroke, accentuates the movement. The extremely natural appearance of the man in the leather jerkin with the portrait medallion has led to the suggestion that this is a portrait. The painting is very unconventional and informal for a portrait, however, and we have no clue as to who it might portray.

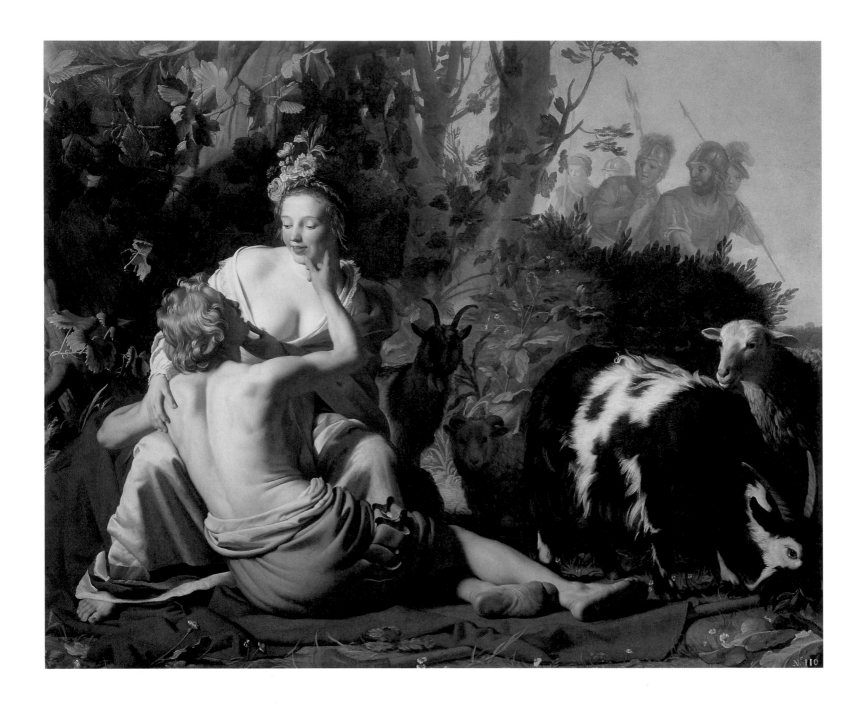

The poet Hooft described how the Persian princess Granida was separated from her companions during a hunting party and met the shepherd Daifilo, who instantly fell in love with her. When Granida returned to her palace, Daifilo resolved to follow her. At court, two princes – Tisiphernes and Ostrobas – were competing for Granida's love. Their rivalry was to be decided by a duel. Daifilo offered to fight in Tisiphernes' place, wearing his armour. The shepherd

killed Ostrobas and the future seemed clear: Daifilo's master Tisiphernes would become betrothed to Granida.

Meanwhile, however, Granida had fallen in love with Daifilo and asked the shepherd to elope with her. During their flight, as they lay in each other's arms, they were surprised by armed men, who wanted to revenge Ostrobas' death by sacrificing the shepherd and the princess on his grave. At this point Tisiphernes intervened.

28

GERARD VAN HONTHORST (1592-1656)
Granida and Daifilo, 1625
Canvas 145 x 178.5 cm
UTRECHT, CENTRAAL MUSEUM
(acquired in 1942, see p. 348)

54

He protected his beloved princess and his helper Daifilo, and decided to let the two lovers go their way and live happily ever after. Honthorst's painting captures the moment when the lovers are discovered by Ostrobas' avengers. Honthorst was not portraying the tension and drama of the story, but rather the idyllic romance of two lovers in a landscape. Honthorst's Caravaggesque manner made way here for a more classicist style with full-length figures and a focus on the landscape in which they were set, all painted in bright colours. However, the artist betrayed his Caravaggesque background in the odd detail, such as the shepherd's dirty feet.

VERTUMNUS AND POMONA

Apart from a brief stay in Italy, the painter Paulus Jansz Moreelse remained faithful all his life to Utrecht, the city of his birth, where he held a great many public posts. He was, for instance, both a member of the town council and a dean of the Guild of St Luke, and he was closely involved in the founding of the University of Utrecht. His social standing and political activities brought him a prominent clientele. Moreelse received many commissions from patrons in court circles, for whom he painted not only portraits, but also pastoral scenes and mythological works. In *Vertumnus and Pomona* Moreelse combined a pastoral idyll with a mythological scene, since this story from Ovid's *Metamorphoses* is also a glorification of the unspoilt rural life.

Vertumnus and Pomona are both guardians of gardens, orchards and fruit. Moreelse therefore depicted the two gods in a garden, surrounded by fruit of all kinds. The young, beautiful Pomona has woven cherries into her hair and holds a pruning knife. The old woman talking to her and unashamedly ogling her décolleté is the god Vertumnus. He tried to pay court to Pomona in various guises, as a reaper, as a herdsman and – when Pomona proved uninterested in men – as an old woman. This metamorphosis by Vertumnus also failed to entice Pomona, however. It was not until the young god revealed himself in his true form that Pomona at last succumbed to his advances.

Moreelse's portrayal of the story is quite confrontational. The young goddess looks directly and seductively at the viewer, as though offering herself just as she offers the bunch of grapes. The loss of her innocence is near. The viewer is warned but at the same time shown an exemplary model: the tree encircled by a vine stands for a faithful relationship in which the man and woman are each other's help and stay. This, Moreelse seems to be saying, is what one should strive for. Youth and beauty are but transient qualities, as witnessed by the stark contrast between the young, beautiful Pomona and the old, wrinkled Vertumnus.

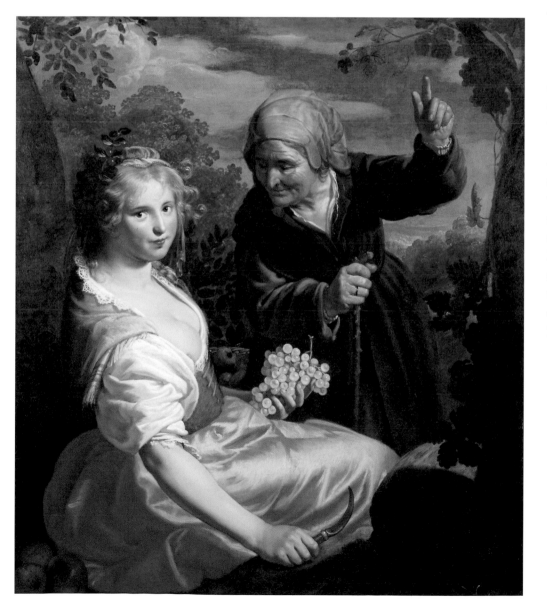

29
PAULUS MOREELSE (1571-1638)
Vertumnus and Pomona, c. 1625-1630
Canvas 130 x 114 cm
ROTTERDAM,
MUSEUM BOIJMANS VAN BEUNINGEN
(acquired in 1865, see p. 345)

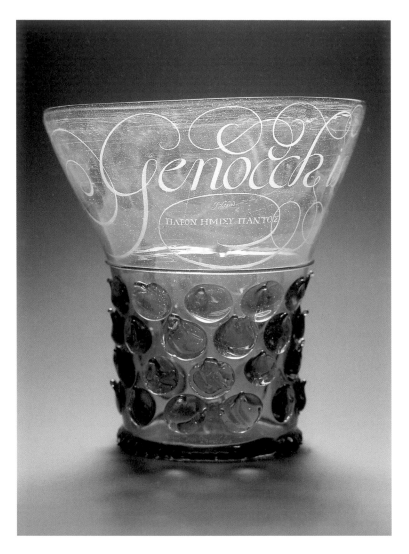

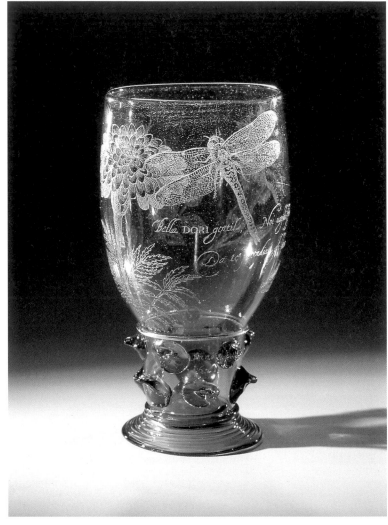

30

Berkemeyer with diamond-point engraving by
Anna Roemers Visscher (1583-1651), 1642
Green glass h. 22 cm
HAMBURG, MUSEUM FÜR KUNST UND GEWERBE
(acquired in 1904, see p. 334)

31

Roemer with diamond-point engraving by
Anna Roemers Visscher (1583-1651), 1621
Clear, dark green glass h. 13 cm
AMSTERDAM, RIJKSMUSEUM
(acquired in 1886, see p. 313)

BERKEMEYER

Glasses appear in several of these paintings, including *The merry fiddler* by Honthorst and *The merry drinker* by Frans Hals. These are *berkemeyers* – goblets with a broad stem and a wide, spreading, funnel-shaped bowl, just like the large green glass [30] which is decorated with an engraving by one of the most gifted glass calligraphers of the age, Anna Roemers Visscher. Anna Roemers Visscher grew up in a cultured milieu and her education included lessons in music, languages, poetry and the use of the diamond point in glass decoration. She was a member of the *Muiderkring*, a circle of lovers of literature and music who met in the Muiderslot, the summer residence of the poet Pieter Cornelisz Hooft. Anna Roemers Visscher had close contacts with the poet Joost van den Vondel and with the powerful Constantijn Huygens, for whom she once engraved a glass as a gift.

She engraved this glass in 1642 for a gentleman of whom there is no longer any record, Ludovicus de Romer, 'as a token of friendship', as she wrote on the foot of the glass. On the bowl she executed calligraphic engraving in three languages. In large, ornate letters there is a line of verse by the Greek poet Hesiod, 'Half is more than the whole', with the text in Greek, *Pleon hemisy pantos*, and in Latin, *Plus est dimidium toto*, below.

ENGRAVED ROEMER

The *roemer* was another popular type of glass in the 17th century. A *roemer* has an ovoid bowl, a hollow cylindrical stem with knob-shaped ornaments known as 'prunts'

and a foot that is often made of spirally wound glass. The name probably derives from the German word Römer, 'Roman', and has nothing to do with the name of the engraver of this 1621 *roemer*, Anna Roemers Visscher. Anna Roemers Visscher was exceptionally skilled in the technique of diamond engraving. Using a tool with a sharp diamond point, she incised a sophisticated decoration of flowers and insects in the fragile curved surface. Here she drew a shell, a dragonfly, a wild rose and a carnation on the glass, and suggested overlapping and depth by means of hatching and stippling.

Anna Roemers also engraved some words in Italian on the glass: *Bella DORI gentil, Noi vaghi fiori, Da te prendiam gli honori*. In translation the poem reads 'Amiable Dora, 'tis you who make us comely blooms', and probably refers to Dorothea van Dorp, the victim of an unhappy love affair with Constantijn Huygens.

GOLD ORNAMENTATION

Gold ornamentation decorates the *roemer* that was once owned by Prince Maurits, son of Willem of Orange. Gilt *roemers* are rare in the Netherlands. In 1606 an artist whose identity is no longer known engraved the *roemer*, probably commissioned by Prince Maurits. The prince's arms are shown over the date, *AN 1606*. Above them the artist placed a crown, while next to the coat of arms is a pollarded tree with three branches. Maurits adopted this emblem after the death of his father: the truncated tree symbolises the murdered stadholder and the three branches stand for his sons, Filips Willem, Frederik Hendrik and Maurits. The symbolism continues in the branch with three roses on the other side of the crown. To the emblem of the budding tree the prince added the motto that can also be seen on the glass, TANDEM.FIT.SURCULUS ARBOR – 'in time the shoot grows into a tree', by which Prince Maurits of Orange expressed his hopes for a happy political future for his country.

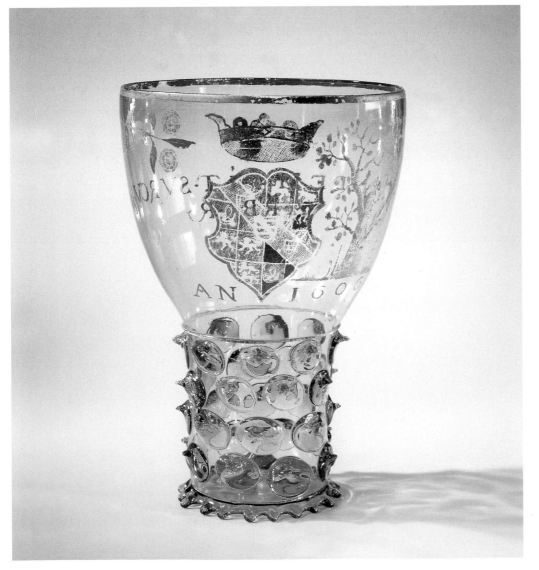

32
Roemer with the coat of arms and motto of Prince Maurits, 1606
Clear, green glass, gilt h. 23.4 cm
AMSTERDAM, RIJKSMUSEUM
(acquired in 1885, see p. 313)

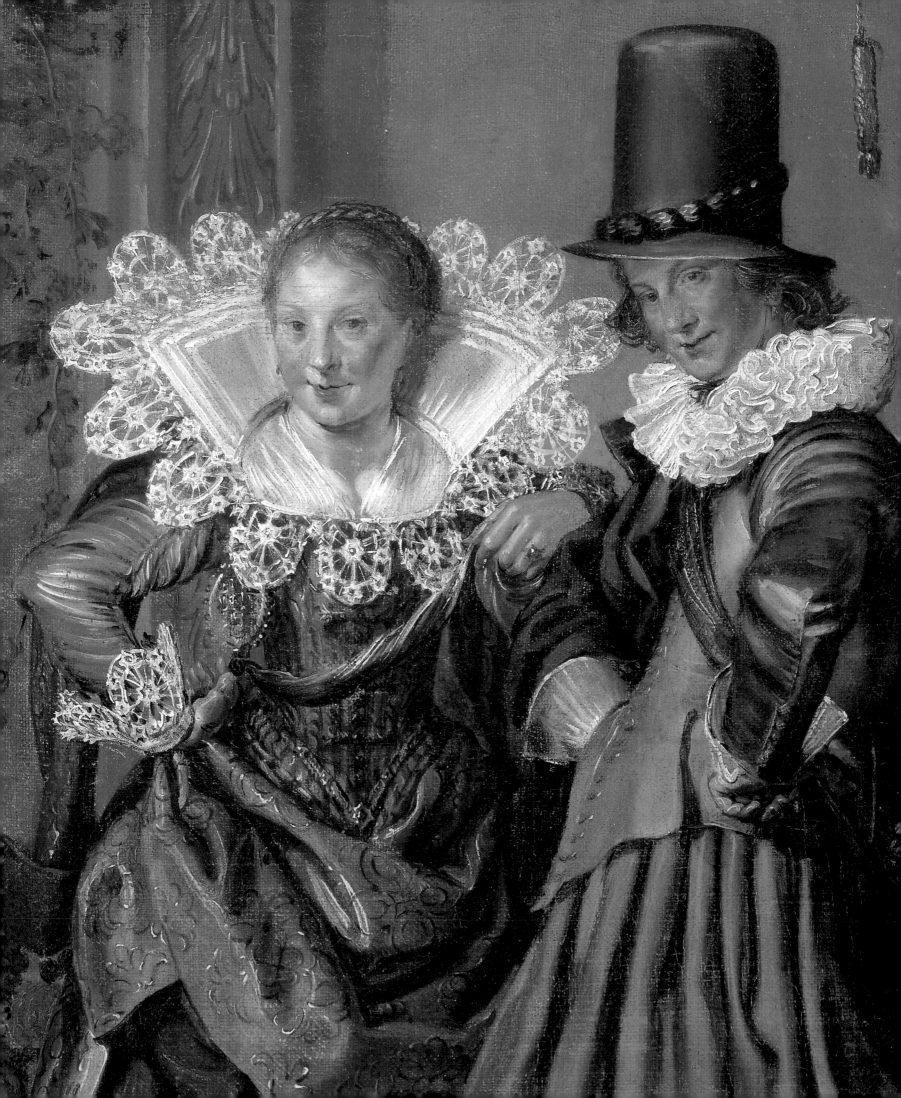

5 EXTRAVAGANTLY DECKED OUT 1620-1640

A LARGE NUMBER of the pictures made by Dutch painters in the Golden Age were produced for the free market. The church was no longer the most important patron and buyer of art. The new clients were ordinary burghers, and they were in the market for a very different sort of painting. Artists therefore sought new and suitable subjects, which they found primarily in their own surroundings. In a very short time artists developed a great variety of genres that answered to the tastes of the middle class, such as landscape, still life, townscapes and the genre piece. With an eye to competition, artists specialised in one of these subjects. By devoting themselves to one particular genre they were able to attain the highest standards, which increased the chances of selling their work. Within the category devoted to portrayals of everyday life – the genre piece – there was a specialisation referred to by the term *geselschapje*, or 'company', which depicted groups of men and women, elegantly dressed, sometimes even extravagantly decked out.

MERRY COMPANIES

This genre flourished for a short time during the first decades of the 17th century. Its most important practitioners were Dirck Hals, Pieter Codde and Willem Buytewech. Buytewech painted this extravagantly dressed couple, a detail of the painting *Elegant couples courting*. Both the man and woman are very fashionably dressed:

she sporting a lace collar that fans out behind her head, and he wearing pleated, puffed breeches and an extremely tall hat. Although the couple seem to be posing, these are probably not portraits. This man and woman are part of a merry company which Buytewech presumably painted for the free market. There are however instances of merry companies consisting of a collection of portraits, in which case the faces clearly display individual features. A painting by Jan Miense Molenaer depicts a wedding party in which the members of the family portrayed are known [38].

The merry company had its roots, once again, in Flanders, where Flemish painters made representations of biblical subjects in which the atmosphere was dominated by lightheartedness and revelry. These biblical scenes had a moral that was abundantly clear to 17th-century viewers: opulence and pleasure-seeking should not be condoned. This warning against extravagance is to be seen in the Dutch merry company, even though it is often subtly concealed in the painting.

BLEACHED COLLARS

A conspicuous part of 17th-century dress was a collar of fine white linen (known as cambric) trimmed with lace. Until around 1625 both men and women wore ruffs; later on limp, flat collars became fashionable. To make a ruff, more than 15 metres of fabric was pleated to form a circumference of 38 centimetres. Every time it was washed, the whole collar was taken apart, bleached and re-pleated. The bleaching of linen, which involved a combination of buttermilk and sunlight, took place outside town. Twice a year horse-drawn barges left Amsterdam for the bleaching fields. Anyone who wanted to wear white collars, therefore, had to own a lot of them.

Stiffening the collar required wheat-meal, a scarce commodity owing to the war with Spain. Nonetheless, collars grew larger and larger, and starch no longer sufficed to make them stand up. Very large ruffs had to be held up with a supportasse, a wire frame wound round with thread of silver, gold or silk.

ELEGANT COUPLES COURTING

Elegant couples courting is the name of the painting by Willem Buytewech in which two fashionably dressed couples are portrayed. The man and woman on the right seem to have found each other: she leans against him nonchalantly. The couple on the left cannot really be said to be courting. She looks at him, but he looks out of the picture. The woman holds two rosebuds in her hands. She plays a game with the man: he may choose, without looking, one of the two roses, whereby he chooses either the lady next to him, or the lady in the red dress. Either way, the woman will decide who wins: she has her arms crossed, so that right may become left and left right. No matter what his answer is, the gentleman will always be hers. In this way the man is caught in the woman's web, like a spider's prey. The spiderweb which Buytewech painted on the barred window, vaguely visible behind the coat of arms, alludes to this.

It is not known whose coat of arms this is. The fountain in the background also functions as a symbol: here love gushes forth, and this is also referred to by the roses in the foreground.

GARDEN PARTY

Like Buytewech, Dirck Hals, the younger brother of Frans Hals, concentrated on depicting elegantly dressed ladies and gentlemen. He painted this merry company in park-like surroundings. The amazing thing is that Buytewech's lady in red also appears in Hals's painting, standing in exactly the same pose, and the dog in Buytewech's painting is also to be seen in Hals's representation.

Hals made his painting some six years after Buytewech painted his *Elegant couples courting*. The practice of 'quoting' images from other artists' paintings was a way of showing that the painter kept abreast of current fashions in art. In this way an artist also showed his admiration for the work of

a colleague, and could even compete with him by demonstrating that he could paint the same thing, only better.

Dirck Hals considered Willem Buytewech a good example. He often borrowed figures from Buytewech's work, and he also imitated his fellow townsman in his compositions and choice of subject matter – the merry company. Dirck had undoubtedly learned the rudiments of painting from his brother Frans, as witnessed by his daringly loose brushwork.

WARNING

In the park surrounding an impressive villa the members of a gallant company amuse themselves at a party. They are all fashionably dressed, just as in Buytewech's painting. Hals also paid careful attention to detail. The pose of the man standing in front on the left is very elegant indeed. His arms are crossed and his right leg is placed forward; he almost seems to perform a

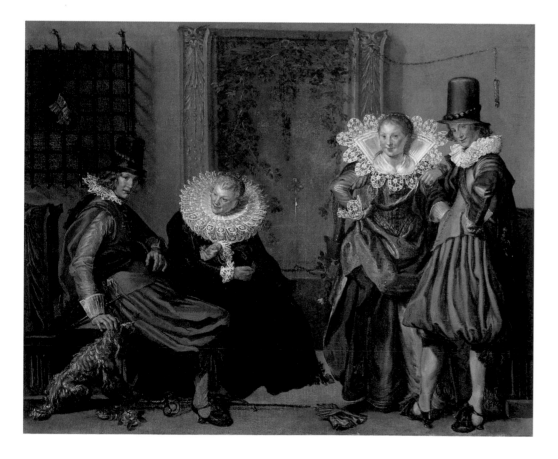

33
WILLEM BUYTEWECH (1591/1592-1624)
Elegant couples courting, c. 1618
Canvas 56 x 70 cm
AMSTERDAM, RIJKSMUSEUM
(acquired in 1926, see p. 315)

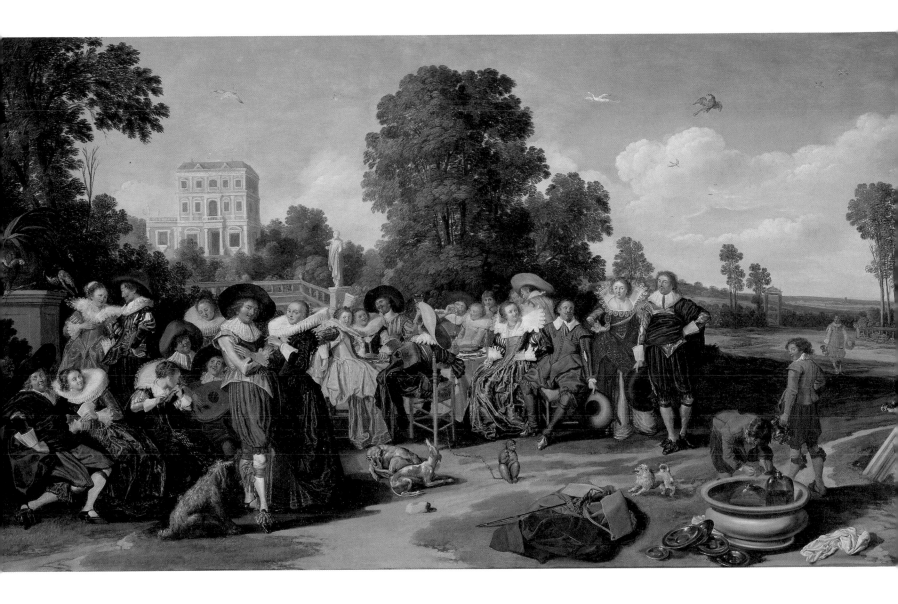

dance step. The woman next to him points to him, as if to say that he is her choice. Although this scene seems to be about nothing more than sensual pleasure, Dirck Hals has taken care to provide a moment of reflection. The key to understanding the depiction is the monkey in the foreground. The monkey on the chain represents humankind, whose sins act as fetters from which it cannot free itself. In its paw the monkey holds a piece of fruit, clearly a reference to the forbidden apple of paradise. The viewer is hereby warned: pleasure should not degenerate into sinful debauchery.

The action takes place in an idyllic garden with parrots and other exotic birds.

The landscape and the house have been idealised. Hals refers here to the theme – which originated in the Middle Ages – of the pleasure-garden, a dream world with various references to love, such as a love castle, the *chateau d'amour*. Dirck Hals could have become acquainted with this motif through his brother Frans, who situated his portrait of Isaac Massa and Beatrix van der Laen in a pleasure-garden [*13*]. Buytewech, Dirck Hals's great example, also placed his elegantly dressed couples in a pleasure-garden. The small fountain depicted there – symbolic of fertility – is one of the classic elements of this motif.

34

DIRCK HALS (1591-1656)
Garden Party, c. 1624
Panel 78 x 137 cm
AMSTERDAM, RIJKSMUSEUM
(acquired in 1899, see p. 314)

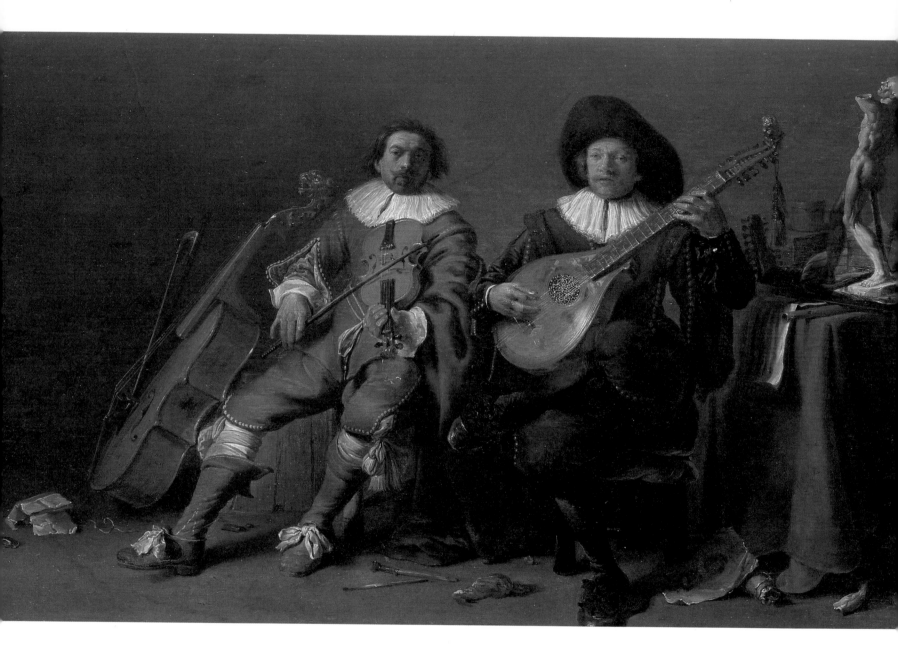

35

CORNELIS SAFTLEVEN (1607-1681)

The duet, c. 1635

Panel 34 x 53 cm

VIENNA, AKADEMIE DER BILDENDEN KÜNSTE

(acquired in 1822, see p. 349)

THE DUET

It is only a small, modest company that the painter Cornelis Saftleven of Gorinchem portrayed. Two gentlemen, with a violin and a zither, make music in a room in which other musical instruments are also to be seen. Next to the violinist stands a viola da gamba; a lute and a flute lie on the table. Saftleven also painted various attributes of the artist: a palette and brush lie on the floor, pieces of paper are scattered around and a plaster cast of a nude muscleman stands on the table. This reference is no

coincidence. The musicians are, in fact, also painters, for Cornelis Saftleven here portrayed himself and his brother Herman, who was also a painter, making music in brotherly fashion. Harmony plays an important role in both music and painting, and perhaps Saftleven wanted to stress its importance by combining both art forms in one painting.

Music plays a role in other of Saftleven's paintings as well. In his many depictions of peasant companies, seated between laughing and drinking peasants are always one or two

people making music. In *The duet* he
replaced the peasants with two smartly
dressed gentlemen, playing instruments that
are in keeping with their status. In addition
to peasant scenes, Cornelis Saftleven painted
scenes from the Bible, historical and allegorical representations and landscapes with
cattle. He was not an especially great artist,
but his extremely varied oeuvre includes
several highlights, including this masterpiece.

YOUNG STUDENT

The young man in Pieter Codde's painting
looks absentmindedly out of the picture
while leaning back in a chair with his elbow
propped on the table. His lace collar is loose
and his jacket is partly unbuttoned, giving
him a nonchalant appearance. The room is
empty, except for the desk with books and
the chair he sits on. Pieter Codde reserved a
large part of his painting for the wooden
floor and the bare back wall of the room.
The bare, whitewashed wall displays here
and there some dents, holes, cracks and a
few nails. These details, which are painted
so well they seem real, break the plainness
of the back wall and bring it to life.

Here Codde probably wanted to portray
more than just a young student in a sober
room. Such a pensive figure, surrounded by
books, usually personifies Melancholy. The
pipe, which the young man holds in his right
hand, is also one of the attributes of Melancholy. Not only dejection but also intellec-
tual musing are associated with this kind of
temperament. This subject gave Codde, who
is mostly known for his merry companies,
the opportunity to concentrate on a simple
composition, painted with a minimum of
colour but with a maximum of tonal
differentiation.

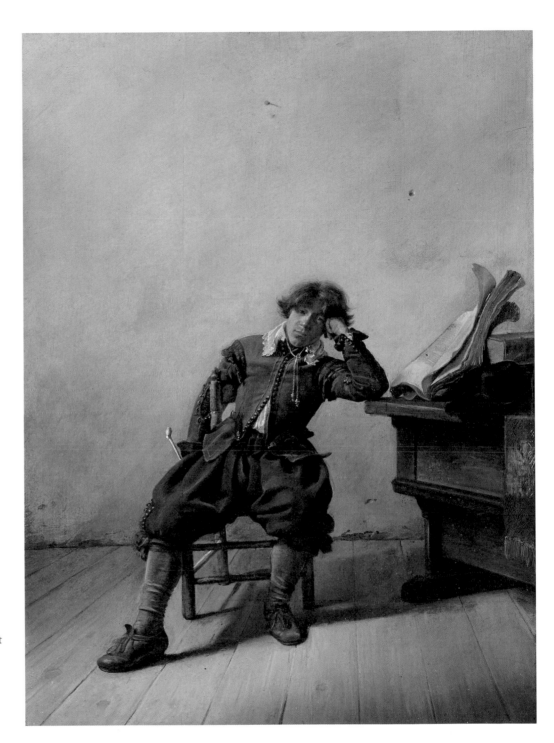

36
PIETER CODDE (1599-1678)
*A young student at his desk:
Melancholy*, c. 1630-1633
Panel 46 x 34 cm
LILLE, MUSÉE DES BEAUX-ARTS
(acquired in 1885, see p. 336)

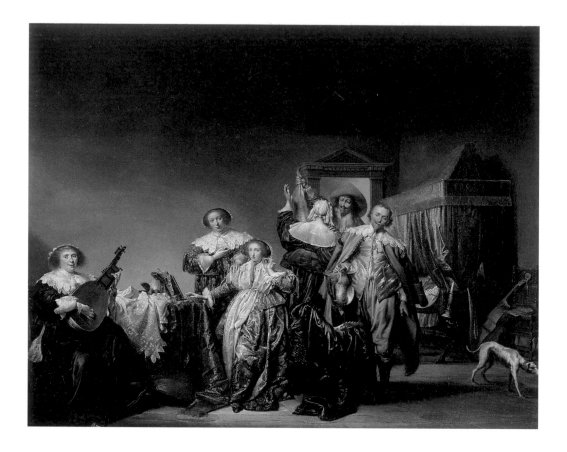

37
PIETER CODDE (1599-1678)
Gallant company, 1633
Panel 54 x 68 cm
AMSTERDAM, RIJKSMUSEUM
(acquired with the aid of the Rembrandt
Society in 1986, see p. 318)

GALLANT COMPANY
Probably some time later Codde painted a
larger company, consisting of six persons, in
which he concentrated on the rendering of
his characters' clothing. With an unerring
hand he painted gleaming fabric, transparent
lace collars, an elegant hat. His fine brush
succeeded in capturing the various materials
and in lending character to the figures.

Two men return from the hunt. One of
them holds up a hare, the other displays two
partridges. A lady stands up to take the
hare. She is the only one among the company who turns her back to the viewer. The
room is sparsely furnished, making the bed
all the more striking. Its curtain has been
opened invitingly. For most 17th-century
viewers it must have been instantly clear
that love comes into play here. Hunting
must be interpreted in the figurative sense:
these hunters are hunting for love. 'Hare-
hunting' meant 'love-making'. The hunter
with the hare seems to be the successful one.

The woman standing opposite him wants to
take the hare from him: she welcomes his
advances. The man with the partridges has
not yet had a nibble, but he is also bent on
finding a woman. The birds, in addition to
standing for bird-catching, were also symbolic of love-making. This erotic symbolism
is intensified by all manner of accessories in
the painting, such as the candle next to the
bed, as well as the dog, which in this context stands for lasciviousness and unchaste
behaviour. In this setting the instruments,
and also the little boxes with jewels, ribbons
and other trinkets, are most likely symbolic
of worldly extravagance.

MARRIAGE PORTRAIT
The large hall in which the celebration of
the wedding of Willem van Loon and
Margaretha Bas takes place resembles a
'perspective box', or peepshow, in which
figures have been placed. The painter Jan
Miense Molenaer kept the architecture –

completely a product of his imagination – in
the dark, while placing the people in the
light. Like Pieter Codde, he concentrated on
the figures, which in Molenaer's case form a
group portrait.

The main characters sit somewhat to the
left of centre. The bride, Margaretha Bas,
dressed in a light-coloured gown, sits next to
the bridegroom, Willem van Loon. They
were married on 6 October 1637. Willem
had previously been married to Maria
Geelvinck, but she died at an early age.
From that marriage Willem had a son, Jan,
whose hand is held here by his stepmother.
Little Jan, not yet three, has blond curls and
wears a long dress. The painter made sure
the viewer knew he was a boy by depicting a
real boy's toy in his hand – a whip.

Next to Willem sits his youngest sister,
Anna, who had married Willem Nieupoort
two months before, which perhaps explains
why this gentleman is depicted in such an
odd way, kneeling before his wife as though

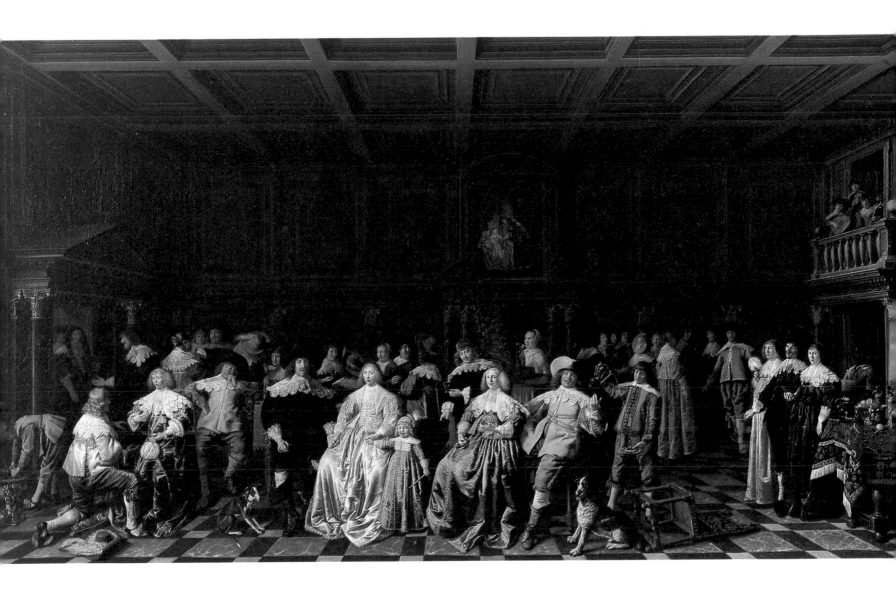

proposing to her. To the right of the bridal couple sit Geertruyd van Loon and her husband Dirck Graswinckel. The overturned chair next to them is symbolic of Hans, the groom's deceased brother. The wedding guests are being served by the groom's unmarried brothers, 21-year-old Arent and 17-year-old Lieven. To the left of the bridal couple sits another brother, Maerten. Finally, standing on the far left is the eldest of the Van Loon brothers, Nicolaas, posing next to the door he holds open for a lady. This is the bride's half-sister, Geertruid Bas, who is a widow. At the far right is a row of people: Nicolaas's wife, Emmerentia van Veen, her brother-in-law, Pieter van Loon and his wife, Anna van Foreest.

JAN MIENSE MOLENAER

In 1637 Jan Miense Molenaer received a commission to record the wedding of Willem van Loon and Margaretha Bas in a painting, in which portraits of all the members of the groom's family were to be included. The painter had just moved to Amsterdam that year. He had come from Haarlem, where he had been apprenticed to Frans Hals. A year earlier Molenaer had married the painter Judith Leyster, who probably assisted him in his work from then on. Molenaer painted various group portraits, including another portrait of the Van Loon family. Otherwise he mainly produced peasant scenes and genre pieces.

38

JAN MIENSE MOLENAER (c. 1610-1668)
The marriage of Willem van Loon and Margaretha Bas, 1637
Canvas 92 x 165 cm
AMSTERDAM, MUSEUM VAN LOON
(in the possession of the Van Loon family since 1637, see p. 321)

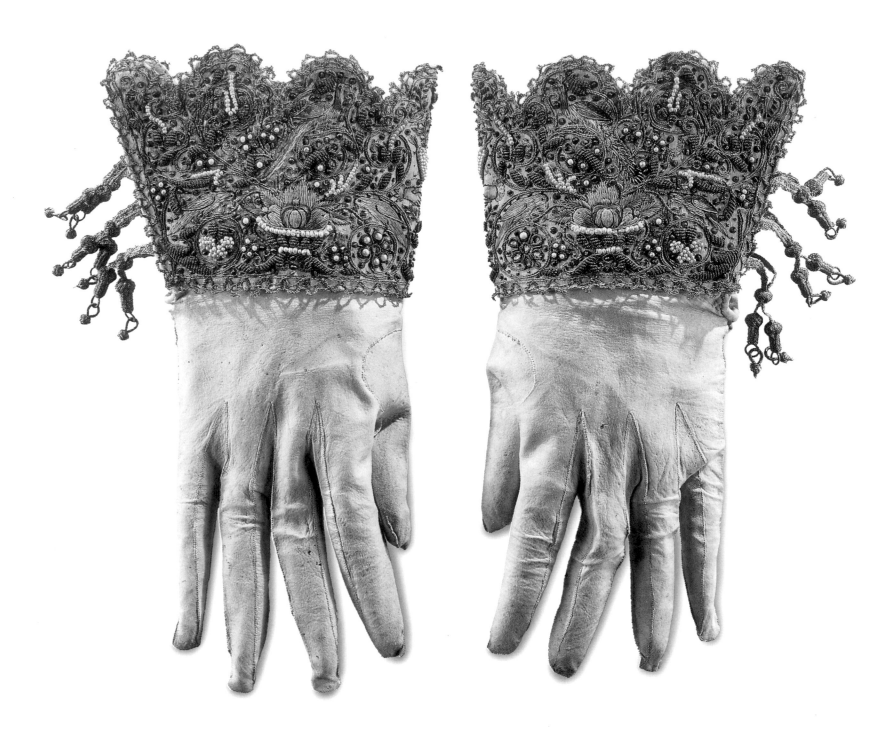

39

Wedding gloves, c. 1622
White leather with embroidered cuffs, l. 24 cm
AMSTERDAM, RIJKSMUSEUM
(acquired in 1978, see p. 318)

GLOVES

It was customary in the 17th century for a man, upon becoming engaged to a woman, to present his bride-to-be with a pair of wedding gloves, which she was to wear on her wedding day. Only when the marriage was actually solemnised in the church were the gloves taken off for a minute, at which time the bride and groom gave each other their right hand.

Johanna Le Maire was given these gloves [39] by her future husband, Pieter van Son, whom she married in June 1622 in the New Church in Amsterdam. She and her husband had their portraits painted by Nicolaes Eliasz Pickenoy. Both of them are probably wearing their wedding clothes. In her right hand Johanna holds the gloves in such a way that the embroidery on the cuffs can be easily seen. It is quite exceptional that both the 17th-century portrait and the pair of gloves have been preserved. The portrait and the gloves remained together in the family's possession until the 1970s.

The gloves are made of thin white leather. The embroidery on the cuffs was executed in multicoloured silk with gold thread, pearls and sequins, displaying various symbols of marriage. The central representation is formed by two hands holding each other and a heart pierced by arrows. The hands represent marital fidelity; they stand for the moment when the marriage is sealed with a handshake. The pierced heart is of course symbolic of love. Between the gold threads various birds may be made out, including a peacock – an attribute of Juno, the goddess of marriage – which symbolises the married state and faithfulness, and a partridge, which in this context stands for fertility. The bowl of fruit embroidered at the top of the cuff represents the sense of taste. In the middle of the bowl is a pomegranate, whose great number of seeds make it a symbol of fertility. Finally, the violet is a symbol of virginity and the rose represents all-conquering love.

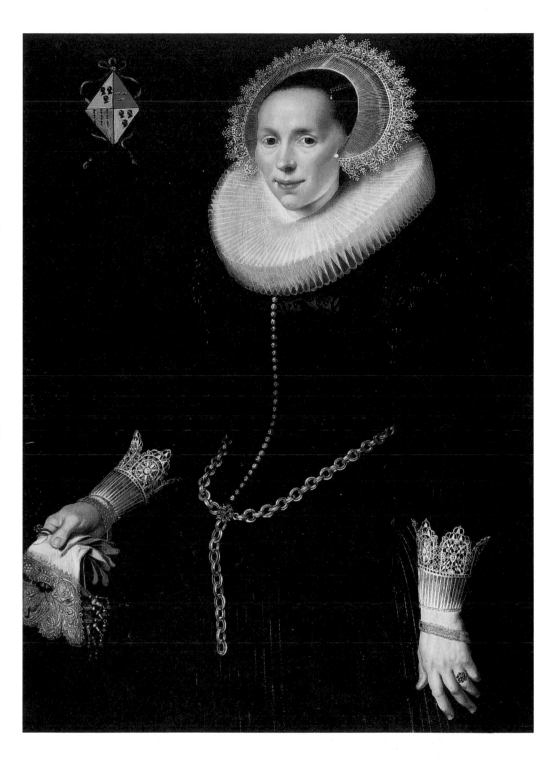

NICOLAES ELIASZ PICKENOY (1588-1650/1656), *Portrait of Johanna Le Maire*, c. 1622
Panel 105 x 78 cm. Present whereabouts unknown

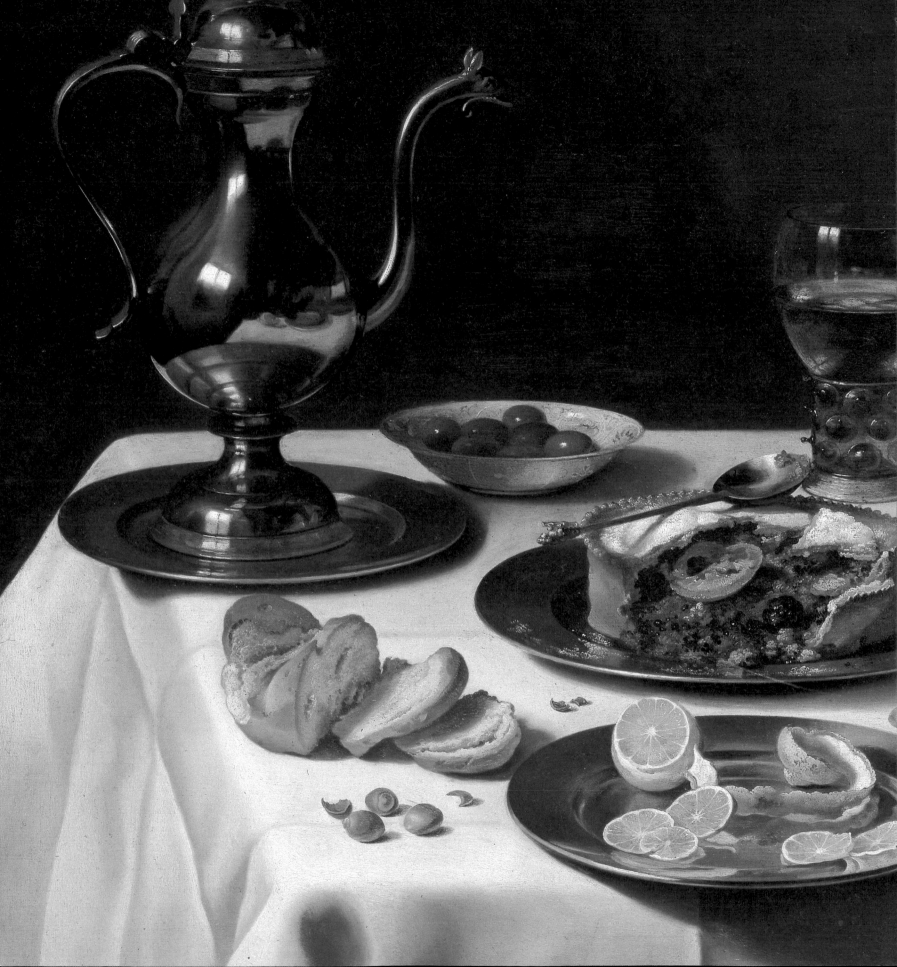

6 DECEPTIVELY REALISTIC 1610-1650

STILL-LIFE PAINTERS of the Golden Age succeeded in making deceptively good imitations of reality. With nothing but paint and brushes they conjured up dozens of different materials on their canvas or panel: a shiny metal jug next to a breakable china dish, the soft skin of a peach next to a grainy crust of bread. Flowers, grapes, jugs and cheeses seem to free themselves from the flat surface. The Dutch still-life painters were unrivalled in this field.

STILL LIFE

A still life is a composition of motionless objects, painted by the artist from life. This does not mean to say, however, that the profuse flower arrangements and artfully laid tables which occur in 17th-century still lifes were actually to be found in Dutch households. The objects were gathered together by the painter and combined in a certain way. The still life was arranged by the artist, and it was this grouping that the painter wanted to depict in as realistic a way as possible. A large number of painters were so skilled at doing this that the 'bestilled' life became nearly palpable. The term 'still life' was not actually used until around 1650, before which time this type of painting was referred to as a 'banquet', a 'breakfast piece', a 'flowerpot', a 'fruit piece', or 'a painting of a jug and smokers' requisites'. The objects depicted determined the name.

The still life was a popular specialisation within the field of painting. Within the still-life specialism painters usually concentrated on one type of still life, such as the fruit piece, the flower painting or depictions of cutlery and drinking vessels. Artists composed their still lifes in such a way as to show off their skills, choosing those objects they were best able to depict. A silver jug with a round body gave the painter an opportunity to imitate the gleam of the material and to show how surrounding objects were reflected in its smooth surface. A half-full glass required the perfect rendering of reflection, transparency and lustre, and a meat pie with a piece cut out of it let the painter show reality at its juiciest and most appetising. Still-life painters concentrated on depicting those objects at which they excelled, which meant that this genre enjoyed especially high standards. The perfect rendering of material, clever compositions and subtle illumination won the admiration of a broad public, who ensured that still lifes sold well. High prices were paid for flower paintings in particular.

TULIPMANIA

Many still lifes feature tulips. This rare and costly flower was imported into the Netherlands from Turkey in the 16th century. Tulip collectors displayed these flowers in small decorative gardens in which the tulips were widely spaced. During the course of the 17th century this flower became immensely popular, giving rise to a tulip craze, or 'tulipmania', that reached its height in 1636, at which time an exclusive bulb could fetch the same price as a house on an Amsterdam canal. Rich merchants and simple artisans alike invested their money – in many cases borrowed – in the tulip trade. After peaking in 1636-1637 the tulip market crashed, causing many buyers and sellers to go bankrupt. The Amsterdam doctor Claes Pietersz kept a lasting memory of his love of tulips: in 1621 he changed his name and has been known ever since as Nicolaes Tulp [58].

< DETAIL OF 45

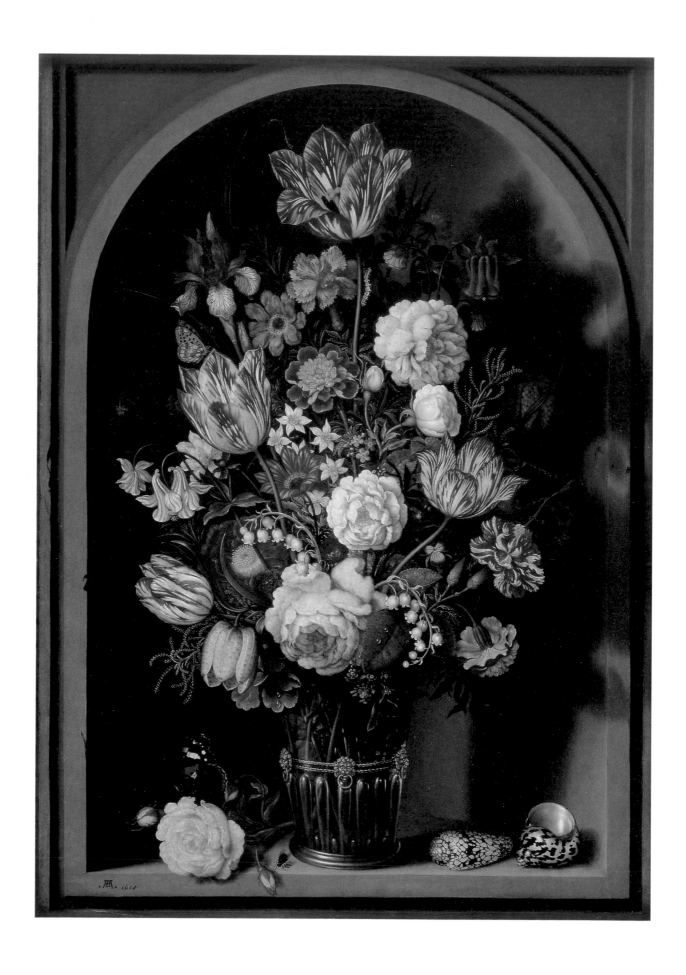

40

AMBROSIUS BOSSCHAERT (1573-1621)
Bouquet of flowers in a vase, 1618
Copper 55.5 x 39.5 cm
COPENHAGEN, STATENS MUSEUM FOR KUNST
(acquired in 1791, see p. 325)

AMBROSIUS BOSSCHAERT

Ambrosius Bosschaert was born in Antwerp but lived and worked for most of his life in the town of Middelburg in the province of Zeeland. At the end of the 16th century Zeeland was the second most important province, after Holland, and Middelburg, the provincial capital, was the country's second-largest trading centre. Many flower-lovers lived in this prosperous town: they laid out gardens with rare plants, corresponded with each other about their horticultural pursuits and had the objects they collected immortalised in paint. Ambrosius Bosschaert catered to this need by specialising in flower still lifes, just as did his three sons and his brother-in-law, Balthasar van der Ast.

Although Bosschaert's magnificent bouquets are rooted in reality, they could never have been observed in real life, for they consist of flowers that bloom at different times of the year. When a flower was at its most beautiful, the painter made a drawing of it. Later on he used these individual 'flower portraits' to compose bouquets.

The arrangement of Bosschaert's bouquets is highly symmetrical and the various flowers scarcely overlap. Each flower is rendered individually and testifies to careful observation. A niche frames the bouquet nicely and closes off the composition. Arched niches are one of the characteristic features of Bosschaert's flower still lifes, as are the exotic shells which he added to this picture. Shells, like unusual flowers, were also a popular collector's item.

This work probably cost a pretty penny. The exact price of this painting is not known, but it is known that the last work Bosschaert ever made – a 'flower pot' – was bought for 1000 guilders.

VAN DER AST

When Balthasar van der Ast was only 15 his father died, and from that time onwards he lived with the family of Ambrosius Bosschaert. Balthasar was the younger brother of Bosschaert's wife, Maria. Van der Ast probably learned to paint from Bosschaert; like his brother-in-law, he specialised in flower still lifes. Like Bosschaert, Van der Ast depicted each flower very precisely with almost no overlapping, though he differed from his teacher in his preference for more complex compositions. In his flower still life of 1618, Van der Ast placed two bouquets against the splendid backdrop of Renaissance architecture, which was probably painted by Bartholomeus van Bassen.

The painting is strikingly asymmetrical. The focal point of the painting is on the left-hand side, where the largest bouquet stands and where the buildings above are more brightly illuminated and depicted in greater detail than those on the right. Moreover, the perspectival vanishing point of the architecture is to be found in the large bouquet. Van der Ast's flower still life is not only remarkable for its composition: it is nearly square, and square formats were a rare occurrence in 17th-century Dutch painting. The picture is also exceptionally large for a still life.

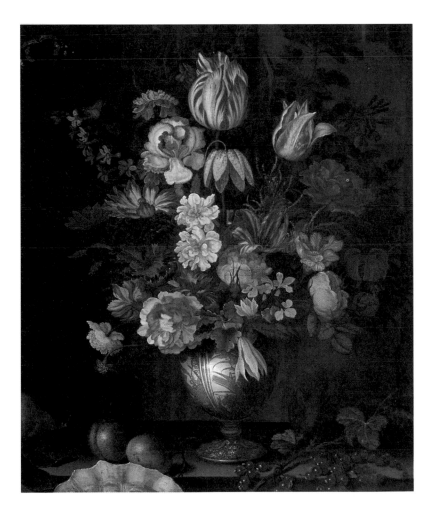

DETAIL OF 41

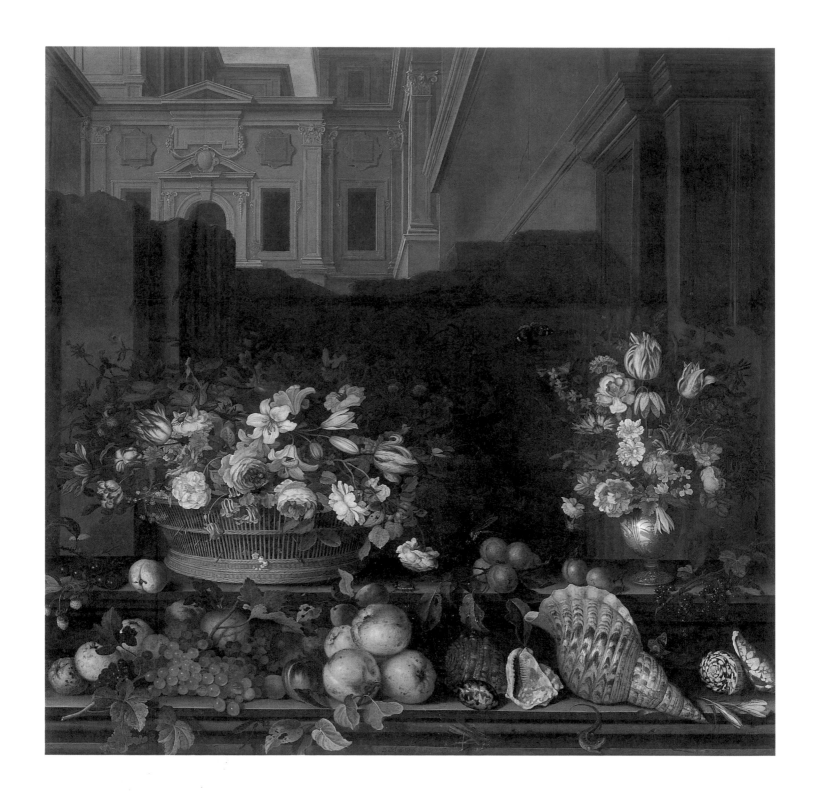

41

BALTHASAR VAN DER AST

(1593/1594-1657)

*Still life with flowers, fruit
and shells,* c. 1640

Panel 134 x 140 cm

DOUAI, MUSÉE DE LA CHARTREUSE

(acquired in 1964, see p. 328)

42

HANS BOULENGER (c. 1600-1672/1675)
Tulips in a vase, 1639
Panel 68 x 54.5 cm
AMSTERDAM, RIJKSMUSEUM
(acquired in 1883, see p. 311)

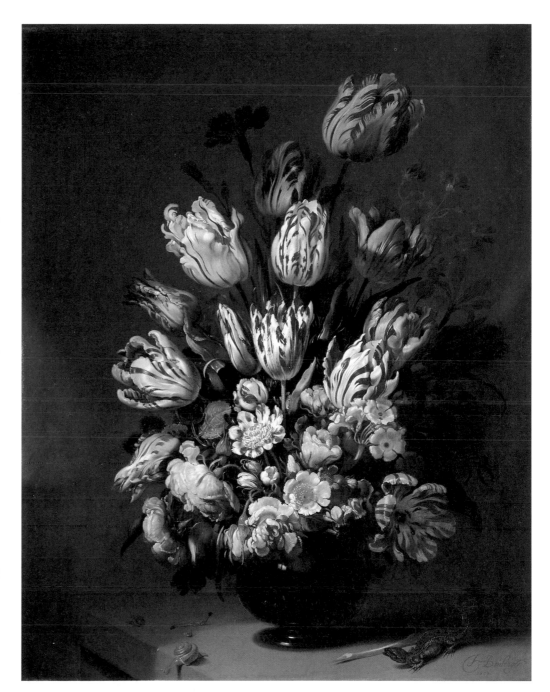

Like Bosschaert, Van der Ast must have worked from drawings of individual flowers. This bouquet also contains flowers that bloom in different seasons. He combined this richly rendered profusion with plums, apples and other fruits, as well as exotic shells and various insects. Every element in Van der Ast's still life, no matter how small, testifies to his feeling for elegance and effect.

TULIPS IN A VASE

A lush bouquet of flowers stands on the table. The glass vase seems barely big enough to hold the profusion of tulips, roses, anemones and carnations. Although the bouquet looks less forced than those of Ambrosius Bosschaert and Balthasar van der Ast, it is still unlikely that this bouquet of flowers was painted from life. The Haarlem painter Hans Boulenger would have worked, just like his colleagues did, from drawings of individual flowers, considering that roses and tulips do not bloom at the same time of year. Boulenger knew how to turn a bouquet of flowers into a unified whole, more so than did Bosschaert and Van der Ast. He achieved this effect by means of a more supple technique, by using less diverse and less exuberant colours, by letting some of the flowers overlap and by the subtle play of light and shadow. Part of this red and white bouquet remains in the shadow, while several flamed tulips catch the full light.

Boulenger might have wanted to show more than just beauty and perfection: he perhaps wanted to make the viewer aware of the transitory nature of all this splendour. After all, a flower in a vase has a very short life: it is destined to wilt or to be eaten by insects. Moreover, at that time the tulip was the pre-eminent symbol of transience, since the bulbs of this popular flower had led to many people's financial ruin in the days of 'tulipmania'. Boulenger painted these *Tulips in a vase* in 1639, two years after the tulip market had crashed.

43

Johannes van der Beeck, called
Torrentius (1589-1644)
*Three vessels with bridle: allegory
of temperance*, 1614
Panel (oval) 52 x 50.5 cm
Amsterdam, Rijksmuseum
(acquired with the aid of the Rembrandt
Society in 1918, see p. 315)

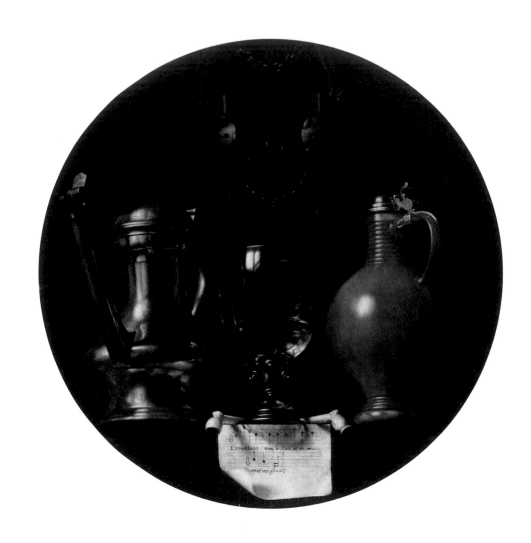

TEMPERANCE

An unambiguous warning was portrayed by the Amsterdam painter Johannes Torrentius: *Wat bu-ten maat be-staat, int on-maats qaat / ver-ghaat* (Those who know no moderation will perish in evil dissipation). This warning on the sheet of music in the lower centre of the painting expresses the message that the painter wanted to impress upon the viewer with this unusual depiction: those who don't know where to draw the line will fare badly. This still life is an allegory of temperance. Each element of the work ties in with this theme: the pitcher, jug and glass, the bridle in the background, the pipes with their bowls turned upside down and the sheet of music with its unmistakable message.

Music and measure are inextricably bound up with each other. The combination of pitcher, jug and glass occurred frequently in this context: the pitcher perhaps contained water and the jug wine. The percentage of alcohol in the glass in the middle could be kept down by adding water to the wine. The same held true with regard to the use of tobacco: one can have too much of a good thing. The bridle, gleaming subtly in the dark, fits in perfectly with the theme of moderation: this instrument serves to hold a horse in check.

TORRENTIUS

Johannes, the son of Sijmon van der Beeck, assumed the name of Torrentius, after the Latin word for a torrent or rushing stream, which is the meaning of his Dutch surname. This still life dedicated to moderation, or temperance, is his only known work. Many works by the artist's hand were burned after he was sentenced to twenty years in the House of Correction for 'heresy and polygamy'. At the intercession of Charles I of England, who was once the owner of this still life, the painter was released after two years.

Torrentius was a controversial figure. Not only is his debauched life well documented, but his incredibly accomplished painting technique was written about while he was still alive. Some thought Torrentius's technique a wonder, so miraculous it bordered on sorcery. They found his naturalism astonishing and his technique unparalleled, for his brushstrokes were nearly invisible. Constantijn Huygens wrote that he suspect-

ed that there would not soon be another painter who was capable of depicting the lustre of objects of glass, pewter, earthenware and iron as subtly as Torrentius could. Torrentius's rendering of reflections is very natural. The slightly concave neck of the pewter pitcher seems just as 'real' as the round body of the earthenware jug. The painter needed only one or two specks and a couple of lines to suggest a *roemer*, the type of glass depicted here. The bridle above it is, if possible, painted with even fewer contours, though it is just as convincing. The shadows on the sheet of music intensify the semblance of three-dimensionality, making the *roemer* seem even more precariously perched on the edge of the narrow shelf. This unique work proves Torrentius to be an undisputed master.

STILL LIFE WITH CHEESE AND FRUIT

The reflection of half an apple in the gleaming pewter plate, the transparency of the *roemer* containing white wine, the nuances of light and shadow in the curling, drooping apple peel: every detail of this still life has been sublimely rendered. Such still lifes are also called 'breakfast pieces'. It displays a selection of simple foods and objects: bread, cheese, fruit, a pewter plate, a jug and a wineglass.

Floris van Dijck presents us here with a sampling of his skills. He managed to render each object and all of the various foods displayed on the table with striking precision: each material shows to advantage. The shiny crust of the bread roll stands out clearly from the glaze of the jug made of Rhineland earthenware. The crumbliness of the various cheeses contrasts with the freshness of the apples next to them, and the Chinese bowl holding the apples is made of translucently thin porcelain. Van Dijck effectively rendered the fragility of eggshell china by painting a thin white line along its upper edge. The white damask tablecloth, its shining fabric displaying patterns woven into it, is nearly tangible. The fold cutting through the woven tulip in the lower centre subtly lends the painting the necessary feeling of depth.

44

FLORIS VAN DIJCK (1575-1651)
Laid table with cheese and fruit, c. 1615
Panel 82.2 x 111.2 cm
AMSTERDAM, RIJKSMUSEUM
(acquired with the aid of the Rembrandt
Society in 1982, see p. 318)

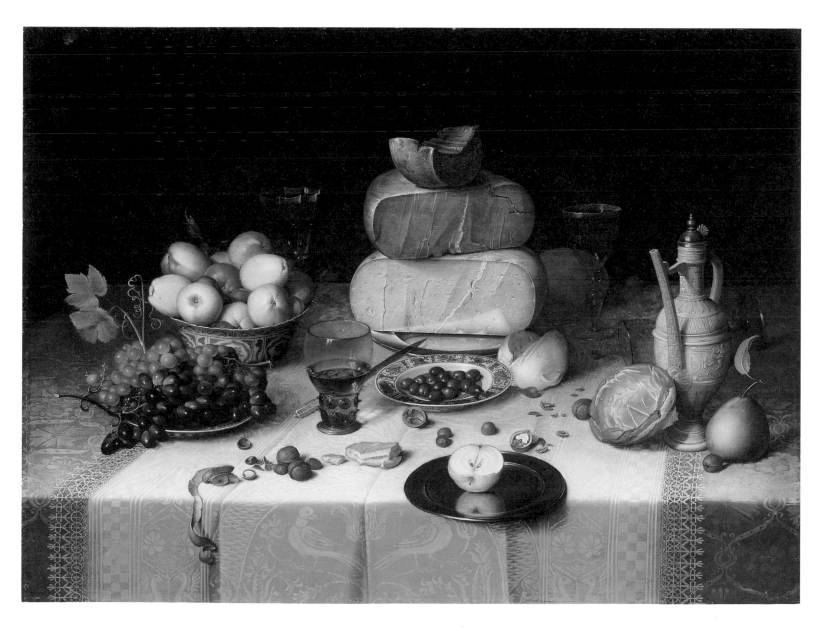

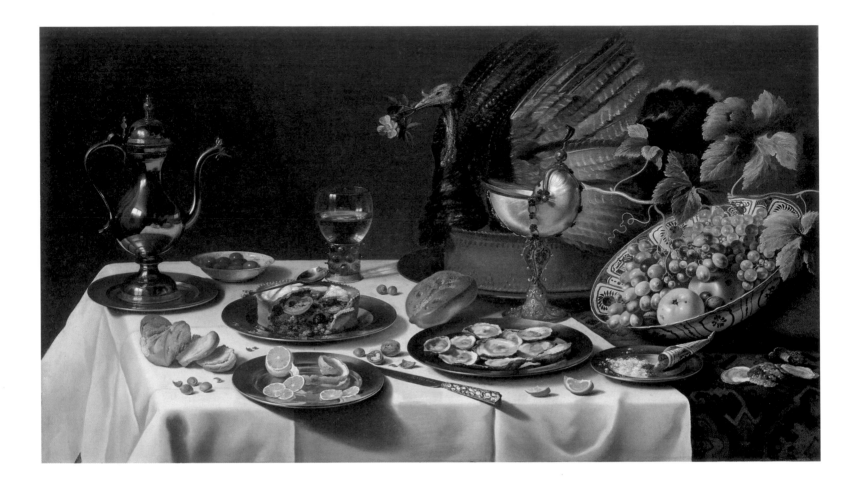

About twelve still lifes by Floris van Dijck are known, all of which were probably painted in Haarlem. They differ from one another only in details. He always made a careful arrangement of objects and food, striving to let each part of the laid table show to advantage. The various objects scarcely overlap, having been placed at a reasonable distance from one another, while the perspective was chosen to make it seem as though the viewer is looking at the table from a point slightly above. These characteristics are a feature of nearly all the 'breakfast pieces' made during this period in Haarlem.

PIETER CLAESZ

The development of the still life is comparable to that of the painted landscape. The colours became more subdued, the composi-

tions more coherent and the 'horizon' lower. While in the landscapes the sky began to occupy more and more space, in the still lifes the wall behind the laid table began to take up a larger part of the canvas or panel. The wall also became increasingly light in colour.

The oeuvre of Pieter Claesz displays the entire development of this specialism. Claesz, born in Berchem near Antwerp, went to Haarlem around 1615 and remained there his whole life. His known works span the period from 1621 to 1660. His early work, which includes the *Still life with turkey pie*, is rather colourful and still somewhat incoherent, whereas his later work is more sober, displaying more naturalness in the composition and more evenness of palette. One innovation which Claesz introduced was showing the left edge of the

45

PIETER CLAESZ (1597/1598-1660)
Still life with turkey pie, 1627
Panel 75 x 132 cm
AMSTERDAM, RIJKSMUSEUM
(acquired with the aid of the Rembrandt
Society in 1974, see p. 317)

table, by which means he increased the feeling of depth in his paintings, leaving behind the rigid horizontal composition which characterises the work of Floris van Dijck. This type of composition became more or less standard; few of the later still-life painters deviated from it.

Even though Pieter Claesz's composition is looser than that of Van Dijck, the structure of *Still life with turkey pie* is still rather traditional. The vantage point from which the painter depicted the table is admittedly slightly lower and therefore somewhat more natural, but because the various objects do not overlap, they seem to be displayed in the same way as in Van Dijck's still life.

Claesz took advantage of this display of mainly precious objects to give a demonstration of his technical skill. The various materials and lighting effects were painted with precision. The plate balanced on the edge of the table casts a shadow on the white tablecloth, whose creases cause a difference in hue; the *roemer*, half-filled with wine, casts a light-yellow shadow onto the cloth. The reflections on the round body of the pitcher are brilliant indeed: not only is the plate on which the pitcher stands reflected in its surface, but also part of the table and even the room in which the painting was made are discernible.

WILLEM CLAESZ HEDA

The *Still life with gilt goblet* by Willem Claesz Heda is a perfect example of the next step in the development of still-life painting. The hues in this painting differ little from one another. Only the partly-peeled lemon provides a bright, colourful accent: it

46
WILLEM CLAESZ HEDA (1593/1594-1680)
Still life with gilt goblet, 1635
Panel 88 x 113 cm
AMSTERDAM, RIJKSMUSEUM
(acquired with the aid of the Rembrandt
Society in 1984, see p. 318)

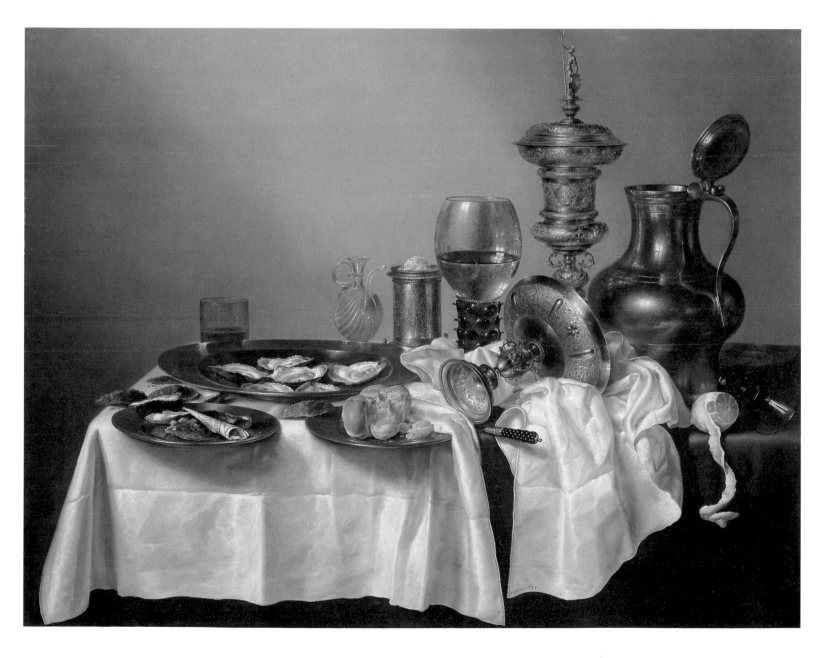

47

JAN DAVIDSZ DE HEEM (1606-c. 1684)
Still life with lobster and nautilus cup, 1634
Canvas 61 x 55 cm
STUTTGART, STAATSGALERIE
(acquired in 1978, see p. 347)

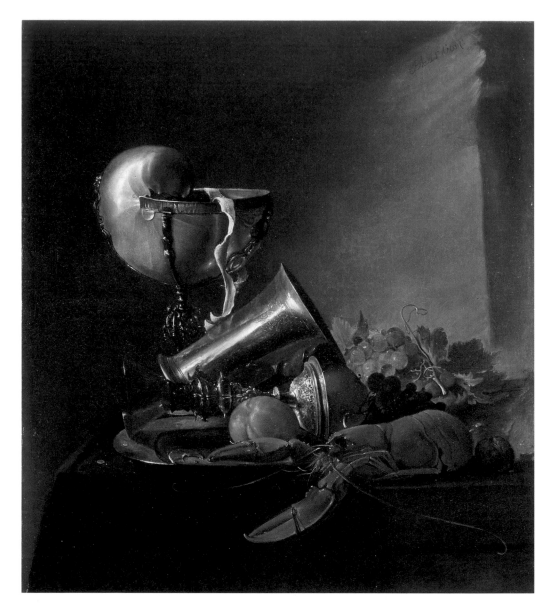

reflects in the foot of the pewter jug with its enticing, opened lid. Moreover, the objects are no longer displayed in isolation; they overlap, forming a unified whole. In addition, the background has become much lighter and the viewpoint lower: the viewer looks at the display from a vantage point on the same level, not from above.

Willem Heda, who spent forty years painting still lifes, is considered the great master of reflection, the mirroring of light in smooth and shining material. The glass *roemer*, gilt goblet, silver *tazza* (shallow drinking vessel on a foot) and pewter jug offer plenty of opportunities to depict reflections in the various materials. The glass and the jug, for example, reflect the leaded windows, while the white of the damask napkin shines in the *tazza*. Each object in the composition exerts an effect on the object next to it. The glass containing red wine reflects in the plate of oysters, the bread roll casts a soft yellow shadow on the tablecloth and even the smaller plate of oysters and the paper cone holding pepper – perched dangerously on the edge of the table – throw a subtle shadow on the tablecloth.

JAN DAVIDSZ DE HEEM

Jan Davidsz de Heem painted various kinds of still lifes: flower and fruit still lifes, as well as book still lifes and arrangements of food and objects in the style of the Haarlem painters Claesz and Heda. After moving to Antwerp in about 1636, De Heem's still lifes became grander and more extravagant. He probably painted the *Still Life with lobster and nautilus cup* during his Dutch period, while still in Leiden. It is more colourful

than was customary at that time, even though the painter tempered the red of the lobster and the orange-pink of the peach with greys and browns, to avoid bright accents and harsh contrasts.

For this still life De Heem chose a vertical format, suitable to the diagonal arrangement he had in mind, in which the precious nautilus cup dominates the composition. De Heem rendered the mother-of-pearl gleam of the exotic nautilus shell with remarkable precision. A long, dried-out lemon peel has been laid over the shell, linking the nautilus cup with the silver beaker in front of it, in

whose engraved silver surface the peel is reflected. This beaker, with its simple decoration, forms in its turn the background for another precious object: the glass-holder, in which a *berkemeyer* has been clamped. The splendour of this still life lies not only in its perfect arrangement within the diagonal composition, but also in the painstakingly chosen gradations of colour which run along the same diagonal. The yellow of the lemon peel is followed by the softer yellow of the glass-holder and the orange of the peach; the red lobster closes off the composition.

GLASS-HOLDER

The glass-holder in De Heem's *Still life with lobster and nautilus cup* was a status symbol owned only by the highest circles of society. Glass-holders existed as early as the 15th century and had one purpose only: to give a simple *berkemeyer*, for example, the status of an ostentatious goblet. Glass-holders were made until the mid-17th century, after which they dropped out of fashion, which resulted in most of them being melted down.

The Amsterdam glass-holder made by Leendert Claesz has survived for centuries because it was part of the Amsterdam municipal silver. Together with four other glass-holders, it was commissioned by the city government. The names of the treasurers who bestowed the commission are engraved on the bottom of the base: Gerrit Jacob Witse and Jan ten Grootenhuis.

The decorations on the glass-holder refer unmistakably to the capital city. The foot is decorated with the coat of arms of Amsterdam, a shield with three X crosses (the attribute of St Andrew) on top of each other in a vertical band. The coat of arms is surmounted by a crown and flanked by two lions. The cog (a ship with rounded prow and stern), which was part of Amsterdam's oldest seal, also decorates the foot. Symbols of fishing and shipping accompany this old type of ship. The decorations on the upper part consist of ships with the wind full in their sails, representing the four points of the compass. The sea monsters that are meant to grip the cup encircle half a globe. These elements symbolise shipping and Amsterdam's dominion of the seven seas. The city government was fond of translating its power, wealth and influence into images.

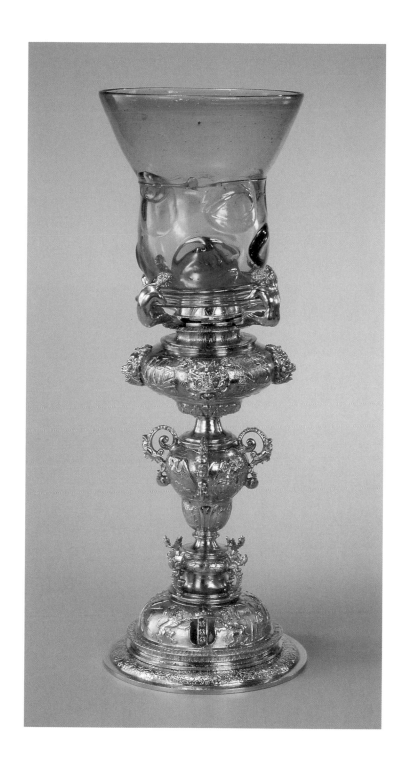

48

ATTRIBUTED TO
LEENDERT CLAESZ (1580-after 1609)
Glass-holder, 1609
Silver-gilt h. 24.8 cm
AMSTERDAM, RIJKSMUSEUM
(on loan from the City of Amsterdam
since 1885, see p. 312)

49
Triangular salt-cellar with cover, 1618
Silver, parcel-gilt, h. 30.2 cm
AMSTERDAM, RIJKSMUSEUM
(acquired with the aid of the Rembrandt
Society in 1988, see p. 319)

SALT-CELLAR

An object displayed in many still lifes is the
salt-cellar. It can have various shapes
– round, triangular, hexagonal – and is
always a conspicuous object in the composition. Salt was considered a special product:
it not only counteracted decay, but was also
essential in preparing meals and even had a
healing, cleansing effect. In those days salt
was considerably more expensive than it is
now. The extraction and processing of sea
salt was not a simple procedure, and this
made it very costly. In short, salt deserved
pride of place on the dinner table, and time
and money were therefore lavished on the
production of salt-cellars. An exceptional
example is this triangular salt-cellar dating
from 1618, not so much because of its form
– this was seen frequently in those days –
but because it is still complete. Similar
salt-cellars are usually missing the loose,
pyramid-shaped lid.

The construction of this ornate table
decoration is clear: the salt-cellar is composed of various parts that fit together like
the pieces of a building kit. The triangular
base rests on curled feet in which griffins'
heads can be discerned. Fantastical figures
have also been worked into the wildly
curling supports of the middle section; each
support ends in a lion's paw which rests on
a ball. In the midst of these winged monsters
sits a gilt female figure next to an anchor:
she is a symbol of Hope. The salt-cellar
proper, the plateau with the well that holds
the salt, is surrounded by delicately adorned
edges. Curled braces at the three corners
support the pyramid-shaped lid. These three
curls are also composed of various fantasy

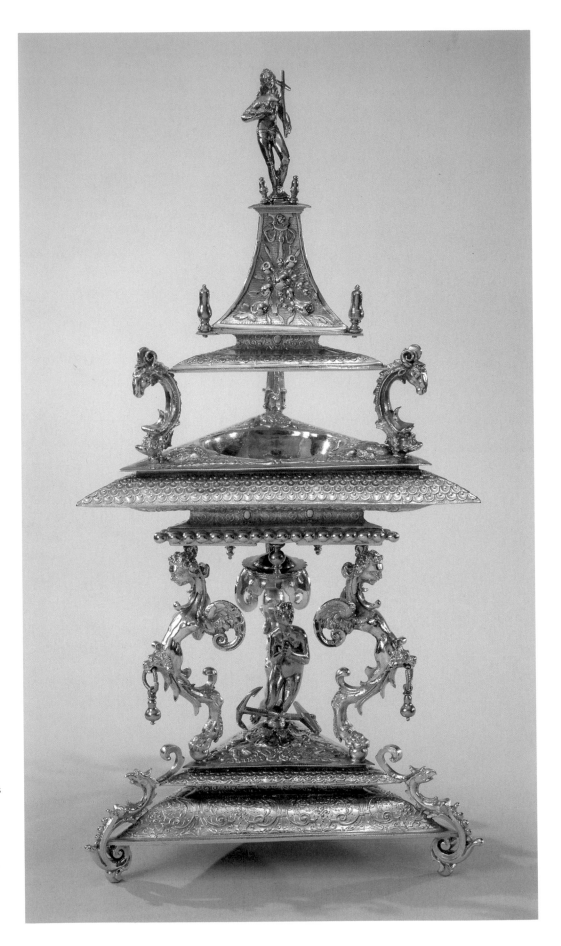

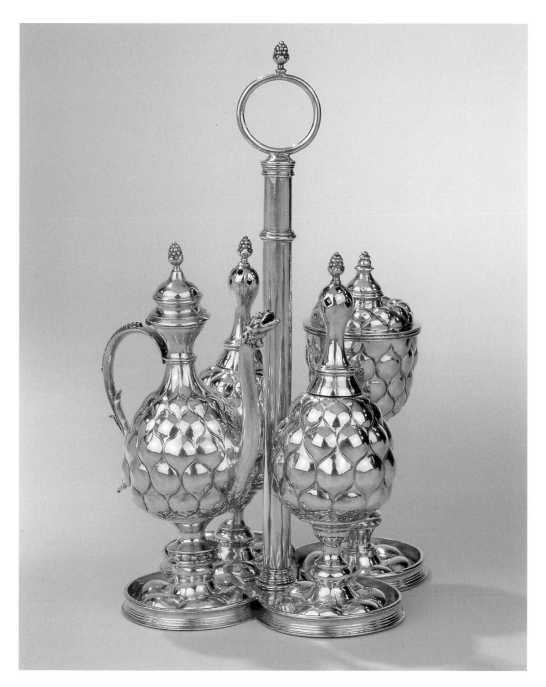

50

ATTRIBUTED TO
ANTHONY GRILL (1609-1675)
Cruet-stand, 1642
Silver with remnants of gilt, h. 27.1 cm
AMSTERDAM, RIJKSMUSEUM
(acquired in 1997, see p. 319)

CRUET-STAND

A salt-cellar of much more modest proportions than the triangular one dating from
1618 is the salt-cellar that was once part of
a cruet-stand. On a holder stands an oil
cruet, two shakers – probably intended to
hold different kinds of pepper – and a salt-
cellar with a lid. This cruet-stand, made by
Anthony Grill, is the only one of its kind: it
is the oldest preserved silver service intended
for secular use. A salt-and-pepper set like
this one would have adorned the table of
well-to-do burghers. There must have been
more of them, for a print exists which
depicts just such a cruet-stand – one, in fact,
which had been the third prize in a lottery
held in Durgerdam, a village near
Amsterdam.

All parts of the set are decorated with
the same motifs: bulging 'fish bladder'
motifs decorate the body and foot of the
shakers, the cruet and the salt-cellar. On the
top of each object – even on the carrying
ring – Grill placed a little pine cone. This
symbol referred to Augsburg, the city where
the silversmith lived before he settled in
Amsterdam.

motifs: each curl consists of a man's head
and the head of a ram. The lid, decorated
with flowers, is also crowned by a symbolic
figure: the woman with a book and cross
stands for Faith. This gilt image forms the
decorative finale of this masterpiece in
silver. It is not known who made this salt-
cellar; the maker's mark is no longer legible.

The clear articulation and structure of
this splendid piece – which is composed of

loose, cast elements – is typical of the art of
the 16th century, which means that this
object was already somewhat old-fashioned
at the time it was made. By then the tone
had already been set by the flowing, organic
forms used by Adam and Paulus van Vianen
and Johannes Lutma. Nevertheless, some
'modern' elements are recognisable in the
details: the plateaus are decorated with
flowing, auricular forms.

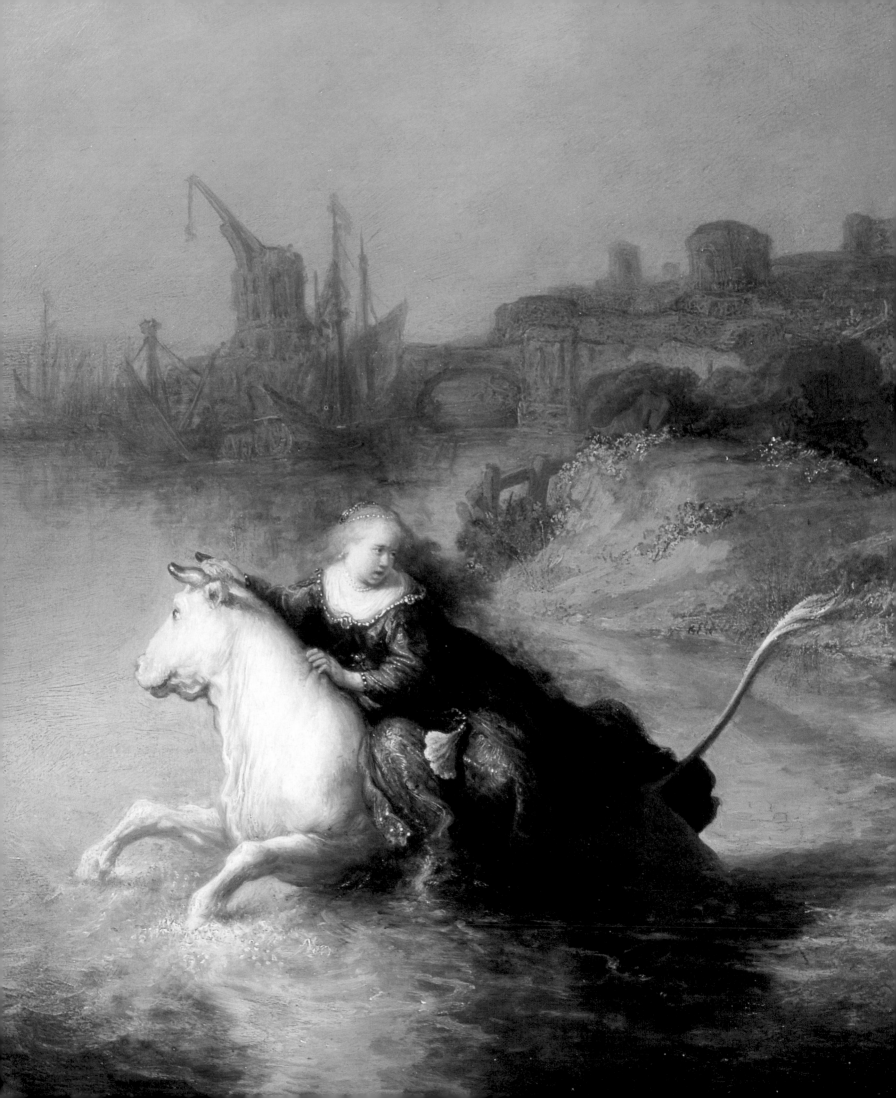

7 EXEMPLARY STORIES 1620-1640

REMBRANDT VAN RIJN enjoyed fame and prestige as a portrait painter, though he himself probably saw history painting as his true calling. High demands were placed on artists working in this genre, who depicted exemplary stories taken from the Bible, classical antiquity and mythology. History painters had to be masters of various specialities, capable of painting everything from landscapes and interiors to people, animals and still lifes. Not only did they avail themselves of the rules of composition and perspective, but they had to know how to dress their figures in the appropriate costumes and they also had to be aware of the literary and visual sources informing the stories they portrayed. Painters of 'histories' had to be capable of lending visual expression to the moral of their story. Artistic theory of the 17th century therefore esteemed history painters more highly than painters of portraits, still lifes or landscapes.

CRUCIAL MOMENT

In the early 17th century, history paintings came to focus more and more on one crucial moment in a story, and artists began increasingly to concentrate on rendering the emotions of the main characters. In his painting of *The abduction of Europa*, for example, Rembrandt portrayed the moment when the white bull abducts the young princess. The frightened Europa clings to the bull, leaving her terrified attendants behind

on the shore. Rembrandt was a master in the choice of the dramatic moment. He seldom depicted the traditional episode of a story, but chose instead a novel perspective which he then portrayed with unerring skill.

Rembrandt received his training as a history painter in Amsterdam from the most important history painter of his time, Pieter Lastman. The way in which Lastman 'told' his stories was innovative; he paid a lot of attention to depicting his protagonists' emotions, which found expression in their faces and gestures. Lastman had a predilection for stories which gave him an opportunity to paint throngs of people, in addition to his leading characters.

At the beginning of his career Rembrandt made history paintings in the style of Lastman, whose compositions he varied in an attempt to improve upon the work of his teacher. His paintings – like Lastman's – were colourful, teeming with people and full of action. The illumination in Lastman's paintings was predominantly uniform, however, without much contrast between light and dark, whereas Rembrandt employed lighting effects to lend added drama to his depictions. His handling of light demonstrates the influence exerted on him by the Utrecht Caravaggisti (see chapter 4) with their chiaroscuro effects. Rembrandt, in his turn, exerted a decisive influence on others.

THE YOUNG REMBRANDT

Rembrandt was born in Leiden in 1606, the fifth son of the miller Harmen Gerritsz van Rijn and Neeltgen Willemsdr van Zuytbrouck. After receiving his primary education at the Latin school, he enrolled in 1620 at Leiden University, which he never actually attended. Around 1621-1623 he was apprenticed to the Leiden history painter Jacob van Swanenburgh (1571-1638), after which, in 1624, he spent six months as a pupil of Pieter Lastman in Amsterdam. Back in Leiden, Rembrandt set up as an independent painter, with his own workshop and his first pupil – Gerard Dou.

In 1631 Rembrandt moved to Amsterdam, where he found lodgings at the house of the art dealer Hendrick van Uylenburgh, whose daughter Saskia he married in 1634. In Amsterdam Rembrandt quickly made a name for himself. Although he had originally specialised in history painting, he also received a large number of important commissions for portraits (see also chapters 8 and 18).

< DETAIL OF 53

BACCHANAL

This remarkable painting – more than two metres wide – by Moses van Uyttenbroeck has all the characteristics of an early 17th-century history painting. It is colourful and displays rather uniform illumination. His focus on the naked body connects Van Uyttenbroeck with Mannerism, while his realistic rendering of skin colour may be

51

MOSES VAN UYTTENBROECK

(1595/1600-1646/1647)

Bacchanal, 1627

Canvas 125 x 206 cm

BRAUNSCHWEIG,

HERZOG ANTON ULRICH-MUSEUM

(acquired in 1776, see p. 323)

traced to Caravaggism. It is not known for whom Van Uyttenbroeck made this painting, but the format and the specific choice of subject suggests that it was a commissioned work.

Sitting on a triumphal chariot, Bacchus, the god of wine, is pulled by two panthers, whose reins are held by a satyr sitting on the box. A crowd of naked and semi-naked youths, men and women accompany the young god: singing, dancing and making music, they parade behind the chariot. The scene portrays an episode from Ovid's *Metamorphoses*, in which it is told how the ecstatic, jubilant Bacchants – the devotees of Bacchus – adorned with ivy and vines, follow Bacchus on his journey around the world. Bacchus himself is young and handsome, sitting in an elegant pose and holding the *thyrsus*, a staff wound round with ivy.

Riding on ahead of Bacchus is his teacher and companion Silenus, the fat and inevitably drunken old man straddling a donkey. Gods of a lesser order than Bacchus also take part in this colourful procession winding its way through the mountainous, Italianate landscape.

Striking indeed are the curious figures in the foreground, all seemingly cast in the same mould, with squat and rather shapeless bodies. The painter created a feeling of depth and distance by placing the figures in rows behind each other.

ORESTES AND PYLADES

Like Van Uyttenbroeck, Pieter Lastman made a definite distinction between the brightly illuminated figures in the foreground, the dimly lit figures in the middle distance and the blue-grey illumination of the group in

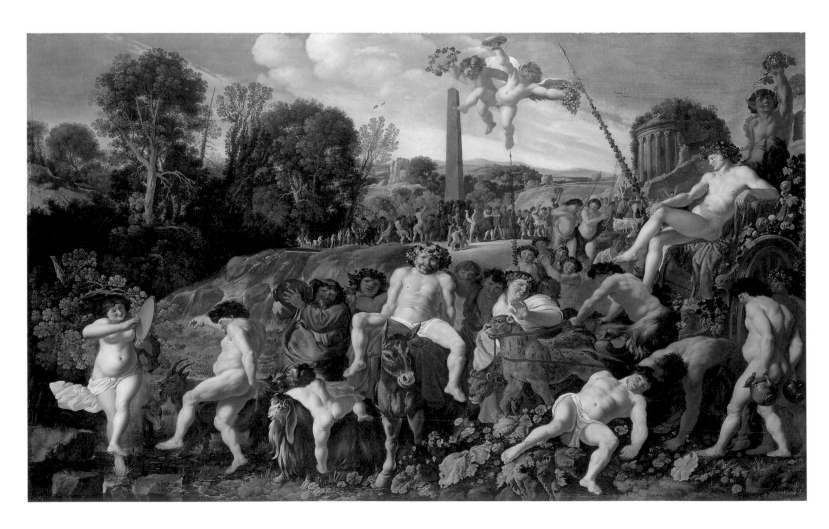

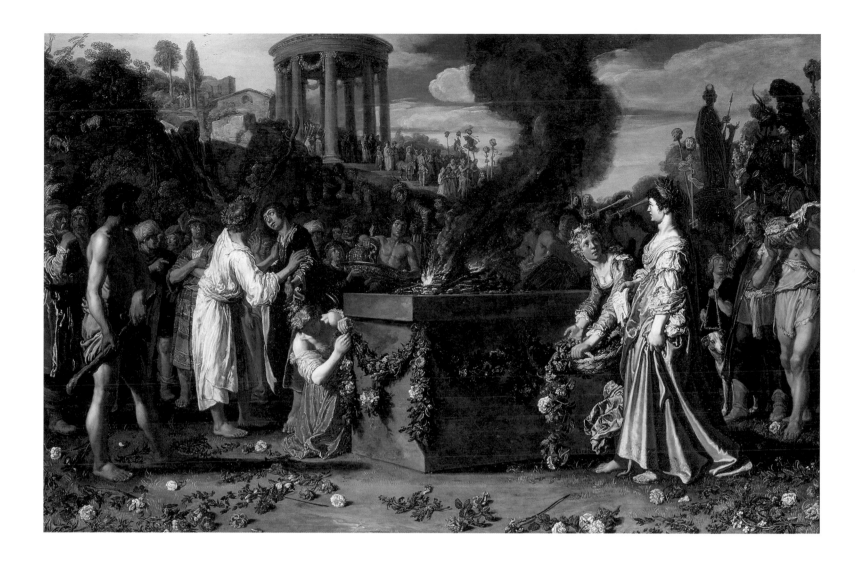

the background. Most of the light falls on the protagonists, Orestes and Pylades, standing to the left of the altar, discussing which of them will have to sacrifice himself. Here Pieter Lastman portrayed the crucial moment in a classic drama.

The Greek writer Euripides (c. 481-406 BC) described how Orestes, son of the hero Agamemnon, travelled to Tauris, together with his faithful friend Pylades, in order to steal the famous cult statue of the goddess Artemis. The priestess of the temple that housed the wooden statue was none other than Iphigenia, Orestes' sister, whom Artemis had secretly brought to Tauris years earlier. Orestes did not know that she was still alive. Before the friends could put their wicked plan into action, however, they were found out

and taken prisoner. Orestes and Pylades were led along to the temple, where they were to be sacrificed – the fate of all strangers who set foot on Tauris. Iphigenia took pity on them and decided that one of them would be allowed to live, leaving it to the men to decide who should be sacrificed. Although each wanted to die to save the other, they finally decided that Orestes would be sacrificed. At the moment he was to die, however, Iphigenia recognised her brother. The sacrificial banquet was called off, and Iphigenia and the young men fled to Mycenae, taking the statue of Artemis with them.

Lastman portrayed this complicated story in a skilful manner. The illumination and colour scheme were used to set off the protagonists from the dozens of supporting

52
PIETER LASTMAN (1583-1633)
*Orestes and Pylades disputing
at the altar*, 1614
Panel 83 x 126 cm
AMSTERDAM, RIJKSMUSEUM
(acquired with the aid of the Rembrandt
Society in 1908, see p. 314)

actors. Typical of Lastman's early work is the crowded composition, in which throngs of people can be distinguished far into the background. They form a colourful procession of spectators, winding their way from the temple to the altar, carrying armour, human heads on poles and the wooden statue of Artemis.

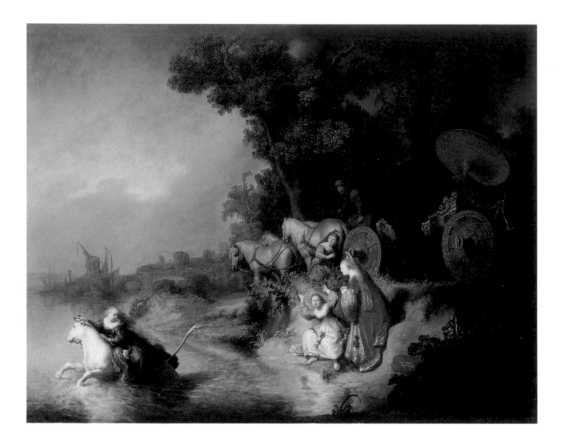

53
REMBRANDT (1606-1669)
The abduction of Europa, 1632
Panel 62.2 x 77 cm
LOS ANGELES, THE J. PAUL GETTY MUSEUM
(acquired in 1995, see p. 338)

54
REMBRANDT (1606-1669)
The wedding of Samson, 1638
Canvas 126.5 x 175.5 cm
DRESDEN, GEMÄLDEGALERIE
(acquired before 1728, see p. 329)

>

Lastman painted this depiction around ten years after his visit to Italy, where he made numerous drawings, including many of classical architecture. This Italian influence is visible in the setting in which he placed the story of Orestes, Pylades and Iphigenia, and in his signature: *Pietro Lastman.*

EUROPA AND THE BULL

Pieter Lastman's most famous pupil was Rembrandt van Rijn. Rembrandt studied only half a year with the Amsterdam history painter, but was nevertheless strongly influenced by him. This is seen in the palette, the rendering of emotions and the choice of subject of Rembrandt's *The abduction of Europa*. As a history painter Rembrandt concentrated mainly on biblical stories, but, inspired by his teacher, he portrayed in this picture a story from Ovid's *Metamorphoses*: the abduction of the princess Europa.

Ovid tells how the supreme god, Jupiter, fell in love with Europa, the daughter of the Phoenician king, Agenor. In order to get close to her, Jupiter disguised himself as a white bull. When Europa and her retinue, out riding in a coach, stopped by the seashore, the affectionate animal fell at her feet. Europa playfully climbed on its back, upon which the bull took off, ran into the sea and bore her off to Crete.

Rembrandt placed the main characters in the light and kept both foreground and background darker in tone, thereby emphasising the spectacle of the central event. The décor is of secondary importance, even though the surroundings are carefully worked out. The shore forms a diagonal line which points to the city in the distance, Tyre, where ships lie in the harbour and a crane stands on an unfinished tower.

SAMSON'S WEDDING FEAST

A masterly example of a history painting with theatrical effects is Rembrandt's portrayal of *The wedding of Samson.*

Rembrandt painted a crucial moment during the wedding feast of Samson and his wife, a woman of the Philistines, the people who had dominion over Israel. According to the story in the Bible (*Judges* 14:10-18), Samson – recognisable by his long hair – proposed a riddle to his Philistine guests on the first day of the week-long wedding feast: 'Out of the eater came forth meat, and out of the strong came forth sweetness.' No one present knew the solution, but after begging him for seven days, Samson's wife finally managed to pry the answer out of him and immediately passed it on to her fellow countrymen. When they answered Samson with 'What is sweeter than honey? and what is stronger than a lion?', Samson instantly saw through the deceit, for only his wife could have known that he had once killed a lion with his bare hands and that he had later found bees swarming in the lion's carcass, and also a honeycomb. In his rage Samson killed thirty Philistines.

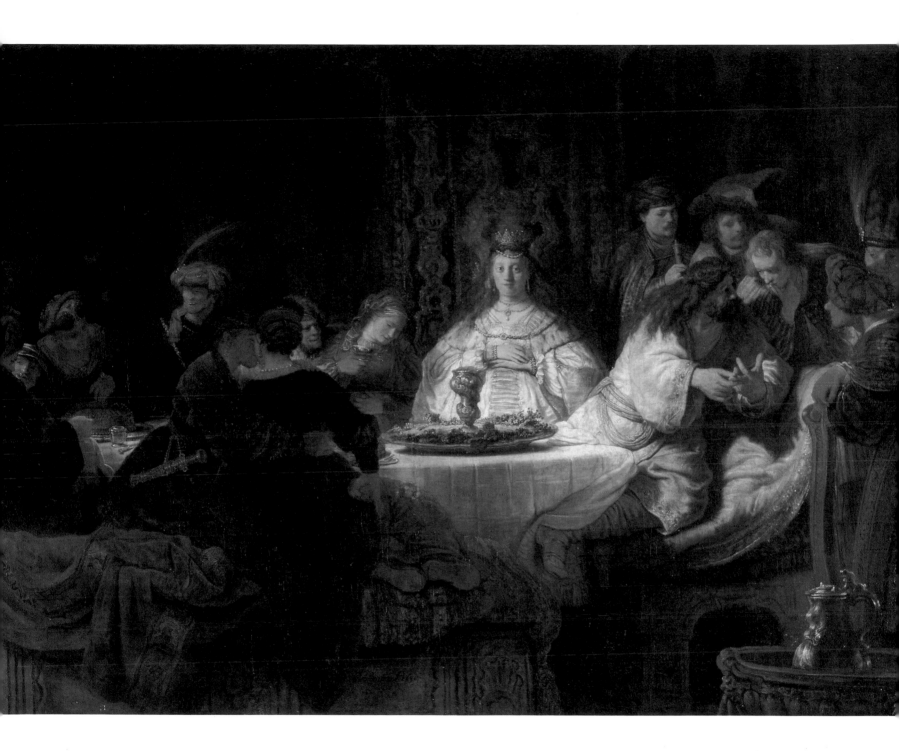

NATURAL GESTURES

Rembrandt placed the bride in full light and made her the central figure of his composition: she was, after all, the one responsible for the turn of events. Her cool glance and reserved demeanour seem to anticipate the dénouement.

One of Rembrandt's contemporaries was quick to recognise the power of this theatrical painting. In a speech delivered in 1641 to the members of the Leiden Guild of St Luke, the Leiden painter and writer Philips Angel praised this painting because the artist had so successfully immersed himself in the story. The guests lie on sofas, for example, as was customary in ancient times, and it is obvious from Samson's natural gestures that he is proposing a riddle to the people gathered round him. Angel also argued that Rembrandt's strength was evident in his depiction of the wedding guests: only some of those present listen to the groom, while others laughingly raise their glasses or are engrossed in conversation. Here the painter made an admirable rendering of a very plausible situation, proving that he had studied Samson's story and plumbed its depths.

55

REMBRANDT (1606-1669)
*Jeremiah lamenting the destruction
of Jerusalem*, 1630
Panel 58.3 x 46.6 cm
AMSTERDAM, RIJKSMUSEUM
(acquired with the aid of the Rembrandt
Society in 1939, see p. 316)

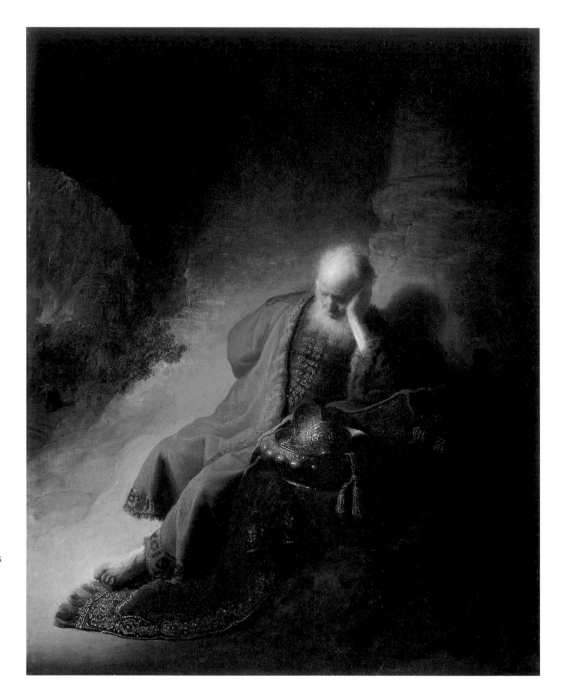

JEREMIAH

A mournful figure, dramatically lit against a dark background: this is how Rembrandt summed up the story of the destruction of Jerusalem. According to the Bible, Jeremiah had predicted the destruction of Jerusalem, the capital of Judah, to King Zedekiah, who would have had to meet the demands of Nebuchadnezzar, the King of Babylon, if Jerusalem were not to go up in flames. Zedekiah paid no heed to the warning and Jeremiah's prediction came true. Nebuchadnezzar captured the city, set fire to it and had Zedekiah's eyes put out.

The old Jeremiah sits at the foot of a pillar, resting his head on his hand, a gesture of sorrow and melancholy. His elbow is propped on a thick book, next to which lie precious vessels. On the left in the distance Jerusalem is being burned and plundered. Nebuchadnezzar's soldiers, armed with lances, march into the city. Above the city flies a figure carrying a flaming torch. Near a stairway stands a man in a long cloak, pressing his fists against his eyes: the blind King Zedekiah.

This small painting, which Rembrandt made while still in Leiden, is one of the high points of his early work. Striking indeed is the contrast between the carefully depicted face, with its deep wrinkles and fluffy beard, and the much coarser brushstrokes defining the background. Rembrandt placed the figure of Jeremiah diagonally across the picture plane; the light falls on his forehead, robe and feet. The background was painted with

a lightly applied, thin layer of paint. In several places Rembrandt used the handle of his brush to draw in the still-wet paint, exposing the canvas's light, ochre-coloured ground. This is visible, for example, in the braiding on Jeremiah's jerkin and in the cursorily rendered vegetation on the left.

GOVERT FLINCK

Govert Flinck worked in Rembrandt's studio in Amsterdam between 1633 and 1636. He completely adopted Rembrandt's style, choice of subject matter and working method. Three years after leaving his master's workshop he made the history painting *Isaac blessing Jacob*, after a story taken from the book of *Genesis*. Rembrandt's influence is still unmistakable in his choice of subject,

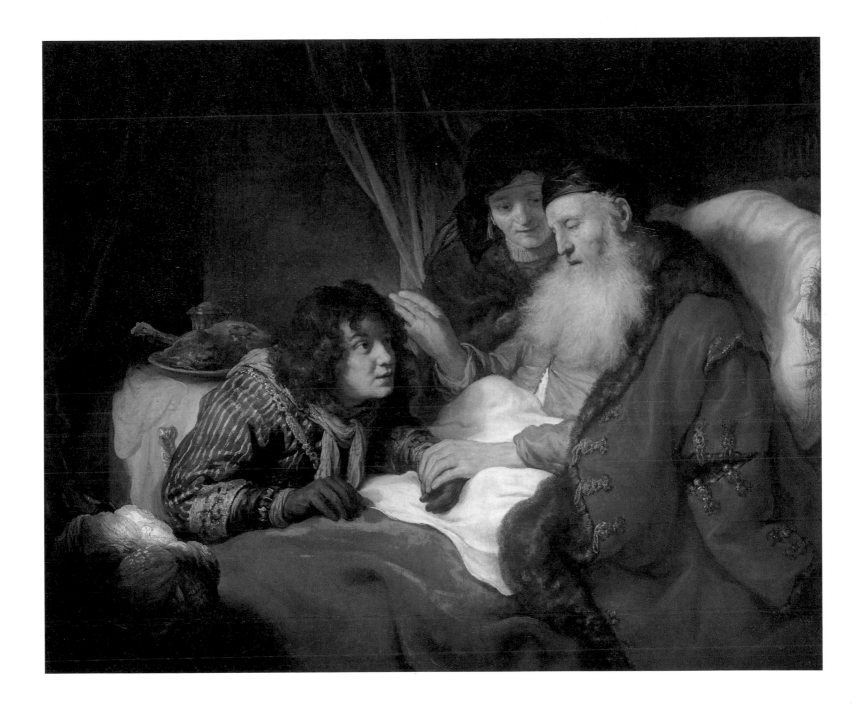

handling of paint, palette and manner of painting. Flinck's old Isaac with his woolly white beard would not be out of place in one of Rembrandt's biblical representations: he bears a strong resemblance to the latter's Jeremiah.

Until around 1640 Flinck continued to produce paintings in the style of Rembrandt. They displayed such a similarity to Rembrandt's that Flinck's paintings were

taken to be works by his teacher and also sold as such. Later on he freed himself from Rembrandt's influence and adopted the elegant, colourful style that was most appreciated in the years around 1650, during which period Flinck was working on paintings intended for Amsterdam's town hall (see chapter 21).

56
GOVERT FLINCK (1615-1660)
Isaac blessing Jacob, 1638
Canvas 117 x 141 cm
AMSTERDAM, RIJKSMUSEUM
(acquired in 1808, see p. 310)

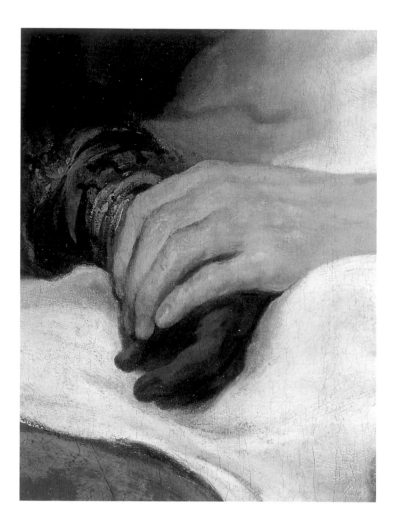

DETAIL OF 56

ISAAC AND JACOB

Like Rembrandt, Govert Flinck was capable of rendering great tension and drama. The old Isaac, his wife and their youngest son are the main characters in this scene. According to the story in the Bible (*Genesis* 27:1-29), Isaac, who was blind, felt his end approaching and decided to give his blessing, which was intended exclusively for the first-born, to his eldest son, Esau. First, however, he commanded Esau to shoot some venison and prepare it for him. Isaac's wife Rebecca heard this and thought of a trick to have Jacob – her favourite son, who was younger than Esau – receive his father's blessing. She ordered Jacob to put on Esau's clothes, then she prepared the

meat of two billy goats, and covered Jacob's hands with the shaggy skin of the two animals. In this way the blind Isaac would think he was feeling Esau's hairy hands. Flinck portrayed the moment in which Isaac is deceived by his wife and youngest son. The blind Isaac, suspecting nothing, gives his blessing to Jacob. Isaac rests his left hand on the hand of Jacob, while with his right hand he blesses his youngest son.

Flinck made the viewer a participant in the event by placing the figures close to the picture plane. The tension is clearly visible in the faces of mother and son. This painting, with its remarkably bright colours, shows Flinck at his best.

FLORA

Rembrandt's brand-new bride, Saskia van Uylenburgh, was probably the model for Flora, the Roman goddess of flowers, springtime and fertility, here crowned with flowers and dressed in a costly gown. On 22 July 1634 Rembrandt married Saskia, and in the same year he painted his *Flora*. It is tempting to see in Flora a portrait of Saskia: the goddess displays a certain similarity to a portrait drawing which Rembrandt made of Saskia on the occasion of their engagement.

Rembrandt portrayed a modest, charming Flora, dressed in a rather oriental costume. Her floral finery includes a red tulip, in those days a flower both costly and popular. Flowers also entwine the stick in her hand. The foliage in the background indicates the outdoor setting.

Although this painting does not portray a story – and is therefore not a true history painting – it has a theatrical appearance. Here as well, Rembrandt achieved this effect by means of illumination, making the goddess seem to break free from the background. Unsurpassed is the variation Rembrandt introduced into his brushstrokes, ranging from minute and meticulous to broad and powerful. The face and hands were painted with a fluent, soft and tender touch; the flowers, the motifs in the material and the embroidery on the sleeves were depicted with rather fine brushstrokes; the heavy folds in the gown were rendered in a broad and pastose manner.

57

REMBRANDT (1606-1669)
Flora, 1634
Canvas 124.7 x 100.4 cm
ST PETERSBURG, HERMITAGE
(acquired between 1770 and 1783,
see p. 346)

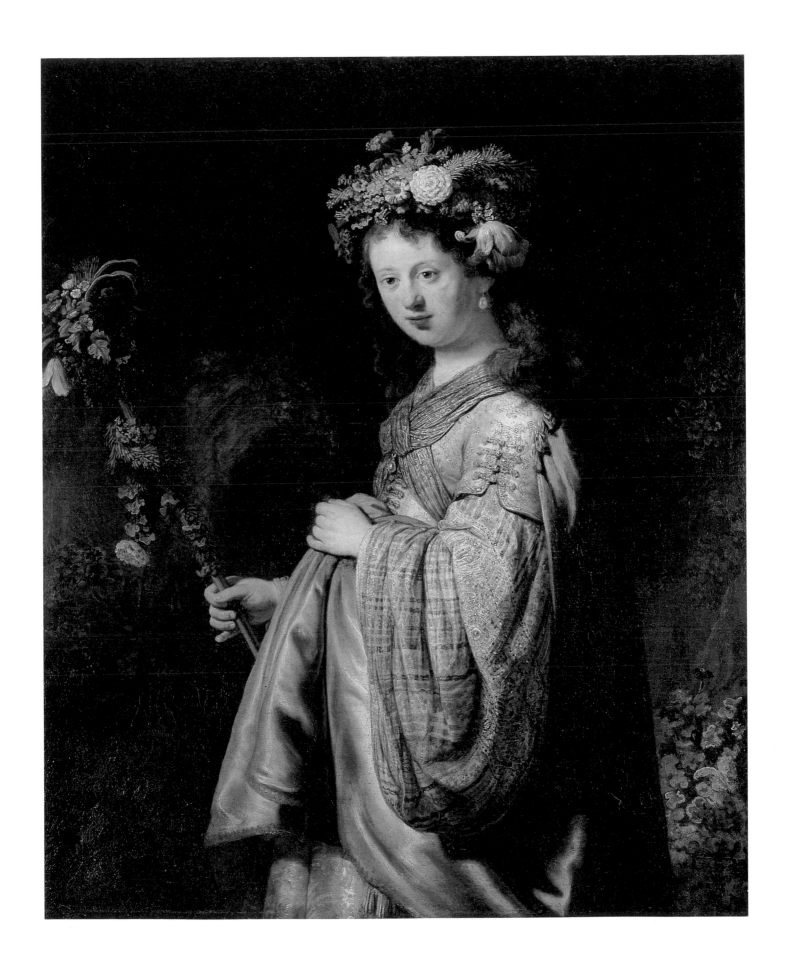

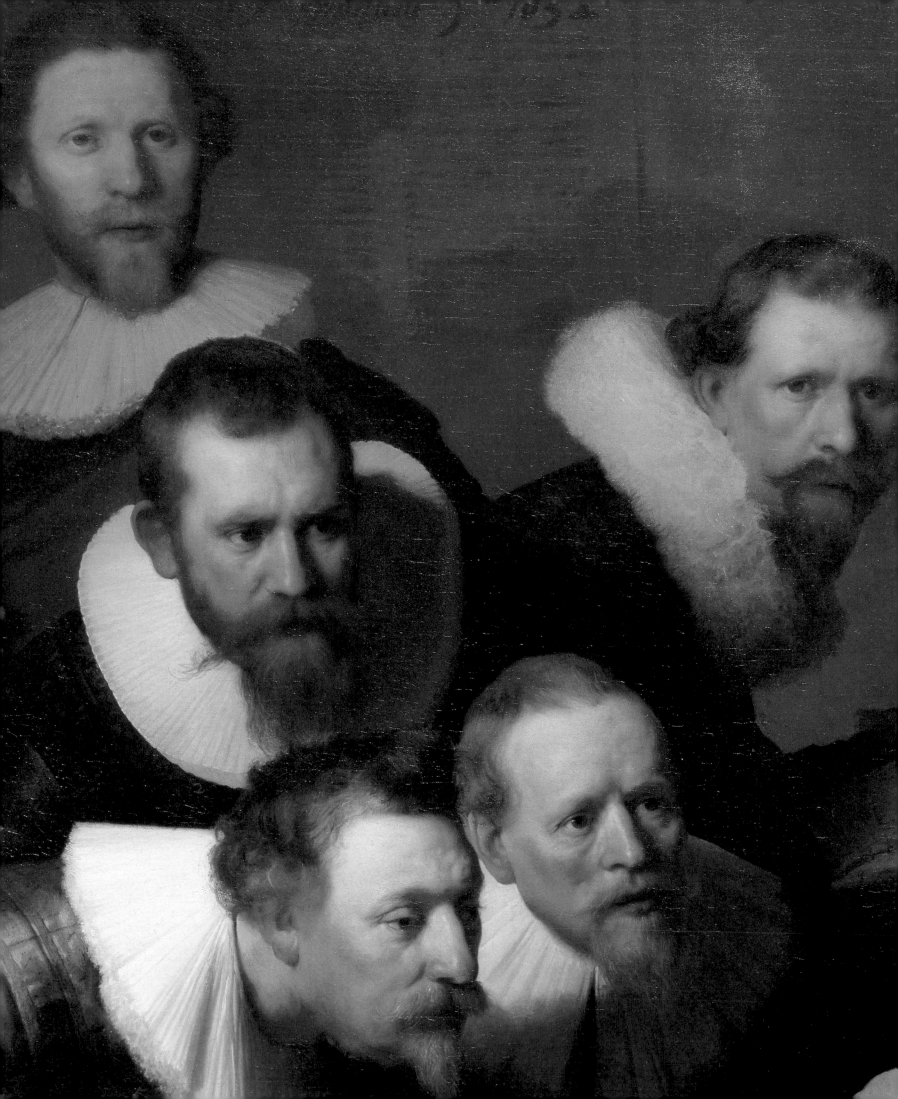

8 IMPORTANT COMMISSIONS 1630-1650

AT THE END of 1631 Rembrandt van Rijn moved from Leiden to Amsterdam. The young, ambitious painter had decided to try his luck in the largest and most prosperous city in the Dutch Republic. This step proved to be of crucial importance for his career. Soon after settling down he received commissions to paint the portraits of wealthy Amsterdam burghers. In no time the Leiden painter earned a place among the respected artists and artisans working in Amsterdam. This prosperous metropolis offered a golden future to talented painters, sculptors, gold- and silversmiths and cabinetmakers.

MAGNIFICENT GROUP PORTRAIT

While Rembrandt was still living in Leiden his talent had already attracted a lot of attention. Constantijn Huygens, the influential secretary of Stadholder Frederik Hendrik, visited Rembrandt and Jan Lievens, who were probably sharing a studio at that time. According to Huygens, Rembrandt was Lievens's superior in precision and the vivid rendering of emotions. He praised Rembrandt highly, and then commissioned both Rembrandt and Lievens to paint his portrait.

During his Leiden period Rembrandt had not executed any large portrait paintings, but in Amsterdam he produced an impressive series of them between 1631 and 1635. He made several individual portraits of

Amsterdam burghers, and in 1632 he received an important commission to paint a group portrait: *The anatomy lesson of Dr Nicolaes Tulp* [58]. The fact that Rembrandt received this commission is remarkable in itself. He had proven his talent, to be sure, but he had never painted such a large group portrait.

The person who commissioned it was probably Nicolaes Tulp himself, the *praelector anatomiae*, lecturer in anatomy, of the Amsterdam surgeons' guild. This doctor, who provided instruction to members of the guild – surgeons, assistants and apprentices – had been appointed by the town council. In Amsterdam it was customary for lecturers to have their portraits painted in the midst of a number of guild members. Paintings were made of various anatomy lessons, portraying Tulp's predecessors as well as his successors. Until some time in the 19th century these group portraits were preserved in the weighhouse, which had long housed the guild. Most of these portraits are now to be found in the Amsterdam Historical Museum.

AMSTERDAM

Dominion over the seven seas was largely in the hands of the Dutch in the 17th century, by which time Amsterdam had taken over the role, previously held by Antwerp, of the world's trading centre. The city functioned as a staple market and exerted a great attraction on anyone with money. The number of inhabitants grew rapidly, increasing from approximately 50,000 people around 1600 to 120,000 in 1630 and 200,000 around 1650. As early as 1610 the municipal government decided on a plan to expand the city by building a ring of canals, along which rich burghers had their houses built.

By the time Rembrandt settled there in 1631, Amsterdam had also gained importance as a cultural centre. This city, with its international orientation and concentration of wealth, held forth interesting possibilities to artists. Not surprisingly, the production of art in the Netherlands was concentrated in Amsterdam.

< DETAIL OF 58

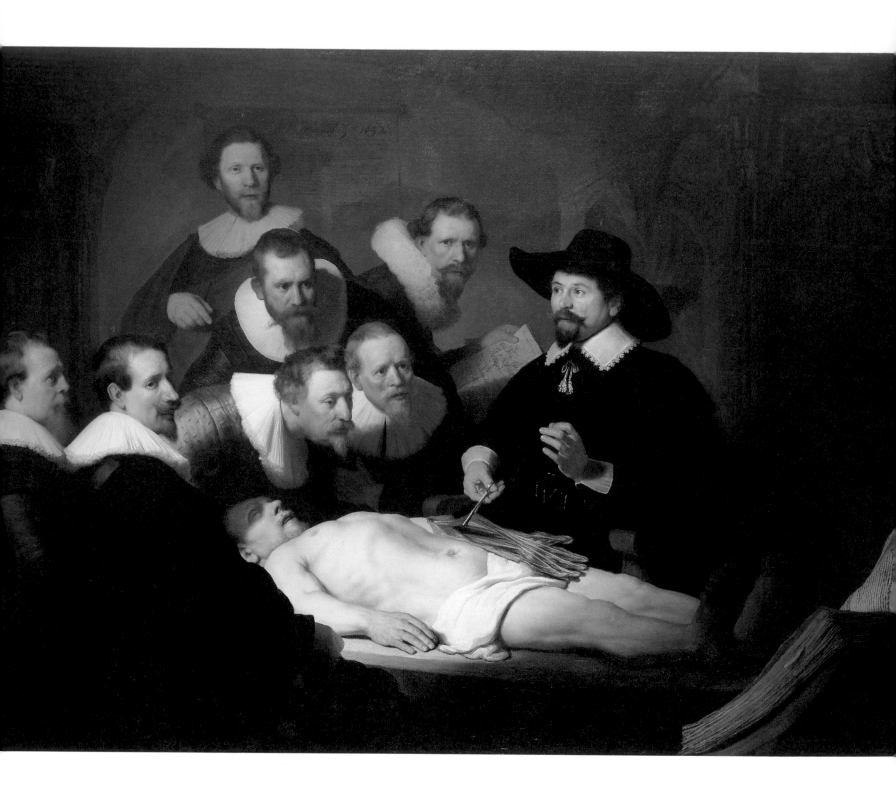

58

REMBRANDT (1606-1669)

The anatomy lesson
of Dr Nicolaes Tulp, 1632

Canvas 169.5 x 216.5 cm

THE HAGUE, MAURITSHUIS

(acquired in 1828, see p. 332)

ANATOMY LESSON

Once a year the Amsterdam surgeons' guild organised an anatomy lesson which was open to the public. Guild members and learned outsiders paid to attend the lesson given by the *praelector*. The event attracted hundreds of interested people. The anatomy lesson usually lasted longer than a day and always took place in the winter, because the cadaver decayed more slowly at lower temperatures. The body of an executed criminal was used for the demonstration. In 1632 the surgeons' guild had at its disposal the body of Adriaan Adriaansz, alias 'The Kid'. On 31 January, the day the anatomy lesson was to begin, Adriaansz had been hanged for committing a robbery. For Tulp, *praelector anatomiae* of the surgeons' guild since 1628, this was the second public anatomy lesson of his career, and to mark the occasion he decided to have his portrait painted by Rembrandt.

Tulp stands behind the dissecting table on which the corpse lies. The doctor is dressed in black and is the only member of the company wearing a large hat. Behind him is a shell-shaped niche, which serves to bring him to the fore. Tulp demonstrates the dissection of an arm, explaining at the same time what he is doing. The audience watches in fascination.

This group portrait, which Rembrandt made when he was 26 years old, differs in every respect from previously painted anatomy lessons. Whereas in all previous paintings the cadaver lay parallel to the picture plane, Rembrandt positioned it somewhat diagonally, with a large anatomy book at its feet. This lent an atmosphere of tension to the scene, with the listeners on the left, grouped around the head of the corpse, and on the right the protagonist, Dr Tulp. By means of this diagonal construction Rembrandt introduced movement into the composition. This effect is further heightened by the fact that several of the gentlemen lean forward curiously, their gaze fixed on the arm, which is the subject of the lesson. In his forceps Tulp holds the forearm flexors.

Here Rembrandt did not depict a realistic situation. In fact the first operation in an anatomy lesson was dissecting the abdomen. The arm was usually the last thing to be dissected, and then mostly an arm that had been cut off the body. As has emerged from technical examination, during the painting process Rembrandt made small changes in the poses of the figures, probably in order to liven up the action.

In the 18th century the names of the eight gentlemen portrayed were written on the piece of paper containing an anatomical sketch, which Hartman Harmansz, to the left of Dr Tulp, holds in his hand.

BACK IN AMSTERDAM

In 1817 Cornelis Apostool, director of the Rijksmuseum, made an appeal to have *The anatomy lesson of Dr Nicolaes Tulp* removed from the damp and leaking Amsterdam weighhouse. According to Apostool, the painting, 'so excellent in truth, power and simplicity', would be better off in the Rijksmuseum. No one listened to his cry of distress, however, and Rembrandt's masterpiece continued to hang in the weighhouse for another 11 years.

In 1828 it was sold for 32,000 guilders to the Dutch state, which financed the purchase largely with the proceeds from a sale of paintings belonging to the Rijksmuseum. King Willem I, to Apostool's great disappointment, decided to have the painting hung in the Mauritshuis in The Hague. During the exhibition *The Glory of the Golden Age* the painting is once again in the city where it was made.

PORTRAIT OF JOHANNES WTENBOGAERT

The young, ambitious Rembrandt received a commission to portray the elderly, assertive Remonstrant minister Wtenbogaert [59]. On 13 April 1633 Reverend Wtenbogaert travelled from The Hague to Amsterdam to have his portrait painted by Rembrandt. The sitting was probably limited to this one day, during which Rembrandt would have concentrated on his model's wrinkled face. Afterwards he would have filled in his impressions and worked them up into a portrait.

Rembrandt placed the minister near a table. The old man seems to be frozen in time, as in a snapshot. The illumination focuses attention on the wrinkled face with its clear gaze, the greyish beard and the snow-white ruff. His left hand rests on his breast; in his right hand he holds his gloves. Just as he had done in *The anatomy lesson of Dr Nicolaes Tulp*, Rembrandt added a touch of action, though here it is minimal: the model turns momentarily in the direction of the viewer. In this subtle way Rembrandt was able to breathe life into the portrait.

Black and brown are the dominant colours in this painting. Rembrandt succeeded, however, in introducing subtle nuances into these dark hues, making a superb distinction between light and dark. For example, he painted the dark-brown fur, with which the cloak is trimmed, as a fuzzy contour against the lighter background.

JOHANNES WTENBOGAERT

Johannes Wtenbogaert (1557-1644) – founder of the Remonstrant Brotherhood, a Protestant congregation – was an important advocate of tolerance within the church. Between 1600 and 1615 he was court pastor to the Princes of Orange. As the leader of the Remonstrants he played an important role in the theological clash with the Gomarists, who were stringent Calvinists. In 1610 Wtenbogaert wrote the *Remonstrantie*. This document was meant to be an instrument of conciliation, but became instead a bone of contention that precipitated an irreparable rift. When things came to a head in 1617 and Prince Maurits sided openly with the Gomarists, Wtenbogaert was forced into exile. From Antwerp and

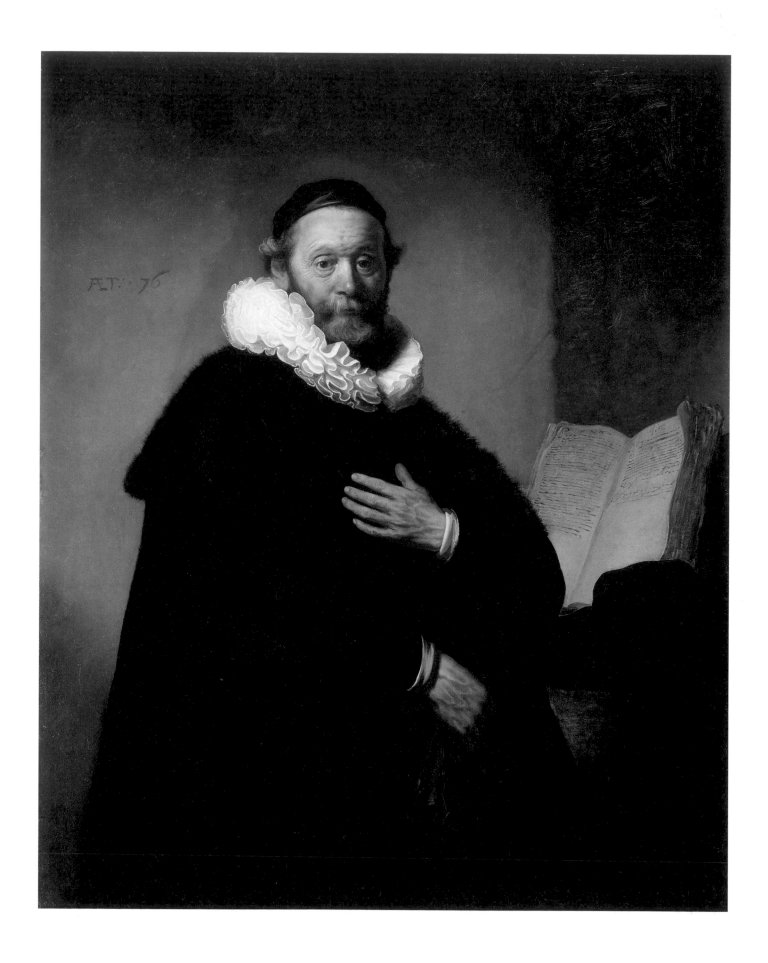

59

REMBRANDT (1606-1669)
Portrait of Johannes Wtenbogaert, 1633
Canvas 130 x 103 cm
AMSTERDAM, RIJKSMUSEUM
(acquired with the aid of the Rembrandt
Society in 1992, see p. 319)

<

60

JAN LIEVENS (1607-1674)
Self-portrait(?) in a yellow robe,
c. 1630-1631
Canvas 112 x 99.4 cm
EDINBURGH,
NATIONAL GALLERY OF SCOTLAND
(acquired in 1922, see p. 330)

>

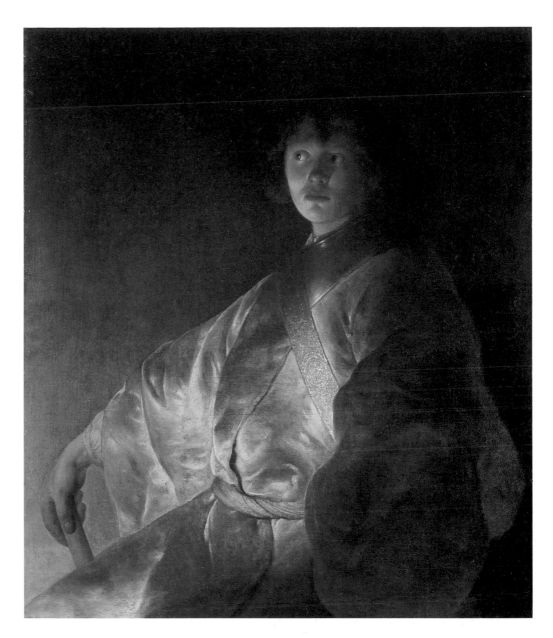

Rouen he worked to organise the Remonstrant Brotherhood. After the death of Prince Maurits he returned secretly to his native country in 1626. Seven years later Rembrandt painted his portrait: it was commissioned by the Amsterdam merchant Abraham Anthonisz Recht, a Remonstrant and follower of Johannes Wtenbogaert. At the age of 76 Wtenbogaert was still thought of as a leader by his fellow Remonstrants.

Abraham Anthonisz Recht (1588-1664) had the painting hanging in his manor house just outside Amsterdam, as emerges from the inventory drawn up after his death. At that time the work was worth 40 guilders. During the 18th century the painting was probably to be found with Recht's heirs. At the beginning of the 19th century the painting surfaced in Italy and was purchased by the English baron Meyer de Rothschild. The portrait remained in the family's possession until 1992, when it was sold at auction in London. The new owners offered to let the Rijksmuseum buy it, as they thought it actually belonged here. And so, after two centuries, the canvas has finally returned to the Netherlands.

YOUNG MAN IN A YELLOW ROBE

The powerful sense of drama and illumination that characterises Rembrandt's portraits is also a feature of the work of his Leiden colleague Jan Lievens, with whom Rembrandt was in close contact. Both 'beardless youths', as Constantijn Huygens called them, experimented with sources of artificial light, which created interesting reflections and shadows.

In the painting of the man in the yellow robe Lievens opted for dramatic illumination from the lower left, fixing all attention on the shining material of the robe and the reflections in the metal decoration around his shoulders. Only part of his face is illuminated. The light coming from below casts a curious shadow on the man's head. It is therefore not likely that this was a commissioned portrait; perhaps the painter himself was the model.

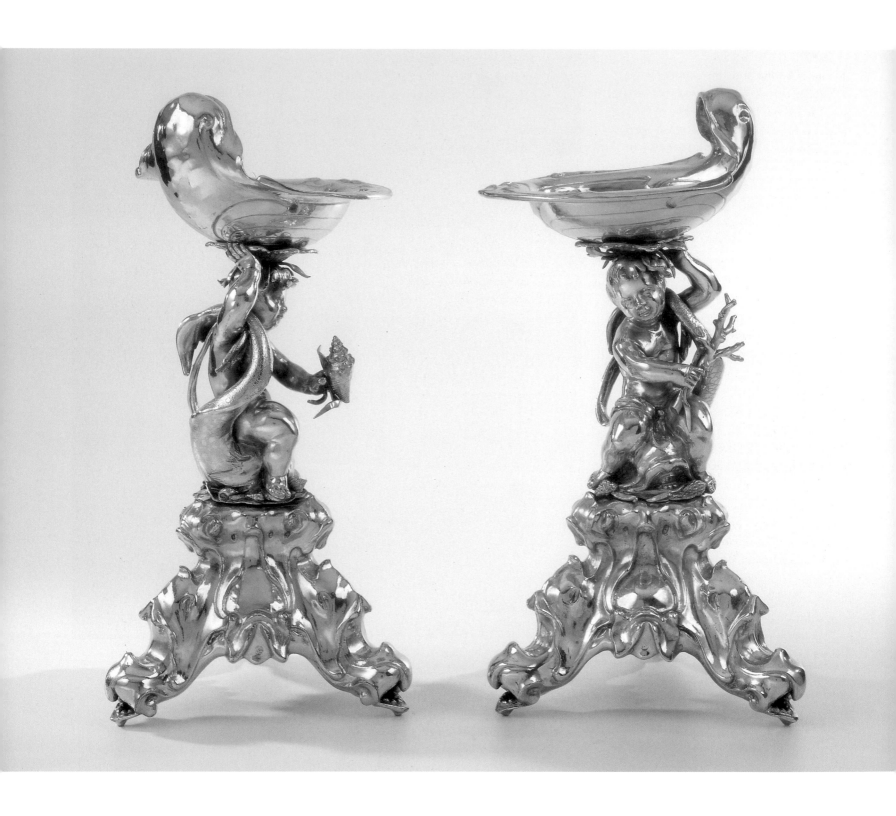

61

JOHANNES LUTMA (1587-1669)
Two salt-cellars, 1639
Silver, parcel-gilt, h. 24.2 cm
AMSTERDAM, RIJKSMUSEUM
(acquired in 1960, see p. 316)

SALT-CELLARS

Johannes Lutma probably considered the salt-cellar that he made in 1639 [61] a high point in his oeuvre. Proudly he had himself portrayed, together with just such a salt-cellar, by the Amsterdam painter Jacob Backer (1608-1651), a pupil of Rembrandt. The salt-cellar in the painting is one of a series of four. Two of them are to be found in the Amsterdam Historical Museum and two in the Rijksmuseum.

The salt-cellars, made as costly table decorations, consist of three parts. The foot, composed of three fabulous sea monsters, is cast and gilt. The middle section, the stem, is also cast and consists – in the case of both salt-cellars displayed here – of a boy sitting on a dolphin, supporting the shell-shaped salt well with one hand and holding a shell and a piece of coral in the other. The fish, shells and coral refer to the source of salt, the sea. Lutma made the salt well itself in another technique. It is not cast but chased,

and – just like the foot of the salt-cellar – gilt. This was a means of introducing variation not just in form, but also in colour.

DISH

Two years after making the salt-cellars, Lutma made a dish for which he also used the technique of chasing, or hammering a sheet of silver into the desired form. With a bit of imagination it is possible to make out an opened mouth in the bottom of this organically formed dish. The handle is formed by a tortoise-like animal which hangs its head into the dish. Here form and decoration flow into one another.

Lutma viewed this dish as a work of art, a sculpture. This is witnessed by his signature: he did not place his maker's mark on the dish, as was customary, but instead engraved his name in full – *J Lutma F.* – on the underside of the dish: J Lutma Fecit, Johannes Lutma made this.

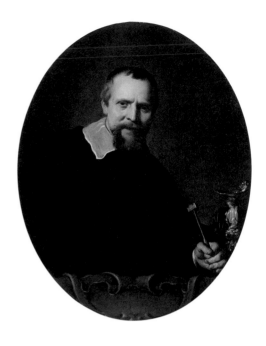

JACOB BACKER (1608-1651)
Portrait of Johannes Lutma, c. 1640
Panel 91 x 71 cm. AMSTERDAM, RIJKSMUSEUM

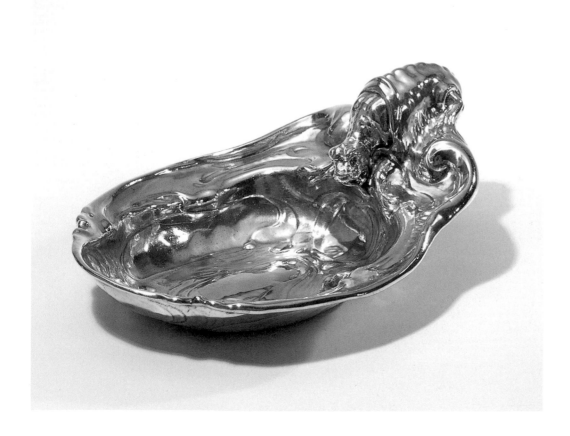

62

JOHANNES LUTMA (1587-1669)
Dish, 1641
Silver w. 20.3 cm
AMSTERDAM, RIJKSMUSEUM
(acquired in 1925, see p. 315)

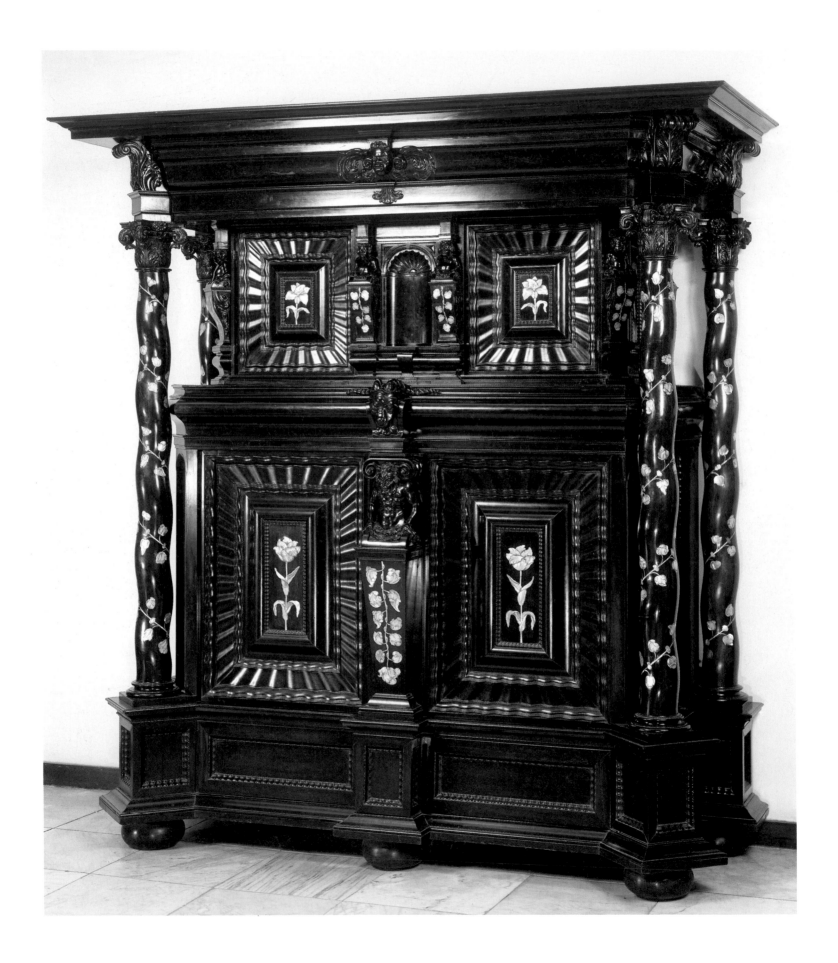

63

ATTRIBUTED TO
HERMAN DOOMER (c. 1595-1650)
OR HIS WORKSHOP
Cupboard, c. 1640-1650
Oak, veneered with ebony, kingwood,
rosewood and partridge wood(?), inlaid with
mother-of-pearl and ivory, 218 x 196 x 84 cm
AMSTERDAM, RIJKSMUSEUM
(acquired in 1975, see p. 317)

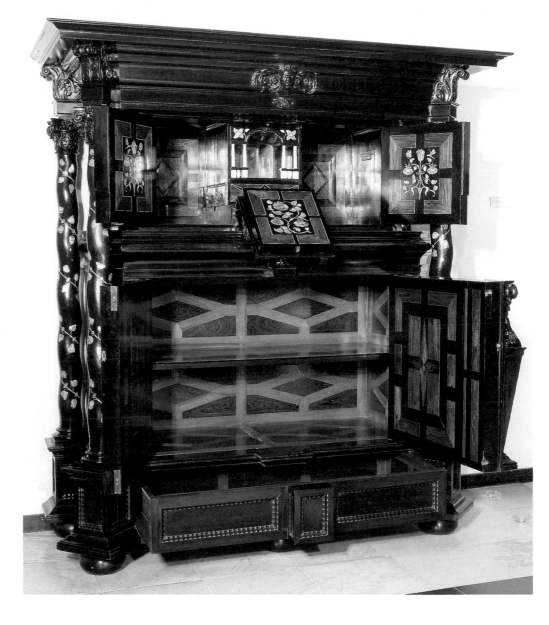

HERMAN DOOMER

A lot is known about 17th-century painters and sculptors; far less is known about cabinetmakers. One exception is the cabinet-maker Herman Doomer, whose life has been relatively well researched. The interest shown in him does not have to do with his work so much as with the fact that Doomer and his wife, Baertje Martens, had their portraits painted by Rembrandt in 1640. This couple could evidently afford to have their portraits painted by one of the most famous portrait painters of the day, an indication that Doomer must have been a successful man.

Herman Doomer, born in Anrath in Germany, lived in Amsterdam from 1613 until his death in 1650. He specialised in working with ebony. In Amsterdam this exotic wood was fairly easy to come by, because returning ships of the Dutch East India Company sometimes brought it back with them. Doomer's workshop specialised in making picture frames. He probably supplied Rembrandt with ebony frames, and this could have been how the two masters became acquainted.

PRECIOUS CUPBOARD

In the inventory of the estate of Herman Doomer's widow, various ebony cupboards are mentioned which had been made in her husband's workshop, including a 'large ebony cupboard with inlaid mother-of-pearl', which was estimated to be the most valuable piece in the inventory. This is probably the cupboard [63] that has been part of the collection of the Rijksmuseum since 1975.

This cupboard testifies to the cabinet-maker's great mastery. The entire oak cupboard has an ebony veneer and is decorated with mother-of-pearl flowers and butterflies. When the cupboard is opened, one sees that it is also completely decorated on the inside. In the upper part of the cupboard there is even an architectural embellishment in perspective. This 'architectural representation' is visible only when the hinged flap in the middle of the upper part is opened.

Judging from the decoration, both inside and out, this cupboard was no ordinary storage cupboard but an art cabinet. An ingeniously built cupboard like this one would have served as a repository for a collector's art treasures, and would have had pride of place in the room where he displayed his collections.

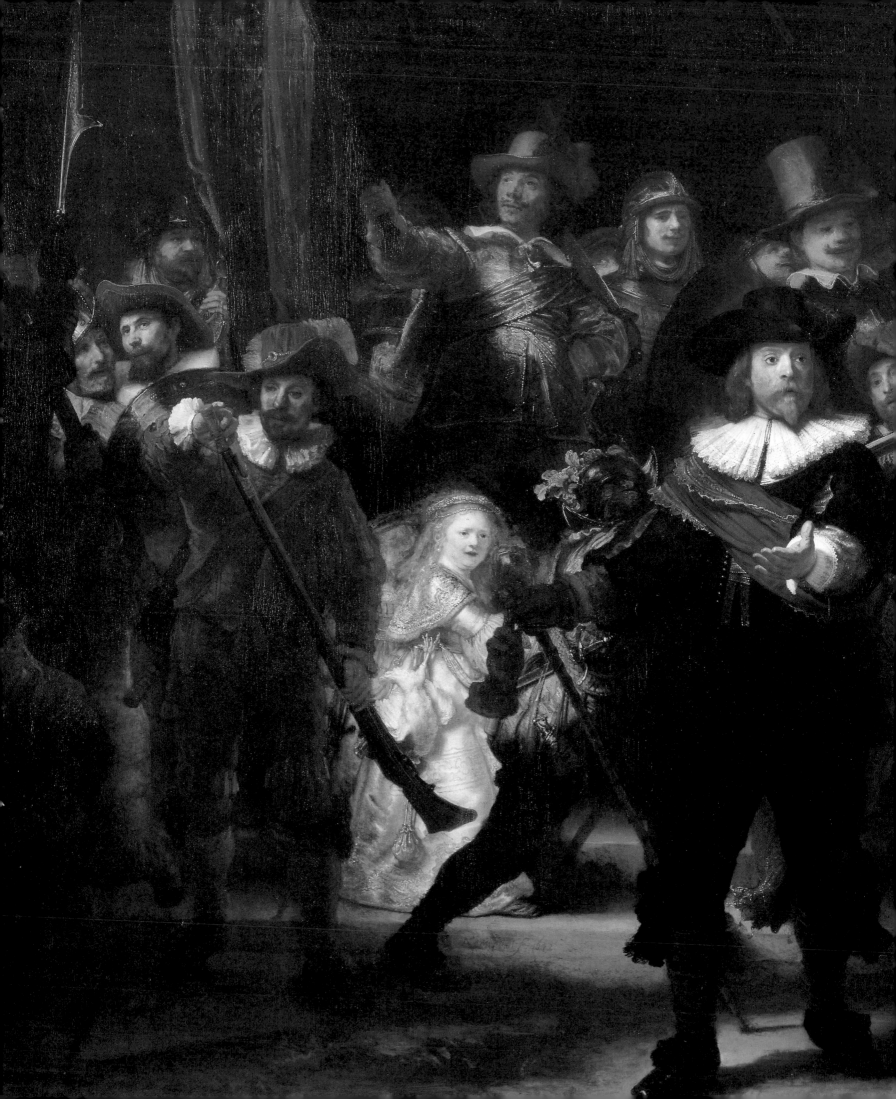

9 MILITIA COMPANIES 1635-1650

FOR PORTRAIT PAINTERS militia companies were lucrative clients. Civic guardsmen regularly commissioned group portraits and the resultant militia piece would be displayed in the company's meeting and banquet hall. Around 125 of these portraits have survived from the 16th and 17th centuries, half of which were commissioned by companies in Amsterdam. The most famous of all these is undoubtedly the portrait of one Amsterdam company, now known as *The Night Watch*.

Painting a large group of people without allowing the composition to become stiff or boring is not always simple. Over the years artists have sought a solution to this problem in a variety of ways. Early militia portraits show the guardsmen in static poses, side by side and in rows, with only a gesture of the hand to suggest any contact. This type of composition is actually just a collection of individual portraits in a single picture. By grouping the various figures around a table, painters tried to create a greater sense of coherence. In the first portraits to employ this form, the men were arranged around three sides of a table. The Amsterdam painter Dirck Barendsz (1534-1592) introduced a new element: following an Italian example, he placed the militiamen all around the table, turning the men at the front to face the viewer. This made the composition more coherent and the figures more lively.

In 16th-century group portraits, the militiamen were generally portrayed half-length and sometimes three-quarter-length. In 1588, however, the officers of the Amsterdam crossbowmen's guild had a full-length portrait painted. Among Amsterdam companies, full-length portraits continued to be popular throughout the 17th century, while artists and patrons in Haarlem remained true to the three-quarter-length portrait.

MASTERS OF GROUP PORTRAITURE

Frans Hals, himself a civic guardsman for many years, painted five portraits of Haarlem militia companies. His robust, rapid brushstrokes captured in brilliant colour the self-confidence and vitality of the militiamen. A commission from the crossbowmen's guild in Amsterdam in 1633 was rather less successful. The full-length portrait was only half finished when a disagreement arose between the painter and the militiamen. Eventually the Amsterdam painter Pieter Codde was asked to complete the group portrait, now known as *The Meagre Company*. Hals's clarity remained intact despite the switch, but Codde was unable to match Hals's robust style.

Bartholomeus van der Helst was as colourful and graceful with the brush as Frans Hals. His portrayal of a civic-guard banquet – *The celebration of the Treaty of Münster at the crossbowmen's headquarters*,

MILITIAS

Every town in the Northern Netherlands had at least one militia company. These citizens' militias, or civic guards, patrolled the city walls and kept the peace, defending the town, maintaining order whenever the mob rioted, appearing on ceremonial occasions and fighting on the front whenever the need arose. Militia companies were organised in guilds named after the weapon they bore: longbow, crossbow or harquebus (a type of firearm). Militia guilds met at their company headquarters, which had an attached shooting range, or 'doelen'.

In theory, all male citizens between the ages of 18 and 60 were obliged to serve in the militia, but not everyone could afford it. Militia membership was reserved for the rich: civic guards had to own property worth at least 600 guilders and were required to pay for their own weapons and armour. The officers of militia companies were often wealthy merchants, who stemmed from the same urban elite as the town councillors.

< DETAIL OF 65

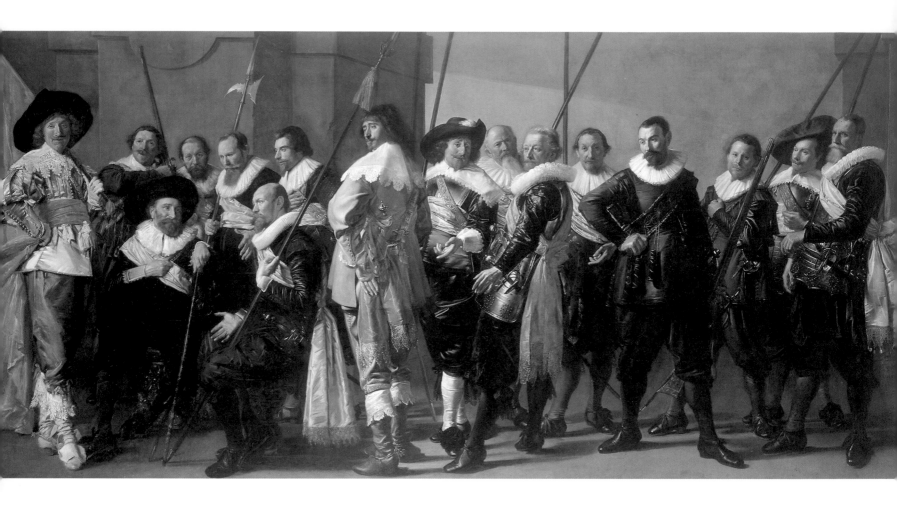

64

FRANS HALS (1582/1583-1666) AND
PIETER CODDE (1599-1678)
*The company of Captain Reynier Reael
and Lieutenant Cornelis Michielsz Blaeuw,
known as 'The Meagre Company'*, 1637
Canvas 209 x 429 cm
AMSTERDAM, RIJKSMUSEUM
(on loan from the City of Amsterdam since 1885,
see p. 311)

made in 1648 for the Amsterdam crossbow-men's hall, is a splendid group portrait in which the painter showed himself to be much more than a portrait painter. His rendering of the various materials and fabrics is masterly.

Van der Helst arranged the composition and handled the light in such a way that all the sitters were seen to advantage. In Rembrandt's *Night Watch* this appears to have been far less of a consideration. In this picture, which was painted in 1642 for the Kloveniersdoelen, Rembrandt created an exciting spectacle which seems to depict a random moment. His theatrically lit picture of militiamen in action was a milestone in the tradition of civic-guard portraits.

THE MEAGRE COMPANY

Art historian and restorer Jan van Dijk found the militia portrait by Frans Hals and Pieter Codde so 'barren and frail', in 1758, 'that they might rightfully be called the meagre company'. Since then this militia portrait has been known by that name. In 1633 Frans Hals was commissioned to paint the portrait of Captain Reynier Reael and Lieutenant Cornelis Michielsz Blaeuw of the Amsterdam crossbowmen's guild together with their militiamen. He was to paint the piece in Amsterdam, where the members of the company lived. For Hals, who lived in Haarlem, this involved regular trips to the capital. In fact he was rarely to make the journey at all. In 1636, three years after receiving the commission, he had still only completed part of the painting. Eventually the militiamen took him to task. In reply he responded, as the preserved documents state,

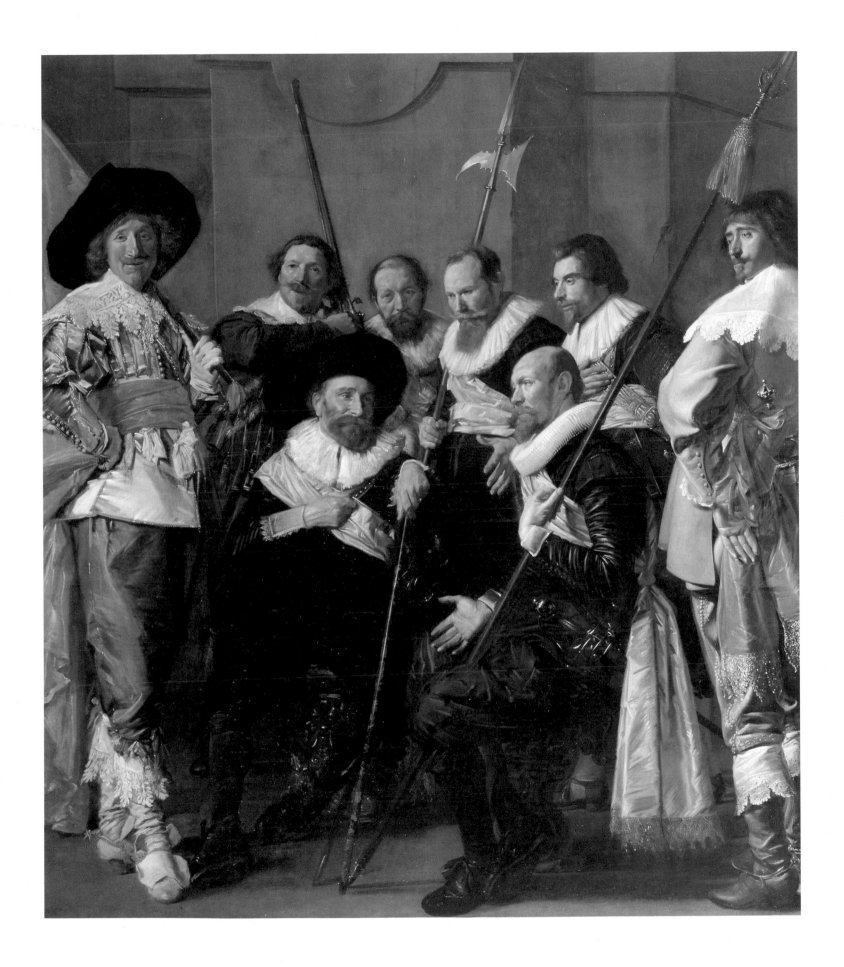

that it had been agreed he would begin the portraits in Amsterdam and complete them in Haarlem. The representatives of the guild, however, claimed that they had even offered six guilders extra per portrait on the condition that Hals travel to Amsterdam to paint the men's bodies as well as their faces. Hals was to receive 66 guilders per person upon completion of the painting, a total of 1,056 guilders for the whole work. Despite the high rate, Hals could no longer be persuaded to make the journey to Amsterdam. He suggested that the unfinished work be brought to Haarlem, where he would complete the sitters' attire. Then he proposed to finish painting the faces, assuming that the militiamen did not object to travelling to Haarlem. By now the dispute had become so heated that the guild decided to ask another artist to complete the painting. The task fell to Pieter Codde, a strange choice since Codde's paintings were usually small and meticulous. Codde lived in Amsterdam, though, and may even have been a member of the militia company.

ROUGH AND SMOOTH

Frans Hals painted the general outlines of the composition and completed some of the faces and hands, but only the ensign on the left, with the shiny satin jacket, is entirely by his hand. The skill with which this figure was painted did not escape the critical eye of Vincent van Gogh, who wrote after visiting the Rijksmuseum in 1885 of the 'orange, white and blue fellow in the left corner ... seldom have I seen a more divinely beautiful figure.'

Pieter Codde painted the costumes and the portraits which Hals had failed to complete. He tried to adapt his own style to that of Hals, but the differences between the painters are vast. Hals's brush is rough and restless; each stroke is clearly visible. Codde's manner is far less robust, more precise and therefore flatter. He sculpted his figures with small, rhythmic, smooth brushstrokes. Yet it is not just the brushwork that

is different. Hals's ensign is a man of flesh and blood, while Codde's officer standing in the centre appears far less natural. His arm is much too long below the elbow, while his limp hand seems not to rest on his hip but to be glued there. His head is like a loose appendage joined to the sloping shoulder. Codde lacked Hals's confident touch. After completing the painting he never attempted to paint a portrait in Hals's style again.

NIGHT WATCH

'Portray the captain and the lieutenant surrounded by their militiamen' is supposed to have been Rembrandt's simple commission to paint the Amsterdam company of the Kloveniers or arquebusiers, the civic-guard company named after the weapon they carried. Although it differed little from most commissions for portraits of militia companies, the result – *The Night Watch* – was more original and exciting than any other civic-guard painting. Instead of portraying his sitters in static poses standing in rows or seated around a table, Rembrandt gave priority to movement and action.

Captain Frans Banning Cocq's arm is outstretched, the heel of his left foot is slightly raised and his mouth is open. The company is about to march off and it is the rather disorderly moment preceding this which Rembrandt depicted. The men are in motion: one militiaman loads his gun, the drummer beats his drum, a dog barks and a girl walks past. *The Night Watch* is a snapshot of a group in action and that is what makes the painting so exceptional.

The portrait was intended for the company's headquarters in Amsterdam, the Kloveniersdoelen – the shooting-range and headquarters of the arquebusiers – to which a new wing had just been added, completed around 1638. This great hall was intended for official receptions and was to be lined with portraits of the various companies of the civic guard. Seven major group portraits were painted between 1638 and 1645. Rembrandt's *Night Watch* of 1642 was

65

REMBRANDT (1606-1669)
The company of Captain Frans Banning Cocq and Lieutenant Willem Jan Ruytenburch, known as 'The Night Watch', 1642
Canvas 363 x 437 cm
AMSTERDAM, RIJKSMUSEUM
(on loan from the City of Amsterdam since 1808, see p. 309)

definitely the odd man out in this series. Unfortunately, no comments by contemporaries have survived. The first serious critique of the work appeared in 1678, some 35 years after it was painted. Samuel van Hoogstraeten, who had once been apprenticed to Rembrandt, wrote that Rembrandt had focused more on the wider picture than on the individual portraits and that he found the *Night Watch* to be so painterly in concept, elegant in composition and so powerful, that it made the other paintings look like playing cards. Van Hoogstraeten then added that he thought Rembrandt could have added a bit more light.

In fact, although Rembrandt's unique treatment of light – the powerful contrast between light and dark – was criticised, it also received considerable praise. After all, the use of highlights – Rembrandt's trademark – are what heighten the tension in the painting. This is how he focused attention on the girl, placing her in the limelight. A dead bird hangs from her belt, the claws of which are clearly visible. These refer to the militia company's name, Kloveniers or 'klauweniers' – *klauwen* are claws in Dutch – so that the girl may be seen as a regimental mascot.

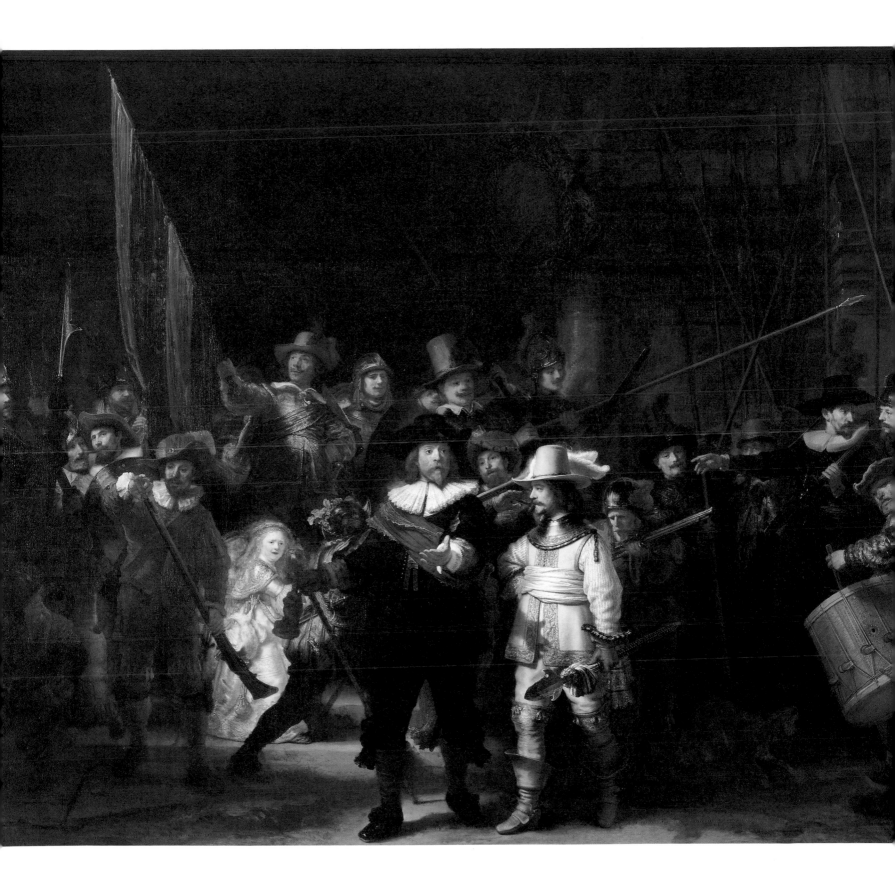

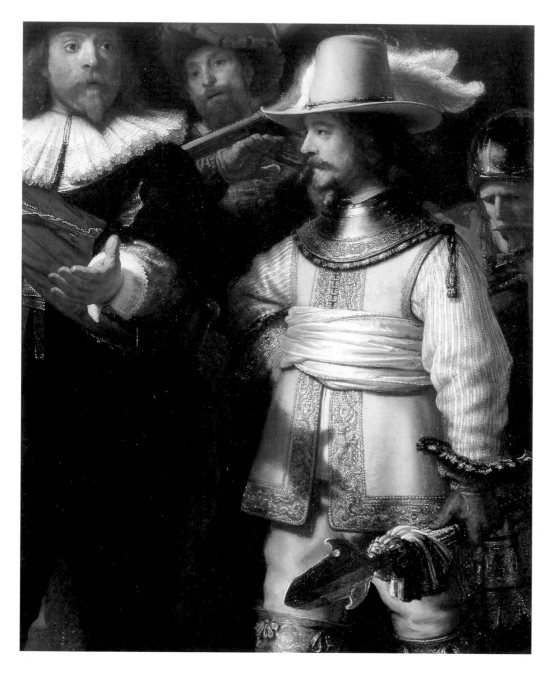

DETAIL OF 65

than Rembrandt had ever intended. This layer of varnish was removed when the work was restored in 1975, returning the picture to its original brilliance. Although the scene appears to be less nocturnal than once thought, the painting has kept its name.

BANQUET

Bartholomeus van der Helst grouped no fewer than twenty-five people around a single table in such a way that he managed to do justice to each individual portrait while preserving the integrity of the group. He portrayed the militiamen in all kinds of poses: standing gallantly and bending slightly forward, as well as seated, talking, gesturing, listening, eating and drinking. The unifying element is the table, which stretches across the length of the canvas, parallel to the picture plane. The leading personalities are the people in front of the table, the others sit or stand behind it, like the woman bringing in the peacock pie and the innkeeper, Christoffel Pook, shown filling a glass. These two are servants; all the other people at the banquet are militiamen. On the right Cornelis Jansz Witsen and Lieutenant Johan Oetgens van Waveren shake hands, symbolising the recently signed treaty. The banquet was held by the men of the Guild of St George – the Amsterdam crossbowmen's guild – to celebrate the signing of the Treaty of Münster, which took place on 5 June 1648, signalling the end of the Eighty Years' War. The captain holds the company's prize possession, a large silver ceremonial drinking horn showing St George on horseback, killing the dragon. More towards the centre is a seated ensign holding a banner showing a woman with the coat of arms of Amsterdam.

Van der Helst painted this group portrait for the crossbowmen's headquarters on Amsterdam's Singel. The painting was hung in the old hall on the first floor and Van der Helst included the view from this hall in the picture. Two façades are visible from the

Another figure highlighted in the painting is the lieutenant. The shadow of Captain Banning Cocq's outstretched hand is cleverly cast on the lieutenant's jacket, the thumb and index finger subtly framing a detail of the embroidery on the band across the coat. This decorative element features a lion bearing the coat of arms of Amsterdam with its three X crosses.

WORLD FAMOUS

The Night Watch became famous as Rembrandt's revolutionary redefinition of the traditional militia piece, as well as for its dramatic lighting effects and the daring manner in which it was painted. The name *Night Watch* originated in the 19th century, by which time the varnish had become yellowed and the work appeared far darker

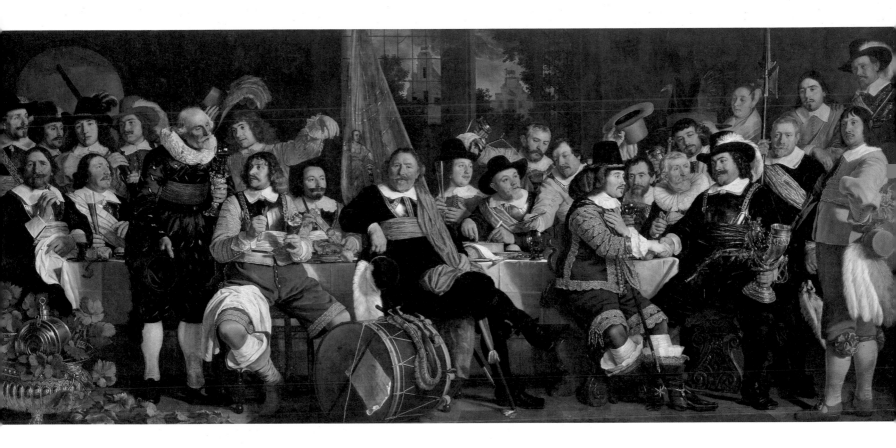

window, both crowned with the image of a lamb: a brewery, 'Het Lam', and beside it a Mennonite church, known as 'Bij het Lam'. Van der Helst painted with such attention to detail that even the background was depicted with meticulous accuracy.

REFLECTIONS

This attention to detail is also visible in the way Van der Helst rendered the various materials. He was able to differentiate subtly between the colour and reflection in a pewter plate, the silver of the drinking horn and the wine barrel on the floor to the left. His rendering of the various fabrics is almost tangible. The ensign wears trousers made of a stiff, heavy material; the linen napkin on his knee is thin and delicate. The man standing next to him wears yellow stockings with a pattern that Van der Helst simply scratched into the wet paint. Equally impressive is the contrast between the rather pale, slim hand of Lieutenant Van Waveren and

the brown, sturdy hand of Captain Witsen. The cuirass Witsen wears is a *tour de force*: the faces of the three men seated near him are reflected in the metal. Without having to resort to painstaking precision, Van der Helst was able to depict details with a masterly touch, as witnessed by the piece of paper under the cord of the drum on which a poem about the recent peace is inscribed.

In his rendering of materials Van der Helst certainly surpassed Rembrandt. During the 18th and 19th centuries, *The Night Watch* and *The celebration* competed for the title of best militia piece. Until the mid-19th century Van der Helst's portrait was generally the favourite, but then the scales began to tip in favour of the *Night Watch*. The appreciation for Rembrandt's powerful lighting effects, broad brushstrokes and exciting composition came to eclipse the admiration for Van der Helst's elegance and his focus on the individual portrait.

66

BARTHOLOMEUS VAN DER HELST (1613-1670)
The celebration of the Treaty of Münster, 18 June 1648, at the crossbowmen's headquarters (St George's Guard), Amsterdam, 1648
Canvas 232 x 547 cm
AMSTERDAM, RIJKSMUSEUM
(on loan from the City of Amsterdam since 1808, see p. 310)

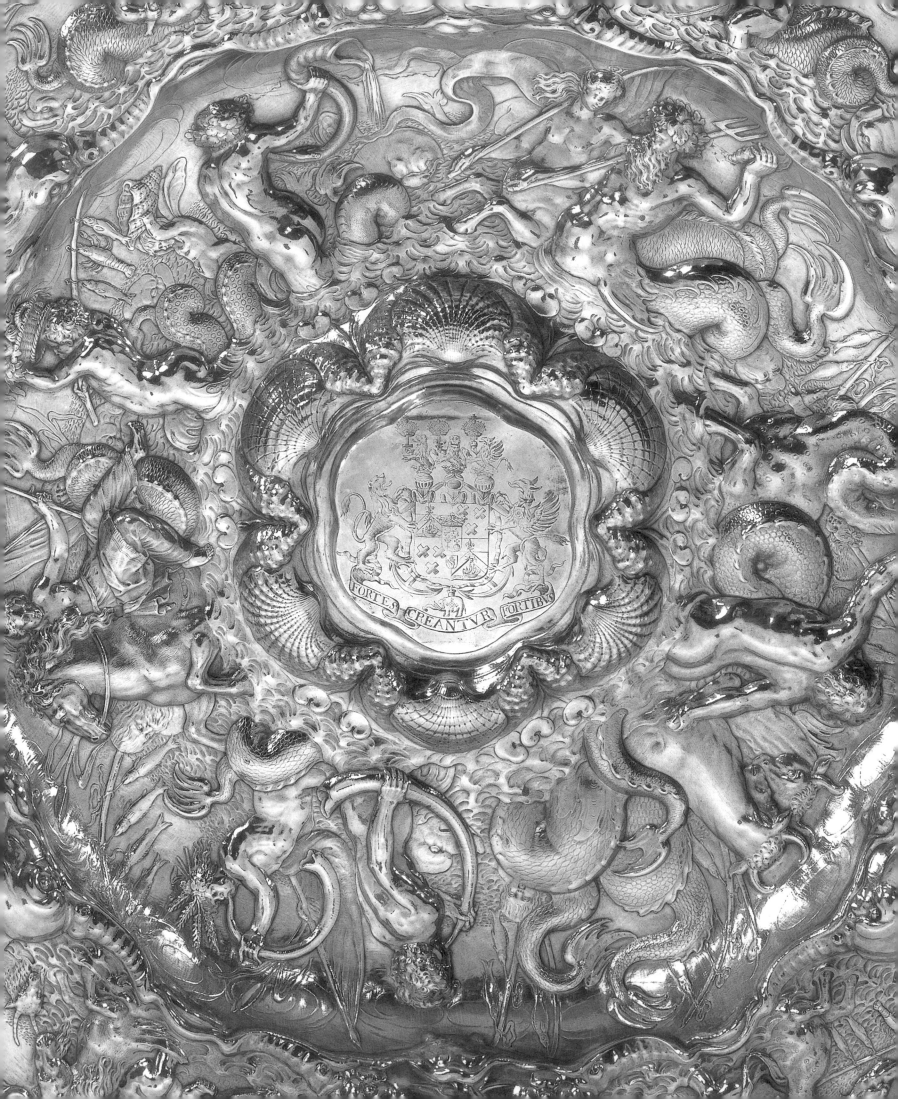

10 WHIMS AND DROLLERIES 1645-1675

FLOWING LINES which call to mind the folds in soft skin or the lobes of a human ear, forms that look like molluscs and monstrous beings – these are the ingredients of the decorative style that was becoming fashionable at the beginning of the 17th century: the auricular style. These lobate forms seem sluggishly fluid, like syrup flowing in all directions. Just where an ornament begins or ends is barely discernible.

The designation 'auricular style' was not used in the 17th century; the term is a later, 19th-century invention. In this chapter the terms 'lobate' and 'auricular' are used interchangeably. In the 17th century, however, such ornaments were referred to as 'whims and drolleries'.

NEW ORNAMENT

Two Utrecht silversmiths, the brothers Adam (c. 1568-1627) and Paulus van Vianen (c. 1570-1613), are considered to be the inventors of the auricular ornament, although its origins probably lie in 16th-century Italian ornamental prints. These prints served as examples for artists and artisans and doubtless inspired the Van Vianen brothers – Adam in Utrecht and Paulus in Prague – to make their most daring and original decorations.

After its introduction by the Van Vianens at the beginning of the 17th century, this form of decoration was adopted by other artists as well. Around 1635 the

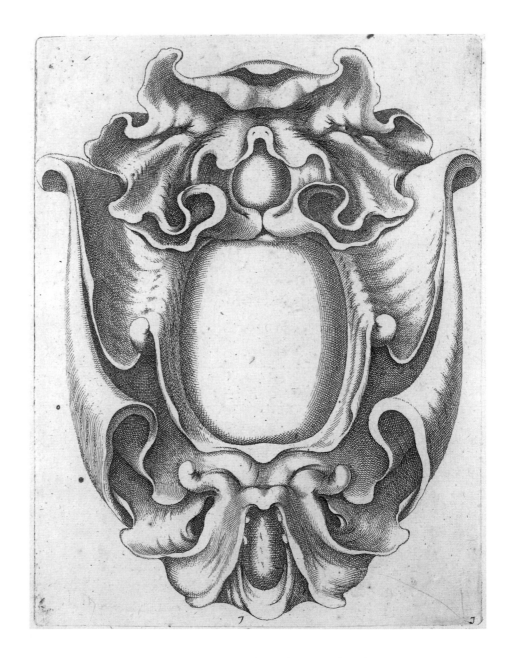

JOHANNES LUTMA (1587-1669), *Cartouche in auricular style*, 1654
Etching and engraving, 22.8 x 17.9 cm. AMSTERDAM, RIJKSPRENTENKABINET

< DETAIL OF 67

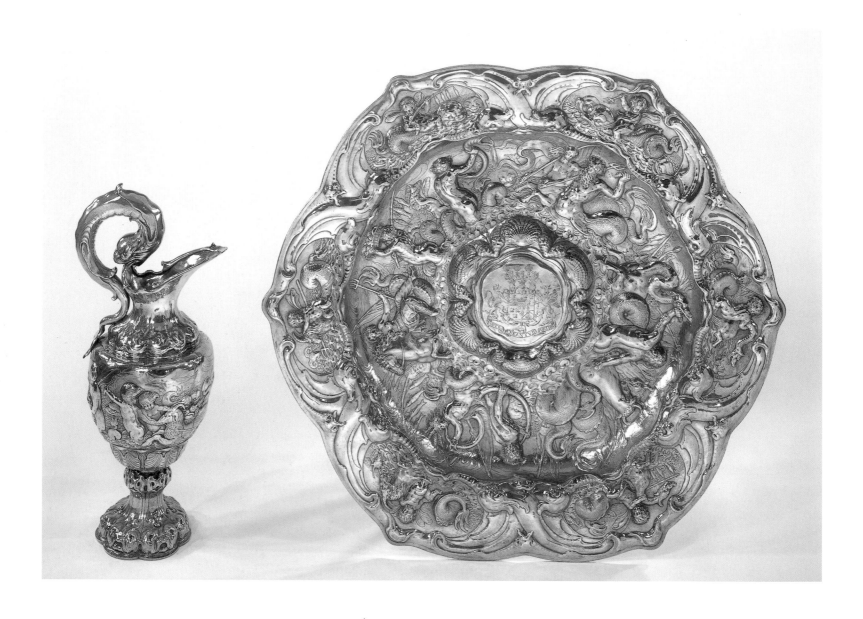

gold- and silversmith Johannes Lutma
started working with auricular ornaments in
Amsterdam, and these motifs subsequently
became more widely known.

It took quite a while before the lobate
ornament – whose malleable, flowing character made it especially suitable to application in chased silver – was adopted by artists
other than gold- and silversmiths. The first
pieces of furniture decorated in this style did
not make their appearance until the mid-
17th century. Lobate ornamentation was
also applied to picture frames. A splendid
example is the gilt frame around the self-
portrait of Ferdinand Bol [74].

LUTMA

A ewer-and-basin set such as this one made
by Johannes Lutma was intended to serve
as a showpiece, the large format offering
an opportunity to apply auricular ornamentation in its most extravagant form. Both
ornamental sets were made to honour
special occasions.

The older of the two sets, which is intri-
cately wrought, dates from 1647 and was
made as a gift for Admiral Maarten
Harpertsz Tromp, who played an important
role in the capture of Dunkirk in 1646. This
victory was quite possibly the reason why the
silversmith Lutma was given a commission to

67

JOHANNES LUTMA (1587-1669)
*Ewer and basin with the coat of arms
of Cornelis Tromp*, 1647
Silver, ewer h. 50.4 cm; basin diam. 74.5 cm
AMSTERDAM, RIJKSMUSEUM
(acquired in 1895, see p. 313)

make a ewer and basin in honour of this naval hero. The coat of arms decorating the middle of the large basin, however, is that of Cornelis Tromp, Maarten's son, and was affixed at a later date. The representation depicting the trident-wielding sea-god Neptune, which surrounds the coat of arms, possibly refers to this naval hero. Lobate ornaments are discernible between the sea monsters; soft forms mark the edge of the basin. Lutma also used these organic forms in his decoration of the ewer, especially in the stylised monster-heads on the foot and in the sinuous snake's tail which forms the handle.

Lutma developed the auricular ornament into a full-fledged Baroque decorative form. The ewer almost has the character of a sculpture, while the basin is perhaps best described as a 'painting' in lobate style.

RESTRAINED FORM

Eight years later, in 1655, Lutma again used the lobate ornament in a ewer-and-basin set, albeit on a more modest scale. Lutma received a commission to make a ewer and basin for the banquet marking the dedication of the new Amsterdam town hall, the present-day Royal Palace on the Dam (see chapter 21). This set is much more austere in shape and more simply decorated than the older ewer and basin. Auricular ornaments are to be seen on the edge of the basin and in the ewer's spout and handle; the curling edges of the engraved cartouches also display flowing, lobate forms.

Engraved in the cartouches on the ewer are the coats of arms of the treasurers who were in office in 1655: Dr Nicolaes Tulp – portrayed in Rembrandt's *Anatomy lesson*

[58] – and Cornelis Dronckelaar. Depicted in the cartouches on the edge of the basin are the coats of arms of the incumbent burgomasters, and engraved in the heart of the basin, on the place where the ewer stands, is the coat of arms of the city of Amsterdam.

68

JOHANNES LUTMA (1587-1669)
Ewer and basin for the Amsterdam town hall, 1655
Silver, ewer h. 21 cm; basin diam. 60.5 cm
AMSTERDAM,
AMSTERDAMS HISTORISCH MUSEUM
(in the possession of the City of
Amsterdam since 1655, see p. 320)

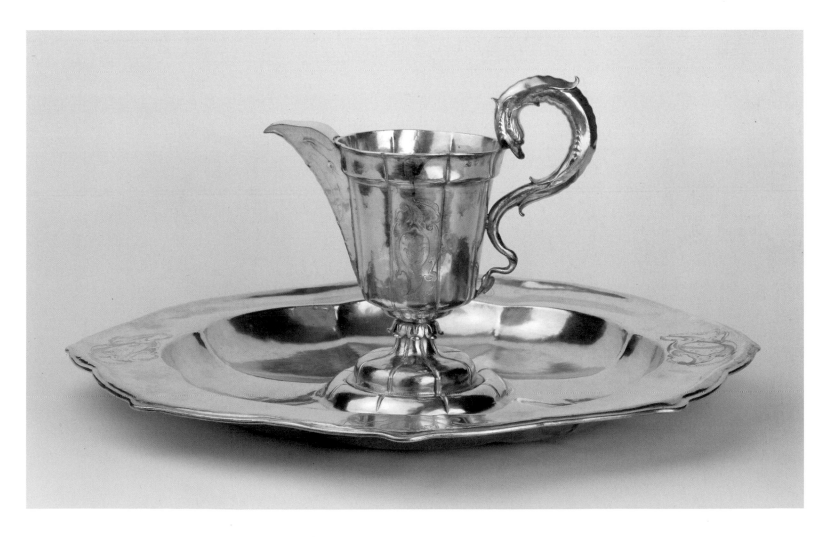

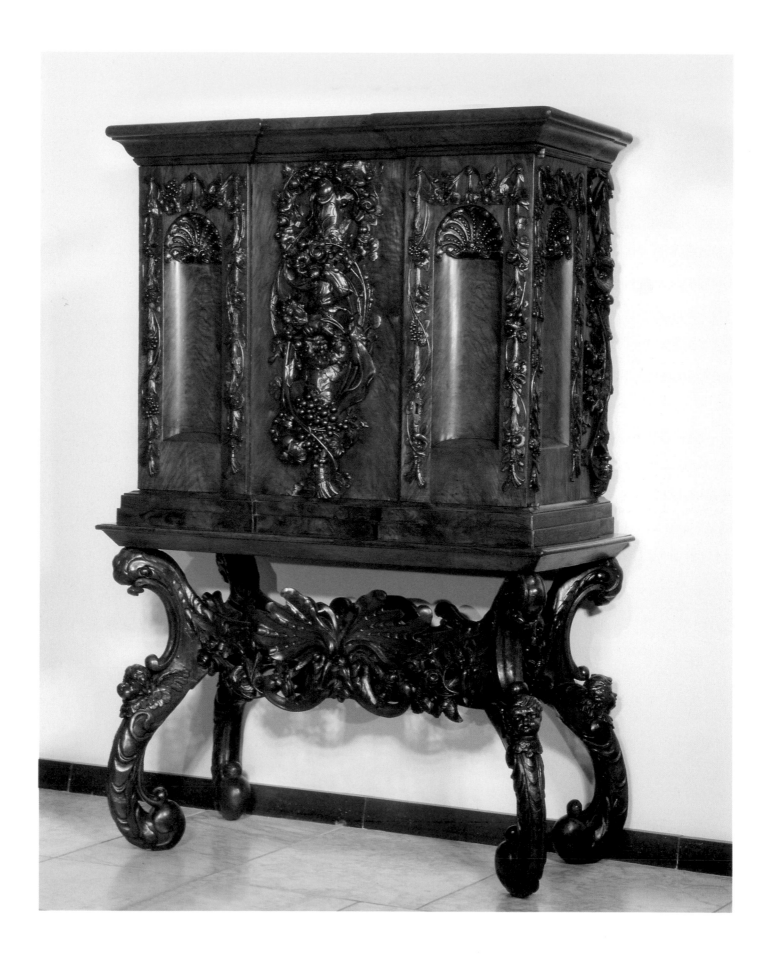

SCULPTED FURNITURE

In the mid-17th century, designs for works in precious metals made by Adam van Vianen – the artist who raised the auricular style to new heights – were published in the form of prints. Shortly afterwards there appeared in Amsterdam prints whose designs were no longer intended only for work in precious metals. In this way designs in the lobate style became widely known and served as examples for artists and artisans in various fields.

In addition to its use in silver and gold objects, the auricular style proved eminently suited to the production of sculpted tables and picture frames. The sculptors who made these objects blended the lobate style with elements derived from other styles. They combined, for example, garlands of flowers, little angels and acanthus leaves – decorative motifs taken from Classicism and the Baroque – with the whimsical, organic forms of the auricular style. The feet of the lobate table and the stand on which the layette cupboard rests both display this new development in the evolution of the auricular style.

In both pieces of furniture the legs consist of large scrolls that gradually flow into a monster-like mask in the middle. The table's stand is carved in such a way as to resemble kneadable material. The cupboard's stand displays sharper carving, but even here all the elements – the angels' heads, for example – have been integrated into a unified whole. The upper part, the cupboard proper, is much more austere in form. The cupboard was made in the classicist style, comparable to that displayed by Dutch architecture in the mid-17th century. The decorative festoons of flowers and fruit are typical of this style.

The profuse decoration of the cupboard's exterior was not carried through to its interior, which was simply provided with shelves. This type of small cupboard resting on a high stand was probably intended for the layette. Such storage cupboards for nappies and baby clothing were described in 17th-century inventories as 'baby-linen cupboards' or 'baby-linen cabinets'.

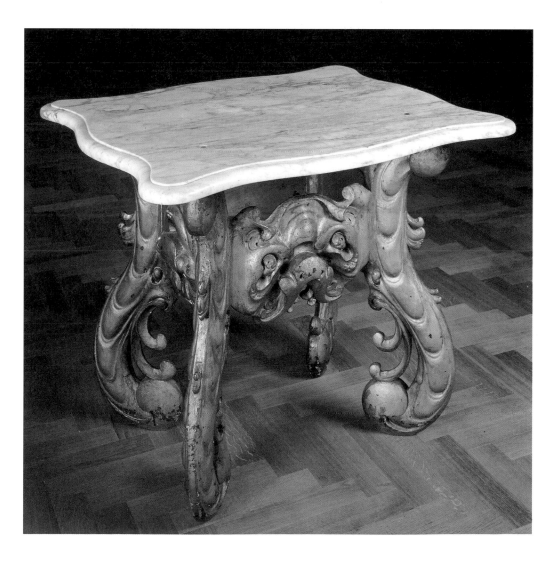

69
Layette cupboard, c. 1650-1675
Oak and walnut 178 x 119 x 57 cm
AMSTERDAM, RIJKSMUSEUM
(acquired in 1985, see p. 318)

<

70
Side table, c. 1660
Gilt wood with marble top
80 x 89 x 72 cm
UTRECHT, CENTRAAL MUSEUM
(acquired in 1923, see p. 348)

>

SCONCE

Characteristic of the lobate style of the mid-17th century is the combination of lobate ornaments with other decorative motifs. The large silver candle-holder, or sconce, made by the Hague silversmith Hans Coenraet Breghtel, is completely decorated with leaf and vine motifs combined with softer, more supple forms characteristic of the auricular style. Breghtel let the leaves and curly tendrils flow organically into each other, by which means he turned the entire sconce into one big ornament.

The parcel-gilt sconce, meant to be fixed to the wall, left the Netherlands shortly after it was made, as part of a pair of sconces taken to Russia as a diplomatic gift from a Dutch delegation visiting Moscow. The Dutch Republic took great pains in the 17th century to maintain relations with Russia. Both countries undertook diplomatic missions in which costly presents played an important part. On the way to the audience, the gifts were pointedly displayed by bearers at the front of the procession. Breghtel's large sconces certainly made a good impression. They are still preserved in the armoury of the Kremlin Museum in Moscow.

CANDELABRUM

The enormous standing candelabrum was made by the brass founder Joost Gerritsz for a similar purpose. It was commissioned by the Dutch East India Company as a present for the shogun, Japan's supreme ruler. It was in the Company's interest to maintain good relations with Japan, as there was a lot at stake. Every year Japan reconsidered its decision to allow the Dutch to keep their trading post, and time after time this proved to be a tense moment. Just how tense is apparent from the fact that after 1641 no other European country was granted admittance, giving the Netherlands a monopoly on trade with Japan until well into the 19th century. To curry favour with the shogun, it was customary to shower him with presents every year. In 1640 the present was this

large candelabrum, together with twelve sconces and two crates of candles.

The candelabrum consists of a stem and a crown. The crown is composed of three tiers of ten branches each. The 31st candleholder at the top of the stem crowns the whole. The crown of candle-bearing branches is supported by six turned columns with Tuscan capitals. The foot of the candelabrum is formed by six volutes, decorated with auricular ornaments.

This standing candelabrum went down very well with the Japanese leader: not only were the Dutch allowed to continue trading with Japan, but the candelabrum was given a place of honour in Nikko, a complex of tombs, temples and treasure-houses.

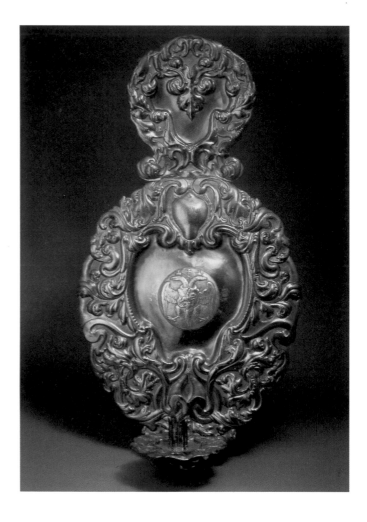

71
HANS COENRAET BREGHTEL (1608/1609-1675)
Sconce, 1647
Silver, parcel-gilt, h. 92.5 cm
MOSCOW, KREMLIN MUSEUM
(acquired in 1648, see p. 340)

72
JOOST GERRITSZ (1598-1652)
Candelabrum, c. 1640
Copper h. c. 350 cm
NIKKO (JAPAN), NEAR THE YOMEIMON ARCH
(presented to the shogun in 1640, see p. 341)

>

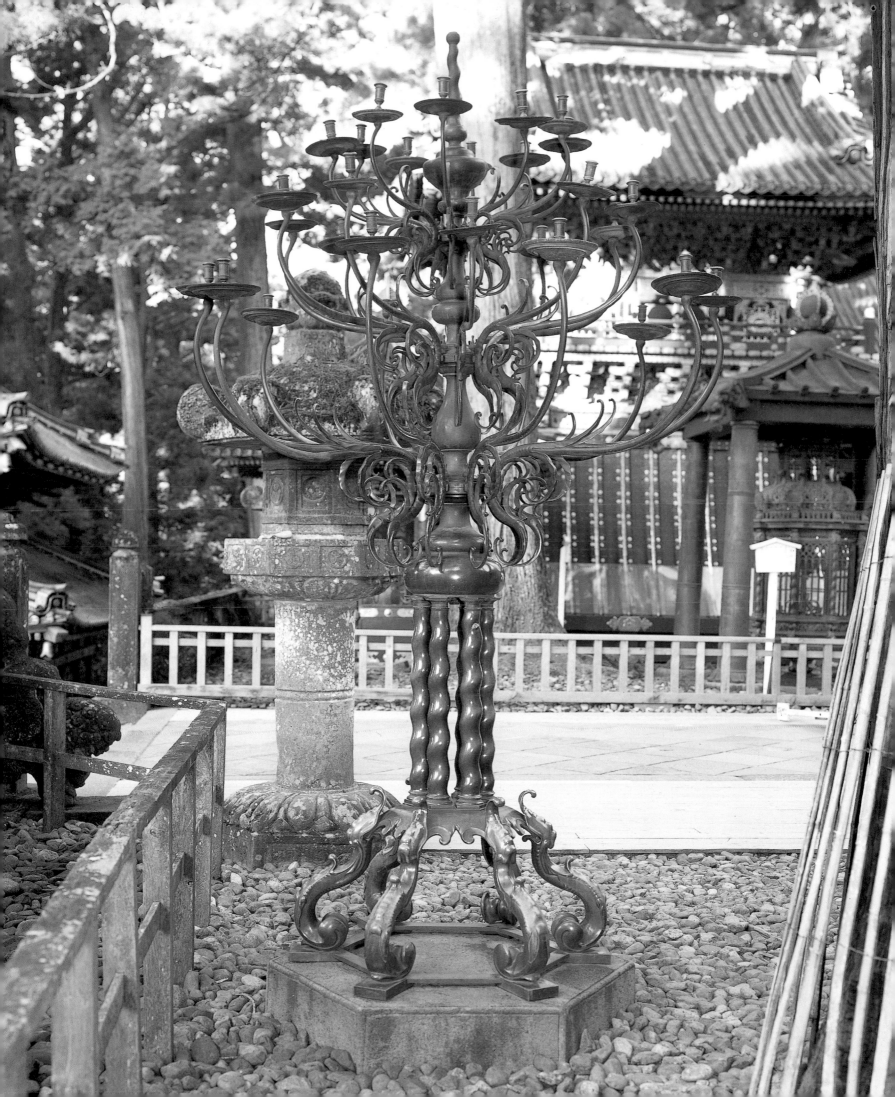

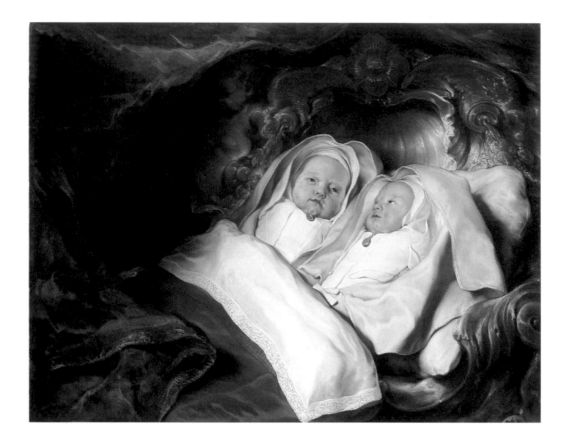

73
SALOMON DE BRAY (1597-1664)
The twins Clara and Aelbert de Bray,
c. 1646
Canvas 82.6 x 64.8 cm
PRIVATE COLLECTION, ON LOAN TO
THE NATIONAL GALLERY OF SCOTLAND,
EDINBURGH
(see p. 351)

CRADLE

Around 1646 Salomon de Bray painted an unusual portrait in which he displayed his knowledge of the auricular style. The two babies portrayed are literally embedded in lobate motifs. They are Clara and Aelbert de Bray, the children of Simon de Bray, a nephew of Salomon. On a sketch which De Bray made as a preparatory study, he wrote the names of the twins and the year, 1648.

The impressive cradle in which the twins lie is profusely decorated with undulating, shell-shaped motifs and horns of plenty. A little angel and a flower have also been incorporated into the flowing form of the whole, which gives the impression of being one big Baroque shell. The shining green cloth surrounding the bed seems to have been momentarily pulled to the side to reveal the treasure within.

Whether such a cradle actually existed is a good question. In the sketch the artist made of the twins, the children lie sleeping peacefully in a simple basket with handles and a hood. The elaborate lobate motifs were perhaps a product of De Bray's imagination, who hoped in this way to make his portrayal of the children even more beautiful.

The painting was probably made to mark the occasion of the twins' baptism. Clara and Aelbert both wear a medallion hanging from a chain. Such ornaments were given to children at their baptism by their godparents. De Bray accentuated the medallions to such an extent that it seems likely he made this painting to honour the occasion. He may even have been their godfather and therefore depicted the babies wearing his present and lying in this exceptionally beautiful cradle in lobate style.

SELF-PORTRAIT

'Whims and drolleries' decorate the frame around the self-portrait that Ferdinand Bol made in 1669. This frame, ordered by Bol himself, is still as it was originally. It is made of gilt limewood and decorated with vines, flowers, grapes and lobate shapes, which ripple across the whole of the frame. In some places the auricular ornaments are overgrown with flowers and leaves, while in other places, such as the upper corners, the frame itself is clearly visible. A prominent place at the upper centre is graced with a large sunflower.

Bol portrayed himself not as a painter with easel and palette, but as a stylish burgher, a man of the world. He wears a long, fashionable periwig which was the custom only in well-to-do circles, as well as a costly dressing gown made of gold-coloured silk brocade. Bol probably painted this self-portrait, honouring the occasion of his second marriage, to present to his new wife, Anna van Erckel. The painting contains various symbols of love, one of which is the sleeping Amor on which Bol leans nonchalantly. A love-god who is asleep refers not just to love, but to the suppression of lust: in other words, to chastity. In the 17th century true love was a chaste concept, certainly in the case of a couple of a certain age. Bol was 53 and his wife 45 when they married, and people of such a respectable age were expected to curb their emotions. By means of this portrait Bol was showing his wife that he would not let himself be seduced by the vagaries of Amor: Cupid's services were no longer required.

In this context the sturdy pillar in the background stands for Bol's steadfastness in love and must be seen as a sign of marital fidelity and a chaste life. Finally, the sunflower on the frame may also be seen in relation to Amor. In the 17th century the sunflower was a common symbol of love: just as the sunflower follows the sun, true lovers follow one another. Bol has clearly shown in this portrait that his was a higher form of love and not just base passion.

FERDINAND BOL

This self-portrait is one of Bol's last works. After marrying Anna van Erckel he practically gave up painting. Bol was well-off even before this time, but his second marriage made him a wealthy gentleman who no longer had to paint for a living.

Ferdinand Bol was born in Dordrecht, the son of a doctor. He probably learned to paint in Utrecht in the workshop of Abraham Bloemaert. Around 1635 he went to Amsterdam to work with Rembrandt, in whose studio he stayed until about 1642, after which he set up as an independent painter in Amsterdam.

When he made this self-portrait at the age of 53, however, he had long since abandoned the style of his teacher. He now worked in a more elegant, colourful and flamboyant style, completely in accordance with the fashions of the day. This is in keeping with the richly ornamented frame in which Bol placed his self-portrait. Many paintings probably had similar gilt frames in those days, but original combinations of frame and painting have rarely been preserved.

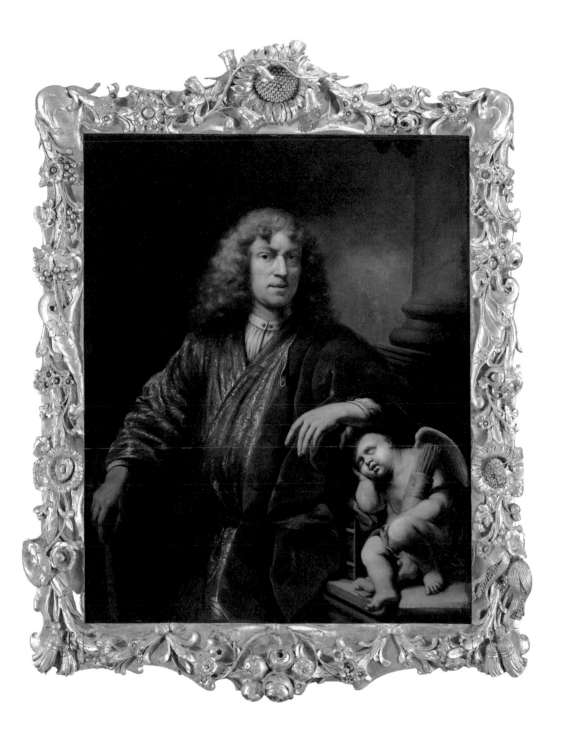

74
FERDINAND BOL (1616-1680)
Self-portrait, c. 1669
Canvas 128 x 104 cm
AMSTERDAM, RIJKSMUSEUM
(acquired in 1849, see p. 311)

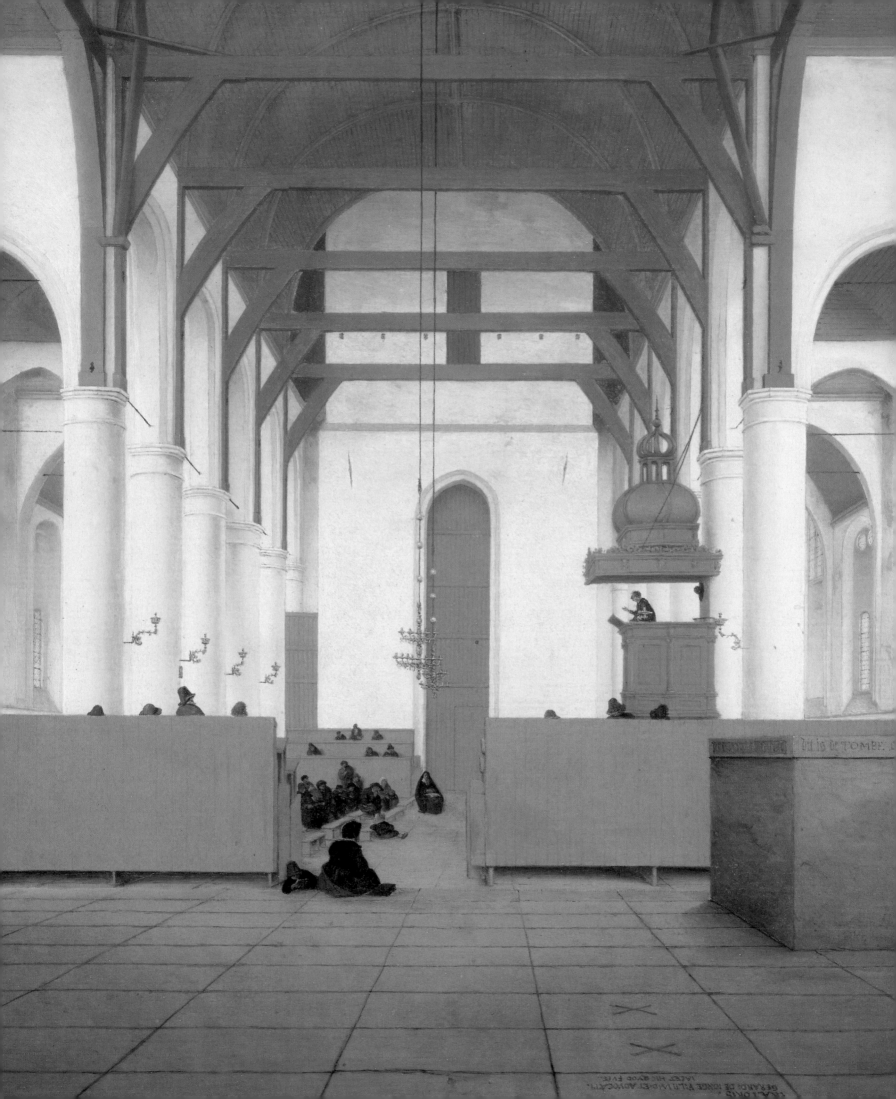

11 CLARITY AND HARMONY
1635-1665

ARCHITECTURAL painters, perhaps more so than all other 17th-century artists, were preoccupied with rendering visible reality. They experimented with various methods of perspective and combined their technical skills with careful observation, which often produced spectacular results, especially in the genre of painted church interiors. Pieter Saenredam, Gerard Houckgeest and Emanuel de Witte – each in his own way – made impressive depictions of church interiors.

PERSPECTIVES

Pieter Saenredam turned the painting of church interiors into a highly respectable specialism, spending endless amounts of time on preparations for a painting. He measured, calculated and made on-the-spot drawings – sometimes for weeks on end – before immortalising his churches in paint. His architectural paintings, accurate with regard to perspective, set the tone for this specialism in 17th-century painting. His balanced interiors radiate an atmosphere of peace, clarity and harmony. No one can disturb the peaceful stillness of his paintings, not even the preacher in the pulpit.

Perspective theory was indispensable for a painter who wanted to render anything as complex as a church interior. A method of perspective, which enabled artists to depict on a flat surface objects which then seemed three-dimensional, had been developed in the Renaissance by Italian artists. They used mathematical calculations to put tiled floors, colonnades and ceilings into perspective, and the invention of the printing press meant that this knowledge quickly spread throughout Western Europe. In the 16th century alone there were 33 different books published on perspective. The first painters who specialised in 'perspectives', as architectural paintings were then called, constructed fanciful buildings which provided them with an outlet for the expression of all their new-found knowledge.

Pieter Saenredam studied perspective theory in order to depict large, existing buildings in a convincing way. In 1627 he received a commission to make a drawing of the interior of the Church of St Bavo for Samuel Ampzing's book describing and praising the city of Haarlem. The later master was not yet so practised in the rendering of perspective, but fortunately he could turn to the Haarlem surveyor Peter Wils for advice, and together they developed a method which Saenredam continued to employ his whole life long. On the basis of site drawings and precise measurements he made construction drawings which laid the groundwork for his paintings. He built up his constructions from a central perspective, with a vanishing point in the distance where all the lines of vision converge.

INNOVATION

Around 1650 two artists in Delft were responsible for an innovation in architec-tural painting. Gerard Houckgeest and Emanuel de Witte painted church interiors based on a perspective construction having two lines of vision and two vanishing points that lie outside the depiction. Their paintings made a more natural, less composed impression, thanks to this method of construction. Houckgeest and De Witte introduced seemingly random views, whereby people come more to the fore than in Saenredam's churches. In Saenredam's work the figures are subordinated to the space, whereas in Houckgeest and De Witte's paintings the people make a real contribution to the picture, breathing life into the architecture and heightening the realistic effect.

SAENREDAM

Pieter Jansz Saenredam was born in the village of Assendelft in the province of North Holland, a son of the engraver Jan Saenredam. He learned to paint from the Haarlem artist Pieter de Grebber. At first Saenredam made portraits, landscapes and book illustrations, but from the age of 30 onwards his specialism was the depiction of church interiors. In order to render convincingly these imposing spaces on a panel of modest dimensions, he nearly always followed the same working method. On the basis of on-site drawings, he constructed a perspective sketch the same size as the panel he would later use. He transposed this sketch by blackening the back, laying it on

< DETAIL OF 75

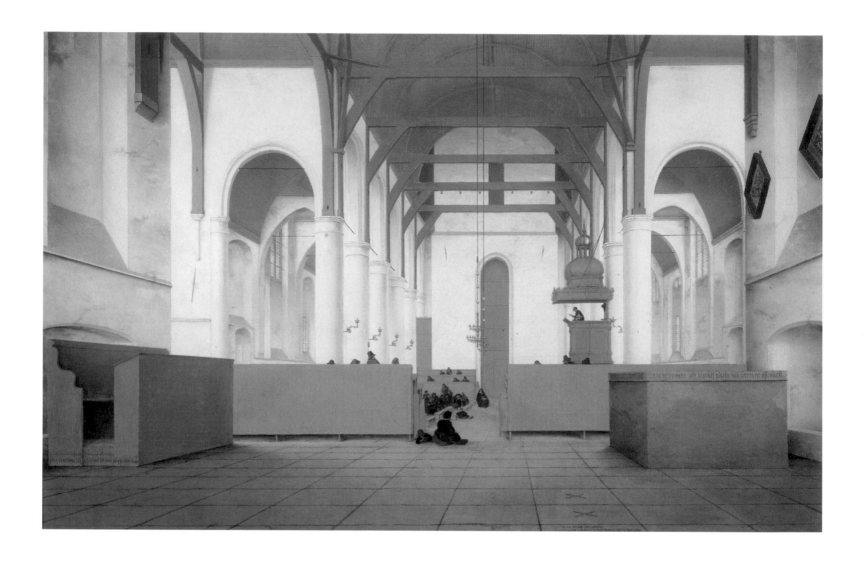

75

PIETER SAENREDAM (1597-1665)
*Interior of the Church of St Odulphus
in Assendelft*, 1649
Panel 50 x 76 cm
AMSTERDAM, RIJKSMUSEUM
(on loan from the City of Amsterdam
since 1885, see p. 311)

the panel and tracing the main lines. Using the impression thus made on the primed panel the artist set about making the painting.

For his church interiors Saenredam usually chose a low viewpoint intended to guide the viewer's gaze into the picture. In Saenredam's interior of St Odulphus in Assendelft, for example, the eye is sucked into the depths of the picture by the tapering lines along the floor, and subsequently directed upwards to the high, narrow niche encircling the door.

CHURCH OF ST ODULPHUS

Saenredam painted the Protestant Church of St Odulphus in his native village around 40 years after he had left it. Names are

engraved in one of the stone tiles in the foreground: it is the grave of Jan Saenredam and several other members of his family. The Latin text reads in translation as follows: *Here lie the bodily remains of Jan Saenredam, the renowned engraver, Petrus the Younger, sheriff of Assendelft for forty-four years, his son Gerard the Younger, doctor in secular and ecclesiastical law, and lawyer.* This gravestone is the only one preserved from St Odulphus, which was torn down in the 19th century. Saenredam's inclusion of this text turned the painting into a family document.

Painting the 'portrait' of the Church of St Odulphus was a long, drawn-out process. As early as 1634 Saenredam made a detailed drawing of the choir and the nave. In 1643,

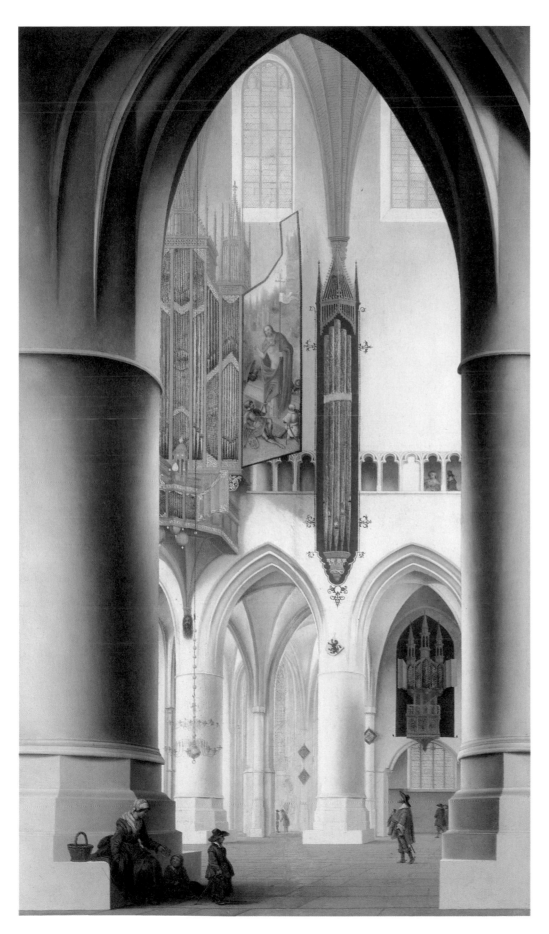

on the basis of this drawing and precise measurements, he made a detailed construction drawing which resulted in the painting. Saenredam wrote the date on which he finally completed the painting on the church pew at the left: *dit is de kerck tot Assendelft, een dorp in Hollandt, van / pieter saenredam, dese geschildert int jaer 1649. den 2. October* (this is the church at Assendelft, a village in Holland, by / Pieter Saenredam, this painted in the year 1649 the 2nd of October).

CHURCH OF ST BAVO

Less than one year elapsed between the first sketches and the finished painting which Saenredam made of the interior of the Church of St Bavo in Haarlem. In August 1635 he made an on-site drawing; on 15 April 1636 he completed the painting. He recorded this date on the small organ, which occupies a modest place in the work compared with the highly detailed rendering of the main organ.

When Saenredam made the painting of St Bavo, prominent Haarlem music-lovers were lobbying for more organ music in the church. The originally Catholic church was being used for Protestant church services, having been stripped of all its Catholic decoration. Calvinist clergymen had an aversion to organ music in the church – the psalms were sung without instrumental accompaniment – and therefore preferred not to have organs in the house of God. Beautifully made musical instruments testified, after all, to ostentation and extravagance. The music-lovers of Haarlem presented a petition to the

76
PIETER SAENREDAM (1597-1665)
Interior of the Church of St Bavo in Haarlem, 1636
Panel 95.5 x 57 cm
AMSTERDAM, RIJKSMUSEUM
(acquired in 1806, see p. 309)

town council, in which they asked for the organ – 'the jewel of the church' – to be played every day. Saenredam may well have depicted the large, 15th-century organ so prominently in support of this campaign. Another possibility is that his painting had been commissioned by a lover of organ music. In any case, he took great pains to produce a detailed depiction of the richly ornamented instrument.

The contrast between the delicate detail of the organ and the smooth, solid shape of the pillar in the foreground is very great indeed. Saenredam also introduced a sharp differentiation in illumination between the arch and the space behind it. Farther back, through to the next view, the painting becomes even lighter. The small figures have scarcely any colour; they were painted in the same hues as the architecture.

The figures in Saenredam's work do not emphasise their presence, yet they serve to indicate the scale of their surroundings and help the viewer to explore the painting. The boy in the foreground thus looks at the man with the sword, who in turn fixes his gaze on the opened organ shutter with the representation of the resurrection of Christ. Saenredam also used the figures to add playful elements: in St Odulphus in Assendelft, for example, a boy lies reading a book during the sermon, while a man and woman meet secretly in the gallery of St Bavo. Saenredam's subtle jokes lighten up his church interiors without disturbing the peace and harmony permeating his paintings.

ST MARY'S SQUARE
Pieter Saenredam lived in Haarlem but made architectural sketches in all parts of the country. Sometimes he did this at the instigation of his friend Jacob van Campen (1596-1657), the painter and architect known mainly for his design of the town hall on the Dam in Amsterdam (see p. 241). The meticulous Saenredam kept careful records, noting on each drawing when and

why he had made it, making it possible for us to follow his journeys day by day.

Saenredam did not limit himself to church interiors, but also drew and painted the exteriors of important buildings and churches. In 1662, three years before his death, he painted a splendid view of St Mary's Square (Mariaplaats) in Utrecht, in which he recorded for posterity a number of characteristic buildings: on the right, St Mary's Church; slightly to the left of centre, the tall tower of the cathedral; and more to the left, the tower of the Buur Church. Saenredam succeeded in conveying the atmosphere of a peaceful summer afternoon. The square is nearly deserted. Soft sunlight bathes the buildings surrounding the square, whereby the blue-grey colour of the façade of the small house in front of the cathedral tower stands out nicely. The composition is closed off on the left by a wall and on the right by the bell tower of the medieval St Mary's. On the façade of this church the painter signed and dated his work: *Pieter Saenredam fecit 1662.*

The painting was finished in 1662, but long before that Saenredam had made preparations for its execution, making an on-site drawing as early as 1636. At that time Saenredam was staying for five months in the city of Utrecht, taking measurements and making drawings of various buildings. The painting with St Mary's Square shows nearly the same view as the drawing, except for a couple of trees on the square which the artist decided to leave out, probably because they obscured the view of the church. Saenredam used the 1636 drawing as the basis for a detailed construction drawing in which he calculated the perspective and drew it accurately. He let all the lines of perspective converge on the same point, the so-called 'eye'. This point is to be found in the dark spot beneath the window of the house farthest to the left. The construction drawing was smaller than the panel on which he made the painting. With the help of a grid, Saenredam applied the construc-

tion drawing to the panel in the scale of the projected painting. Here and there the lines of this grid shine through the paint: for example, below the round window on the façade of St Mary's.

ST MARY'S CHURCH
The building of St Mary's began around 1085 under the leadership of Conrad, bishop of Utrecht from 1076 to 1099, with the support of Henry IV (1050-1106), king and later emperor of the large East Frankish kingdom, by then the Holy Roman Empire. The first part of the church was consecrated in 1099.

Until well into the 16th century St Mary's functioned as a chapter church, but the political domination of the Protestants meant a turning point in its history. Public profession of the Catholic faith was banned, and starting in 1585 Reformed services were held in the church. In the following centuries parts of the church were taken down and sold, or demolished, until the whole building was razed to the ground in the 19th century and replaced by the present Building of Arts and Sciences. St Mary's Square and the cloisters have survived the centuries, but the medieval church with its rounded, Romanesque arches has survived only in Saenredam's paintings.

HOUCKGEEST
Two artists, both active in Delft, caused a small revolution in architectural painting: Gerard Houckgeest and Emanuel de Witte. Around 1650 Houckgeest introduced the oblique view in his church interiors. This was an important change with respect to the static, spacious church interiors of Pieter Saenredam. In Houckgeest's paintings the viewer looks into the church from a seemingly arbitrary angle, whereby it seems to make no difference whether or not a pillar is standing in the middle of the field of vision – on the contrary, this seems almost to be a prerequisite. This technique, which enabled Houckgeest to lend a feeling of depth to his

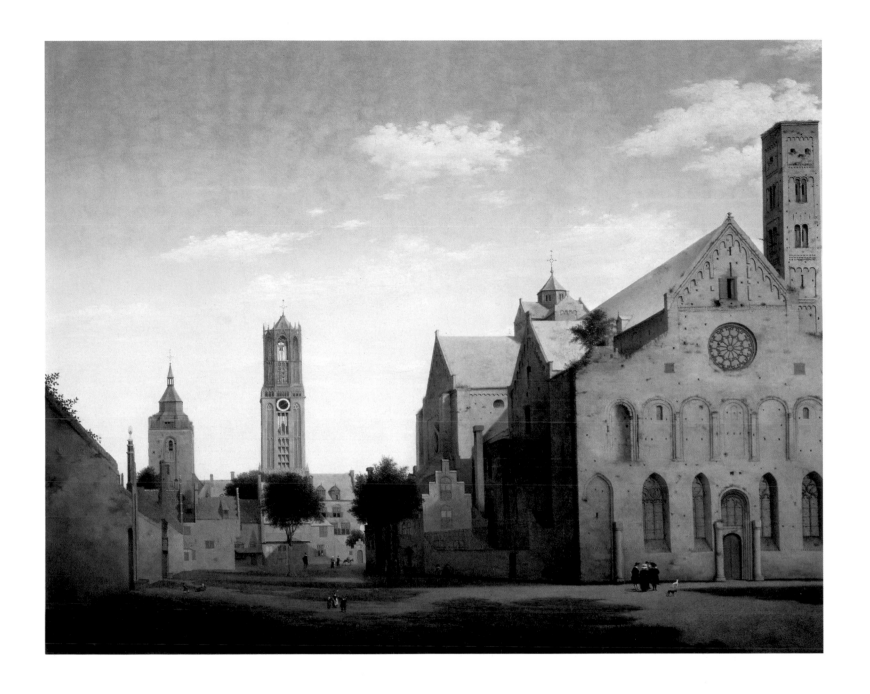

77

PIETER SAENREDAM (1597-1665)
View of St Mary's Square with the
Church of St Mary in Utrecht, 1662
Panel 109.5 x 139.5 cm
ROTTERDAM, MUSEUM
BOIJMANS VAN BEUNINGEN
(acquired in 1872, see p. 345)

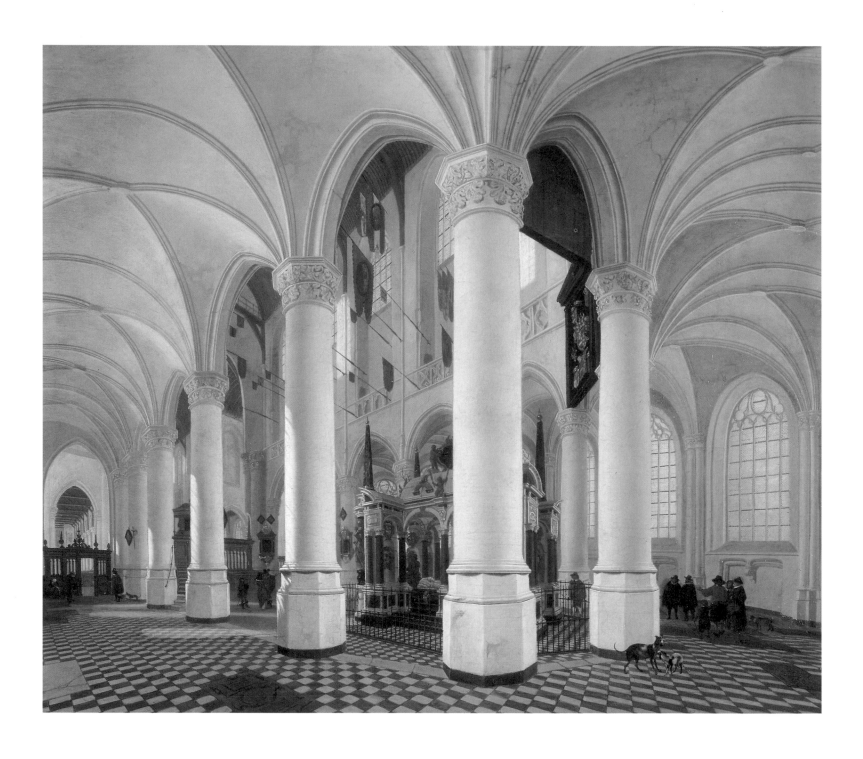

78

GERARD HOUCKGEEST (c. 1600-1661)
*Ambulatory of the New Church
in Delft, with the tomb of
Willem the Silent*, c. 1651
Panel 65.5 x 77.5 cm
THE HAGUE, MAURITSHUIS
(acquired in 1816, see p. 332)

paintings, is different from Saenredam's method. In the latter's church interiors all lines of perspective converge on one point, whereas Houckgeest chose a perspective construction with two vanishing points: one on the left-hand edge of the painting and one on the right in the picture. Houckgeest employed this so-called 'diagonal perspective' in nearly all his works.

Houckgeest was born in The Hague and moved to Delft when he was about 35. There he first devoted himself to painting fantasised church interiors, inspired by prints dating from the beginning of the century. In 1650 he decided to concentrate on portraying existing church interiors. He made various 'portraits' of the interior of the New Church in Delft, all of which include depictions – some more conspicuous than others – of the tomb of Willem I of Orange, known as Willem the Silent. In the painting from the Mauritshuis [78] the impressive monument stands modestly amidst a forest of pillars. The bright light accentuates the surroundings more than the tomb, but anyone looking at the figures in the painting gradually becomes aware, almost accidentally, of the presence of the silent monument.

DE WITTE

Emanuel de Witte painted the tomb from approximately the same angle as Houckgeest, though the atmosphere of the two paintings is very different. De Witte's style is looser and he paid more attention than Houckgeest did to the depiction of people, which is not surprising for someone who began his career as a figure painter. Around 1650 De Witte decided to specialise in church interiors, but even in this genre he continued to exhibit a remarkable interest in the human figure. Here he painted men, women and children in the immediate vicinity of the monument. A wealthy couple in the foreground give alms to a begging child, who serves as a poignant contrast to the well-dressed rich child looking through the railing at the tomb. Just as in Houckgeest's paintings, dogs run around the church. Both painters were hereby drawing attention to an everyday situation that sometimes got out of hand: records show that churches often employed people to chase out dogs.

De Witte also paid close attention to the play of light. The persuasive power of his architecture owes more to the beautiful lighting effects than to the precision of the perspective construction. The technical side was not De Witte's strong point; he was not a true master of the art of perspective, and was wont to make use of compositional diagrams made by his colleague Houckgeest. When De Witte began painting church interiors both artists were living in Delft, which explains why they were both so fond of portraying Delft's New Church. De Witte, however, continued to make paintings of the New Church, even after his move to Amsterdam in 1652. This undoubtedly had something to do with the political overtones inherent in portrayals of the tomb of Willem the Silent. Such depictions were a tribute to the House of Orange and probably in vogue among Orangist sympathisers.

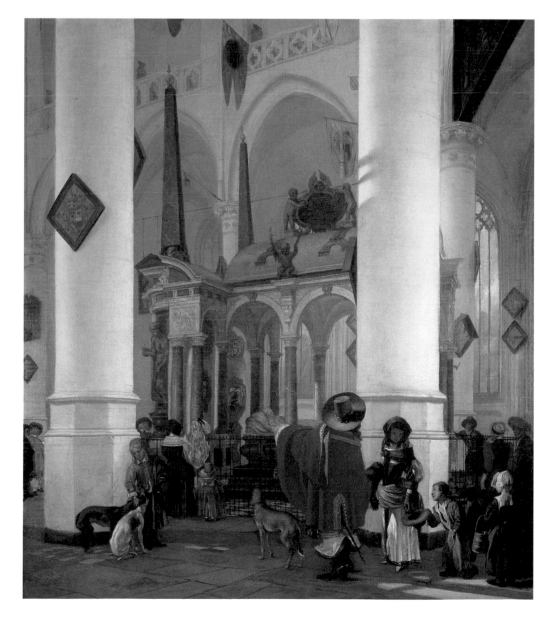

79

EMANUEL DE WITTE (c. 1616-1691/1692)
*View of the tomb of Willem the Silent
in the New Church in Delft*, 1656
Canvas 97 x 85 cm
LILLE, MUSÉE DES BEAUX-ARTS
(acquired in 1890, see p. 336)

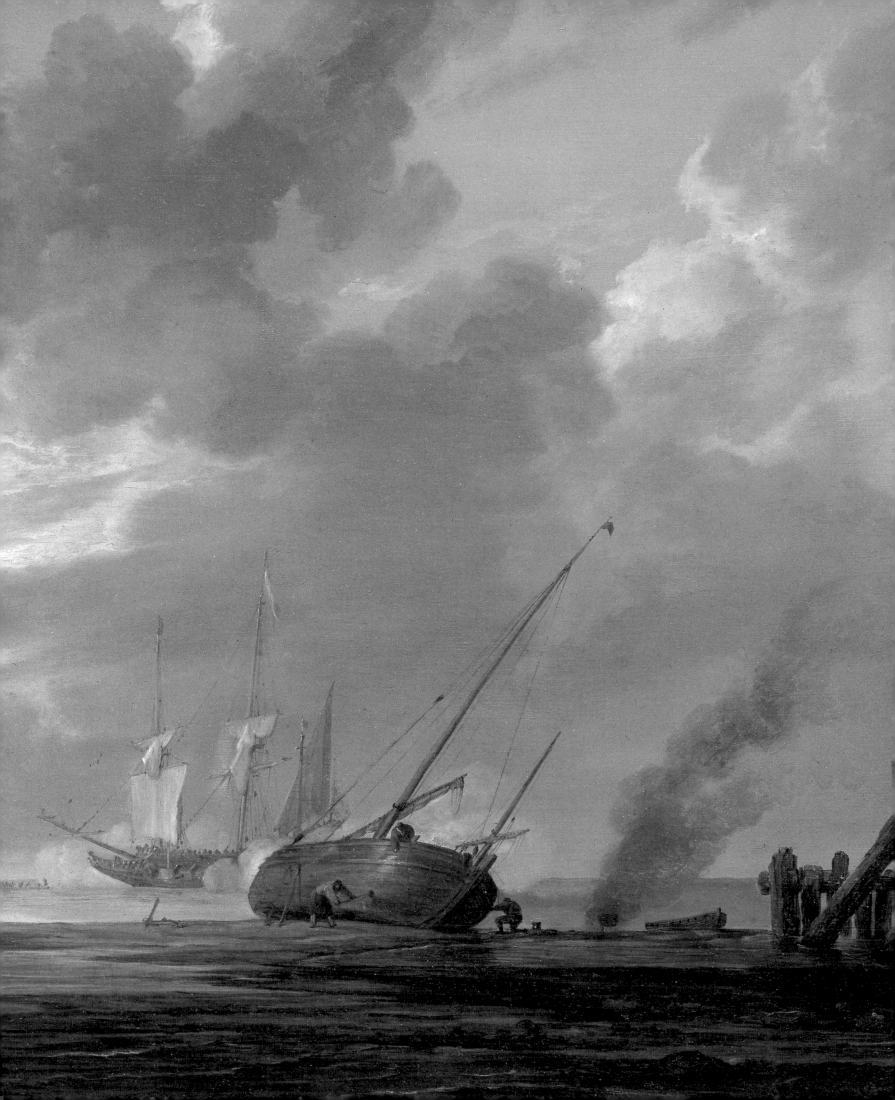

12 SKY AND WATER 1630-1650

THE COLOURFULNESS of early 17th-century landscapes (see chapter 3) made way after 1630 for a more sober palette in which the colours were closely related to one another. Painters now began to concentrate more particularly on the atmospheric rendering of the natural setting. They placed the horizon lower, thereby creating more room for impressive, cloud-filled skies. Whereas the narrative element was seldom missing from earlier landscapes, now the human figure was assigned a subordinate role. The beginnings of these developments were already apparent in the early work of Jan van Goyen and Salomon van Ruysdael [21, 22], and it continued in their later work and that of their contemporaries.

Within the genre of landscape painting there was ever greater specialisation. Hercules Segers, for example, was a specialist in rugged mountain landscapes, Jan van Goyen concentrated on river and polder scenes, Aert van der Neer dedicated himself to making nocturnal pieces and Jan Porcellis became a specialist in portraying the tempestuous sea. Everything points to the existence of a great demand for landscapes, a demand which was gladly met by hundreds of specialised landscape painters.

PANORAMA

The panorama, or distant view, affords a broad view of a primarily flat landscape, often from a high vantage point. It seems to be typically Dutch: where else could it have its origins but in the flat landscape of Holland? In terms of composition the panorama is an unusual type of depiction. The foreground was left empty as a rule, while the horizon was usually rendered as one continuous line, scarcely interrupted by either trees or houses. Not surprisingly, it took some time for Dutch landscape painters to take such a daring step.

The first panoramas appeared in drawings. Shortly after 1600 the Haarlem artist Hendrick Goltzius drew the first panoramas. Hercules Segers, who lived for a short while in Haarlem, followed suit with several etchings of distant views. The painted landscapes he had made in Amsterdam were still traditional mountain landscapes, completely a product of his imagination [81]. His first painted panoramas did not appear until years later.

These bear a striking resemblance to the drawings Goltzius had made several decades earlier. A true specialist in this type of distant view was Philips Koninck [152].

In the 1630s such artists as Salomon van Ruysdael and Jan van Goyen [83] contributed to the development of the painted panorama. These artists often placed a hill or other accentuated object in the foreground for the purpose of leading the viewer's gaze into the painting.

A new development in panorama painting came from an unexpected quarter. In an etching made around 1643, Rembrandt introduced a new type: a panorama in which the silhouette of a city clearly stands out against the sky. Until that time the horizon was interrupted at most by a tower or a couple of trees. It is this type of panorama that Jacob van Ruisdael would further develop several decades later into his so-called 'Haarlempjes', or small views of Haarlem (see chapter 19).

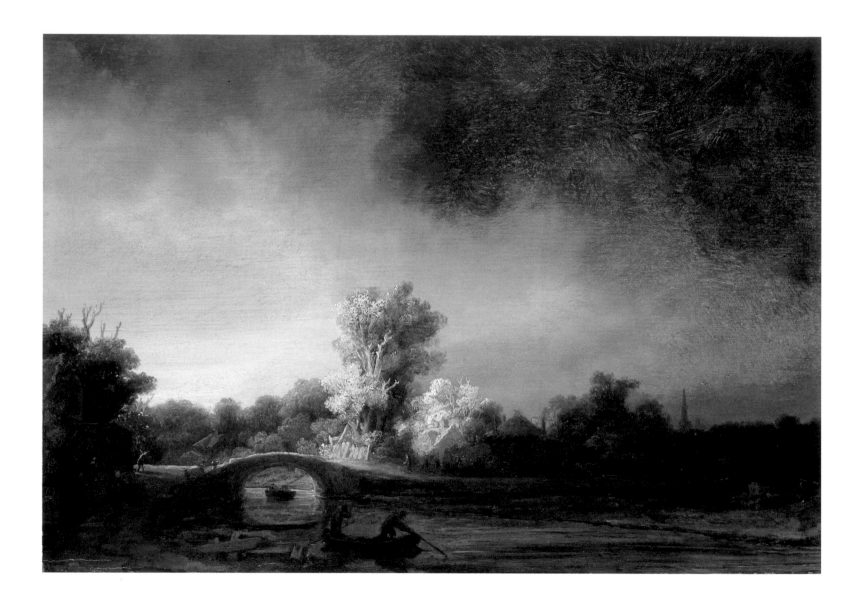

80

REMBRANDT (1606-1669)
The stone bridge, c. 1638
Panel 29.5 x 42.5 cm
AMSTERDAM, RIJKSMUSEUM
(acquired with the aid of the Rembrandt Society
in 1900, see p. 314)

COARSELY PAINTED

A rough-hewn storm cloud dominates Rembrandt's dramatic landscape with a stone bridge. A black sky darkens land and water, while an intense beam of light skims across the road, the bridge and the tall trees. Beneath the threatening clouds tiny figures

continue on their way: fishermen punt their boats down the canal, a wagon stops at an inn and to the left a man carrying a pole on his shoulder plods on towards the bridge, his bent back lit up by the sunlight.

Rembrandt's handling of the paint follows the apportionment of light in the scene: in the dark areas the paint is thinly applied, whereas in the lighter areas it is laid on more thickly. The storm cloud at the upper right is composed of coarse brushstrokes, using little paint, so that the underpainting shows through in places. Where the light is brightest, near the tall trees in the middle, Rembrandt used a fine brush, painting in a rather pastose manner.

Rembrandt regularly worked out of doors, making drawings of the landscape, but the few landscape paintings he made must have originated in his studio. This small Dutch landscape painting with its dramatic chiaroscuro is unique in Rembrandt's oeuvre. His other landscapes are mountainous fantasy landscapes in the manner of Hercules Segers.

MOUNTAINOUS LANDSCAPE

This *Mountainous landscape* by Hercules Segers was possibly owned at one time by Rembrandt, who possessed seven landscapes by Segers. In 1839, when this painting became part of the collection of the Uffizi in

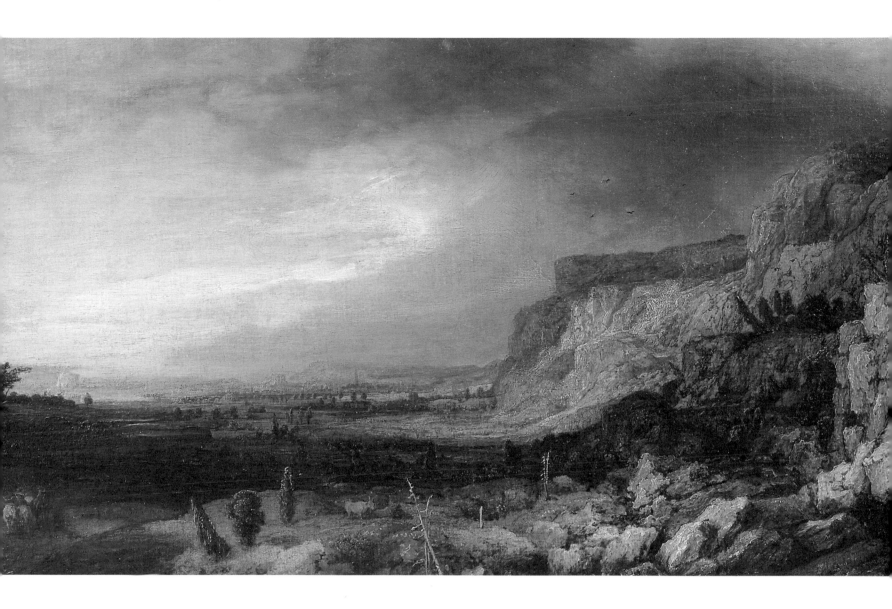

Florence, it was attributed to Rembrandt. This is hardly surprising, as Rembrandt's landscapes are painted in the style of Segers. Moreover, Rembrandt probably painted over parts of Segers's *Mountainous landscape,* adding on the left a wagon with a man on the box, horses and a man walking, thus introducing a human element into an otherwise desolate – and for Segers so typical – landscape. The sky at the upper left was painted over with bluish white paint, and the mountains on the right were made a bit higher. These changes were made in order to heighten the drama of the scene, which calls to mind Rembrandt's landscape with the stone bridge.

Segers's parents came from the Southern Netherlands, but he himself was born in Haarlem. During his apprenticeship to Gillis van Coninxloo he came into contact with the Flemish landscape tradition, and eventually contributed personally to its perpetuation. The rugged mountains, the dark foreground and the blue-grey distance are reminiscent of Flemish examples, but Segers's panorama is grander, producing a more majestic landscape.

Segers's sketchy manner of painting, by which the brushstrokes remain clearly visible, was exceptional in his day, just as were his simple, tonal colour schemes.

81

HERCULES SEGERS
(1589/1590-in or before 1638)
Mountainous landscape, c. 1620-1630
Canvas on panel 55 x 99 cm
FLORENCE, GALLERIA DEGLI UFFIZI
(acquired in 1839, see p. 330)

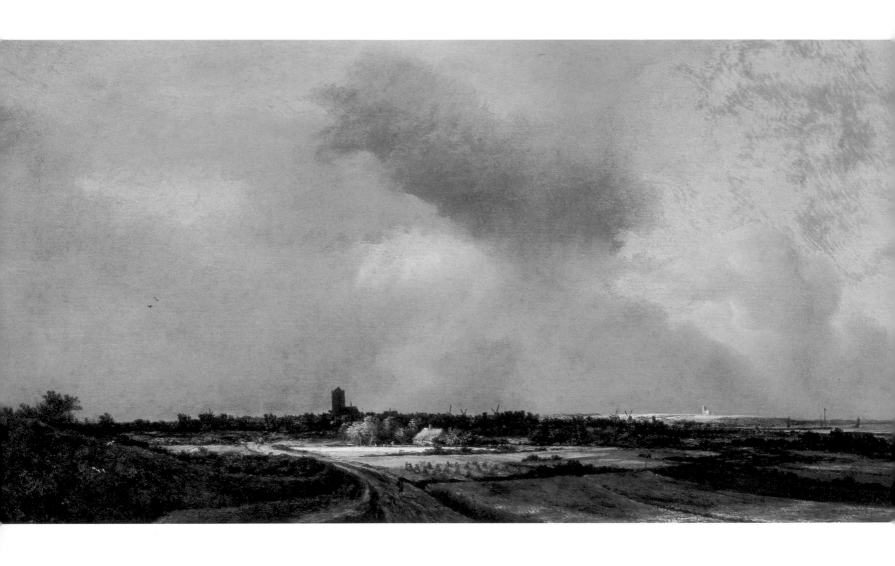

82

JACOB VAN RUISDAEL (1628/1629-1682)
View of Naarden, 1647
Panel 34.8 x 67 cm
MADRID, MUSEO THYSSEN-BORNEMISZA
(acquired in or before 1928, see p. 339)

NAARDEN

Around 1620 Hercules Segers introduced the panoramic view into Dutch painting, anticipating the landscape painters of the 1630s and 1640s, including Jacob van Ruisdael. The latter probably learned to paint from his father Izaack – frame-maker, painter and art dealer – and from his uncle Salomon van Ruysdael, the landscape painter. In his native town of Haarlem he saw the very best landscape painters of his time at work, which undoubtedly acted as a stimulus. Jacob van Ruisdael developed into a versatile painter, who mastered many variations within the genre of landscape painting, including the panorama.

The *View of Naarden* of 1647 is one of his first paintings, made when he was 18 or 19 years old. Ruisdael chose a low horizon, which left him a lot of room for the sky. This painting is more than just a view of Naarden: more than anything, it is a 'view' of a typical Dutch sky with cumulus clouds. The little hill on the left, a means of accentuating the foreground, was derived from Ruisdael's predecessors. An invention of his own is the meandering road, which leads the viewer, as it were, through the painting all the way to the town in the distance, where the church of Naarden towers above the surrounding countryside. Windmills stand out against the cloudy sky and at the right, on the horizon, lies the church of Muiderberg, brilliantly lit by the sun. At the far right is the Zuiderzee, with a boat sailing on it.

HAARLEMMERMEER

The small panoramic landscapes of Jan van Goyen are looser and much more schematic than those of Ruisdael. This painting offers a view of the watery area near Haarlem called the Haarlemmermeer. On the land one sees some windmills and haystacks, cows grazing and two figures sitting on a little hill at the left. Smoke curls upwards from a limekiln. On the horizon, to the right of centre, the Church of St Bavo in Haarlem is dimly visible.

Like Ruisdael, Van Goyen painted sky for the most part, in this case a sombre mass of clouds. The landscape is painted in several closely related shades of brown, ochre-yellow, blue and green. The tonal colour scheme contributes to the specifically Dutch atmosphere of this landscape, in which sky and water form the most important 'elements'. Van Goyen's high productivity was a result of his working method. He repeated successful compositions again and again, making only small changes each time. This was described by Samuel van Hoogstraeten in his treatise on the art of painting (1678): 'By "swaddling" the whole canvas all at once – here light, there dark, more or less like a multicoloured agate or marbled paper – he was able, with barely any effort, to apply with tiny brushstrokes all manner of drolleries, so that over yonder a distant view looms up with peasant hamlets, while elsewhere appears an old fort with a gate and landing-stage, reflected in the rippling water, as well as various kinds of ships and barges, loaded with passengers and freight. In short, his eye – as though in search of the forms that lay hidden in the chaos of his paint – skilfully guided his hand, so that one saw a perfect painting.'

83

JAN VAN GOYEN (1596-1656)
View of the Haarlemmermeer, 1646
Panel 34.6 x 50.5 cm
NEW YORK,
THE METROPOLITAN MUSEUM OF ART
(acquired in 1871, see p. 342)

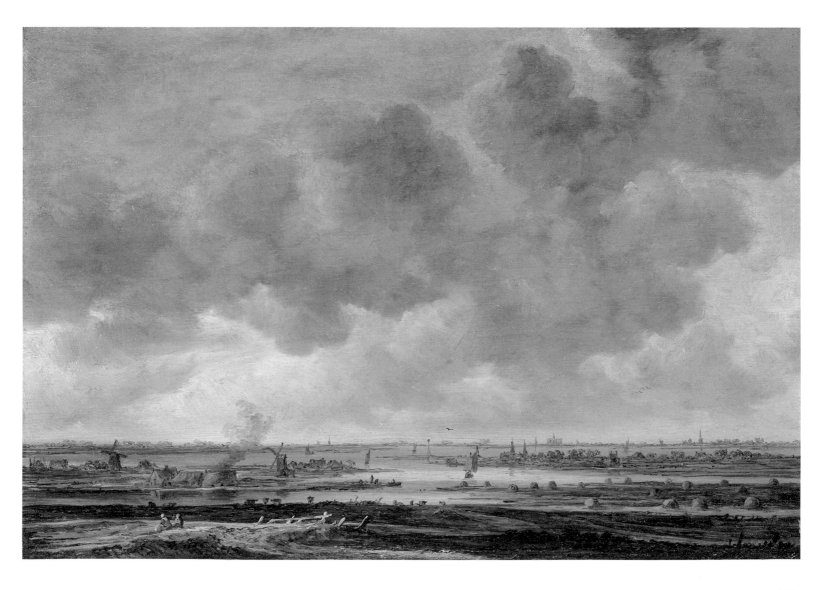

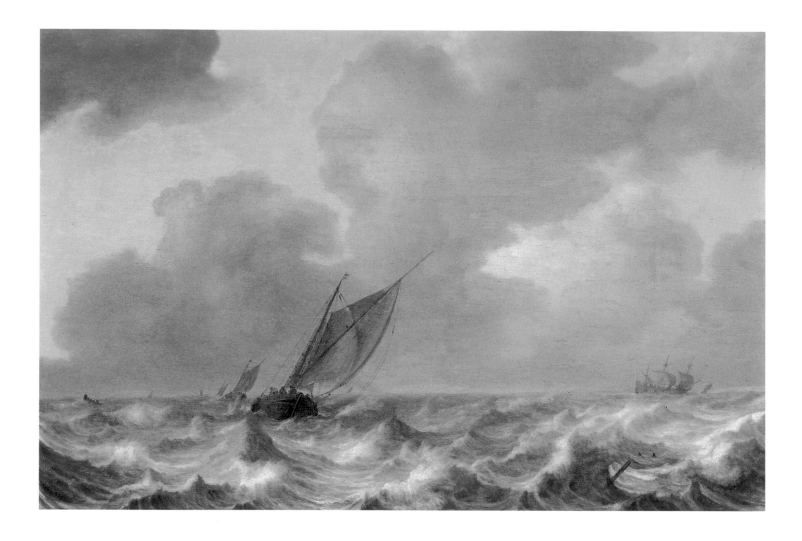

According to Van Hoogstraeten, this is how Van Goyen set to work during a painting competition that was supposedly held around 1630. Three painters – Jan van Goyen, François Knibbergen and Jan Porcellis – were supposed to make a painting in only one day, at the end of which it would be decided whose was the best. Van Hoogstraeten not only described the competition, but also explained why painting quickly was so important: 'At the beginning of this century Dutch walls were not so thickly hung with paintings as they are nowadays. This became more and more common, however, which prompted some painters to assume a quick manner of painting, so that they could complete a piece, large or small, every day.'

PORCELLIS

Regarding Jan Porcellis's participation in the competition Van Hoogstraeten wrote the following: 'The third was our Porcellis, the great Raphael of marine painting! His supporters practically gave up hope, however, when they saw how slowly he set to work with his brush. At first it even seemed as though he was wantonly wasting time, or else could not decide how to start. This was because he first imagined in his mind the whole design of his painting, before ever dipping his brush in the paint. However, the results clearly showed that this was the correct way of working, because even though he persevered in his slowness, he did everything with a sure hand, and was finished with his painting in the evening, just as were his two opponents... and this

84

JAN PORCELLIS (1580/1584-1632)
Vessels in a strong wind, c. 1630
Panel 41.5 x 61.7 cm
MRS EDWARD CARTER, UNITED STATES
(see p. 351)

piece was declared by the judges to be better than the other two.'

The painting *Vessels in a strong wind* shows the marine painter Jan Porcellis at his best. Three freighters of the same type, with one mast and a spritsail, fix their course on a place on the horizon, of which only a church tower is visible. On the right sail an East Indiaman and a small sailing boat, on the left a rowing boat.

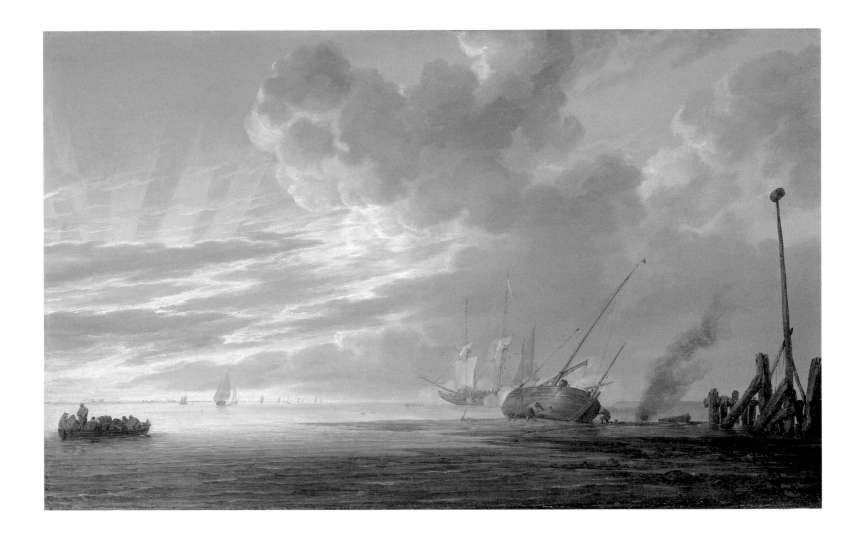

Porcellis lent the necessary depth to the painting by placing the three freighters in a row behind each other. The depiction is dominated by the magnificently rendered cloud formations and the white crests on the waves. Whereas the traditional seascape was usually a 'portrait' of a ship or a historical account of a naval battle, the important element here is the portrayal of sky and water.

DE VLIEGER

Porcellis influenced various marine and landscape painters, one of whom was Simon de Vlieger, who initially painted in a colourful, illustrative manner, but began to concentrate more and more on the atmospheric rendering of the sea, lakes and rivers. This *Seascape in the morning* represents an

intermediate stage in his development. Here the painter was interested not only in the atmosphere, but also in the story. On the right a ship has been hauled onto dry land; a pot of tar stands on the fire, to be used in caulking: stopping up the ship's seams with oakum and sealing them with tar.

The colours are subdued. The grey dominating the foreground becomes lighter towards the horizon, changing there into the impressive sky in shades of blue. Towards the horizon the forms also become more vague. The depth and grandeur thus suggested by the painter lend the work an unprecedented monumentality.

85

SIMON DE VLIEGER (1600/1601-1653)
Seascape in the morning, c. 1640-1645
Panel 36.8 x 58.4 cm
WASHINGTON, NATIONAL GALLERY OF ART
(acquired in 1997, see p. 350)

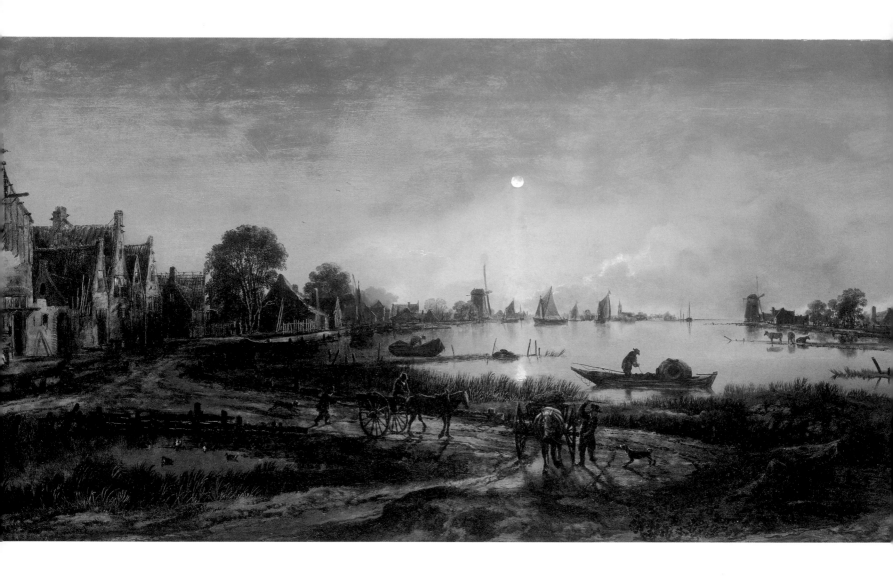

86

Aert van der Neer (1603/1604-1677)

River view by moonlight, c. 1645

Panel 55 x 103 cm

Amsterdam, Rijksmuseum

(acquired in 1936, see p. 316)

MOONLIGHT

Aert van der Neer specialised in subjects eminently suited to depiction in a tonal, monochrome palette: winter scenes and nocturnal pieces. In both genres the painter normally gave water an important place. In the nocturnal scenes he usually displayed some sort of activity in the foreground, as in the *River view by moonlight*. This painting affords a view of a river stretching to the horizon. The moon illuminates the scene so brightly that the water reflects its surroundings: the man in the boat in the foreground, the cows on the shore to the right and the boats and windmills along the left shore. Van der Neer's palette consists of ochres, white, black, brown and shades of blue. He used ochre for the ground – the prepared

surface on which the scene was painted – which shines through the paint layers, helping to define the tonality of the painting. The whole was cursorily painted; only the foreground is somewhat more detailed. With white paint he rendered the reflection of light on the horse's back, the dogs' snouts and the ducks' feathers. He made scratches in the still-wet paint with a sharp object, probably the handle of his brush, causing the light, ochre-coloured ground to show through. In this way he suggested the reflection of the moonlight on the road, near both pairs of horse and cart, and, more to the background, in front of the fence by a farmhouse. In addition to using both ends of his brush, the painter also used his fingers. He rendered the reflection of the trees on the right by means of a thumbprint, and he shortened the sail arm of a windmill, which had turned out too long, simply by wiping the paint away with his fingers. All in all, the painter managed in subtle ways to lend nuances of light and depth to this nocturnal scene.

TRAVELLERS AT AN INN

Isack van Ostade constructed his *Travellers at a country inn* in accordance with a clear pattern: two diagonal lines divide the picture plane; at the point where they intersect stands a large tree. The triangle thus formed at the right was then filled with houses, people and animals. The people gather around a dilapidated inn. A horse and cart stop, a cripple seems to propel himself forward, men loiter at the entrance to the inn and others carry on working. The corresponding section opposite, however, was left practically empty. A pollarded willow stands out against the sky; only two rustic figures and a little boy form the counterbalance to the large group of people on the other side of the sandy road. The little group at the left serves as a *repoussoir*: it lends depth to the painting and guides the viewer's gaze into the depiction. The scene is so crowded with people that the painting can be viewed not only as a landscape, but also as a genre piece. The lively naturalness of the picture is strengthened by the fluent and direct manner of painting, while the unity of the composition is preserved by the use of closely related colours. The talented younger brother of the better-known Adriaen van Ostade died at the age of 28, having been active as a painter for about 10 years.

87

ISACK VAN OSTADE (1621-1649)
Travellers at a country inn, 1645
Panel 75 x 109 cm
THE HAGUE, MAURITSHUIS
(acquired with the aid of the Rembrandt Society
in 1925, see p. 333)

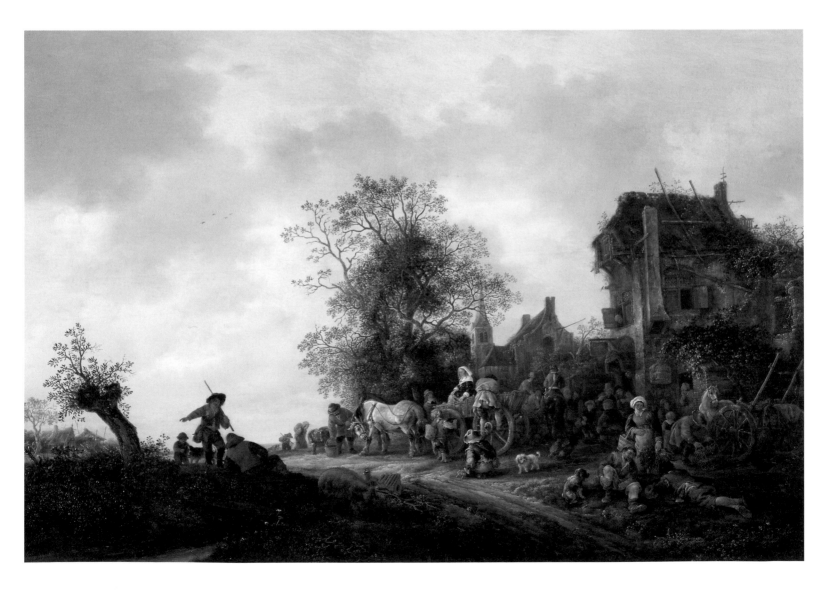

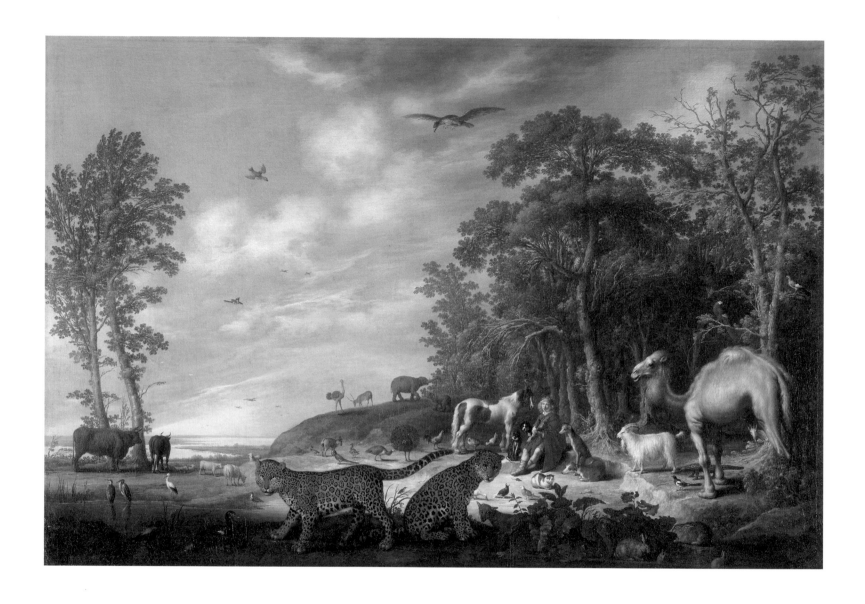

88

AELBERT CUYP (1620-1691)
Orpheus with animals in a landscape,
c. 1640
Canvas 113 x 167 cm
PRIVATE COLLECTION, BOSTON
(see p. 351)

AELBERT CUYP

In the midst of animals Orpheus plays on his violin. According to classical literature, his singing and lyre-playing had a magical effect. Wild animals followed him, trees and plants bent towards him and rivers stopped flowing for him. Even people came under the spell of his music. In short, he was capable of taming nature. This subject was portrayed frequently in the 17th century, probably because it offered the artist an opportunity to paint all kinds of animals.

Aelbert Cuyp was born in 1620 to a painters' family in Dordrecht. Under his father's guidance Aelbert developed into a painter of sun-drenched landscapes inhabited by animals. This painting with Orpheus is an early work. The landscape consists of a wooded hill on the right and a distant, watery view to the left, the whole seeming very Dutch indeed. A curious collection of animals inhabits the landscape. Close to Orpheus are the house pets and farm animals: dog and cat, horse and goat, peacock, chicken and a monkey. Somewhat farther away from him are the wild and exotic animals: dromedary, elephant, ostrich, parrot and two jaguars. Some of these beasts seem to have been painted from life; indeed, it is quite possible that Cuyp actually studied living specimens. In the 17th century there existed menageries or small private zoos which belonged to country estates. In addition, ships returning from the East sometimes brought home exotic animals, which were then exhibited in Dutch towns. This of course gave artists an excellent opportunity to observe and record these extraordinary animals. Sketches are known

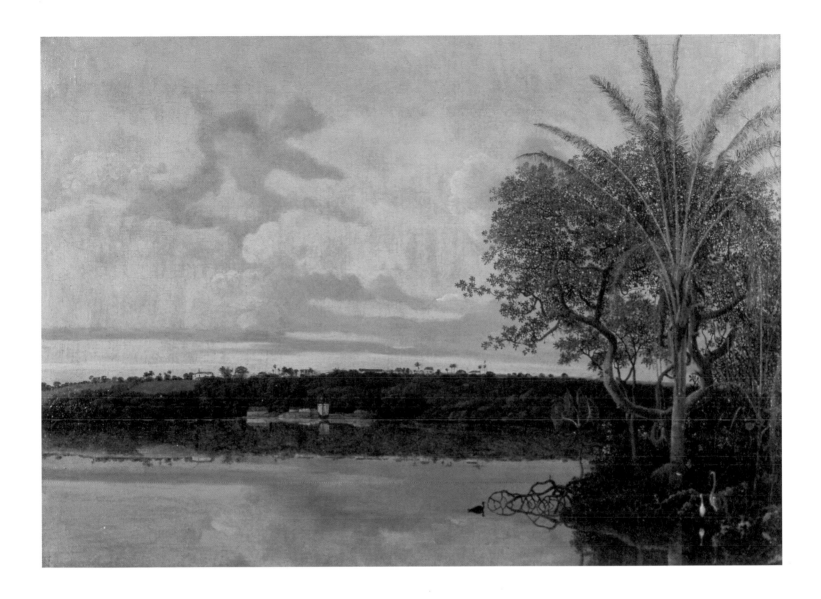

by Rembrandt's hand of an elephant, a lion and a camel, made on just such an occasion. Handbooks urged painters to make use of such opportunities. 'One should, no matter what, seize the opportunity to study exotic animals, such as lions, tigers, bears, elephants, camels and such animals, which one seldom sees but nevertheless needs occasionally for use in an invention,' wrote Willem Goeree in his 'Introduction to the Practice of General Painting', which was published in 1670. It is not easy to say whether Cuyp based his depiction on his own observations or on the examples of other artists.

POST

Frans Post was one of the few artists in a position to study exotic animals in their natural surroundings. Between 1637 and 1644 the Haarlem painter lived in Brazil, part of which was ruled by the Dutch. Post was employed in the service of Johan Maurits of Nassau-Siegen, the governor of Brazil appointed by the Dutch West India Company. The painter was given the unique commission to portray the land and its inhabitants. He made at least 18 paintings, thereby becoming the first to capture the New World on canvas. This landscape belongs to a series of paintings by Post which Johan Maurits presented to the

89

FRANS POST (c. 1612-1680)
*View of Frederiksstad
in Paraíba, Brazil*, 1638
Canvas 60.3 x 84.5 cm
CARACAS, COLECCIÓN PATRICIA
PHELPS DE CISNEROS
(see p. 351)

French king, Louis XIV, in 1678-1679. Most of these works are now in the Louvre in Paris, but this painting disappeared sometime after 1765 and did not surface again until quite recently.

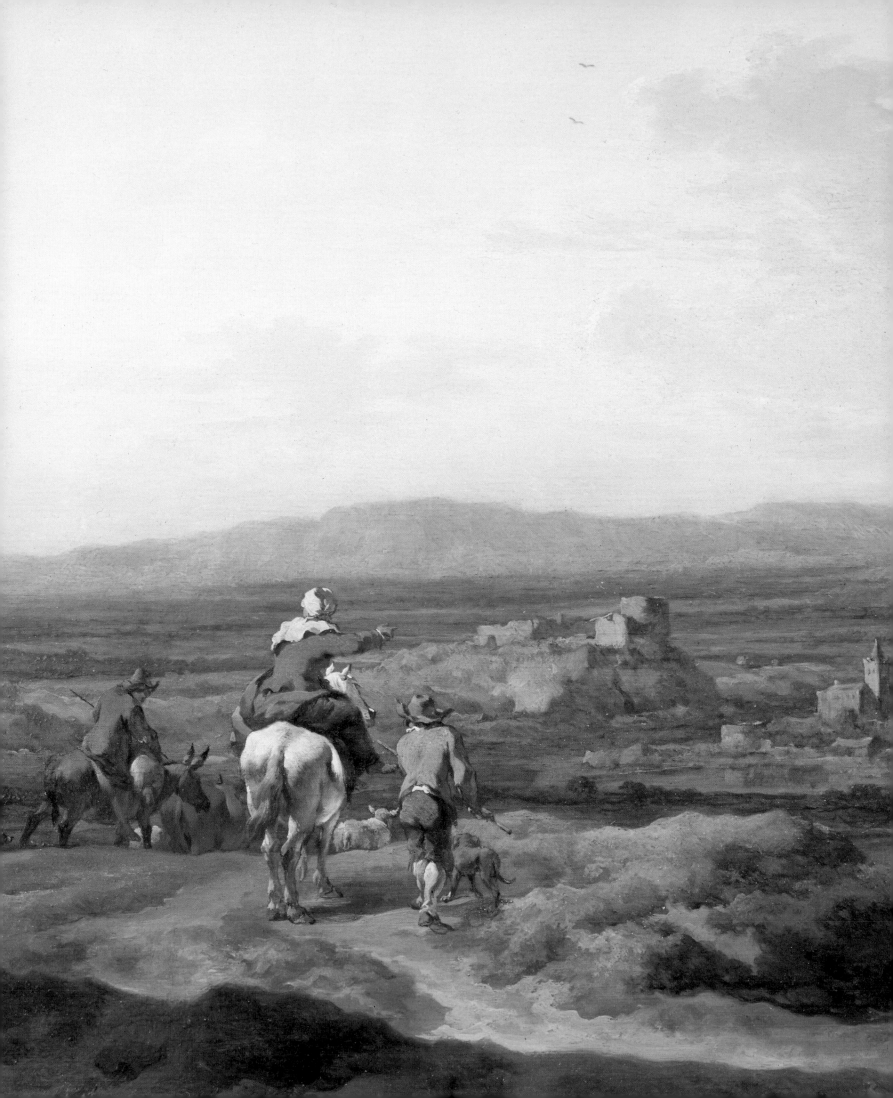

13 GOLDEN LIGHT 1620-1660

As EARLY as the 16th century a trip to Italy, and to Rome in particular, was considered an important part of an artist's training. The goal of this trip was to see with one's own eyes the famous art works of classical antiquity and the Renaissance. Once in Italy, some of these artists were deeply impressed by the work of contemporaries, such as Caravaggio and his followers (see chapter 4), while others were inspired by the Italian landscape. The latter group continued to paint such landscapes after returning to the Netherlands, and these artists became known as the Italianate landscape painters.

TWO GENERATIONS

The Italianate painters may be divided into two groups. The first generation consisted of artists whose Italian sojourn took place sometime between 1620 and 1640. Its most important representatives were Cornelis van Poelenburch and Bartholomeus Breenbergh. The second generation, which included Jan Both, Jan Asselijn, Nicolaes Berchem, Jan Baptist Weenix, Adam Pynacker and Karel Dujardin, stayed in Italy some time between 1640 and 1675.

The artists of the first generation usually painted landscapes with classical ruins and tiny figures who portrayed a biblical or mythological story. In the works of second-generation Italianate painters we still see ruins, but they no longer occupy a central place in the depiction. Their landscapes are peopled with shepherds, travellers, merchants and draughtsmen. These painters' main source of inspiration was the warm, golden Southern light.

APPRECIATION

The Italianate painters did not make realistic landscapes. Reality was their point of departure, but it was not slavishly copied. The same held true for their colleagues who painted the Dutch landscape. These landscape paintings were not produced out of doors, but put together in the studio, and their compositions were based on drawn studies that had been done from nature, sometimes years earlier.

Although Italianising landscapes were highly valued in the 17th and 18th centuries, they later went out of fashion. At a lecture given in 1836 the English painter John Constable (1776-1837) characterised the Italianate painters as 'men who have lost sight of nature'. In his view the natural rendering of the landscape was of prime importance. Only in the second half of the 20th century did the Italianate painters again rise in popularity. The significance, quality and influence of this group of artists were once again recognised and their works became popular among collectors.

CAMPO VACCINO

The *View of the Campo Vaccino* is the earliest dated painting by Cornelis van Poelenburch. He made it in Rome in 1620,

THE BENTVUEGHELS

In 1623 there were so many artists from the North living in Rome that they decided to found a society: the 'Schildersbent'. They called themselves the Bentvueghels. An important stimulus for the founding of this society was the decision of the Italian Accademia to make all foreign artists pay membership fees, even if they were not members. The Dutch artists refused to do this, and strengthened their position by uniting to form a block against the Accademia.

The Bentvueghels had various customs: new members, for example, were subjected to an elaborate initiation ceremony that was a parody of official Church ceremonies. On this occasion the newcomers were given their 'bent names', which often contained derisive references to their outward appearance. Cornelis Poelenburch, for example, was baptised 'Satyr' and Jan Asselijn, who had a misshapen hand, 'Crab'.

< DETAIL OF 93

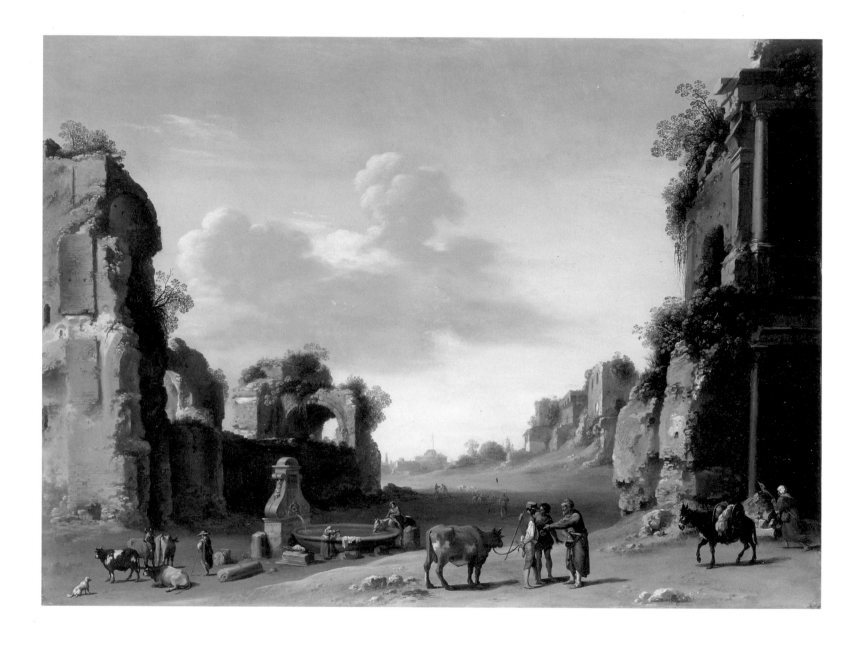

90

CORNELIS VAN POELENBURCH
(c. 1594-1667)
View of the Campo Vaccino, 1620
Copper 40 x 54.5 cm
PARIS, MUSÉE DU LOUVRE
(acquired in 1794, see p. 344)

when he was 26 years old. Poelenburch was born in Utrecht and was apprenticed there to Abraham Bloemaert. In 1617 he left for Italy, where he stayed until 1625.

This painting shows the cattle market held on the Roman Forum. Between the ruins of ancient buildings on both left and right are traders with their cattle and a woman doing the washing at a public fountain from which cattle also drink. The Castel Sant' Angelo is recognisable in the background. The painting does not depict an existing situation. Poelenburch arranged the buildings and ruins to suit his own vision: the Castel Sant' Angelo, for example, is not visible from the Roman Forum. Poelenburch was obviously much more interested in producing a Southern impression; he was the first

Netherlandish painter to render the atmosphere and sunlight of Italy in a convincing way. While the work of his predecessors, such as the Flemish painter Paul Bril, usually displays an accumulation of individual motifs, Poelenburch succeeded in moulding the ruins and landscape into a unified whole, with the Southern light as the binding element.

Poelenburch was highly successful: after his stay in Rome he worked in Florence for Cosimo II de' Medici, in England for Charles I and in the Netherlands for Prince Frederik Hendrik. For the rest of his life

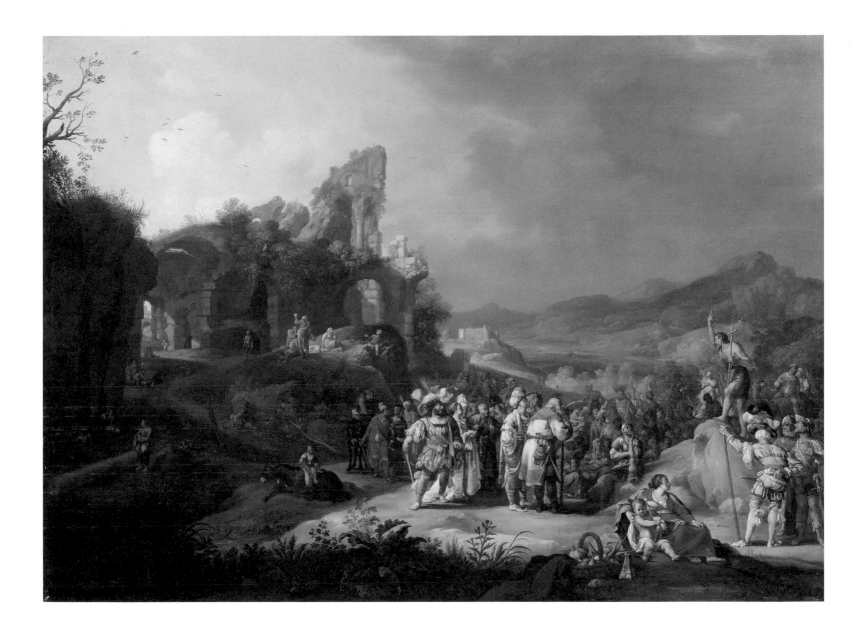

91

BARTHOLOMEUS BREENBERGH (1599-1657)
The preaching of John the Baptist, 1634
Panel 54.5 x 75 cm
NEW YORK,
THE METROPOLITAN MUSEUM OF ART
(acquired in 1991, see p. 342)

Poelenburch continued to cook up paintings according to this successful recipe, painting ruins set in Italian landscapes and enlivened with little figures.

JOHN THE BAPTIST

In 1619 Bartholomeus Breenbergh arrived in Rome, two years after Poelenburch. There, under Poelenburch's influence, he developed into one of the most important painters of Italian landscapes. Later on, after returning to the Netherlands, he used the many drawings he had made in Italy as the basis for his paintings. A good example is this biblical scene of *The preaching of John the Baptist*, painted in Amsterdam in 1634, which he situated in an Italian landscape. The ruin at the left is strongly reminiscent of the Colosseum.

In the centre Breenbergh placed a large group of people who listen to the preaching of John the Baptist. The way in which this group of figures is arranged reveals the influence of the history painter Pieter Lastman (see chapter 7), in whom Breenbergh must have been greatly interested. Here Breenbergh skilfully incorporated into the landscape the people flocking to hear the sermon. No studies of the individual figures are known; Breenbergh probably borrowed them from the work of others.

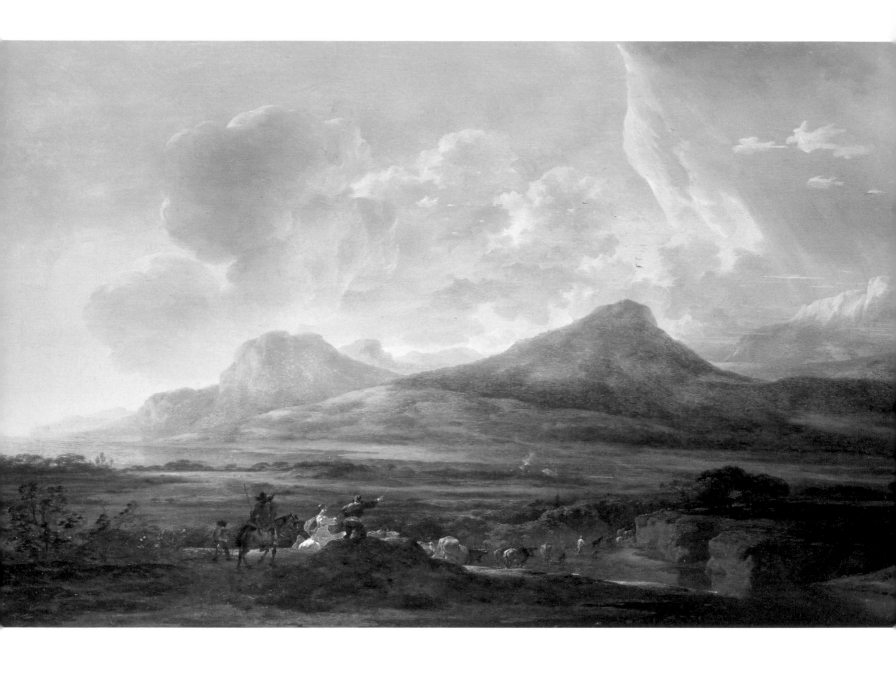

92

Jan Asselijn (c. 1615-1652)
River bank with herdsmen, c. 1650
Panel 43 x 67 cm
Vienna, Akademie der bildenden Künste
(acquired in 1822, see p. 349)

TWO LANDSCAPES

Mountains rise up on the horizon of a vast landscape; in the foreground shepherds drive their flocks down into the valley. This description fits both the painting by Nicolaes Berchem and the one by Jan Asselijn. There are even more similarities: both are tonal paintings with colourful accents in the clothing of the shepherds in the foreground. Moreover, the same gesture occurs in both paintings: an extended arm pointing to the right.

ASSELIJN

Jan Asselijn probably stayed in Rome from 1636 to 1644. After returning to Amsterdam he continued to paint Italian landscapes. The *River bank with herdsmen* was painted around 1650. At that time he had been back from Italy for three years, but he was none theless able to produce a powerful rendering of the Italian atmosphere. The alternation of light and shadow on the expansive land-scape is especially beautiful, as are the gradations of colour in the clouds.

In addition to panoramic landscapes such as this, Asselijn also painted harbour views. An exception in the oeuvre of this Italianate painter is his famous *Threatened swan* in the Rijksmuseum (see p. 10), which depicts a life-size swan taking flight in defence of its nest. It was the first painting bought by the Nationale Konst-Gallerij (the National Art Gallery), the forerunner of the Rijksmuseum.

BERCHEM

Nicolaes Berchem, son of the still-life painter Pieter Claesz, was active as an independent painter and a member of the Haarlem painters' guild already in 1642. It

is possible that he was in Italy between 1653 and 1656, though this is not certain. It is however clear that Berchem's painting of an *Italian landscape with mountain plateau* was influenced by Jan Asselijn.

Berchem left a large oeuvre: more than 850 paintings are attributed to him. He also painted figures as staffage in other painters' landscapes. His characteristic figures are recognisable in various paintings by Jacob van Ruisdael, Meindert Hobbema and Jan Baptist Weenix. The many copies made after his work testify to Berchem's renown: he was popular already during his lifetime, but especially so in 18th-century France.

93
NICOLAES BERCHEM (1620-1683)
Italian landscape with mountain plateau, 1655
Panel 33 x 44.1 cm
COLLECTION OF HER MAJESTY
QUEEN ELIZABETH II
(acquired in 1814, see p. 337)

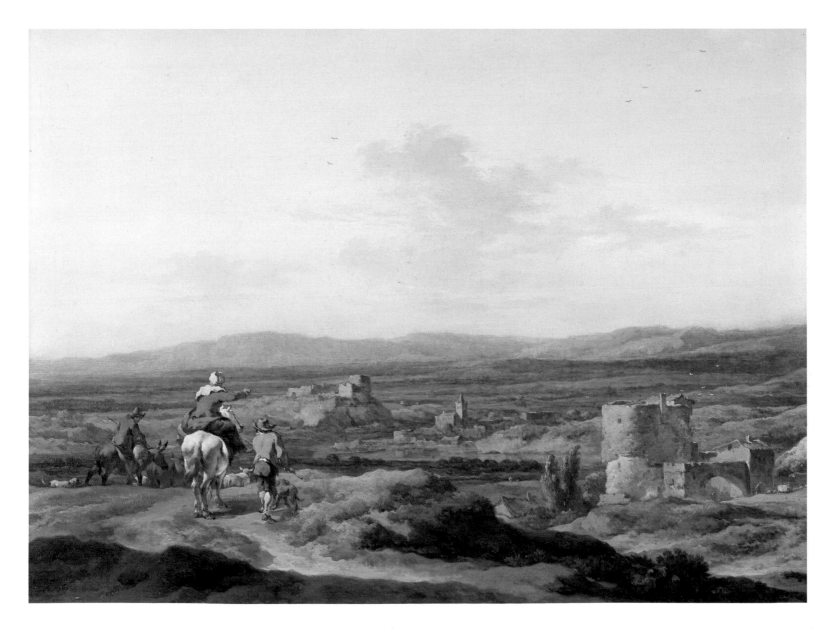

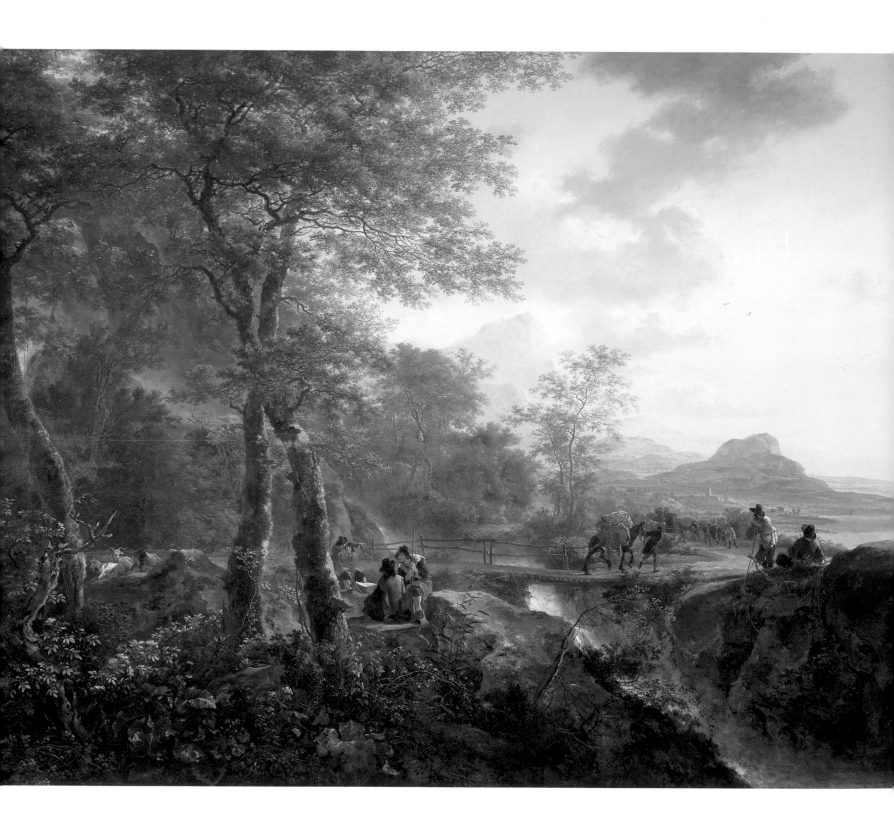

94

JAN BOTH (?-1652)

Italian landscape with draughtsman, c. 1650

Canvas 187 x 240 cm

AMSTERDAM, RIJKSMUSEUM

(on loan from the City of Amsterdam

since 1885, see p. 311)

LANDSCAPE WITH DRAUGHTSMAN

This large painting by Jan Both is cleverly composed: the picture plane is divided in two, with a wooded landscape on the left and a distant view of mountains on the right. The picture is divided by a rushing waterfall that flows under a bridge, which in turn connects the two halves of the painting. Travellers, shepherds and a draughtsman populate the landscape. The painting's imposing format contributes to its allure. Formats such as this were not common in Holland, though perhaps the painting was originally part of some decorative panelling.

The draughtsman's sheet of paper is lit up by a beam of sunlight. The shepherd next to him looks over his shoulder, following his artistic endeavours. Would a travelling artist in those days actually have stopped to record a beautiful view with a rushing mountain stream? It seems likely, considering the great number of preserved drawings that were made out of doors. These drawings served to refresh the artist's memory while painting in the studio.

Both's painting originated in his studio in Utrecht around 1650, years after his trip to Italy. It is remarkable that Jan Both was able to reproduce so convincingly the light and heat of the Italian sun, long after he had actually seen and felt it. The entire scene is bathed in light coming from the background. Both did not paint ruins or temples; he was primarily interested in nature, seen in a nearly supernatural light. There is also a nice balance in Both's work between the precisely rendered plants and massive trees in the foreground and the panorama stretching into the background. This composition of the landscape served as an example to Adam Pynacker.

LAKE SHORE

Although Adam Pynacker mainly painted Italianate landscapes, it is not known whether he ever visited Italy. *Boatmen moored on a lake shore* exudes a characteristic Italian atmosphere: a golden light lends the land colour, brushing past the white bark of the birch tree and the moss-covered tree trunks and creating sharp accents. A crooked, broken-off tree trunk in the foreground and an equally crooked tree on the right close off the composition.

On the shore of the lake a woman sits with her child; on one side of her stands a man with a large hat and on the other an ox and a donkey. The combination of figures has caused this scene to be interpreted as a biblical representation: the Rest on the Flight into Egypt – the point at which Mary, Joseph and the baby Jesus stop to rest, tired out by their journey. It is not at all clear, however, whether Pynacker actually intended to portray this story. The main subject seems to be the Italian countryside, the warm sunlight and the hazy atmosphere.

95

ADAM PYNACKER (c. 1620-1673)
Boatmen moored on a lake shore,
c. 1660
Canvas on panel 97.5 x 85.5 cm
AMSTERDAM, RIJKSMUSEUM
(acquired in 1808, see p. 310)

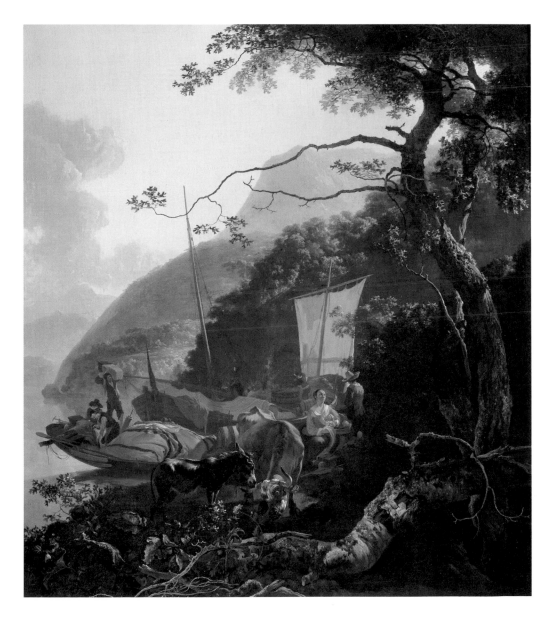

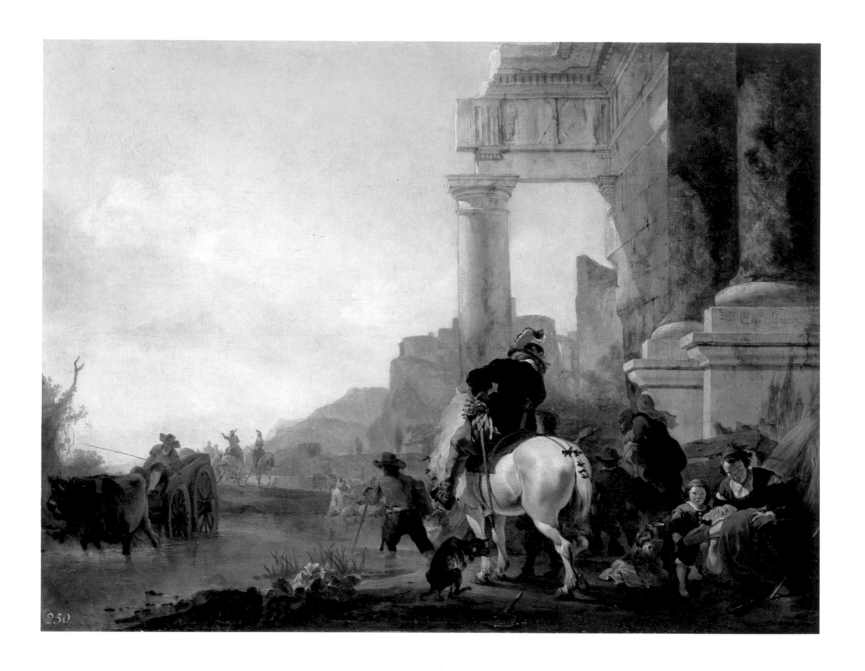

96

JAN BAPTIST WEENIX (1621-1659)
The ford in the river, 1647
Canvas 100 x 131.5 cm
ST PETERSBURG, HERMITAGE
(acquired in 1922, see p. 347)

THE FORD IN THE RIVER

Shortly after his return from Italy, Jan Baptist Weenix painted *The ford in the river*, in which he gave a striking depiction of all the activity taking place at the foot of the ruins of a majestic temple with large pillars. The most salient feature is the gleaming white horse with decorated tail. Animals regularly appeared as staffage in landscape paintings, but here an individual specimen was given an especially prominent place.

The painting is teeming with anecdotal detail. The horseman sits with his back to the viewer, talking with another man standing to the side. On his right a woman removes her red stocking; the boy next to her is already barefoot. Behind them a man carries a woman on his back, ready to ford the river. Finally, a striking detail is the dog in the foreground, blatantly answering nature's call.

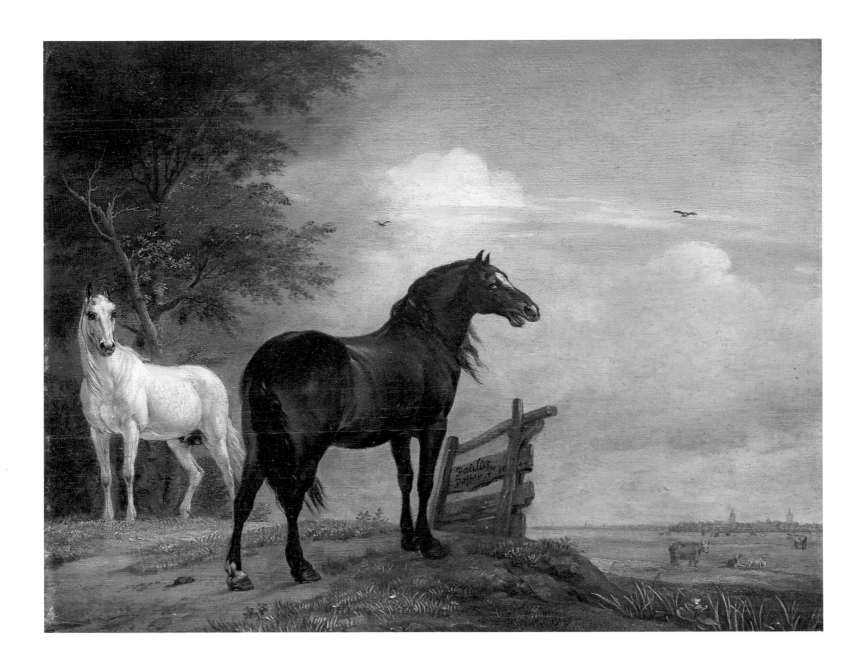

HORSES AS THE FOCAL POINT
If the white horse in Weenix's painting received a great deal of attention, those in Paulus Potter's work were given the principal role. In *Two horses near a gate in a meadow* the depiction of the animals is truly lifelike. They stand on a rise where the mane and tail of the dark horse apparently catch a lot of wind. The gate is an essential element of the composition: it forms the transition between the high foreground and the low-lying background. It was also the perfect place for Potter to place his signature: with

pompous precision he wrote his name and the date – *Paulus Potter f 1649*.

This is a typical Dutch landscape. On the right, meadows with grazing cattle stretch into the distance, where a city is visible. Its profile is recognisable as that of Delft, with the sturdy tower of the Old Church on the right and that of the New Church on the left. In 1646 Potter registered in this city as a master painter, though it is not clear whether he ever lived there. It is certain, however, that in 1649 he became a member of the Guild of St Luke in The

97
PAULUS POTTER (1625-1654)
Two horses near a gate in a meadow, 1649
Panel 23.5 x 30 cm
AMSTERDAM, RIJKSMUSEUM
(on loan from the City of Amsterdam
since 1885, see p. 311)

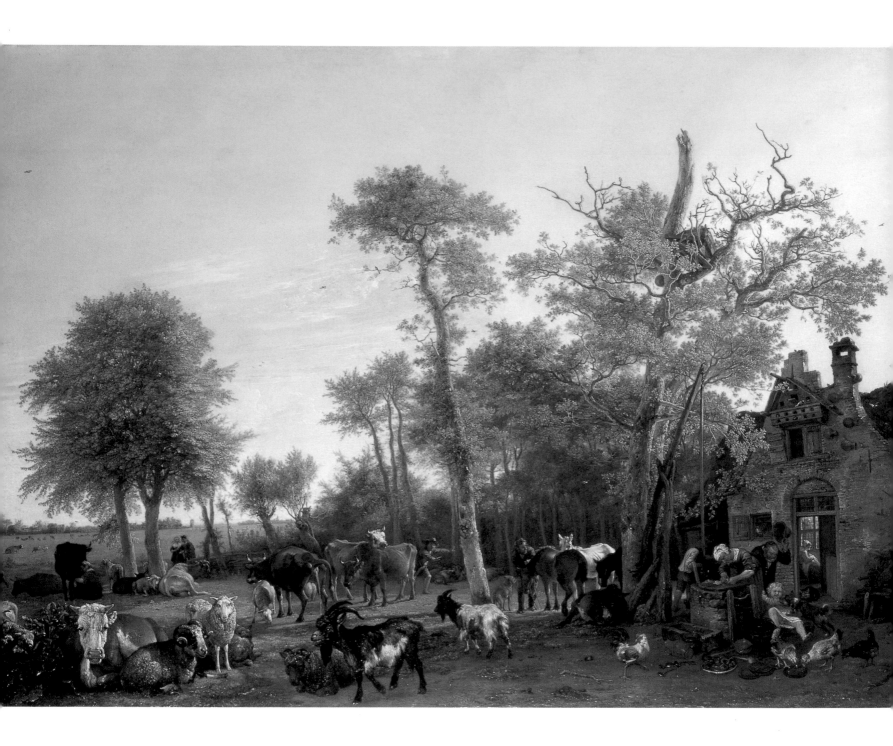

98

PAULUS POTTER (1625-1654)
The farmyard, 1649
Panel 81 x 115.5 cm
ST PETERSBURG, HERMITAGE
(acquired in 1815, see p. 346)

Hague, where he was living with his family. In 1652 Potter was again living in Amsterdam, where he was active until his death, shortly after his twenty-eighth birthday. Potter never travelled to Italy. The golden sunlight bathing his paintings must have been something he saw in the work of his fellow painters.

'MUCH TOO BASE A SUBJECT'
Potter's strength lay in the painting of animals. Horses, cows, sheep, goats, chickens, dogs and cats – he painted all these animals very true to life, paying great attention to their hide or skin, coat of fur or plumage, as well as to their various stances. *The farmyard* is a genre-like scene with a variety of animals and a great deal of anecdotal detail.

A man wearing a red cap shoves bread into an oven; next to a well a farmer's wife wrings out the washing. Through an open door one glimpses a woman, seated by a window with her mending. Outside, above the upper window, is a dovecote, near which hang earthenware pots in which birds nestle.

Striking indeed are some of the details: the boy sitting with his legs wide apart, for example, as well as the urinating cow. This cow was apparently the reason why Amalia van Solms, widow of the stadholder Frederik Hendrik, ended up refusing to buy this painting, which she had ordered for her palace. It was, after all, 'much too base a subject... for Her Highness to view daily', according to the artists' biographer Arnold Houbraken. Several years later, in 1652, an envoy of the Swedish queen, Christina, admired the painting in Potter's studio, reporting that the painter had worked on it uninterruptedly for five months, and that it was admired by all painters. His offer of 300 francs was however refused: the painter wanted 400.

COWS AND SHEEP

The animal paintings by Karel Dujardin bear many similarities to those of Potter. Like Potter, he succeeded in rendering animals in a masterly way. In *Cows and sheep at a stream* he depicted sheep and a lamb, two cows and a donkey in a Dutch meadow, surrounded by a mountainous Italianate landscape. The transitions between light and shadow were subtly painted. Dujardin

hereby conjured up the atmosphere of a warm summer day. This painting, which was especially popular in the 18th century, was bought by the French king, Louis XVI.

Dujardin had been a pupil of Nicolaes Berchem, and probably worked between 1640 and 1652 in Italy, after which he lived in Amsterdam. In 1675 he again travelled to

Italy, where he died in Venice in 1678. His paintings excel in the rendering of the Mediterranean light, but otherwise there are few elements in his work that refer to Southern sojourns. In addition to painting landscapes, Dujardin was also a skilful portraitist and painter of biblical scenes [173].

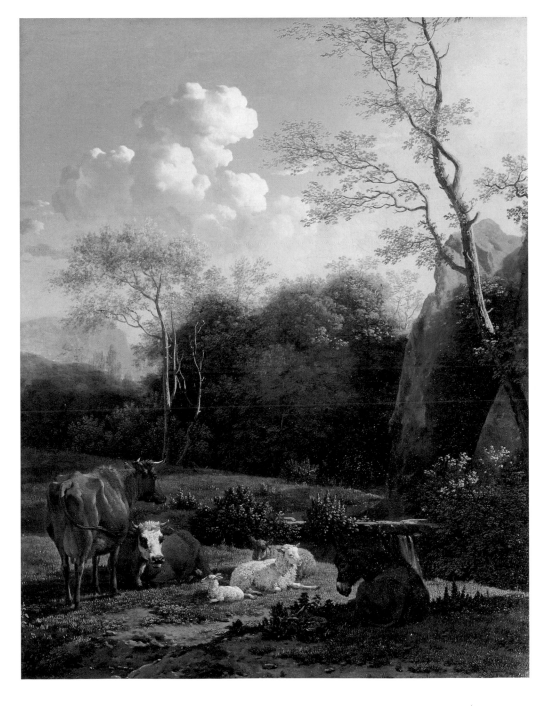

99

KAREL DUJARDIN (1622-1678)
Cows and sheep at a stream,
c. 1655-1656
Canvas 52 x 43 cm
PARIS, MUSÉE DU LOUVRE
(acquired in 1783, see p. 344)

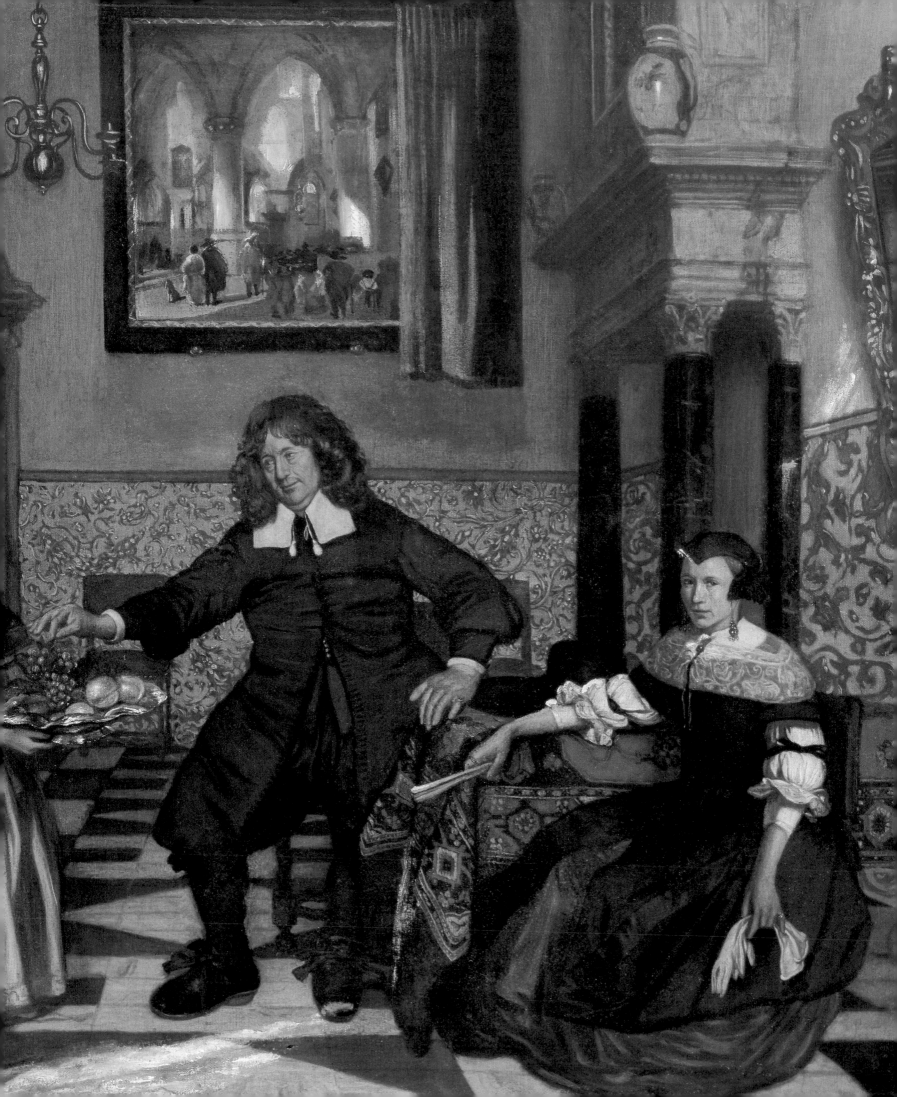

14 THE DUTCH INTERIOR
1650-1670

MANY OBJECTS of the Golden Age which are now proudly displayed in museums originally furnished the homes of well-to-do burghers. Exactly what these interiors looked like – and which parts were common to most homes – is information which has seldom been passed down, but there have nevertheless been many attempts to reconstruct the ambience of the middle-class home. Various sources offer clues on this score: inventories provide descriptive summaries of the objects present in a house at a given time, and a few, rare 17th-century doll's houses display interiors in miniature. Paintings also offer glimpses of Dutch interiors, though it is highly unlikely that Pieter de Hooch, Johannes Vermeer and Emanuel de Witte depicted existing interiors. Their paintings give an impression of what things were like, but not a faithful picture of reality.

RICHLY FURNISHED INTERIOR

The two unidentified burghers, depicted in the detail of the painting by Emanuel de Witte, had their portraits painted in a richly furnished room. There are marble tiles on the floor, the walls are covered with gold-leather wallpaper, a painting and a mirror hang on the wall and Chinese vases stand on the mantel. The interior seems to suit this couple, and it is therefore tempting to reconstruct the Dutch interior on the basis of such a painting. It appears, however, that marble floors were quite rare. Such floors were, admittedly, a coveted status symbol, but in living quarters, where the inhabitants' comfort was of primary importance, wooden floors were preferred to cold, stone floors. Many artists nonetheless chose to depict marble floors with black and white tiles arranged in complicated patterns. From the painter's point of view such floors were interesting, owing to the effect produced by perspective. They also served to lend a richer ambience to the interior.

In 17th-century paintings of interiors, Oriental carpets play a comparable role. If marble floors were a rarity, so were hand-knotted Turkish rugs which were used as tablecloths. Inventories reveal that only the very affluent possessed Oriental carpets. The fact that painters often depicted tables covered with such rugs probably has something to do with their decorative effect: for a painter a Turkish carpet meant added colour.

Emanuel de Witte depicted many costly accessories in the portrait he made of this man and woman. Examples of most of these objects have been preserved, but if inventories and descriptions of buildings are anything to go by, they were seldom seen together in one room.

DOLL'S HOUSE

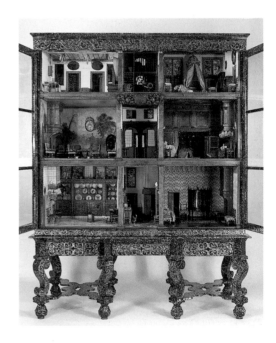

By studying the doll's house once owned by Petronella Oortman (1656-1716) some idea may be formed of the interior of the houses of Amsterdam's patrician families. It also gives a good idea of how one kept house in those days.

< DETAIL OF 110

CUPBOARD

Great wealth and variety characterised the decorative arts in the 1660s and 1670s. Lavishly decorated Baroque furniture was made at this time, as well as simple, elegant objects of costly materials. A good example of furniture in this simple yet refined style is this cupboard with black ebony accents.

The cupboard is constructed along the lines of a classical building. On a sturdy base rest Corinthian columns, which accentuate the corners and the central axis. A cornice, whose horizontality is emphasised by the black bands of ebony, closes off the cupboard at the top. Geometrical forms and bands in contrasting woods form the most prominent ornamentation; the rippled mouldings are especially subtle.

Not one functional detail disturbs the total picture. The designer decided to do without handles and knobs, which did not make opening the drawers in the base any easier. Furthermore, the key hole has been cleverly concealed: it is to be found behind the central embedded column. In order to open the cupboard the column must first be pushed to the side. This ingenious detail testifies in particular to the master craftsmanship of this cabinetmaker, whose name is not known. He made this cupboard for the Trippenhuis, the home built for the extremely wealthy merchant Louis Trip on the Kloveniersburgwal in Amsterdam.

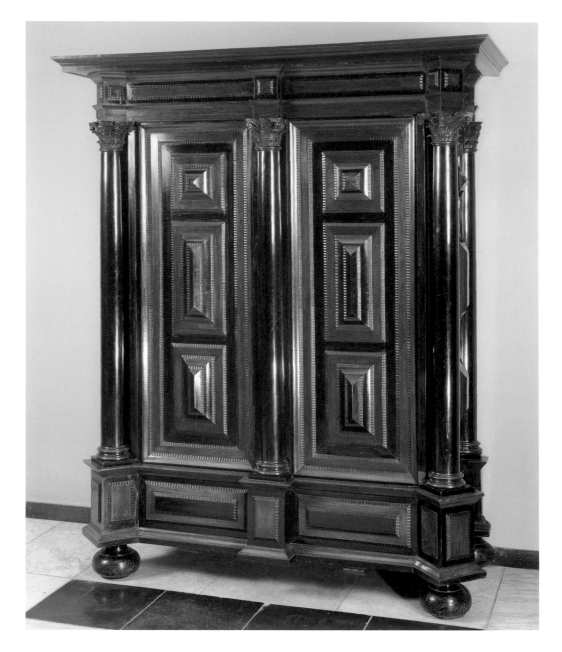

TABLE TOP

Travel guides published in the 17th century informed visitors to Amsterdam of the possibility of visiting the workshop of Dirck van Rijswijck, an artist who was famous for his mother-of-pearl inlay work. Amsterdam imported great quantities of mother-of-pearl shells, and incorporating them into utensils or objects of art had become one of the specialities of this city. Van Rijswijck, who was presumably born in Kleve in present-day Germany, spent most of his life in Amsterdam.

A masterpiece by Van Rijswijck is this table top with flowers and insects [*101*]. The large, octagonal table top is made of Lydian stone, a black variety of jasper used as a touchstone to test the quality of gold, silver and other precious metals. This was done by rubbing the stone with the alloy in question and noting the colour of the mark it made [*see 10 and 11*]. The matt black table top is inlaid with countless pieces of mother-of-pearl which Van Rijswijck cut, polished,

100

Cupboard, c. 1660-1680
Oak, veneered with ebony and rosewood,
217 x 176 x 77 cm
AMSTERDAM, RIJKSMUSEUM
(acquired in 1944, see p. 316)

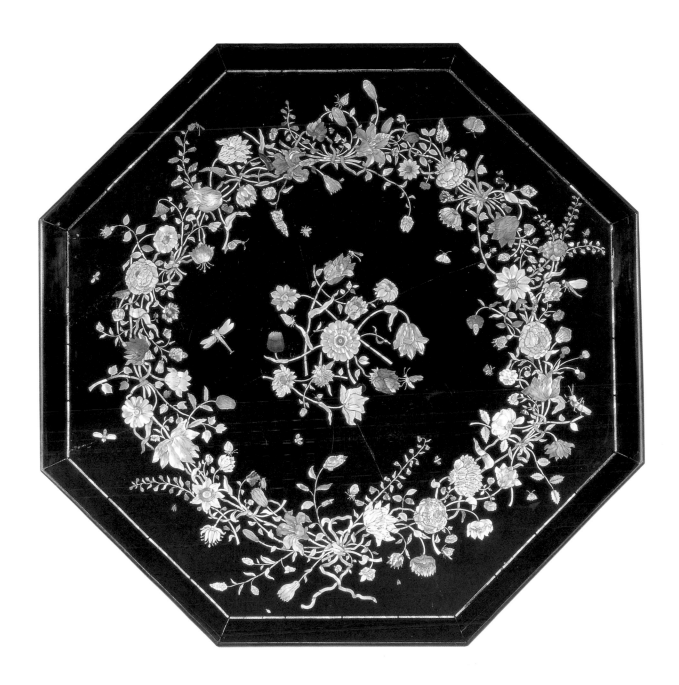

and engraved. This artist was already famous in his own day for the natural effect he produced without the use of added pigments. He combined mother-of-pearl of various colours to create exceedingly refined, decorative depictions, such as this garland of tulips, roses, lilies and other flowers, held together by a ribbon.

Around the garland he placed flies, beetles, butterflies, dragonflies and a grasshopper. The detail in both flowers and insects borders on the impossible. One of

the Netherlands' greatest poets, Joost van den Vondel (1587-1679), was so fascinated by Van Rijswijck's craftsmanship that he sang its praises in several of his poems. In 1660 he wrote a long ode to this octagonal table top, which he called 'On the touchstone banqueting table of the gods'.

Van Rijswijck probably never sold his 'table of the gods'. Since 1904 it has been part of the Rijksmuseum's collection. Here it is displayed on a modern base, as no old base for this table has survived.

IOI

DIRCK VAN RIJSWIJCK (1596-after 1679)
Table top, c. 1650-1660
Touchstone, inlaid with mother-of-pearl, in an ebony border, diam. 138.5 cm
AMSTERDAM, RIJKSMUSEUM
(acquired in 1904, see p. 314)

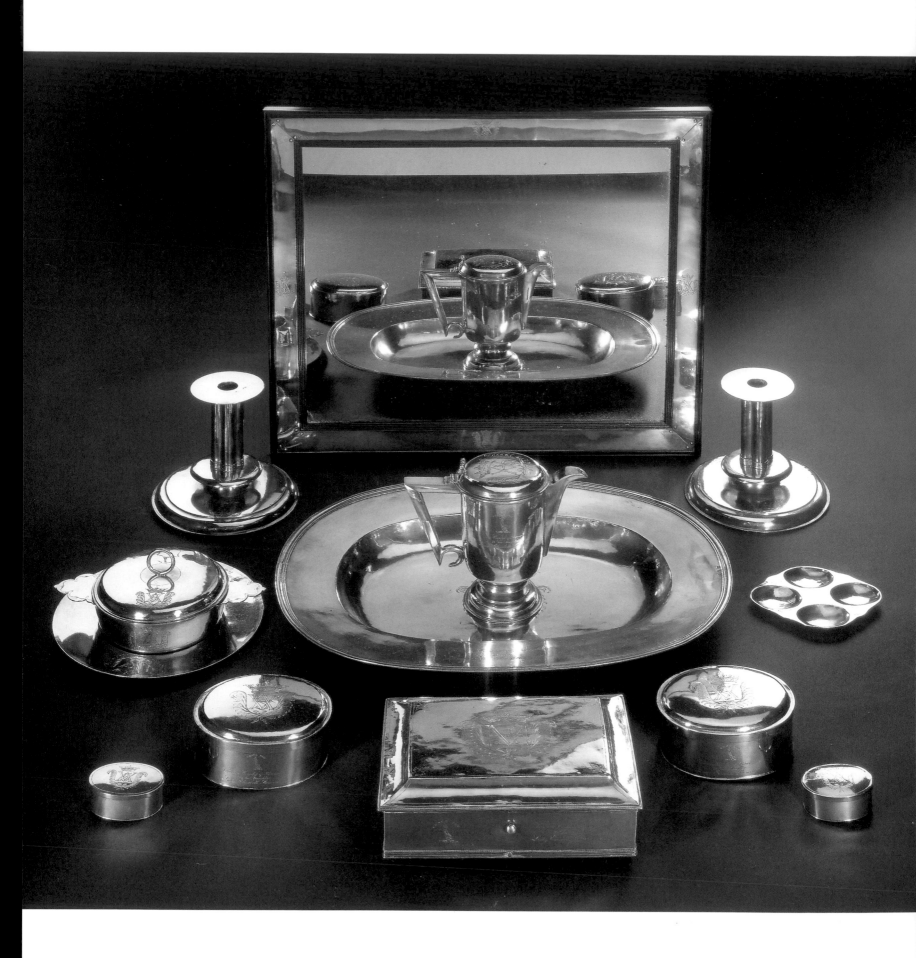

102

Toilet set belonging to Veronica van Aerssen
van Sommelsdijck, 1651-1658
Silver-gilt, mirror: h. 51.5 cm
THE HAGUE, GEMEENTEMUSEUM DEN HAAG
(acquired between 1960 and 1976, see p. 331)

<

103

Pair of candlesticks, 1668
Silver h. 28.4 cm
AMSTERDAM, RIJKSMUSEUM
(acquired in 1968, see p. 317)

>

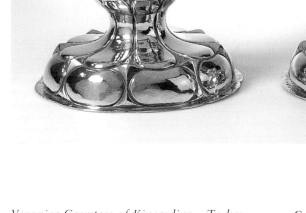

TOILET SET

Many of the objects used to furnish Dutch interiors during the Golden Age did not survive the centuries. Common utensils wore out, or fell into disuse and were thrown away. Objects made of precious metals which were no longer used or had gone out of fashion were often melted down to make new objects.

This silver toilet set belonging to Veronica van Aerssen van Sommelsdijck [102] was spared, however, undoubtedly because it remained in the family for several generations. The various objects comprising the set are decorated with the owner's monogram. A text was later engraved on each object, which shows that Veronica, meanwhile married to Alexander Bruce, Second Earl of Kincardine, had given the toilet set to her daughter Elizabeth:

Veronica Countess of Kincardine – To her Daughter Lady Elizabeth Boswell.

The toilet set consists of a ewer and oval basin, a toilet case, a porridge bowl and lid, two small boxes, two slightly larger oval boxes, two candlesticks, a mirror and a pin tray. The objects are made of silver, some of them gilt, and all are decorated sparingly. Clean shapes and harmonious proportions were of more importance than profuse ornamentation. Even though all the pieces belonging to this set display a uniform style, various artists took part in its production, as witnessed by the makers' marks on the objects. Johannes Voest made the ewer, the basin, the toilet case and the round and oval boxes. The candlesticks are attributed to Arentsz van Rheenen, and the porridge bowl is the work of Gerrit Vuystinck I.

CANDLESTICKS

Not all 17th-century makers' marks may be linked to a name. This pair of silver candlesticks from the Rijksmuseum's collection [103] are marked with a heart, though it is not known whose mark this was. The silversmith must have worked in Amsterdam, however, as evidenced by the city's hallmark on the foot.

The candlesticks have a simple form, with an unusual, abstract decoration. The elongated, oval sections, divided by 'diamond heads', produce a constant play of reflections. The decoration of the drip-pan, with eight slightly concave, petal-like sections, is reminiscent of a stylised flower. These Amsterdam candlesticks are much less soberly decorated than those made by the Hague silversmith Arentsz van Rheenen [102].

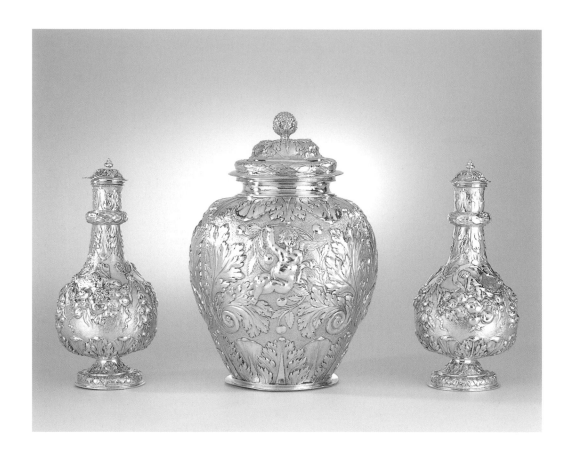

104

ATTRIBUTED TO
BARENT VAN MILANEN
(active c. 1663-1680)
Vase and two flasks, 1678-1679
Silver h. 41.9 cm and 35.6 cm
PRIVATE COLLECTION, UNITED KINGDOM
(see p. 351)

<

105

Dish with diamond-point engraving by
Willem Jacobsz van Heemskerk
(1613-1693), 1685
Clear glass diam. 32.3 cm
AMSTERDAM, RIJKSMUSEUM
(acquired in 1885, see p. 312)

>

VASE AND TWO FLASKS

Exceptional, both in form and decoration: this describes the three silver objects – a vase and two flasks – with detailed decoration made by a Dutch silversmith. The accumulation of bulbous forms was probably inspired by Chinese and Japanese porcelain objects, great numbers of which were imported into the Netherlands in the 17th century. Silver objects displaying this form were highly unusual in the Netherlands; the artist may well have been inspired by English examples.

In the thin silver of which the flasks and vase are made, the silversmith embossed delicate garlands, some of which are composed of tulips and others mainly of fruit. It is not known who commissioned these objects. The makers' marks show that the special decorative objects were made in The Hague, probably by Barent van Milanen.

WEDDING PRESENT

In 1685 the Leiden glass-engraver Willem van Heemskerk engraved this dish [105] for his son Joost, who married Anna Coninck in December of that year. Van Heemskerk was 72 years old at the time, a fact he recorded with his signature on the back.

Using graceful whorls Van Heemskerk engraved suitable sayings around the couple's monogram. The text on the edge reads as follows: *Bestand 'ge, noit-besweken Trouw, Werkt lyvelijk- en ziel-behouw* (Faith, unwavering and steadfast, will make both soul and body last). Beneath the monogram the words *iuste* and *syncere* enjoin one to exercise justice and honesty; occurring again in the crown above the monogram are the initials of Joost van Heemskerk and Anna Coninck.

The dish on which Van Heemskerk engraved his wishes for the bridal couple was made in the Netherlands in the Venetian manner, *à la façon de Venise*.

Venetian glass was renowned in the 16th century for its hardness, thinness and clarity, and served as an example to glassblowers in other European countries, including the Netherlands. Venetian engravers preferred to use a diamond point, capable of engraving delicate decorations on hard glass.

When glass engraving began to flourish in the Netherlands in the Golden Age, artists working in this medium adopted the Venetian method of diamond engraving. This technique was used to produce works of very high quality and was used by a large number of engravers, some of whom specialised in engraving representations, while others devoted themselves to calligraphy. Various Leiden engravers, including Willem Jacobsz van Heemskerk, concentrated on calligraphy. Van Heemskerk was probably inspired by the engravings of Anna Roemers Visscher [30, 31], who lived in Leiden at the time Van Heemskerk engraved his first glasses.

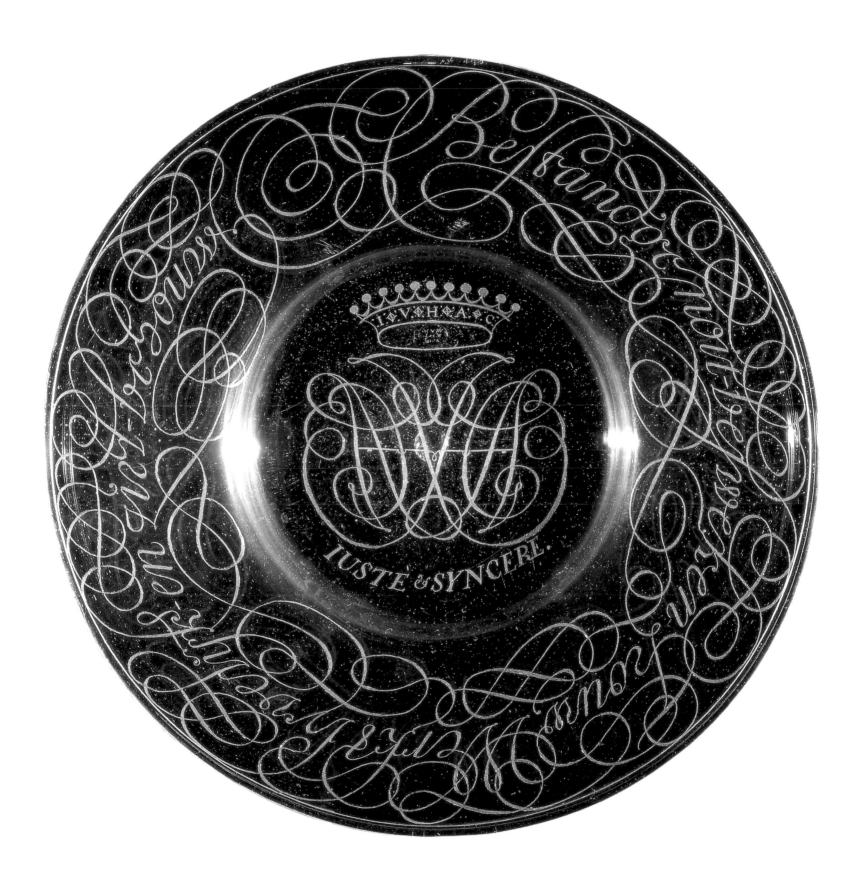

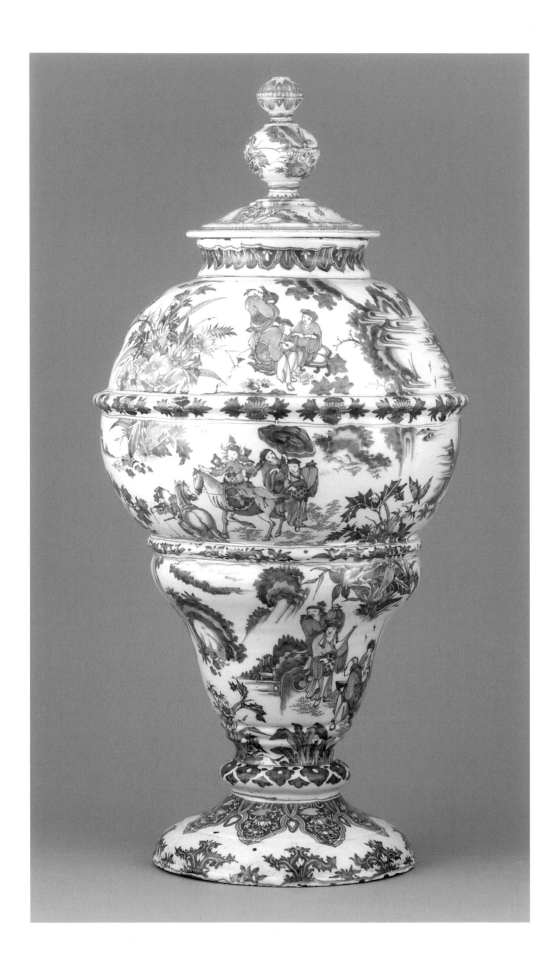

106

Large covered vase, c. 1680-1690
Blue-painted faience h. 95.5 cm
KASSEL, HESSISCHES LANDESMUSEUM
(acquired in 1927, see p. 335)

<

107

Large covered jar, c. 1635
Blue-painted faience h. 50 cm
LUND, MUSEUM OF CULTURAL HISTORY,
KULTUREN
(acquired in 1915, see p. 339)

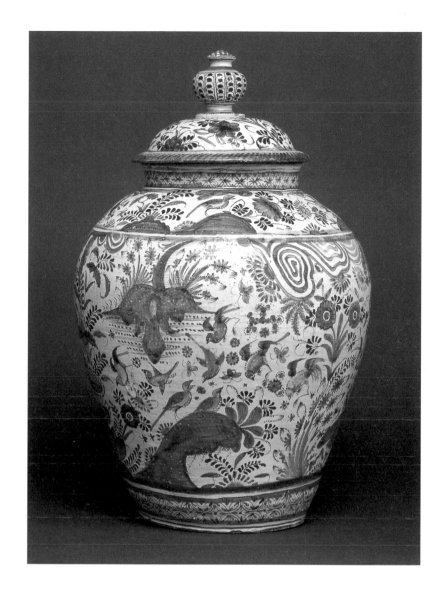

DELFT BLUE

Costly earthenware objects decorated many 17th-century Dutch interiors. At the beginning of the 17th century dozens of majolica potteries, mainly in Delft, were able to meet the demand for earthenware vessels, intended both for decoration and everyday use. Their position was greatly endangered, however, when the Dutch East India Company began to import Chinese porcelain into the Netherlands. These porcelain objects with their exotic painted decorations soon became popular among rich collectors, who exhibited them as showpieces in their interiors. The Delft potters attempted to regain their position by imitating this porcelain. They did not succeed, however, in discovering the secret of making Chinese porcelain, and their imitations were limited to the outward appearance of their objects. These looked Chinese as regards form, glaze and decoration, but the thinness and through-and-through whiteness of Chinese porcelain defied imitation.

A few potteries did succeed in glazing their earthenware in such a way that it was barely discernible from porcelain. They covered the entire object on all sides with a white tin glaze, on which the decoration was applied before the object was fired for the last time. Such tin-glazed earthenware is called *faience*, after Faenza, one of the Italian cities in which this kind of earthenware was made in the 14th and 15th centuries. The decoration of Delft *faience* was often taken directly from Chinese examples.

VASE

The large covered vase [*106*] contains three bands of Chinese depictions. The bottommost painting depicts various figures, including a mother breastfeeding her child. Above them a master and his valet ride horses through a landscape, followed by two servants with a parasol. Above this scene a group in a rugged landscape sit on a bench conversing, surrounded by plants and trees.

COVERED JAR

The ornamentation on this large covered jar [*107*] was also inspired by the decorations on Chinese porcelain. The Delft painter made use of a popular motif: a bird sitting on a rock in a watery landscape. In addition to his painstaking rendering of the birds, the painter also devoted a lot of attention to the sprigs of flowers that fan out gracefully over the vase. As in the case of the large covered vase [*106*], the decoration is composed of various bands above one another, separated by ridges.

TULIP VASE

A luxury item that was made in all shapes and sizes in the 17th century is the flower pot, a receptacle for cut flowers. Its requisite parts included the water reservoir and the spouts in which the cut flowers were put. Nowadays such flower pots are usually called tulip vases, because the spouts are frequently filled with tulips.

A striking feature is formed by the monster-like heads on the lid of this rare, round tulip vase from the Hamburg Museum for Arts and Crafts [108]: with bared teeth they hold the spouts in their jaws. Like the handles in the form of dragon's heads on both sides of the flower pot, these monsters evoke associations with Chinese ornamentation. On the other hand, the decorations in the glaze – garlands of flowers and a hunting scene in which stags are besieged by hunters and hounds – have nothing to do with China.

108

Round tulip vase, c. 1680-1690
Blue-painted faience h. 35 cm
HAMBURG, MUSEUM FÜR
KUNST UND GEWERBE
(acquired in 1891, see p. 334)

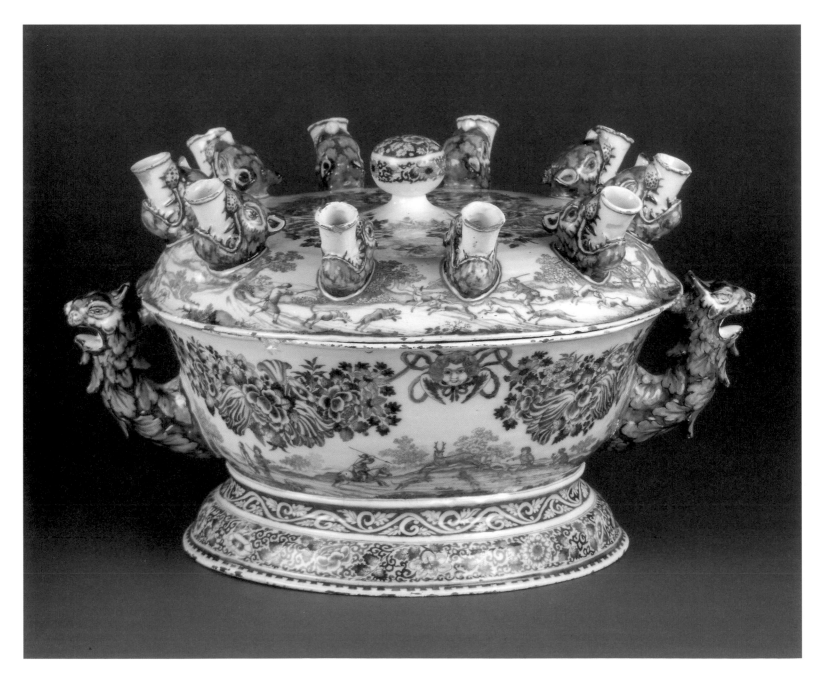

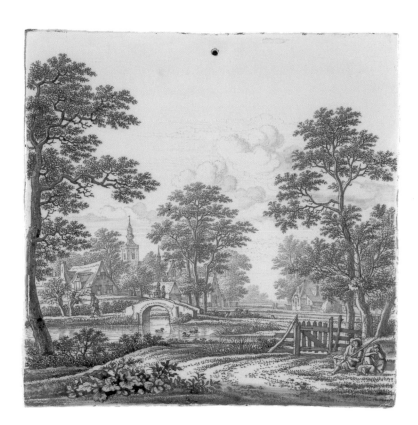
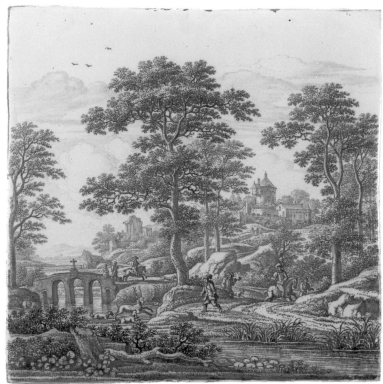

109

FREDERIK VAN FRYTOM (c. 1632 1702)

Two plaques with depictions of landscapes,

c. 1690

Blue-painted faience

34.8 x 34.3 cm and 34.6 x 34.2 cm

DOORN, HUIS DOORN

(since 1919, see p. 327)

PLAQUES

Until 1680 most Delft *faience* was painted with Chinese representations: Delft-blue earthenware had originated, after all, as an imitation of Chinese porcelain. Later on, more and more earthenware acquired a Dutch appearance, such as these two plaques by Frederic van Frytom [*109*]. One plaque bears a depiction of a hunting scene in a hilly landscape with a castle in the background. The castle was once incorrectly identified as Castle Bentheim in Germany. The other plaque offers a view of Overschie, in the vicinity of Delft. In 17th-century inventories such plaques were described as 'porcelain paintings', which tells us to what use they were put: they were usually framed and hung on the wall.

Frederik van Frytom was the best *faience* decorator of his time. He presumably worked for the pottery *De Doppelde Schenckan*, which existed from 1661 to 1777, the heyday of Delft earthenware. Frytom was able to rise above the purely decorative, and went further than many of his colleagues, who often repeated fixed decorative patterns. He painted entire landscapes of his own invention, which was exceptional for *faience* decorators at that time. Most of his colleagues worked from prints or drawings that had been prepared as stencils. It should therefore come as no surprise to learn that Van Frytom was more than just a decorator of earthenware: he made paintings in oil as well. Most of his works are unsigned, as is most *faience*, but these plaques bear his name in full, from which we may infer that he considered them to be exceptional pieces.

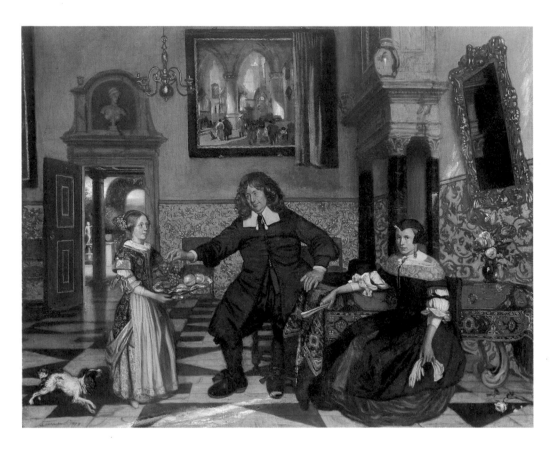

110

EMANUEL DE WITTE (c. 1616-1691/1692)
Portrait of a family in an interior, 1678
Canvas 68.5 x 86.5 cm
MUNICH, ALTE PINAKOTHEK
(acquired in 1972, see p. 340)

<

VAN DER HELST

This family portrait by Bartholomeus van der Helst [111] was painted more than twenty-five years before De Witte's, but it is more than just time that separates the two. Van der Helst painted this life-size portrait of a man, woman, child and greyhounds with much more bravura. Theatrical illumination ensures that all attention is directed at the family; their surroundings are only cursorily indicated.

This unusually large family portrait was commissioned by Pieter van de Venne, a wealthy burgher of Amsterdam, when he was 28 years old. He had his portrait painted with his wife, Anna de Carpentier, the daughter of a high-ranking official of the Dutch East India Company. In 1652 the couple had one child, two-year-old Lucas. In this portrait the toddler shines in his red satin clothes, wearing ostrich feathers on his head and dangling a crystal teething-ring on a gold chain.

The painting demonstrates the artist's ability to form an impressive ensemble with only a few figures. It is therefore hardly surprising that Van der Helst was one of the most sought-after portraitists of his time.

EMANUEL DE WITTE

Emanuel de Witte, who is known mainly for his paintings of church interiors [see 79], painted this portrait of a man, woman and girl in a richly furnished interior [110]. Various attempts have been made to discover the identity of the sitters, though up to now none has been successful. De Witte paid a great deal of attention to the arrangement of the décor. He not only wanted to depict the couple's prosperity (see p. 153), but probably also incorporated into the painting clues as to their identity.

The rose at the lower right, for example, could indicate a deceased member of the family, perhaps a dead child or the wife's previous husband. At the same time, the rose is also a more general symbol of the fragility and fleeting nature of life. It is uncertain whether the bunch of grapes and the dog should be seen as symbols, and the same holds true for the mirror and the painting on the wall in the background, which has a curtain to shield it from light and dust. This painting depicts the interior of Amsterdam's Old Church, and is a schematic rendering of an existing painting by De Witte which is now to be found in a private collection in South Africa. There is a great difference in style between the *Portrait of a family in an interior* and the *Interior of the Old Church*, the painting within the painting. The church interior is loosely depicted with a great deal of feeling for light and space, whereas the portrait seems rather stiff and displays completely uniform illumination.

Did the family portrayed have something to do with the Old Church, or did De Witte include it solely as a reference to his own work? Although the painting still cries out for interpretation, it nonetheless provides a treasure trove of information: it depicts well-to-do burghers in ideal surroundings.

111

BARTHOLOMEUS VAN DER HELST (1613-1670)
Pieter Lucaszn van de Venne with Anna de Carpentier and child, 1652
Canvas 187.5 x 226.5 cm
ST PETERSBURG, HERMITAGE
(acquired before 1774, see p. 346)

>

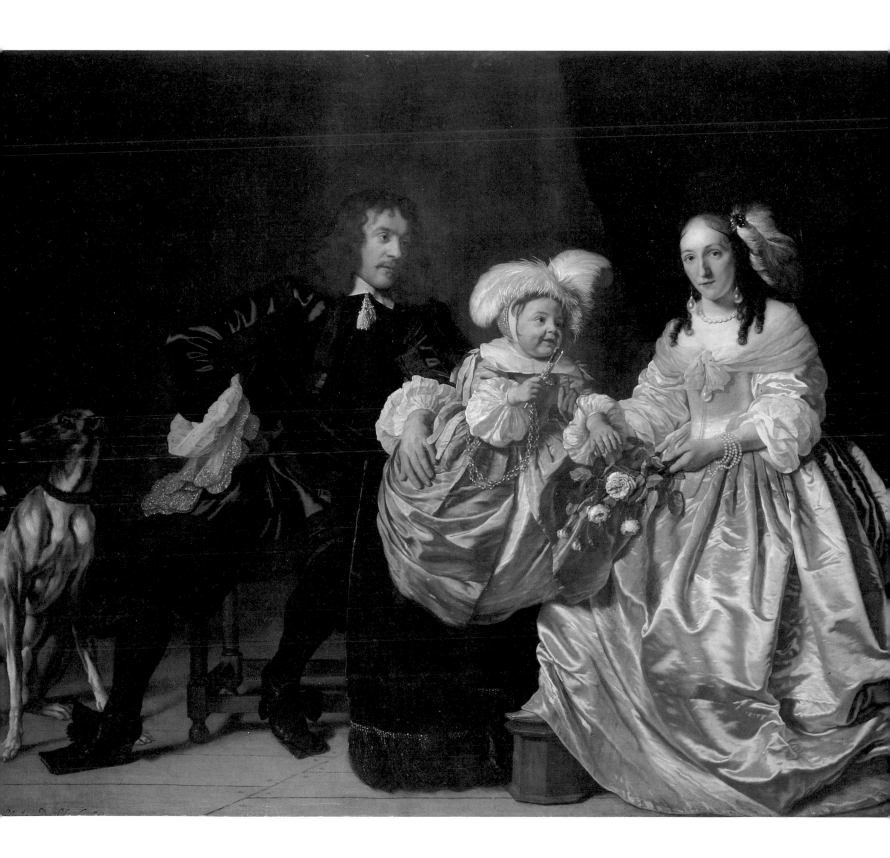

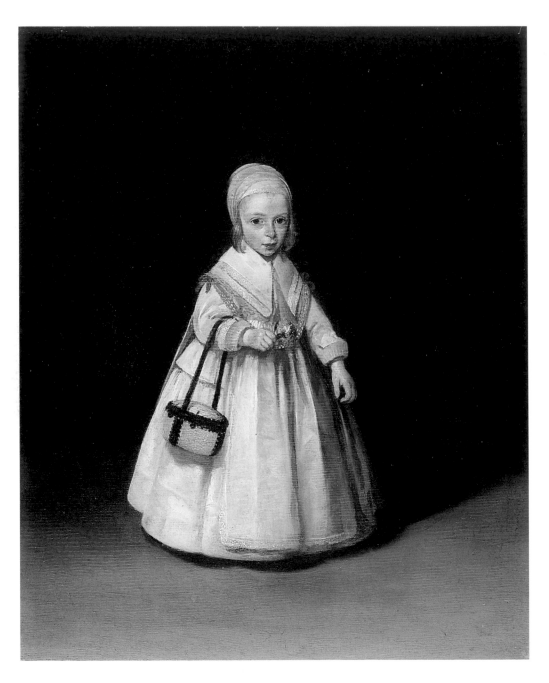

II2

GERARD TER BORCH (1617-1681)
*Portrait of Helena van der Schalcke
(1646-1671), c. 1648*
Panel 34 x 28.5 cm
AMSTERDAM, RIJKSMUSEUM
(acquired with the aid of the Rembrandt Society
in 1898, see p. 314)

the transition from the floor to the back wall almost invisible. Only very gradually does the light foreground flow into the dark background, against which Helena's portrait stands out brightly.

The girl in blue, painted by the Haarlem portraitist Johannes Verspronck [113], also stands in front of an empty wall, breaking free from it by means of the subtle play of light and shadow. Even though she also looks like a grown-up, she could not have been much older than ten years old when this portrait was painted. Verspronck had a great eye for detail, giving a very precise rendering of the dress trimmed in gold lace, the feather fan, her face and thin hair, her clear eyes and her rosy cheeks. Transparent greyish brushstrokes in the shadowed areas of her face and blue-grey brushstrokes on her nose and lips lend the portrait great vitality.

The girl wears clothing that was extremely modern in those days. The dress is trimmed with lace cuffs and has a neckline of transparent lace, over which falls a collar consisting of three layers of lace. Jewellery completes the picture: a pearl necklace and earrings, bracelets, a brooch and a hair ornament. Everything points to her being a member of a very well-to-do family, even the mere fact that an individual portrait was painted of her.

YOUNG LADIES

Two girls from wealthy families have been immortalised at their loveliest. The little girl, Helena van der Schalcke, was approximately two years old when the artist Gerard ter Borch painted her portrait. She was the daughter of Johanna Bardoel and the cloth merchant Gerard van der Schalcke, both of whom also had their portraits painted by Ter Borch. Helena looks like a little grown-up, wearing a long, white silk dress and carrying a lady's handbag. In her right hand she holds a red carnation, a flower that frequently occurs in portraits as a symbol of the resurrection and the hope of eternal life – serious symbolism indeed for the portrait of a toddler.

Ter Borch placed Helena in an empty room. There are no toys to be seen, nor does any furniture divert our attention from the modest little figure. The artist reduced her surroundings to a minimum, and made

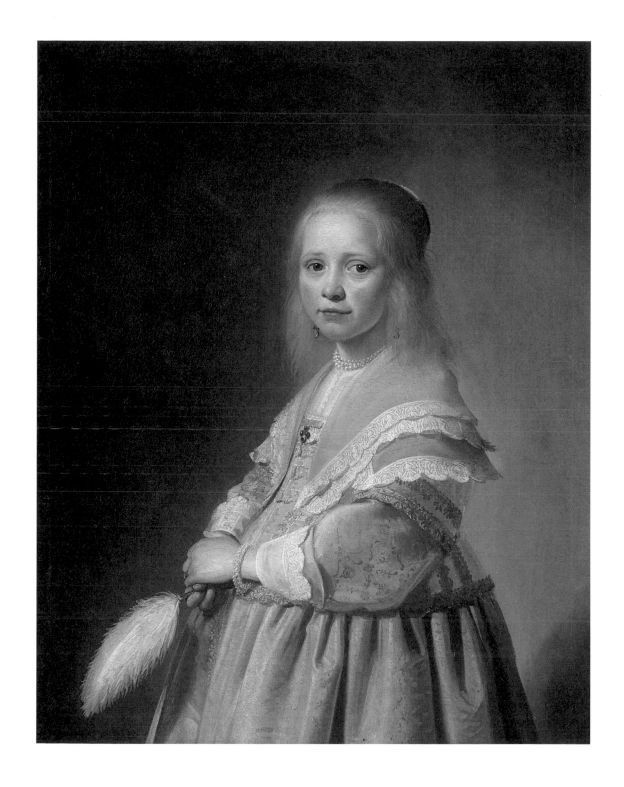

113

Johannes Verspronck (1597-1662)
Portrait of a girl dressed in blue, 1641
Canvas 82 x 66.5 cm
Amsterdam, Rijksmuseum
(acquired with the aid of the Rembrandt Society
in 1928, see p. 315)

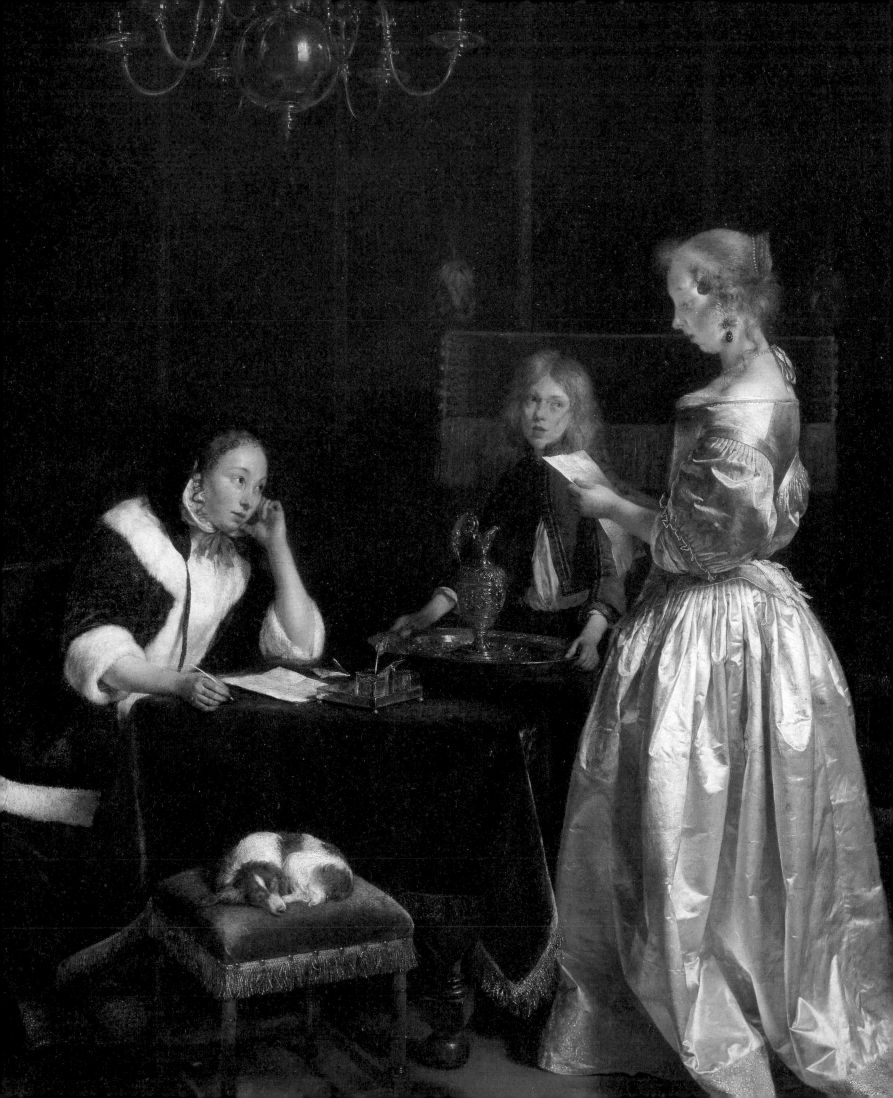

15 SEEMINGLY EVERYDAY 1650-1670

MERRY COMPANY, outdoor party, conversation piece, brothel scene, soldiers in an alehouse: in the 17th century, paintings representing scenes of everyday life were named after their depictions. The collective name of 'genre painting' has existed only since the 19th century. This generic term can refer to very diverse paintings, though all of them depict recognisable situations taken from daily life. As a rule the painter did not portray real people, but rather characteristic types and situations: an old man seducing a young girl, peasants brawling and drinking, industrious housewives, loose women in a brothel.

Art theorists in those days, who valued history painting most highly, did not waste words discussing this rather unexalted branch of painting. The vast number of genre paintings produced, however, is convincing evidence of the great demand that must have existed in the 17th century for these seemingly everyday scenes.

DEVELOPMENT

Since time immemorial artists have taken motifs from their own surroundings, but until the 17th century everyday actions or events were almost never the main subject of a painting. In the 15th and 16th centuries genre scenes were often part of a series depicting a specific subject: representations of the four seasons featured scenes of peasant life, and depictions of the five senses included scenes of eating and music-making. Such themes as the seven deadly sins or the seven virtues, as well as biblical stories and proverbs, provided an opportunity to depict scenes of everyday life.

In the 17th century, life in and around the home became an independent subject of paintings. These genre pieces seem like snapshots, as though the painter had recorded them on the spot. Like most 17th-century paintings, however, they were carefully composed and did not actually represent a faithful picture of reality.

HIDDEN MEANING

Often a deeper meaning lies hidden in these renderings of reality which seem at first glance so true to life. Sometimes the symbolism is difficult to unravel, at other times the solution is laid on with a trowel. Frequently the painter showed the viewer a bad example or depicted the sinful world. Some artists provided the key to the symbolism by including a text in the painting, while others hid the message in a detail of the representation – in an object, for example, or in a painting within the painting. However, not all genre painters were attempting to convey a message, and various artists immortalised scenes of everyday life without any intention of including a hidden meaning.

SYMBOLISM

It may not always be clear to the contemporary viewer whether or not a painting contains a symbolic meaning. One aid in deciphering 17th-century symbolism is emblematic literature, a genre in which prints were supplied with a motto and a short moralising text. An emblem displayed a message in a concrete yet symbolic way: a boy blowing bubbles, for example, stood for the transience of earthly existence. Roemer Visscher (1547-1620) and Jacob Cats (1577-1660) are two of the best-known authors of such texts. Cats in particular was very popular in his day among broad segments of the population.

Books of emblematic prints were a source of inspiration to artists. By incorporating emblematic representations in their own paintings, artists could lend their work a certain tenor. Didactic messages of this nature could also provide the painter with an excuse to portray dubious subject matter.

< DETAIL OF 121

THE BROTHEL

Women with bared breasts and men in a drunken stupor feature in this *Brothel scene* by Nicolaus Knupfer. This painter of German extraction worked in Utrecht from 1630 onwards. He was the teacher of Jan Steen, who also made paintings which alluded to sexuality, though not so bare and brazen as those of Knupfer. One of the women in the large four-poster bed balances a hat with feathers on her foot and grabs a man beneath his tunic. He raises his glass to the woman on his other side. Two men have climbed onto the table and stand there

looking outside, where something worth seeing is apparently going on. Knupfer used this group of profligates enjoying liquor, gambling, sex and music to portray a sinful existence.

It seems paradoxical that this kind of painting was in vogue in the Calvinist Netherlands, but representations of licentiousness were meant to serve as negative examples. Indeed, since the 16th century there had been a lively tradition of portrayals of brothel scenes, alehouses and inns. Their origins lay in the biblical story of the Prodigal Son, who squandered his

money on carousing and whoring.

It is possible that this painting, too, represents the 'Prodigal Son among the Harlots'; then again, Knupfer may have been portraying an episode from a play, which would explain the fantasised clothing and the step – possibly the edge of the stage – in the foreground. Even a combination of the two is a possibility. The Prodigal Son was a popular subject of plays at the time, and Knupfer frequently painted theatre-like scenes, even though the majority of his works are history paintings.

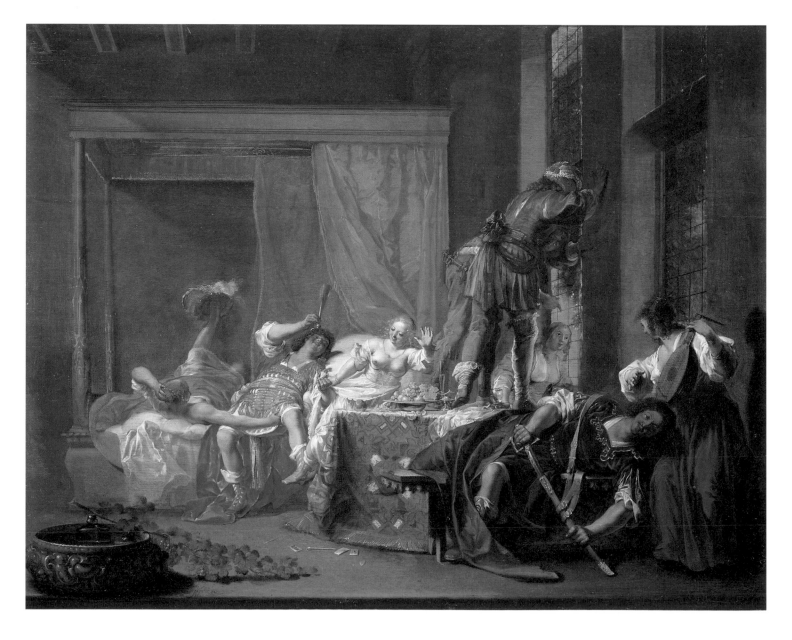

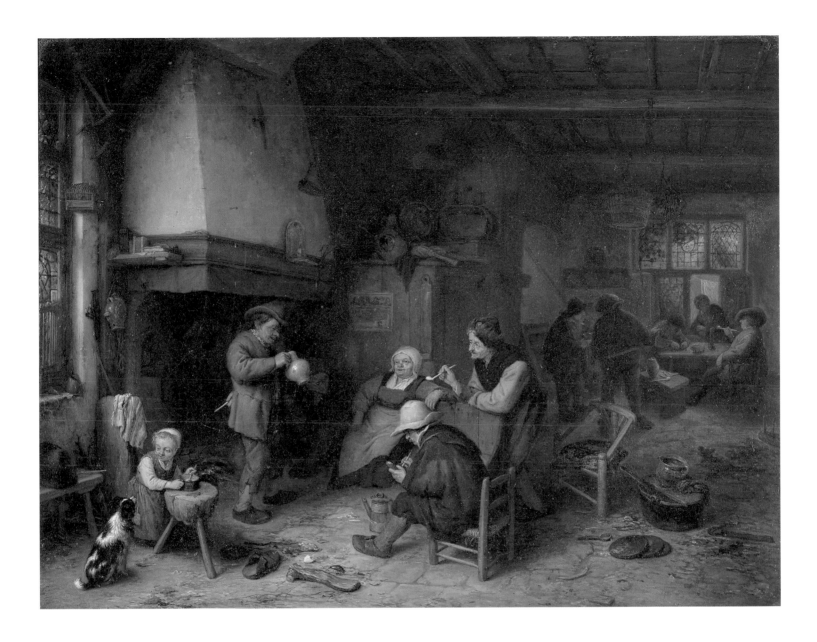

115

ADRIAEN VAN OSTADE (1610-1685)
Peasants in an interior, 1661
Copper 37 x 47 cm
AMSTERDAM, RIJKSMUSEUM
(on loan from the City of Amsterdam
since 1885, see p. 312)

114

NICOLAUS KNUPFER (c. 1609-1665)
Brothel scene, c. 1650
Panel 60 x 74.5 cm
AMSTERDAM, RIJKSMUSEUM
(acquired in 1981, see p. 318)

<

COMPANY OF PEASANTS

This painting by Adriaen van Ostade of a
peasant company is much less theatrical.
Peasants sit together in an inn, smoking
their pipes. In the foreground, near a large
fireplace, a man with a jug in his hand tells
a story while the others listen. In the background a second group sits at a table.
Adriaen van Ostade, a painter from
Haarlem and a pupil of Frans Hals,
specialised in scenes featuring peasants
drinking and smoking.

At the beginning of his career Van
Ostade painted mainly rough, uncivilised

peasants: his paintings displayed drinking,
squabbling and brawling men, who served
as an example of how *not* to behave. Later
his views of peasant life changed, and his
representations became less coarse and even
tended towards the charming. In these later
paintings the cautionary motifs are less
obvious. In *Peasants in an interior* he
painted a cosy inn with a touching scene in
the foreground: a girl eating a bowl of porridge and a dog looking on beggingly.

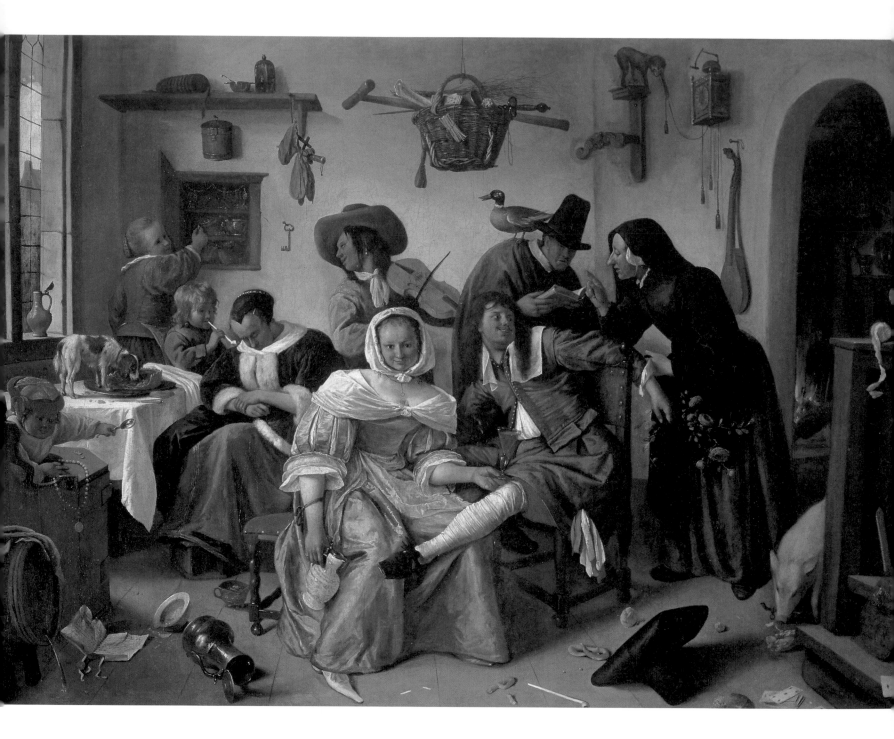

JAN STEEN

Jan Steen's paintings seem light-hearted and unpretentious, intended exclusively to amuse the viewer, yet they often contain a message, wrapped up in texts or subtle references. Jan Steen was a storyteller *par excellence* and a great painter to boot. He was a master at arranging figures and rendering atmospheres. Steen is most famous for his genre pieces, but he also painted biblical and mythological subjects, portraits and landscapes. His technique also displayed great variety: sometimes he painted very precisely, paying great attention to detail, while at other times he used broad, loose brushstrokes. He alternated between large theatrical canvases and small, painstakingly painted panels.

In addition to studying with Nicolaus Knupfer, Steen was probably also a pupil of

116

JAN STEEN (1626-1679)
'In luxury beware', c. 1663
Canvas 105 x 145 cm
VIENNA, KUNSTHISTORISCHES MUSEUM
(acquired in 1783, see p. 349)

Adriaen van Ostade in Haarlem. In 1648, having completed his training, he registered as a master painter in Leiden. He then went to work in the studio of the landscape painter Jan van Goyen, where he undoubtedly contributed to the latter's prolific production. Steen himself painted only a few landscapes, and there is little in his work that is reminiscent of Van Goyen. His passion for storytelling seems to have been what motivated him most; people were clearly the most important element in his stories.

A 'JAN STEEN HOUSEHOLD'

While mother sleeps, children, grown-ups and animals all run riot. A girl raids the cupboard, a boy smokes a pipe and the child in the highchair throws everything on the floor. The couple in the foreground display extremely bold behaviour: he has flung his leg over her lap and she provocatively holds a glass of wine between his legs. Even the animals are behaving like animals: a dog sinks his teeth into a meat pie, a monkey stops the clock and a pig makes off with the spigot from the wine barrel. This last motif portrays a Dutch proverb which literally says 'here the sow pulls out the spigot', meaning that the housewife has lost all control of her household. Steen wrote another proverb on the slate at the lower right: *In weelde siet toe* (In Luxury Beware), for those living in the lap of luxury must take care not to succumb to debauchery and wastefulness. The basket hanging from the ceiling, containing a switch, a beggar's crutch and a leper's clapper – the instrument lepers were required to carry to warn healthy people of the contagious disease they carried – predicts that this dissolute family can expect nothing but punishment, sickness and poverty. A strange element in this depiction is the hunched-over man with a duck, or 'quacker', on his shoulder. This was Steen's way of telling the viewer that this man is a Quaker, a member of a Protestant sect. He and the woman next to him, perhaps a nun, are lecturing this unruly company.

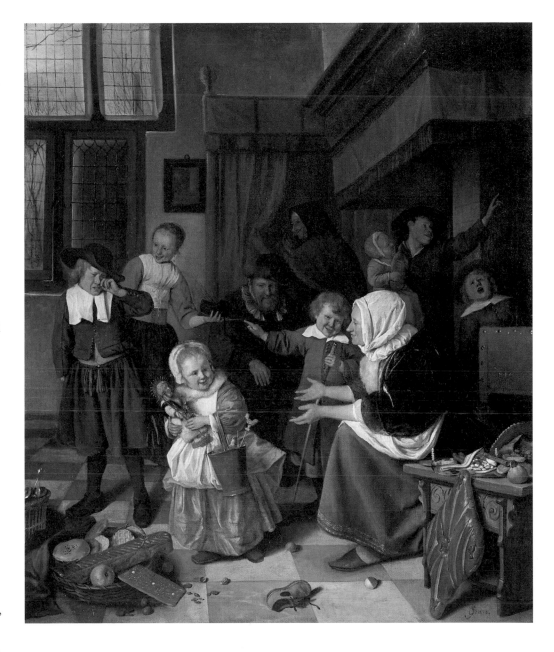

Jan Steen depicted so many dissolute households that they became proverbial. By the 18th century the saying a 'Jan Steen household' was already current, and this expression still denotes a household that is a perfect shambles.

THE FEAST OF SAINT NICHOLAS

The Feast of Saint Nicholas was and still is one of the most important family holidays in the Netherlands. On the evening of 5

117

JAN STEEN (1626-1679)
The feast of Saint Nicholas, c. 1665-1668
Canvas 82 x 70.5 cm
AMSTERDAM, RIJKSMUSEUM
(acquired in 1809, see p. 310)

December Saint Nicholas hands out presents and sweets, at least to the good children. Naughty children are given a switch – a bundle of twigs, symbolic of a beating. This subject was eminently suited to Jan Steen, who was the first Dutch painter to concentrate on the portrayal of such festivities.

Steen's *Feast of Saint Nicholas* displays all kinds of things that are still part of Saint Nicholas celebrations: putting out a shoe (in the hope of finding sweets or a present in it), singing around the fireplace and teasing other members of the family. The children in this picture have just received their presents. The little girl holds a doll and a bucket filled with toys and sweets. A little boy has received a *kolf* club (something like a hockey stick) from Saint Nicholas. He laughs and points at his tearful brother who has been given a switch. The maidservant behind him pointedly displays the shoe containing the bundle of twigs.

Here Jan Steen demonstrates his immense talent for storytelling. He makes clear what is happening by spinning a web of glances and gestures between the figures. In addition to the clever arrangement of the figures, the skilfully painted still lifes in the foreground are striking: on the left the basket with cakes, gingerbread, fruit and nuts, and on the right the chair against which leans a *duivenkater*, a diamond-shaped bread eaten on festive occasions.

SLEEPING MAIDSERVANT

Unlike Steen's busy paintings full of anecdotal detail, the genre pieces of Nicolaes Maes are peaceful and still. Around 1650 Maes was a pupil of Rembrandt, whose influence is clearly present in his work. Maes's palette, for example, bears strong similarities to Rembrandt's. The deep black and the use of chiaroscuro betray his training. Nonetheless, Maes's paintings differ greatly from Rembrandt's as regards atmosphere and choice of subject matter. There are no known paintings by Rembrandt which depict domestic scenes, although he did make many drawings of this subject, which Maes may have seen while working in the master's studio.

Many of Maes's figure paintings portray

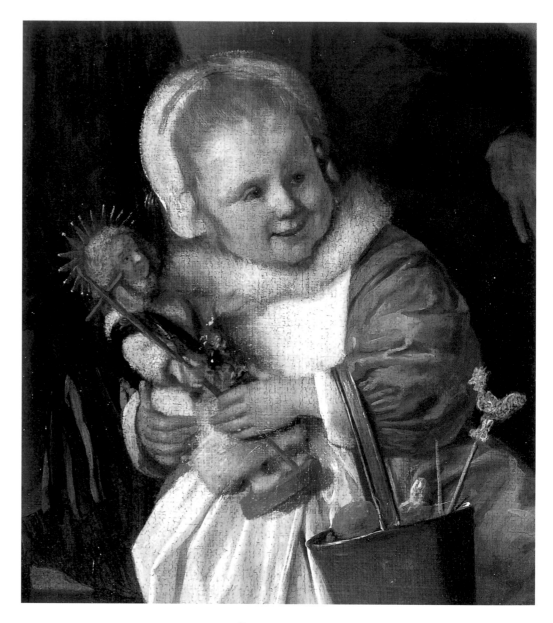

DETAIL OF 117

the same subject: domestic life. He usually depicted a woman, busy indoors with some virtuous task like preparing a meal, praying, making lace or reading out loud to the children. In this painting the protagonist is a kitchen maid who has fallen asleep. The woman next to her, the lady of the house, points at her maid while addressing herself directly to the viewer, in whom she confides the laziness of her servant. In the meanwhile the cat sees its chance and polishes off a bird.

The view on the left gives on to another room in which people are sitting around a table. Maes hereby created an illusion of depth, which is strengthened by the tiled floor, to which a great deal of space has been devoted. From the point of view of perspective, however, the floor is less successfully rendered: the pots and pans in the foreground seem unstable on the sloping tiles.

118

NICOLAES MAES (1634-1693)
The sleeping kitchen maid, 1655
Panel 70 x 53.3 cm
LONDON, NATIONAL GALLERY
(acquired in 1847, see p. 337)

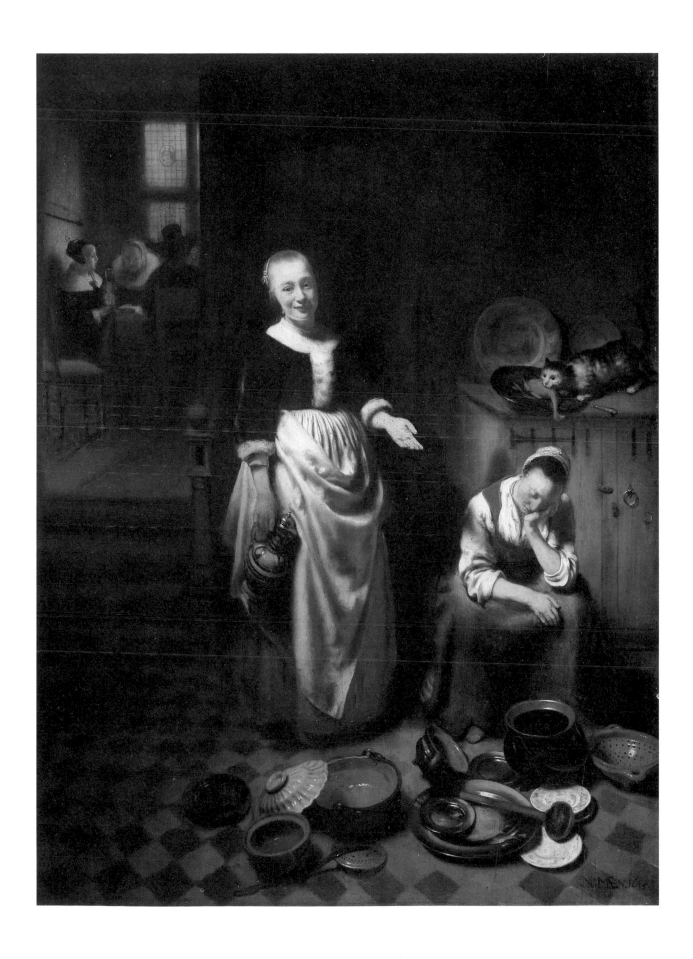

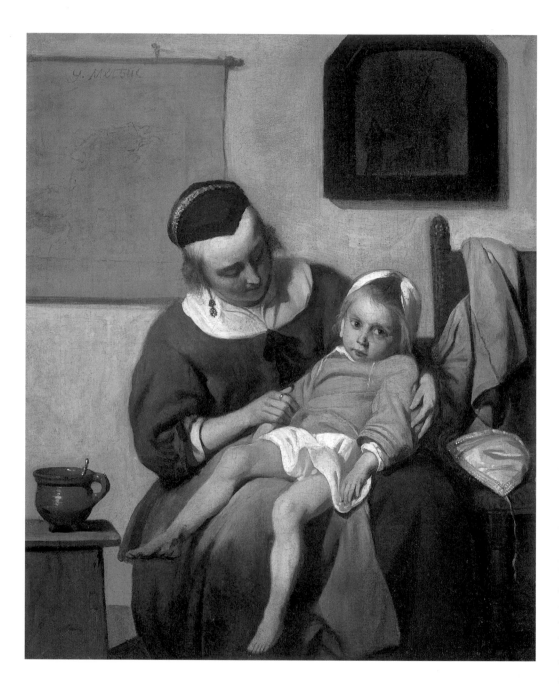

119
GABRIËL METSU (1629-1667)
The sick child, c. 1660
Canvas 32.2 x 27.2 cm
AMSTERDAM, RIJKSMUSEUM
(acquired with the aid of the Rembrandt Society
in 1928, see p. 315)

<

120
GERARD TER BORCH (1617-1681)
Boy de-fleaing a dog, c. 1655
Canvas 34.4 x 27.1 cm
MUNICH, ALTE PINAKOTHEK
(acquired before 1742, see p. 340)

>

Not very much is known about the life of Gabriël Metsu. He was born in 1629 in Leiden, where he was one of the founders of the Guild of St Luke. His work reveals the influence of various artists, from Nicolaus Knupfer and Jan Baptist Weenix to Johannes Vermeer and Pieter de Hooch. Metsu's painting of *The sick child* recalls the work of the last two artists in particular. The peace and quiet exuded by the painting and its concentration on only a few persons, as well as the light, uniform back wall, are strongly reminiscent of Vermeer and De Hooch (see chapter 17).

THE SICK CHILD
Leaning listlessly against the mother, the child stares with sad, dark eyes past the viewer into nothingness. The mother bends tenderly over her sick child. On the cupboard stands an earthenware bowl with porridge, which will probably remain untouched.

Through his distribution of colour Gabriël Metsu achieved a balanced composition. The painter divided the picture plane diagonally in two by drawing an imaginary line from lower left to upper right. To the left of this line he used only subdued colours, such as grey, light brown and yellow, while to the right of the diagonal the colours are much more vivid. The eye-catcher is the woman's red skirt, against which Metsu placed the blue of her apron, the white and yellow of the child's clothing and the green accent of the garment hanging over the chair.

BOY WITH HIS DOG
Just as Metsu's solicitous mother bends over her child, this boy by Gerard ter Borch bends over the dog he is de-fleaing. This painting exudes the same peace and quiet as that of Metsu. With great concentration the boy picks through the animal's fur, in search of anything suspicious. The dog looks up from under his master's arms, docilely undergoing the examination.

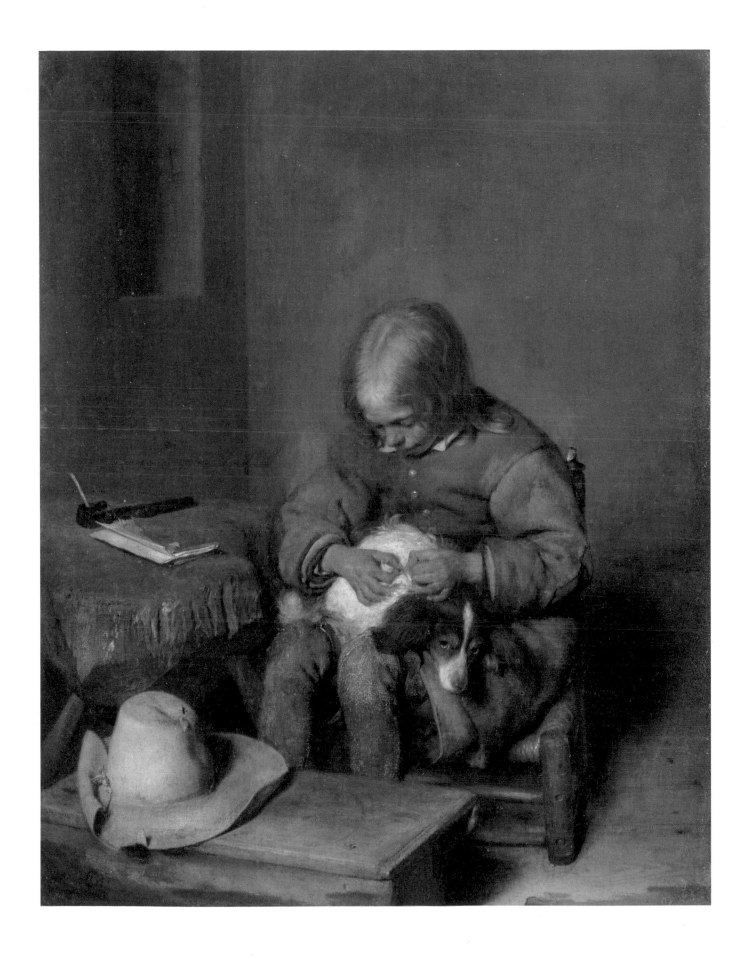

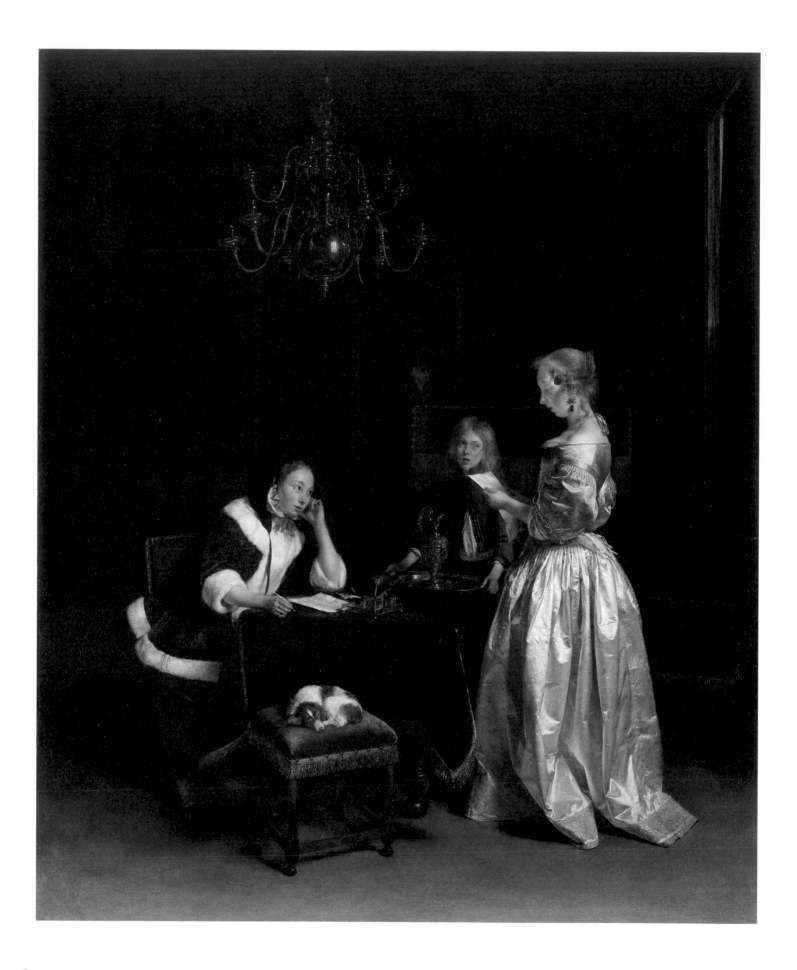

The scene takes place in the corner of a room, with a niche or window at the left. The boy sits near a table. In the foreground stands a bench on which lies a large slouch hat. The whole depiction is painted in the same shades of brown, green and yellow. A few accents catch the eye, such as the white collar of the blouse and the blue of the trousers. The painting was done with loose, rapid, transparent brushstrokes. It is highly likely that the boy portrayed here is Gerard ter Borch's younger brother Mozes, who posed as a model more than once, as did other members of the family.

GERARD TER BORCH

Gerard ter Borch came from a well-to-do, artistic family. He was born in 1617 in Zwolle. His father, Gerard ter Borch the Elder, took a great interest in art and urged his children to develop their talents. Gerard was not the only artistic one: Gesina and Mozes also practised the arts of drawing and painting. Mozes would undoubtedly have become a good artist, had he not died young. Gesina recorded many family gatherings and events in albums, to which she often added accompanying poems. Gerard, however, was the most talented of the family. His father saved the children's drawings, once in a while recording his remarks on them, which provides us with a nice overview of the progress made by these prospective artists.

GENRE PAINTER

Gerard ter Borch learned the rudiments of painting from his father. In 1633 he was apprenticed to the Haarlem artist Pieter de

121
GERARD TER BORCH (1617-1681)
The letter, c. 1660-1662
Canvas 81.9 x 68 cm
COLLECTION OF HER MAJESTY
QUEEN ELIZABETH II
(acquired in 1814, see p. 337)

Molijn, who made landscapes and figure paintings. After two years Ter Borch's training was complete and he became a master painter. He made long trips to England, Italy, Spain, France, and the Southern Netherlands, though scarcely any traces of these sojourns are to be seen in his work. Only in 1648 did Gerard ter Borch return to the Netherlands for good, and from that time on he concentrated on painting genre pieces. At first he mainly painted scenes of the soldier's life, but later he switched over to elegant scenes depicting one or more persons in an interior. Ter Borch's paintings display a minimum of action; his figures are completely absorbed in their own thoughts and activities.

THE LETTER

Gerard ter Borch's painting *The letter* shows a cursorily indicated interior in which three people are grouped around a table. A woman, standing, reads a letter while a youth and a seated woman watch to see how she will react. It is difficult to say what is going on between these three people. The woman could be reading a love letter, but there is nothing in the painting to confirm this. The standing woman, dressed in blue and yellow and fully illuminated, is the protagonist. Her fashionable clothing, made of shiny fabric with small pleats, is meticulously painted. Here as well, the models who posed for this painting were probably members of Ter Borch's family. The woman reading the letter strongly resembles Ter Borch's drawings of his sister Gesina. The boy, who resembles the flea eradicator [120], was probably his brother Mozes. The dog lying on the stool in the foreground must have been Gerard ter Borch's own dog or one that frequented the area, since it figures again and again in his works. Ter Borch repeatedly used more or less the same ingredients to compose other paintings, all of which are very similar in atmosphere.

ILLUSION OF REALITY

A separate school of painting developed in Leiden around the mid-17th century, that of the 'fine painters' (*fijnschilders*), who are recognisable by their very fine, meticulous style of painting. Gerard Dou was the founder of this school. During his apprenticeship to Rembrandt, around 1630, he had already distinguished himself by producing perfect imitations of daily life. In the following years he was able to perfect his technique to such an extent that his brushstrokes were practically invisible. This won him a lot of praise and he soon had numerous followers, of whom the most talented and well-known was Frans van Mieris. Dou and the other *fijnschilders* were concerned with creating the illusion of reality. They attained a high degree of perfection in the rendering of the most diverse materials, from gleaming copper to hard stone. This they combined with subtle lighting effects and a passion for depicting detail. The brushstrokes are scarcely visible: they were disguised by being smoothed over with extra soft brushes. The result was an especially smooth painting, practically bereft of a personal 'handwriting'.

THE DOCTOR

A high point of 'fine painting' is Gerard Dou's portrayal of *The doctor* [122], which was painted so evocatively that it seems real. The painted, arched window framing the depiction and the relief underneath it seem to be made of stone, and this illusion is strengthened by the tip of the rug which hangs over the relief. Moreover, the curtain hanging in the niche has been pushed to the side as though to unveil the scene. These are tricks which Gerard Dou used to give the illusion of three-dimensionality. Depicted on the relief at the lower edge of the painting is a goat being deceived by a mask, which one of the putti holds up to his face. The goat lets itself be taken in, and such is the fate of the viewer who lets himself be fooled by the semblance of reality in this painting.

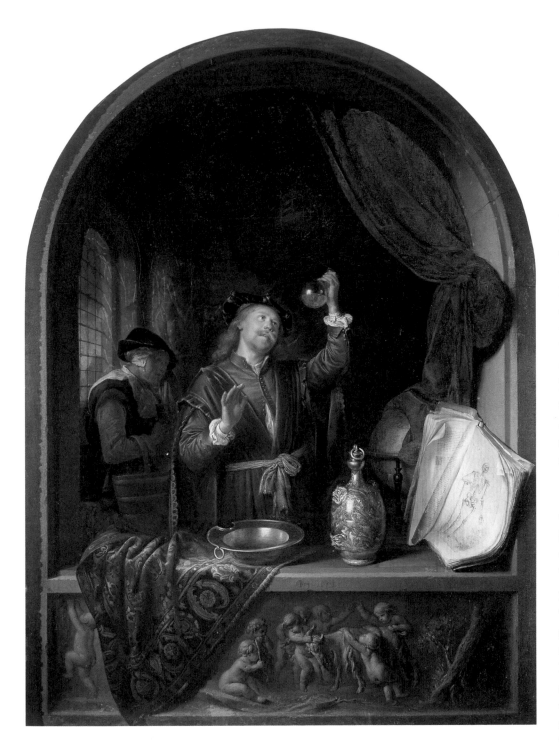

122

GERARD DOU (1613-1675)
The doctor, 1653
Panel 49.3 x 36.6 cm
VIENNA, KUNSTHISTORISCHES MUSEUM
(acquired before 1662, see p. 349)

123

FRANS VAN MIERIS (1635-1681)
Brothel scene, c. 1658-1659
Panel 42.8 x 33.3 cm
THE HAGUE, MAURITSHUIS
(acquired in 1960, see p. 333)

>

the semblance of reality in this painting. The doctor wears a fantasised costume, which could indicate that he is a quack. In the 17th century not everyone who called himself a doctor had a bona fide practice, and artists often ridiculed quacks by portraying them in old-fashioned costumes. The doctor holds up a phial of urine, undoubtedly that of the woman who dries her eyes by the window on the left. Perhaps she is pregnant, or at the very least lovesick. An open cage, such as the one hanging from the ceiling of the room portrayed, often symbolised lost virginity.

VAN MIERIS

Gerard Dou was exceptionally adept at imitating lifeless things, but as a storyteller he was surpassed by his pupil Frans van Mieris. Van Mieris made deceptively illusionistic paintings, rendering people and their actions with extreme accuracy. Dou therefore had good reason to call Van Mieris 'the prince' of his pupils. In his *Brothel scene* Frans van Mieris proves himself to be extraordinarily skilful at staging a scene. The man and woman in the foreground exchange meaningful glances, while she fills his glass yet again. The intentions of the soldier who pulls a woman to him by her apron cannot be misconstrued. In the doorway on the right a man converses with a young woman. The bedclothes hanging over the balustrade are a very revealing detail, and the coupling dogs also underscore the eroticism in this scene. In the past not everyone was amused by this: in the 19th century the strait-laced English owner of this work had the male dog painted

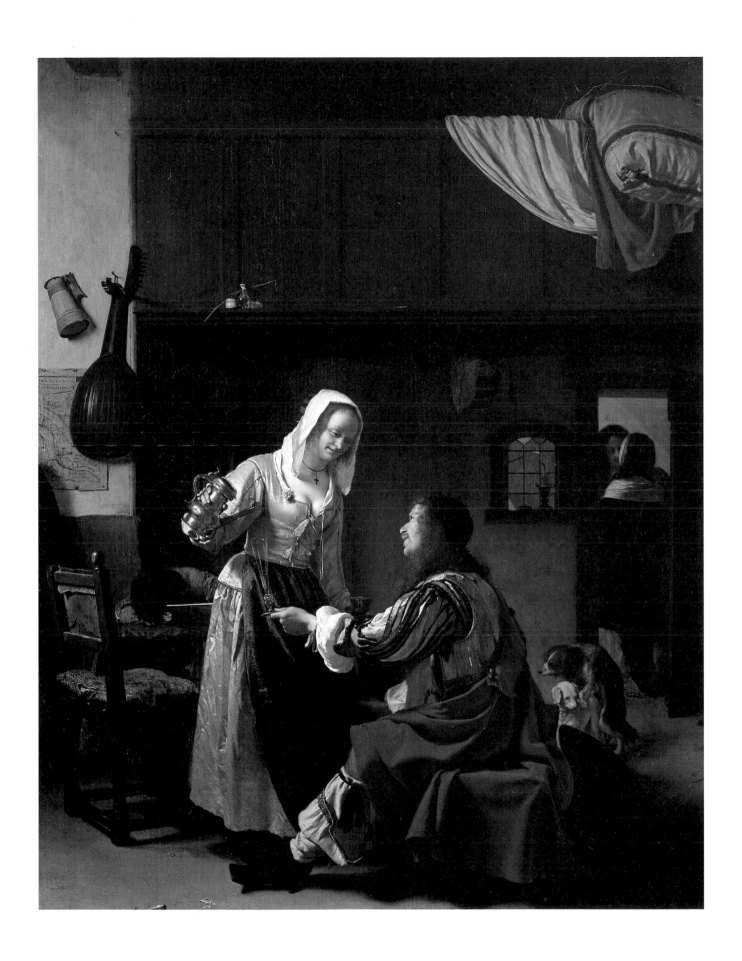

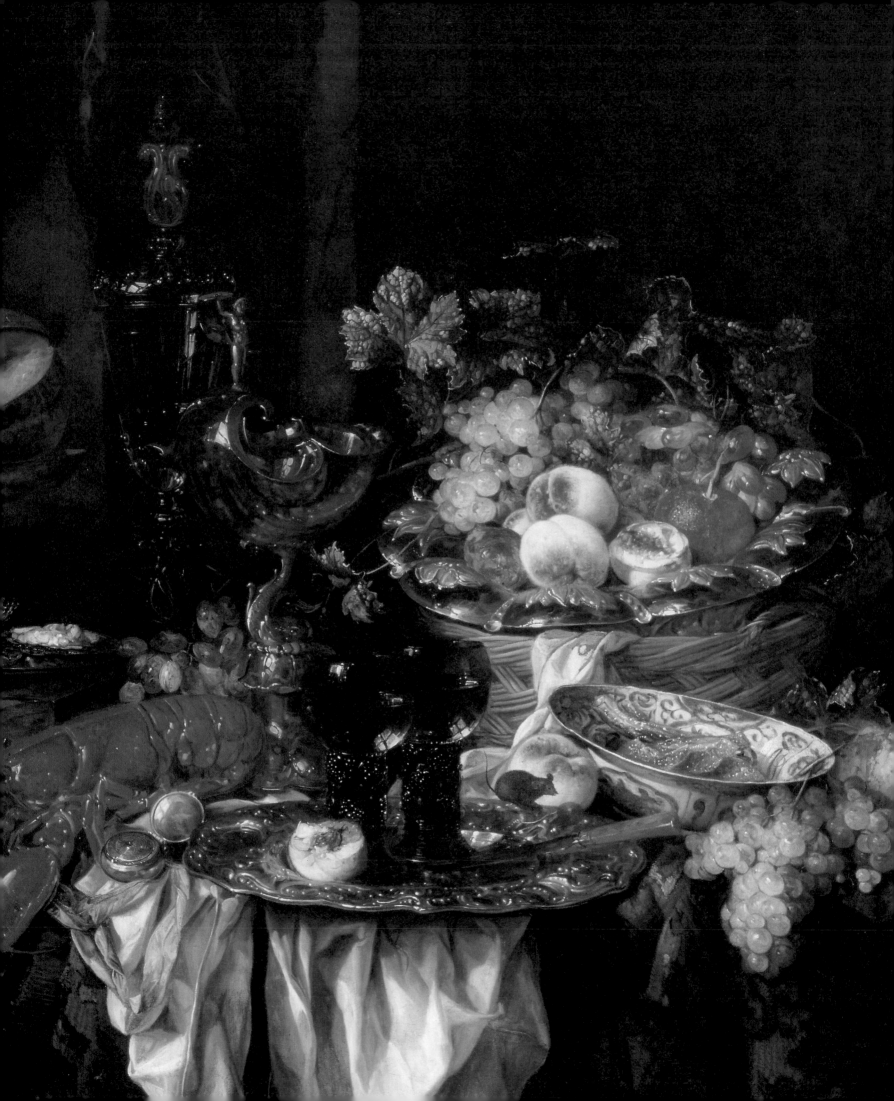

16 IN THE LAP OF LUXURY 1640-1700

Dᴜʀɪɴɢ ᴛʜᴇ ᴄᴏᴜʀꜱᴇ of the 17th century, still lifes became ever more diversified. Some artists continued to concentrate on simple 'breakfast pieces', while others painted lavishly laid tables with exotic foods. Alongside luxuriant, colourful bouquets there were now intimate little paintings with a single flower or piece of fruit, and next to still lifes with precious objects from far-off lands, paintings were made which featured a few of the artist's personal possessions. In the second half of the 17th century all these variations of the still life existed side-by-side.

Abraham van Beyeren was one of the masters of the richly laid table. His sumptuous still lifes, as this type of painting is called, consist of compositions of fruit, lobster, shells and costly tableware made of silver, gold, porcelain and glass. He arranged various objects on wrinkled tablecloths and crumpled napkins. The diversity of materials offered the painter of sumptuous still lifes a choice opportunity to demonstrate his mastery of composition and skill at rendering various materials. The hardness of a lobster's shell and the softness of the skin of a peach, the fragility of Chinese porcelain and the resilience of wickerwork, the stiff folds of a knotted carpet and the suppleness of a wrinkled damask napkin – all these material qualities are united in one single painting.

Still lifes remained popular until the end of the 17th century, proving to be a very lucrative genre for artists. Although there was certainly no decrease in quality, saturation of the market and changing tastes led in the early 18th century to a rather abrupt end to still-life painting. Only flower still lifes remained very much in demand, especially among foreign collectors. One or two specialists in fruit still lifes managed to hold their own, such as the Zeeland painter Adriaen Coorte. Far from the main artistic centres, he continued to paint – into the first decade of the 18th century – extremely simple, idiosyncratic compositions in which the main role was reserved for a bundle of asparagus, a sprig of gooseberries or a couple of medlars.

STILL LIFES IN AMSTERDAM

Haarlem was the city of the monochrome banquet piece: a laid table, painted in closely related colours. Pieter Claesz and Willem Claesz Heda had been the masters of this genre, and had exerted a great deal of influence on a large number of still-life painters, both in Haarlem and elsewhere (see chapter 6). Two artists were responsible for the flourishing of this genre in Amsterdam: Jan Jansz van de Velde and Jan Jansz Treck. Van de Velde was born in Haarlem and probably received his training in that city. Treck learned to paint from his Amsterdam brother-in-law Jan Jansz den Uyl, whose style he also adopted.

DRINKING GAMES

Many still lifes contain depictions of glasses. In the 17th century there were many kinds of glasses, some of which were made especially for drinking games. The 'passglas', for example, as depicted in the painting by Jan Jansz Treck [124], is a tall, narrow glass with equidistant horizontal rings. The filled glass was passed around and everyone had to drink it down to the next ring in one gulp. Anyone unable to do this had to continue drinking down to the following ring.

Another example is the 'mill glass', a glass with the sails of a windmill on the bottom. The player had to blow on the sails to make them turn, then drink the contents of the glass before the sails stopped turning. If he failed to do this, he was forced to drink the number of glasses shown on the windmill's clock.

< DETAIL OF 128

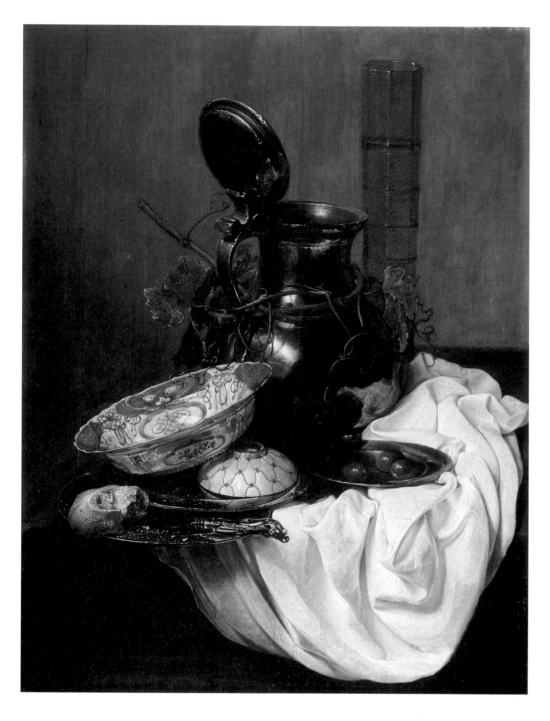

124

JAN JANSZ TRECK (c. 1606-1652)
*Still life with pewter jug
and Chinese bowl*, 1645
Panel 66.5 x 50.5 cm
BUDAPEST, SZÉPMÜVÉSZETI MÚZEUM
(acquired in 1894, see p. 324)

TRECK

The objects in Treck's still life occur in various other paintings by his hand. The pewter jug, tall beer glass and perhaps also the porcelain bowl were probably his own possessions, which enabled him to take all the time he needed to arrange and study them, painting them in various combinations and compositions. The central place is occupied by the pewter jug wound round with vines. With true feeling for the rendering of material, Treck painted the pewter in bluish, dark-grey tones. He must have looked long and hard at the arrangement, which was set up in his studio, for he depicted the reflections in the jug's round body with unerring precision: the yellow-green olives, the light tablecloth, the bright blue of the porcelain bowl. Such Chinese porcelain had been imported into Holland since around 1640 and was very popular among collectors.

VAN DE VELDE

In Jan van de Velde's still life a *passglas* forms the highest point in the composition, from which a diagonal runs to the oyster shell on the right, whose white lining lends a bright accent to the painting. There are more objects in this still life than in Treck's. The meal of oysters seems just to have finished. In addition to the leftover oyster shells, Van de Velde painted the requisite lemons and a sliced orange on a pewter plate. Peppercorns lie on and around the china plate, next to which are some chestnuts, both peeled and unpeeled. The background is formed by a glass with knob-shaped ornaments and an overturned pewter flagon. The tall beer glass marks the transition to the objects in the background: a clay pipe, some tobacco in a small paper bag, and a coal pan. The pan of coals is slightly damaged; the chipped edge gleams subtly.

This still life might be more than just a beautifully arranged and painted collection of objects: perhaps it contains a warning. In the 17th-century visual arts, drinking, smoking and eating oysters were often connected with loose living and sinfulness. For example, in several of his cautionary genre pieces, Jan Steen painted oysters and smoker's and drinker's requisites in the proximity of his undisciplined and licentious burghers. Viewed in this way, Van de Velde's restrained still life could also be said to contain a warning: avoid excessive use of the things displayed here.

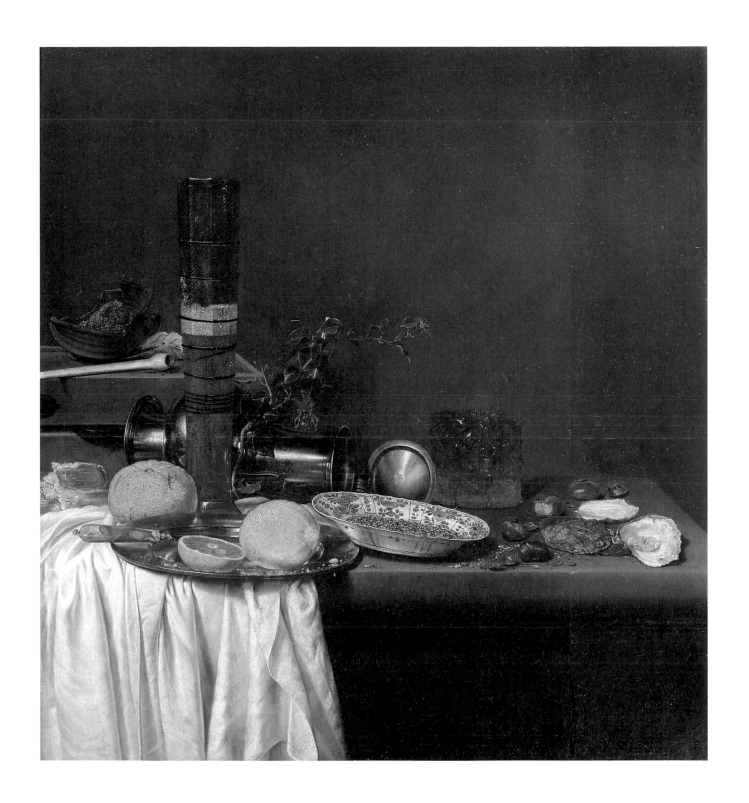

125
JAN JANSZ VAN DE VELDE (c. 1620-1662 or 1664)
Still life with beer glass, 1647
Panel 64 x 59 cm
AMSTERDAM, RIJKSMUSEUM
(acquired in 1908, see p. 315)

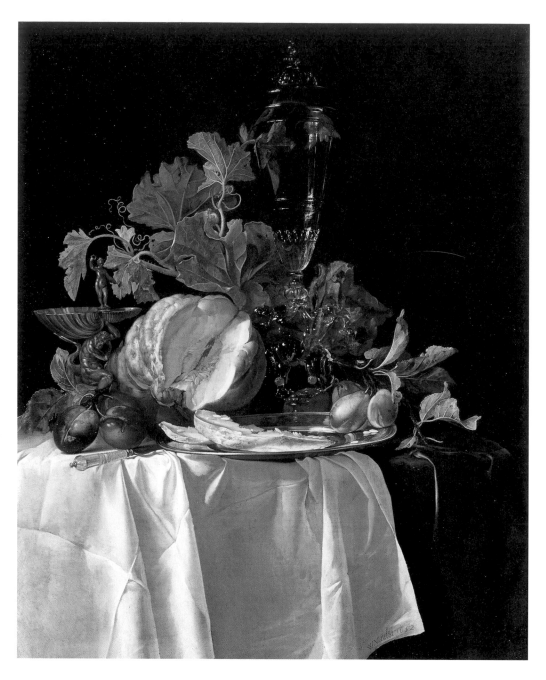

126

WILLEM VAN AELST (1626-c. 1683)
Still life with fruit and crystal vase, 1652
Canvas 73 x 58 cm
FLORENCE, PALAZZO PITTI,
GALLERIA PALATINA
(acquired in 1652, see p. 330)

TWO PAINTERS ABROAD

Intense colours characterise the still lifes of
Willem van Aelst [*126*] and Jan Davidsz de
Heem [*127*]. In Van Aelst's painting the
intense blue of the tablecloth catches one's
eye; in De Heem's festoon of flowers it is
the deep red of various tulips and pieces of
fruit. Both painters developed their styles
outside Holland. Van Aelst worked for a
time in France and Italy, and De Heem spent
a large part of his career in Antwerp.

Nevertheless, they both exerted an influence
on Dutch still-life painting. Van Aelst
returned in 1657 to Amsterdam, where he
lived and worked until his death. Even
though De Heem remained in Antwerp, he
nonetheless kept in touch with his Dutch
colleagues and also made several lengthy
visits to his home town of Utrecht.

VAN AELST

After receiving his training in his home town
of Delft, Willem van Aelst travelled to
France and from there to Italy, where he
became court painter to Ferdinand II de'
Medici, Grand Duke of Tuscany. His *Still
life with fruit and crystal vase* was
commissioned by Cardinal Giovan Carlo de'
Medici, a relative of Ferdinand. Van Aelst
turned this still life into a veritable showpiece.

The top of the composition is formed by
a large crystal vase which was probably in
the possession of the Medici family. The
transparency of the vase was convincingly
rendered by means of the subtle play of
glimmering light against the dark background. Cleanly drawn vine leaves form a
graceful transition to another precious
object: the gilt dish in the form of a shell,
which is carried by a bent sea-god and
crowned by a naked goddess. A real eye-
catcher is the melon next to it, a slice of
which is presented on the silver plate.
The oval melon seeds stand out subtly
against the gleaming metal of the plate.
With the same precision the artist painted
the wrinkles and folds in the white tablecloth, placing his signature and the date on
its hem: *W.V.Aelst. 1652.*

DE HEEM

The panel with festoons of flowers was
signed by Jan Davidsz de Heem at the
upper right, in dark brown on the dark
background, against which all the floral
splendour stands out. The work is not
dated, but he must have painted it in the
1660s, around thirty years after he had left

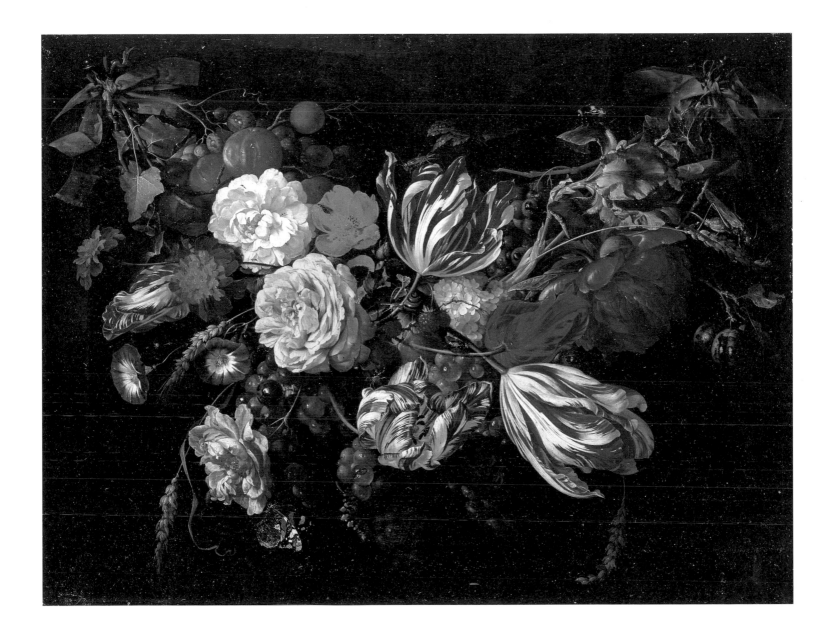

127

JAN DAVIDSZ DE HEEM (1606-c. 1684)
Festoon with flowers and fruit,
c. 1660-1670
Panel 26.2 x 47.5 cm
SCHWERIN, STAATLICHES MUSEUM
(acquired between 1792 and 1821, see p. 346)

for the Southern Netherlands. De Heem emigrated to the South at a time when many artists and artisans were moving to the North. Antwerp's attraction was probably the group of important still-life painters who lived and worked there, including Frans Snijders, Adriaen van Utrecht and Daniël Seghers. They were all in close contact with Rubens and made still lifes as they were not made in Holland – magnificent, spectacular and virtuosic.

De Heem was inspired by their works: even this small panel with the festoon of flowers displays an un-Dutch elegance,

wealth of colour and naturalness. A choice selection of flowers and insects has been gathered together here. On closer inspection the festoon appears to consist not only of tulips, roses, grapes and ivy, but also includes viburnum, grape hyacinth, a peony, irises, raspberries, plums, and some wheat. Furthermore, nine insects may be discerned, some of them extremely tiny but nonetheless depicted with great precision. The snail and the butterfly are easily found, but the yellow ant, earwig and daddy longlegs are more difficult to detect.

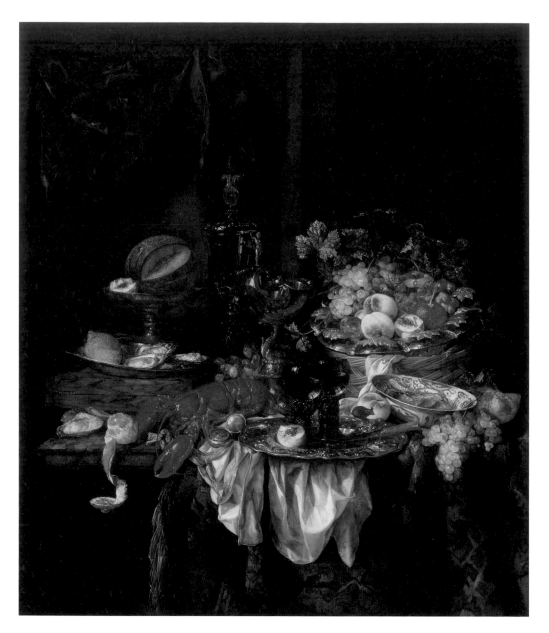

SUMPTUOUS STILL LIFE

Greater profusion than that seen in this still life by Abraham van Beyeren is scarcely imaginable. Sumptuous still lifes such as this one came into fashion after 1640. Van Beyeren had specialised in this genre, following in the footsteps of Jan Davidsz de Heem, who was responsible for inventing this type of still life, which overwhelms the viewer with its wealth of lavishly displayed objects.

The Hague artist Van Beyeren gathered together a colourful collection of exclusive objects on a marble table top, most of which is covered with an Oriental rug. A sliced melon graces a gilt *tazza*; oysters with lemon are presented on a silver plate. The two *roemers*, filled with white wine, stand on a silver plate decorated with a fish-scale pattern, and the fruit is also piled up on a silver plate, which in turn lies in a woven basket. In the midst of this are a dazzling gilt beaker with a curling rim and a crystal goblet. The exuberance of this specimen derives from the curious combination of a shell-like form standing on a foot shaped like a fish. It is not at all clear how Van Beyeren, who was anything but rich, managed to get hold of such precious objects, which have the allure of princely possessions. In the midst of all this profusion a mouse merrily climbs over the edge of a silver dish – Van Beyeren obviously had a sense of humour. For a long time the mouse was invisible: a former owner had had it painted out. Perhaps he had an aversion to mice, or perhaps he was aware of – and did not wish to view daily – the symbolism traditionally attached to this animal. Mice supposedly led a gluttonous, sinful life, and were unclean animals that seldom escaped punishment. It is possible that Van Beyeren added the mouse, as well as the pocket watch to the left of the dish, as an exhortation to temperance.

WILLEM KALF

In his *Still life with Chinese bowl and nautilus cup* Willem Kalf displays a predilection for depicting exotic dinnerware, as well as his ability to render the various materials with the appropriate transparency and lustre. Here the artist made a subtle arrangement of citrus fruit, a nautilus cup in a splendid mount, a Venetian glass, a silver dish in auricular style, a *roemer*, a drinking bowl and a Chinese bowl with a lid. This unusual porcelain bowl is decorated with gilt figures in relief. Eight male Chinese

128
ABRAHAM VAN BEYEREN (1620/1621-1690)
Sumptuous still life, 1667
Canvas 141.5 x 122 cm
LOS ANGELES,
LOS ANGELES COUNTY MUSEUM OF ART
(acquired in 1986, see p. 338)

129
WILLEM KALF (1619-1693)
*Still life with Chinese bowl
and nautilus cup,* 1662
Canvas 79.4 x 67.3 cm
MADRID, MUSEO THYSSEN-BORNEMISZA
(acquired in 1962, see p. 339)

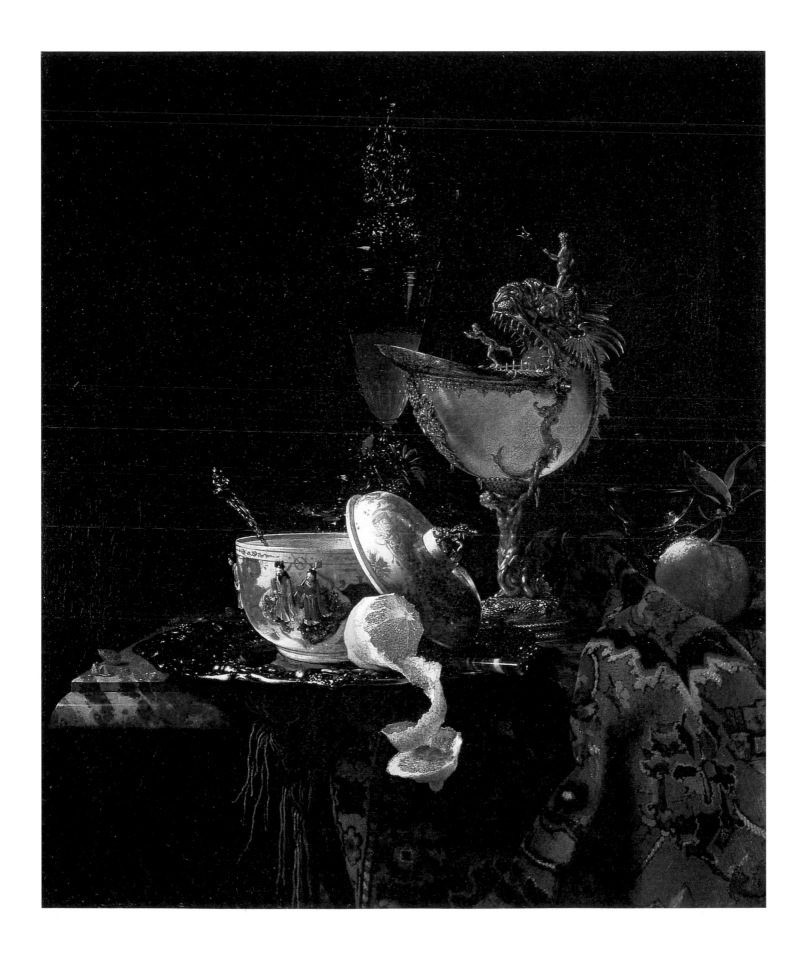

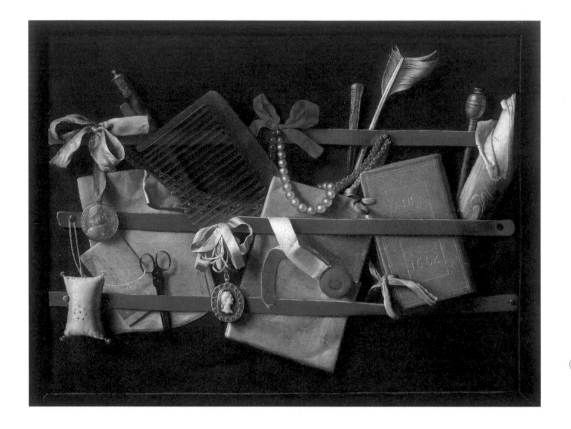

130
SAMUEL VAN HOOGSTRAETEN (1627-1678)
Trompe-l'oeil still life, 1664
Canvas 45.5 x 57.5 cm
DORDRECHT, DORDRECHTS MUSEUM
(acquired with the aid of the Rembrandt Society
in 1992, see p. 327)

figures, in four groups of two, depict the eight 'Immortals', who were Taoist philosophers. Kalf may have had the pot, a favourite collector's item, in his possession for a while, as he was an art dealer as well as a painter.

SAMUEL VAN HOOGSTRAETEN

The life, work and ideas of the painter, art theorist and poet Samuel van Hoogstraeten are well documented, and this is due in large part to the artist's own contributions to the sources. Van Hoogstraeten was born in 1627 in Dordrecht. He moved to Amsterdam to become apprenticed to Rembrandt and worked in the master's studio from 1640 to 1642, together with other pupils, including Carel Fabritius. By 1648 he was back in Dordrecht. Three years later he travelled to Vienna, where he was received by Ferdinand III, Emperor of the Holy Roman Empire. The emperor admired the deceptive realism of one of Van Hoogstraeten's still lifes, and rewarded him for it in 1651 by presenting him with a gold

medal and chain. After a stay in Vienna (1651-1654) and a stay in London (1662-1666), he lived alternately in The Hague and Dordrecht.

Van Hoogstraeten practised various genres of painting. He made portraits, architectural paintings, history and genre paintings, as well as so-called *bedriegertjes* – *trompe-l'oeil* still lifes which are deceptively realistic – and 'perspective boxes'. The latter were small wooden peepshows, the insides of which were painted in such a way as to conjure up the illusion of a spacious interior. Van Hoogstraeten himself described them as follows: 'the curious perspective box, when properly painted with the necessary understanding, makes a finger-long figure appear to be life-size'. In addition to painting, Van Hoogstraeten left his mark on art history as the writer of the *Inleyding tot de Hooge Schoole der Schilderkonst* (Introduction to the Advanced School of Painting) (1678), in which he laid down the rules of history painting.

TROMPE-L'OEIL

The life of Samuel van Hoogstraeten is largely known through archival documents, his ideas on artistic theory are recorded in his 'Introduction' and his personality is revealed in several of his deceptively realistic still lifes. The objects the artist depicted in his *trompe-l'oeil* still lifes reflect his life and social standing. Van Hoogstraeten's *Trompe-l'oeil still life* [130] shows a letter rack, a flat shelf on which three strips of leather have been nailed to hold letters. In this rack Van Hoogstraeten placed other trophies as well. One of these is the gold medal with which Emperor Ferdinand III had decorated the artist, which is attached with a ribbon to a long gold chain. Next to this Van Hoogstraeten painted a nice arrangement of other personal possessions, with a sealed document in the middle on which the artist placed his signature and the date. This document, together with the leather journal bearing the year 1664, the little book rolled up in marbled paper, the penknife and the quill, refer to Van Hoogstraeten's literary

activities. The antique cameo and the large
tortoise-shell wig comb indicate wealth,
honour and high social standing. The meaning of the pin cushion, the scissors and the
pearl necklace is not clear. Perhaps these
feminine objects have something to do with
Sara Balen, Van Hoogstraeten's wife, who
accompanied him on his trip to England.

This *bedriegertje* by Samuel van Hoogstraeten lent added weight to advice aimed at
his pupils. He urged them to apply themselves to the rendering of flat objects on a flat
surface, for a painter could win fame and
honour with these *trompe-l'oeil* effects. Here
Van Hoogstraeten provided a convincing
demonstration of his skills and his acquired
status. Viewed in this way, the still life may
also be seen as a masterly self-portrait.

MEDLARS

At the turn of the 18th century, at a time
when only a few still-life specialists were
still active in the Netherlands, Adriaen
Coorte was painting little gems in this genre.
He kept well clear of extravagance and
luxury, never painting opulent decorations,
lavish drapery or heaps of precious objects.
Coorte found strength in simplicity. This
painter, who was active in Middelburg in
the province of Zeeland, made simple compositions containing extremely convincing
depictions of everyday objects, fruit and
vegetables. In this still life with three medlars the illumination is subtle; the light
brushes past the front of the stone plinth.
Coorte's medlars are almost palpably present. The red-brown skin gleams and curls up
at the top. A dark variant of this brown
recurs in the shadow, and the colours mingle
where the pieces of fruit touch each other.
The butterfly stands out brightly against the
dark background. Coorte gave a bafflingly
realistic rendering of the fragility of this
insect. Adriaen Coorte's artistry and skill
was not fully appreciated until the second
half of the 20th century. Coorte was not
famous in his own day either, which perhaps
explains why so little is known of his life.

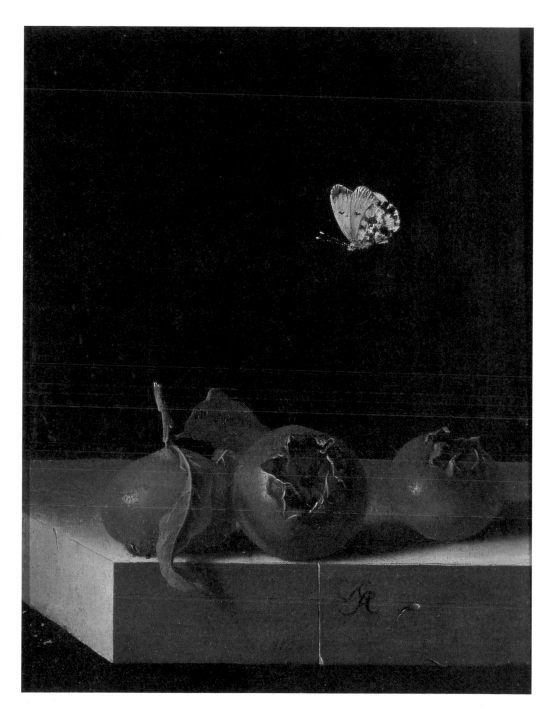

131

ADRIAEN COORTE (active c. 1683-1707)
Still life with three medlars, c. 1696-1700
Paper on panel 26.8 x 20.4 cm
PRIVATE COLLECTION
(see p. 351)

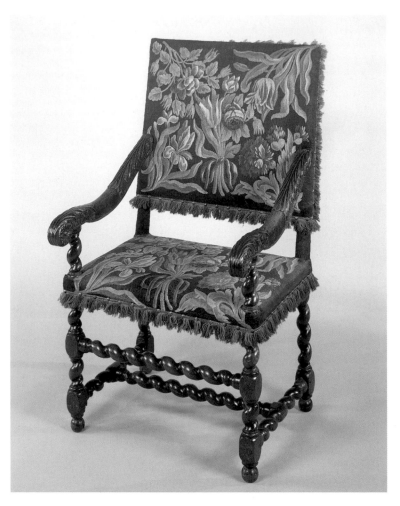

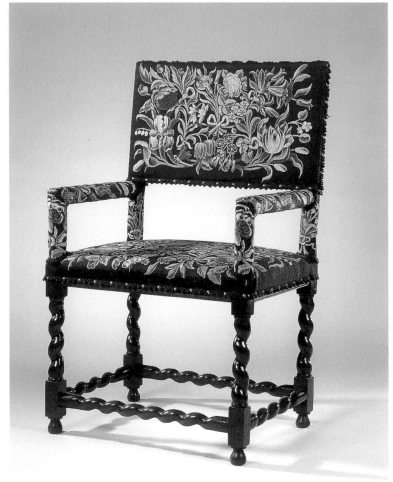

132

Armchair, c. 1650-1675

Walnut, upholstered with tapestry

112.5 x 60.5 x 67 cm

AMSTERDAM, RIJKSMUSEUM

(on loan from the Koninklijk Oudheidkundig

Genootschap since 1899, see p. 314)

133

Armchair, c. 1650

Walnut, upholstered with tapestry

105 x 62 x 47 cm

PRIVATE COLLECTION, AMSTERDAM

(see p. 351)

STILL LIFES IN WOOL AND SILK

Tapestry tablecloths with floral patterns were a genre typical of Northern Netherlandish tapestry production. They generally date from the second and third quarters of the 17th century. Workshops in Delft and Gouda, as well as Amsterdam and Schoonhoven, produced these floral tapestries. Many pieces of furniture were also covered with tapestry from the middle of the century onwards, at which time it was fashionable to decorate a room *en suite*. The same pattern and material were therefore used for chair-coverings and tablecloths. Few tapestry-covered chairs have been preserved from the Golden Age, the main reasons being changing tastes and wear and tear.

These two beautifully upholstered chairs [132 *and* 133] are therefore exceptional. The tailor-made tapestries display highly elaborate combinations of flowers tied together with a ribbon. The seat of the chair belonging to the Rijksmuseum [132] shows a strikingly large pattern which continues into the corners. The fabric has withstood the ravages of time; the flowers still have their natural colours, which stand out nicely against the dark-blue background. The armrests are decorated with carving into which leaf patterns have been incorporated.

The armrests of the other chair [133] are completely covered with tapestry, as are the vertical struts supporting the armrests and running between the seat and back of the chair. Insects may be discerned here and there among the flowers. This chair was one of a set of 12 upholstered chairs which an Amsterdam patrician bequeathed to a home for needy women. This chair, still in excellent condition, belonged to the furnishings in the governors' meeting room.

TABLECLOTH

The colours of this woven tablecloth with a large cartouche in the middle have been well preserved [134]. Flora, the ancient Italian goddess of flowers, is portrayed in a landscape with classical buildings. Large quantities of flowers fan out from the middle to cover the whole tablecloth. They are arranged in such a way that in each row alternate stalks point to the outside edge, the others towards the middle. The designers of such motifs imitated nature in the same painstaking manner as the still-life painters, and the tapestry weavers succeeded in introducing just as many nuances of colour with their wool and silk as the painters did with their paint.

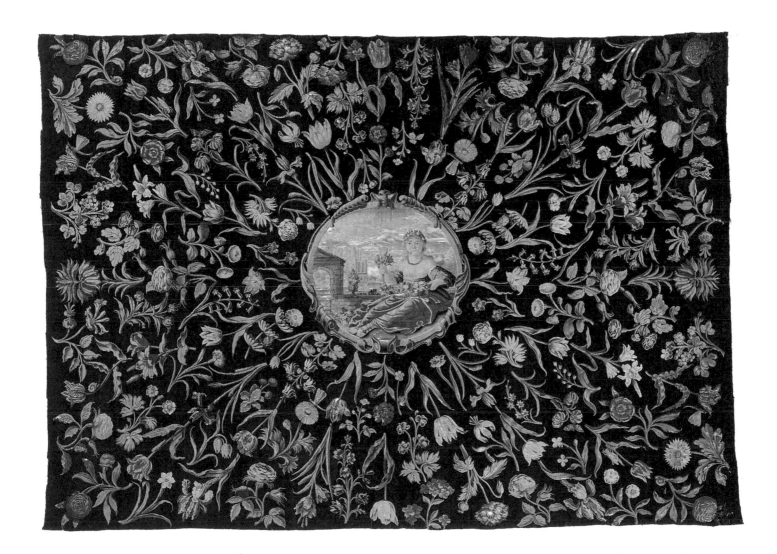

134
Tablecloth with Flora in
oval cartouche,
c. 1660-1680
Wool and silk, 194 x 275 cm
AMSTERDAM, RIJKSMUSEUM
(on loan from the Koninklijk Oudheidkundig
Genootschap since 1885, see p. 312)

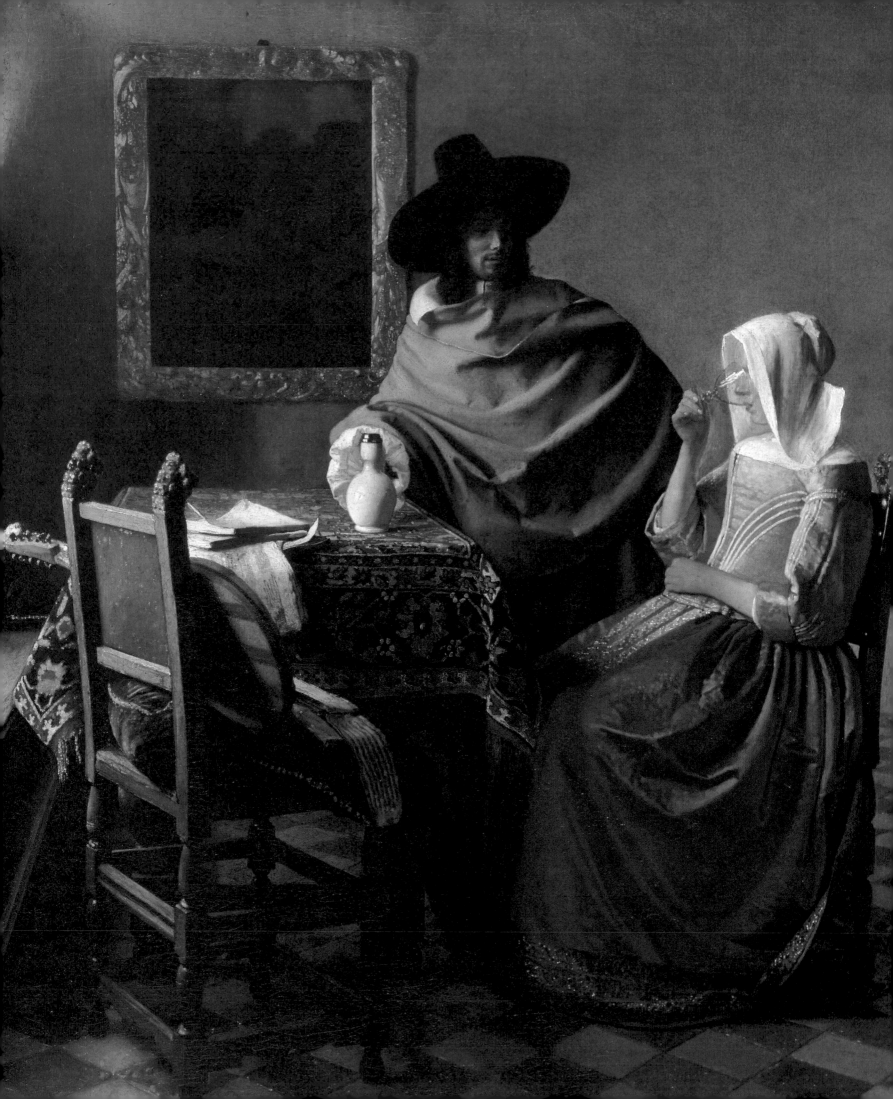

17 THE DELFT LIGHT 1650-1670

Ⅾuring the course of the 17th century, Delft became more conservative, both politically and culturally. Various Delft artists worked for the nearby stadholder's court in The Hague; their rather traditional, internationally oriented style was in keeping with the conservative taste of their patrons.

In the 1650s, however, great changes took place: architectural painting received a new impulse from Gerard Houckgeest and Emanuel de Witte (see chapter 11), and the unsurpassed genre paintings of Carel Fabritius, Johannes Vermeer and Pieter de Hooch put Delft back on the map. Without exception, their paintings are characterised by a feeling for perspective and superb rendering of daylight.

BLOSSOMING

The reason for this sudden blossoming of painting in Delft is not entirely clear. The focus on light and perspective of the two Delft innovators, Houckgeest and De Witte, certainly contributed to these new developments. Their interiors radiated a feeling of naturalness, owing to their discoveries and skills in the field of perspective. Houckgeest's perspective in particular, with its two vanishing points, was a significant development, both for the specialism of interiors and for Delft genre painting as a whole.

The Delft school of painting received another impulse from Carel Fabritius, who moved to the city around 1650. Fabritius

was enormously interested in the effect of perspective. He was a pupil of Rembrandt, but he abandoned his teacher's typical chiaroscuro contrasts in favour of a more natural rendering of light. Fabritius's subtle handling of light was a determining factor in the development of the Delft school of painting.

ILLUSION OF SPACE

The most important masters of the Delft school of painting in the second half of the 17th century were Pieter de Hooch and Johannes Vermeer. Both artists painted the same, rather simple subjects – a few figures in an interior – and had an unparalleled feeling for natural light and the illusion of space. Nevertheless, their works can be clearly distinguished from one another. Vermeer generally painted a small part of one room, often only a corner of it, whereas De Hooch usually portrayed a whole room, frequently with a view to adjacent rooms. While Vermeer zoomed in on a couple of figures in his interiors, De Hooch concentrated on the very precise rendering of one, mostly complex area. In nearly all of his paintings, Vermeer had the light coming from one side, whereas De Hooch played an ingenious game with light coming from various angles. These two Delft masters undoubtedly influenced each other, though Vermeer probably looked more to his slightly older colleague De Hooch than the other way around.

DELFT

The city of Delft has always played an important role in Dutch history. When Willem the Silent (1533-1584) had his headquarters there, Delft was an important political centre. During the first half of the 17th century the city also underwent rapid growth in trade and industry. By mid-century Delft had become an important centre of commerce and consequently one of the most influential cities of Holland. Delft housed chambers of both the Dutch East India Company and the Dutch West India Company, and the city was for a long time the entrepôt of the English trading company Merchant Adventurers. Important industries strengthened the city's economy. In addition to beer breweries and the textile industry, it was the potteries producing earthenware that were most important in this respect. Starting in the 1640s they grew into the most important industry in Delft, producing the Delft-blue earthenware which became the city's most important export.

< DETAIL OF 137

135

CAREL FABRITIUS (1622-1654)
The goldfinch, 1654
Panel 33.5 x 22.8 cm
THE HAGUE, MAURITSHUIS
(acquired in 1896, see p. 332)

GOLDFINCH

Carel Fabritius's depiction of a single bird in front of its feeding tray is unusually simple. This small painting is comparable in various respects to Johannes Vermeer's *Kitchen maid*. Although the subjects are widely different, the power of both paintings lies in the same elements: the bright, natural light, the simplicity of the composition, the solid brushwork and the balanced use of colour. Fabritius made *The goldfinch* in 1654, a few years before Vermeer painted his *Kitchen maid*. The work of the young Fabritius certainly influenced Vermeer.

Fabritius painted *The goldfinch* on a rather thick panel, whose edges are not bevelled in the usual way, from which one may deduce that the painting was not meant to be framed. Nail holes in the upper and lower edges have led to the theory that the panel was part of an object in which reality and illusion merged almost imperceptibly. In the 17th century goldfinches were popular household pets which generally spent their lives tied to their feeding trays underneath a birdhouse. Beneath the feeding tray a minia-ture mechanism enabled the goldfinch to draw its own drinking water from a well by lowering a tiny bucket into the water reser-voir. It is now assumed that a real birdhouse was once attached to the top of the painting and a small well to the bottom.

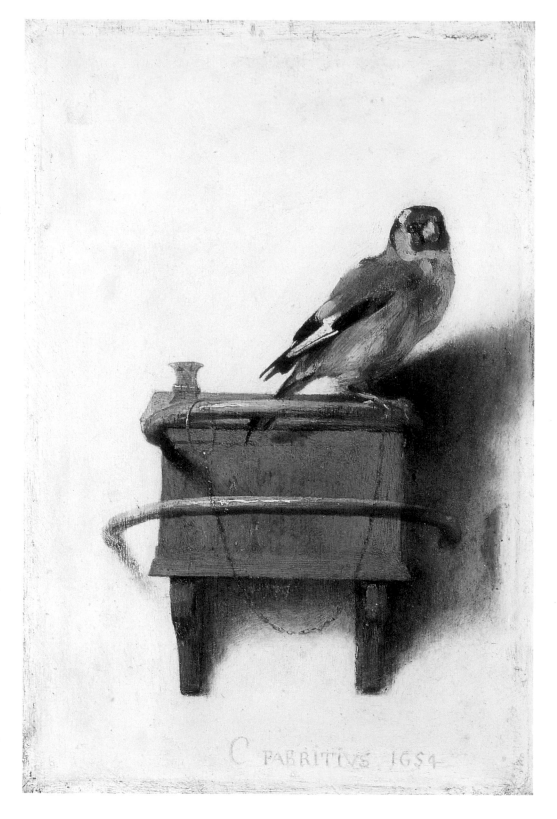

PREMATURE DEATH

Carel Fabritius died on 12 October 1654 when an underground gunpowder magazine in Delft accidentally exploded. Two hundred houses were wiped out and there were dozens of casualties. This explosion and the ensuing fire must have destroyed a great deal of Fabritius's work, since so few paintings are known by his hand. These however testify to Fabritius's exceptional qualities, which were recognised early on. A poem published upon his death praised the 'most renowned' Fabritius, at the same time proclaiming which artist would henceforth carry the torch: Johannes Vermeer.

RENOWNED MILKMAID

As early as 1696 Johannes Vermeer's painting of *The kitchen maid* was praised in a sale catalogue with the words 'exceedingly good'. In 1719 the painting was again described, this time as 'the renowned milkmaid'. Now, at the beginning of the 21st century, this work is one of the most famous paintings of the Golden Age.

A perfectly ordinary kitchen maid is busy carrying out an everyday task. Extremely carefully, with her head tilted slightly, the girl pours milk from a jug into a bowl. She has a robust appearance, which is emphasised by the low viewpoint – the viewer looks up at her from slightly below. The composition, illumination and solid brushwork enabled Vermeer to turn this ordinary subject into a powerful painting.

The light in the picture was painted very meticulously in Vermeer's characteristic manner. He made use of subtle alternations of light and shadow: the girl's right hand, upon which the light shines, contrasts with the shadowed wall behind it, whereas the shadowed side of the girl stands out against the illuminated wall. Along her shoulder and arm Vermeer painted a bright, white contour, which further strengthens the silhouette effect. In the still life on the table – a basket of bread rolls, a Cologne-ware jug and a bowl – the reflection of light was

painstakingly rendered by means of small, light-coloured dots. In heightening the illusion of reality Vermeer paid attention to the smallest details, such as a broken pane and the light falling through it on to the window frame, and the subtle shadows emanating from the nails and holes in the dilapidated wall.

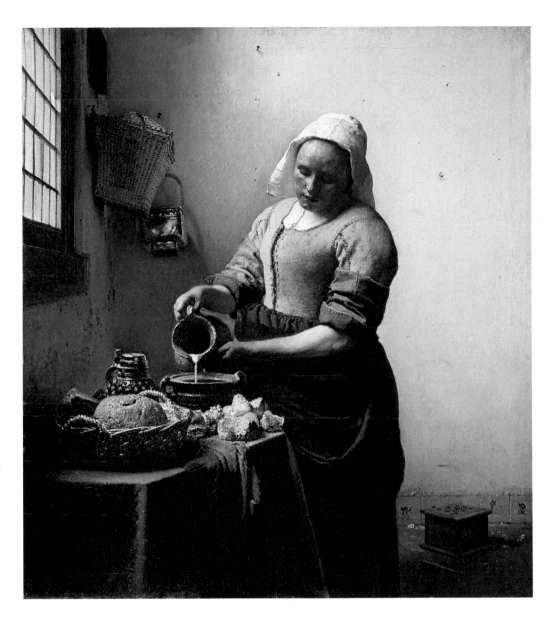

136

JOHANNES VERMEER (1632-1675)
The kitchen maid, c. 1658-1660
Canvas 45.5 x 41 cm
AMSTERDAM, RIJKSMUSEUM
(acquired with the aid of the Rembrandt
Society in 1908, see p. 314)

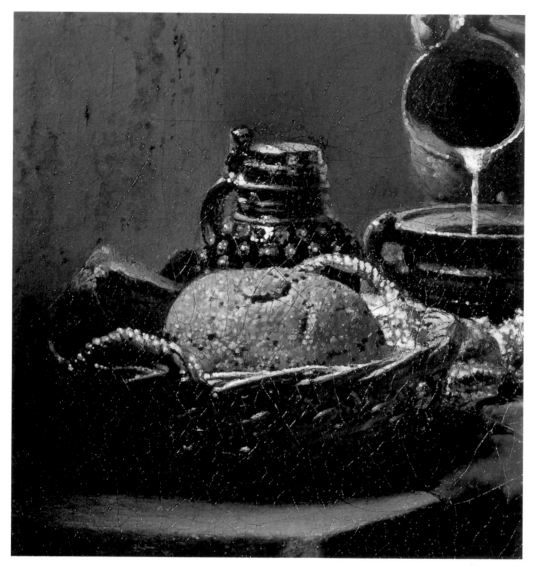

DETAIL OF 136

JOHANNES VERMEER

Johannes Vermeer spent his whole life in Delft. His father was not only a satin weaver and innkeeper, but also an art dealer, which means that the young Vermeer must have come into contact with painting early in life. It is not known who his teacher was, but some think it may have been Leonaert Bramer, who was at that time a reputable Delft painter.

In 1653, at the age of 21, Vermeer became a member of the Guild of St Luke and set up as an independent artist. He began his career as a history painter, but

around 1656 he began to concentrate on making genre pieces featuring one or more figures in an interior. Vermeer's brushwork became more refined and he developed the *pointillé* technique, using small dots of paint to create the illusion of reflected light.

Vermeer was not very productive: he made only about two paintings a year. There must have been a total of approximately 40, of which 34 have survived. His most important customers were citizens of Delft. The local baker, for example, owned two paintings by Vermeer. The majority of his paintings – no fewer than 21 – were

137
JOHANNES VERMEER (1632-1675)
The glass of wine, c. 1661-1662
Canvas 66.3 x 76.5 cm
BERLIN, GEMÄLDEGALERIE
(acquired in 1901, see p. 322)

purchased by Pieter van Ruyven, a good friend and patron of the artist.

GLASS OF WINE

The glass of wine shows a more spacious interior than that seen in *The kitchen maid*, though it contains the same ingredients. In this painting as well, the light enters through a window on the left; again there is a table, this time with two people. The soberness of the kitchen has made way for the richness of a distinguished interior. The lady and gentleman have apparently been making music or are just about to do so, when the woman finishes drinking her wine. The man watches her emptying her glass and is ready to fill it up again; remarkably enough, he has no glass himself. For his informed viewers Vermeer incorporated a moralising commentary in the stained-glass window. It contains, in addition to a coat of arms, a depiction of a female figure with a bridle in her hand: a personification of temperance. To be sure, temperance is not being practised in this painting, in which Vermeer splendidly portrayed how *not* to behave.

As in all of Vermeer's paintings, light plays an important role here. Exquisite indeed is the narrow, gleaming vertical edge of the window frame, upon which even the shadow of the lead strips is depicted. Vermeer also demonstrated his deftness at painting materials, as evidenced by his magnificent rendering of the transparent glass, the coarse texture of the tablecloth and the gleaming silk dress.

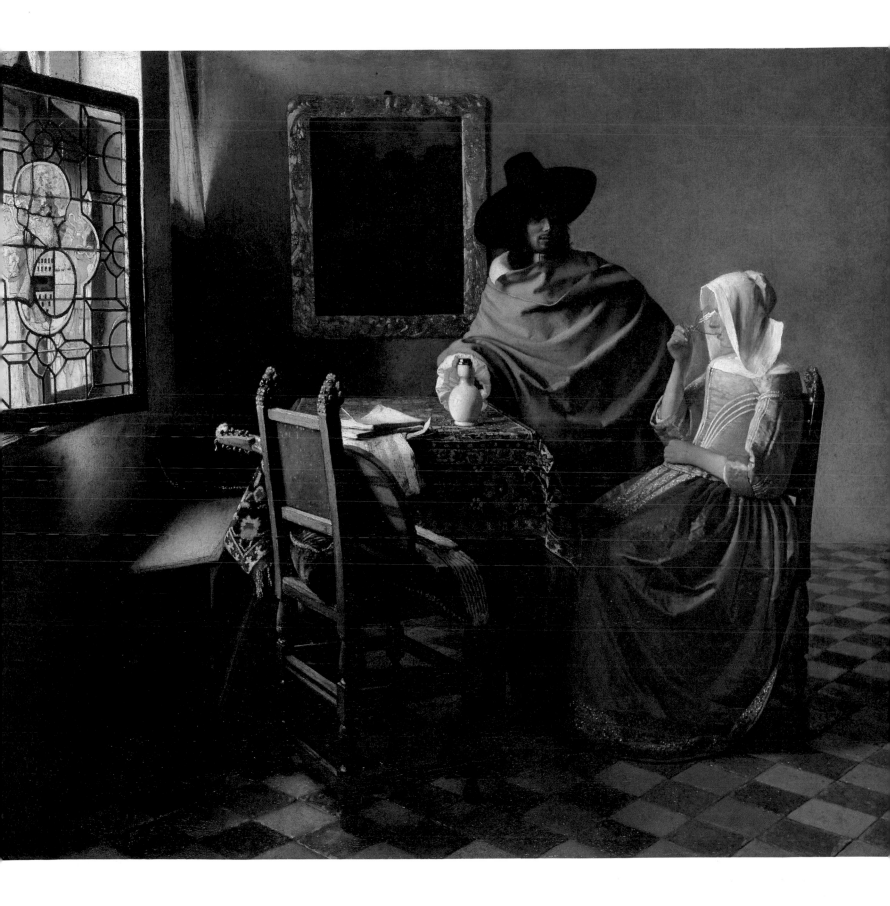

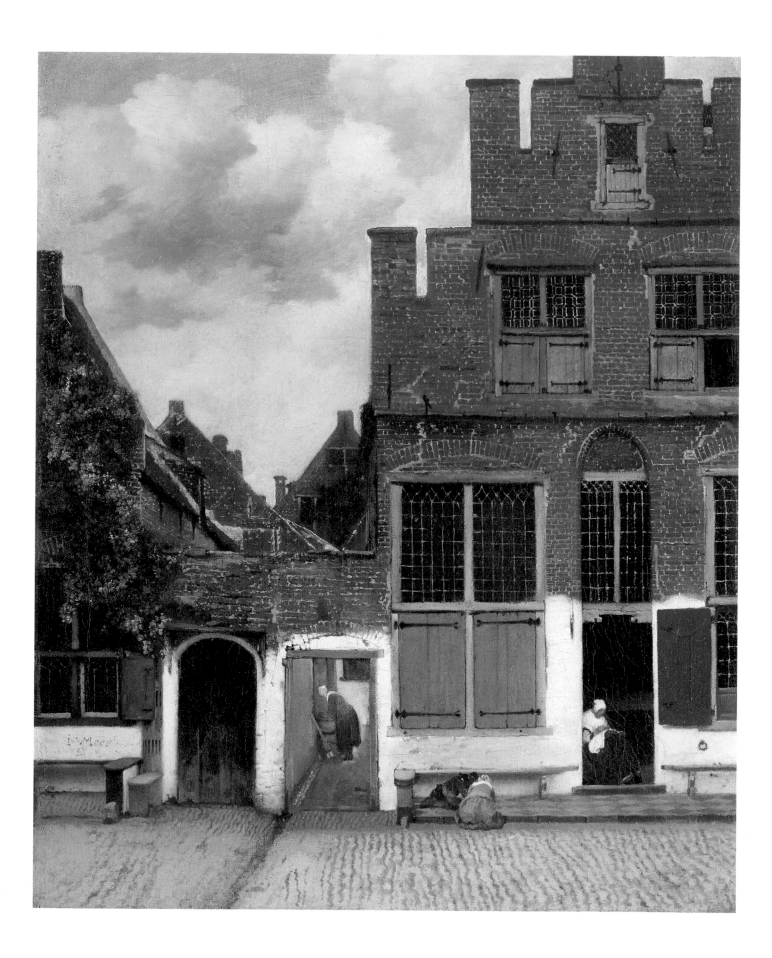

138

JOHANNES VERMEER (1632-1675)
The little street, c. 1658
Canvas 54.3 x 44 cm
AMSTERDAM, RIJKSMUSEUM
(acquired in 1921, see p. 315)

<

THE LITTLE STREET

A woman has scrubbed the street in front of her house; the water glistens as it runs along the gutter. A boy and girl play on the pavement, while a woman sits in the doorway, busy with her sewing. The peacefulness of everyday life in a 17th-century Dutch town was convincingly rendered by Johannes Vermeer in *The little street*.

This simple scene was expertly painted in every respect. The various building materials – the leaded window panes, the wooden shutters, the whitewashed walls and the raw, red brick – were all evocatively rendered. Vermeer did not depict each individual brick, but created instead an overall impression of a weathered façade, which is uniformly illuminated. He painted *The little street* in rather subdued colours. Only here and there, distributed over the picture plane, do accents of colour catch the eye: the red and green shutters, the yellow sleeve of the woman sewing and the girl's blue skirt. Like Vermeer's other paintings, this work also testifies to his strong sense of composition. He placed the row of houses parallel to the picture plane. The view alongside the house to an inner courtyard – with the gutter and yellow paving stones in the foreground – lies at right angles to the picture plane, thereby giving the work a feeling of depth. The unusual, seemingly cut-off upper and right-hand edges add an element of tension to the composition.

The little street is exceptional in Vermeer's oeuvre. Only two cityscapes are known by his hand: the *View of Delft* and this painting. *The little street* undoubtedly originated in competition with Pieter de Hooch, the painter of 'through-views' (door-

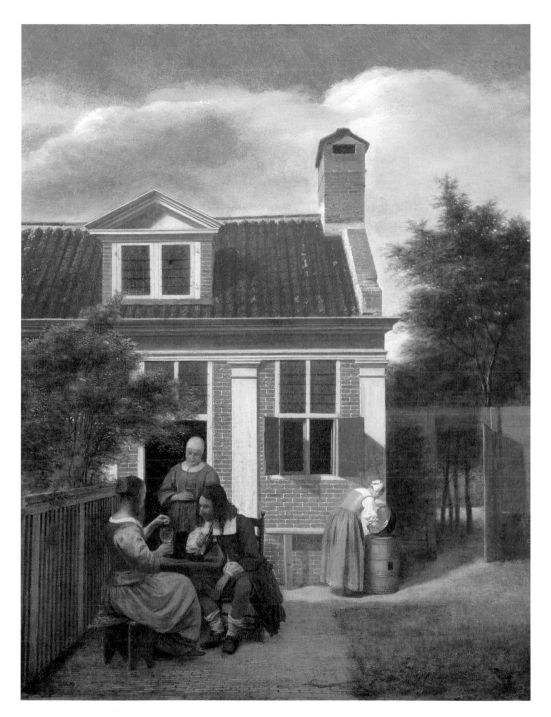

kijkjes), views from one room to another, or from a room into a courtyard or vice versa. De Hooch, who had settled in Delft in 1652, was specialised in interiors, though he occasionally painted an everyday scene taking place in a back garden or inner courtyard. The work of the slightly older De Hooch must have impressed Vermeer.

139

PIETER DE HOOCH (1629-1684)
Three women and a man in a courtyard,
c. 1663-1665
Canvas 60 x 45.7 cm
AMSTERDAM, RIJKSMUSEUM
(on loan from the City of Amsterdam
since 1885, see p. 312)

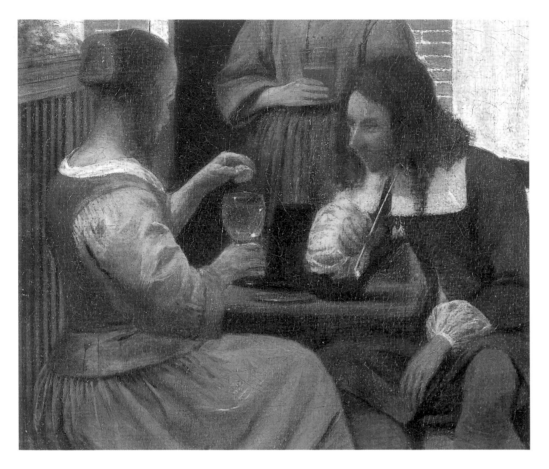

DETAIL OF 139

THE COURTYARD BEHIND THE HOUSE

The house in the painting by Pieter de Hooch [139] looks newer and less weather-beaten than that painted by Vermeer. The red-brick walls are decorated with austere white pilasters. In the courtyard behind the house a man and a woman sit at a table. She squeezes a piece of lemon above her glass, while he watches with interest, as does the woman standing, who holds a glass of beer in her hand. Pieter de Hooch was possibly alluding to a Dutch proverb: Two beloveds are quite a treat, for after the sour, one takes the sweet.

This painting clearly testifies to the attention De Hooch paid to perspective and spatial effect. The fence on the left forms a diagonal which leads the viewer's gaze into the scene, while the view on the right, with its beam of sunlight on the ground, guides the viewer's gaze further into the background.

PIETER DE HOOCH

In 1652 Pieter de Hooch, who was born in Rotterdam, settled in Delft. He probably received his training in Haarlem in the studio of the landscape painter Nicolaes Berchem. At the beginning of his career De Hooch mainly painted soldiers drinking and playing cards in dark barracks, but after the mid-1650s he switched over to genre pieces in which women often play the principal role. The rendering of sunlight falling into complicated spaces, complete with views through to other rooms, became increasingly important.

During his Delft years De Hooch made around 50 paintings with carefully com-posed interiors such as this. Like many promising young artists in the 17th century, Pieter de Hooch went in 1661 to seek his fortune in Amsterdam, where there were many more potential clients.

INTERIOR

Shortly after moving to Amsterdam, De Hooch began to paint interiors that were remarkable for their precision and refinement, one example of which is the painting *Interior with women beside a linen cupboard*. The lady of the house puts linen back in the cupboard, while the maidservant holds a pile of clean wash. A child plays *kolf* in the doorway. The interior depicted is that of a well-to-do family, as indicated by the magnificent cupboard made of oak with inlaid ebony, the windows and doorway which are framed by ornate pilasters, the paintings on the wall and the statue of the Greek hero Perseus.

De Hooch built his composition out of vertical and horizontal lines and forms, along which he guides the viewer's gaze into the background. Behind the child the entrance hall is visible. The open front door affords a glimpse of the canal and a house on the other side, which De Hooch also rendered with crystal clarity: the white accents of natural stone stand out against the red-brick wall of the house, which was built in early 17th-century Dutch Renaissance style.

De Hooch excelled in the careful application of the rules of perspective, by means of which he obtained a splendid feeling of depth, as well as in his handling of light, which testifies to careful observation. The subdued light in the foreground, which bestows the depiction with warmth, plays over the cupboard and the two women and illuminates the laundry basket. Light from another source falls into the stairwell on the right, whereas bright daylight is seen in the background.

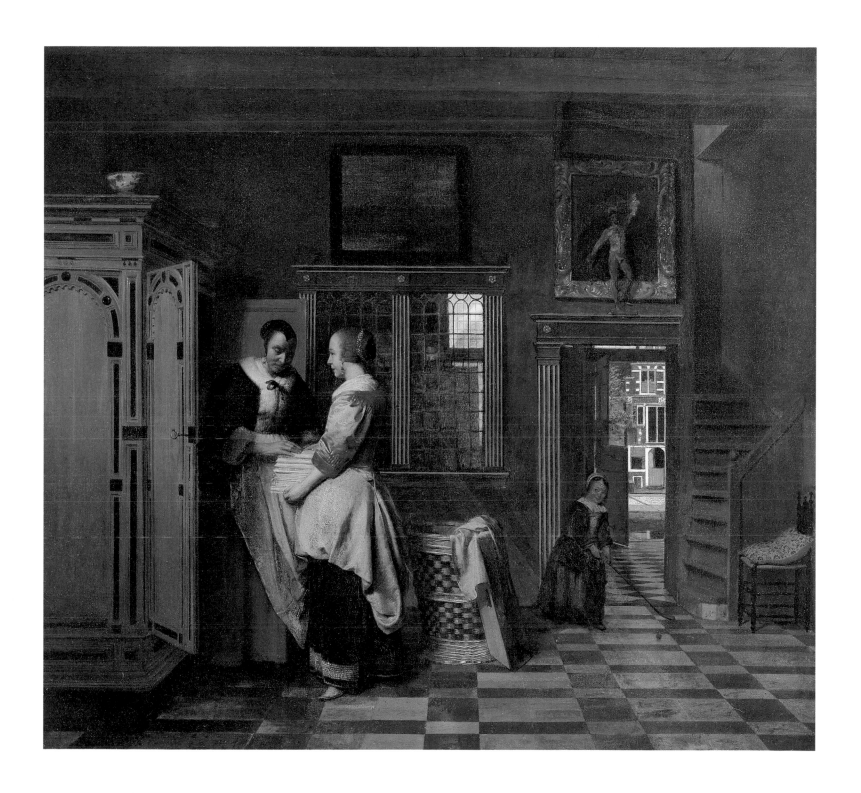

I40

PIETER DE HOOCH (1629-1684)
Interior with women beside
a linen cupboard, 1663
Canvas 70 x 75.5 cm
AMSTERDAM, RIJKSMUSEUM
(on loan from the City of Amsterdam
since 1928, see p. 315)

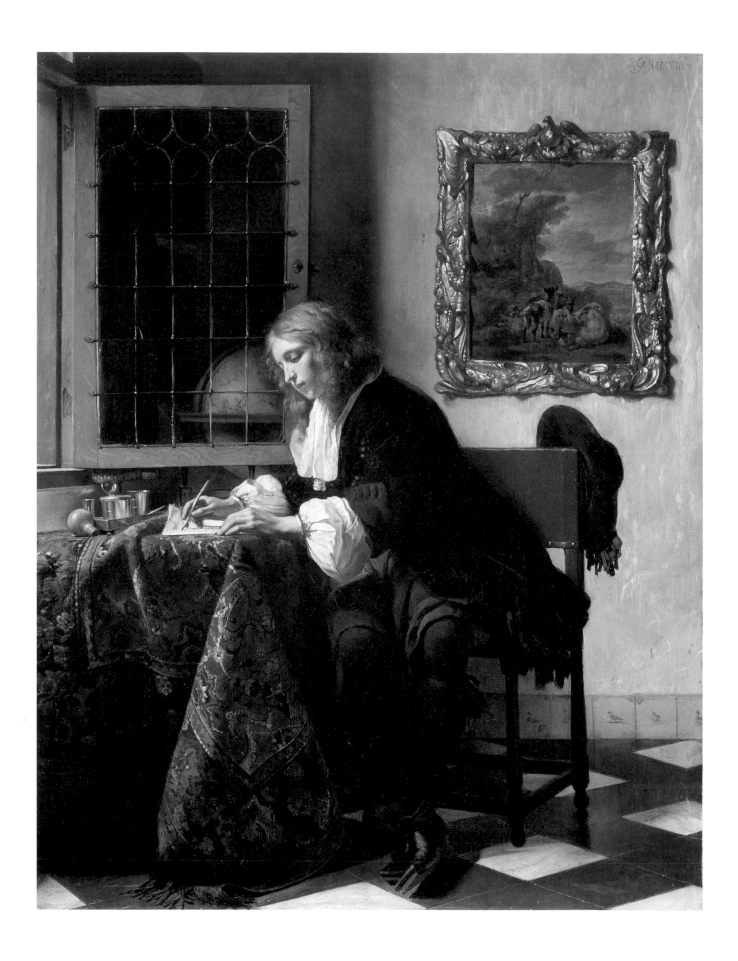

141A

GABRIËL METSU (1629-1667)
Gentleman writing a letter, c. 1662-1665
Panel 52.5 x 40.2 cm
DUBLIN, NATIONAL GALLERY OF IRELAND
(acquired in 1987, see p. 329)

<

LOVE LETTER

These phenomenal masterpieces by Gabriël Metsu clearly belong together, telling a story which is easy to read. On one panel an elegantly dressed man writes a letter, which the young woman in the other painting reads attentively. The influence of Johannes Vermeer and Pieter de Hooch is unmistakable. Although Gabriël Metsu lived in Amsterdam, his familiarity with the Delft school is evidenced by his accurate rendering of natural light, his balanced compositions and his distribution of colour over the picture plane. Metsu's *Gentleman writing a letter* and *Lady reading a letter* both exude the atmosphere of Vermeer and De Hooch.

The silvery daylight lends these two richly furnished interiors a clarity that allows all the details to show to advantage: the man's clothing, the delicacy with which he holds his pen, the silver ink well on the table, the globe standing behind the open window with leaded panes and the gilt Baroque picture frame. The woman puts down her mending to devote her entire attention to the letter, which she holds up to the light. The patiently waiting maid, who holds the letter's wrapper between her fingers, pulls a curtain back to reveal a painting. The seascape with its tempestuous waves probably contains the key to understanding the painting: the letter is a love letter, for love is as fickle as the sea.

Metsu's subtle use of colour is visible in both paintings. A striking element in the painting of the man is the glowing red of the inside of the window frame, which recurs in the red of the Oriental carpet and the back of the chair. In the painting of the woman he again used this colour, but in a more subtle way, on the underside of the sewing pillow lying on the woman's peach-coloured satin dress. The balanced use of colour and the carefully thought-out composition lend an atmosphere of perfect peace to these two masterpieces of the Golden Age.

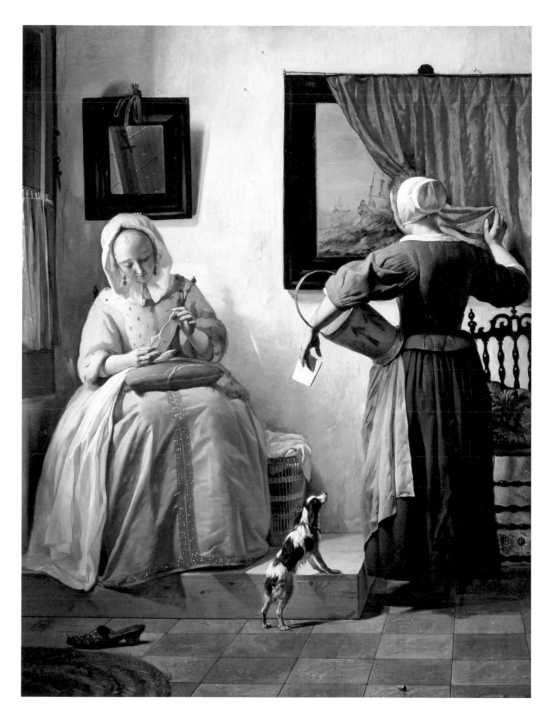

141B

GABRIËL METSU (1629-1667)
Lady reading a letter, c. 1662-1665
Panel 52.5 x 40.2 cm
DUBLIN, NATIONAL GALLERY OF IRELAND
(acquired in 1987, see p. 329)

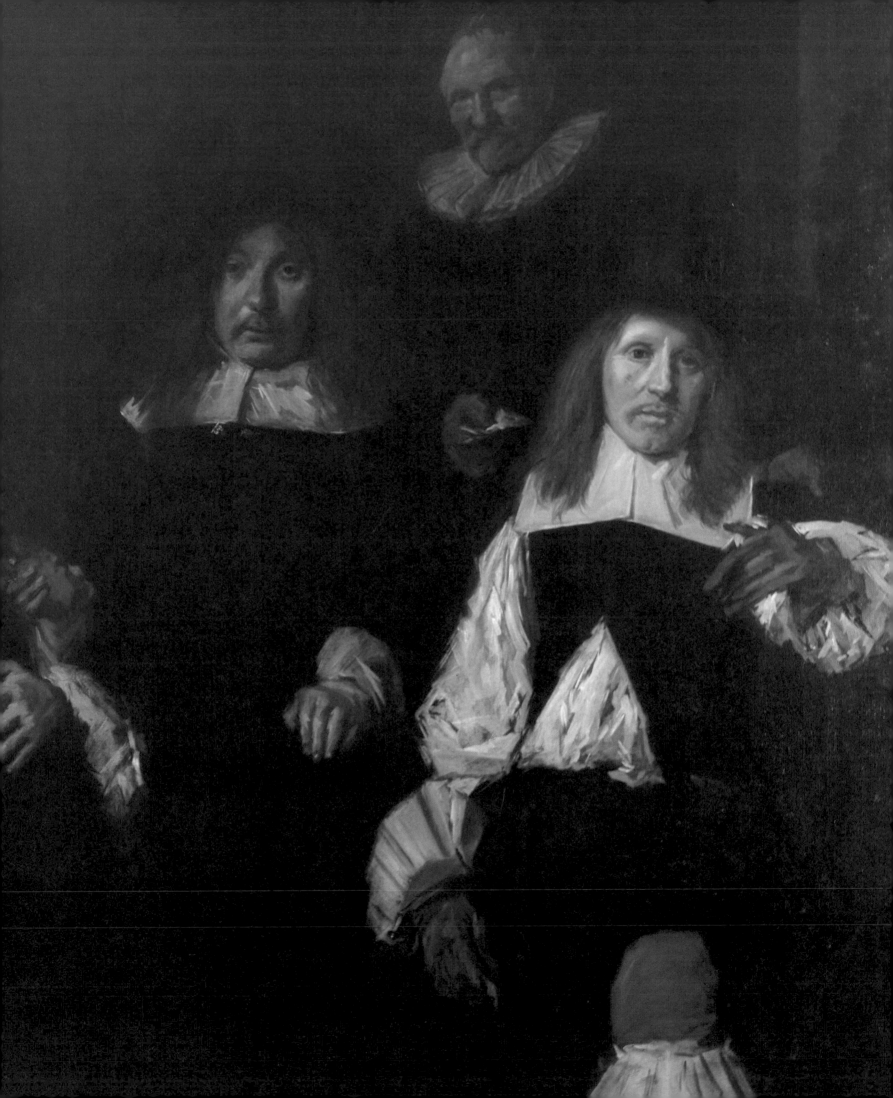

18 REMBRANDT AND FRANS HALS 1650-1670

R EMBRANDT and Frans Hals are the undisputed great masters of the Golden Age. Their work has been described in glowing terms in the hundreds of publications devoted to these two artists. Renowned art historians waxed lyrical in the catalogues appearing at the last retrospectives devoted to Rembrandt and Hals, in 1991 and 1989, respectively. Rembrandt is called a 'giant', whose painting technique was inimitable: '... one gets the impression that it was not the artist who painted but the painting that painted itself, that it appears to be the outcome of a geological process rather than paint applied by a human hand...'. Frans Hals is described as 'the painter whose naturalism breathed new life into Dutch painting'. The group portraits of the regents and regentesses of the Old Men's Almshouse in Haarlem, which he painted when he was in his eighties, are 'the most searching portraits he ever painted'.

Vincent van Gogh voiced his sentiments regarding these two masters in an even more expressive way. He stood 'rooted to the spot' in front of Hals's *Meagre Company* [64], and referring to Rembrandt's *Jewish bride* [148] he wrote: 'Would you believe it – and I honestly mean what I say – I should be happy to give ten years of my life if I could go on sitting here in front of this picture for a fortnight, with only a crust of dry bread for food.'

PHENOMENAL TECHNIQUE

It is these artists' unparalleled painting technique that unleashed this string of superlatives. Although their manner of painting differed on various points, they both achieved magnificent effects by alternating loose, powerful brushstrokes with thin and delicate ones. In the words of 20th-century connoisseurs, Hals painted with 'short strokes of colour' and Rembrandt with 'clots and flakes'.

During the course of their careers, both artists, neither of whose styles had ever been smooth and delicate, began painting in a looser and coarser manner, increasingly leaving out elaborate detail. In the paintings they made towards the end of their lives, they approached their subjects with unerring confidence. From close up, the brushstrokes appear to criss-cross each other randomly, but from a distance the suggestion of form in both artists' work is very convincing. Rembrandt and Hals were both unsurpassed in employing this manner of painting to suggest life and movement on the flat canvas.

REPUTATION

Although nowadays the mastery of Rembrandt and Frans Hals is undisputed, this was not always the case in past centuries. Rembrandt's work was criticised early on: the paint was said to drip off his canvases 'like filth'. Tastes changed, and many had begun to prefer smooth and precisely rendered paintings with uniform illumination. For almost two centuries Hals's paintings in particular were scarcely valued as works of art, and even those who recognised his genius lamented the sloppiness of his workmanship. The English painter and theoretician Sir Joshua Reynolds (1723-1792) admired Hals's ability to portray a 'strong-marked character of individual nature', but found it a pity that Hals had not 'joined to this most difficult part of the art, a patience in finishing what he had so correctly planned'. After 1850 Hals's star rose rapidly, and Rembrandt, whose reputation had never sunk so low as that of Hals, also gained in renown. Both of them ultimately became known as the great masters of the Dutch Golden Age.

< DETAIL OF 146

GIRL AT A WINDOW

Girl at a window is a good example of Rembrandt's transition from fine brushwork to a coarser manner of painting. Her red jacket and white blouse were rendered with broad, accurate brushstrokes. Although the girl looks at the viewer, she nonetheless seems withdrawn and dreamy, leaning slightly forwards out of the window, catching the full light. Rembrandt kept the background dark, underscoring the play of light on her hair, which glances off her cap and turns some of her curls golden. The red of the jacket recurs in her lips and cheeks, as well as in her hair. A girl at a window is a subject that often occurs in Rembrandt's oeuvre. The French painter and art theoretician Roger de Piles (1635-1709), who stayed in Holland in 1693, told an anecdote about a similar painting that Rembrandt had made in 1645. According to De Piles, that work was intended to be a *trompe-l'oeil*. Rembrandt had placed the painting as a joke in front of the window, with the result that passers-by mistook the painted image for Rembrandt's maidservant. Only after several days did they notice that she never changed her position, and the joke was found out. It is not certain whether the girl in the red jacket was meant to be a *trompe-l'oeil*, though it is tempting to think so.

REMBRANDT'S STYLE

The *Self-portrait* by Carel Fabritius, Rembrandt's gifted pupil (see chapter 17), is comparable stylistically with the *Girl at a window*. The wall, as well as his face and hair, were executed with broad brushstrokes. The thickly applied colours – olive green and dark brown – are clearly traceable to Rembrandt. The same is true of the face: like Rembrandt, Fabritius modelled it by alternating areas of light and dark. Strong daylight falls on his forehead and the left side of his face, whereas his eye sockets, chin and the right side of his face are concealed in shadow. Unlike his teacher, Fabritius made less contrast between the figure and the background, so that his lighting seems less theatrical than Rembrandt's.

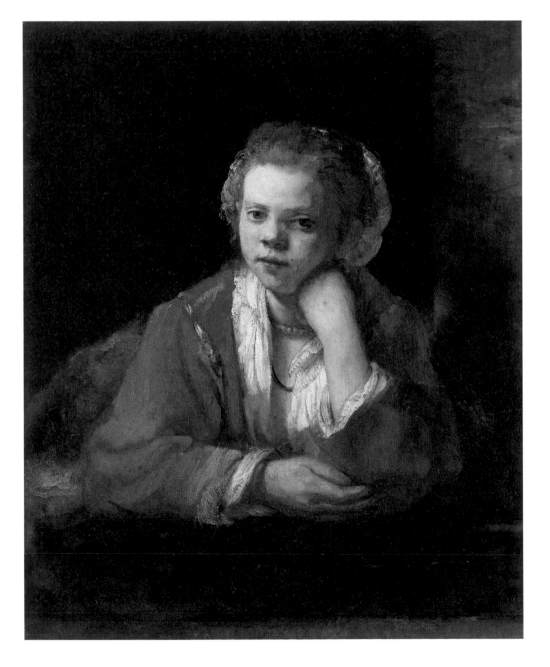

142

REMBRANDT (1606-1669)
Girl at a window, 1651
Canvas 78 x 63 cm
STOCKHOLM, NATIONALMUSEUM
(acquired in 1773, see p. 347)

FABRITIUS

Carel Fabritius probably learned to paint from his father, but by the age of 20 he was working in Rembrandt's workshop, where he most likely executed commissions under the master's name. He had evidently mastered his teacher's style so well that he could function as a stand-in. Fabritius moved several times after completing his training in Amsterdam. In 1650 he was living in Delft, where he helped to lay the foundations of the Delft school of painting. In the self-portrait he made around this time, the young artist looks out confidently at the world. His unfortunate death in 1654 put an abrupt end to the career of this promising and talented artist.

The *Self-portrait* bears witness to Fabritius's original vision as regards this genre. Adopting elements from the various kinds of self-portraits current in the 17th century, he managed to combine them into one convincing composition. A popular type of portrait was that in which the painter presented himself as a well-dressed and authoritative personage, posing in fact as an important patron. Another type of self-portrait showed the painter in his studio, standing in front of a canvas, for example, and dressed in working gear. Fabritius combined the dignity of the first type with the working clothes of the second to produce a sober self-portrait in which he shows neither his surroundings nor his painting implements. The composition of this portrait is also remarkable. The painter placed his face more or less in the centre of the panel, which left a lot of room for the bare, worn wall behind him. In most portraits of this time the head is placed higher in the picture plane.

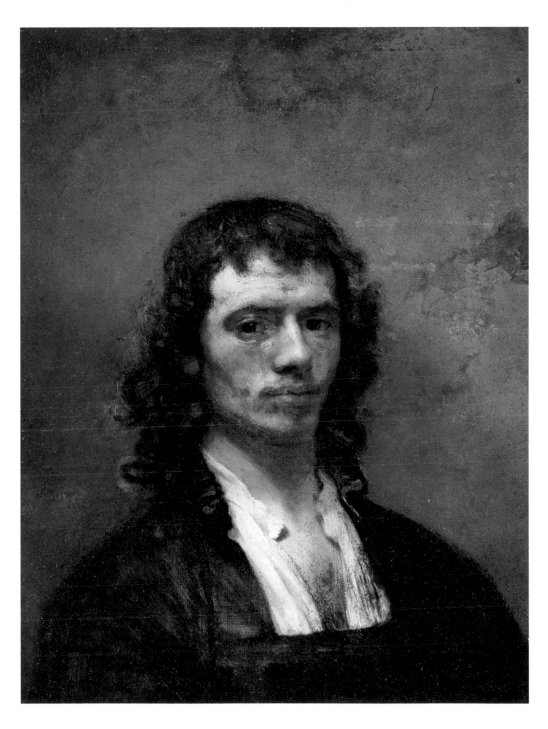

143

CAREL FABRITIUS (1622-1654)

Self-portrait, c. 1648-1650

Panel 65 x 49 cm

ROTTERDAM,

MUSEUM BOIJMANS VAN BEUNINGEN

(acquired in 1847, see p. 345)

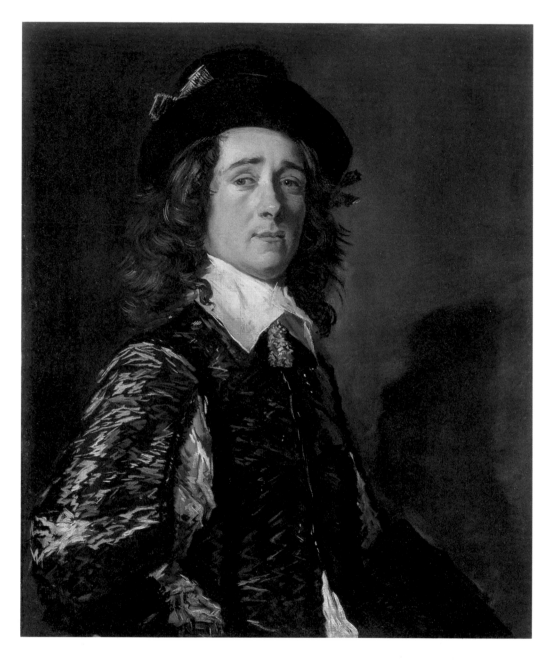

I44
FRANS HALS (1582/1583-1666)
Portrait of Jaspar Schade, c. 1645
Canvas 80 x 67.5 cm
PRAGUE, NÁRODNÍ-GALERIE
(acquired in 1890, see p. 344)

JASPAR SCHADE

The zigzag lines on the sleeve and front of Jaspar Schade's jacket are highly intriguing. Frans Hals rendered in a remarkably effective way the play of light on the folds of the gleaming silk jacket. Above the flat white collar a supercilious gent turns towards the viewer, giving the impression of a self-confident and vain man.

Jaspar Schade came from a patrician family of Utrecht. He was squire of Tull and 't Wael, and later became deacon of the chapter of Oudmunster at Utrecht, representative of the province of Utrecht to the States General and president of the Court at Utrecht. This man of standing had his portrait painted at a young age: he was probably 22 years old at the time. Here Frans Hals proved himself to be a formidable portraitist, possessing psychological insight and the ability to find an original solution to the rendering of materials. Jaspar is dressed according to the latest fashion, and this corresponds to the picture of him given by a letter of 1645, the year in which this portrait was most likely painted, which warns Jaspar's cousin in Paris not to do what Jaspar had done and run up such high tailor bills.

Schade hung this portrait in his country house in the vicinity of Utrecht, where it continued to hang until well into the 19th century, even though the house had long since passed out of the family's possession. Each subsequent owner had bought the painting along with the house: according to legend, the house would collapse if the painting were removed. In 1865 the owner had the courage to sell the painting, on the condition that the buyer have a copy made of the portrait, to ensure Jaspar Schade's continued presence in the house.

145

REMBRANDT (1606-1669)
Portrait of Titus, c. 1653-1655
Canvas 77 x 63 cm
ROTTERDAM,
MUSEUM BOIJMANS VAN BEUNINGEN
(acquired with the aid of the Rembrandt
Society in 1940, see p. 345)

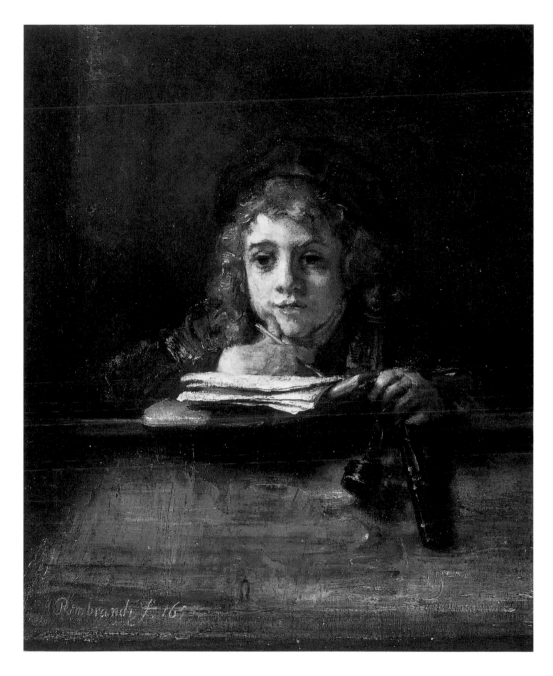

TITUS

The pensive young man behind the lectern is approximately 14 years old. He is Rembrandt's son, Titus, who was born in September 1641. He was the fourth child born to Rembrandt and his wife Saskia Uylenburgh; the first son and two daughters all died within months after birth. Less than a year after the birth of Titus, Saskia died, and Geertje Dircks came to care for little Titus in Rembrandt's house on the Jodenbreestraat. The relationship between Rembrandt and Geertje developed to the extent that a promise of marriage was made, but Rembrandt broke his promise and had Geertje locked up in the *Spinhuis*, a House of Correction for women. In the meantime he had started a relationship with Hendrickje Stoffels, with whom he shared his life until she died in 1663. Titus married in 1668, but died in the same year; his daughter Titia was born half a year after his death. Rembrandt did not live to celebrate her first birthday; he died on 4 October 1669.

The portrait Rembrandt made of his son captures the intimacy of domestic life. Titus is sunk in thought, staring out over his papers. The thumb of his right hand jabs his cheek; the pen in that hand is temporarily out of use. His pencil case dangles from his left hand. It seems that Titus is occupied with a writing exercise, his momentary musing having been captured with a couple of unerring brushstrokes by his father.

The portrait of Titus is a beautiful example of Rembrandt's skill at composing a painting. The white of the paper on which Titus's hand rests recurs in a subtle way in the glimmer of light on his right sleeve and in his hair. Titus's carmine red cap and sleeves provide colourful accents in a solid composition. The portrait is set in a triangle, the bottom half of which is taken up by the front of the lectern.

In the lower left on a loosely painted area scratched with a palette knife, Rembrandt's name is legible. Examinations have revealed that Rembrandt did not place it there himself. It is not known when or by whom his name was added, but there is no doubt whatsoever that this exceptionally fine portrait of the artist's son was done entirely by Rembrandt's own hand.

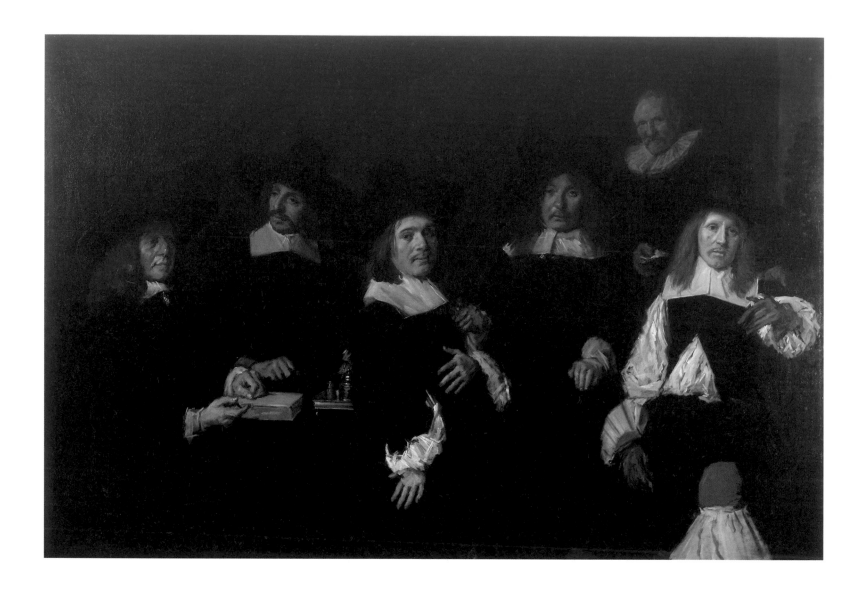

REGENTS

The breathtaking, red-stockinged knee of a fashionably dressed regent forms a surprising and daring element in the *Portrait of the regents of the Old Men's Almshouse in Haarlem*, which was executed primarily in shades of black and white.

When Frans Hals made this painting, around 1664, he was more than 80 years old, yet there is no sign here of a washed-out octogenarian, as witnessed by his sure touch and original style. With a minimum of contours and only a few rapid brushstrokes, he succeeded in suggesting such striking details as hands and gloves.

As in all of Hals's portraits, this regents' portrait also bears witness to his tendency towards the informal. The man, for example, with the crooked hat, lank hair and tired eyes makes a remarkably nonchalant and mercilessly realistic impression. Nevertheless, this portrait must have met with his patrons' satisfaction, as they are not known to have voiced any criticism.

OLD MEN'S ALMSHOUSE

The regents' portrait is still to be found in its original place in the Old Men's Almshouse in Haarlem, which is now the Frans Hals Museum. The Old Men's Almshouse was built at the beginning of the 17th century, offering a home to some 60 old men. In order to be admitted, one had to be at least 60 years old, a bachelor

146

FRANS HALS (1582/1583-1666)
The regents of the Old Men's Almshouse in Haarlem, c. 1664
Canvas 172.5 x 256 cm
HAARLEM, FRANS HALSMUSEUM
(on loan from the City of Haarlem since 1862, see p. 331)

or a widower, a resident of the city and, moreover, known to have led a virtuous life. The Old Men's Almshouse was not meant for the poorest people. Upon taking up residence, the men were expected to bring along a few essentials: a bed, three blankets,

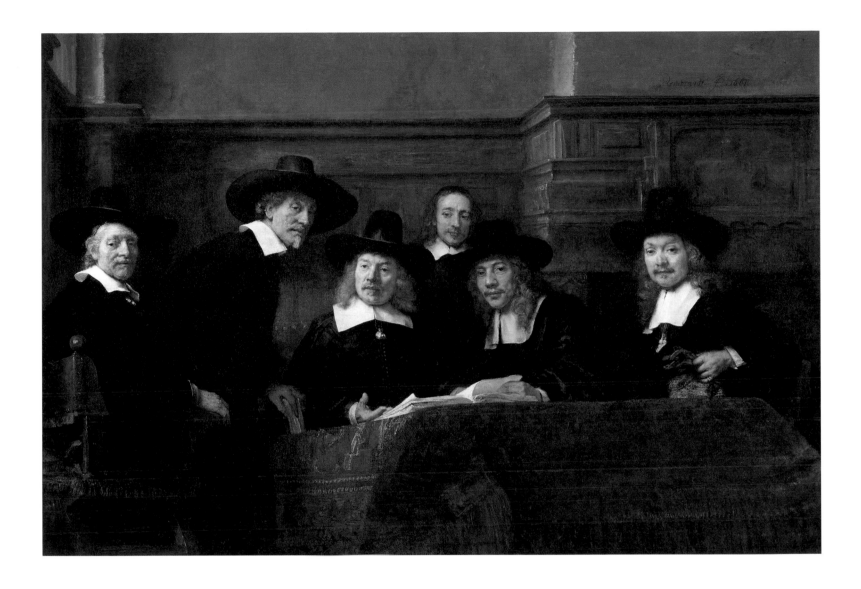

two pillows, six sheets, six pillowcases, six nightcaps, twelve shirts, a chair with a cushion, a curtain with a valance and two guilders.

Frans Hals painted portraits of both the regents and the regentesses of the Old Men's Almshouse. These two portraits were Hals's last important commissions. He died two years later.

THE SYNDICS
A couple of years before Frans Hals made his regents' portraits, Rembrandt painted his portrait of *The syndics*, which was to be his last large group portrait. The Amsterdam drapers' guild commissioned Rembrandt to paint a portrait of their sampling officials

and their manservant, the man without a hat. Sampling officials were responsible for supervising the quality of dyed worsted, a thickly woven woollen fabric, and for this purpose they used sample pieces of cloth. The officials met three times a week to carry out their inspections; careful supervision was necessary to ensure that only worsted of the highest quality was traded in Amsterdam. These men held their posts for one year, from Good Friday to Good Friday. The sampling officials in office from 1661 to 1662 were, from left to right, Jacob van Loon, Volckert Janszoon, Willem van Doeyenburg, Jochem de Neve and Aernout van der Mye. Their manservant was Frans Hendrickszoon Bel.

147
REMBRANDT (1606-1669)
The syndics, 1662
Canvas 191.5 x 279 cm
AMSTERDAM, RIJKSMUSEUM
(on loan from the City of Amsterdam
since 1808, see p. 310)

STAALHOF
The portrait was intended for the Staalhof, the building in the Staalstraat in Amsterdam where the drapers had their headquarters and the cloth was tested. The panelling that Rembrandt painted behind the sampling officials probably corresponds to the

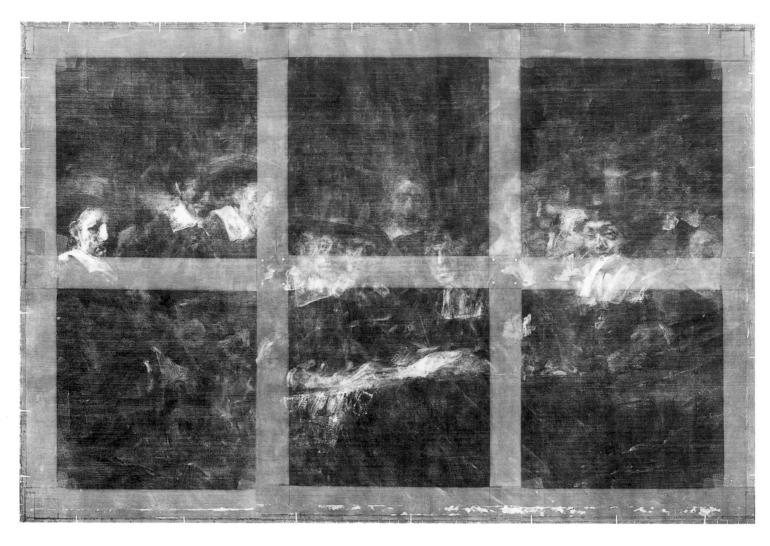

X-RADIOGRAPH OF 147

building's interior. The portrait's measure-ments had been determined beforehand, as well as the place where it would hang – rather high, above the panelling. These stipulations, with which Rembrandt was required to comply, explain the striking perspective, whereby the table is seen from a point slightly below. The strong light falling into the room from the left could mean the presence of a window there.

Rembrandt was also required to keep to a prescribed formula: the sampling officials had to be seated and their manservant was supposed to stand. These rules were not strictly observed by Rembrandt: the man second from the left, Volckert Janszoon, is in motion. Rembrandt portrayed him in the

act of either standing up or sitting down, in this way preventing the portrait from becoming stiff or boring, as it would be with five men in a row, all wearing hats. From x-radiographs it emerges that Rembrandt wrestled with this problem during the paint-ing process. The half-standing man was originally standing upright; only later did Rembrandt turn him into a half-bent figure. The manservant was also shifted around, having first stood at the far right.

LIGHTHOUSE

Rembrandt signed the painting on the table-cloth, using dots that make it seem as though his signature is woven into the deep-red cloth. The signature and date have

faded and become less legible. In the 18th century a second signature was placed at the upper right, where the date reads 1661. Rembrandt himself, however, gave *The syndics* the date 1662.

Directly below the falsified signature hangs a painting, framed by the panelling, depicting a lighthouse with beacons. This picture symbolises vigilance, a quality that sampling officials must possess in great measure. Revealing in this respect is the gesture of Van Doeyenburg, the third offi-cial from the left, who, with palm upwards and thumb raised, wants to emphasise the reasonableness and honesty of his opinion on the quality of the cloth.

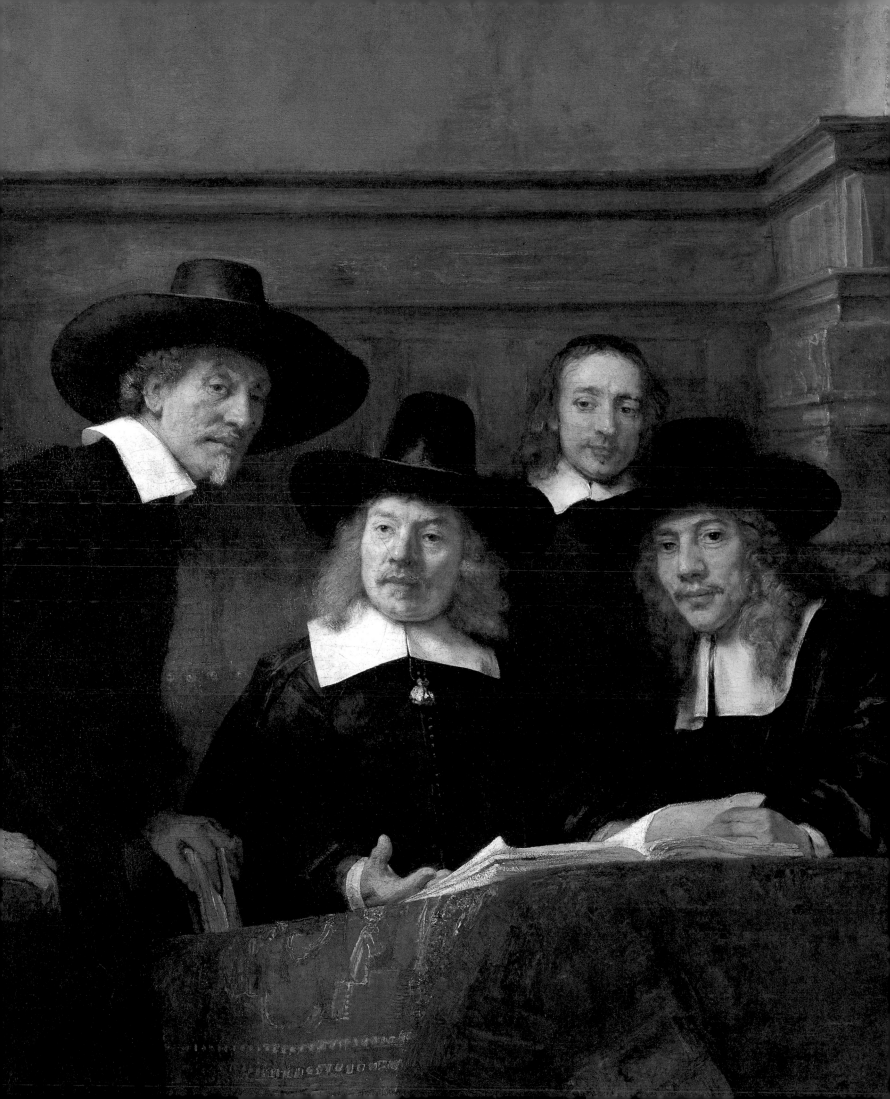

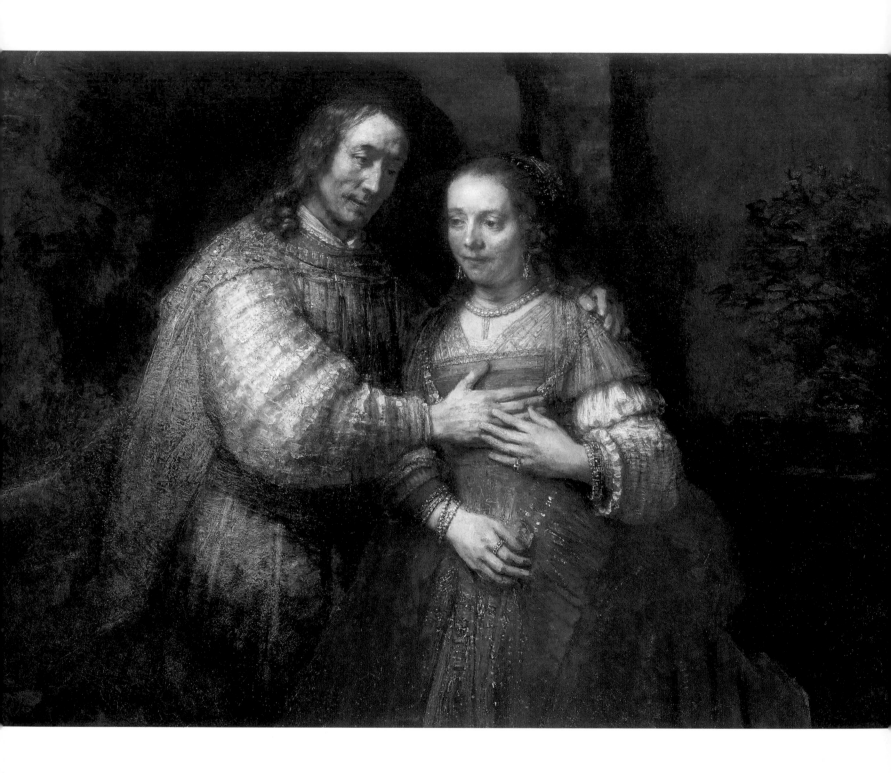

148

REMBRANDT (1606-1669)

Isaac and Rebecca

('The Jewish bride'), c. 1665

Canvas 121.5 x 166.5 cm

AMSTERDAM, RIJKSMUSEUM

(on loan from the City of Amsterdam

since 1885, see p. 312)

THE JEWISH BRIDE

If it is the unique composition that attracts one's attention in *The syndics*, in *The Jewish bride* the first thing one notices is the unbelievably rich and varied handling of paint. The painting provides a distinct sampling of painting techniques. The faces and hands, consisting of thin layers of paint of various colours, were painted in a rather smooth and restrained way. The paint on the man's sleeve, on the other hand, is rough, lumpy and thickly applied. Here the master possibly used a palette knife, with which he pressed the paint onto the canvas, scraping it off again in places. With a few brushstrokes and streaks of paint, Rembrandt rendered the costly materials such as the transparent fabric around the woman's shoulders. In a few places the artist made scratches in the paint, such as on the left next to the man's arm. Rembrandt thus used paint not only for its colour – deep red, bronze-green and golden ochre – but also to lend texture to the painting.

LOVING SCENE

It is a loving scene, depicting a man embracing a woman. Whether it takes place in an interior or out of doors is not entirely clear. The woman leans against a wall or balustrade; a plant is seen on her right, though otherwise the background remains vague. The emphasis is on the sumptuously dressed couple. At first glance it is not clear who this man and woman represent.

The title of the painting dates from the 19th century. The facial expressions and the gesture of the hands have led to many speculations as to the couple's identity. Is it a father escorting his daughter to her wedding – the Jewish bride – or is it a loving couple, either contemporary or biblical?

Nowadays they are assumed to represent the biblical couple Isaac and Rebecca. The source of this attribution is a drawing from which the context of the depiction may be deduced. The drawing depicts a passage from *Genesis* (26:6-7), in which Isaac and Rebecca are unmasked as a married couple. Isaac, son of Abraham, was staying at that time in the land of the Philistines: '...and the men of the place asked him of his wife; and he said, She is my sister: for he feared to say, She is my wife; lest, said he, the men of the place should kill me for Rebecca; because she was fair to look upon.' One day, however, King Abimelech looked out the window and saw 'brother and sister' in a loving embrace. He asked the couple for an explanation and then offered Isaac and Rebecca protection. In the drawing Rembrandt sketched a man and woman on a bench, being spied on from a window.

Rembrandt did not depict these surroundings in his painting. He portrayed both figures from close up, three-quarter-length, concentrating in this way on the two persons. It is possible that a married couple had their portraits painted as Isaac and Rebecca: such *portraits historiés* were popular in those days. No matter what their identity, Rembrandt portrayed this couple lovingly in a masterly painting.

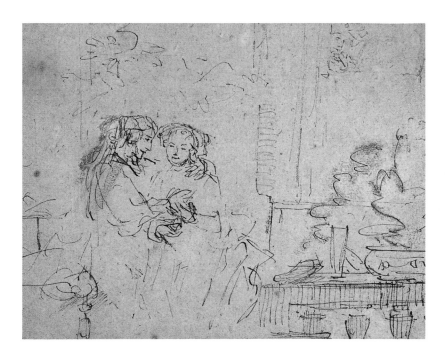

REMBRANDT (1606-1669), *Isaac and Rebecca spied on by Abimelech*,
c. 1655-1656. Pen and ink, 14.5 x 18.5 cm. PRIVATE COLLECTION

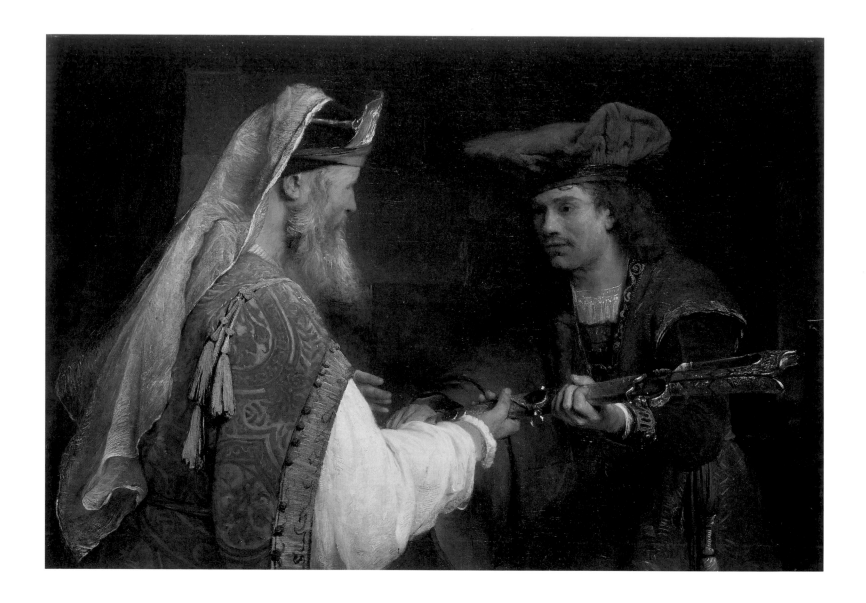

149

AERT DE GELDER (1645-1727)

Ahimelech giving the sword of
Goliath to David, c. 1680-1690

Canvas 90 x 132 cm

LOS ANGELES, THE J. PAUL GETTY MUSEUM

(acquired in 1960, see p. 338)

ARENT DE GELDER

Around 1661 Arent de Gelder went to
Amsterdam to complete his training with
Rembrandt. There he would have seen the
master working on a painting like *The*
syndics. After his apprenticeship De Gelder
returned to his home town, Dordrecht,
where he continued to paint in the master's
style. While most of Rembrandt's pupils
turned, during the course of their careers, to
a smoother and more elegant style of painting, De Gelder remained faithful to his great
example until the end of his life. Like
Rembrandt, he used the handle of his brush
to make scratches in the wet paint, a palette
knife to lay the paint on thickly and distrib-

ute it over the canvas, and his fingers to
smear the paint around or wipe it off. De
Gelder left no technique untried in his
striving to achieve the desired effect.

THE SWORD OF GOLIATH

De Gelder followed his master not only in
painting technique, but also in his attention
to costumes and accessories. He built up a
collection of robes, head-coverings, armour
and weapons, all of which he used in his
biblical representations. It seems as though
De Gelder expended all his energy painting
glittering fabrics with splendid patterns and
embroidery: the deftly painted costumes
show to advantage when contrasted with the

facial expressions and poses of his characters, which are not always portrayed with equal skill. In his depiction of *Ahimelech giving the sword of Goliath to David* he portrayed the greenish tassels on the priest's back in a fascinating way. The pattern in the grey-green robe and the sword also testify to De Gelder's concentration on the rendering of materials. Here De Gelder portrayed a rather unknown biblical story. *I Samuel* 21 tells the story of David, who, poor and alone, was fleeing from King Saul. He took refuge with the priest Ahimelech, whom he asked for bread and a sword with which to defend himself, upon which the priest gave David the sword of the giant Goliath. Using his favourite composition, De Gelder depicted the moment at which the sword was handed over, portraying two half-length figures against a dark, neutral background. This intimate scene is one of the high points of De Gelder's oeuvre.

DE LAIRESSE

Even at the end of his life Rembrandt made impressive portraits. This less than handsome man [150] is his fellow painter Gerard de Lairesse (see chapter 24). De Lairesse greatly admired Rembrandt's technique at first – it is no coincidence that he posed for him – but later rejected his work on art-theoretical grounds, characterising Rembrandt's rough manner of painting as 'daubing'.

Gerard de Lairesse's portrait was painted when he was 24 years old. The fashionably dressed man sits in front of a table, holding some papers in his hand. There is nothing to indicate that this man is an artist. Rembrandt made no attempt to flatter his model; he portrayed De Lairesse with his outward imperfections. It was more usual for portrait painters to camouflage their models' flaws, without of course losing sight of the likeness they were meant to be portraying. Painting portraits required the artist to perform a constant balancing act between striving for as close a likeness as possible

and embellishing the plain truth. If De Lairesse had wanted an idealised portrait, then Rembrandt was not the man to ask. The result, however, was a powerful and probing painting.

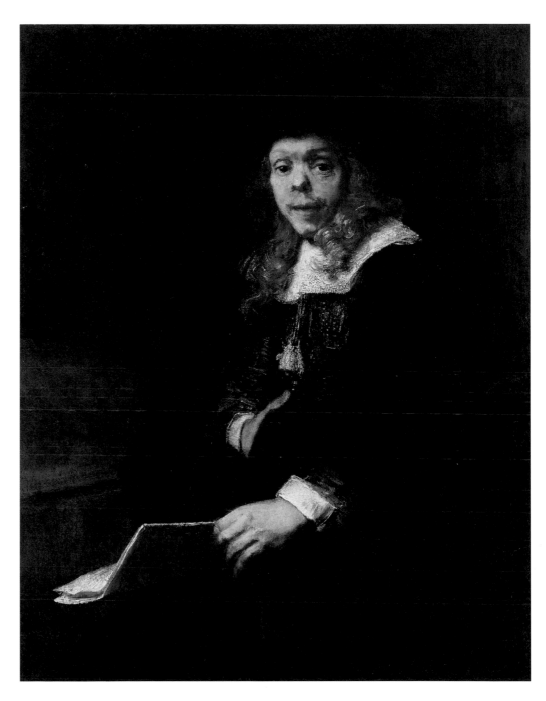

150
REMBRANDT (1606-1669)
Portrait of Gerard de Lairesse,
c. 1665-1667
Canvas 112.7 x 87.6 cm
NEW YORK, THE METROPOLITAN MUSEUM
OF ART, ROBERT LEHMAN COLLECTION
(acquired in 1975, see p. 342)

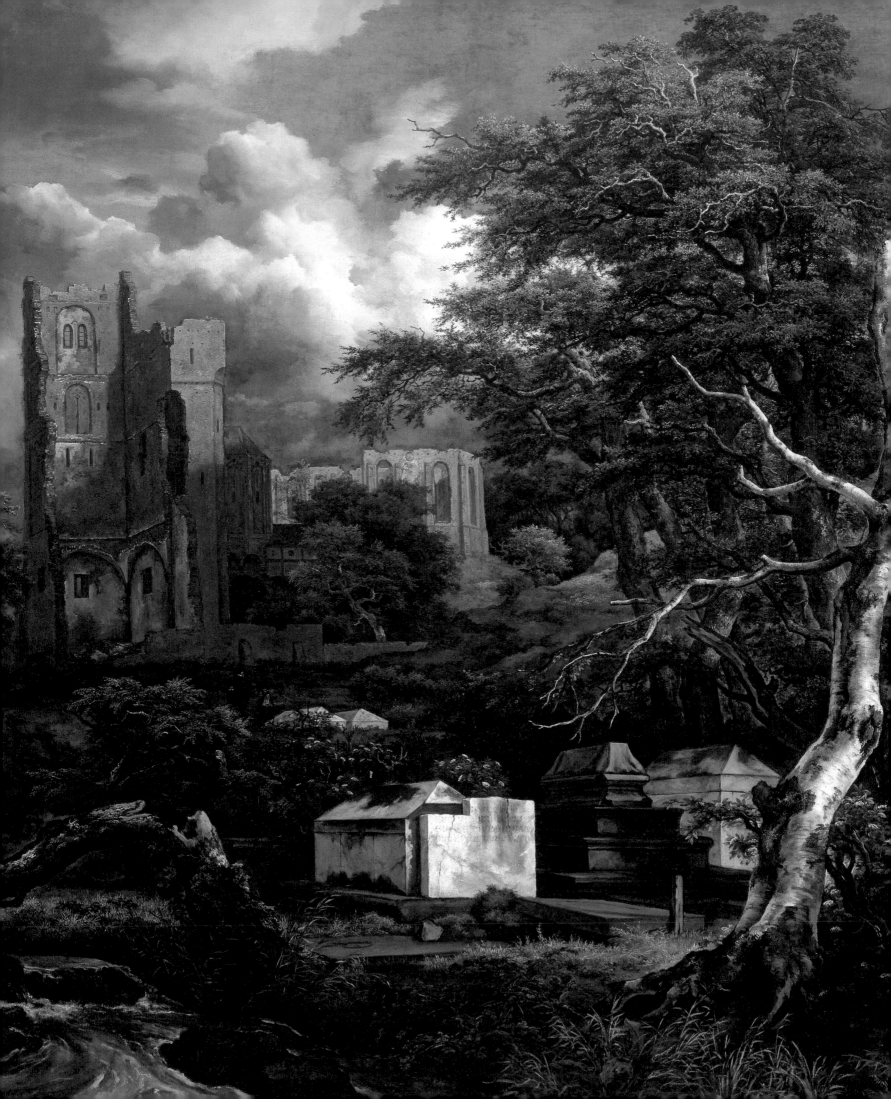

19 MASTERS OF LANDSCAPE 1650-1670

In the mid-17th century the limited, somewhat pale palette of subdued colours that characterised early 17th-century landscape painting started to make way for a more varied and powerful use of colour. Sharper contrasts between light and dark, more vibrant colours and more robust forms began to appear in the compositions of young landscape painters, such as Aelbert Cuyp and Jacob van Ruisdael. These new masters, whose works determined the face of Dutch landscape painting, created a manner of painting that was both magnificent and monumental.

INNOVATORS

Aelbert Cuyp of Dordrecht and Philips Koninck of Amsterdam provided the stimulus for these innovations in landscape painting, but the greatest innovator was Jacob van Ruisdael. He lent grandeur to groups of trees or to architecture in a landscape by adopting a low viewpoint, dramatic illumination and vivid colours. In *The Jewish cemetery* Ruisdael leads the viewer's gaze upwards to the imposing ruin of the church, and focuses attention on the tomb by illuminating it brightly against the dark background. In this way he was able to dramatise recognisable locations, his predilection for dark colours serving to heighten the dramatic effect. Ruisdael's skies are always covered with clouds, with the sun breaking through in a few places. Ruisdael portrayed both flat Dutch landscapes and mountainous, foreign-looking landscapes. Until that time artists had painted mostly charming landscapes; Ruisdael's were heroic and must have made quite an impression.

POWERFUL COMPOSITIONS

The vast, sun-drenched landscapes of Aelbert Cuyp represent the transition from the tonal landscapes of Jan van Goyen, for example, to the grandiose work of Jacob van Ruisdael. Cuyp's landscapes combine a poetic atmosphere with a powerful composition, often bestowing animals with a fully fledged role in the depiction.

Cuyp could characterise animals with amazing exactitude, as witnessed by his *River landscape with horsemen* [151]. The silvery-white grey horse and the cows, for example, are more convincingly rendered than the people. In 1897 the poet Jan Veth – like Cuyp, a native of Dordrecht – described Cuyp's cows as follows: 'His cows are not dozy, good-natured beasts who do nothing but eat and rustically chew their cud; they are bold, robust beings who stick up their snouts and bellow to the skies.'

In the 17th century Cuyp's landscapes were imitated by only one or two artists, but in the 18th century they became very popular. In England Cuyp was all the rage, resulting in whole shiploads of his paintings being exported to England. This was also the fate of his *River landscape*, which the Rijksmuseum was fortunately able to buy in 1965 from its English owner.

CLOUD-FILLED SKIES

The 17th-century Dutch landscape painters are famous for their cloud-filled skies. It is indeed remarkable that they portrayed clouds in such a strikingly conspicuous way: some artists almost went so far as to make the sky the subject of their paintings. In the early 19th century the sky was once again treated as an essential part of the painted landscape, and the Dutch example must have played an important role in this revival. The English painter John Constable (1776-1837), for example, made sketches in oil with studies of clouds, many of which have been preserved.

Some 17th-century painters made very true-to-life depictions of clouds, but neglected to combine them with the rest of the picture in a convincing way. Hendrick Avercamp [17], for example, painted people skating merrily beneath a threatening sky, and Jacob van Ruisdael combined a sunset with a sky full of fleecy clouds, just the sort that disappear around sunset [153].

< DETAIL OF 155

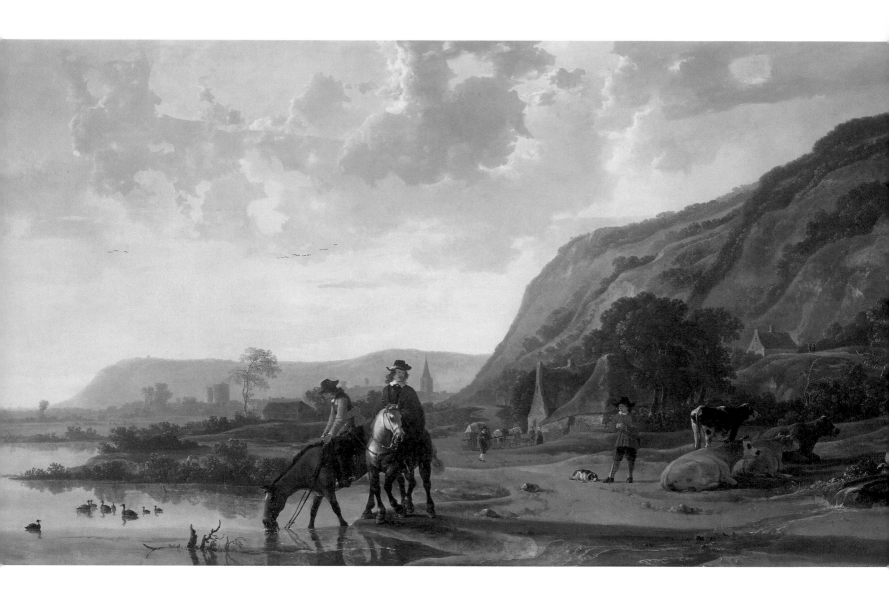

RIVER LANDSCAPE

A hazy, sun-drenched river landscape is
edged by steep hills. A horseman lets his
horse drink, watched by a shepherd with
some cows and sheep. The sun is low on
the horizon, casting long shadows over the
land, while the golden glow of the sunlight
creates a warm atmosphere. Aelbert Cuyp's
powerfully composed landscapes are usually
bathed in this un-Dutch golden light. The
19th-century French art critic Eugène
Fromentin aptly described Cuyp's ability
'to paint the light and to render the
pleasant and invigorating sensation caused
by a warm atmosphere which envelops
and penetrates us.' Cuyp could only have
observed this typically Southern light in the
work of the Italianate painters (see chapter
13). Cuyp himself never made the trip to
Italy, but the work of Jan Both, who returned from Italy in 1641, unmistakably
influenced Cuyp [see 94]. The *River landscape with horsemen* has been identified as
the hilly area between Nijmegen and Kleve.
In 1652 Cuyp took a trip along the Rhine to
Kleve, and the drawings he made at that
time formed the basis for this painting.

151

AELBERT CUYP (1620-1691)
River landscape with horsemen, c. 1655
Canvas 128 x 227.5 cm
AMSTERDAM, RIJKSMUSEUM
(acquired with the aid of the Rembrandt Society
in 1965, see p. 317)

152

PHILIPS KONINCK (1619-1688)
Panorama with farmhouses along a road, 1655
Canvas 133 x 167.5 cm
AMSTERDAM, RIJKSMUSEUM
(acquired with the aid of the Rembrandt Society
in 1967, see p. 317)

>

PANORAMA

Between 1650 and 1665 Philips Koninck painted panoramic landscapes whose composition and focus on the cloudy sky are comparable with Ruisdael's paintings of the bleaching fields near Haarlem. In *Panorama with farmhouses along a road*, he painted a magnificent view of a river landscape, seen from a high vantage point. The horizon, which lies slightly below the middle of the picture, is not interrupted by trees, church towers or the silhouette of a city. The painting is composed of horizontal strips, emphasised by the long bands of shadow falling on the land. It was inspired by the countryside in the province of Gelderland, even though this flat river landscape probably did not exist exactly in this form. The country road on the left leads the viewer's gaze past the farmhouses further into the picture, where a city looms up behind the bridge. More towards the background a river meanders through the landscape as far as the eye can see. Here and there Koninck added a person, such as the fisherman at the lake shore in the foreground, who has just had a bite: the glistening fish thrashes about on the line.

Koninck painted the landscape with small brushstrokes and thickly applied paint; the sky, on the other hand, is very thinly applied. This loose manner of painting, in which the brushstrokes are visible, is reminiscent of Rembrandt. His palette, with its many earthy shades of brown and the occasional red accent – such as the red roof tiles and the red jacket of the fisherman – also betrays Rembrandt's influence. Koninck was possibly a pupil of Rembrandt, though this has not been verified. The two artists were certainly acquainted, however, and it is obvious that Rembrandt's work, like that of Hercules Seghers [81], was of great importance for Koninck.

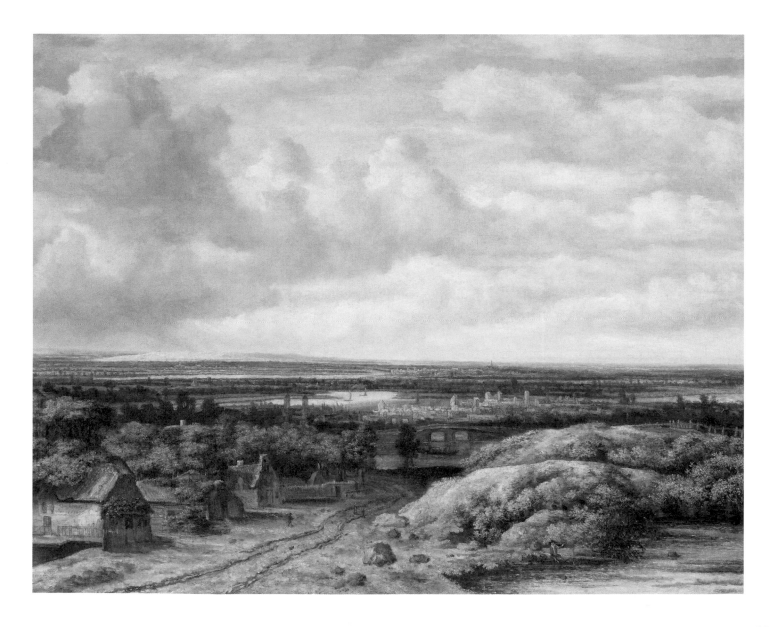

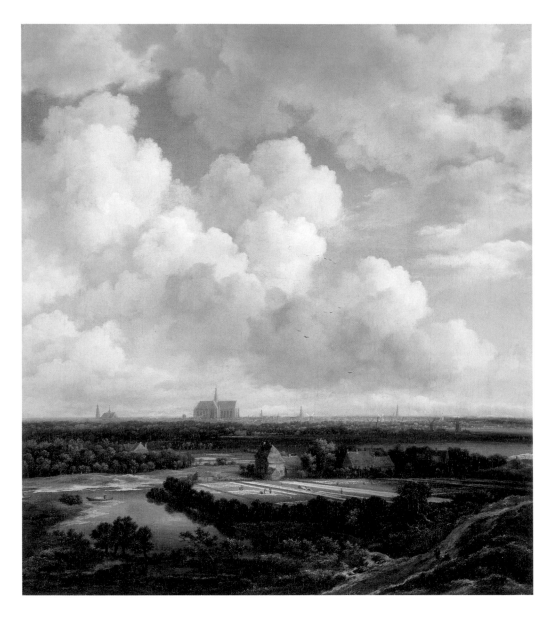

153

JACOB VAN RUISDAEL (1628/1629-1682)
View of Haarlem with bleaching fields,
c. 1670
Canvas 62.2 x 55.2 cm
ZÜRICH, KUNSTHAUS,
STIFTUNG PROF. DR. L. RUZICKA
(acquired in 1949, see p. 350)

SMALL VIEWS OF HAARLEM

Jacob van Ruisdael was a versatile landscape painter, who painted wooded landscapes, rushing waterfalls, landscapes with ruins, Dutch panoramas, cityscapes, and a few seascapes and dune landscapes. An unparalleled panorama is his view of the bleaching fields near Haarlem, which he made around 1670. These *Haarlempjes* ('little views of Haarlem'), as these works by Ruisdael were called in the 17th century, provide apt characterisations of the Dutch landscape with its beautiful cloud formations. In this landscape, in which the Haarlem Church of St Bavo is visible in the background, the painter used light and colour to introduce variation. The pieces of linen lying in the water and on the fields are gleaming in the sun. Bleaching linen was an important industry in Haarlem, and the poetic picture painted by Ruisdael was a sight often seen in those days.

WINDMILL

Just as in the *Bleaching fields near Haarlem*, in his depiction of *The windmill at Wijk bij Duurstede* Ruisdael made use of a low horizon, which left a lot of room for the threatening sky. Here and there the sunlight pierces the clouds, lending a yellow hue to the stone windmill. Shadows from the clouds are cast on the water. The three women also catch the light, as does the sailing boat on the water. Ruisdael placed the windmill on a hilly rise and rendered the view of it from below, thereby giving the simple stone windmill a majestic aspect.

Here Ruisdael probably depicted the calm before the storm. The boat's sails hang straight down, the water is calm and the windmill's sails seem to stand still. The calm will soon be over, though; the threatening sky signals an oncoming storm.

154

JACOB VAN RUISDAEL (1628/1629-1682)
The windmill at Wijk bij Duurstede, c. 1670
Canvas 83 x 101 cm
AMSTERDAM, RIJKSMUSEUM
(on loan from the City of Amsterdam
since 1885, see p. 312)

DATING

It is uncertain whether the windmill Ruisdael painted still exists. In the 17th century there were two windmills quite close to each other, only one of which has survived. It is not known which one Ruisdael depicted. The late medieval castle of Wijk, to the left of the windmill in the painting, no longer exists, whereas the truncated tower of St Martin's Church is still standing. This church was the key not only to identifying the location but also to dating the painting: archival documents state that the tower was provided with a clock in 1668. The painting, in which a clock-face is visible, could not have been painted before that year. It is now dated to around 1670.

The spot where Ruisdael painted the three women was actually the site of the *Vrouwen Poort*, or 'Women's Gate'. Ruisdael replaced this gate with the women, enabling him to devote more attention to the windmill, which otherwise would have been largely obscured by the gate.

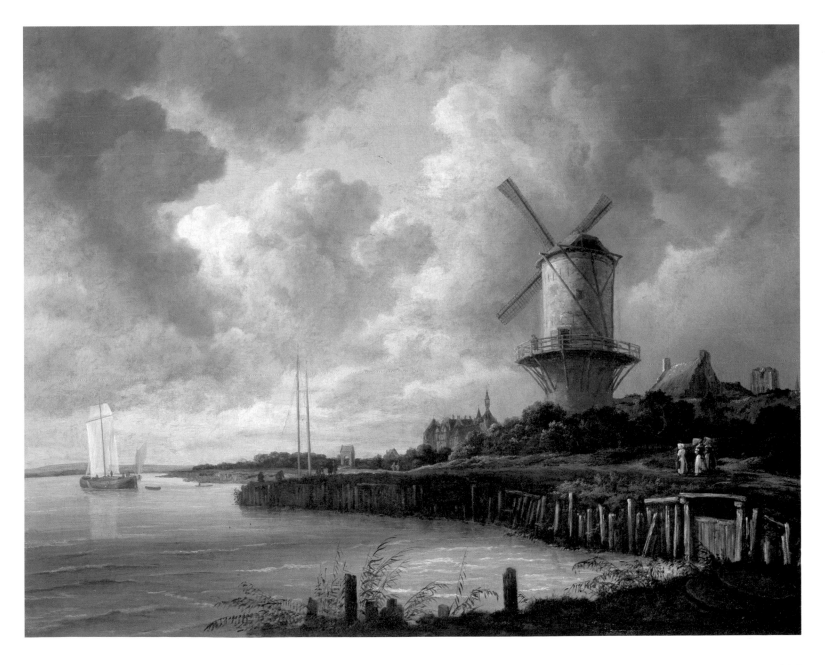

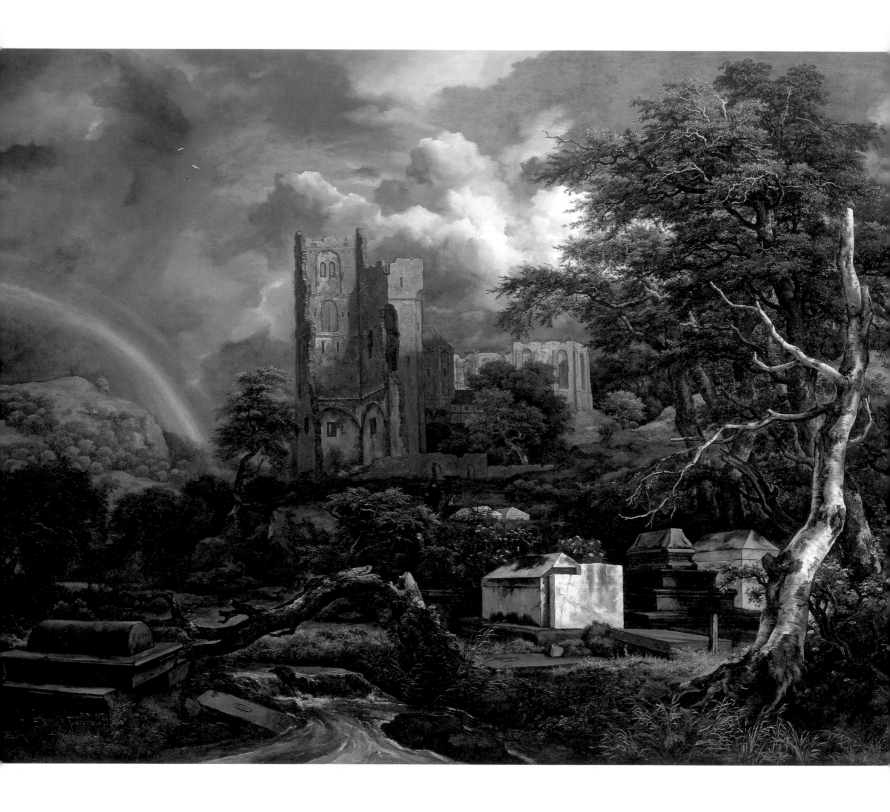

155

Jacob van Ruisdael (1628/1629-1682)

The Jewish cemetery, c. 1660-1670

Canvas 141 x 182.9 cm

Detroit, The Detroit Institute of Arts

(acquired in 1926, see p. 326)

THE JEWISH CEMETERY

A dead, broken-off tree lies across a rushing stream which flows through a hilly landscape. Here and there in the landscape lie tombs, surrounded by trees and vegetation. In the centre, on higher ground, stands a ruin, above which dark clouds gather. A rainbow appears on the left. Jacob van Ruisdael's *Jewish cemetery* portrays an intriguing and dramatic scene. The tombs depicted here are still to be seen at Ouderkerk on the river Amstel near Amsterdam, where the Portuguese-Jewish cemetery Beth Haim has been located since 1616.

The large, white marble tomb in the foreground is that of Eliahu Montalto, a well-known physician who died in 1616. Next to his tomb stands a sarcophagus whose reddish marble is so elaborately worked that it seems as though a cloth has been draped over the tomb. This is the grave of Issak Uziel, who died in 1622, next to whom lies Israel Abraham Mendez, who died in 1627. The other tombs are also identifiable.

Ruisdael made two on-site drawings, which display a fairly accurate rendering of the tombs. The other elements in the painting were his own additions. The tombs are situated in a hilly landscape, for example, whereas in reality the cemetery can be said at most to be on slightly uneven terrain. A rushing mountain stream does not actually flow alongside or through the cemetery, and the ruins, in fact, never stood at Ouderkerk on the Amstel. Ruisdael was not interested in a realistic rendering of the graveyard, but rather in the drama and power of the composition. He very likely saw these ruins in Egmond, some 40 kilometres from Ouderkerk. The Romanesque abbey there was in a deplorable state, as was the Gothic church in Egmond-Binnen. No drawings by Ruisdael are known of these ruins, though he did make a sketch in oil of one of them.

Much discussion has focused on the possible symbolic content of the painting.

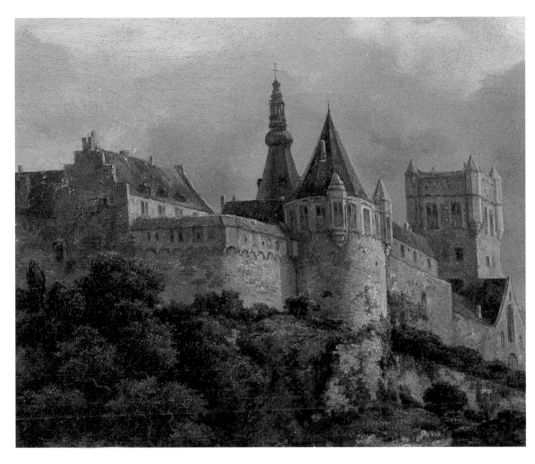

DETAIL OF 156

The unmistakable references to the transience of earthly existence – the tombs, dead trees and ruins – are combined with the allusion to hope symbolised by the sun bursting through the clouds and the appearance of the rainbow. It is difficult to say, however, just how important this symbolism was, either to Ruisdael or to the person who perhaps commissioned the painting.

BENTHEIM CASTLE

To gain inspiration Jacob van Ruisdael undertook several short trips. Around 1650 he travelled with his fellow painter and friend Nicolaes Berchem [*see* 93] to the region around the German border, where he must have seen Bentheim Castle. The castle is the subject of at least a dozen paintings, but the painting in Dublin [*156*] is without doubt the most impressive of all.

The castle towers above the wooded, mountainous landscape. In reality it is a modest structure situated in a gently rolling landscape, but Ruisdael turned it into a nearly impregnable fortress. He chose a low viewpoint, causing the castle to stand out against the sky. The viewer's gaze is then led along the back of the hill, past a windmill, to the horizon. This distant view contrasts beautifully with the precise depiction of the foreground. The rocks covered with vegetation, the sawn-off log and the tree trunk bending right out of the picture are all meticulously rendered. In the middle distance Ruisdael painted a few tiny figures, further emphasising the grandeur of nature.

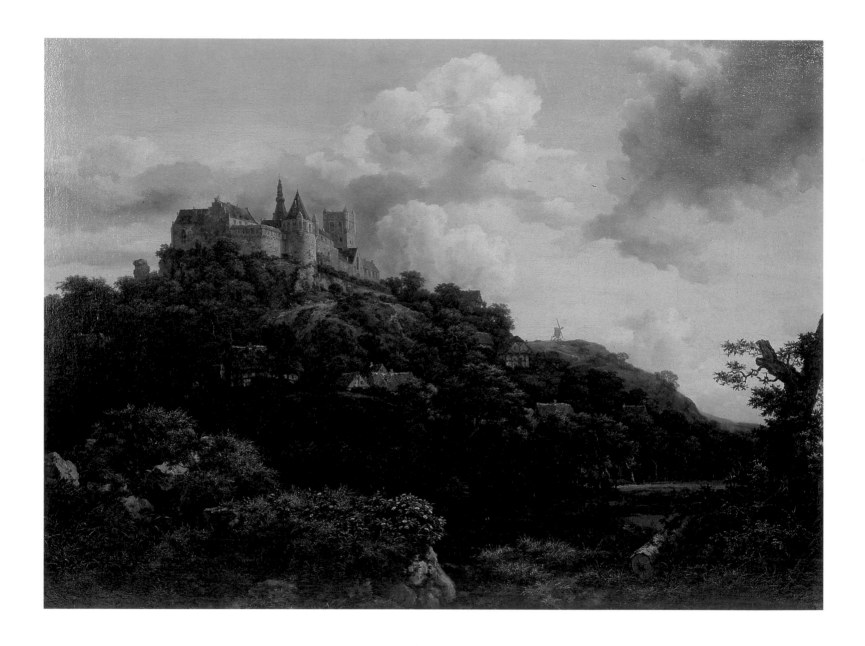

156

JACOB VAN RUISDAEL (1628/1629-1682)

Bentheim Castle, 1653

Canvas 110.5 x 144 cm

DUBLIN, NATIONAL GALLERY OF IRELAND

(acquired in 1987, see p. 329)

MEINDERT HOBBEMA

In July 1660 Jacob van Ruisdael declared in the presence of a notary that Meindert Hobbema 'served and learned with him for several years' and that he had 'not spent his money badly or frivolously, but honestly and frugally paid his rent'. Hobbema was an orphan, and this statement was probably made at the request of his guardian. Jacob van Ruisdael undoubtedly exerted a lot of influence on the young painter; together they undertook short study trips to the east of the country, where they made sketches from nature. They both used these sketches in their paintings, which explains why the same motif sometimes occurs in both their work.

Hobbema's landscapes are more airy than those of Ruisdael. His later paintings in particular display bright, sunny scenes, but his early landscapes – such as *Wooded landscape with cottages* – also testify to the painter's predilection for wooded landscapes with sunlight filtering through the trees.

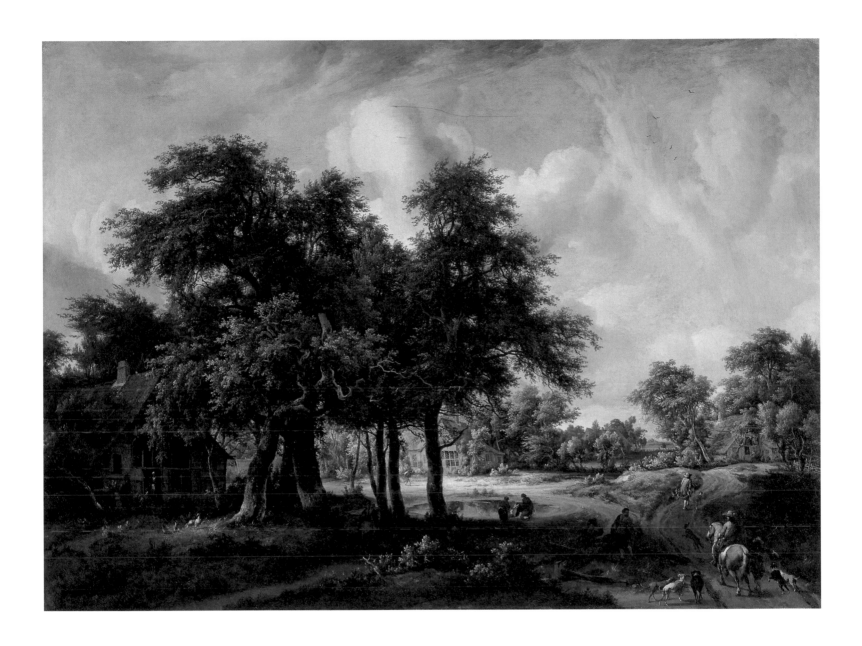

Hobbema often painted variations on a theme: again and again he painted trees along sandy roads or around a water mill, always from a different perspective.

The composition of the *Wooded landscape with cottages* is dominated by a group of trees in the foreground. Hobbema gave these trees a monumental allure, just as Ruisdael had done with the windmill and Bentheim Castle. Behind the trees is a pond, at the side of which a couple dallies, and behind this a sun-drenched glade, which gives a suggestion of depth. The dark tree trunks act as a *repoussoir:* by placing them against the light landscape in the background the painter created a feeling of spaciousness. Depth is also created by the winding path, running from the lower right – where a horseman and his hounds return from the hunt – to the cottage hidden in the woods on the right.

157
MEINDERT HOBBEMA (1638-1709)
Wooded landscape with cottages, c. 1655
Canvas 88 x 120.7 cm
THE HAGUE, MAURITSHUIS
(acquired with the aid of the Rembrandt Society in 1994, see p. 333)

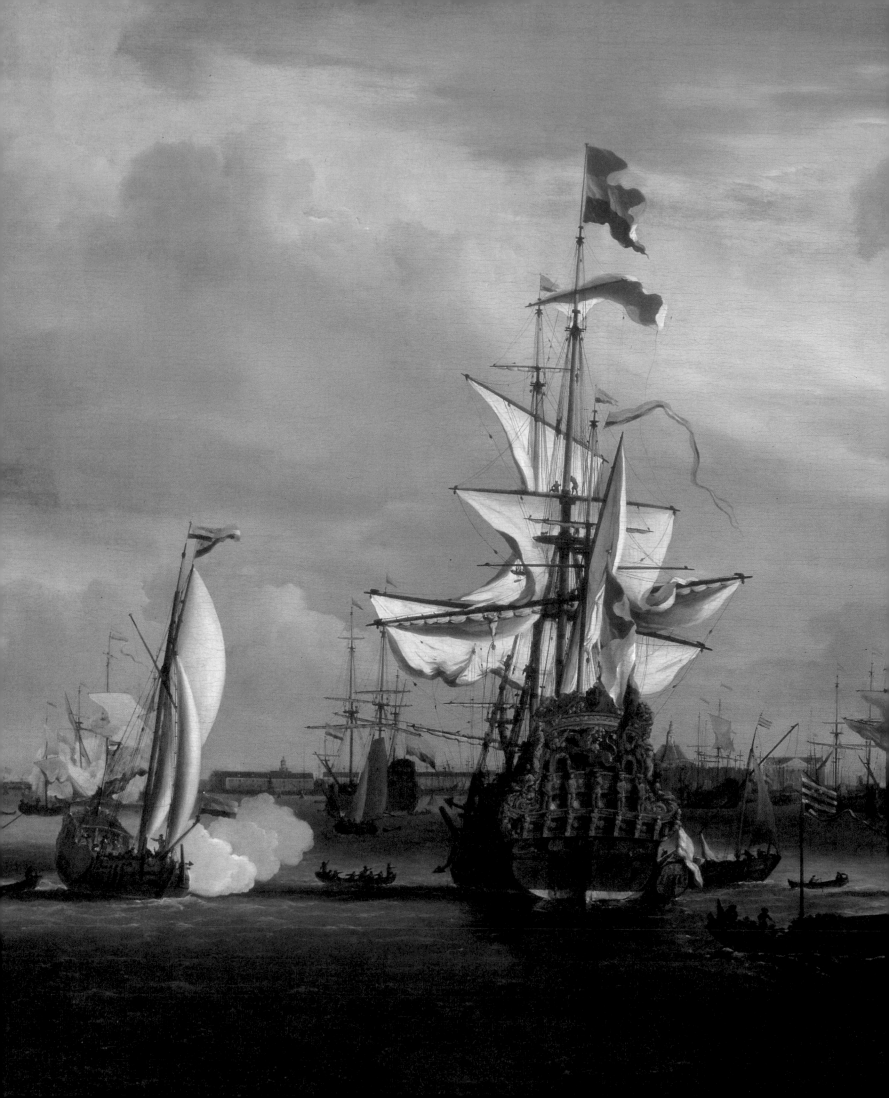

20 MARINE PAINTINGS 1650-1690

Duʀɪɴɢ the 17th century, Dutch shipping experienced its heyday. The navy scored numerous military victories, and overseas trade flourished as never before. All these marine activities were naturally reflected in Dutch artistic production. The state, for example, had successful naval battles immortalised, commanding officers commissioned artists to record their heroic deeds for posterity and captains had portraits of their ships painted.

'WAR CORRESPONDENT'

Willem van de Velde the Elder was a 'war correspondent', and was often present at naval battles, sent on assignment by the States of Holland. He was given a capable first mate who manoeuvred his ship – a galliot – between the warring ships, giving him a good view of the battle. At sea Van de Velde drew 'from life', later working up his drawings into 'pen paintings'. His recordings of battles, however, are not comparable with present-day news coverage. Sometimes Van de Velde did not work up his drawings until years after the event, and by no means did he always give an accurate rendering of reality.

DEVELOPMENT

In the mid-17th century, Amsterdam was the centre of marine painting. A decisive role in the development of this speciality was played by Simon de Vlieger [85], who lived first in Amsterdam and later in nearby Weesp. De Vlieger exerted a great deal of influence on various marine painters. Willem van de Velde the Younger, the son of Van de Velde the Elder, was a pupil of De Vlieger, and Jan van de Cappelle, a great master of seascapes, owned a number of works by De Vlieger.

The various specialists in marine painting all display the same development: over the years their paintings increasingly made room for ships. The marine painters made precise portraits of the various ships, often grouped together, creating a beautiful contrast between vast panoramas and the ships' portraits.

Every marine painter had a predilection for a specific type of weather. In Van de Cappelle's work, the sea is always calm and a silvery light causes an atmosphere of peace and well-being to settle over the water. The paintings of Ludolf Bakhuysen, on the other hand, are dominated by rough and turbulent water. It is said of this artist that he often went out in a boat in bad weather to observe first-hand the effect of a storm on the sky and water. It is therefore hardly surprising that the atmosphere in his paintings is superbly rendered. Bakhuysen remained productive until his death in 1708 and is considered the last important representative of Dutch marine painting.

WAGING WAR AT SEA

In the 17th century, England and the Dutch Republic waged war against each other three times: from 1652 to 1654, from 1665 to 1667 and from 1672 to 1674. Rivalry between these two trading nations and political power struggles were the main causes of the Anglo-Dutch Wars. During the course of these three wars, which were largely fought at sea, the Dutch navy scored illustrious victories.

During the Second Anglo-Dutch War, England was supported by France. The end of the war was expedited by the unexpected attack of the Dutch war fleet on the English naval base at Chatham in June 1667. One month later the peace treaty was signed. The Dutch Republic lost New Amsterdam (later to become New York) to England and received in exchange Suriname.

< DETAIL OF 161

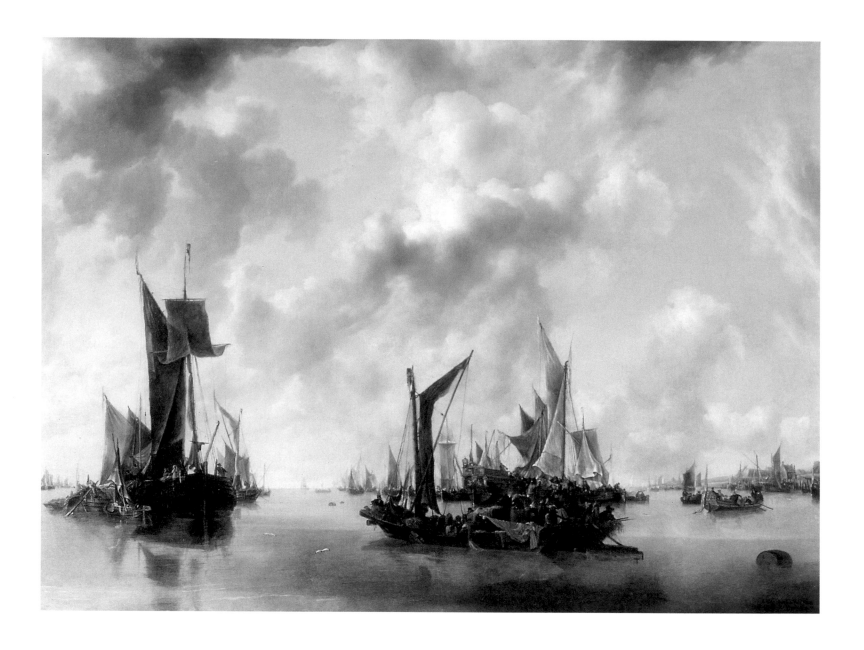

158

JAN VAN DE CAPPELLE (1624/26-1679)

A calm, 1654

Canvas 110 x 148.2 cm

CARDIFF, NATIONAL MUSEUMS &
GALLERIES OF WALES

(acquired in 1994, see p. 324)

CALM SEA

A calm by the Amsterdam marine painter
Jan van de Cappelle is one of the very few
dated paintings by his hand: he painted it in
1654. The sea is extremely placid, the ships
reflecting in the calm water. The sky is predominantly silver-grey, and the groups of
ships floating on the smooth sea provide
accents of brown. Its peacefulness and
simplicity bestow this seascape with a certain grandeur. In particular, the brilliance
of the sunlight on the beautifully rendered
cloud formations make this painting one of
the most beautiful of its kind.

VAN DE CAPPELLE

Jan van de Cappelle was probably an auto-
didact. Although he made and sold many
works, he was not a full-time artist. Van de
Cappelle was a merchant by profession and
ran a dye-works which enabled him to
amass a great fortune. When he died he left
92,000 guilders, and his estate included
several houses, a pleasure yacht and an
impressive art collection.

Van de Cappelle possessed some 200
paintings, including works by Rubens,
Van Dyck, Goltzius, Buytewech, Jan and
Esaias van de Velde, Porcellis, Van Goyen,

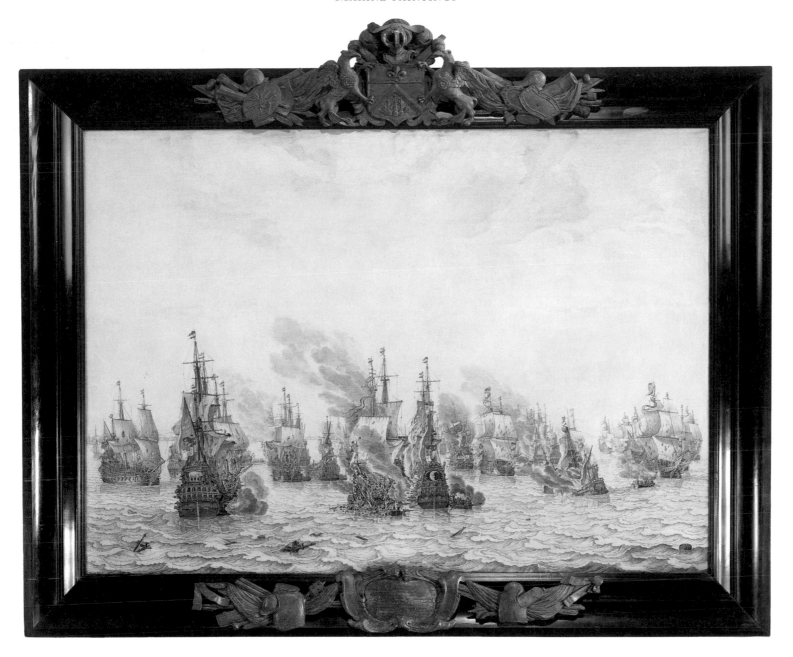

De Vlieger and Willem van de Velde, as well as several thousand drawings. Works by Rembrandt were the high point of his collection: Van de Cappelle owned 6 paintings and 500 drawings by the master. No other collector ever had this many drawings by Rembrandt in his possession.

THE BATTLE OF LIVORNO

The calm that characterises Van de Cappelle's painting is nowhere to be seen in *The battle of Livorno*, which Willem van de Velde the Elder recorded in black and white. For the precise depiction of this naval battle he used a special technique called 'pen painting'. These were drawn with pen and ink on a panel which had been prepared with a white ground. Only some of the darker parts – the clouds or waves, for example – were done with a brush. This technique had the great advantage of allowing him to depict minute detail.

159

WILLEM VAN DE VELDE THE ELDER
(c. 1611-1693)
The battle of Livorno, c. 1655
Panel 114 x 160 cm
AMSTERDAM, RIJKSMUSEUM
(acquired in 1885, see p. 312)

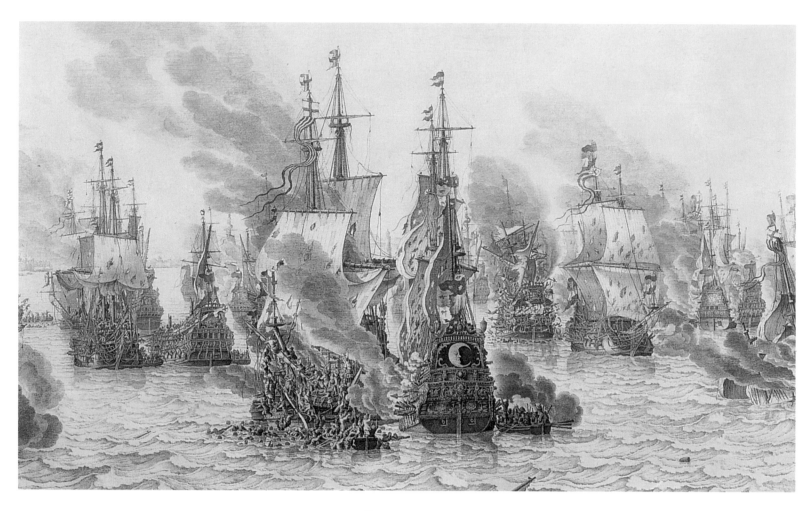

DETAIL OF 159

With a very fine pen it was possible to draw sharply and precisely, and this was ideal for what Van de Velde and his patrons had in mind: the most exact rendering possible of the ships, from the stern to the mast-top, as well as the clearest possible picture of the scene of battle. Van de Velde did not in fact call himself a painter; he signed his letters with his name and the appellation 'ship's draughtsman'.

At the battle of Livorno (Leghorn), where the Dutch Republic and England fought in 1653, an important role was played by Cornelis Tromp, son of Maerten Tromp [see also 67]. He commanded a ship that had been captured from the English a short time before. While the Dutch and English fleet lay at anchor in the neutral harbour of Livorno for the purpose of protecting trade in the area, the English saw the chance to recapture their ship. Van de Velde was commissioned by Cornelis Tromp to portray the ensuing battle on the open sea, with Tromp playing the hero's role as commander of *De Halve Maan* (The Half-Moon). The ship, clearly recognisable from the half-moon on her stern, is in the centre of the painting; the burning English ship *Samson* is being grappled. In this battle the British were overwhelmingly defeated, but this was due not so much to Tromp as to the commander Jan van Galen, whose brilliant tactical move was responsible for the victory. Van Galen was severely wounded in the action, but had himself tied to the mast to enable him to carry on giving orders on

his ship *De Olifant* (The Elephant). In Van de Velde's painting, however, this flagship sails aimlessly around at the left, while Tromp's ship does all the work. The artist twisted reality to suit his purpose, giving his patron what he wanted – honour, fame and victory.

ORNATE GOBLET
The battle of Livorno took place during the First Anglo-Dutch War (1652-1654), the main cause of which was commercial rivalry. During the Second Anglo-Dutch War, another war fought for mercantile reasons between 1665 and 1667, the Dutch and English again did battle at sea. The end of this war was hastened along in June 1667 by the Dutch fleet's attack on the English ships

laid up in the river Medway near Chatham, to the east of London. The Dutch attack came as a surprise to the British. A chain across the river, which was supposed to block the entry of enemy ships, was broken by the Dutch ship *Pro Patria*. Two English ships were seized and six others burnt. The English admiral's ship, the *Royal Charles*, was sailed back to Holland as a trophy. One month later the treaty between Holland and England was signed.

At a banquet held in November 1667 the States of Holland presented this golden goblet to Admiral Michiel de Ruyter as a token of gratitude for the part he played in the successful attack on the naval base at Chatham. On the body of the goblet the entire story is painted in multicoloured enamel, from the chain over the river to the burning ships of the English. This ornate golden goblet, made by the Hague goldsmith Nicolaas Loockemans, is further decorated with inlay work of black and white enamel.

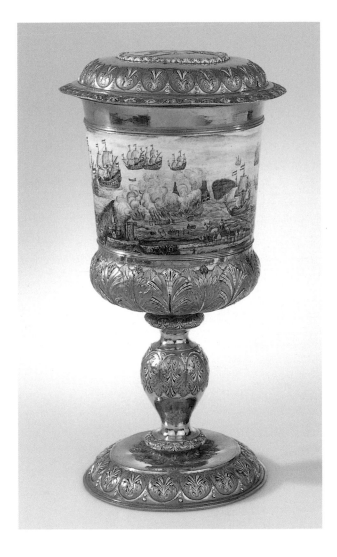
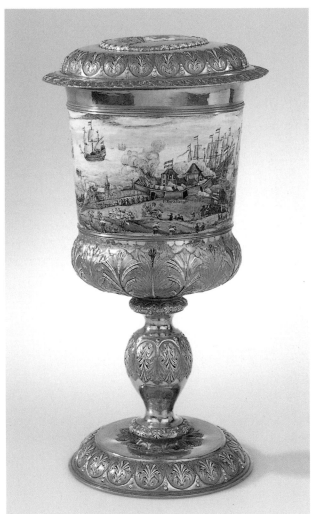

160

NICOLAAS LOOCKEMANS (?-1673)
Covered goblet, 1668
Gold and enamel h. 30 cm
AMSTERDAM, RIJKSMUSEUM
(acquired in 1893, see p. 313)

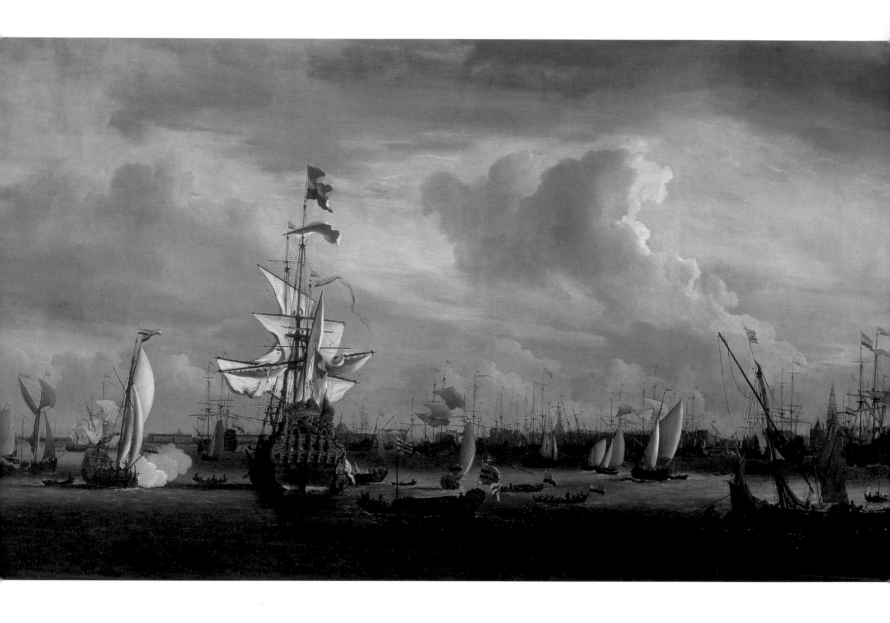

161

WILLEM VAN DE VELDE THE YOUNGER
(1633-1707)
*The 'Gouden Leeuw' on the IJ
at Amsterdam,* 1686
Canvas 179.5 x 316 cm
AMSTERDAM,
AMSTERDAMS HISTORISCH MUSEUM
(since 1975, previously in the Rijksmuseum,
1808-1975, see p. 320)

HOLLAND'S GLORY

This giant painting by Willem van de Velde the Younger shows Holland's glory: the harbour of Amsterdam, the beating heart of the Dutch Republic. It was here that the Dutch fleet set sail for the East Indies or laid anchor upon returning from America, fully laden with merchandise. The large frigate *De Gouden Leeuw* (The Golden Lion) dominates the painting. On the right a forest of masts – most of them with the Dutch national flag at the top – stands out against the profile of Amsterdam. At the far right is the tower of the Old Church and next to it the Schreierstoren. More to the left the Montelbaanstoren is visible, as well as the

façade of the Admiralty Depot – the present-day Maritime Museum – the roof and spire of a church, the Oosterkerk, and at the far left the elongated façade of the warehouse of the Dutch East India Company. The painter gave a precise rendering of the city's profile, even though it only served to add detail to the depiction. His main concern, of course, was the ships. The sails of the *Gouden Leeuw* stand out brightly in the evening light. It looks as though the ship is furling her sails: two sailors, occupied with the sail, stand on the yard of the middle mast. Apparently the ship is returning to her home harbour, and the anchor might be lowered at any moment. The state yacht to the left of

236

the *Gouden Leeuw* fires a salute to welcome the ship home.

The viewer looks at this scene from a short distance away. The painter left the foreground open, apart from the *waterschip*, a kind of fishing craft, at the far right. The rippling water, a broad band of which lies in shadow in the foreground, forms the overture to the rest of the painting. Only afterwards does the visual commotion begin: ships and boats, masts, yards and sails, flapping flags and pennants form the main motifs. In addition, an important part of the painting is devoted to the typical, cloud-filled Dutch sky.

ENGLAND

Willem van de Velde the Younger learned the rudiments of painting from his father, who afterwards placed him 'under the supervision of the artful ship painter Simon de Vlieger', according to the artists' biographer Arnold Houbraken. The young Van de Velde was therefore instructed in the same specialism his father practised. Around 1672 both father and son left for England, where they went to work for Charles II. Both Van de Veldes received a yearly stipend of 100 pounds, the father for 'taking and making Draughts of Seafights' and the son for 'putting the draughts into colour'. The painters were highly successful in England, where they continued to live until their death.

Nevertheless, the young Willem would have gone to the Netherlands from time to time to execute commissions there. The majestic painting of The *'Gouden Leeuw' on the IJ at Amsterdam* was most likely commissioned by the Chief Commissioners of the Harbour Works, whose office was in the Schreierstoren, where the painting is known to have hung for a long time.

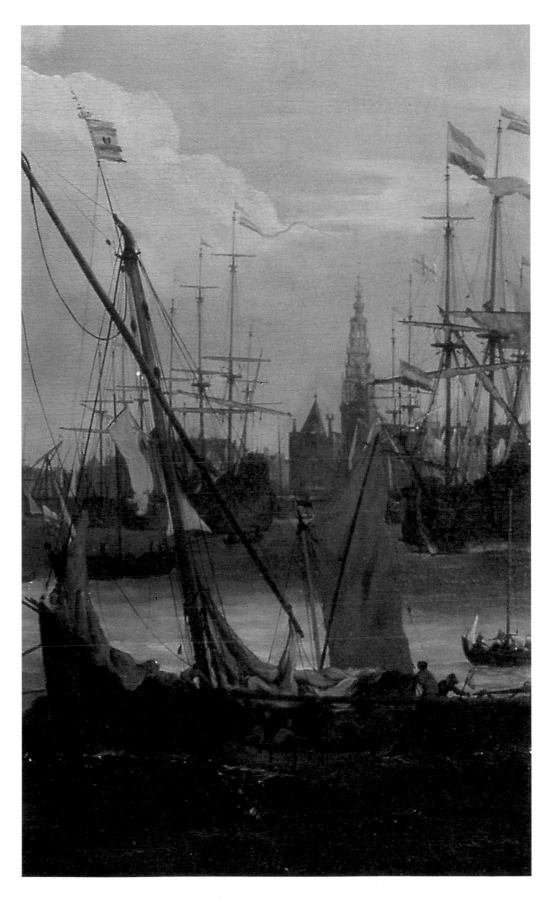

DETAIL OF 161

STRONG WIND

Willem van de Velde the Younger [*162*] and Ludolf Bakhuysen [*163*] both depicted the same subject: ships on a stormy sea. Van de Velde's ships are coping all right – the seamen still seem to be in control – but in Bakhuysen's seascape the situation is dire.

Van de Velde painted his *Ships on a stormy sea* around 1671, shortly before leaving for England. He was so successful in depicting the violence of the storm that the force of the wind and the pounding of the waves are almost palpable. The sun has just broken through the heavy, threatening clouds and shines on the sail of the small ship in the foreground. The pennant at the top of the mast is the flag of the islands of Terschelling and Vlieland. The scene perhaps takes place near the coast of these West Frisian islands.

Around 1800 this seascape was in the possession of the third Duke of Bridgewater, who commissioned the English artist Joseph Turner (1775-1851) to make a pendant. The composition of his version resembles that of his 17th-century predecessor, but Turner added an important dramatic element: the collision of the two ships in the foreground seems unavoidable (see pp. 298-299).

162

WILLEM VAN DE VELDE THE YOUNGER
(1633-1707)
Ships on a stormy sea, c. 1672
Canvas 132.2 x 191.9 cm
TOLEDO, THE TOLEDO MUSEUM OF ART
(acquired in 1977, see p. 348)

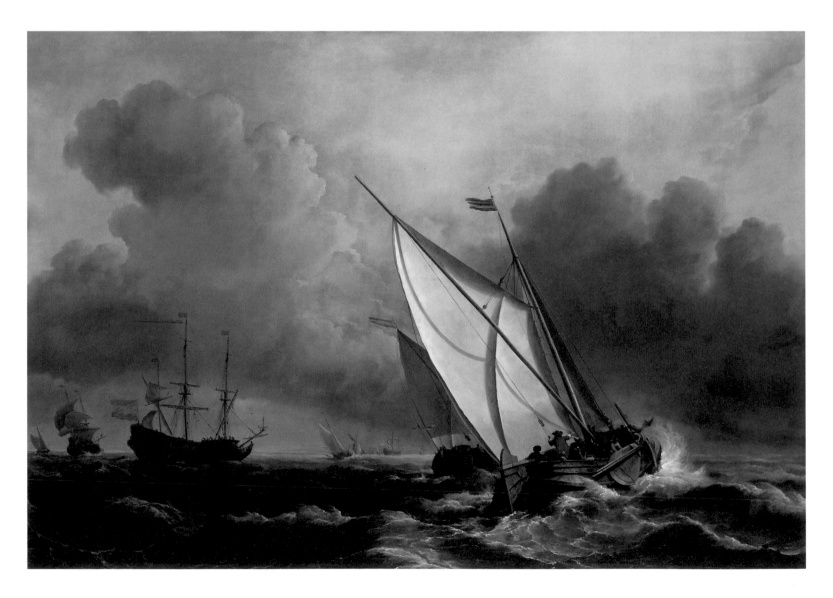

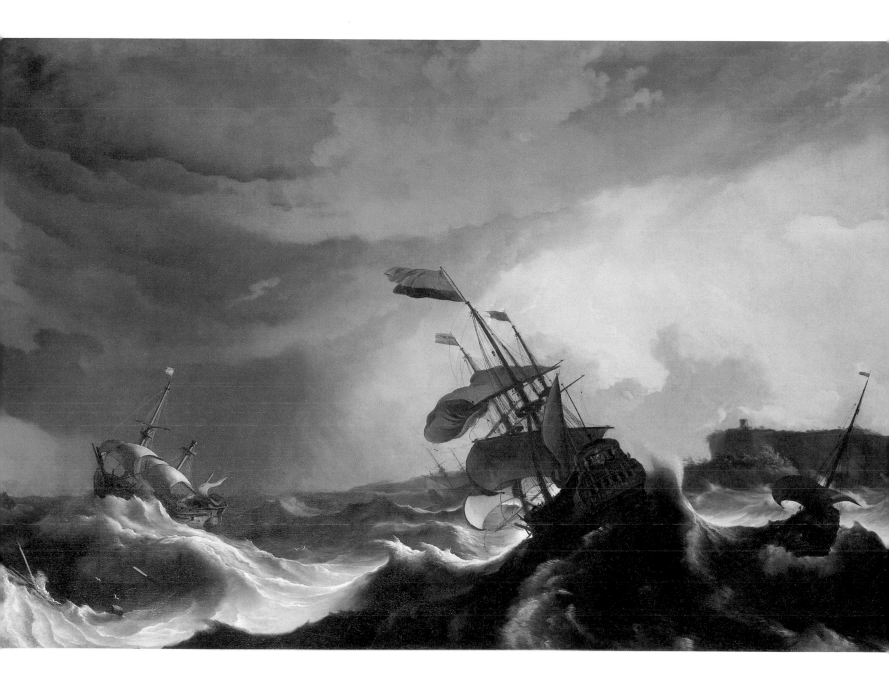

RAGING STORM

After the Van de Veldes moved to England, Ludolf Bakhuysen became the most celebrated marine painter in the Dutch Republic during the last quarter of the 17th century. The violence of nature is the main focus of Bakhuysen's painting. He concentrated – even more than Van de Velde did – on the high waves lashing against the ships. The frigate in the foreground attempts to lower her sails before it is too late. Two masts of the ship on the left have nearly been swept overboard. The wild sea finds its echo in the racing clouds. One cannot be certain these ships will reach the coast safely.

Most of Bakhuysen's seascapes were painted in a smooth style, but in *Ships in distress in a raging storm* he pulled out all the stops and made a truly ambitious composition. This impressive painting dating from c. 1690 is one of the last masterpieces produced in this genre in the 17th century.

163

LUDOLF BAKHUYSEN (1631-1708)
Ships in distress in a raging storm, c. 1690
Canvas 150 x 227 cm
AMSTERDAM, RIJKSMUSEUM
(acquired with the aid of the Rembrandt Society in 1988, see p. 319)

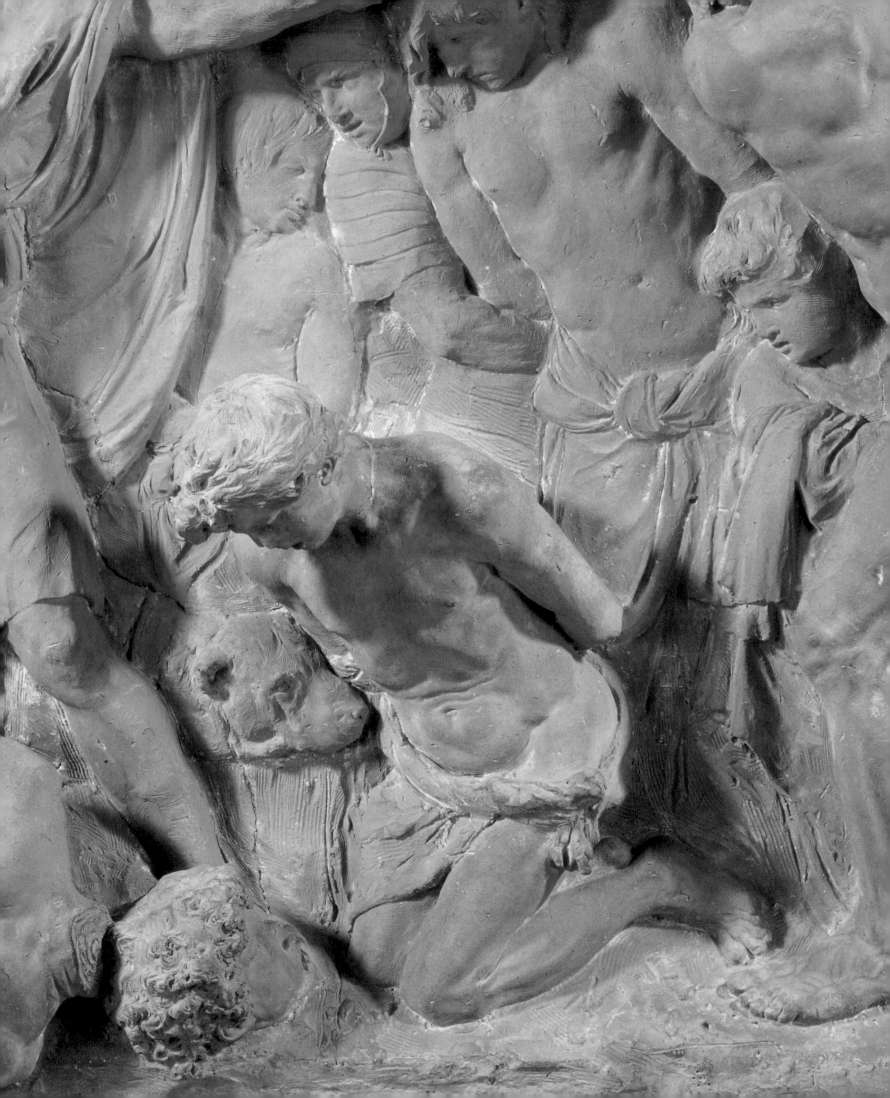

21 IMMORTALISED IN STONE 1650-1680

IN THE FIRST twenty years of the 17th century Dutch sculpture was dominated by the Amsterdam sculptor and architect Hendrick de Keyser (see chapter 1). His tomb for Willem of Orange in Delft reflected the prevailing international style and put the Dutch Republic on the map as far as sculpture was concerned. For several decades after De Keyser's death there were no sculptors working at this elevated level. The situation changed halfway through the century, when highly skilled sculptors from the Southern Netherlands came to the North in response to the growing demand for sculpture in the prosperous Dutch Republic.

The Flemish portrait sculptor François Dieussart, for instance, spent several years working in The Hague, where he received commissions from the stadholder's court. Dieussart, who had been trained in Rome, introduced a new, classicist portrait style reflecting the latest developments in Italy. He worked in Italian marble, which was shipped from Carrara to Amsterdam in large quantities from the 1640s onwards, and this material accentuated the classical feel of his sculpture. The use of the white Carrara marble gave Dutch sculpture a very different look. Until then artists had used this material only very occasionally; they generally worked in sandstone, English alabaster or Belgian marble.

MAJOR UNDERTAKING

The large-scale import of Italian marble was associated with the most ambitious Dutch sculptural undertaking in the Golden Age: the decoration of Amsterdam town hall. The Antwerp sculptor Artus Quellinus was commissioned for this project. He, like Dieussart, had received part of his training in Italy. Between 1650 and 1665 Quellinus and dozens of assistants worked on an impressive number of sculptures for the façades and public rooms of the new town hall.

During his stay in Amsterdam the celebrated sculptor also undertook other commissions, so that his Dutch oeuvre consists of more than just his work on the town hall. Quellinus also left an indelible mark on Dutch sculpture through the influence he had on his pupils and close associates. This influence is clearly visible in the work of Rombout Verhulst, although his statues are less idealised than those of his master Quellinus.

During the second half of the 17th century, artists concentrated on tombs, portraits and, at the end of the century, on garden statuary. Throughout the 17th century there was, of course, a continuing demand for architectural ornamentation. More 17th-century sculpture can be found in and on buildings than on display in museums.

THE AMSTERDAM TOWN HALL

In 1639 the Amsterdam town council decided to have a new town hall built; the existing town hall was demolished owing to its dilapidated state. Amsterdam wanted a large, monumental town hall that would symbolise the power of this metropolis. The architect chosen for the job was Jacob van Campen (1595-1657), who designed a large building in classicist style in keeping with the grandeur attributed to the city by its leaders. The interior was decorated by the best architects and painters. Building began after the signing of the Treaty of Münster in 1648. The new town hall was famous even before it was completed: the poet Joost van den Vondel (1587-1679) called it 'the eighth wonder of the world'.

In 1808 Louis Bonaparte turned the Amsterdam town hall into a palace. The 'Palace on the Dam' still functions today as a royal palace, although for a large part of the year it is open to the public.

< DETAIL OF 167

DIEUSSART

The Flemish sculptor François Dieussart was the 'court artist' *par excellence*. He received commissions from several European rulers and moved his workshop from court to court. He worked in London and Copenhagen and spent some time in The Hague, where his patrons included the Princes of Orange, Maurits and Willem II. During his stay in The Hague he also made portrait sculptures of Pieter Spiering and his wife Johanna. Dieussart immortalised them in an understated, natural style. By portraying the faces turned towards each other, the artist created an expressive link between the two busts. Dieussart had seen examples of this artistic solution during his apprenticeship in Italy.

Pieter Spiering, the youngest son of the Delft tapestry-maker François Spiering [see 3], was an important art collector whose collection included work by Gerard Dou. He even paid Dou an annual stipend to ensure that the painter would give him the right of first refusal of every new work. Working for his father as an agent, Spiering had dealings with other countries, including Sweden. His many transactions with the Swedish royal house led to his appointment as Swedish ambassador to the Dutch Republic in 1635. He also acted as art agent for Queen Christina of Sweden (1626-1689). It was probably in this capacity that Spiering came into contact with Dieussart, whom he commissioned to make portraits of himself and his wife Johanna Doré. According to surviving documents, Dieussart also made a portrait sculpture of Queen Christina, though this work is no longer known.

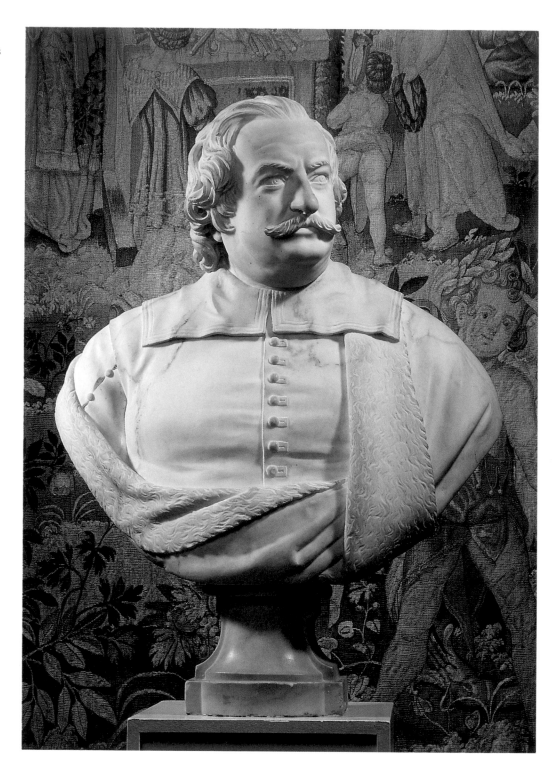

164A
FRANÇOIS DIEUSSART (c. 1600-1661)
Portrait of Pieter Spiering (?-1652), c. 1645-1650
Marble h. 89 cm
AMSTERDAM, RIJKSMUSEUM
(acquired in 1971, see p. 317)

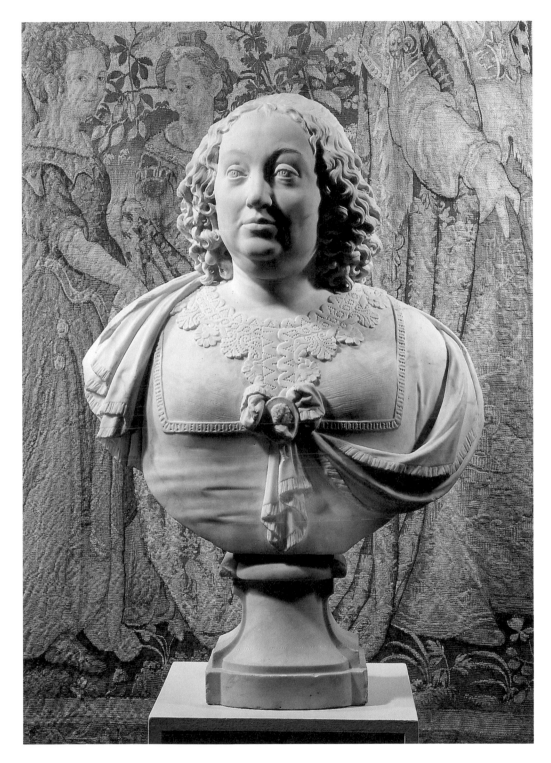

PORTRAIT SCULPTURES

In the 17th-century Netherlands there were
more portraits painted than sculpted. A
sculpted portrait was not an obvious choice
for the ordinary burgher, since sculptures
were more generally associated with royal
patrons. Nevertheless, marble portrait busts
of burghers were made throughout the
17th century which strongly resemble classical portrait busts in style and material.
François Dieussart naturally drew inspiration from Italian examples. He had trained
in Rome and had worked with the master
of Baroque sculpture, Gianlorenzo Bernini
(1598-1680). Bernini, unsurpassed in his
handling of marble, made stone statues
which seem to come alive. Nonetheless,
according to a 17th-century anecdote it
was Bernini who maintained that it was
impossible to create a perfect likeness in
marble. To prove this – wrote a young
English sculptor who visited the master – he
took a servant out of the room and pow-
dered his face and hair with flour. When he
brought the servant back again, none of his
pupils recognised the man. It was Bernini's
way of demonstrating just how important
the colour of skin, hair, eyes and lips are in
making a recognisable portrait. True likenesses in marble or bronze would appear to
be among the impossibilities of art. It is only
through the careful use of light and shade
and by exploiting the spatial qualities of a
statue that a sculptor can portray his model
convincingly.

164B

FRANÇOIS DIEUSSART (c. 1600-1661)

Portrait of Johanna Doré, c. 1645-1650

Marble h. 82 cm

AMSTERDAM, RIJKSMUSEUM

(acquired in 1971, see p. 317)

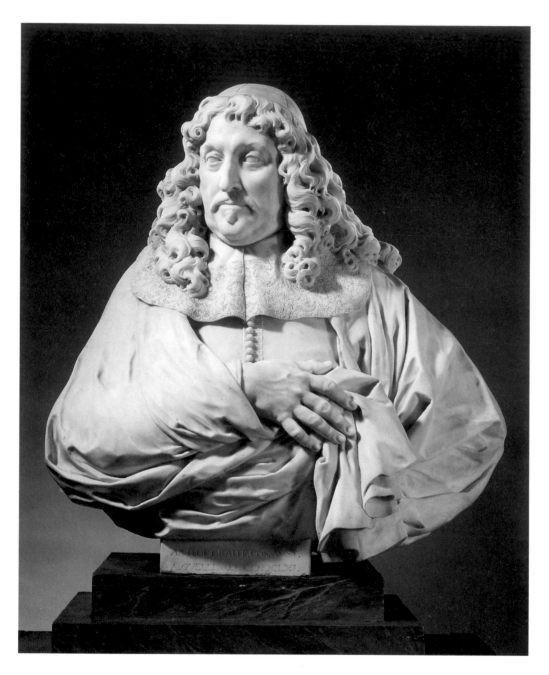

165
ARTUS QUELLINUS (1609-1668)
Portrait of Andries de Graeff
(1611-1678), 1661
Marble h. 75 cm
AMSTERDAM, RIJKSMUSEUM
(acquired in 1817, see p. 310)

brows, moustache and wig. Quellinus rendered the sitter's clothes in minute detail. The flat collar of Flemish lace appears to lie loose on De Graeff's shoulders, and the buttons on his jerkin have a natural irregularity. Again following the Italian example, Quellinus concealed the unnaturally sharp transition between bust and plinth with a cloak draped from the shoulders and around the chest. He reinforced the natural look of the statue by incorporating one arm in the bust, with the hand holding part of the cloak. Quellinus could not have immortalised De Graeff more impressively than this. In this life-size bust, he created one of the most important Baroque portrait sculptures of the Dutch Golden Age.

JOHAN DE WITT

Shortly before Quellinus returned to Antwerp, his birthplace, this Flemish sculptor made a masterly portrait of Johan de Witt (1623-1672), Grand Pensionary of Holland. The bust of the politician, who at this time was still powerful and influential, is stately and yet it also exudes a natural nonchalance. As in the bust of Andries de Graeff, Quellinus added an arm, with the hand emerging from the loose folds of the cloak. The natural effect was enhanced by putting a pair of gloves in the sitter's hand.

Quellinus portrayed De Witt's face, the lips slightly parted, with the utmost care. He undoubtedly made a good likeness, although the commission was certainly not easy to execute. From the sculptor's letters to his client it is evident that the busy statesman had virtually no time to sit for him.

LIFELIKE

Artus Quellinus was well aware of the problem that Bernini had so convincingly illustrated. He had also received his training in Italy, and he was familiar with the stylistic devices that had been developed there – particularly by Bernini – to make portrait sculptures more lifelike. One of the tricks of the trade employed to give a statue greater expression was the apparent freezing of a movement. The sitter was shown with his head turned a little to one side, perhaps with his mouth slightly open. The artist thus created the impression of having captured a moment in time. Quellinus used this solution for the first time in the marble portrait of Andries de Graeff [165]. He succeeded in creating an extraordinarily realistic likeness of the expression and features of this burgomaster of Amsterdam. He made an effective distinction between the smooth, polished skin and the rougher surface of the eye-

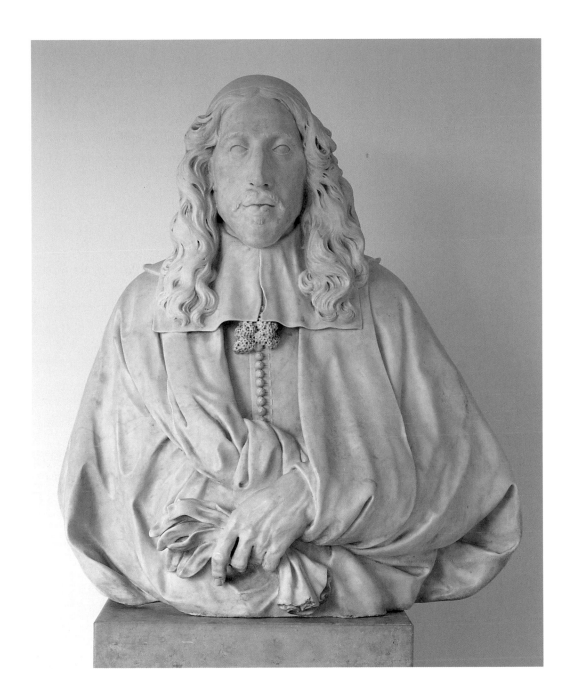

166
ARTUS QUELLINUS (1609-1668)
Portrait of Johan de Witt
(1623-1672), 1665
Marble h. 95 cm
DORDRECHT, DORDRECHTS MUSEUM
(acquired in 1871, see p. 327)

Quellinus expressed some mild annoyance about the limited number of sessions that the Grand Pensionary had granted him.

Johan de Witt played an important role in the 'stadholderless period' (1650-1672). In his capacity as Grand Pensionary, he was for many years the most powerful statesman in the Dutch Republic. His downfall was imminent when France and England turned against the Republic and calls for the return of the stadholder became increasingly insis-tent. The young Prince of Orange, Willem III, was appointed stadholder and the services of Johan and his brother Cornelis were no longer required. Cornelis de Witt was accused of conspiring against Prince Willem III. He was imprisoned in The Hague and convicted. When Johan went to visit him in prison on the day of the verdict, an Orangist mob gathered outside. They dragged the brothers out of the prison and tore them limb from limb.

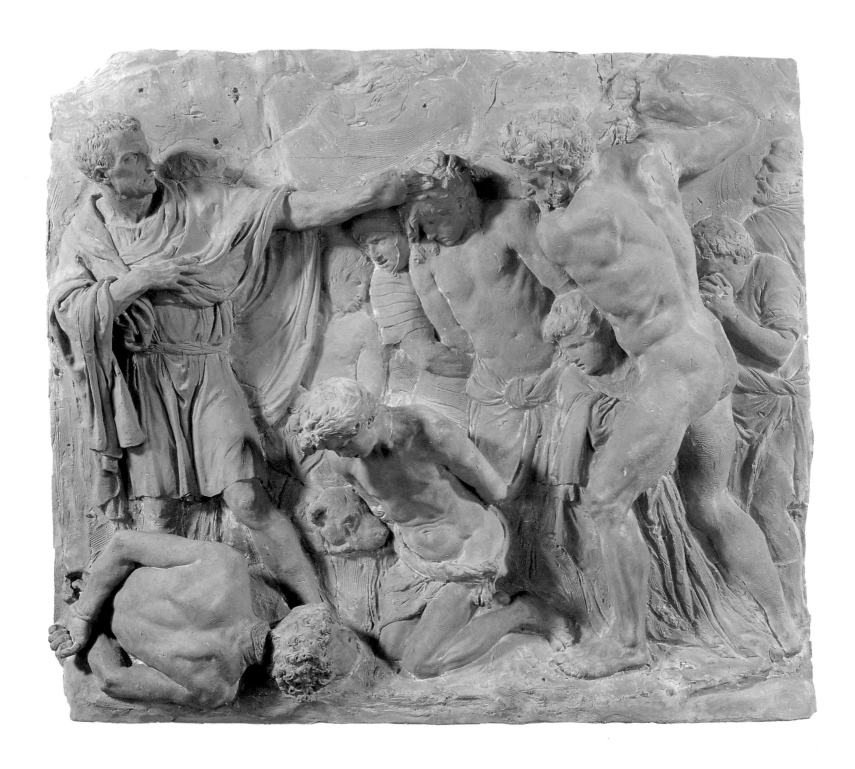

167

ARTUS QUELLINUS (1609-1668)
The judgement of Brutus: Justice,
c. 1651-1654
Terracotta 73 x 83 cm
AMSTERDAM, RIJKSMUSEUM
(on loan from the City of Amsterdam
since 1887, see p. 313)

SCHOLARLY SERIES OF STATUES

Amsterdam's new town hall was unrivalled in prestige, size and cost. The building was to be a symbol of the city's power and riches. This wealth was reflected not just in its magnitude and building materials – it was made of costly foreign stone – but in the extensive ornamentation that its creators designed for the town hall. Many of the carved decorations, for example, have an obvious meaning: they depict the wisdom of the Amsterdam city government and symbolise the central position which – in the eyes of those who commissioned the work – Amsterdam occupied in the world and in the universe.

It is impossible to say for certain who was responsible for the extensive and scholarly series of sculptures. The designs were probably selected in close consultation between architect Jacob van Campen and the building committee. One of the erudite members of this committee was Andries de Graeff [165], a burgomaster known for his wide cultural interests. In designing the programme for the ornamentation, Van Campen and the committee members drew inspiration from the history of the 'fatherland', the Bible and classical Roman art. In Artus Quellinus they found a sculptor who could translate their concept into marble and bronze in a truly brilliant manner.

Once Jacob van Campen's designs had been approved by his clients, Quellinus made small-scale models, which were likewise submitted for approval. Some of these preparatory studies in terracotta have been preserved, and even the fees paid for some of the clay models have survived. Quellinus received 24 guilders for a small terracotta pump crown, while for the model of the tympanum – which was more than four metres wide – he was paid 600 guilders. These were sizeable sums, compared with the wage for a skilled tradesman – about a guilder a day.

EXEMPLARY JUSTICE

The judgement of Brutus is a terracotta design for a marble relief in the Amsterdam town hall. This relief was destined for the Tribunal, the chamber in which justice was administered. All the carved ornamentation in this room is associated with justice, punishment and death. In the west wall there are three carved reliefs showing examples of the administration of justice taken from Roman and biblical history. The terracotta studies for all three have survived. An entry in the town hall accounts states that Quellinus was paid 200 guilders for the modelled 'flat history representing Junius Brutus'. The sculptor worked out the figures with considerable accuracy in classicist style. He portrayed Brutus in a Roman tunic, while the executioner, as if he were a classical god, is naked. The background was so loosely and sketchily rendered that the marks of the palette knife can still be seen.

Lucius Junius Brutus, the Roman consul, is the central figure in the story. His gesture indicates to the executioner that the sentence can be carried out. The executioner stands ready to cut off the head of the kneeling youth. In front of the young man lies the head of the previous victim. Brutus was the consul in Rome when a group of young Romans conspired against him. The plot was discovered and the conspirators, including Brutus's own sons, were sentenced to death. Brutus was not prepared to make an exception for his sons – justice must be impartial – and so they too were beheaded. This is the dramatic moment depicted by Quellinus. This cruel scene took place in Rome in the 6th century BC and stood as an example of justice and integrity for the 17th-century judges who pursued their calling in the Amsterdam Tribunal.

WALL OF THE TRIBUNAL IN THE AMSTERDAM TOWN HALL, 1652

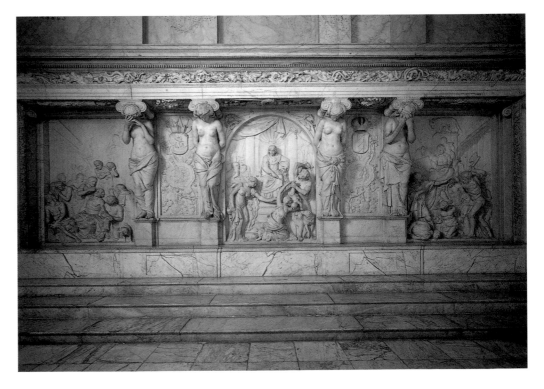

CLAY AND MARBLE

Rombout Verhulst, born in Mechelen in Flanders and trained in Quellinus's workshop in Amsterdam, benefited from the favourable climate for sculpture that prevailed in the Dutch Republic in the second half of the 17th century. The presence of the gifted Antwerp sculptor Quellinus had given sculpture a huge boost and was the decisive factor in Verhulst's development. After completing his work for the town hall, Verhulst concentrated on monumental sculpture, portraits and garden statuary. Even more than Quellinus, he strove to achieve a strong sense of realism in his portraits. The portrait of Jacob van Reygersbergh (1625-1675) is a prime example of Verhulst's naturalistic style.

There are two extant versions of the statue: the Rijksmuseum has a terracotta bust [168a], while the marble was purchased by the Getty Museum in Los Angeles in 1984 [168b]. The terracotta figure served as the *modello*: Verhulst modelled it in clay as the study for the marble bust. His preparatory work was extremely meticulous and the *modello* is worked out in minute detail. It is a mark of Verhulst's ability that he was able to carve all these details – which are a good deal easier to achieve in clay than in marble – so accurately in the marble portrait. When he actually embarked on the marble sculpture, he used a cast of the terracotta portrait as a plaster working model. He was able to mark specific points and make minor adjustments on the plaster bust without damaging the terracotta portrait. The terracotta bust was regarded not simply as a study, but as a finished work of art in its own right. It was probably delivered to the client when the marble portrait was completed.

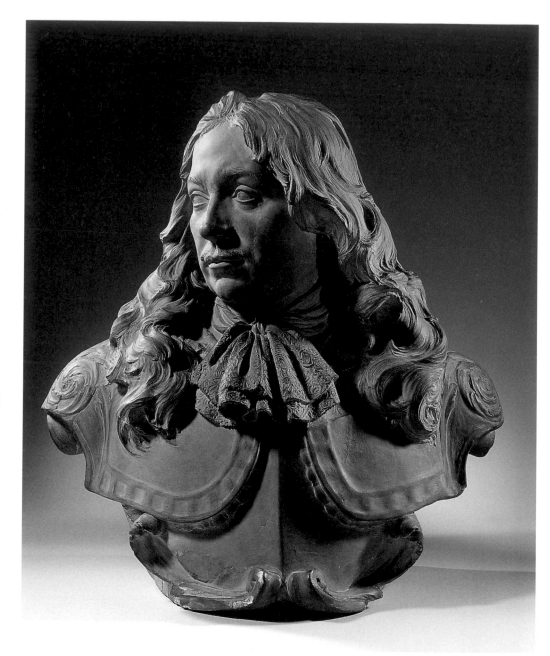

168A
ROMBOUT VERHULST (1624-1698)
Portrait of Jacob van Reygersbergh
(1625-1675), 1671
Painted terracotta h. 55 cm
AMSTERDAM, RIJKSMUSEUM
(acquired with the aid of the Rembrandt Society
in 1896, see p. 313)

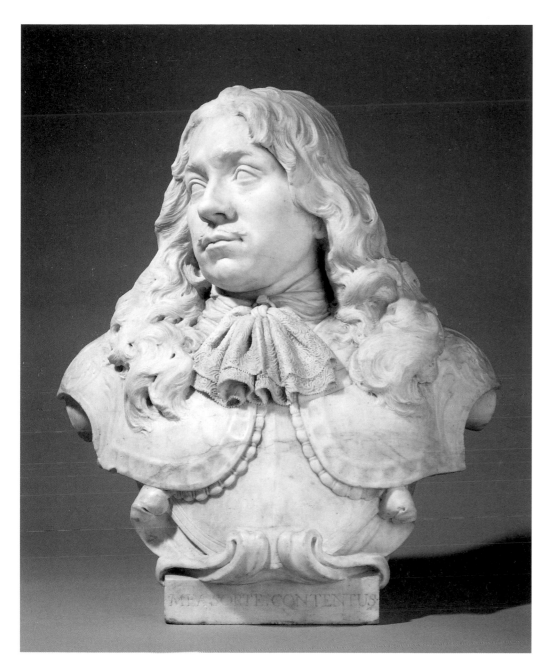

168 B

ROMBOUT VERHULST (1624-1698)

Portrait of Jacob van Reygersbergh

(1625-1675), 1671

Marble h. 63 cm

LOS ANGELES, THE J. PAUL GETTY MUSEUM

(acquired in 1984, see p. 338)

VAN REYGERSBERGH

Jacob van Reygersbergh, born in Middelburg, was the Zeeland delegate to the States General and consequently spent a considerable amount of time in The Hague. He was an important client of Rombout Verhulst, acting as intermediary in commissions for monuments and tombs that the sculptor undertook for the nobility of Holland, Zeeland and Groningen, with whom Van Reygersbergh had either professional relations or family ties.

Verhulst gave Van Reygersbergh a relaxed, almost dreamy expression. He portrayed his sitter with great realism, even indicating the iris and pupil in the eyes of the marble portrait. The small bump between the nose and the right eye also bears witness to a high degree of naturalism. Verhulst used a variety of textures in the finish of the different parts of the work. The skin of the face contrasts with the roughness of the hair, and the surface of the metal armour has a very different feel from the loosely knotted lace jabot.

A striking feature is the transition from the sitter's body to the plinth. Whereas Quellinus opted for a natural solution with the plinth almost entirely concealed under the flowing folds of a cloak, Verhulst actually emphasised the transition with two scrolls. Verhulst did not indicate any arms on this bust, but allowed the shoulders to rest on large scrolls, filling the cavities with large, stylised leaves. One reason for this decorative solution might be that the piece was not intended as an individual work. It is possible that Verhulst designed it as part of a tomb that was never built, in which the bust would have been placed in a niche surrounded by scrollwork.

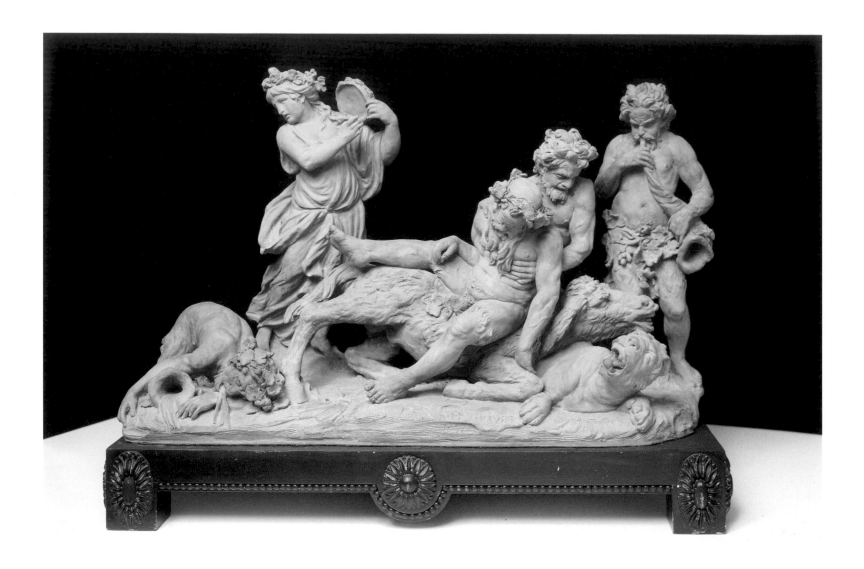

169A

PIETER XAVERY (c. 1647-1673)

Bacchanal, 1671

Terracotta 36.5 x 61.5 x 23 cm

THE HAGUE, MUSEUM
MEERMANNO-WESTREENIANUM

(acquired in 1840, see p. 333)

BACCHANTS

Like Quellinus, the Flemish sculptor Pieter Xavery came from Antwerp. He left the city in 1670 and settled in Leiden. In the same year he got married and enrolled as a student of mathematics at the University of Leiden. Aside from a record of the birth of a child, no facts about Xavery's life have been found. All of his known dated works were done between 1670 and 1674. Some of these works serve to ornament buildings in Leiden, but he really made his name as a modeller of small terracotta groups. His sculptures are more exuberant than was customary in 17th-century Holland. It is therefore likely that Xavery received his training in Antwerp, where the influence of the Baroque painter Pieter Paul Rubens (1577-1640) meant that styles in painting and sculpture were more theatrical than they were in the North.

A subject like the Bacchants offered the sculptor an opportunity to indulge himself in a scene of debauchery. The followers of Bacchus, the Greek god of wine, were drunken nymphs, satyrs and other creatures of the woods. They made music and carried wine and sacrificial offerings. The group of Bacchants was traditionally led by Silenus, a wise but inevitably drunken old man who was considered to be responsible for Bacchus' education, and it is he who is the central figure in Xavery's Bacchanal. The donkey which Silenus traditionally rides has stumbled over a panther, which is also part of Bacchus' entourage. The panther snarls, the donkey brays, a satyr holds up the drunken Silenus. Xavery created an effective contrast between the limp body of the fat old man and the savagely roaring panther as it endeavours to free itself. Behind them a

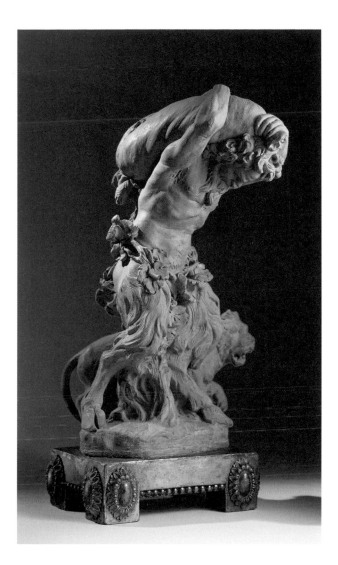
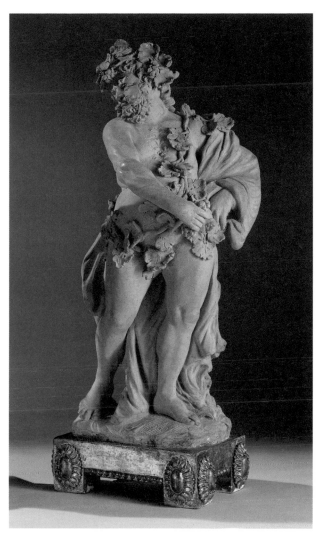

satyr blows a horn, while a naiad on the left plays a tambourine. The composition is completed by a prostrate satyr on the far left. Being violently sick, he forgets the flask of wine he was carrying. Immoderation and waste are combined in the figure of this satyr.

The statuettes of Faun and Bacchus were made in the same lively, fluid style. Their build is rather squat, like that of the Bacchants around the fallen donkey. Although they are now separated from the main group, it is highly likely that they belonged to the same ensemble. The three groups have the same late 18th-century wooden bases, which would indicate that they were not separated until after this.

Together the three groups form a procession, which would probably have taken pride of place on a table or a cabinet. It is not known whether additional figures from this group of Bacchants have been preserved.

The sculptor captured the revellers with their fat bodies and flaccid poses very effectively. The Faun with the goat's legs is more muscular than his companions; he carries a large winesack on his shoulders. The lion at his feet is also part of the Bacchanalian procession. The other figure, Bacchus, is crowned with vine leaves, and has garlands of vine leaves and elegant drapery hanging down behind his plump legs. His head turns in the opposite direction to his feet;

with these opposing movements Xavery breathed some life into the scene, at the same time lending a certain elegance to Bacchus.

169 B

PIETER XAVERY (c. 1647-1673)
Faun and Bacchus, 1671
Terracotta h. 35 and 42 cm
PRIVATE COLLECTION, ATLANTA
(see p. 351)

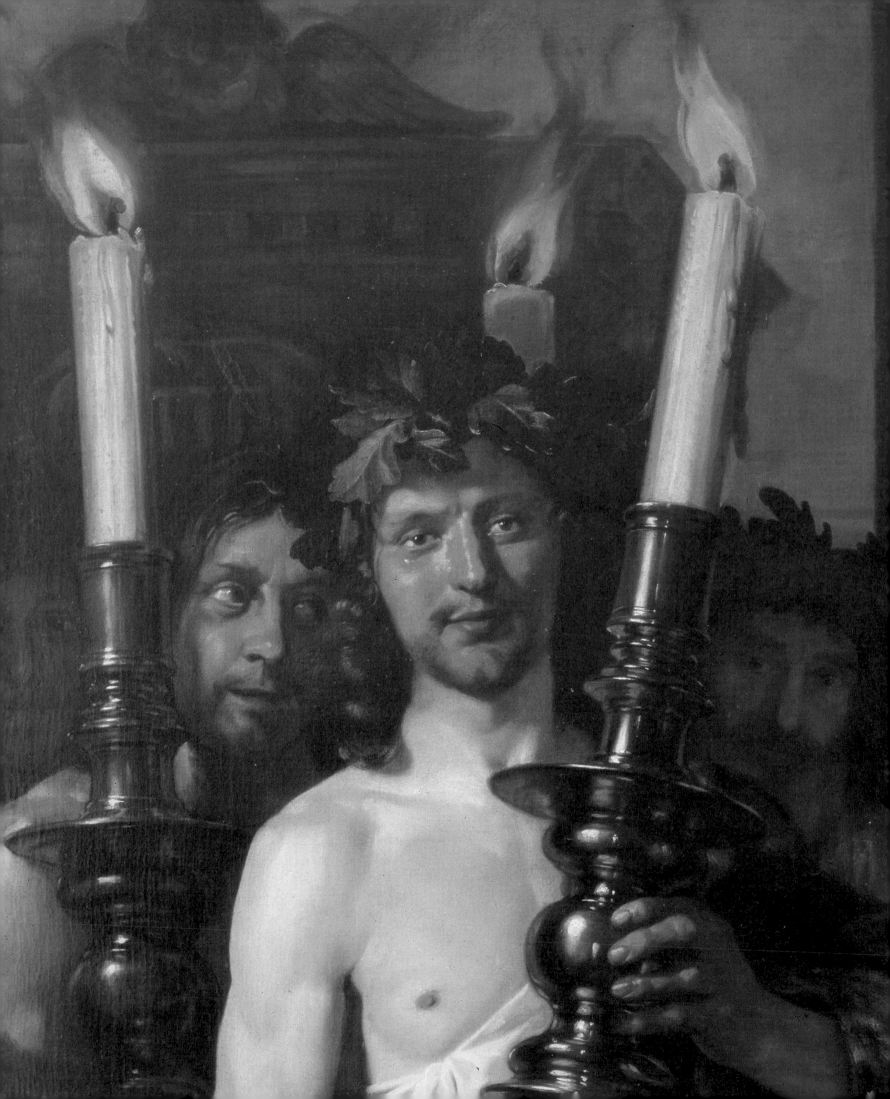

22 IMPRESSIVE HISTORY PAINTINGS 1650-1670

A NUMBER of significant developments in Dutch history painting took place around 1650, with changes in style, the use of colour and the treatment of light. The coarse manner of painting and strong chiaroscuro of Rembrandt and his school fell out of fashion, giving way to clear, cool colours and a glossy, fluid style of painting. Artists returned to the classicist principles of clarity and harmony, taking the art of antiquity and the Renaissance as their example. The extreme realism that characterised the art of the first half of the 17th century was regarded as an aberration by the theoreticians of the day. In 1719 the artists' biographer Houbraken wrote that even 'before Rembrandt's death, eyes had already been opened', 'Italian brushwork' had been reintroduced and 'fine painting had appeared again'.

COURT STYLE

Classicism was a typical court style that reflected the magnificence of the sovereign and of all those who associated themselves with him. The court of Stadholder Frederik Hendrik in The Hague consequently encouraged Classicism in Holland. After 1650, when Frederik Hendrik's death ushered in the first stadholderless period, Amsterdam's wealth made it the main centre of power. Amsterdam's regents were not princes, to be sure, but they nonetheless assumed a certain princely style and embraced Classicism.

OTHER SITES

Many history pieces from this classicist period in Dutch painting were intended for palaces, country houses and government buildings and are consequently very large. Two major building projects dating from the mid-17th century gave history painters the opportunity to let themselves go in a thoroughly un-Dutch way: the Huis ten Bosch in The Hague and the new town hall in Amsterdam were elaborately decorated with works answering to a carefully thought-out programme. This was the first time in the Northern Netherlands that the walls of monumental buildings had been covered with magnificent paintings on such an ambitious scale. The subjects chosen for the decorations were taken from classical antiquity, the Bible and history. The stories were chosen for their symbolic significance, but above all they illustrated the grandeur of the people who commissioned them.

ORANGE HALL

Frederik Hendrik (1584-1647), Prince of Orange, became stadholder in 1625 – initially of five provinces and later of seven. The prince's universally recognised strength lay in conquests of a predominantly military nature, yet he was also an important patron of the arts and a man who commissioned buildings of royal status. He built several palaces, including the palaces of Noordeinde and Huis ten Bosch in The Hague. The latter was originally intended as

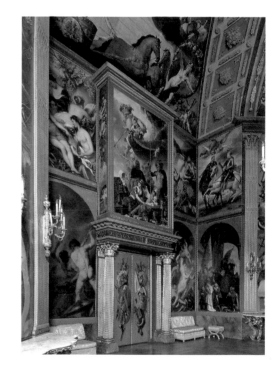

THE 'HUIS TEN BOSCH', ORANGE HALL

a modest country house in the woods for his wife, Amalia van Solms. When Frederik Hendrik died in 1647, Amalia decided to turn the central hall, the Orange Hall, into a memorial to her husband. This hall, which is some 19 metres high, is painted from floor to ceiling. Painted on wood inside the dome are the heavens, with a portrait of Amalia van Solms in the centre, and there are celestial scenes painted between each of the ribs. On the walls below are thirty enormous canvases depicting events in the life of the stadholder. Most of them are allegorical works in which Frederik Hendrik is

< DETAIL OF 172

compared with the great figures of antiquity and classical mythology. The paintings honour him as the spiritual father of the Treaty of Münster (1648), which brought an end to the Eighty Years' War, and as the man who had made possible the economic prosperity of the Golden Age.

The decorative programme for what by Dutch standards was an extremely large project was conceived by the stadholder's former secretary, Constantijn Huygens, in close consultation with the architect, Jacob van Campen. The paintings had to be able to stand comparison with the great Baroque decorations elsewhere in Europe – works like the cycle that Peter Paul Rubens had painted in Paris in honour of Marie de' Medici. To carry out this immense task Huygens and Jacob van Campen together selected eight painters, including Van Campen himself. The other 'seven best painters in the country' – in Huygens's words – were Jacob Jordaens, Theodoor van Thulden, Pieter de Grebber, Gerard van Honthorst, Jan Lievens, Salomon de Bray and Cesar van Everdingen. It was Van Everdingen who received the commission to paint an overmantel depicting the birth of Frederik Hendrik.

THE LITTLE PRINCE

In the shield of Minerva, the Roman goddess of war, sits the infant Frederik Hendrik, looking out at the viewer from under his ermine-lined cap. Mars, the god of war, hands the little Prince his lance, thus investing him with his worldly power. The winged Cupid places his quiver around the little boy's shoulders. Willem of Orange, Frederik Hendrik's father, stands behind Minerva, with a skeleton beside him. The skeleton holds an arrow in his right hand and throws his left arm around the stadholder: the death of the 'Father of the Fatherland' is at hand. Willem of Orange was murdered in 1584, the year of Frederik Hendrik's birth. The veiled woman on the left could be Willem's wife, Louise de

Coligny. It would be a logical place for the young mother, but the features do not correspond with those in known portraits of her, and this has cast doubt on the identification. Another possibility is that this is the sibyl who had predicted the dawn of a Golden Age as described by the Roman poet Virgil in antiquity. A third possibility is that this veiled woman is a goddess watching over the birth. Whoever she is, she attracts attention – Willem, Minerva and Mars all look at her and not at the new baby.

The appearance of both gods – Mars and Minerva – as personifications of the art of war, the sciences and statecraft, clearly indicates the fields in which the future ruler will win fame and honour. Mars is accompanied by a strong wolf. The lion in the foreground represents the Netherlands, and also the kingly virtue of vigilance. The putti in the sky hold up a baldachin, a traditional ceremonial attribute of a ruler. They enthusiastically celebrate the arrival of Frederik Hendrik with great baskets of fruit and flowers. The celestial light and the chain of putti connecting heaven and earth illustrate the celestial powers' approval of this happy event.

VAN EVERDINGEN

The Alkmaar-born painter Cesar van Everdingen was an old friend of Jacob van Campen. They became acquainted in Alkmaar, where Van Everdingen painted the great organ that Van Campen had built there. After this, from 1641 to 1643, Van Everdingen worked in Amersfoort under Van Campen's guidance. Van Everdingen's paintings are characterised by compositions full of commotion, in which the figures are crowded together close to the picture plane. This approach means that the effect of depth is very limited. Cool, clear colours, lit by blue and red accents, are also characteristic of Van Everdingen's work, and he was a master in rendering different materials. His work represents a high point in Dutch Classicism.

FERDINAND BOL

Like Rembrandt, who was his teacher, Ferdinand Bol devoted himself to painting portraits and history pieces (see also 74). Initially he worked so much in Rembrandt's style that confusion regularly arose regarding the attributions of some of his paintings. After 1650, however, his work became more colourful and more elegant, and he exchanged Rembrandt's broad touch for more refined brushwork.

His large work *Venus and Adonis* [171], which he painted around 1657, is a superb example of Bol's classicist work. The finish is smooth and the work is painted in clear shades of red, white and blue, but Rembrandt's influence can still be recognised in the way the painter plays with light and shade. The face of the young hunter, Adonis, is in shadow, and the shadow cast by his body falls on Venus' face. The manner in which Bol rendered the cloak next to Venus, with white highlights that make the fabric gleam, also bears witness to the influence of his master.

170

CESAR VAN EVERDINGEN (c. 1617-1678)
Allegory of the birth of
Frederik Hendrik, c. 1650
Canvas 373 x 243 cm
THE HAGUE, HUIS TEN BOSCH, ORANGE HALL
(in situ since c. 1650, see p. 332)

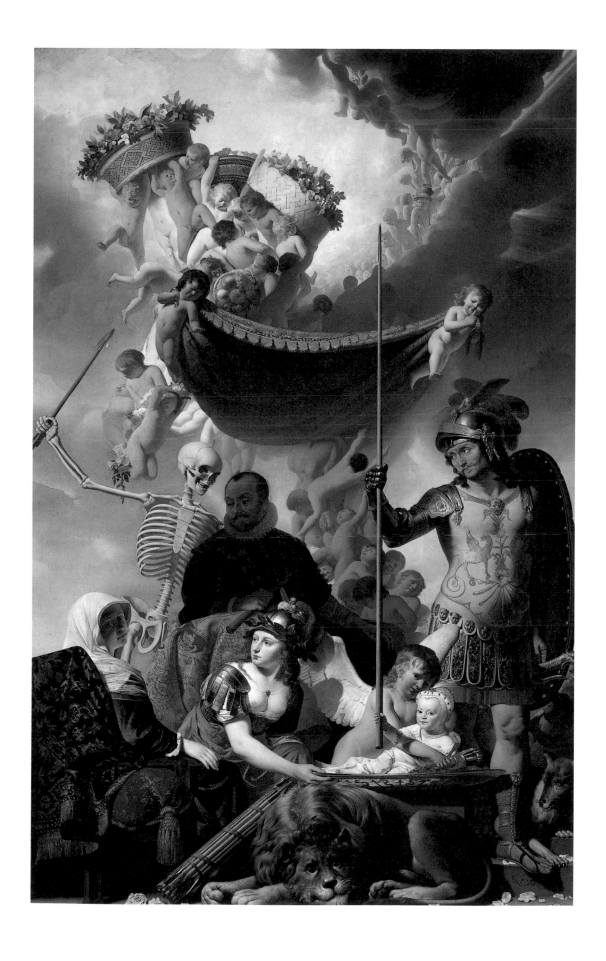

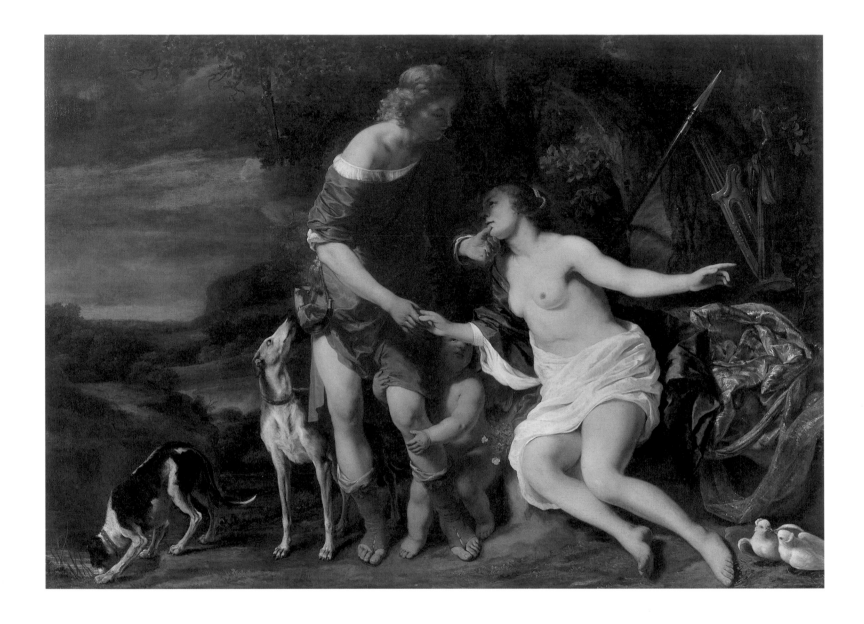

171

FERDINAND BOL (1616-1680)
Venus and Adonis, c. 1658
Canvas 168 x 230 cm
AMSTERDAM, RIJKSMUSEUM
(acquired in 1983, see p. 318)

The story of Venus and Adonis is taken from
the tenth book of Ovid's *Metamorphoses*.
Venus, the goddess of love, becomes
enamoured of the beautiful young huntsman, Adonis. In Bol's painting Venus and
the young Cupid try in vain to prevent

Adonis from going hunting, as the goddess
has had a premonition that the hunting
party will have fatal consequences, and
indeed the hunter is killed by a wild boar.

The story of Venus and Adonis was
a favourite in the Netherlands. Rubens
painted the subject several times and Bol
later painted another picture of the same
theme. It was probably the moral compo-
nent that made the story popular: Adonis
was seen as the epitome of reckless youth,
whose rejection of Venus' advice led him to
his death.

JAN DE BRAY

Jan de Bray – a son and probably also a
pupil of the painter and architect Salomon
de Bray – was one of the most important
representatives of Classicism in Haarlem.
Although he mainly painted portraits, he
was also a very skilled history painter. De
Bray could immerse himself totally in a
story, and this enabled him to capture
historical scenes on canvas in a highly
original way. A good example of one of his
successful history paintings is *David playing
the harp*. David, King of Israel, can be
identified by the crown, the harp he plays
and his white linen garment as described in

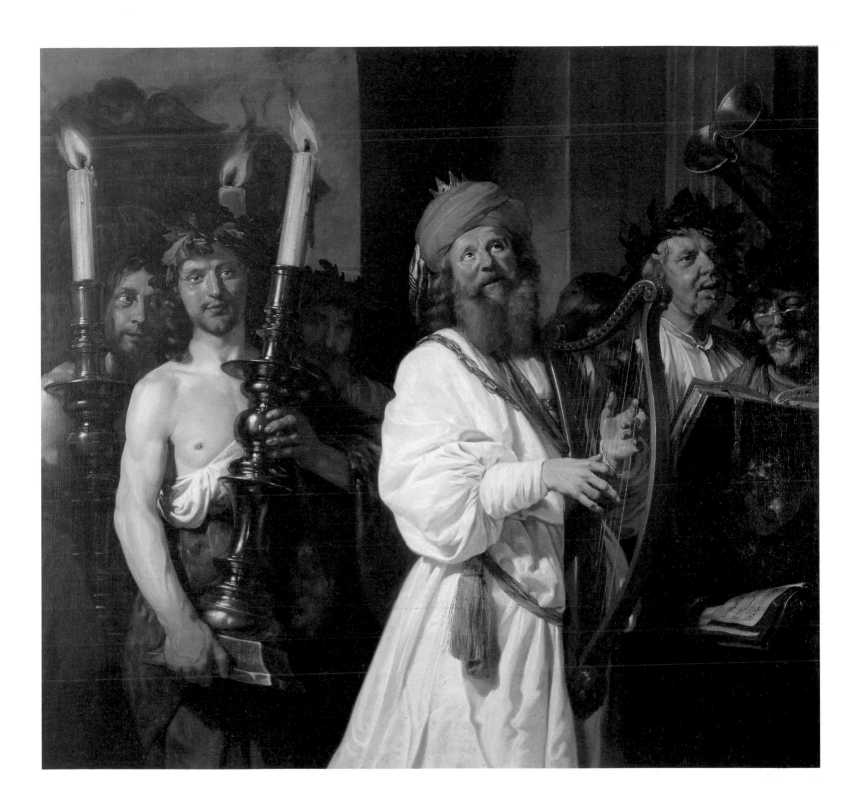

the Bible. As he plays, he raises his eyes to heaven. It is just possible to see the Ark of the Covenant being borne in behind him. The Ark, a magnificently decorated chest, contained the Jews' holy objects. The Philistines had captured it, but it brought

them so much misfortune that they longed to be rid of it. Here David and 'all the Israelites' bear the Ark back to Jerusalem, accompanied by 'shouting and blowing of trumpets' (*II Samuel* 6).

172
JAN DE BRAY (c. 1627-1697)
David playing the harp, 1670
Canvas 142 x 154 cm
THE EARL OF WEMYSS AND MARCH,
SCOTLAND (see p. 351)

The men stand close together and are portrayed half-length. Remarkable indeed is the fact that two men and a boy fix their gaze on the viewer. The man with the candlestick looks brazenly at the beholder. The man just behind him also looks out of the picture and so too does the boy on the extreme right, who emerges under the singers' lectern, supporting the heavy book on his head.

De Bray cleverly combined the individuality of the different characters with a more idealised, timeless rendering of the scene as a whole. This gives his history paintings a more down-to-earth character than those of Dujardin, Bol and Van Everdingen.

DUJARDIN

Around 1660 Karel Dujardin, known for his Italianate landscapes [see 99] also started to paint large biblical scenes in a smooth, elegant and colourful style. *St Paul healing the cripple at Lystra* is an impressive example of a history painting in classicist style.

The apostle Paul is the central figure in the composition. He towers over a crowd of sick and kneeling people. The scene depicted here is taken from the story of Paul, who had fled with Barnabas to Lystra – in present-day southern Turkey – (*Acts* 14:9-10). When Paul was preaching in Lystra, among those listening to him was a man who had been a cripple since birth. Paul 'saw that he had the faith to be cured, so he said to him in a loud voice, "Stand up straight on your feet"; and he sprang up and started to walk'. After this miraculous cure, the crowd took Paul and Barnabas to be heathen gods, and the people even wanted to make sacrifices to them. Appalled, the Christian apostles shouted that they were not gods and begged the people not to offer them sacrifices. In desperation they tore their own clothes. This last event was often depicted in the 17th century, but Karel Dujardin chose a more original moment.

The apostle Paul was painted from a low viewpoint, his form looming against the cloudy sky. He stands in an elegant pose, with his weight on his left leg as he gestures expansively with his arms. Paul, dressed in a brown robe and a bright red cloak, looks at the cripple beside him. The strong red is balanced by the bright blue of the clothes worn by the women on the left. The woman in the foreground on the right, with her immaculate white headdress, is also striking. She grasps the hem of Paul's cloak in her hand in the hope of receiving some of his power.

The needy people standing behind Paul look not at him but at the point where Barnabas once stood. Dujardin had originally portrayed Barnabas behind Paul, but later – for reasons unknown – removed him from the picture. The faint outlines of Barnabas' head are still dimly visible.

DETAIL OF 173

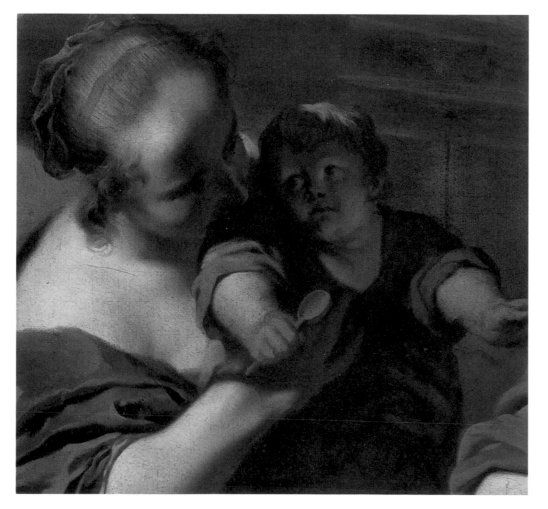

173

KAREL DUJARDIN (1622-1678)
St Paul healing the cripple at Lystra,
1663
Canvas 179 x 139 cm
AMSTERDAM, RIJKSMUSEUM
(acquired with the aid of the Rembrandt Society
in 1997, see p. 319)

>

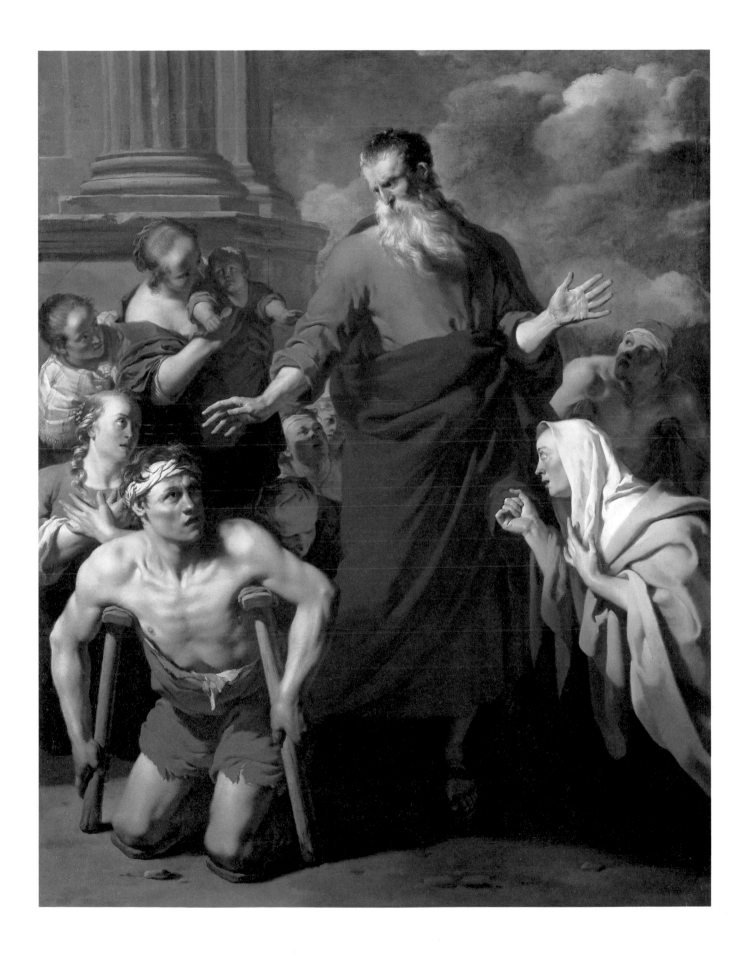

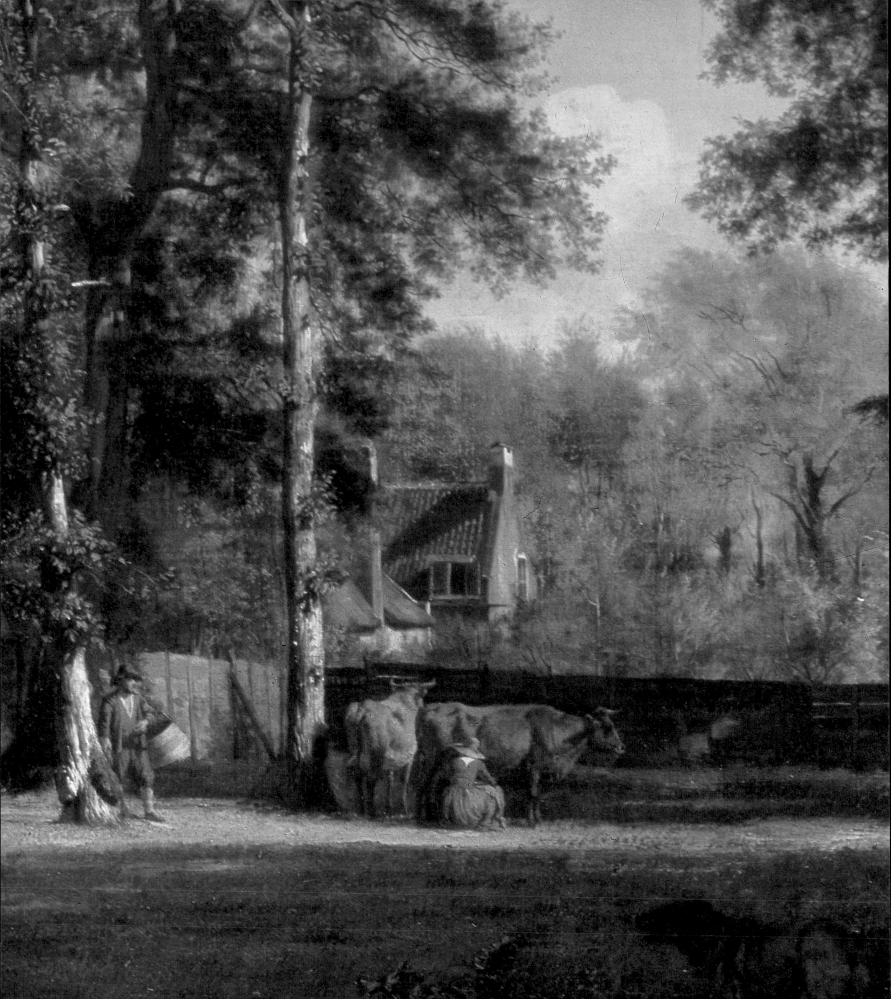

23 ELEGANCE AND REFINEMENT 1660-1690

IN THE second half of the 17th century there was growing criticism of the unedifying subjects chosen by the artists of the first half of the century. 'One saw almost nothing but groups of beggars, crippled, scrofulous and tattered, brothels full of filth, gluttonous peasants in drunken carousals, repugnant in various respects and too foul for words', wrote the art theoretician, artist and lawyer Jan de Bisschop (1628-1671). In his view this was beyond the pale, 'because it is an evident error of judgement to believe that things which are hideous in life are sweet and pleasant when depicted in art.'

THE EXAMPLE OF ANTIQUITY

The beauty that Johan de Bisschop had in mind could be found in the art of antiquity. He drew attention to the classical model in Holland in two influential publications, *Icones* (1668) and *Paradigmata* (1671), in which he elevated idealised, classical art to the norm. He illustrated these books with etchings after Greek and Roman sculptures and after drawings by the great Italian artists of the Renaissance, who had also followed the antique example. De Bisschop's works were rapidly taken up by artists as a source of models. It is possible, for example, to detect in the work of Caspar Netscher and Adriaen van der Werff various classical elements derived from De Bisschop's *Icones*.

REFINEMENT

The extremely precise style is well suited to the classical elements in the paintings of this period. This refinement is seen not only in the work of Netscher and Van der Werff, who can be counted among the 'fine painters' (see chapter 15), but also in that of the landscape painters Adriaen van de Velde and Philips Wouwermans and the architectural artists Gerrit Berckheyde and Jan van der Heyden. A more classical and hence more timeless elegance and refinement can be discerned in almost every genre. In general it can be said that the era of great innovations was over. The craftsmanship, however, was undiminished. Be they portraits or history paintings, landscapes or genre pieces, there are innumerable paintings that bear witness to great skill, displaying, in addition, a certain ease: technical barriers in painting seem to have disappeared.

RICH AND POWERFUL

In the third quarter of the 17th century the gap between rich and poor became wider, with the rich becoming richer and more powerful. In municipal affairs things were run by a small number of wealthy families, who managed, by means of intermarriage and mutual agreements, to hold the reins of power for a long time.

The lifestyle of wealthy burghers bordered on the regal. Stone from abroad was imported to build their large houses, and materials from the Orient to make their clothes. Their interiors became increasingly costly and exotic, and the number of servants grew. This bourgeois culture with its courtly allure was reflected in particular in the genre painting of the second half of the 17th century, and it is also evident in the hunting scenes painted by such artists as Philips Wouwermans.

< DETAIL OF 176

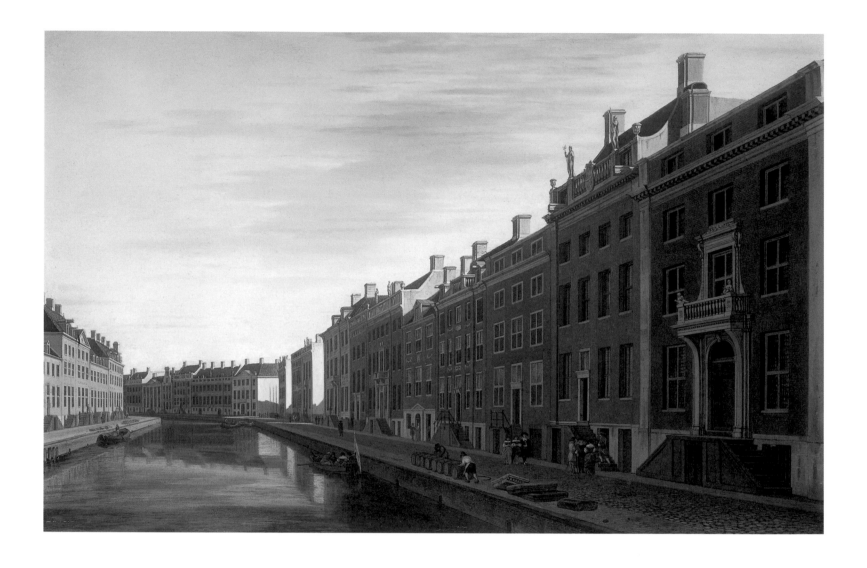

174

GERRIT BERCKHEYDE (1638-1698)
The 'golden bend' in the Herengracht,
Amsterdam 1672
Panel 40.5 x 63 cm
AMSTERDAM, RIJKSMUSEUM
(acquired in 1980, see p. 318)

GROWING CITY

The Gorinchem painter Jan van der Heyden and the Haarlem-born Gerrit Berckheyde are among the painters who raised the cityscape to new heights. Both artists found a superb subject in Amsterdam, which was undergoing explosive growth; no other city in the world was changing as fast as Amsterdam was at that time.

In 1672, when Berckheyde painted the 'golden bend', the section of the Herengracht between the Leidsestraat and the Vijzelstraat, it had just been completed. The 'canal belt', or semi-circle of parallel canals around the city centre, was constructed in two stages. The first part was built around 1610, the second around 1660. Berckheyde painted part of the second expansion,

recording the latest fashion in domestic architecture. The traditional canal house, three windows wide with a top gable, had become less popular. During the second half of the 17th century rich burghers preferred to buy two adjacent lots, each seven metres wide, on which they built double-fronted houses. The tops of the gables were finished with classical cornices, sometimes crowned with balustrades, statues or pediments.

BERCKHEYDE

Perspective, the fall of light and geometric accuracy are the most striking features of Berckheyde's *The 'golden bend' in the Herengracht, Amsterdam*. The geometric effect is created by the vertical lines of the houses, the horizontal cloud banks and the sharp diagonals of the canal. It is heightened still further by the contrast between the façades that are lit and the ones in shadow, and by the bright light that streams into the empty lots on the southern side.

There is not a tree to be seen in the painting of this newly built section of Amsterdam, though there were in fact trees on this site in 1672. We know this from a drawing that Berckheyde probably made as a study for the painting, which shows low trees a few years old on the north side of the canal and young, recently planted trees on the south. By omitting the trees Berckheyde was able to do full justice to the buildings, but in so doing he gave this small area of Amsterdam a much more austere and calculated look than was actually the case.

VAN DER HEYDEN

In his painting *Dam Square in Amsterdam, with a view of the New Church* Jan van der Heyden focused not so much on the buildings as on the activity in the square. Van der Heyden believed that the atmosphere was more important than the architecture. He painted no more than a corner of Jacob van Campen's new town hall and only showed the façade of the transept of the New Church – with its soaring window – in detail; the nave of the church is essentially left in shadow. The boy bowling his hoop, the townspeople sauntering across the square, the horse pulling the sled and the dog in the foreground on the right, coupled with the lively style in which the architecture is painted, give the central square of Amsterdam a wholly natural look. Van der Heyden himself was responsible for the architecture, but the figures and animals were painted by Adriaen van de Velde, one of the most brilliant figure and landscape painters of the third quarter of the 17th century.

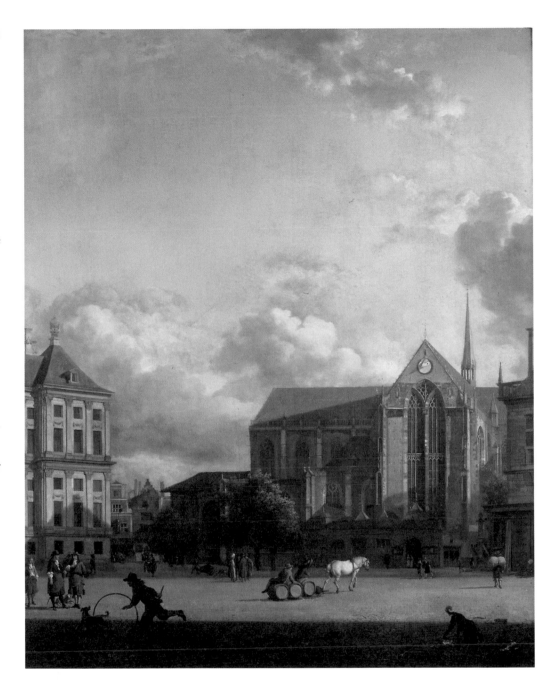

175
JAN VAN DER HEYDEN (1637-1712)
Dam Square in Amsterdam, with a view of the New Church, c. 1668-1670
Panel 68 x 55 cm
AMSTERDAM,
AMSTERDAMS HISTORISCH MUSEUM
(bequeathed to the City of Amsterdam in 1893,
see p. 320)

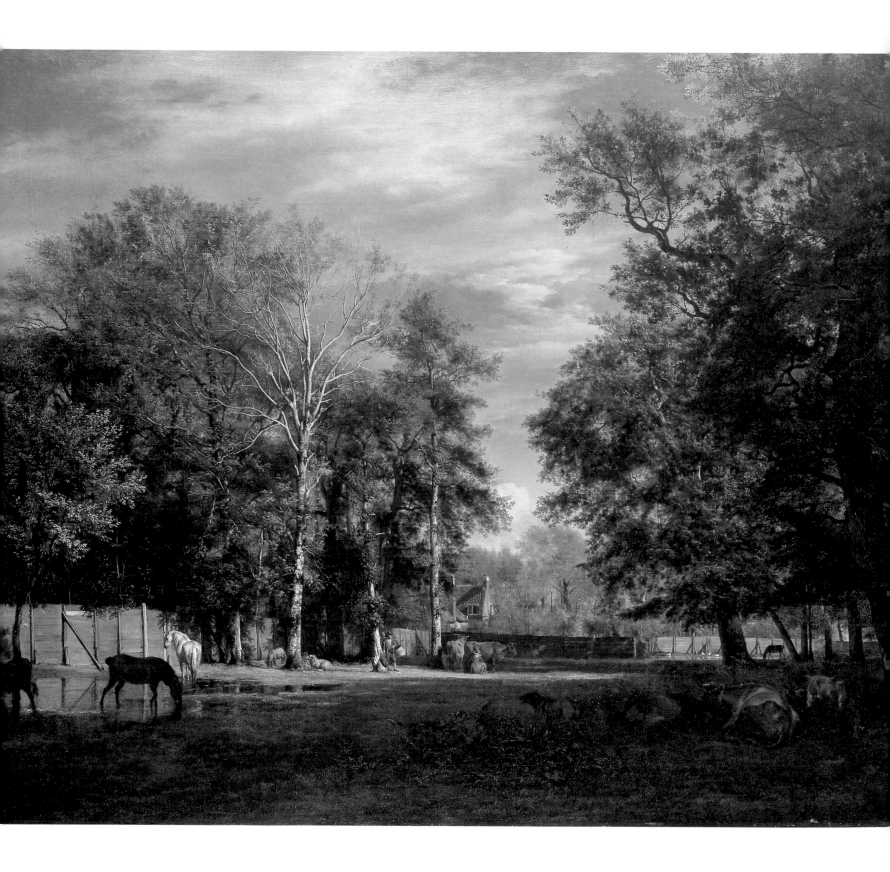

176

ADRIAEN VAN DE VELDE (1636-1672)

The farm, 1666

Canvas on panel 63 x 78 cm

BERLIN, GEMÄLDEGALERIE

(acquired in 1899, see p. 322)

<

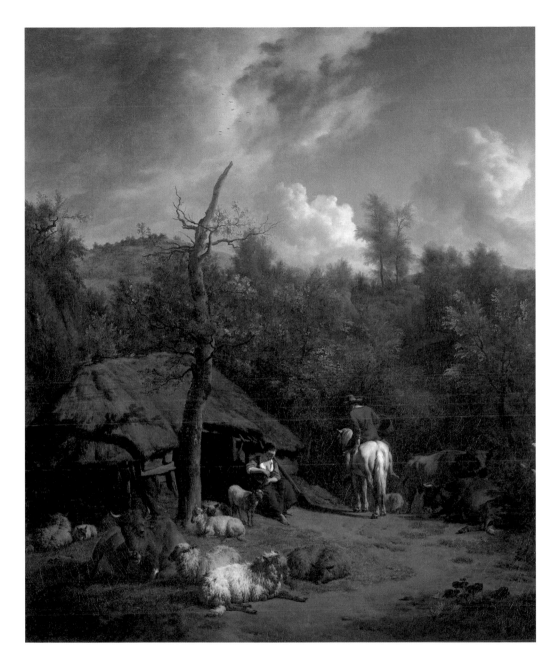

ADRIAEN VAN DE VELDE

Adriaen van de Velde was the son of the marine painter Willem van de Velde the Elder (*see 159*). Although he certainly studied with his father, Adriaen devoted himself to landscapes with people and animals. The figures in his landscapes were so well executed that several of his fellow artists asked him to paint the staffage in their work. Adriaen's figures consequently appear not only in the work of Jan van der Heyden [*175*], but also in paintings by Jacob van Ruisdael, Meindert Hobbema, Philips Koninck, Allaert van Everdingen and his brother Willem van de Velde the Younger.

According to the artists' biographer Arnold Houbraken (1660-1719) Adriaen van de Velde took to the out of doors and painted nearly every day from nature. Many of these sketches have survived. A comparison of his drawings and paintings reveals how the artist set about his work. He probably started by making a rough compositional sketch. He would then draw various figure studies of both people and animals. Finally, Van de Velde made a detailed design drawing, which served as the starting point for the painting. There are several surviving preparatory studies of this kind for his painting *The hut* [*177*]. Van de Velde drew the woman with the basket several times, and there are also separate sketches of the animals and the hut.

The drawing on which his masterpiece *The farm* [*176*] is based has also been preserved. The painting demonstrates Van de Velde's versatility and talent. Each element

was carefully worked out: the different types of trees, the cows peacefully chewing their cud, the well-proportioned horses reflected in a puddle, the watchful dog in the foreground and the woman milking a cow in the middle distance. All the elements together form an entity, further heightened by the exceptionally fine interplay of light and shade, with the brightly lit trunk of the tree in the centre providing a striking accent.

177

ADRIAEN VAN DE VELDE (1636-1672)

The hut, 1671

Canvas 76 x 65 cm

AMSTERDAM, RIJKSMUSEUM

(acquired in 1822, see p. 310)

265

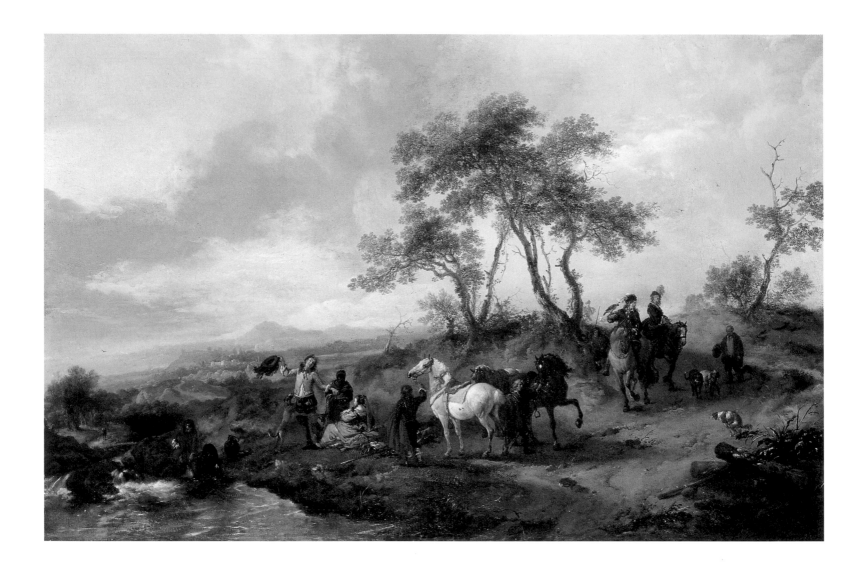

178

PHILIPS WOUWERMANS (1619-1668)
Halt of a hunting party, c. 1665
Canvas 55.6 x 82.9 cm
LONDON, DULWICH PICTURE GALLERY
(acquired in 1811, see p. 336)

MAGNIFICENT HORSES

The Haarlem painter Philips Wouwermans was one of the most successful artists of the Golden Age. He was also extraordinarily prolific, leaving an oeuvre of around a thousand works. His paintings – usually of a manageable size – are of hunting parties, battles, stables, smithies and army encamp-

ments. Horses are always a prominent feature. The colours in Wouwermans's paintings are delicate and the works are technically perfect.

Wouwermans's picture of the hunting party [*178*] features two opulently dressed couples and their servants, stopping to rest by a river. While one couple has already settled down to rest, the other couple still sit on their horses. Wouwermans reserved a small area for genre-like scenes in many of his paintings. Here the little dog on the right seems to be thumbing its nose, so to speak, at the aristocratic elegance of the scene.

Wouwermans also incorporated a narrative element in *The grey* [*179*], one of his early works. The horse which the young

man holds by the bridle has a chance to rest because his rider – the man concealed behind the hillock on the right – has dismounted to relieve himself. The grey, placed in the limelight in this splendid pose, bestows the scene with a monumental allure.

179

PHILIPS WOUWERMANS (1619-1668)
The grey, c. 1646
Panel 43.5 x 38 cm
AMSTERDAM, RIJKSMUSEUM
(acquired with the aid of the Rembrandt Society in 1894, see p. 313)

>

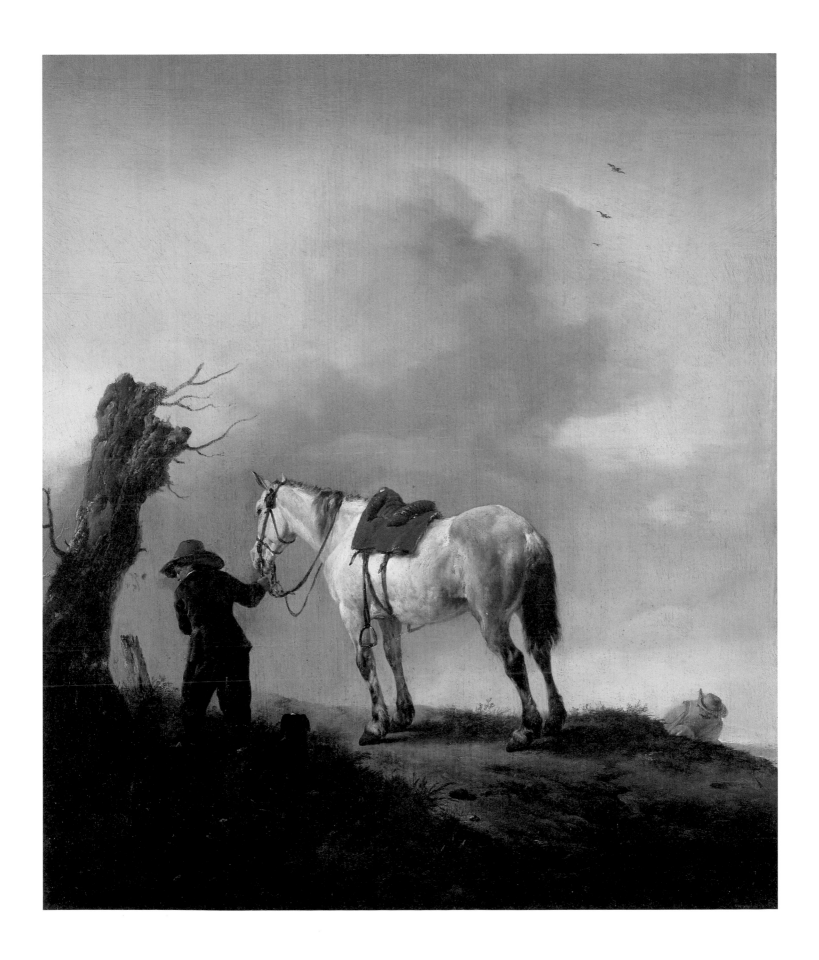

APPRECIATION

Wouwermans's paintings were highly sought after; few painters earned as much money from their work as he did. His paintings remained popular after his death. His work was represented in all the royal collections amassed in the 18th and 19th centuries, and the great museums that grew out of these collections have dozens of paintings by this equestrian painter. The list is headed by the Gemäldegalerie in Dresden, with more than 60 works, and the Hermitage in St Petersburg, which has over 50 paintings by Wouwermans. In the 18th century *Halt of a hunting party* was in the collection of the Duc d'Orléans. Wouwermans's paintings were much sought after by noble collectors; already in those days hunting was a favourite pastime in aristocratic circles.

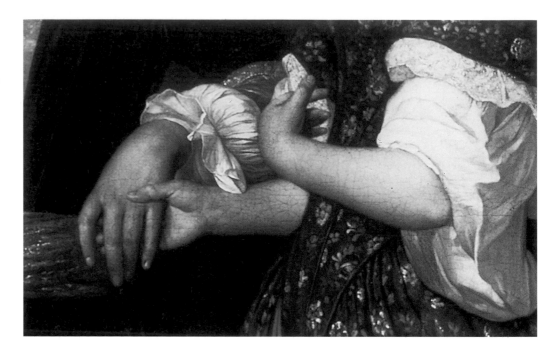

DETAIL OF 180

'FINE PAINTERS'

The 'fine painters' Godfried Schalcken, Eglon van der Neer and Caspar Netscher all worked in the tradition of Gerard Dou, the founding father of 'fine painting'. Like Dou, they endeavoured to capture the visible world as faithfully as possible, but unlike Dou – whose paintings sometimes give the impression of being a collection of cleverly painted details – they tried to create a convincing entity. The start of this development can be seen in the work of Dou's most gifted pupil, Frans van Mieris (*see 123*).

EGLON VAN DER NEER

Eglon van der Neer devoted a great deal of attention to the minutest details in his genre paintings – from the foreground to the most distant point in the background – though this did not always serve to heighten the natural effect of these scenes. The very precise and accurate rendering of the various materials sometimes gives his paintings a cool, distant feel. Nevertheless, Van der Neer was highly successful: the opulent interiors and the extremely costly materials he so accurately depicted must have appealed

to the imagination of his clients. He was admired by many of the crowned heads of Europe and worked as court painter to the Elector Palatine Johann Wilhelm.

The rich, fashionably dressed burghers who are the subject of *Elegant couple in an interior* are shown surrounded by several servants. Van der Neer paid great attention to the costly fabrics of the clothes of the elegant couple in the foreground. He rendered the sheen and transparency of ribbons, embroidery and lace with the utmost care, and the man's beautifully coifed wig received the same meticulous attention to detail. The various elements in the painting have not been forged into a unified whole, however. Eglon van der Neer probably wanted to demonstrate his technical skill in the depiction of details. The great variety of materials is certainly no coincidence.

We cannot say with any certainty whether the painting depicts anything more than two people in a stylish interior. The fact that the couple in the background are drinking and their rather too intimate behaviour might indicate that this is a brothel scene.

GODFRIED SCHALCKEN

Godfried Schalcken was the only one of the three to have studied with Gerard Dou in Leiden. This was around 1660, the period when Dou was concentrating on painting nocturnal scenes. These paintings, lit with scant candlelight, were universally praised; the representation of a light source and its associated reflections was regarded as a great artistic feat. The young Schalcken accepted the challenge and elected to specialise in scenes illuminated by candlelight, achieving an unequalled standard in this singular genre in a remarkably short space of time.

180

EGLON VAN DER NEER (1635/1636-1703)
Elegant couple in an interior, 1678
Canvas 85.5 x 70.1 cm
PRIVATE COLLECTION, COURTESY OF
WADSWORTH ATHENEUM, HARTFORD
(see p. 334)

>

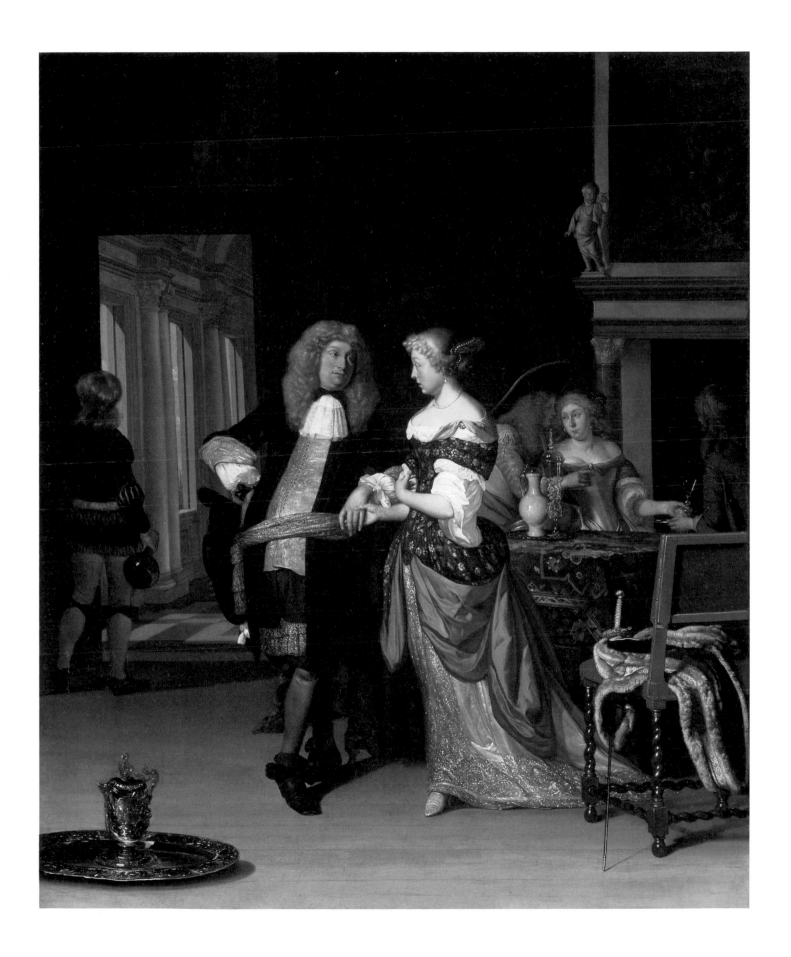

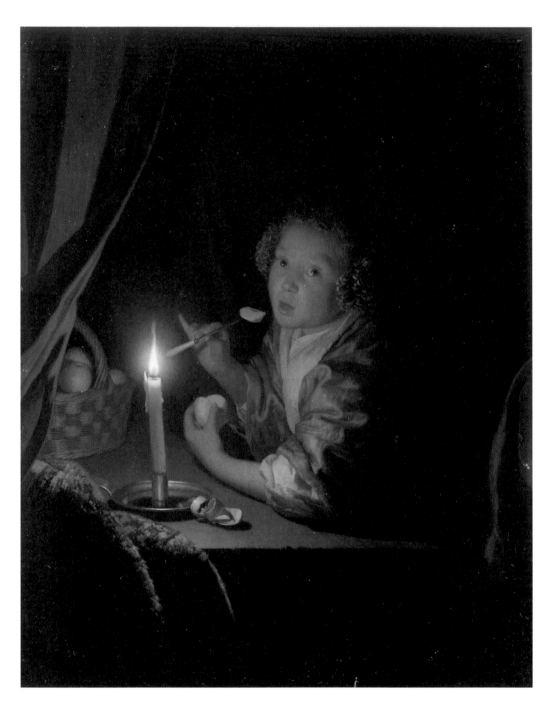

181

GODFRIED SCHALCKEN (1643-1706)
Girl eating an apple, c. 1675-1680
Panel 32.2 x 24.8 cm
SCHWERIN, STAATLICHES MUSEUM
(acquired between 1735 and 1792, see p. 346)

<

182

CASPAR NETSCHER (1635/1636-1684)
Portrait of Abraham van Lennep, 1672
Canvas 55 x 45.3 cm
PARIS, COLLECTION FRITS LUGT,
INSTITUT NÉERLANDAIS
(acquired with the aid of the Rembrandt Society
in 1976, see p. 343)

>

Schalcken's painting is not so minutely detailed as his teacher's. This is evident from the rendering of the Turkish carpet in the foreground. Dou would have painted it down to the tiniest detail, but Schalcken depicted it in small, powerful strokes in bright red, blue and yellow. The illusion of real knotted wool is in no way diminished by this – Schalcken's imitation of reality is at least as convincing as that of his illustrious predecessor.

NETSCHER

The work of Gerard ter Borch was also an important source of inspiration for the 'fine painters'. Eglon van der Neer and Caspar Netscher were pupils of his and their early work in particular is strongly reminiscent of Ter Borch's. Both artists gradually distanced themselves from their teacher's style, however. They laid increasing emphasis on painterly details and costly fabrics, while their models became increasingly elegant. Caspar Netscher painted genre scenes and history paintings and was, like Godfried Schalcken, much in demand as a portrait

Girl eating an apple is a fine example of one of Schalcken's candlelit works. The subject is a mundane, domestic one: a girl, seated at a table, puts a piece of apple into her mouth. The scene is lit only by the flame of a candle. With extraordinary effectiveness Schalcken captured the phenomenon of the candlelight, with just a few reflections of the orange glow. Admirers wondered how the

artist managed to pull off this feat. In the 18th century, an Englishman actually suggested that Schalcken had installed an enclosed cabin in his studio, lit only by a burning candle, where his model would sit. The painter was then said to have looked in through a peephole to paint the dimly lit scene.

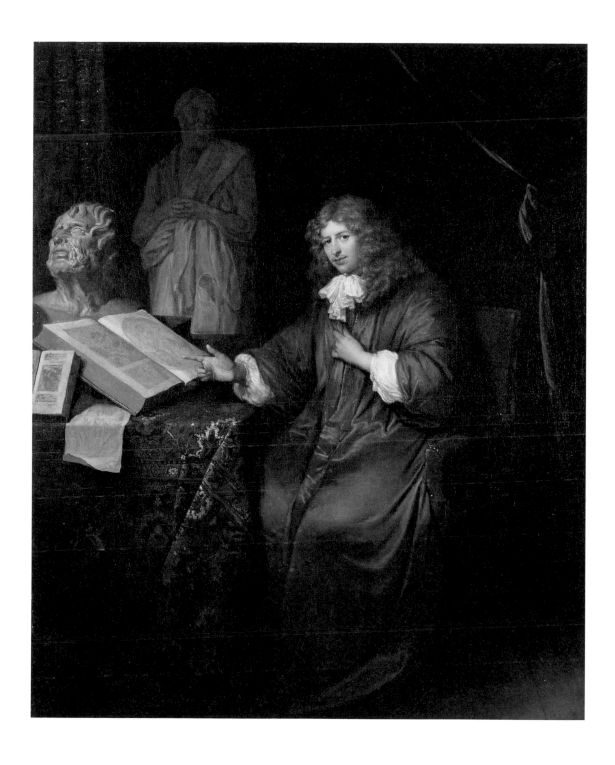

painter. His *Portrait of Abraham van Lennep* is typical of his work [*182*]. Abraham van Lennep (1627-1678) was known as a lover of the arts and sciences, and Netscher included in his portrait attributes that leave no room for doubt as to the sitter's interests. The distinguished Van Lennep, wearing a satin-trimmed dress-ing gown, points emphatically at a valuable object in his collection – one of the 34 books containing mainly Italian prints and drawings, a collection that Van Lennep had built up over many years. The classical statuary – a head of Seneca and a statue of Homer – refers to Van Lennep's interest in antiquity. The statue of Homer was not in fact in Van Lennep's collection; Netscher depicted it after a print which Jan de Bisschop had published shortly before in his *Icones* of 1668 (see p. 261).

271

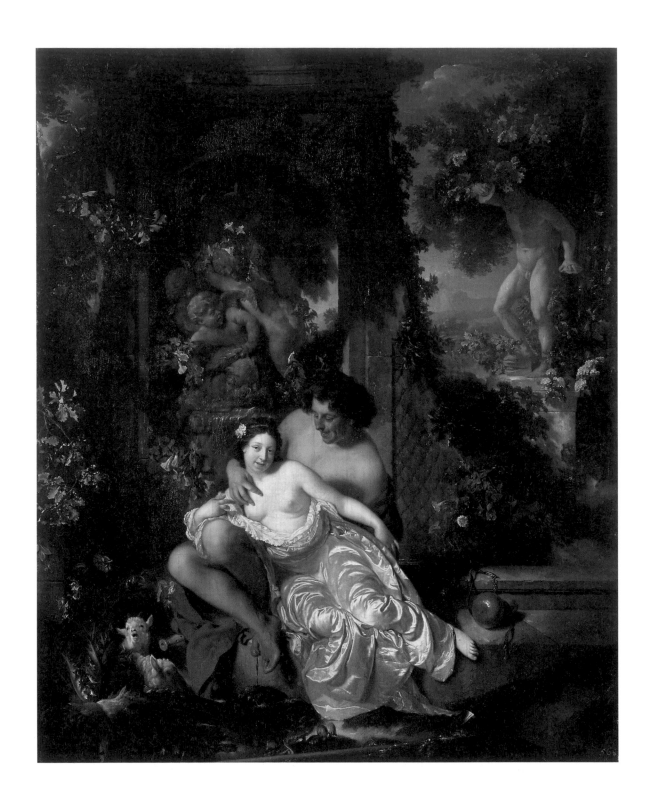

183

ADRIAEN VAN DER WERFF (1659-1722)

Shepherd and shepherdess, 1689

Panel 58.5 x 47.5 cm

DRESDEN, GEMÄLDEGALERIE

(acquired in 1710, see p. 329)

ADRIAEN VAN DER WERFF

The most renowned artist at the end of the Golden Age was the Rotterdam painter Adriaen van der Werff. His extremely elegant works with their enamel-smooth finish were sold for huge sums and were sought after by royal collectors. Van der Werff learned the technique of 'fine painting' from Eglon van der Neer, and his early works are highly reminiscent of the work of his master. Van der Werff began his career painting genre pieces, but soon turned to history paintings and allegories in a classicist style, in which ideal beauty and harmony prevail.

The painting of the pastoral scene depicting the shepherd and the gracefully reclining shepherdess is an example of his early work. It already contains many classical elements, but still bears a strong resemblance to the work of his teachers. All the themes are worked out in great detail, and as a result the painting makes a rather incoherent and overloaded impression. Van der Werff actually made a sort of apology for it later on, when he described it as 'cleverly done, but of an earlier time'. Van der Werff surrounded the couple with all sorts of accessories, including plants, flowers, trees, architecture, a fountain and classical statues. All this was intended to show that the couple are in a pleasure-garden and have decidedly amorous intentions, as unambiguously symbolised by the flute lying near the shepherd.

Shepherd and shepherdess was purchased by the Elector Palatine, who also ordered a series of no fewer than 15 paintings from Van der Werff. This series occupied Van der Werff's time to such an extent that he had to turn down a commission from the Elector of Saxony. When the latter complained, the Elector Palatine magnanimously presented him with two paintings by Van der Werff, including the *Shepherd and shepherdess*. The Elector of Saxony's collection is the nucleus of the collection in the Gemäldegalerie in Dresden, the current home of this work.

VAN BOSSUIT

The Brussels sculptor Francis van Bossuit spent several years studying in Rome, where he joined the group of Dutch and Flemish artists known as the Bentvueghels. His Italian experiences left an indelible stamp on his development. Around 1680, when Van Bossuit settled in Amsterdam, he worked in an international Baroque style which was strongly influenced by classical examples.

The superb ivory statue of Mars, the god of war, which Van Bossuit made in Amsterdam, was probably based on a classical statue that the sculptor saw in Rome. The classical Mars also reaches for his sword and is shown naked, as was customary in classical sculpture. This statue of Mars proves that Van Bossuit had total mastery of the idealised classical style. The god's pose – with the slight twist of the torso, the details of muscles and veins, and the threatening look on his face – have been captured with consummate skill. Van Bossuit was a master in handling ivory, which is hard and very difficult to work. He followed the original line of the material, the tusk, as Mars' pose reveals. In this statue there is no trace of the angularity that so often characterises ivory carving. It seems almost to have been modelled in wax or clay. Van Bossuit gave the individual elements of the statue a character of their own. The shield, for example, decorated with the terrifying head of Medusa, rests lightly against Mars' calf, and the rough ground he stands on contrasts with the polished body of the god. The subtle treatment of this exceptionally large ivory carving makes this sculpture one of the great works of the Golden Age.

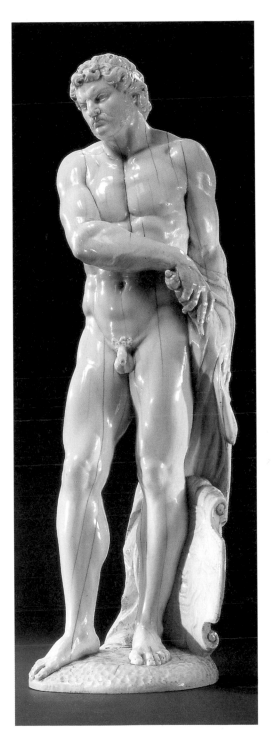

184

FRANCIS VAN BOSSUIT (1635-1692)
Mars, c. 1680-1692
Ivory h. 44 cm
AMSTERDAM, RIJKSMUSEUM
(acquired with the aid of the Rembrandt Society
in 1998, see p. 319)

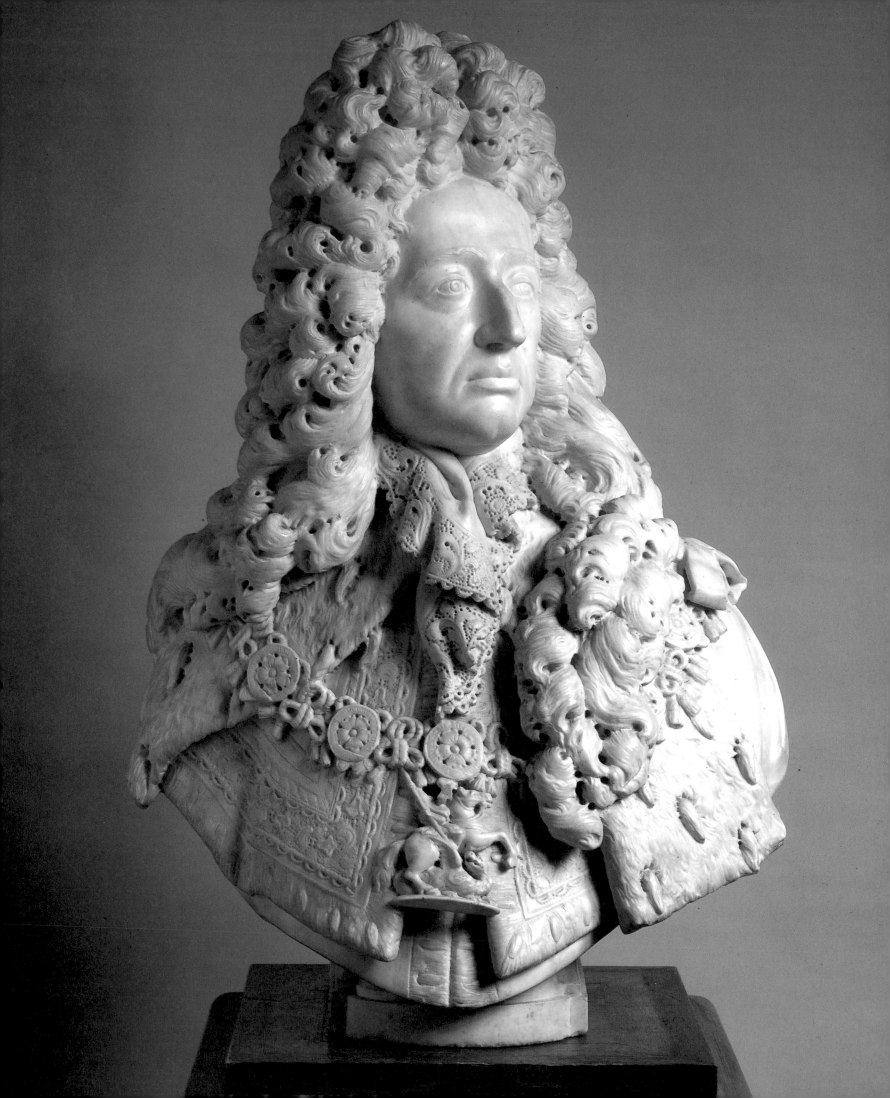

24 COURT ART UNDER WILLEM III
1680-1700

WILLEM III (1650-1702) was a statesman, soldier, passionate huntsman and art lover. With his English wife Mary Stuart (1662-1694) he built, furnished and decorated palaces and laid out gardens in both the Dutch Republic and England. The royal couple gave numerous artists the opportunity to display their skills. Following French examples, all the artistic forms were harmonised to form a coherent entity. Architecture, sculpture, painting, crafts and landscaping were used in combination to express the power and status of the stadholder-king.

FRENCH EXAMPLES
At the end of the 17th century Louis XIV (1638-1715), the Sun King, set the tone for all the courts of Europe. The decorative style which developed in his palace at Versailles became the model even for Willem III, the arch-rival of the French king.

185
JAN BLOMMENDAEL (1650-1702)
Portrait of Stadholder-King Willem III
(1650-1702), 1699
Marble h. 80 cm
THE HAGUE, MAURITSHUIS
(acquired in 1816, see p. 332)

<

French art was nothing new at the court in Holland – Willem's grandfather, Frederik Hendrik, had a French mother who had extended commissions to artists from her native country on more than one occasion, while Willem's father, Willem II, had had furniture made in Paris. There had also been close ties with France during the stadholder-less period before Willem III came to power (1650-1672). Dutch artists and their patrons kept a close eye on developments in France, and French ornamental prints, which were used as models by craftsmen, found their way to the Dutch Republic. The most important French influence, however, came in about 1685 when the Catholic Sun King turned against the Huguenots – the French Calvinists. As a result they fled the country by the thousand. Many of them, including craftsmen, went to the tolerant Low Countries, where they continued to work in the style they had developed in their own country. One of these émigrés was Daniel Marot (1661-1752), a man who was to have a significant influence on the arts in the Dutch Republic.

THE END OF THE CENTURY
Three years before the death of Willem III, Jan Blommendael portrayed the stadholder-king in marble [185]. He showed him as a powerful sovereign, wearing the royal ermine cape and the chain of the Order of the Garter. The stadholder-king's clothes and his wig are in the French mode, and the whole style of this sculpture is based on French Baroque portrait sculpture.

The fashions at the court of Willem III dictated in their turn the taste of the well-to-do in the Netherlands. In their spacious homes, rich burghers surrounded themselves with French furniture, as well as ceiling and wall decorations in the French style. These foreign influences can also be identified in painting. The 17th century ended on as eclectic and international a note as it had begun.

PALACE 'HET LOO'
In 1684 Willem III bought the castle 'Het Loo' near Apeldoorn, and work on the building of a new palace started immediately. The French artist Daniel Marot was responsible for the decoration of the interior

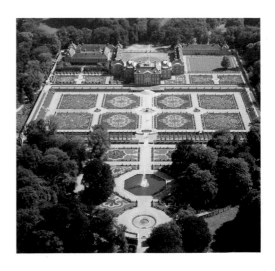

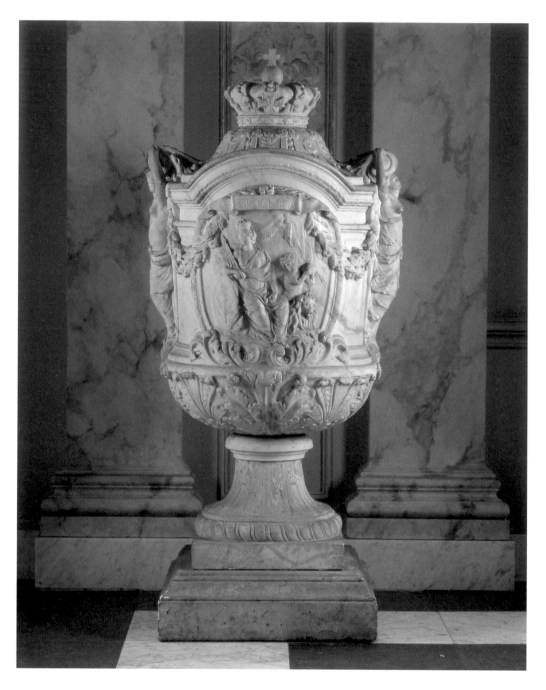

186

JAN EBBELAER (1666-1706) AFTER
DANIEL MAROT (1661-1752)
Scotia-Virtus vase, 1696-1697
Marble h. 160 cm
APELDOORN,
PALEIS HET LOO NATIONAAL MUSEUM
(in situ since 1696-1697, see p. 321)

URNS

There were four urns on the terrace at the back of 'Het Loo', two of which have survived. One was made by Jan Blommendael and the other by Jan Ebbelaer, both after designs by Daniel Marot. The urns bear a king's crown on their covers and each one depicts a virtue and a part of Willem III's kingdom. Ebbelaer's urn represents Scotland; the urn showing the Dutch Republic is by Blommendael. The other two urns, which have been lost, symbolised Ireland and England.

The urn depicting the Dutch Republic shows the Maid of Holland under the inscription *Je Maintiendrai*, accompanied by two winged female figures: one with the orb and the other with the crowned Dutch lion. On the other side of the urn is Fortitude; behind her is a pillar symbolising steadfastness. The second urn [*186*] depicts Virtue, holding aloft a laurel wreath while two winged genii bear a globe. Scotland is represented by a crowned woman with a sceptre in her hand and a putto holding an orb. The cover of the urn bears the Tudor rose, the French lily, the Scottish thistle and the Irish harp. The scrolls are supported by caryatids – women with their hands above their heads, holding the ornamentation.

TWO TILES

In 1689, when Willem III and his wife became William and Mary, king and queen of England, they commissioned rebuilding work at Hampton Court Palace, the royal country residence near London. Although the plans were confined to the improvement of the existing building and the addition of a new wing, the works did not proceed swiftly. Since the king and queen wanted to stay at Hampton Court, private apartments were furnished for Mary in the Water Gallery, the garden pavilion on the bank of the River Thames. The rooms were attractive and comfortable: there was hot and cold water in the bathroom, for instance, and the decorations of the dairy included

and probably also for the layout of the new palace, which was built after a design by Jacob Roman (1640-1716). Marot also designed the gardens and their pavilions.

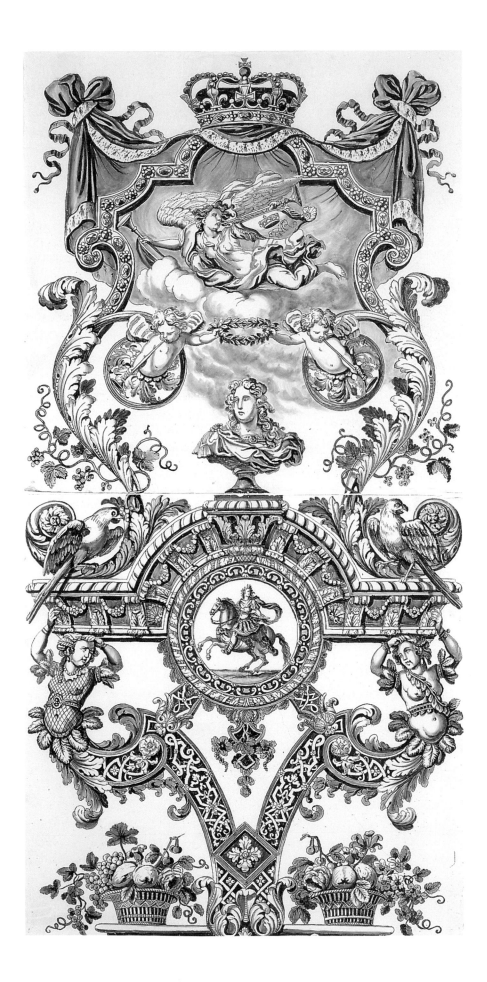

Delftware tiles made after a design by Daniel Marot.

Marot's designs are based on the Louis XIV style, with S- and C-shaped scrolls, acanthus leaves, pilasters, herms and caryatids, always arranged in a symmetrical pattern. Such elements can also be found in the earthenware tiles that Marot designed for the Water Gallery.

Mary Stuart was a passionate collector of *objets d'art* and owned a very large collection of Delftware. Thanks to Mary, people in court circles – both in the Netherlands and in England – developed a taste for this blue-and-white earthenware. This provided a significant boost for the Delft potteries, particularly for the pottery known as *De Grieksche A*, which was Mary's favoured supplier.

A GILT TABLE

Daniel Marot supplied designs for virtually all forms of decorative art. The gilt wood table now in the Rijksmuseum [*188*] was made in his style. He published many of his designs as series of prints, classified according to type and material. These series included designs for objects in silver, as well as carved tables, for even furniture was made in silver at the court of Louis XIV. In 1689, however, the Sun King was forced to melt down his silver furniture to pay for his military campaigns. He had it replaced with carved wooden furniture, which was then gilt.

187

POTTERY 'DE GRIEKSCHE A'
UNDER THE SUPERVISION OF ADRIAEN KOCKS,
AFTER DANIEL MAROT (1661-1752)
Two tiles, c. 1690
Blue-painted faience, 62 x 62 cm
AMSTERDAM, RIJKSMUSEUM
(acquired in 1955, see p. 316)

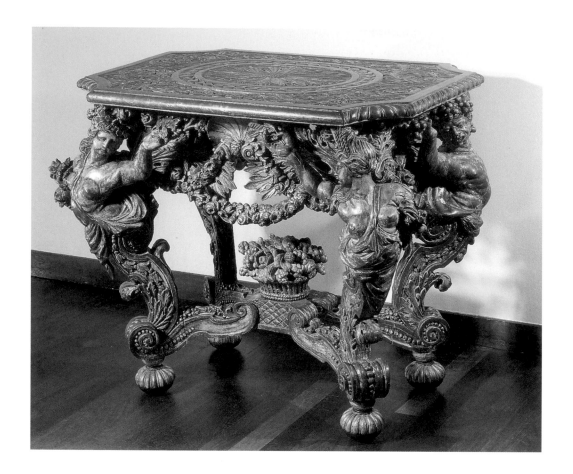

188

Table, c. 1700
Gilt limewood and oak,
87.5 x 108.5 x 73.5 cm
AMSTERDAM, RIJKSMUSEUM
(acquired in 1937, see p. 316)

190

ATTRIBUTED TO JAN VAN MEKEREN
(1658-1733)
Cabinet, c. 1690-1710
Oak, veneered with kingwood, ebony,
rosewood, olive, sycamore and other woods
205 x 173 x 61 cm
AMSTERDAM, RIJKSMUSEUM
(acquired in 1964, see p. 317)

>

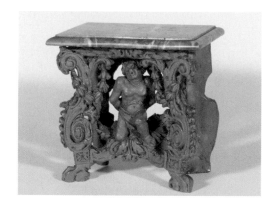

189

HENDRIK NOTEMAN (1656-1734)
Model for table, c. 1700
Terracotta 17.2 x 17.8 x 12 cm
DORDRECHT,
MUSEUM MR. SIMON VAN GIJN
(acquired in 1933, see p. 328)

This side table in the French court style was originally gilt, but most of the gilding has worn off so that it is now the reddish-brown ground, the 'bole', that gives the piece its colour. The forward-leaning herms and caryatids forming the legs of the table are typical of Marot's style. These figures, linked by festoons of flowers, represent the four seasons.

When furniture as lavish as this was commissioned, preliminary terracotta models were made, exactly as they were for sculptures, and submitted to the client for approval. The little table by Hendrik Noteman is one of these terracotta models [189]. It is a design for a table with a marble top supported on elaborate scrolls with a chained figure in the centre. The table for which this model was made is now to be found in an institution in Haarlem.

FLORAL MARQUETRY CABINET

The large two-doored cabinet-on-stand is a typically Dutch piece of furniture. Cabinets like this have a simple interior with just a few shelves and a couple of drawers. They were generally used to store household linen. The cabinet attributed to Jan van Mekeren is simple in form, so that all the attention is focused on the superb floral marquetry decoration. The oak cabinet has been entirely covered with various kinds of wood, which the cabinetmaker used to create still lifes of vases overflowing with flowers of all kinds.

Van Mekeren worked not only with the different colours of the woods but also with the direction of the grain. The sophisticated composition of the still lifes in the inlaid work was inspired by French examples and is reminiscent of the work of the Parisian cabinetmaker André-Charles Boulle (1642-1732).

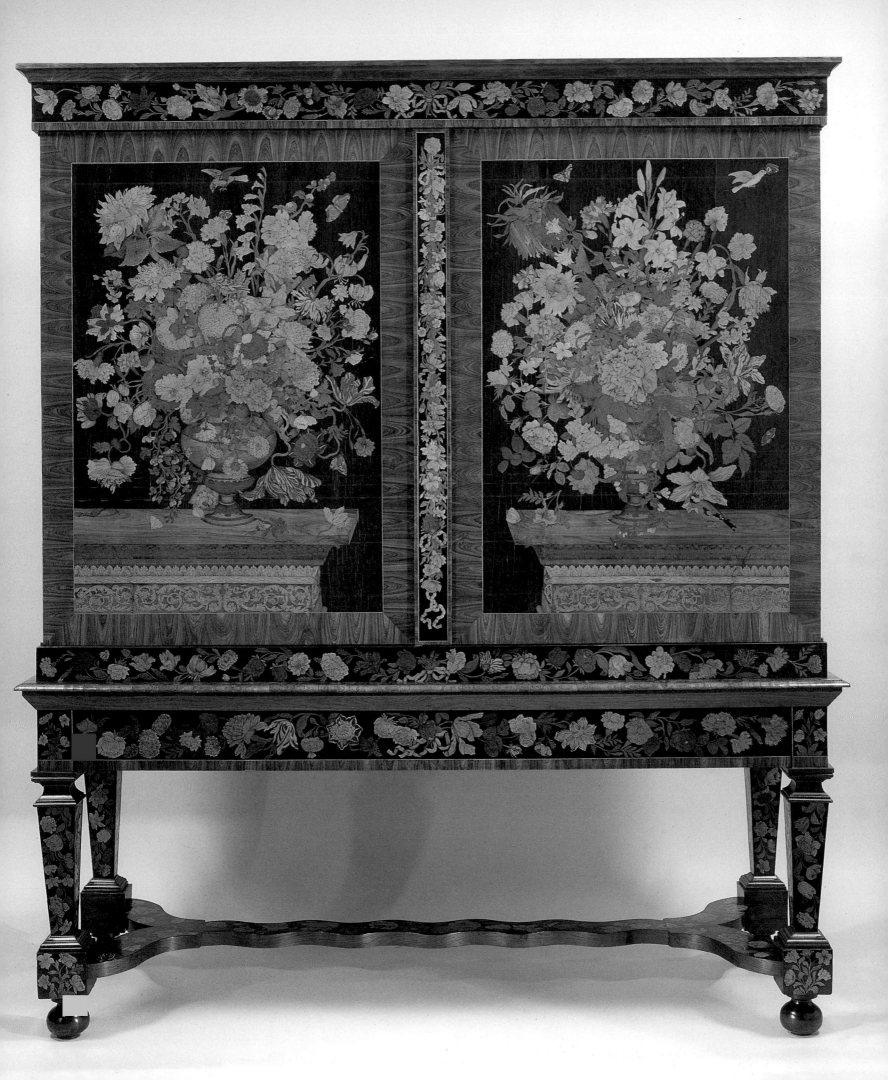

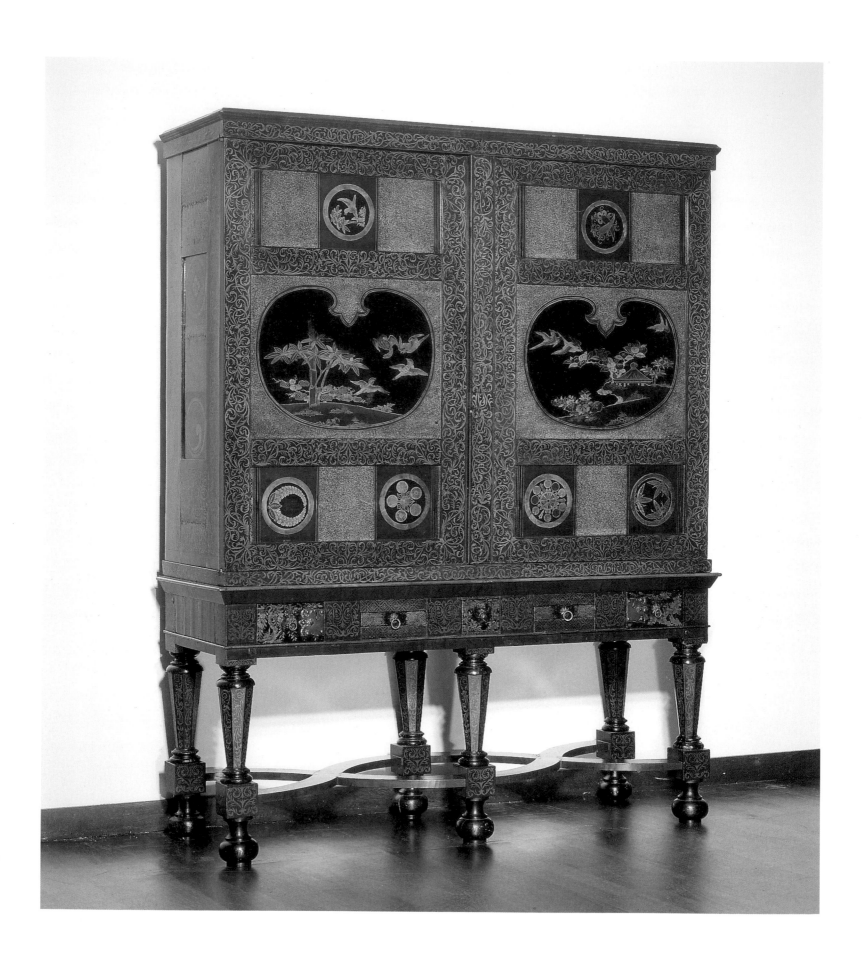

191

Cabinet, c. 1690-1710

Oak, veneered with walnut, palm and purple-wood, inlaid with Japanese lacquer panels, decorated with polished rayfish skin (same-nuri), 202 x 158.5 x 54 cm

AMSTERDAM, RIJKSMUSEUM

(acquired in 1979, see p. 318)

192

Cabinet, c. 1700

Oak, lacquer in black and gold, embroidery in coloured wool

147 x 117 x 47 cm

AMSTERDAM,

AMSTERDAMS HISTORISCH MUSEUM

(acquired in 1938, see p. 320)

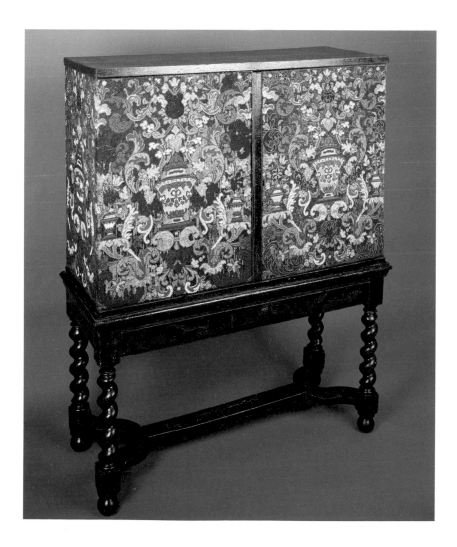

JAPANESE LACQUER WORK

The exotic materials used to decorate the lacquer-work cabinet [191] are remarkable. This lacquer work was originally part of a Japanese chest dating from the early 17th century. Seamen sailing for the Dutch East India Company brought chests like this back to the Netherlands, where they were regarded as a curiosity. When they went out of fashion later in the century they were broken up and used in other pieces of furniture – as in the panels of this cabinet.

The Japanese lacquer worker had combined the lacquer work with shagreen, another typically Japanese material. The technique used to process this is called *same-nuri*. It involved polishing the dried skin of a shark or ray to bring out the characteristic decorative texture of the light skin. Cutting up the Japanese chest destroyed the original coherence of the decorative pattern. The front of the chest comprised the large panels showing Japanese landscapes, surrounded by shagreen, while the circular lacquer-work ornaments, reminiscent of Japanese coats of arms, originally decorated the side of the chest.

The Dutch cabinetmaker used the old Japanese decoration, and also added whimsical marquetry to it. The cabinetmaker appears to have taken his inspiration for this inlay work from examples of English furniture decoration.

EMBROIDERY

Another curiosity is the small cabinet in the collection of the Amsterdam Historical Museum [192]. This cabinet is not decorated with marquetry – its two small doors are covered with embroidery in coloured wool and its sides are similarly decorated. The pattern is of colourful, curling vines in a vase. The piece reflects the late 17th-century trend towards more colourful and imaginative decoration. The cabinet itself is simple: inside it has just one deep and one shallow shelf above three drawers. The wood is lacquered in black and gold in imitation of Oriental lacquer work. Around 1700, fire screens, table tops and seats of various kinds were often covered with embroidery, but it is extremely unusual to find it on a piece of furniture used for storage. Only one other Dutch example has been preserved. Sadly, nothing is known about the owner or the maker. The cabinet may have been made by an amateur: decorative techniques like embroidery and lacquering were also mastered by enthusiasts, though in this case the amateur-decorator was obviously highly skilled.

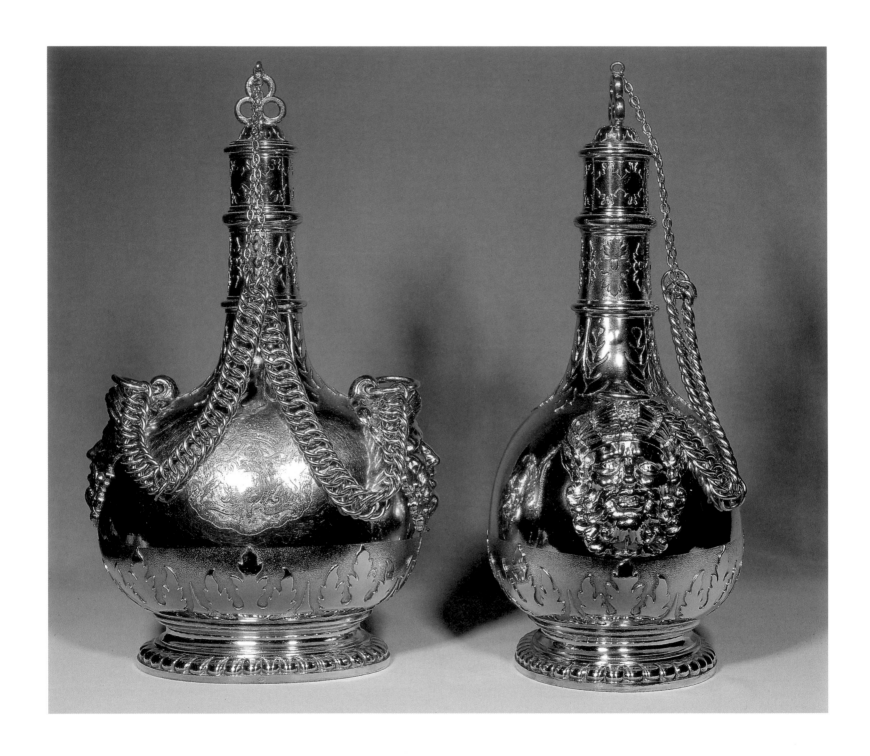

193

ADAM LOOFS (c. 1645-1710)
Two pilgrim bottles with the coat of arms of
William, the first Duke of Devonshire, 1688
Silver-gilt h. 47 and 48.2 cm
DEVONSHIRE COLLECTION,
CHATSWORTH SETTLEMENT
(probably commissioned by Willem III and given
by him to the first Duke of Devonshire,
see p. 325)

SILVER

In 1679 the silversmith Adam Loofs brought two tables, two large mirrors and four large candlesticks – all made of silver – from Paris to the Netherlands. These pieces were made by an unknown French silversmith, with whom Loofs had probably worked.

Loofs, who was born in The Hague, worked in Paris for several years and became familiar with the Louis XIV style. In 1680 he became silver steward at the court of Willem III in The Hague. Loofs made silver furniture, and silver bowls, plates, wine coolers, goblets and bottles, including these pilgrim bottles [193], for the stadholder-king. The shape of these silver-gilt bottles derives from the leather bottles carried by pilgrims in the Middle Ages. The French influence can be seen in the stylised acanthus leaves around the body and the foot of the bottles. This pair was probably a gift from King Willem III to the first Duke of Devonshire in 1694.

CANDLESTICK

The W under the foot of the candlestick by Adam Loofs [194] may indicate that the piece was made for Willem III, or that it was owned by him. The candlestick was made in Louis XIV style. The stem is formed by a standing female figure holding on her head a drip-pan, on which the candleholder proper rests. The decoration of the candlestick, with palmettes, acanthus leaves and 'fish bladder' motifs, is typical of the style of the French court. Loofs had become familiar with this style during his years in Paris and was thus a link between the French court and that of the stadholder.

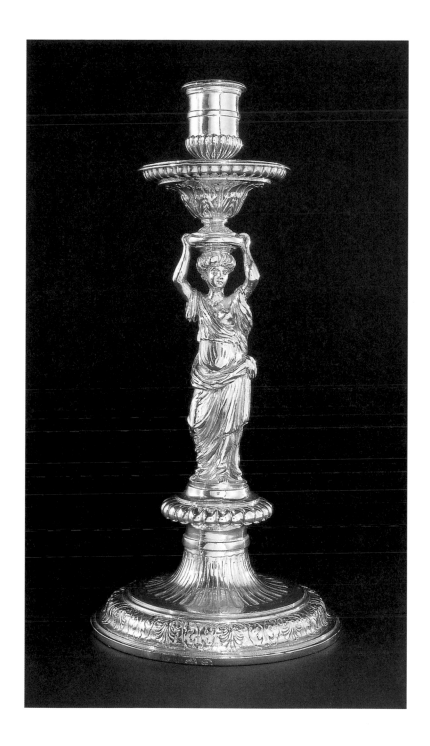

194

ADAM LOOFS (c. 1645-1710)
Candlestick with a female figure as stem,
1687
Silver h. 28.6 cm
AMSTERDAM, RIJKSMUSEUM
(acquired in 1966, see p. 317)

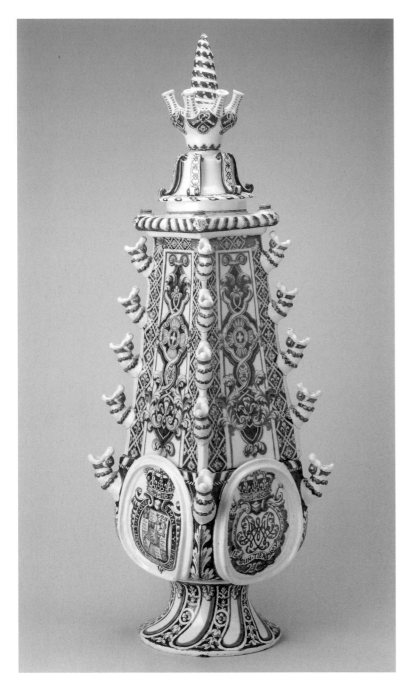
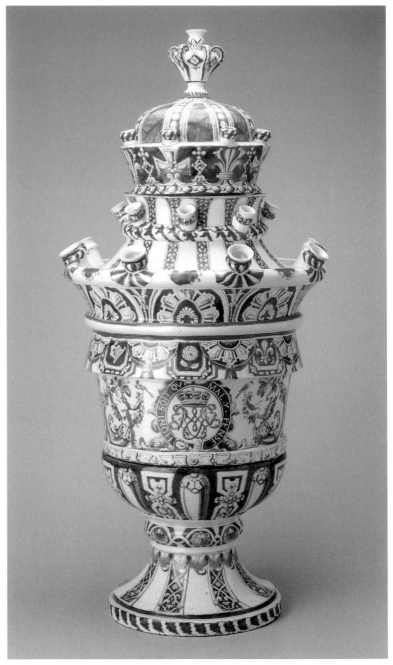

195
POTTERY 'DE GRIEKSCHE A'
UNDER THE SUPERVISION OF ADRIAEN KOCKS
Two tulip vases with the arms
of Willem III, c. 1690-1700
Blue-painted faience, h. 102 and 98 cm
HER MAJESTY QUEEN ELIZABETH II
(commissioned by Willem III for
Hampton Court Palace, see p. 337)

FAIENCE

At the end of the 17th century Delft *faience* became increasingly popular in the Netherlands. The Delft potteries were commissioned by Willem III and his court to make impressive tulip vases and other imposing pieces. The King of England ordered pieces of Delftware to decorate the palaces in his kingdom.

The large flower vases made in the Delft pottery *De Griecksche A* for the stadholder-king [*195*] are still owned by the British royal family. Adriaen Kocks, who was in charge of *De Griecksche A* during this period, supervised their manufacture. The vases have a lid in the shape of a king's crown. The arms are those of the English monarch and the inscription *honi soit*

qui mal y pense (evil be to him who evil thinks) is the motto of the Order of the Garter.

The way vases like these were used, with a flower in each little spout, can be seen on two octagonal Delft vases from the pottery run by the widow of Wemmers Hoppesteyn and her son Rochus [*196*]. The design is a Chinese scene as viewed through the eyes of a Dutchman. Large porcelain vases filled with flowers stand on and beside the balustrade of a terrace. The exuberant, multi-coloured decoration refers to Chinese examples. The decorative motifs above and below the scene are comparable with those on Chinese pieces of the Wan-Li period (1563-1620). These vases are the pinnacle of the Hoppesteyn pottery's output.

196

POTTERY 'HET JONGE/OUDE MORIAENSHOOFD'
UNDER THE SUPERVISION OF
THE HOPPESTEYNS
Two octagonal vases, c. 1680-1685
Polychrome faience, h. 75 cm
DOUAI, MUSÉE DE LA CHARTREUSE
(acquired before 1877, see p. 328)

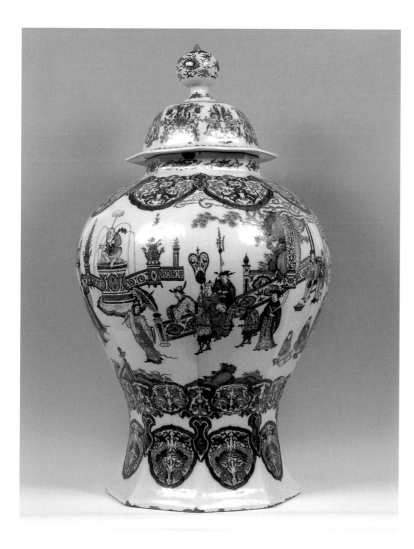
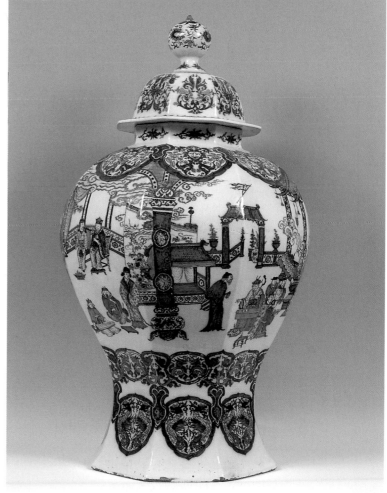

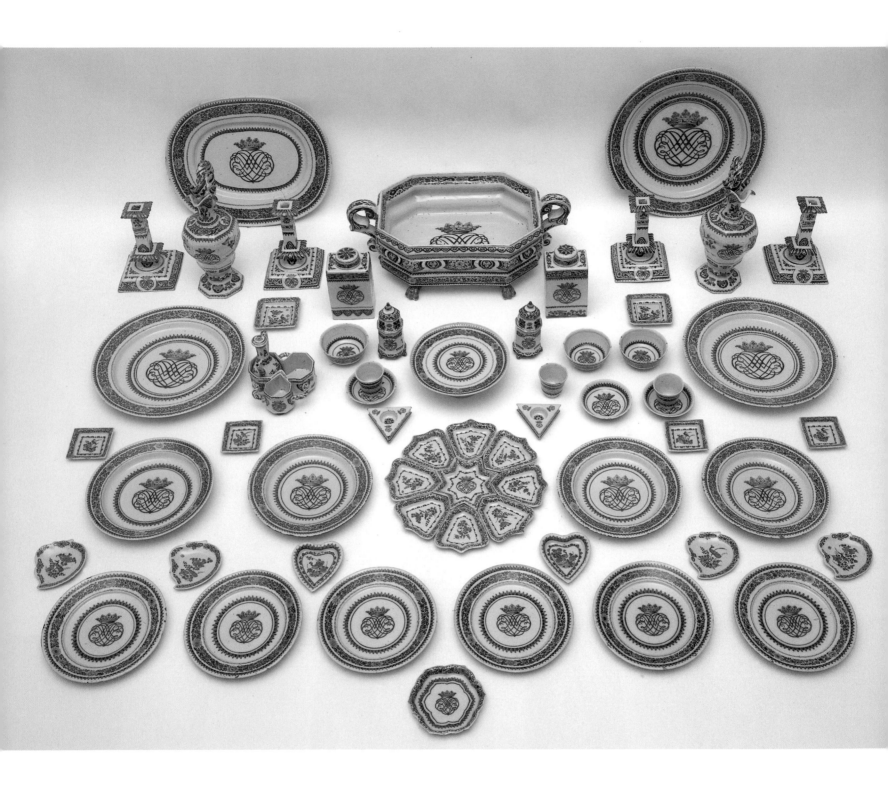

197
Pottery 'De Metalen Pot' under
the supervision of Lambertus Cleffius
Selection from the Lobkowicz service, c. 1685
Blue-painted faience
Nelahozeves (Czech Republic),
Nelahozeves Castle,
The Lobkowicz Collections
(acquired c. 1685, see p. 341)

LOBKOWICZ SERVICE

De Metalen Pot (c. 1670-1691), the Delft pottery run by Lambert Cleffius (?-1691), ·was also honoured with a royal commission when Wenzel Ferdinand Prince Lobkowicz of Bilina in Bohemia (1656-1697) ordered this service. This is a very unusual service in a number of ways. To begin with, no other 17th-century service has survived with so many pieces intact – there are still 125 items. The size alone gives it a royal air. It is also probably one of the earliest examples of a set of dinnerware made entirely of earthenware. It must have been made in about 1685; prior to this similar sets were probably made in silver. It is therefore not surprising that the shapes of the various pieces echo the shapes found in a silver service. The modern feel of the whole thing is also striking; in fact this service set the standard for the china and porcelain services we still use today. The decoration on many of the pieces displays motifs borrowed from Chinese porcelain. The plates and dishes are decorated only with the monogram WL (Wenzel Lobkowicz) enclosed in simple borders. The monogram of the owner of the pottery, LC, can be found on almost every piece.

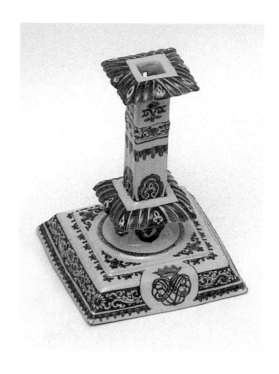

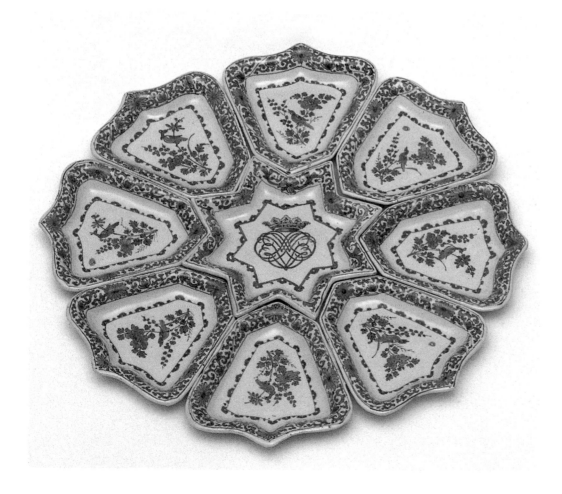

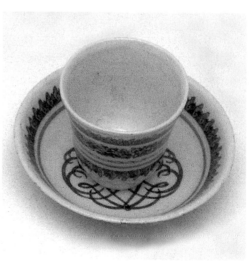

DETAILS OF 197

THE FLOATING FEATHER

Painted wall-coverings depicting views over park-like landscapes are among the most characteristic forms of art in late 17th-century Holland. The decorative paintings by Melchior d'Hondecoeter – sometimes mounted as wall-coverings in panelling, sometimes framed – fitted extremely well in these interiors. Stadholder-King Willem III and his architect and designer Daniel Marot were evidently impressed by d'Hondecoeter's massive canvases. D'Hondecoeter was commissioned to make paintings for the palaces of Honselaersdijk and Het Loo and for Willem III's hunting lodge, Soestdijk.

For this hunting seat, the present-day Palace of Soestdijk, d'Hondecoeter painted 'a pelican and other birds by a pool', known as *The floating feather*. D'Hondecoeter specialised in painting birds, having started his career by painting chickens and ducks in farmyards and later concentrating on exotic birds in stately park-like landscapes. Such idyllic scenes lent themselves perfectly to decorating the canal houses of Amsterdam's patricians and Willem III's palaces.

FROM LIFE

D'Hondecoeter painted from life: he studied the poultry in his own barnyard, and the more exotic birds he would have seen in the menageries kept by the wealthy owners of country houses. Willem III also kept birds at Het Loo and had an extensive menagerie at his residence at Honselaersdijk. The artists' biographer Arnold Houbraken maintained that d'Hondecoeter had trained a cockerel so that it would remain in the desired pose at the painter's command. This unlikely tale served primarily, of course, to emphasise the astonishingly lifelike quality of d'Hondecoeter's work.

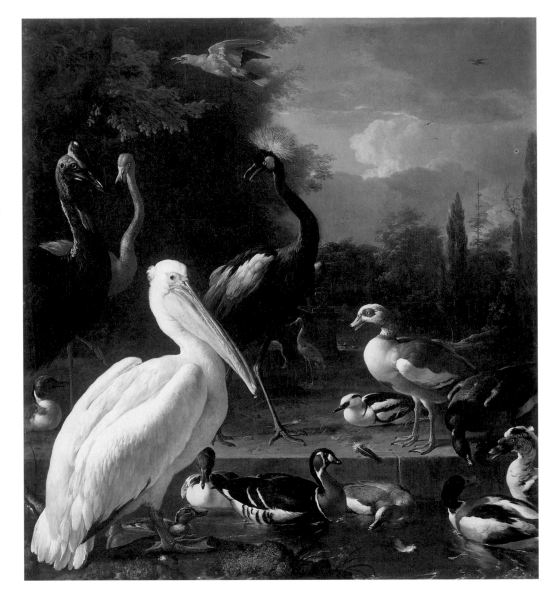

WEENIX

Jan Weenix, emulating d'Hondecoeter, also concentrated on painting huge canvases with depictions of animals, although Weenix painted primarily game – dead animals as trophies of the hunt. He was the son of Jan Baptist Weenix, the painter of Italianate landscapes [*see 96*], from whom he learned the painter's trade. Jan Weenix liked to place his still lifes of dead game animals and birds in a park-like setting or, as in the *Landscape with huntsman and dead game*, against a wooded vista. Classical details like garden urns and statues are characteristic of his work.

198

MELCHIOR D'HONDECOETER (1636-1695)
The floating feather, c. 1680
Canvas 159 x 144 cm
AMSTERDAM, RIJKSMUSEUM
(acquired in 1800, see p. 309)

199

JAN WEENIX (1640-1719)
Landscape with huntsman and dead game, 1697
Canvas 344 x 323 cm
EDINBURGH, NATIONAL GALLERY OF SCOTLAND
(acquired in 1990, see p. 330)

>

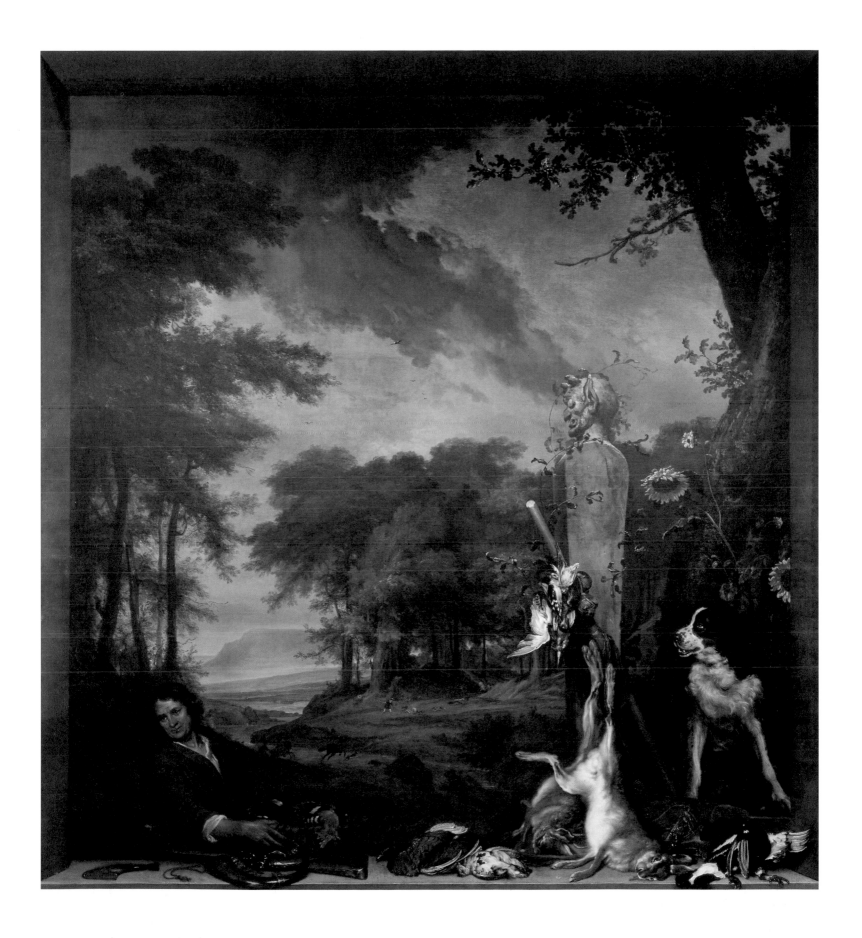

The massive *Landscape* was originally part of a series of five decorative wall-paintings representing the five senses: taste, sight, smell, touch and hearing. This painting symbolises the sense of smell, illustrated by the dog, which traditionally represents this sense. The huntsman has set out on a stone balustrade the game he has just shot. Weenix accurately painted the plumage of the birds and the hare's gleaming fur. A striking feature is the large stone window, framing the rural prospect. The hunt continues in the distance.

The series of five, each with a similar stone frame, may have been commissioned by Jacob Henriques de Granada for his house on the Nieuwe Herengracht in Amsterdam. There the paintings were incorporated in the panelling in the salon. In 1920 the whole set was purchased by the American newspaper magnate William Randolph Hearst. The paintings were subsequently dispersed and this one came into the possession of Paramount Picture Studios. The immense canvas appeared in 1946 as part of the décor in a Bob Hope film.

DE LAIRESSE

Gerard de Lairesse was a leading painter and theoretician at the end of the Golden Age. He painted in a classicist style, with sharp outlines and clear, cool colours, a style that was much esteemed by wealthy patricians and those in the circle of the stadholder-king. Commissioned by Willem III, De Lairesse produced murals and ceiling paintings for Soestdijk, Het Loo and the Binnenhof in The Hague. De Lairesse had few words of praise for Rembrandt's dark, more robustly painted works, which were renowned in the first half of the 17th century. 'Away with fiddling, rootling and messing about: touch your work with a cunning hand. However not in the manner of Rembrandt or Lievens, who dragged the pigment like muck across the Piece; but smoothly and evenly, so that your objects appear round and raised through Art alone, and not by daubing.'

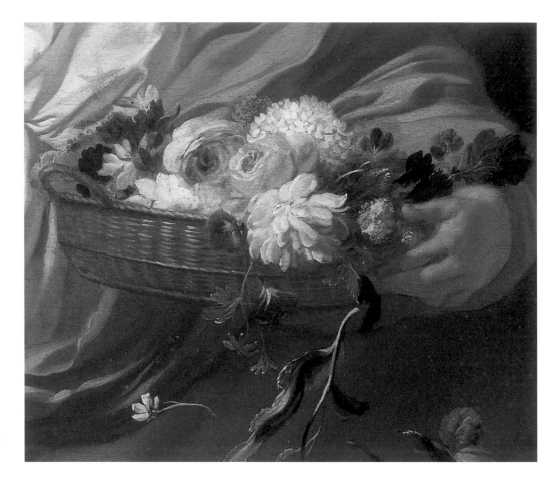

DETAIL OF 200

He probably made his smoothly painted *Apollo and Aurora* for a large Amsterdam canal house, possibly commissioned by a burgomaster of Amsterdam. It is one of the first and most impressive examples of De Lairesse's work as a decorative painter in Amsterdam. Standing on his chariot Apollo drives the four-in-hand. Apollo, the sun god, is identified by the aureole around his head. His red cloak billows up so that the aureole is subtly lit. On a cloud sits Aurora – Dawn. She wears a white gown with golden stars and a copper-coloured stole. In her hair she has a pearl diadem surmounted by the eight-pointed morning star. The pearls in her hair and around her neck represent dewdrops that come from her eyes. The flowers she strews around are those that open at dawn. Gerard de Lairesse must have had unshake-

able confidence in the future of art in the classical mould. Not so long ago De Lairesse's work and that of his contemporaries was seen as marking the definitive end of the glory of the Golden Age, a judgement contrasting sharply with the ambition radiated by this monumental *Aurora*.

200
GERARD DE LAIRESSE (1640-1711)
Apollo and Aurora, 1671
Canvas 204.5 x 193 cm
NEW YORK,
THE METROPOLITAN MUSEUM OF ART
(acquired in 1943, see p. 342)

>

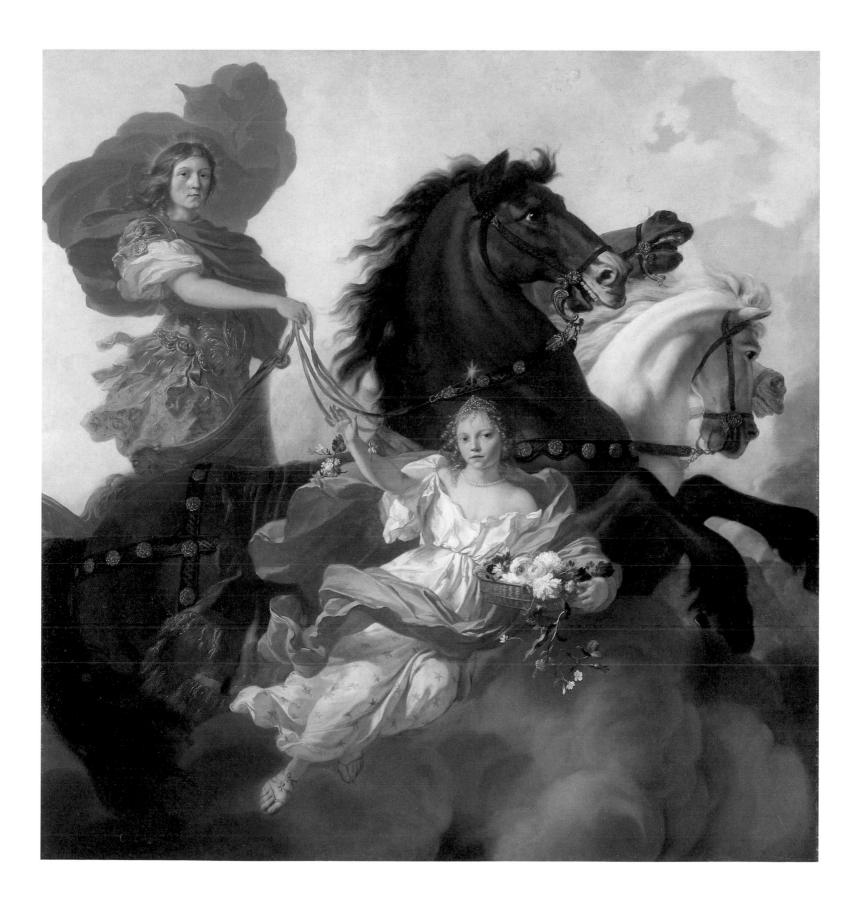

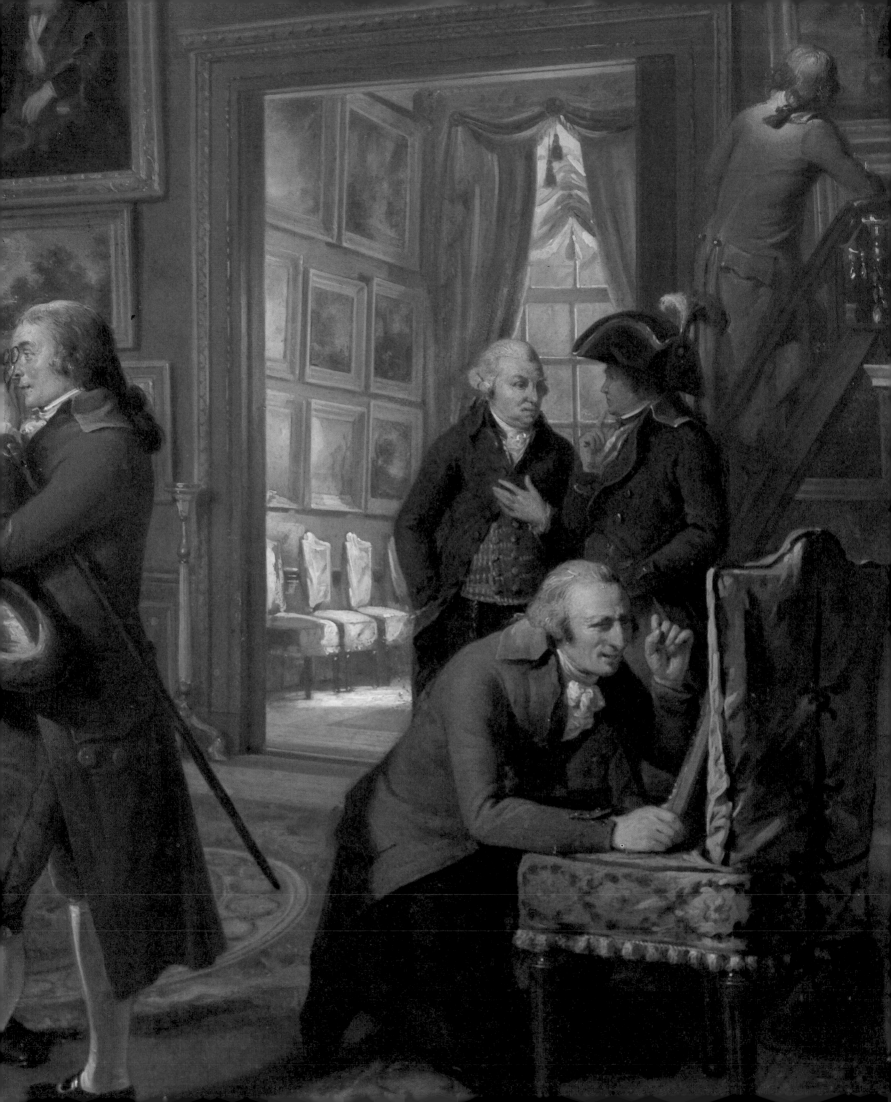

EPILOGUE

COLLECTING ART OF THE GOLDEN AGE

As WE SAID in the introduction, the exhibition *The Glory of the Golden Age* is a homage to the great collectors of 17th-century Dutch art. The caption to each work of art consequently states the year in which the work was acquired by its present owner. The catalogue at the back of this book examines the provenance of the individual works and the history of the museums in which they now reside. In some museums the collection dates back to the 17th or 18th century, whereas other collections only came into being in the latter part of the 20th century. This analysis creates a vivid picture of the shifting interest in Dutch art of the Golden Age.

Although there were collectors in the 17th century who brought together both paintings and works of art, each field has its own collecting tradition. The royal art collections acquired in the 18th century live on in the national museums in Berlin, Munich, Stockholm and Vienna. Another category is the essentially 19th-century museum of decorative arts (usually including sculpture), such as the Victoria & Albert Museum in London and comparable museums in Berlin, Hamburg and Vienna. The Rijksmuseum exhibits paintings and works of art in the same building, albeit displayed separately. In *The Glory of the Golden Age* the fields of painting, sculpture and the decorative arts have not been segregated, although the three-dimensional pieces are shown in a different way and are generally in the minority.

THE CABINET

Collecting in the Dutch Republic in the 17th century was not confined to paintings and valuables, it also encompassed objects from the natural world, curiosities, antiquities and albums of prints and drawings. A collection could contain examples of any or all of these categories, with each collector having his own individual preferences. Collections like these were almost always broken up on the death of the owner and, as a rule, auctioned off.

We know what Rembrandt kept in his 'cabinet' in his house in the Jodenbreestraat from the inventory which was drawn up in 1656 and which formed the basis for a reconstruction in the Rembrandt House that was completed in 1999. His collection was extraordinarily eclectic and must have been worth a considerable sum. In addition to prints and drawings, he owned objects from the natural world, ethnic African artefacts, works of art from Asia, antique statues, musical instruments, costumes and weapons. Valuable items included silver, Venetian glass and Oriental porcelain.

Paintings made in Antwerp with representations of such 'cabinets' reveal that paintings, antiquities, sculpture and other valuable objects were all a permanent part of collections of this kind, which could also include seashells, coins and instruments (fig. 1). Objects of this kind would also have been part of Dutch 'cabinets'.

The majority of the works of art in this exhibition, however, must have had a place in a contemporary interior. Works of art of the 17th-century Netherlands were usually utilitarian – cupboards, chairs, glasses, salt-cellars, jugs and bowls, plates and dishes were made to be used. However, there were also objects whose sole function was ornamental [106, 195, 196], and there were decorative pieces that were made to commemorate important events in history [4, 67].

Goldsmiths and silversmiths like Paulus and Adam van Vianen and Johannes Lutma had an international reputation, and their

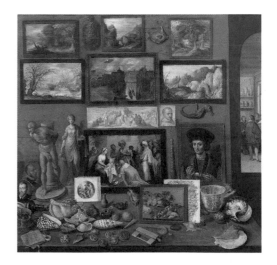

1. FRANS FRANCKEN THE YOUNGER, *Cabinet of art and curiosities*, c. 1620. Panel 74 x 78 cm. VIENNA, KUNSTHISTORISCHES MUSEUM

< DETAIL OF FIG. 6

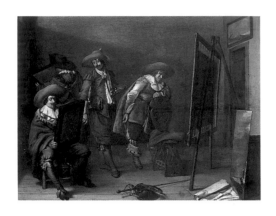

2. PIETER CODDE, *Art-lovers in an artist's studio*,
c. 1630. Panel 38.3 x 49.5 cm.
STUTTGART, STAATSGALERIE STUTTGART

work was highly collectable in their own lifetimes. In the 17th century the silver-gilt ewer that Adam van Vianen made in memory of his brother Paulus in 1614 for the Amsterdam silversmiths' guild [5] was displayed in the guildhall.

Examples of applied art – some of them quite spectacular – were given to allies or other foreign nations as diplomatic gifts. Hendrick de Keyser, for instance, designed a copper candlestick that was presented to the Shah of Persia in 1619, and similar gifts were made to the Mogul princes in India. The temple at Nikko in Japan still houses the Dutch East India Company's gift to the shogun: a large lantern, 12 wall sconces and a candelabrum. The latter has returned to the Netherlands for this exhibition [72]. The silver wall sconces by Breghtel in the Kremlin were also diplomatic gifts [71].

COLLECTING PAINTINGS IN THE 17TH CENTURY

The extraordinary flowering of 17th-century Dutch painting was undoubtedly related to the country's economic prosperity, which meant that many Dutch burghers were in a position to buy paintings. Paintings were traded in a flourishing open market governed by supply and demand. A painting could be had for just a couple of

guilders, while works of slightly higher quality cost only 20 or 30 guilders. Prices could however reach several hundred guilders, depending on the subject, the degree of detail and the fame of the painter. Paintings were on sale everywhere – at markets and auctions, in shops and from the artists themselves (fig. 2). In addition to professional art dealers, there were painters who dealt in art on the side.

As well as producing paintings for the free market, the better-known painters derived a significant part of their income from commissions, with portraits being the most common kind of commission. Couples often had their portraits painted for their children, and these paintings were usually passed on to their descendants by inheritance. The portraits of people in influential Amsterdam regents' families, such as the Van Loons [38] and the Six family, are consequently still in the families' possession. Group portraits of militia companies, regents and civic administrators remained in the institution to which the sitters belonged, such as government buildings, militia headquarters and almshouses.

In many cases, history paintings were also commissions. Many of these works were to be seen in more or less public buildings like the East India House, the West India House and the town hall.

Although there was no actual royalty in Holland, the stadholders, particularly Frederik Hendrik and Amalia van Solms [170] and Willem III (see chapter 24), were also important patrons of the arts. It was not until late in the 17th century that monumental painted decoration graced the ordinary burgher's domestic interior [199, 200].

Most paintings were on a small scale, however, and were a standard feature of many 17th-century interiors. They were usually sold after the owner's death. There was a particularly lively trade in works of art in Amsterdam, providing a rich source

of works by both contemporary and 'old' masters.

In Holland only a small group of collectors, including the Reynst brothers in Amsterdam, were interested in Italian paintings, which fetched high prices at auction. Most art-lovers collected contemporary Dutch art, which they often bought directly from the painter. The wealthy Hague collector Pieter Spiering [164a], for example, paid Gerard Dou an annual stipend of 1000 guilders in return for the right of first refusal of the artist's latest works.

17TH-CENTURY ROYAL COLLECTIONS

The paintings of Flemish art collections by such artists as Francken and Teniers reveal what the collections owned by the general public and by royalty were like at that time (figs. 1 and 3). The huge collection owned by Archduke Leopold Wilhelm of Austria, governor from 1646 to 1656, for example, was dominated by 16th-century Italian painting but contained a fair proportion of contemporary Flemish works by Van Dyck, Rubens and others. Dutch paintings were rather poorly represented [122]. When he stepped down as governor he took his collection back to Vienna, where it is now the nucleus of the collection of paintings in the Kunsthistorisches Museum.

In the collection assembled by Frederik Hendrik and Amalia van Solms there is a predominance of work by contemporary Flemish and Dutch painters: Rubens and Van Dyck are well represented, as are Utrecht painters like Abraham Bloemaert, Gerard van Honthorst [28], Paulus Moreelse and Cornelis van Poelenburch. Commissioned by the stadholder, Rembrandt produced seven Passion paintings between 1633 and 1646 (these works are now in Munich). The stadholder's collection was short-lived; it was split up after the death of Frederik Hendrik and his wife, with most of the paintings ending up in royal collections in Germany.

CONTEMPORARY DUTCH ART ABROAD

In the first half of the 17th century, paintings were produced primarily for the local Dutch market, although gifts of paintings to royal relations were also customary. Around 1630, for example, Charles I of England acquired paintings by Rembrandt and Lievens that probably came from Willem II. International commissions appear to have picked up gradually as the century progressed, and by 1700 there were several artists working for foreign courts.

The Florentine Grand Duke Ferdinand II (who ruled from 1621 to 1670) had a particular fondness for still lifes and brought still-life painters such as Otto Marseus van Schriek and Willem van Aelst to Italy. Between 1652 and 1656, Van Aelst was commissioned by Ferdinand's brother Giovanni Carlo to paint a number of still lifes that are still in Florence today [126]. Ferdinand's son Cosimo de' Medici came to Holland twice between 1667 and 1669. On both occasions he visited various collectors and artists' studios, including those of Rembrandt, Willem van de Velde and Gerard Dou. He also bought paintings by Jan Davidsz de Heem, Jan van der Heyden, Willem van de Velde and others. It was probably in 1669 that he acquired a late self-portrait by Rembrandt for his uncle's collection of self-portraits. This work is now in the Uffizi. Cosimo's later acquisitions reveal his liking for the *fijnschilders*, including Dou, Netscher, Van Mieris and Van der Werff. Most of the 17th-century Dutch paintings now in museums in Florence – the Uffizi and the Pitti – are contemporary purchases.

Equally noteworthy is the fact that in 1652 the Sicilian collector Antonio Ruffo commissioned Rembrandt to portray *Aristotle* (fig. 4). This was followed in 1661 by a painting of *Alexander* (now in Glasgow) and in 1662 by a portrayal of *Homer* (now in the Mauritshuis). Later in

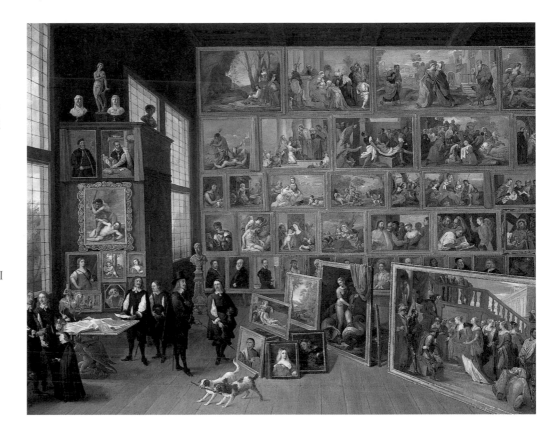

3. DAVID TENIERS THE YOUNGER, *The art collection of Archduke Leopold Wilhelm in Brussels*, c. 1651.
Canvas 123 x 163 cm.
VIENNA, KUNSTHISTORISCHES MUSEUM

the century Louis XIV acquired a Rembrandt self-portrait for his collection, which already contained works by Dou, Mignon and others. In 1678-1679 he also acquired a series of Brazilian landscapes by Frans Post [89] from Johan Maurits of Nassau-Siegen.

The first royal collector to collect Dutch art on a large scale was Johann Wilhelm in Düsseldorf, Elector Palatine from 1690 to 1716. His father Philipp Wilhelm already owned works by Gerard Dou and Frans van Mieris. 'Fine painters' like Eglon van der Neer, Schalcken and Van der Werff and still-life painters like Jan Weenix and Ruysch profited from the son's collecting activities: they all supplied him with paintings – Van der Neer and Van der Werff as court painters. Flemish artists were strongly represented in his collection, with 40 works

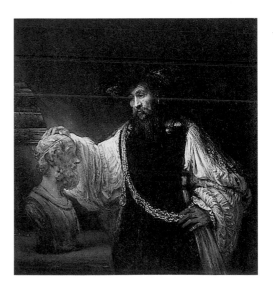

4. REMBRANDT, *Aristotle*, 1652.
Canvas 143.5 x 136.5 cm. NEW YORK,
THE METROPOLITAN MUSEUM OF ART

by Rubens, 17 by Van Dyck and 7 by Adriaen Brouwer. As far as the Dutch school was concerned, the emphasis was on the *fijnschilders*, the Italianate landscape painters, Rembrandt and Wouwermans. The Düsseldorf collection, which was opened to the public in 1756, became part of the Alte Pinakothek in Munich in 1807.

HOUBRAKEN

Arnold Houbraken's *Groote schouburgh der Nederlantsche konstschilders en schilderessen* (3 volumes, 1718-21) was *the* handbook for the 18th-century lover of 17th-century Dutch painting. The book contains more than 600 biographies of 17th-century Dutch painters. The book's highly anecdotal approach has provoked a great deal of criticism since the 19th century, and its reliability has been called into question repeatedly, yet it gives us a good idea of the knowledge and appreciation of 17th-century painting at the beginning of the 18th century. Houbraken devoted considerable attention to the popular painters of the time: the *fijnschilders* and the Italianate painters, De Lairesse, Potter, Wouwermans, Brouwer, Van Ostade, Steen and Rembrandt. He also covered Frans Hals, Van Goyen, Ruisdael, most of the Caravaggisti and the classicist history painters. Curiously, however, Meindert Hobbema and Johannes Vermeer were not included in the *Groote schouburgh*.

Later in the century, when the French connoisseur d'Argenville reduced Houbraken's 600 biographies to around 100 in his *Abrégé de la vie des plus fameux peintres* (1753-64), Hals, Van Goyen, Cuyp, Van de Cappelle, Steen and most of the still-life painters did not appear, and neither did Hobbema and Vermeer. In 18th-century French collections, the *fijnschilders* and Italianate artists were the fashion, and d'Argenville's selection reflects this. In the same period, art-lovers in England were discovering (or rediscovering) the impor-

tance of landscape painters like Cuyp and Hobbema.

18TH-CENTURY FRENCH COLLECTIONS OF DUTCH ART

Dutch painting was not highly regarded in 17th-century French classicist art theory, but towards the end of the century there was a reversal, and its emphasis on colour and realism was once more appreciated. The theoretician Roger de Piles, who rejected overly stringent classicist theory at the end of the century, praised Rembrandt's use of chiaroscuro and colour. During a stay in Holland at the end of the 17th century he acquired a *Girl at a window* by Rembrandt, which he described as a perfect *trompe-l'oeil*. This was probably the earlier painting of the subject dating from 1642 (now in Dulwich) and not, as was thought for many years, the later version in Stockholm being exhibited here [142].

Soon after this, French painters like Chardin turned to Dutch painting for inspiration, and Dutch paintings became popular among collectors. The *fijnschilders*, such as Dou, Van Mieris, Schalcken, Netscher and Van der Werff, Italianate artists like Van Poelenburch, Breenbergh, Both and, above all, Berchem and Adriaen van de Velde, landscape painters such as Wijnants and Wouwermans, and Rembrandt too, were all extremely popular.

Dutch artists acquired a place in major art galleries alongside Italian, French and Flemish painters. The famous collection owned by Philippe Duc d'Orléans, the brother of the French king, included numerous works by the *fijnschilders*, the Italianate painters, Wouwermans [178] and Rembrandt (among them the now disputed *Windmill* in Washington and the workshop piece *The Holy Family at night* in the Rijksmuseum). Curiously enough, the collection also contains Knupfer's *Brothel scene* [114] under the name Jan Baptist Weenix. Not only was the Palais Royal

open to the public, but a descriptive catalogue was published in 1727 and the collection was reproduced in print later in the century, all of which combined to make it in many respects the standard for later collectors.

Whereas Dutch painters occupied a modest place in the collection of the Duc d'Orléans as a whole, they dominated later collections, some of which contained nothing but Dutch works. A famous example is the collection owned by the Comtesse de Verrue, whose paintings by Berchem, Wouwermans and Adriaen van de Velde (the latter now in the Wallace Collection) fetched the highest prices at the auction after her death (1737). The boom in Dutch masters continued in a series of sales between 1760 and 1784. One of the collections to go under the hammer was that of the Duc de Choiseul, and many of the works in his collection were published in print in 1771. It gives us an idea of his preference for small cabinet pictures, genre pieces (Van Ostade [115] and Teniers) and landscapes with figures (Wouwermans, Potter, Berchem). Rembrandt seems meanwhile to have been pushed somewhat into the background.

18TH-CENTURY GERMAN COLLECTIONS OF DUTCH ART

The situation in Germany in the 18th century differed from that in France and Holland in that it was primarily the local rulers who were responsible for building up collections in which Dutch painting occupied a prominent place. Since most of them found their way into museums in the late 18th and 19th centuries, it is quite easy to identify the preferences of the people who amassed them. The collections created in Braunschweig (see p. 323), Dresden (see p. 329), Munich (see p. 340) and Schwerin (see p. 346) in the 18th century are represented in the exhibition by works on loan.

Regrettably, there are no paintings from the museum in Kassel, which is to reopen in the summer of 2000 following an extensive renovation and was therefore unable to send any works to this exhibition. The collection in Kassel was assembled between 1722 and 1756 by Prince Wilhelm of Hesse – Count Wilhelm VIII after 1730. Rembrandt occupied an even more prominent place in the collection (12 works, including *Jacob blessing Isaac*) than Rubens. A number of these works came from the cabinet of Valerius Röver in Delft, whose collection was bought in its entirety by the count in 1750. A striking feature is the presence of five paintings by Frans Hals.

The largest royal collection of the 18th century was that of Catherine the Great (1729-1796) in St Petersburg. In amassing the huge collection of 17th-century Dutch art, her advisers targeted French, German and English collections, which were acquired *en bloc*. Whereas the cabinet picture prevailed in private French and Dutch collections, the royal collections were dominated by Rembrandt, who was clearly regarded as the equal of Rubens, Van Dyck, Raphael and Titian.

18TH-CENTURY DUTCH CABINETS OF PAINTINGS

The 17th-century Dutch masters continued to be prized by collectors at home too. The German painter Wilhelm Tischbein, who lived in Holland between 1771 and 1773, described the composition of a good Dutch cabinet of paintings thus: 'a *tronie* by Rembrandt; a Rubens cartoon; a painting by Dou; one by Van Mieris the Elder; two by Wouwermans, an early and a late work; a Berchem; Cuyp; Van Ostade; Teniers; Brouwer; Metsu; Ter Borch; a church interior by Neefs; a fruit still life by De Heem; flowers by Van Huysum; cows by Potter; a pastoral piece by Adriaen van de Velde; a stormy sea by Bakhuysen; a painting by Slingelandt; one by Schalcken; a

portrait by Van Dyck; a *tronie* by Lievens; Brueghel; d'Hondecoeter; Van der Werff; Van Poelenburch; Elsheimer; Snijders; Both, Lairesse; and others'.

We find a similar mixture in many auction catalogues of 18th-century Dutch collections. Sadly, when Cornelis Troost painted Jeronimus Tonneman and his flute-playing son in 1736, he showed them not amidst Tonneman's collection but in his drawing-room (fig. 5). The vellum-bound copy of Karel van Mander's *Schilder-boeck* on the table does, however, mark Tonneman out as a connoisseur. In addition to a large collection of drawings, pastels by Troost and some 50 paintings, he owned silver by Van Vianen and an ivory *Mars and Venus* by Francis van Bossuit [184]. At the sale of his collection in 1754, the two ivories by Van Bossuit together fetched 1000 guilders.

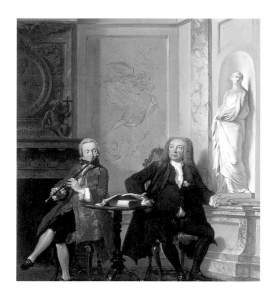

5. CORNELIS TROOST, *Portrait of Jeronimus Tonneman and his son*, 1736. Canvas 68 x 57.5 cm. DUBLIN, NATIONAL GALLERY OF IRELAND

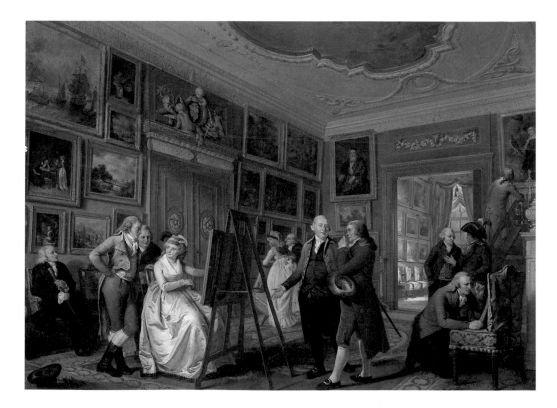

6. ADRIAAN DE LELIE, *The art gallery of Jan Gildemeester Jansz in Amsterdam*, 1794-1795. Panel 64.3 x 84.5 cm. AMSTERDAM, RIJKSMUSEUM

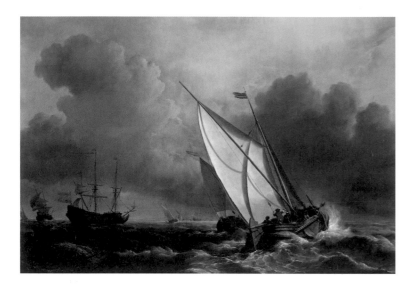

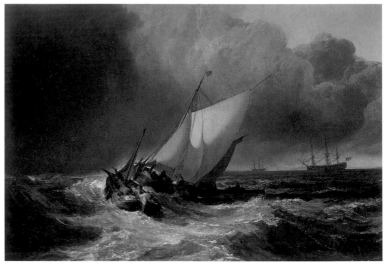

7. WILLEM VAN DE VELDE THE YOUNGER, *Ships on a stormy sea*, c. 1672.
Canvas 132.2 x 191.9 cm.
TOLEDO, THE TOLEDO MUSEUM OF ART [162]

8. JOSEPH MALLORD WILLIAM TURNER, *Dutch fishing boats in a storm*, 1801.
Canvas 162.5 x 221 cm.
PRIVATE COLLECTION, ON LOAN TO THE NATIONAL GALLERY, LONDON

The valuable paintings were by Paulus Potter (3110 guilders, later owned by Braamcamp), De Lairesse (1550 guilders, now in the Rijksmuseum), Adriaen van de Velde (1500 guilders) and Gabriël Metsu (1405 guilders, now in Kassel).

Gerrit Braamcamp also had a famous collection, which was sold in Amsterdam in 1771. Braamcamp owned several paintings by all the Dutch masters who were most in vogue at the time: Adriaen van Ostade (17), Wouwermans (17), Metsu (10, including [141a] and [141b]), Berchem (9), Adriaen van de Velde (8), Rembrandt (8), Gerard Dou (7), Jan Steen (6), Frans van Mieris (6), Potter (5), Dujardin (4, including [99]). Catherine the Great paid top prices for a triptych by Gerard Dou (14,100 guilders) and for the Potter (9050 guilders), both of which were lost when the ship in which they were travelling was wrecked on the voyage to Russia. An early Rembrandt, *Christ on the Sea of Galilee* (Boston), fetched 4360 guilders.

A slightly later collection was that of Jan Gildemeester, whose cabinet was painted by Adriaan de Lelie (fig. 6). The Rijksmuseum bought Asselijn's *Threatened swan* (fig. p. 10) at the auction of the Gildemeester collection in 1800, where the highest prices were paid for a Rembrandt (8050 guilders), a Potter (10,000 guilders) and a Gerard ter Borch (5200 guilders) [121], all of which came into the possession of the English king. At the same sale Vermeer's *Astronomer* (Louvre) and Hals's *Laughing cavalier* (Wallace Collection) went for 340 and 300 guilders respectively.

Most of the paintings in the Tonneman, Braamcamp and Gildemeester collections ended up in museums, and these collections are therefore among the most important in a long series of private Dutch collections of works by Dutch masters. Two 18th-century Dutch cabinets of paintings formed the basis of the Rijksmuseum's collection. In 1808 Louis Bonaparte purchased 65 paintings at the Van der Pot sale, followed in 1809 by more than 130 paintings from the Van Heteren Cabinet.

When he bought Govert van Slingelandt's cabinet in 1767-1768, Stadholder Willem V acquired one of the finest collections of 17th-century Dutch paintings ever assembled. Because Van Slingelandt deliberately limited his collection to 40 paintings, every purchase was made with a view to improving the quality of the collection. With these and other purchases, Willem V transformed the stadholder's collection into an exceptionally fine collection of Dutch cabinet pieces. In 1775 his paintings were moved to a gallery built especially for them in the Buitenhof in The Hague. This gallery was open to the public at set times until French occupying forces took the paintings to Paris in 1795. When they were returned in 1816 they were housed in the Mauritshuis.

THE TASTE FOR DUTCH ART AMONG ENGLISH COLLECTORS

The renewed appreciation of the monumental landscapes by Cuyp, Philips Koninck, Hobbema and Ruisdael is due almost entirely to English collectors of the late 18th century. Without doubt the larger dimensions of these paintings fitted better in English stately homes than they did in 18th-century French and Dutch cabinets of paintings. English landscape painters like Gainsborough, Constable and Turner greatly admired their Dutch predecessors. The extent of this appreciation can be seen in the picture that Turner painted in 1801 for the Duke of Bridgewater, as a pendant to his seascape by Willem van de Velde (figs. 7 and 8).

In 1802 the art dealer Noel Desenfans, founder of the museum in Dulwich, recounted the story of the rediscovery of Cuyp's paintings, which had been consigned to oblivion in Holland because they were too large for cabinets. A Swiss pedlar dealing in English watches in Holland around 1740 exchanged his wares for paintings by Cuyp, which he could sell for a good price in England. This, according to

Desenfans, was the start of the export of paintings by Cuyp, who soon became known as the Dutch Claude Lorrain.

This interest was not confined to Cuyp, but extended to painters like Jan van de Cappelle, Meindert Hobbema and Philips Koninck. One English collector of such paintings was Sir Lawrence Dundas, who had his portrait painted with his grandson in his London house by Johan Zoffany (fig. 9). This portrait displays Jan van de Cappelle's painting *The calm*, currently in this exhibition [158], hanging above the mantelpiece. It is interesting to note that until recently the monumental work of these painters was absent from Dutch museums. Recent purchases from English owners have rectified this situation [151, 152, 157].

The French revolution caused a number of important Italian and French collections to appear on the market in the late 18th century, among them the collection of the Duc d'Orléans, and it was consequently at this time that the great English collections were formed.

The Dulwich Picture Gallery in London (see p. 336) provides a fascinating view of English taste around 1800. Alongside cabinet pieces by painters like Rembrandt, Dou and Wouwermans [178] there are also large landscapes by Cuyp and Pynacker.

THE DEVELOPMENT OF PUBLIC MUSEUMS

In the course of the 18th century the ideas of the Enlightenment regarding the universal significance of art and science resulted in greater access to royal collections. In the 16th and 17th centuries these collections were generally shown only to the royal family, members of the aristocracy and important foreign guests (fig. 3), but in the second half of the 18th century a number of them were opened to a wider public at set times. The paintings were also hung in a more systematic and edifying manner, and it was also at this time that the first descrip-

tive catalogues appeared.

In 1756 the paintings in the collection in Düsseldorf were rehung. The walls were arranged to decorative effect: the largest paintings in the centre with smaller works placed symmetrically around them (fig. 10). The smaller Dutch paintings were generally hung at eye level, often in groupings with larger Flemish, French and Italian works. Rubens was the only artist to be honoured with a separate gallery to himself.

In Vienna, too, the imperial collections in the Belvedere Palace were drastically reorganised at the end of the 1770s according to national and regional schools of painting, displayed more or less chronologically. The Italian school was divided into Venetians, Romans, Florentines, Bolognese and Lombards, whereas the Northern artists – the Dutch, the Flemish and the Germans – were seldom separated. A similar arrangement according to school was also used in other royal collections.

After the French Revolution, the French royal collection in the Musée National in the Louvre was also opened to the public. When the refurbished museum was reopened as the Musée Napoléon around 1800, the Northern paintings were exhibited in the first part of the Grande Galerie, while the Italian paintings were displayed in the second part. Masterpieces from the nations conquered by Napoleon augmented the collection for a time. In the field of Dutch painting the museum could draw on the collection of Stadholder Willem V. During these years *The bull* by Paulus Potter was one of the most popular paintings in the Louvre.

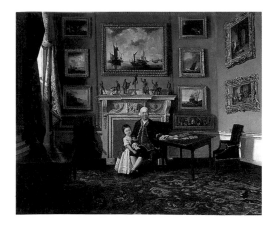

9. JOHANNES ZOFFANY, *Lord Dundas with his grandson in his London house*, 1769. Canvas, 102 x 127 cm. THE MARQUESS OF ZETLAND, ASKE HALL

THE NATIONALE KONST-GALLERIJ

The creation of the Dutch Nationale Konst-Gallerij was discussed in the introduction (p. 9). As we saw, the collection consisted primarily of art from the former stadholders' collections, including works from the palaces of Het Loo and Soestdijk [198], with the occasional piece that belonged to the national government. As a result of acquisitions and gifts, the number of objects grew from 200 to 315 in the space of five years. The purchases in the museum's early years were aimed both at strengthening the historical element in the collection and at giving the work of painters like Ruisdael, Cuyp, Steen, Rembrandt and Rubens a place in the Konst-Gallerij. It was exceptional for high prices to be paid in achieving this ambition. As we saw in the introduction (pp. 9-10), Asselijn's *Threatened swan* was bought two weeks after the opening of the Konst-Gallerij – primarily on historical grounds. The painting, which came from Jan Gildemeester's renowned collection, cost a mere hundred guilders. At the same auction, Rembrandt's *Portrait of a shipbuilder and his wife* was purchased for the English sovereign for 8050 guilders. To make good the lack of a work by Rembrandt, *The beheading of John the Baptist* was bought for 775 guilders in 1801, a painting that is now attributed to Carel Fabritius. The *Hippopotamus hunt*, bought as a Rubens for 3300 guilders in 1804, later proved to be a copy. The museum paid even more – 3500 guilders – for a monumental *Storm* by Ludolf Bakhuysen (fig. 11). This painting was sold again in 1826 for a comparable sum and is now in the Royal Museum in Brussels.

The Nationale Konst-Gallerij in the Huis ten Bosch was short-lived. When Grand Pensionary Schimmelpenninck went to live in the Huis ten Bosch in 1805, the gallery was forced to move to the Buitenhof.

THE ROYAL MUSEUM IN THE FORMER TOWN HALL ON THE DAM

When Louis Bonaparte, the brother of the French emperor Napoleon Bonaparte, became King of Holland in 1806, he changed the name of the Konst-Gallerij to the Royal Museum. On 21 April 1808 the king decided to move the museum to Amsterdam. The Royal Museum was housed temporarily in the former town hall on the Dam, which had meanwhile become the Royal Palace. The painter Cornelis Apostool was appointed director, a post he filled until his death in 1844.

The Royal Museum was opened on 15 September 1808 (fig. 12). It was accommodated in various rooms on the second floor of the Palace, including the Large and Small Council Chambers, where numerous paintings owned by the City of Amsterdam had hung during the period when the building had been the town hall. At Louis Bonaparte's insistence, seven of these were given a place in the Royal Museum, including *The civic guard banquet* by Van der Helst [66], *The 'Gouden Leeuw' on the IJ at Amsterdam* by Van de Velde [161], and Rembrandt's *Night Watch* [65] and

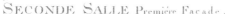

SECONDE SALLE Première Façade.

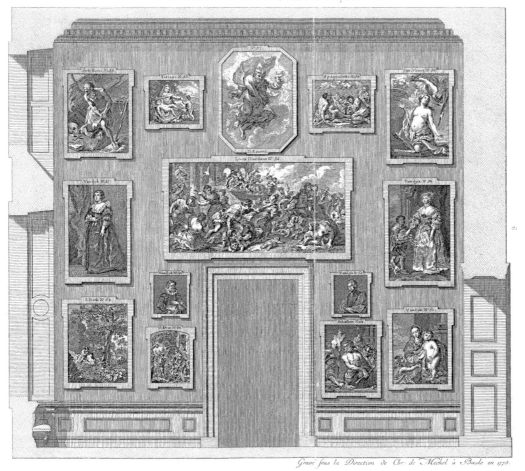

Gravé sous la Direction de Chr. de Mechel à Basle en 1778.

10. ENGRAVING IN NICOLAS DE PIGAGE, *La Galérie Electorale de Dusseldorf*, 1778 (WALL ARRANGEMENT OF THE GERARD DOU ROOM IN THE ART GALLERY IN DÜSSELDORF)

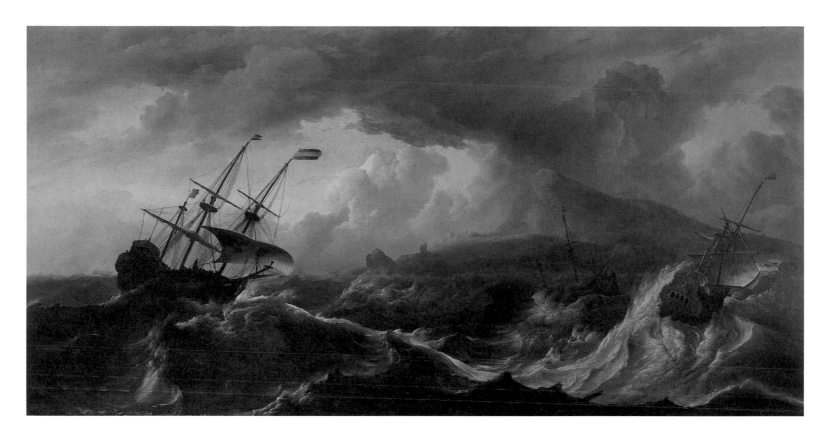

11. LUDOLF BAKHUYSEN, *Storm off a mountainous coast*, c. 1670-1675. Canvas 173.5 x 341 cm.

BRUSSELS, MUSÉE ROYAL DES BEAUX-ARTS

The syndics [147]. Despite its brevity, Louis Bonaparte's reign (1806-1810) was a period of unparalleled growth for the muscum; an unprecedented number of purchases meant that the collection of paintings more than doubled in number.

The loans from the city and the acquisitions from the Van der Pot and Van Heteren collections considerably changed the look of the collection, with the emphasis shifting towards the Dutch school. Sixty-five paintings were purchased at the Van der Pot auction for over 100,000 guilders. The accent was on the classical masters of the Golden Age. The most expensive painting was *The night school* by Gerard Dou (17,500 guilders), followed by *Herdsmen with their cattle* by Paulus Potter (10,500 guilders). In June 1809, the Van Heteren Gevers collection, comprising 137 paintings,

was acquired for 100,000 guilders. This collection, created in the 18th century, also concentrated on 17th-century Dutch and Flemish cabinet pieces. It included Rubens's fine oil sketch of *The carrying of the cross*. Works by Dutch artists included several paintings by Jan Steen, Van der Heyden, Potter, Dujardin, Willem van de Velde, d'Hondecoeter and Wouwermans. Among the public's favourites were Ter Borch's *The fatherly admonition* and Jan Steen's *The feast of Saint Nicholas* [117]. These acquisitions, together with the loans of monumental works by the City of Amsterdam, form the nucleus of the current overview of Dutch painting in the Rijksmuseum.

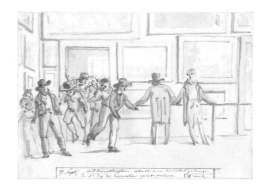

12. CHRISTIAAN ANDRIESSEN,
'People are being crushed here for love of art', the 3rd day of the Exhibition at the Palace, 17 Sept. 1808.
Chalk and brush, 22.6 x 17.9 cm.
AMSTERDAM, RIJKSMUSEUM

RIJKS MUSEUM FOR PAINTINGS IN THE TRIPPENHUIS

Following the restoration of the House of Orange, it was decided in 1815 to house the museum in the Trippenhuis together with the Royal Academy. The building had very little space for the more than 500 paintings, which were exhibited on the first and second floors. Displayed in the front gallery on the first floor, the largest room, were 'the most excellent paintings relating to the country's history and the portraits of the most famous men of our fatherland'. Rembrandt's *Night Watch* and *The civic guard banquet* by Van der Helst hung facing each other on the side walls. The other six museum galleries were on the second floor. Earlier pictures and other larger history paintings were exhibited in the front gallery (fig. 13), while the small galleries at the back housed the still lifes, landscapes and genre pieces. Few changes were made to the layout over the years (fig. 14). Up to 1830, the year of Belgian independence, paintings were still being acquired regularly, even though many wishes of the director, Cornelis Apostool, remained unfulfilled. Furthermore, the Rijks Museum was no longer the only museum of paintings in the Netherlands, as it had been in Louis Bonaparte's time; the stadholders' collection that had returned from Paris was housed in the Mauritshuis. Both museums were dependent for their purchases on the support of Willem I, who had an evident preference for the Mauritshuis. Against Apostool's advice, for example, he decided

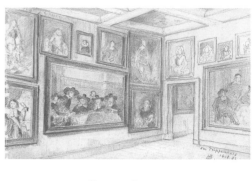

14. HENRI DE BRAEKELAER,
The syndics room, 16 August 1883.
Page from a sketchbook, black chalk, 15.2 x 24 cm.
AMSTERDAM, RIJKSMUSEUM

to exhibit Vermeer's *View of Delft*, purchased for 2900 guilders in 1822, in the Mauritshuis. The same thing happened to Rembrandt's *Anatomy lesson of Dr Nicolaes Tulp* [58], bought from the Amsterdam surgeons' guild. The price of 32,000 guilders was paid mainly from the proceeds of a sale of paintings from the Rijks Museum.

Both institutions aimed to own one good work by every Dutch master, and a number of good 17th-century paintings were purchased to this end: Frans Hals's *The merry drinker* [27] in 1816 for 325 guilders, a Moreelse in 1817 for 2130 guilders, a Rubens in 1822 for 5300 guilders and Honthorst's *Merry fiddler* [26] in 1824 for 600 guilders. A top price of 8290 guilders was paid for *The hut* by Adriaen van de Velde [177], which came from Josephus Augustinus Brentano's famous cabinet. One exceptional purchase was the bust of Andries de Graeff by Quellinus [165] in 1817 for 599 guilders. After Willem I's abdication in 1840, purchases effectively ground to a halt. His successor, Willem II, was interested only in his private collection, while the Dutch government confined its efforts to looking after the collections that already existed. The period up to 1875 was consequently a time of stagnation for the

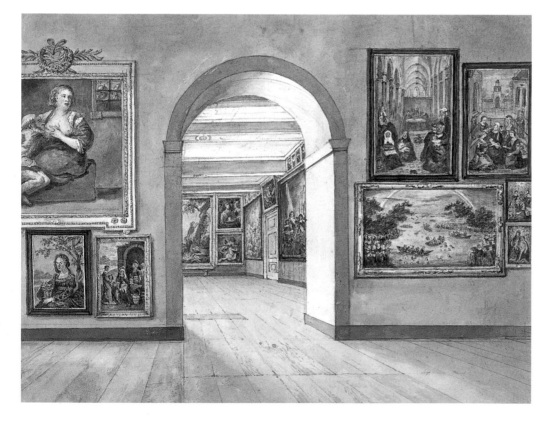

13. GERRIT LAMBERTS, *Interior of the Rijks Museum in the Trippenhuis:*
the front gallery on the second floor, 1838. Watercolour, 25.5 x 32 cm.
AMSTERDAM, MUNICIPAL ARCHIVES

Rijks Museum. There were a few exceptions – the *Self-portrait* by Bol [74], which was bequeathed to the museum, and the *Marriage portrait* by Frans Hals, bought in 1852 for 646 guilders [13].

THE SALE OF DUTCH ART

Sadly, virtually nothing remains in the Netherlands of the magnificent private collection assembled by the Dutch prince and later king Willem II in the first decades of the 19th century. This traditional royal gallery of paintings, with important works by great names like Jan van Eyck and other Flemish primitives, Raphael, Titian, Rubens, Van Dyck, Claude, Murillo and Rembrandt, would have given a Dutch museum an international allure that is lacking to this day. Moreover, his 17th-century Dutch paintings by Rembrandt, Ruisdael, Hobbema and Van der Helst were of a size that we encounter only in the English collections discussed above. The collection was sold in The Hague after the death of the king in 1849, and almost everything went to foreign buyers, among them the museum in Brussels, the Hermitage, the Louvre and the Marquess of Hertford (later the Wallace Collection). The Rijks Museum's Board of Trustees had suggested to the minister that two outstanding paintings by Teniers and Hobbema should be purchased, but again the government was not prepared to make the money available. The Minister of Home Affairs at that time was the liberal Thorbecke, who thought the arts and sciences did not need government support.

The sale of numerous Dutch masterpieces to foreign buyers had started back in the 17th century. In 1871 the Berlin museum director Wilhelm von Bode described the situation as follows: 'Everything in the innumerable Dutch private collections that was not nailed down, apart from a small fraction of paintings, was peddled abroad.' Institutions also sold their collec-

tions. In 1860 the city of Delft auctioned off its collection of 16th-century altarpieces, which had been kept in the town hall since the iconoclasm. When the regents of the Beresteyn Almshouses in Haarlem felt compelled to sell three portraits by Frans Hals in 1876, a public subscription was opened to preserve the portraits for Haarlem. When this did not produce the desired result, the portraits of Paulus Beresteyn and his wife and the large family portrait (now attributed to Pieter Soutman) were sold to the Louvre for the record sum of 100,000 guilders.

Despite all this, the tide turned during this period. In 1870 the Rijks Museum acquired the substantial bequest of the Dordrecht collector L. Dupper Wz: 64 17th-century Dutch paintings, predominantly cabinet pieces, including *The two oaks* by Jan van Goyen and the *Self-portrait* by Gerard Dou. This was the first in a series of gifts which strengthened the emphasis on the 17th-century Dutch school. Moreover, in 1870 the prospect of a new building for the Rijks Museum presented itself.

THÉOPHILE THORÉ

The cramped and poorly organised arrangement of the Rijks Museum in the Trippenhuis attracted growing criticism. The opinion of the museum expressed by the eminent connoisseur of Dutch painting Théophile Thoré in his *Musées de la Hollande* (1858) is uncompromisingly negative. He maintained it would take a new building, a new arrangement of the paintings and a new, detailed catalogue to do justice to the Dutch art of the glorious 17th century.

In fact Thoré's book was a heartfelt plea for 17th-century Dutch painting, whose democratic and humane character he praised. His preferences differed greatly from those of previous generations: in Thoré's view Frans Hals and Johannes Vermeer, both of whom he had rediscovered, were – along with Rembrandt –

the great heroes. Like Cuyp, Metsu, De Hooch, Steen and Hobbema, they had been sadly underestimated. Thoré believed that the flowering of Dutch art had come to an end around 1670 with the loss of an intrinsically Dutch identity. 'Fine painters' and the Italianate artists were not among his favourites. He described De Lairesse – with a distinctly pejorative undertone – as the 'Poussin of the North', and he thought that the work of Van der Werff signalled a definite decline. Thoré's influential views meant a conclusive break with tradition. In the second half of the 19th century this new vision became an increasingly important factor in collecting: the Louvre's purchase of the Van Beresteyn portraits by Frans Hals bears witness to this.

ADRIAAN VAN DER HOOP

In his *Musées de la Hollande* Thoré gave an exhaustive description of Adriaan van der Hoop's collection, which at that time was kept in the Oudemannenhuispoort, known as the Van der Hoop Museum. The collection amassed by the Amsterdam banker was left to the City of Amsterdam in 1854 and housed in the new Rijksmuseum building in 1885. In the very years when the Rijksmuseum was effectively starved of acquisition funds, Van der Hoop used his extensive resources to put together an exceptionally fine collection of 17th-century paintings, many of which still occupy a central position in the Rijksmuseum. Vermeer's *Interior with lady reading a letter*, Rembrandt's *Jewish bride* [148], Ruisdael's *Windmill at Wijk bij Duurstede* [154] and many other paintings [75, 94, 97, 115, 139] all came from Van der Hoop's collection. It was he who, at the sale of Willem II's collection in 1850, paid almost 14,000 guilders for the Teniers that the Rijksmuseum had urged the minister to buy, to no avail. His most expensive purchase was Jan Both's *Italian landscape with a draughtsman* [94], which he bought for 17,200 guilders from the

London dealer John Smith, who supplied Van der Hoop with a great many paintings. The collector did not shy away from large-scale works and this, in conjunction with the outstanding quality, elevated his collection to a level generally unmatched by other Dutch art collections.

BERLIN, LONDON AND AMSTERDAM

The 19th century was the century in which monumental buildings were built for the great national museums in Europe. The building of the Alte Museum (1830) and the Neue Museum (1855) in Berlin confirmed the status of the Prussians as a major power. The same was true of Munich as the capital of Bavaria, where the Alte Pinakothek was opened in 1838. Whereas these two German museums could build on the foundations of a royal collection, the National Gallery in London, which owed its foundation in 1824 to the new liberal government, had to build up its collection of paintings entirely through gifts and purchases, whereby the quality of the paintings acquired was always the key consideration. In terms of Dutch artists, the 18th-century English collecting tradition prevailed. Cuyp, Van de Cappelle, Ruisdael, Hobbema and Rembrandt were already well represented by the latter part of the century – the result of the acquisition of a number of 19th-century collections that had been created according to what was essentially 18th-century taste. Works by Saenredam and Vermeer were added around the turn of the century, but little attention was paid to the minor masters.

In Berlin, Wilhelm von Bode, himself a connoisseur of Dutch art, brought together a much broader overview of Dutch painting, doing justice to the great variety of genres and to the many lesser and greater masters. He generally shared the preferences of Théophile Thoré.

At the beginning of the 1870s, there was growing interest in the Netherlands in the art of the glorious past. Victor de Stuers was an important factor in this trend. In 1873, in his article 'Holland at its narrowest', he called for greater government commitment to the preservation of the nation's cultural heritage. From 1875 onwards, De Stuers was the senior official at the Ministry of Home Affairs responsible for museums and monuments – a job he set about with immense determination. He was concerned with cultural heritage in the broadest sense of the term: in addition to painting, drawing and graphic art, he also devoted his full attention to architecture, sculpture, the decorative arts and Dutch history. After the Lower House of the Dutch parliament voted to build a new Rijksmuseum in 1872, an active acquisitions policy gradually emerged, with a place for all the areas that De Stuers found so important.

THE DEVELOPMENT OF MUSEUMS OF DECORATIVE ART IN THE 19TH CENTURY

As we have seen, in the 17th century valuables and *objets d'art* were kept in 'cabinets' generally belonging to the upper echelons of society. In the 18th century, objects in silver and porcelain, in particular, were part of any royal inventory. In the 17th and 18th centuries, for example, a great deal of Delftware was sold to rulers in Germany, Bohemia and Sweden, who used it to decorate their castles and palaces to impressive effect. When these royal collections were opened to the public they were usually part of an encyclopedic presentation, not founded on any real art-historical considerations.

Shortly after 1850 museums of the decorative arts were founded in London, Vienna, Berlin, Hamburg and elsewhere. The purpose of these museums was to improve the taste of the artisan and the public and to act as model collections for craftsmen and artists. The modest museum at the School of Applied Arts in Haarlem

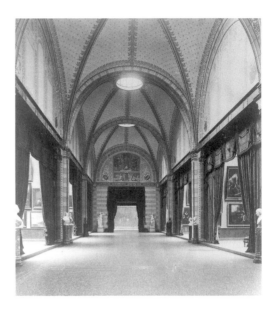

15. THE GALLERY OF HONOUR, c. 1900

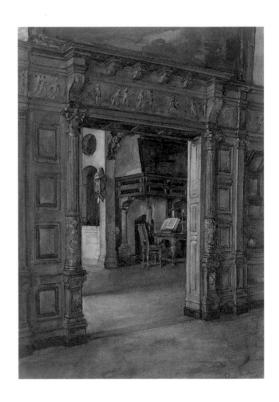

16. GEORG REUTER, *17th-century period room in the Netherlands Museum*, 1893. Watercolour, 63.6 x 45.2 cm. AMSTERDAM, RIJKSMUSEUM

was opened in 1880 with similar goals. The interest in the decorative arts that was reflected in the Rijksmuseum's collection from 1885 onwards had a more antiquarian character, although the museum's function as an example was certainly not ignored.

In 1858 a number of 'practising antiquarians', among them Jonkheer J.P. Six, Abraham Willet, Daniel Franken Dzn and David van der Kellen, Jr., founded the Royal Antiquarian Society in Amsterdam with the aim of 'promoting the knowledge of antiquity, specifically as a source for History, Art and Crafts'. The ultimate objective was the establishment of a national museum of applied arts. In its first decades, the society's collection grew steadily as a result of purchases and bequests.

In 1875 Victor de Stuers founded the Netherlands Museum of History and Art, which was accommodated in a house in The Hague awaiting completion of the new Rijksmuseum building, and transferred to Amsterdam in 1883. The nucleus of this museum was made up of the objects of Dutch origin from the Royal Cabinet of Curiosities, which was kept in the Mauritshuis in The Hague. The non-Western (chiefly Japanese and Chinese) objects in this collection found a home in the Leiden Ethnographic Museum. In 1875 Victor de Stuers put many 'antiquities' he came across in the Netherlands – extremely diverse in terms of both importance and quality – in this new museum. Added to purchases and gifts this meant a significant expansion of the collection. David van der Kellen, Jr. (1827-1895), one of the founders of the Royal Antiquarian Society, became Director of the Netherlands Museum. The two collections came together in the new Rijksmuseum building.

A NEW BUILDING FOR THE RIJKSMUSEUM

The ornamentation on the exterior of the Rijksmuseum building depicts the development and flowering of Northern Dutch culture in the form of reliefs, tile tableaux and inscriptions, with the glorious Golden Age as the central theme. Art of the 17th century was also given the most prominent place in the layout of the museum.

Paintings of the 15th to 19th centuries were exhibited on the whole of the top floor. Rembrandt's *Night Watch* had a central position in the room at the end of the Gallery of Honour (fig. 15).

On the lower floor the Netherlands Museum of History and Art provided a picture of the various aspects of the history of Dutch art and culture. Casts, reconstructions and copies of murals were used in the galleries of church architecture to give an impression of the Middle Ages. This was followed by a series of period rooms (fig. 16), wood panelling, furniture, carpets, glass and silver. There were separate rooms containing textiles, ceramics and porcelain, while paintings of naval battles, battle scenes and portraits of admirals were displayed in the Admirals Gallery.

The State Teacher Training College for teachers of drawing and the State School of Applied Art were based in the Rijksmuseum building, underscoring the museum's function as a model collection. Given the views of the founders of the Royal Antiquarian Society and the provenance of the collection in the Netherlands Museum, it is not surprising that the collection had a strong historical bias towards the 17th century.

Bequests and gifts made before 1900 had contributed to an extremely fine collection of glass, while furniture and the work of silversmiths and goldsmiths were reasonably well represented. The gift of an exceptional collection of Delft pottery by the heirs of John F. Loudon in 1916 meant an overnight improvement of this aspect of the collection, which suddenly acquired outstanding representation. The gift filled a gap that would otherwise probably never have been filled – good pieces of Delftware had already become extremely rare and costly by the time the collection was donated. Delftware had been rediscovered several decades previously and had rapidly become *the* Dutch national symbol. It is therefore understandable that the collection was shown in the Gallery of Honour until the Second World War (fig. 17).

Although there were rather more international purchases at the beginning of the century, acquisitions in the area of the decorative arts were still essentially confined to historically important pieces dating from the 17th century, so that even the French-inspired court art of Willem III's time was completely neglected.

THE RIJKSMUSEUM FOR PAINTINGS

From 1875 onwards, the collection of paintings grew steadily as a result of loans, bequests and purchases. The number of paintings housed in the new Rijksmuseum building tripled (from 700 to 2000) – the permanent loan from the City of Amsterdam included not only the Amsterdam civic-guard pieces, but also the entire Van der Hoop collection.

The tour through the museum began on the left of the Night Watch room. The walls were completely covered with paintings, as they had been in the Trippenhuis. A large gallery containing international art led into two rooms covering the 15th and 16th centuries, followed by numerous galleries and cabinets of 17th-century art, with the Dupper and Van der Poll bequests and the Van der Hoop Museum loaned by the city each having a gallery to itself.

The purchases in this period reflect the art-historical insights of the last decades of the 19th century. This was a time when the approach to art history was centred around

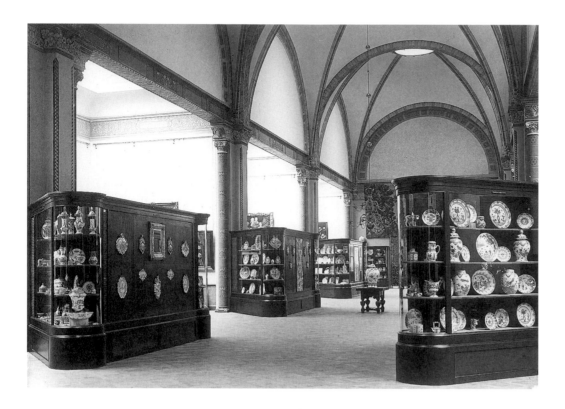

17. THE GALLERY OF HONOUR, c. 1930

archival research, which was bringing a great deal of new information to light. The museum sought to buy signed and dated works by painters often unknown until this time, laying the foundations for the reconstruction of the oeuvre of the artist concerned.

Many purchases were of documentary importance. The purchase of *The ferryboat* by Esaias van de Velde [*19*] in 1885 for 755 guilders was an exceptional stroke of luck. High prices were rarely paid for acquisitions. Exceptions to this were the purchase of Vermeer's *Love letter* for 45,000 guilders in 1893 (the most expensive 19th-century acquisition) and a classic cabinet piece like *The grey* by Wouwermans [*179*], which cost 16,500 guilders. The first Rembrandt ever purchased was *The stone bridge* [*80*], bought for 28,000 guilders at an auction in London in 1900. These three

purchases were made possible by substantial contributions from the Rembrandt Society. In 1907, again with the support of the Rembrandt Society and with government assistance, the museum bought 39 paintings from the Six collection, including Vermeer's *Kitchen maid* and a number of cabinet pieces by such masters as Van Ostade and Metsu. Shortly before his retirement, Van Riemsdijk, senior director since 1897, saw the acquisition of the Rijksmuseum's fourth Vermeer: in 1921 the oil magnate H.W.A. Deterding donated *The little street*, which he had acquired only shortly before from the Six collection.

The continual additions of newly acquired works meant that the galleries made an extremely muddled and unbalanced impression on visitors. Frederik Schmidt-Degener, senior director from 1922 to 1941, put an end to this situation.

A LASTING IMAGE OF DUTCH ART

Under the guidance of Frederik Schmidt-Degener the accent shifted from historical completeness to selection according to quality. The two decades before the Second World War saw the creation of a totally new layout, with works of art presented in a more spacious and evocative way, with art and history separated for the first time.

Schmidt-Degener believed that the aesthetic appreciation of art was central. His concern was to display a 'lasting image of Dutch art', in which the great masters – Hals, Steen, Rembrandt, Saenredam, Vermeer and Ruisdael – played the main part. 'Natural' realism was what he valued, whereas foreign influences were taboo: as long as Dutch painters 'avoided the mainstream of European art, their creations were always new and fresh'.

Mannerists, Caravaggisti, the Italianate painters, 'fine painters' and classicists did not fit into this picture and at best were given a place among the decorative painters who were exhibited along with the Delft pottery in the Gallery of Honour (fig. 17). One departure was that Schmidt-Degener displayed the best examples of sculpture (De Keyser, Verhulst and Quellinus), as well as the decorative arts (silver by Van Vianen and Lutma), close to the 17th-century paintings.

It should come as no surprise to learn that Schmidt-Degener was much more discriminating in his purchases than his predecessors had been. The modest budget available for purchases, which was reduced to a minimum during the Depression, severely limited his opportunities, but fortunately the Rembrandt Society and a number of collectors were prepared to lend their assistance for important acquisitions. They came to the museum's aid for *Rembrandt's mother as the prophetess Anna* by Rembrandt and *Portrait of a girl dressed in blue* by Verspronck [113], which were bought from the Van Oldenburg collection in 1922. Like the Verspronck, Gabriel Metsu's painting *The sick child*

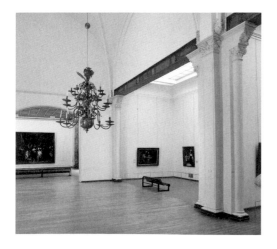

18. THE GALLERY OF HONOUR VIEWED TOWARDS
THE NIGHT WATCH ROOM, 1994

[119], purchased in 1928 for 135,000 guilders, further strengthened the 'lasting image'. The purchase of no fewer than seven paintings by Rembrandt was also the result of Schmidt-Degener's efforts. The last acquisition in this series was Rembrandt's early masterpiece *Jeremiah lamenting the destruction of Jerusalem* [55], which was acquired for 150,000 guilders in 1939 with the aid of the Rembrandt Society and the Photography Commission. One purchase that fell outside the traditional picture of the Golden Age was the acquisition in 1926 of *Elegant couples courting* by Willem Buytewech [33], a work Schmidt-Degener had admired since his youth.

THE NIGHT WATCH RETURNS TO ITS OLD PLACE

When the Rijksmuseum was reorganised after the Second World War, the aesthetic approach continued to prevail. The acquisition after the war of Dr F. Mannheimer's superb collection of decorative art and sculpture brought the quality of the sculpture and decorative arts department up to international standards and also made it possible to exhibit Dutch works of art and sculpture in a more international context. In the postwar years a great deal of work went into improving the quality of the collections over a considerably broader period than had been the case before the war. The Dutch collection was extended to take in the period 1680-1830, and the court art of Willem III also found a place in the museum. At the same time purchases were made to strengthen the 17th-century Dutch sculpture and decorative arts collections. Important silver pieces by Adam and Paulus van Vianen [2, 5] and Johannes Lutma [61], the layette cupboard [69], a cupboard attributed to Herman Doomer [63] and a cabinet attributed to Jan van Mekeren [190], were all acquired after 1945.

The comprehensive overview of Dutch painting started with the Northern

Netherlandish primitives in the eastern galleries and ended in the Night Watch room, an arrangement maintained until the 1980s. In the Gallery of Honour hung the 17th-century Flemish works, in addition to the Italian and Spanish paintings, and – until the 1970s – the Haarlem Mannerists and Utrecht Caravaggisti. When the Gallery of Honour and the Night Watch room were renovated in 1983-1984, the Night Watch regained its place of honour in the centre of the gallery (fig. 18), while from 1986 onwards the later 17th-century Dutch paintings – generally the larger works – were again displayed in the Gallery of Honour.

Over the past few decades, the museum's exhibition and collection policy has focused on undervalued aspects of the painting of the Golden Age, such as Mannerism, genre pieces, history painting, 'fine painting' and framing. All these exhibitions resulted in purchases that enhanced the multifaceted picture of 17th-century art. Numerous 17th-century masterpieces were acquired, including paintings by Rembrandt [59], large still lifes by Claesz and Heda [45, 46] and monumental landscapes by Cuyp and Philips Koninck [151, 152].

Jan Piet Filedt Kok

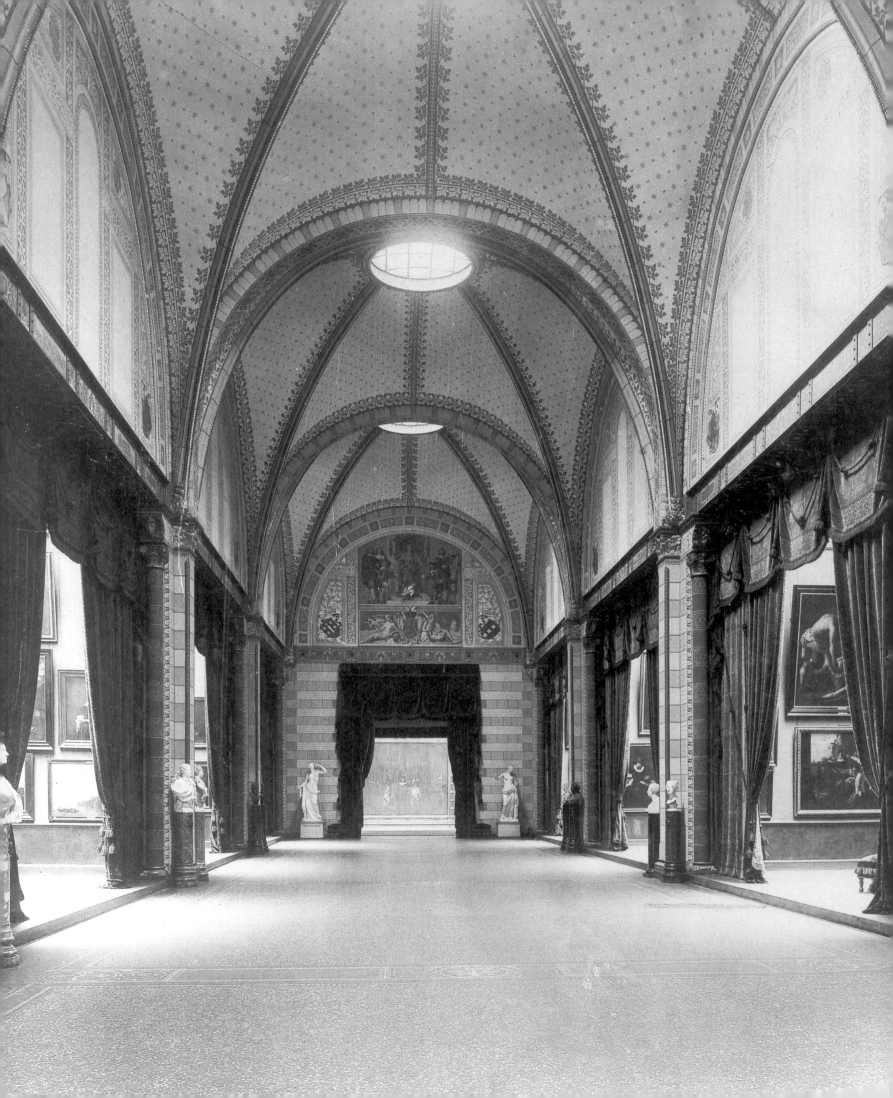

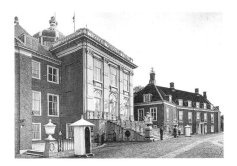

Nationale Konst-Gallerij, The Hague, 1800-1807

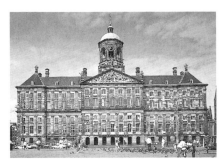

Koninklijk Museum, Amsterdam, 1808-1810

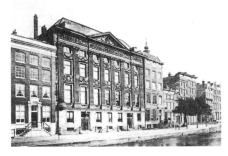

Amsterdam, Rijksmuseum, 1815-1885

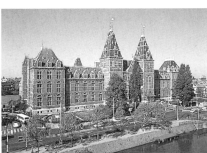

Amsterdam, Rijksmuseum, 1885-2000

AMSTERDAM, RIJKSMUSEUM

1800-1885

The 'Nationale Konst-Gallerij' (The National Art Gallery), the immediate predecessor of the Rijksmuseum, opened its doors to the public on 31/V/1800 in the Huis ten Bosch in The Hague. Most of the art works on display had been in the possession of the stadholders and had been in the Palaces Het Loo and Soestdijk. King Louis Bonaparte moved the museum to Amsterdam in 1808 and had the new 'Koninklijk Museum' (Royal Museum) housed in the former town hall on the Dam. In addition to a loan of seven large paintings from the City of Amsterdam, which included Rembrandt's *Night Watch* and Willem van de Velde's *The 'Gouden Leeuw' on the IJ at Amsterdam* (see p. 236), the number of paintings was almost doubled to more than 500. The paintings, together with the contents of the Print Room, were housed between 1815 and 1885 in the Trippenhuis and baptised the Rijks Museum.

1885-2000

In 1885 the museum moved to the new building on the Stadhouderskade, where the historical collection and the collection of decorative arts of the Nederlandse Museum van Geschiedenis en Kunst (Netherlands Museum of History and Art) were also housed, the basis of the latter being the Royal Cabinet of Curiosities. These were added to the collections of the Koninklijk Oudheidheidkundig Genootschap (Royal Antiquarian Society). Loans from the City of Amsterdam, including the renowned collection of 17th-century Dutch paintings belonging to Adriaan van der Hoop (1778-1854), were given a place in the Rijksmuseum. These loans and bequests, as well as an active acquisitions policy, were responsible for nearly tripling the number of paintings in the collection. In the 20th century this number was again doubled. During the period after the Second World War the aim was to diversify the overview offered by the collection by purchasing works representing underappreciated aspects of 17th-century Dutch painting.

LITERATURE: cat. Amsterdam 1952a; cat. Amsterdam 1952b; cat. Amsterdam 1973; cat. Amsterdam 1976; Van Thiel 1983b; Grijzenhout 1984; cat. Amsterdam 1992; Bergvelt 1998; Van der Ham 2000; exhib. cat. Amsterdam 2000

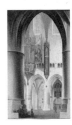

198
[*see p. 288*]
Melchior d'Hondecoeter
(Utrecht 1636-Amsterdam 1695)
The floating feather, c. 1680
Canvas 159 x 144 cm
In the middle, on the edge of the urn:
M.D. Hondecoeter
Inv. no. SK-A-175

LITERATURE:
Plietzsch 1960, p. 161: cat. Amsterdam 1976, p. 282; Vlieger 1995; Stumpel 1995, p. 39

PROVENANCE:
(?) inventory Paleis Het Loo 1713; Paleis Soestdijk, until 1799; moved to Huis ten Bosch, 1799

1800

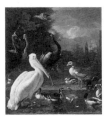

76
[*see p. 123*]
Pieter Saenredam
(Assendelft 1597-Haarlem 1665)
Interior of the Church of
St Bavo in Haarlem
Panel 95.5 x 57 cm
On the lower edge of the small organ:
P. Saenredam. 1636; on the upper edge
of the balustrade: *E ORGEL PSALM.;*
on the lower edge of the balustrade:
NDE ZANGEN EN GEESTELYCKE
LIEDEKENS.
Inv. no. SK-A-359

LITERATURE:
cat. Amsterdam 1976, p. 491; Biesboer 1985, pp. 80, 85, 87-88; Schwartz and Bok 1989, no. 38

PROVENANCE:
purchased in 1806

1806

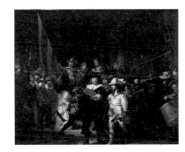

65
[*see p. 107*]
Rembrandt
(Leiden 1606-Amsterdam 1669)
The company of Captain Frans
Banning Cocq and Lieutenant
Willem Jan Ruytenburch, known as
'The Night Watch'
Canvas 363 x 437 cm
Lower left: *Rembrandt f 1642;* on the escutcheon on the gate, probably a later addition: *Frans Banning Cocq, heer van purmerlant en Ilpendam, Capiteijn, Willem van Ruijtenburch van Vlaerdingen' heer van Vlaerdingen, Lu[ij]tenant, Jan Visscher Cornelisen Vaendrich, Rombout Kemp Sergeant, Reijnier Engelen Sergeant, Barent Harmansen, Jan Adriaensen Keyser, Elbert Willemsen, Jan Clasen Leydeckers, Jan Ockersen, Jan Pietersen bronchorst, Harman Iacobsen wormskerck, Jacob Dircksen de Roy, Jan vander heede, Walich Schellingwou, Jan brugman, Claes van Cruysbergen, Paulus Schoonhoven*
Inv. no. SK-C-5

LITERATURE:
cat. Amsterdam 1976, pp. 469-70; Haverkamp Begemann 1982; Bruyn *et al.* 1982-89, vol. 3, no. A 146

PROVENANCE:
Large Hall, Kloveniersdoelen, Amsterdam; Small Armoury of the Old Town Hall, 1715; the Trippenhuis, 1815; on loan from the City of Amsterdam since 1808

1808

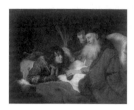

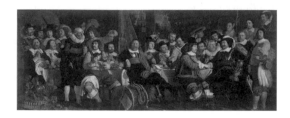

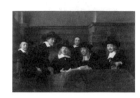

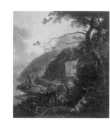

56

[see p. 89]
Govert Flinck
(Kleve 1615-Amsterdam 1660)
Isaac blessing Jacob
Canvas 117 x 141 cm
Previously above Isaac's shoulder:
G.Flinck 1638 (both signature and date
disappeared after cleaning; facsimile in
cat. Amsterdam 1880, no. 87)
Inv. no. SK-A-110

LITERATURE:
Von Moltke 1965, no. 8; cat.
Amsterdam 1976, p. 227; Sumowski
1983-94, vol. 2, no. 614

PROVENANCE:
sale G. van der Pot van Groeneveld,
Rotterdam, 6/VI/1808, no. 37

1808

66

[see p. 109]
Bartholomeus van der Helst
(Haarlem 1613-Amsterdam 1670)
*The celebration of the Treaty of
Münster, 18 June 1648, at the
crossbowmen's headquarters
(St George's Guard)*
Canvas 232 x 547 cm
Lower centre: *Bartolomeus Van der
Helst fecit Ao 1648*; inscription on the
paper under the cord on the drum:
*Belloone walgt van bloedt / ja Mars
vervloeckt het daveren / Van't zwangere
metaal, / en't zwaardt bemint de scheê: /
Dies biedtde dapp're Wits / aan d'eedele
van Waveren / Op't eeuwige verbondt, /
den hooren van de Vreê*
Inv. no. SK-C-2

LITERATURE:
De Gelder 1921, no. 836; cat.
Amsterdam 1976, p. 268; exhib. cat.
Haarlem 1988, no. 189

PROVENANCE:
Voetboogdoelen, Amsterdam; Large
Armoury of the Old Town Hall, 1683;
the Trippenhuis, 1815; on loan from the
City of Amsterdam since 1808

1808

95

[see p. 147]
Adam Pynacker
(Schiedam c. 1620-Amsterdam 1673)
Boatmen moored on a lake shore,
c. 1660
Canvas on panel 97.5 x 85.5 cm
Lower left: *APijnacker* (AP in ligature)
Inv. no. SK-A-321

LITERATURE:
exhib. cat. Utrecht 1965, no. 116; cat.
Amsterdam 1976, p. 458; exhib. cat.
Amsterdam-Boston-Philadelphia 1987-
88, no. 66; Harwood 1988, no. 74

PROVENANCE:
sale Amsterdam, 8/VI/1763, no. 13;
Pieter Fouquet (in 1786 purchased from
Neufville; sold to Van der Pot); sale G.
van der Pot van Groeneveld, Rotterdam,
6/VI/1808, no. 105

1808

147

[see p. 213]
Rembrandt
(Leiden 1606-Amsterdam 1669)
The syndics
Canvas 191.5 x 279 cm
In the middle, on the tablecloth:
Rembrandt f. 1662 and at the upper
right on the wall, presumably an addition
by a later hand: *Rembrandt f. 1661*
Inv. no. SK-C-6

LITERATURE:
Van de Waal 1956, pp. 61-107; Haak
1968, pp. 308-10, 334, 336; cat.
Amsterdam 1976, p. 472; Tümpel 1993,
no. 256; exhib. cat. Berlin-Amsterdam-
London 1991-92, no. 48

PROVENANCE:
commissioned by the sitters and hung in
the Staalhof, the headquarters of the
drapers' guild in the Staalstraat in
Amsterdam; moved to the town hall in
1771; the Trippenhuis, 1815; on loan
from the City of Amsterdam since 1808

1808

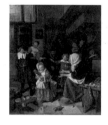

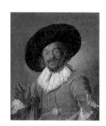

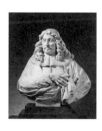

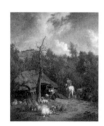

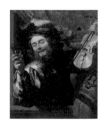

117

[see p. 173]
Jan Steen
(Leiden 1626-Leiden 1679)
The feast of St Nicholas, c. 1665-1668
Canvas 82 x 70.5 cm
Lower right: *JSteen* (JS in ligature)
Inv. no. SK-A-385

LITERATURE:
Van Thienen 1957; cat. Amsterdam
1976, p. 522; De Vries 1977, no. 151;
Boer 1994; exhib. cat. Washington-
Amsterdam 1996-97, no. 30; Kloek
1998, pp. 23-25, 43, 45, 82

PROVENANCE:
sale Seger Tierens, The Hague,
23/VII/1743, no. 178; Hendrik van
Heteren, The Hague 1743-49; Adriaan
Leonard van Heteren, The Hague 1749-
1808; Adriaan Leonard van Heteren
Gevers, The Hague and Rotterdam,
1809; acquired with the latter's cabinet,
1809

1809

27

[see p. 53]
Frans Hals
(Antwerp 1582/1583-Haarlem 1666)
The merry drinker, c. 1628-1630
Canvas 81 x 66.5 cm
Right centre: *FH* (in ligature)
Inv. no. SK-A-135

LITERATURE:
Slive 1970-74, vol. 3, no. 63; cat.
Amsterdam 1976, p. 256; exhib. cat.
Washington-London-Haarlem 1989-90,
no. 30

PROVENANCE:
sale widow of C.P. baron van Leyden
van Warmond, née H.J. de Thomas,
Leiden, 31/VII/1816, no. 13

1816

165

[see p. 244]
Artus Quellinus
(Antwerp 1609-Antwerp 1668)
*Portrait of Andries de Graeff
(1611-1678)*
Marble h. 75 cm
On the socle: *AND.DE.GRAEFF.COS.AMST.
A.QUELLINO.F.CICICLXI*
Inv. no. BK-18305

LITERATURE:
cat. Amsterdam 1973, no. 301; cat.
Amsterdam 1995a, no. 18

PROVENANCE:
sale Amsterdam, 6/IV/1812, no. 1;
Jeronimo de Bosch, Leiden; sale
A.M. Hogguer-Ebeling, Amsterdam,
18/VIII/1817, no. 1 (sold to Jeronimo de
Vries for the Dutch state); Trippenhuis;
moved at the suggestion of the sculptor
P.J. Gabriel to the Academie van Schone
Kunsten (seen by Victor de Steurs in
1875 in the Old Men's Almshouse); since
1885 in the Rijksmuseum

1817

177

[see p. 265]
Adriaen van de Velde
(Amsterdam 1636-Amsterdam 1672)
The hut
Canvas 76 x 65 cm
Lower left: *A.v.Velde f. 1671*
Inv. no. SK-A-443

LITERATURE:
Schatborn 1975; cat. Amsterdam 1976,
p. 558; exhib. cat. Dordrecht-
Leeuwarden 1988-89, no. 32

PROVENANCE:
Wouter Valckenier, Amsterdam; sale E.
Valckenier-Hooft, Amsterdam,
31/VIII/1796, no. 39; sale J.A. Brentano,
Amsterdam, 13/V/1822, no. 344 (sold to
Jeronimo de Vries for the Rijksmuseum)

1822

26

[see p. 52]
Gerard van Honthorst
(Utrecht 1592-Utrecht 1656)
The merry fiddler
Canvas 108 x 89 cm
In the middle, on the parapet:
G. Honthorst fe. 1623 (GH in ligature)
Inv. no. SK-A-180

LITERATURE:
Judson 1959, no. 168; cat. Amsterdam
1976, p. 285; exhib. cat. Philadelphia-
Berlin-London 1984, no. 48; exhib. cat.
Utrecht-Braunschweig 1986-87, no. 64

PROVENANCE:
sale J.G. Eimbke, Berlin, 21/IX/1761, no.
18; sale J. Viet, Amsterdam, 12/X/1774,
no. 106; sale M.M. van Sluijpwijk,
Countess of Moens, Amsterdam,
20/IV/1803, no. 32; sale Van Terburg
family, Amsterdam, 16/VII/1819, no. 74;
purchased from C. Josi, 1824

1824

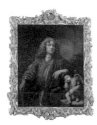

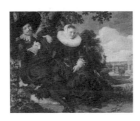

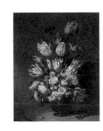

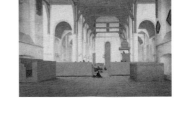

74

[see p. 119]
Ferdinand Bol
(Dordrecht 1616-Amsterdam 1680)
Self-portrait, in or before 1669
Canvas 128 x 104 cm
Inv. no. SK-A-42

LITERATURE:
cat. Amsterdam 1976, p. 123; De Jongh
1981-82; Blankert 1982, no. 103;
exhib. cat. Amsterdam 1984, no. 61;
exhib. cat. Haarlem 1986, no. 9

PROVENANCE:
presumably identical with the self-
portrait of Bol which is recorded in the
division of the estate of Bol's son Elbert
Bol who died a bachelor, the document
drawn up on 17/III/1709: 'a portrait of
Mr Ferdinand Boll in a gilt frame,
Dfl 45 -'; sale Wreesman, Amsterdam,
17/VIII/1818, no. 9 (sold to Albertus
Brondgeest); bequest Albertus
Brondgeest, 1849

1849

13

[see p. 32]
Frans Hals
(Antwerp 1582/1583-Haarlem 1666)
*Marriage portrait of Isaac Massa and
Beatrix van der Laen*, c. 1622
Canvas 140 x 166.5 cm
Inv. no. SK-A-133

LITERATURE:
De Jongh and Vinken 1961; Slive 1970-
74, vol. 3, no. 17; cat. Amsterdam 1976,
p. 256; exhib. cat. Haarlem 1986,
no. 20; exhib. cat. Washington-London-
Haarlem 1989-90, no. 12

PROVENANCE:
sale Jan Six, Amsterdam, 6/IV/1702
(withdrawn); sale H. Six van Hillegom,
Amsterdam, 25/XI/1851, no. 15; acquired
in 1852

1852

42

[see p. 73]
Hans Boulenger
(Haarlem c. 1600-Haarlem 1672/1675)
Tulips in a vase
Panel 68 x 54.5 cm
Lower right: *HBoulenger*. 1639
(HB in ligature)
Inv. no. SK-A-799

LITERATURE:
cat. Amsterdam 1976, p. 127; exhib. cat.
The Hague 1992, no. 7; exhib. cat.
Amsterdam 1994, pp. 90, 101; exhib.
cat. Amsterdam-Cleveland 1999-2000,
no. 24

PROVENANCE:
sale widow of P.C. Baron Nahuys-
Hodgson, Amsterdam, 14-15/XI/1883

1883

75

[see p. 122]
Pieter Saenredam
(Assendelft 1597-Haarlem 1665)
*Interior of the Church of
St Odulphus in Assendelft*
Panel 50 x 76 cm
Left on the choir stall: *dit is de kerck tot
Assendelft, een dorp in hollandt, van
Pieter Saenredam, dese geschildert int
jaer 1649. den 2. October.*; on the
tombstone of Jan Saenredam (at the top):
*IOHANNIS SAENREDAM / SCULPTORIS
CELEBERRIMI. / PETRI DE IONGE XLIV
ANNOS ASSENDELPHI / PRAETORIS. /
GERARDI DE IONGE FILLII I.V.D. ET
ADVOCATI. / IACET HIC QUOD FVIT.*; on
the upper edge of the tomb: *dit is de
TOMBE ofte begraefplaets van heeren
tot assendelft*; on the lower part of the
tomb, overpainted: *en...kerck Assendelft
een ...p in Hollant...Saenredam 1649
volschildert*
Inv. no. SK-C-217

LITERATURE:
cat. Amsterdam 1976, p. 492; Schwartz
and Bok 1989, no. 19; exhib. cat.
Rotterdam 1991, no. 16

PROVENANCE:
sale Zoeterwoude, 11/IX/1766, no. 79;
sale Jeronimo de Bosch, Amsterdam,
6/IV/1812, no. 51; Jeronimo de Vries,
from whom it was acquired by Adriaan
van der Hoop, 17/I/1848; bequest Van
der Hoop to the City of Amsterdam,
1854; on loan from the City of
Amsterdam since 1885

1885

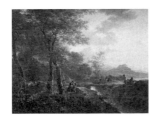

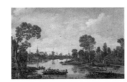

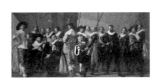

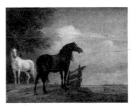

94

[see p. 146]
Jan Both
(Utrecht ?-Utrecht 1652)
Italian landscape with draughtsman,
c. 1650
Canvas 187 x 240 cm
Lower right on rock: *JBoth f.*
(JB in ligature)
Inv. no. SK-C-109

LITERATURE:
exhib. cat. Utrecht 1965, no. 56; cat.
Amsterdam 1976, p. 137; Burke 1976,
no. 1; exhib. cat. Amsterdam-Boston-
Philadelphia 1987-88, no. 15; exhib. cat.
Amsterdam-London 1991

PROVENANCE:
sale Quiryn van Biesum, Rotterdam,
18/X/1719, no. 127; sale Richard
Pickfatt, Rotterdam, 12/IV/1736, no. 57;
Thomas Hamlet, Denham Court, 1829;
sale, London, 27/VII-3/VIII/1833, no.
201 (bought back); John Smith, 1834,
from whom it was bought by Adriaan
van der Hoop; bequest Van der Hoop to
the City of Amsterdam, 1854; on loan
from the City of Amsterdam since 1885

1885

19

[see p. 42]
Esaias van de Velde
(Amsterdam 1587-The Hague 1630)
The ferryboat
Panel 75.5 x 113 cm
Lower right: *E.V. VELDE 1622*
Inv. no. SK-A-1293

LITERATURE:
cat. Amsterdam 1976, p. 558; Keyes
1984, vol. 2, no. 104; exhib. cat.
Amsterdam-Boston-Philadelphia
1987-88, no. 106

PROVENANCE:
sale P. Verloren van Themaat,
Amsterdam, 30/X/1885, no. 100;
C.F. Roos & Co., Amsterdam; acquired
in 1885

1885

64

[see p. 104]
Frans Hals and Pieter Codde
(Antwerp 1582/1583-Haarlem 1666;
Amsterdam 1599-Amsterdam 1678)
*The company of Captain Reynier Reael
and Lieutenant Cornelis Michielsz
Blaeuw, known as 'The Meagre
Company'*, 1637
Canvas 209 x 429 cm
On the right in the middle: *A° 1637*
Inv. no. SK-C-374

LITERATURE:
Slive 1970-74, vol. 3, no. 80; cat.
Amsterdam 1976, p. 257; exhib. cat.
Washington-London-Haarlem 1989-90,
no. 43

PROVENANCE:
Voetboogdoelen, Amsterdam; the Old
Town Hall, 1683, in the Large Armoury
and subsequently in the Burgomasters'
Chamber, on loan from the City of
Amsterdam since 1885

1885

97

[see p. 149]
Paulus Potter
(Enkhuizen 1625-Amsterdam 1654)
Two horses near a gate in a meadow
Panel 23.5 x 30 cm
On the fence: *Paulus/Potter f. 1649*
Inv. no. SK-C-205

LITERATURE:
cat. Amsterdam 1976, p. 454; exhib. cat.
The Hague 1994-95, no. 18; exhib. cat.
Perth-Adelaide-Brisbane 1997-98, no. 5

PROVENANCE:
Goll van Franckenstein family, before
1785 until 1833; sale Pieter Hendrick
Goll van Franckenstein, Amsterdam,
1/VII/1833, no. 61 (sold to Jeronimo de
Vries); Adriaan van der Hoop, 1833;
bequest Van der Hoop to the City of
Amsterdam, 1854; on loan from the City
of Amsterdam since 1885

1885

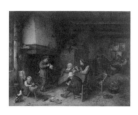

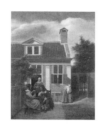

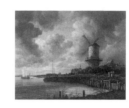

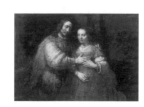

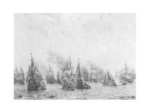

115
[see p. 171]
Adriaen van Ostade
(Haarlem 1610-Haarlem 1685)
Peasants in an interior
Copper 37 x 47 cm
Lower right: *A.V. Ostade 1661*
Inv. no. SK-C-200

LITERATURE:
Hofstede de Groot 1907-28, vol. 3, no. 620; cat. Amsterdam 1976, p. 430

PROVENANCE:
sale Willem Lormier, The Hague, 4/VII/1763, no. 207; sale De Julienne, Paris, 30/III-22/V/1767, no. 153; sale Duc de Choiseul, Paris, 6/IV/1772, no. 42; sale Claude Tolozan, Paris, 23-26/II/1801, no. 79; Duchesse de Berry, Paris, 1829; sold privately, London, 1834 (sold to Albertus Brondgeest for Adriaan van der Hoop); bequest Van der Hoop to the City of Amsterdam, 1854; on loan from the City of Amsterdam since 1885

1885

139
[see p. 201]
Pieter de Hooch
(Rotterdam 1629-Amsterdam 1684)
Three women and a man in a courtyard,
c. 1663-1665
Canvas 60 x 45.7 cm
On the bench at the left: *P D HOOCH*
Inv. no. SK-C-150

LITERATURE:
cat. Amsterdam 1976, p. 287; Sutton 1980, no. 59; exhib. cat. Delft 1996, pp. 119-121; exhib. cat. London-Hartford 1998-99, no. 30

PROVENANCE:
brought by Chaplin to England; O'Neil, 1832; Adriaan van der Hoop, Amsterdam, 1842; bequest Van der Hoop to the City of Amsterdam, 1854; on loan from the City of Amsterdam since 1885

1885

148
[see p. 216]
Rembrandt
(Leiden 1606-Amsterdam 1669)
Isaac and Rebecca ('The Jewish bride'),
c. 1665
Canvas 121.5 x 166.5 cm
Lower right: *Rembrandt f 16..*
Inv. no. SK-C-216

LITERATURE:
Haak 1968, pp. 320-22; exhib. cat. Amsterdam 1969, no. 22; cat. Amsterdam 1976, p. 472; Tümpel 1993, no. 32; Hoekstra 1996; Van de Wetering 1997, pp. 155-60

PROVENANCE:
purchased by John Smith from the Vaillant Collection at Amsterdam, 1825; bought from John Smith by Adriaan van der Hoop, 1833; bequest Van der Hoop to the City of Amsterdam, 1854; on loan from the City of Amsterdam since 1885

1885

154
[see p. 225]
Jacob van Ruisdael
(Haarlem 1628/1629-Amsterdam 1682)
The windmill at Wijk bij Duurstede,
c. 1670
Canvas 83 x 101 cm
Lower right: *Ruisdael*
Inv. no. SK-C-211

LITERATURE:
Rosenberg 1928, no. 70; cat. Amsterdam 1976, p. 487; Kauffmann 1977; exhib. cat. The Hague-Cambridge 1981-82, no. 39; exhib. cat. Amsterdam-Boston-Philadelphia 1987-88, no. 88

PROVENANCE:
sale J. Juriaans, Amsterdam, 28/VIII/1817, no. 55; bought from John Smith by Adriaan van der Hoop, 1833; bequest Van der Hoop to the City of Amsterdam, 1854; on loan from the City of Amsterdam since 1885

1885

159
[see p. 233]
Willem van de Velde the Elder
(Leiden c. 1611-London 1693)
The battle of Livorno, c. 1655
Panel 114 x 160 cm
On a barrel floating at the lower right:
W.V. Velde
Inv. no. SK-A-1364

LITERATURE:
cat. Amsterdam 1976, p. 560; exhib. cat. Amsterdam 1984, no. 42; Robinson 1990, vol. 1, no. 337

PROVENANCE:
originally owned by the Tromp family; sale Cornelia van Kinschot, Amsterdam, 11/VIII/1788, no. 4; sale J. Cramer, Amsterdam, 22/VII/1811, no. 58; purchased for the Rijksarchief (National Archives), c. 1863; Nederlandse Museum van Geschiedenis en Kunst, The Hague, 1875; the Rijksmuseum, 1885 (from 1921 until 1931 on loan to the Scheepvaartmuseum, Amsterdam)

1885

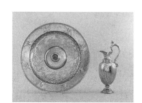

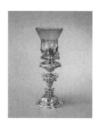

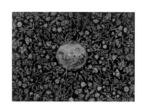

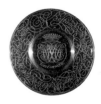

4
[see p. 18]
Adam van Vianen
(Utrecht 1568/1569-Utrecht 1627)
Ewer and basin
Silver-gilt and glass, ewer: h. 38.5 cm; basin: diam. 52.5 cm
Marked on the upper side of the foot of the ewer and on the underside of the basin: assay office mark Utrecht, year letter T = 1614, maker's mark AV in monogram on shaped shield = Adam van Vianen; engraved above the three scenes on the ewer: *ALCMAR.18.SEPTEM.1573.,* *.BOSSV.12.OCTOBRIS.1573.* and *.LEYDEN.3.OCTOBRIS.1574.;* engraved above the eight representations around the edge of the basin:
.SCHEEPSTRYT.29.IANV.1574..MIDDELBOR CH.20.FEBRV.1574., *.SPAENSCHE.VLOOT.7.AVGVS.1588.,* *.BREDA.4.MARTIVS.1590.,* *.GEERTRVYDENBERCH.24.IVNY.1593.,* *.TVRNHOVT.24.IANVARY.1597.,* *.S.ANDRIES.6.MAY.1600..BOMMEL.4.MAY.1 599., .GRAEF.19.SEPTEMBRIS.1602.* and

.GIBRALTAR.25.APRILIS.1607.; engraved beneath the scene on the plateau of the basin: *.VLAENDEREN.2.IVLY.1600.;* on the 'umbo', a medallion with a glass face behind which appears the crowned coat of arms of Amsterdam, held by lions, painted in gold, black, red and white, with a cartouche on the socle dated:
ANNO 1614
Inv. no. BK-Am-17a/b

LITERATURE:
cat. Amsterdam 1952b, no. 81; Ter Molen 1984, vol. 2, no. 408; cat. Utrecht 1984-85, no. 60; exhib. cat. Amsterdam 1993-94, no. 111

PROVENANCE:
probably commissioned by the City of Amsterdam as a gift for Prince Maurits; on loan from the City of Amsterdam since 1885

1885

48
[see p. 79]
Leendert Claesz
(Emden 1580-? after 1609), attributed to
Glass-holder
Silver-gilt h. 24.8 cm
Marked on the underside of the base: assay office mark Amsterdam; year letter V = 1609; maker's mark LC interlaced, attributed to Leendert Claesz; engraved on the underside of the foot: *Deze schroeven syn doen maecken zyde f Gerrit Jacob Witse & Jan ten Grooten-huis Tresorieren van den Jaere 1606*
Inv. no. BK-Am-16c

LITERATURE:
cat. Amsterdam 1952b, no. 75; exhib. cat. Amsterdam 1993-94, no. 97; cat. Amsterdam 1999, no. 5

PROVENANCE:
in 1606 ordered by the City of Amsterdam; on loan from the City of Amsterdam since 1885

1885

134
[see p. 193]
Tablecloth with Flora in oval cartouche,
c. 1660-1680
Wool and silk, 194 x 275 cm
Inv. no. BK-KOG-41

LITERATURE:
exhib. cat. Amsterdam 1971-72, no. 22

PROVENANCE:
gift of A.J. Enschedé to the Koninklijk Oudheidkundig Genootschap, 1859; on loan from the KOG since 1885

1885

105
[see p. 159]
Dish with diamond-point engraving by Willem Jacobsz van Heemskerk
(1613-1693)
Clear, uncoloured glass, diam. 32.3 cm
On the edge: *Bestand'ge noit-besweken Trouw, Werkt lyvelijk-en seel-behouw.;* in the middle: *IVHAC* (Joost Van Heemskerk Anna Conink), beneath a crown in which the same letters are repeated; below the monogram: *Iuste & Syncere;* on the back, in the crown: *W.V.H. AEs 72 3/4 A01685*
Inv. no. NG-NM-764

LITERATURE:
cat. Amsterdam 1995b, no. 87

PROVENANCE:
Van Heemskerk family, Leiden; sale Leiden, 2/IX/1771, no. 192; Koninklijk Kabinet van Zeldzaamheden, The Hague, 1875; Nederlandsch Museum voor Geschiedenis en Kunst, The Hague; in the Rijksmuseum since 1885

1885

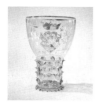

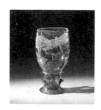

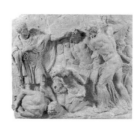

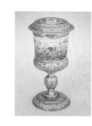

32

[see p. 57]
*Roemer with the coat of arms and
motto of Prince Maurits*
Clear green glass with gilt, h. 23.4 cm
On the bowl of the *roemer: AN 1606* and
TANDEM.FIT.SURCULUS ARBOR
Inv. no. NG-NM-697

LITERATURE:
cat. Amsterdam 1993a, no. 400

PROVENANCE:
Koninklijk Kabinet van Zeldzaamheden,
The Hague, 1875; Nederlandsch
Museum voor Geschiedenis en Kunst; in
the Rijksmuseum since 1885

1885

31

[see p. 56]
*Roemer with diamond-point engraving
by Anna Roemers Visscher
(1583-1651)*
Clear, dark-green glass, h. 13 cm
Between two thistle-prunts on the stem:
Anna Roemers and between two others:
Anno 1621; on the bowl of the *roemer:
Bella DORI Gentil, Noi uaghi fiori /
Da te prendiam gli honori*
Inv. no. BK-NM-8188

LITERATURE:
Smit 1990, pp. 43-44; cat. Amsterdam
1995b, no. 14

PROVENANCE:
A.D. Schinkel; sale The Hague,
24/XI/1864, no. 131; bequest J.
Kneppelhout, 1886

1886

167

[see p. 246]
Artus Quellinus
(Antwerp 1609-Antwerp 1668)
*The judgement of Brutus: Justice,
c. 1651-1654*
Terracotta 73 x 83 cm
Inv. no. BK-Am-51/21

LITERATURE:
Fremantle 1959, pp. 157-64; cat.
Amsterdam 1973, no. 279

PROVENANCE:
Kunstkamer in the town hall; in 1808
probably moved with the rest of the
Rijksacademie voor Beeldende Kunsten
to the upper-storey rooms of the former
stock exchange; Old Men's Almshouse,
1837; on loan from the City of
Amsterdam since 1887

1887

160

[see p. 235]
Nicolaas Loockemans
(?-The Hague 1673)
Covered goblet
Gold and enamel, h. 30 cm
Marked: assay office mark The Hague, a
lion rampant; year letter Q = 1668;
maker's mark and crowned anchor =
Nicolaas Loockemans; in the lid: *Extraxt
Compendiens den 2 July's 1667. Opt
geproponeerde van Heeren G. Raeden is
bij Staten goedt gevonden dat anden
Lt.Adme. de Ruyter Slandts Vlote als
generael gecommandeert hebbende over
en ter saecke van het fameuse exploict
den 21' 22' en 23 Junys 1667 op
rivieren van London en van Rochester
int werck gestelt vereert sal worden een
gouden Cop doerop't voorsz exploict
uitgebeelt. Zij en dat tot een
gedenckteecken in sijne familie en
voorde posteriteyt. Accordeert in
Substantie met de resolutie van Staten.
Herbt. van Beaumont*
Inv. no. NG-NM-9659

LITERATURE:
cat. Amsterdam 1952b, no. 161; exhib.
cat. Amsterdam-Vlissingen 1957, no.
181; exhib. cat. The Hague 1967, no. 56

PROVENANCE:
made as the result of a resolution taken
by the Gedeputeerde Staten van Holland
on 2/VII/1667 and presented by this body
to Admiral M.A. de Ruyter on 7/XI/1667;
Margaretha de Ruyter; bequest Von der
Goltz, 1893

1893

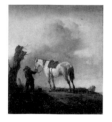

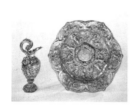

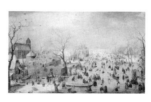

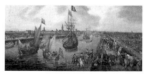

179

[see p. 267]
Philips Wouwermans
(Haarlem 1619-Haarlem 1668)
The grey, c. 1646
Panel 43.5 x 38 cm
In the foreground: *PH W* (PH in ligature)
Inv. no. SK-A-1610

LITERATURE:
Hofstede de Groot 1907-28, vol. 2, no.
207; cat. Amsterdam 1976, p. 615;
Duparc 1993

PROVENANCE:
sale Dirk Versteegh, Amsterdam,
3/XI/1823, no. 47 (sold to Van de Berg);
W.P. van Lennep, Amsterdam; sale
Messchert van Vollenhoven, Amsterdam,
29/III/1892, no. 15; purchased with the
aid of the Rembrandt Society, 1894

1894

67

[see p. 112]
Johannes Lutma
(Emden 1587-Amsterdam 1669)
*Ewer and basin with the coat of arms
of Cornelis Tromp*
Silver, ewer: h. 50.4 cm;
basin: diam. 74.5 cm
Marked on the neck of the ewer and on
the underside of the basin: assay office
mark Amsterdam, year letter Q = 1647;
maker's mark, a heart in a shield =
Johannes Lutma
Inv. no. BK-NM-10244

LITERATURE:
cat. Amsterdam 1952b, no. 121; exhib.
cat. Amsterdam 1984-85, no. 38; cat.
Amsterdam 1999, no. 14

PROVENANCE:
(?) Maarten Harpertsz Tromp; Cornelis
Tromp; Johanna Maria Gans-Tromp or
Dyna Tromp; Van Beresteyn van Maurick
family; Van den Bogaert family; bought
from Steinmetz-van den Bogaert, 1895

1895

168a

[see p. 248]
Rombout Verhulst
(Mechelen 1624-The Hague 1698)
*Portrait of Jacob van Reygersbergh
(1625-1675), 1671*
Painted terracotta, h. 55 cm
Inv. no. BK-NM-10557

LITERATURE:
cat. Amsterdam 1973, no. 314; Scholten
1991; cat. Amsterdam 1995a, no. 23

PROVENANCE:
Jonkheer D.T.A. van den Bogaerde van
TerBruges; Heer van Moergestel,
Heeswijk Castle; purchased with the aid
of the Rembrandt Society, 1896

1896

17

[see p. 40]
Hendrick Avercamp
(Amsterdam 1585-Kampen 1634)
Winter landscape with skaters, c. 1609
Panel 77.5 x 132 cm
On the right, on a wooden shed:
HAENRICVS AV (HA in ligature)
Inv. no. SK-A-1718

LITERATURE:
cat. Amsterdam 1976, p. 91; Welcker
1979, no. S10; exhib. cat. Amsterdam-
Boston-Philadelphia 1987-88, no. 5;
exhib. cat. Amsterdam 1993-94, no. 305

PROVENANCE:
(?) sale E.A. van Ourijk *et al.*,
Rotterdam, 19/VII/1748, no. 1; G. de
Clerq; sale Amsterdam, 1/VI/1897, no. 1;
purchased with the aid of the Rembrandt
Society, 1897

1897

18

[see p. 41]
Adriaen van de Venne
(Delft 1589-The Hague 1662)
*The departure of a dignitary from
Middelburg*
Lower centre: *AV VENNE 1615*
(AV in ligature)
Panel 64 x 134 cm
Inv. no. SK-A-1775

LITERATURE:
cat. Amsterdam 1976, p. 565; Bol 1989,
pp. 50-53; Kluiver 1995

PROVENANCE:
bequest D. Franken Dz, 1898

1898

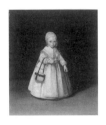

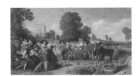

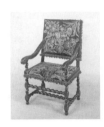

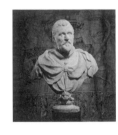

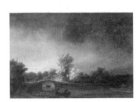

112
[see p. 166]
Gerard ter Borch
(Zwolle 1617-Deventer 1681)
Portrait of Helena van der Schalcke
(1646-1671), c. 1648
Panel 34 x 28.5 cm
Inv. no. SK-A-1786

LITERATURE:
Gudlaugsson 1959-60, vol. 2, no. 30;
Bol 1962, no. 32; Kruimel 1971; exhib.
cat. The Hague 1974, no. 6; cat.
Amsterdam 1976, p. 130

PROVENANCE:
Hendrik Christiaan Kleinpenning (1834-
1904), descendant of the sitter;
purchased from Antiquair Francke,
Amsterdam, with the aid of the
Rembrandt Society, 1898

1898

34
[see p. 61]
Dirck Hals
(Haarlem 1591-Haarlem 1656)
Garden party, c. 1624
Panel 78 x 137 cm
Inv. no. SK-A-1796

LITERATURE:
De Jongh 1969; cat. Amsterdam 1976, p.
255; exhib. cat. Amsterdam 1976, no. 27

PROVENANCE:
Sträten, Rheine, beginning of the 19th
century; purchased from the widow of P.
Driessen-Hooreman, Delft, 1899

1899

132
[see p. 192]
Armchair, c. 1650-1675
Walnut, upholstered with tapestry,
112.5 x 60.5 x 67 cm
Inv. no. BK-KOG-1799

LITERATURE:
cat. Amsterdam 1952a, no. 218; exhib.
cat. Amsterdam 1971-72, no. 37; cat.
Amsterdam 1993b, no. 20

PROVENANCE:
on loan from the KOG since 1899

1899

9
[see p. 25]
Hendrick de Keyser
(Utrecht 1565-Amsterdam 1621)
Portrait of Vincent Coster
(1553-1608/1610)
Marble h. 75 cm
On the back: *HDK* and *F.AO 1608*
Inv. no. BK-NM-11452

LITERATURE:
cat. Amsterdam 1973, no. 224; exhib.
cat. Amsterdam 1993-94, no. 59; cat.
Amsterdam 1995a, no. 9

PROVENANCE:
purchased from Frankfort, a dealer at
Deventer, with the aid of the Rembrandt
Society, 1900

1900

80
[see p. 130]
Rembrandt
(Leiden 1606-Amsterdam 1669)
The stone bridge, c. 1638
Panel 29.5 x 42.5 cm
Inv. no. SK-A-1935

LITERATURE:
cat. Amsterdam 1976, pp. 468-69; exhib.
cat. Amsterdam-Boston-Philadelphia
1987-88, no. 76; Bruyn et al. 1982-89,
vol. 3, no. A 136; Schneider 1990, no. 1;
exhib. cat. Berlin-Amsterdam-London
1991-92, no. 31; exhib. cat. Melbourne-
Canberra 1997-98, no. 11

PROVENANCE:
(?) sale [Aubert], Paris, 17-18/IV/1806,
no. 38; sale Lapeyrière, Paris,
14/IV/1817, no. 46; James Gray,
Versailles, 1863; Marquess of
Lansdowne, Bowood, 1883; sale James
Reiss, London (Christie's), 12/V/1900,
no. 63, purchased with the aid of Dr A.
Bredius and the Rembrandt Society

1900

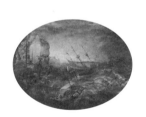

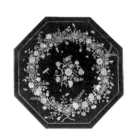

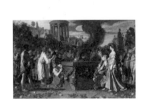

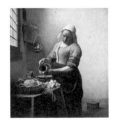

16
[see p. 39]
Adam Willaerts
(Antwerp 1577-Utrecht 1664)
Shipwreck off a rocky coast
Panel 65 x 86.5 cm (oval)
On the edge of the lifeboat:
A Willa..A⁰ 1614
Inv. no. SK-A-1955

LITERATURE:
cat. Amsterdam 1976, p. 605; Goedde
1989, pp. 171-180; exhib. cat.
Amsterdam 1993-94, no. 207

PROVENANCE:
sale Amsterdam (F. Muller),
16/IV/1901, no. 165

1901

101
[see p. 155]
Dirck van Rijswijck
(Kleve? 1596-Amsterdam after 1679)
Table top, c. 1650-1660
Touchstone, inlaid with mother-of-pearl
in an ebony border, diam. 138.5 cm
Inv. no. BK-NM-1916

LITERATURE:
cat. Amsterdam 1952a, no. 306; cat.
Amsterdam 1993b, no. 15

PROVENANCE:
Around 1664 at the home of Van
Rijswijck; Gerard Jonckheer, Rotterdam,
1710; heirs of the bailiff De Groet, 1762;
J. van Kuyk, Delft, 1819; sale
Amsterdam, 11-13/X/1904, no. 1126;
after the sale acquired directly from the
heirs of Van Kuyk

1904

52
[see p. 85]
Pieter Lastman
(Amsterdam 1583-Amsterdam 1633)
Orestes and Pylades disputing
at the altar
Panel 83 x 126 cm
On the altar: *Pietro Lastman fecit 1614*
Inv. no. SK-A-2354

LITERATURE:
Freise 1911, no. 98; cat. Amsterdam
1976, p. 338; exhib. cat. Amsterdam
1991, no. 7; exhib. cat. Amsterdam
1993-94, no. 248

PROVENANCE:
Reinier van der Wolf, 1657; sale Van der
Wolf, Rotterdam, 15/V/1676, no. 15; sale
Jan Six, Amsterdam, 6/IV/1702, no. 32;
sale Taets van Amerongen, Amsterdam,
3/VII/1805, no. 104 (sold
to Toselli); Consul Meyer-Puhiera;
Generaal Von Bredow; purchased by
F. Gerstel with the aid of the Rembrandt
Society, 1908

1908

136
[see p. 197]
Johannes Vermeer
(Delft 1632-Delft 1675)
The kitchen maid, c. 1658-1660
Canvas 45.5 x 41 cm
Inv. no. SK-A-2344

LITERATURE:
Blankert 1975, no. 7; cat. Amsterdam
1976, p. 572; exhib. cat. Washington-
The Hague 1995-96, no. 5

PROVENANCE:
(?)Van Ruijven family, Delft, before
1674-1682; Jacob Dissius, Delft, 1682-
1695; sale Dissius, Amsterdam,
16/V/1696, no. 2; sale Rooleeuw,
Amsterdam, 20/IV/1701, no. 7; sale Van
Hoek, Amsterdam, 12/IV/1719, no. 20;
Pieter Leendert de Neufville, Amsterdam,
before 1759; sale Leendert Pieter de
Neufville, Amsterdam, 19/VI/1765, no.
65 (sold to Yver); sale Dulong,
Amsterdam, 18/IV/1768, no. 10; Jan
Jacob de Bruyn, Amsterdam, 1781; sale

De Bruyn, Amsterdam, 12/IX/1798, no.
32; sale Muilman, Amsterdam,
12/IV/1813, no. 96 (sold to Jeronimo de
Vries for Lucretia van Winter); Lucretia
van Winter (Six-van Winter after 1822),
Amsterdam, 1813-45; Six family, 1845-
1905; purchased from the heirs of Six
van Vromade, with the aid of the
Rembrandt Society, 1908

1908

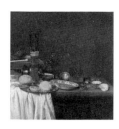

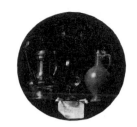

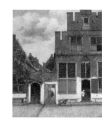

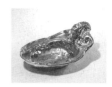

125
[see p. 185]
Jan Jansz van de Velde
(Haarlem c. 1620-Enkhuizen 1662
or Amsterdam 1664)
Still life with beer glass
Panel 64 x 59 cm
On the table: *Jan van de Velde 1647*
Inv. no. SK-A-2362

LITERATURE:
cat. Amsterdam 1976, p. 559; Ebert-
Schifferer 1998, pp. 128-29

PROVENANCE:
sale widow of F. Lemker-Muller,
Kampen, 7/VII/1908, no. 48

1908

43
[see p. 74]
Johannes van der Beeck, called
Torrentius
(Amsterdam 1589-Amsterdam 1644)
*Three vessels with bridle: allegory
of temperance*, 1614
Panel 52 x 50.5 cm (oval)
On the bridle: *JT 1614* (JT in ligature);
on the sheet of music: *ER wat bu-ter
maat be-staat, int on-maats qaat ver-
ghaat*; on the back of the panel the
collector's mark of Charles I of England
Inv. no. SK-A-2813

LITERATURE:
De Jongh 1967; cat. Amsterdam 1976,
p. 543; exhib. cat. Amsterdam 1993-94,
no. 277; Brown 1997; exhib.
cat. Amsterdam-Cleveland 1999-2000,
no. 11

PROVENANCE:
in Lisse in 1629, Charles I of England;
acquired with the aid of the Rembrandt
Society, 1918

1918

138
[see p. 200]
Johannes Vermeer
(Delft 1632-Delft 1675)
The little street, c. 1658
Canvas 54.3 x 44 cm
On the left, below the window:
i VMeer (VM in ligature)
Inv. no. SK-A-2860

LITERATURE:
Blankert 1975, no. 9; cat. Amsterdam
1976, pp. 571-72; exhib. cat.
Washington-The Hague 1995-96, no. 4

PROVENANCE:
(?)Van Ruijven family, Delft, before
1674-1682; Jacob Dissius, Delft, 1682-
1695; sale Dissius, Amsterdam,
16/V/1696, no. 32 or no. 33; Gerrit
Willem van Oosten de Bruyn, Haarlem,
before 1797; sale Van Oosten de Bruyn,
Haarlem, 8/IV/1800, no. 7 (sold to Van
Winter); Pieter van Winter, Amsterdam,
1800-1807; Lucretia van Winter (Six-van
Winter after 1822), Amsterdam, 1807-
1845; Six family, 1845-1921; sale Six,
Amsterdam, 12/IV/1921 (bought back);
Sir Henry Deterding; his gift to the
Rijksmuseum, 1921

1921

62
[see p. 99]
Johannes Lutma
(Emden 1587-Amsterdam 1669)
Dish
Silver w. 20.3 cm
Marked on the underside: year letter K =
1641; two illegible marks; engraved on
the underside: *J Lutma f.*
Inv. no. BK-NM-13258

LITERATURE:
cat. Amsterdam 1952b, no. 109; exhib.
cat. Amsterdam-Toledo-Boston 1979-80,
no. 40; exhib. cat. Amsterdam 1984-85,
no. 30; cat. Amsterdam 1999, no. 11

PROVENANCE:
sale A. Vosmaer, The Hague, 17/III/1800,
no. 53; sale Van Schuylenburch van
Bommenede, The Hague, 10/III/1820; art
dealer J. Morpurgo, Amsterdam; gift
of the Commissie voor Fotoverkoop,
1925

1925

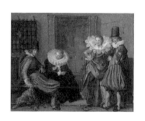

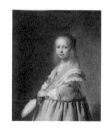

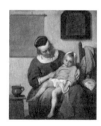

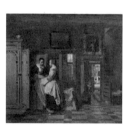

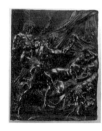

33
[see p. 60]
Willem Buytewech
(Rotterdam 1591/1592-Rotterdam 1624)
Elegant couples courting, c. 1618
Canvas 56 x 70 cm
Inv. no. SK-A-3038

LITERATURE:
Haverkamp Begemann 1959, no. 4; cat.
Amsterdam 1976, p. 159; exhib. cat.
Amsterdam 1976, no. 10; exhib. cat.
Amsterdam 1993-94, no. 297

PROVENANCE:
J. van der Linden van Slingelandt,
Dordrecht; sale Dordrecht, 22/VIII/1785,
no. 167 (as Frans Hals); private
collection or art dealer, Paris; N. Beets,
Amsterdam; acquired with the aid of the
Commissie voor Fotoverkoop, 1926

1926

113
[see p. 167]
Johannes Verspronck
(Haarlem 1597-Haarlem 1662)
Portrait of a girl dressed in blue
Canvas 82 x 66.5 cm
Lower left: *J.VSpronck An⁰ 1641*
Inv. no. SK-A-3064

LITERATURE:
cat. Amsterdam 1976, p. 575; Ekkart
1979, no. 33; Van Thiel 1983c

PROVENANCE:
(?) Von Hendorf, postmaster of the Duke
of Oldenburg; Duke Peter Friedrich
Ludwig van Oldenburg, 1805;
Augusteum, Oldenburg, 1881; M.P.
Voûte, Amsterdam, on loan to the
Rijksmuseum, 1922; bequeathed by M.P.
Voûte to the Rembrandt Society and
given by the latter to the museum, 1928

1928

119
[see p. 176]
Gabriël Metsu
(Leiden 1629-Amsterdam 1667)
The sick child, c. 1660
Canvas 32.2 x 27.2 cm
Above the map: *G. Metsue*
Inv. no. SK-A-3059

LITERATURE:
Meyer 1958, no. 29; Robinson 1974,
pp. 16, 52, 62, 194; cat. Amsterdam
1976, pp. 379-80; exhib. cat.
Amsterdam 1976, no. 41

PROVENANCE:
sale Goll van Frankenstein, Amsterdam,
1/VII/1833, no. 50; sale Steengracht,
Paris, 6/VI/1913, no. 43 (sold to
Kleinberger); sale Huldschinsky, Berlin,
10/V/1928, no. 20; purchased with the
aid of the Rembrandt Society, 1928

1928

140
[see p. 203]
Pieter de Hooch
(Rotterdam 1629-Amsterdam 1684)
*Interior with women beside a
linen cupboard*
Canvas 70 x 75.5 cm
On the stairs: *P D HOOCH/1663*
Inv. no. SK-C-1191

LITERATURE:
cat. Amsterdam 1976, p. 287; Sutton
1980, no. 52; exhib. cat. Delft 1996,
pp. 154-55

PROVENANCE:
Baron Lockhorst, Rotterdam, 1726; sale
Amsterdam, 8/VI/1763, no. 138; sale
Rendorp, Amsterdam, 16/X/1793 and
9/VII/1794, no. 25 (sold to Coclers);
Smith; Stanley, 1828; Six family,
Amsterdam, 1833-1928; sale Six,
Amsterdam, 16/X/1928, no.15;
purchased by the Rembrandt Society for
the City of Amsterdam; on loan from the
City of Amsterdam since 1928

1928

I
[see p. 14]
Adriaen de Vries
(The Hague 1556-Prague 1626)
Bacchus finding Ariadne on Naxos,
c. 1610-1612
Bronze 52.5 x 42 cm
Inv. no. BK-14692

LITERATURE:
cat. Amsterdam 1973, no. 205; exhib.
cat. Amsterdam 1993-94, no. 181;
exhib. cat. Amsterdam-Stockholm-Los
Angeles 1998-99, no. 26

PROVENANCE:
gift of the N.V. Internationale
Antiquiteitenhandel, Amsterdam, 1935

1935

86
[see p. 136]
Aert van der Neer
(Amsterdam 1603/1604-
Amsterdam 1677)
River view by moonlight, c. 1645
Panel 55 x 103 cm
Near the lower edge, in the middle:
AV DN
Inv. no. SK-A-3245

LITERATURE:
cat. Amsterdam 1976, p. 410; Bachmann
1982, p. 103; Zeldenrust 1983

PROVENANCE:
Jonkheer Jan Six, Amsterdam; sale Six,
Amsterdam, 16/X/1928, no. 30; gift of
Sir Henry Deterding, London, 1936

1936

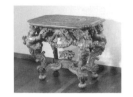

188
[see p. 278]
Table, c. 1700
Gilt limewood and oak,
87.5 x 108.5 x 73.5 cm
Inv. no. BK-14980

LITERATURE:
cat. Amsterdam 1952a, no. 315;
exhib. cat. New York-Pittsburgh
1988-89, p. 21; cat. Amsterdam 1993b,
no. 31

PROVENANCE:
gift of the Commissie voor
Fotoverkoop, 1937

1937

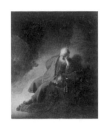

55
[see p. 88]
Rembrandt
(Leiden 1606-Amsterdam 1669)
*Jeremiah lamenting the
destruction of Jerusalem*
Panel 58.3 x 46.6 cm
On the rock in the middle: *RHL 1630*
Inv. no. SK-A-3276

LITERATURE:
exhib. cat. Amsterdam 1969, no. 1; cat.
Amsterdam 1976, p. 467; Bruyn *et al.*
1982-89, vol. 1, no. A 28; exhib. cat.
Berlin-Amsterdam-London 1991-92,
no. 8; exhib. cat. Melbourne-Canberra
1997-98, no. 5

PROVENANCE:
sale Margaretha Helena Graafland,
Amsterdam, 10/VI/1767, no. 13; Count
Sergei Stroganoff, St Petersburg, later
Paris; H. Rasch, Stockholm; purchased
with the aid of friends of the museum, the
Rembrandt Society, the Dutch State and
the Commissie voor Fotoverkoop, 1939

1939

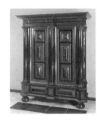

100
[see p. 154]
Cupboard, c. 1660-1680
Oak, veneered with ebony and
rosewood, 217 x 176 x 77 cm
Inv. no. BK-15982

LITERATURE:
cat. Amsterdam 1952a, no. 108;
cat. Amsterdam 1993b, no. 21

PROVENANCE:
R. May; purchased in 1944

1944

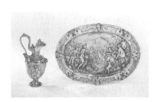

2
[see p. 15]
Paulus van Vianen
(Utrecht c. 1570-Prague 1613)
*Ewer and basin with episodes
from the stories of Diana*
Silver, ewer: h. 34 cm;
basin: 6.5 x 52.3 x 40.5 cm
On the front of the basin: *PV* and *1613*
Inv. no. BK-16089

LITERATURE:
cat. Amsterdam 1952b, no. 79; exhib.
cat. Amsterdam-Toledo-Boston 1979-80,
no. 20; Ter Molen 1984, vol. 2, no. 19;
Utrecht 1984-85, no. 32; exhib. cat.
Amsterdam 1993-94, no. 190

PROVENANCE:
(?) Nicolaes Snouckaert van Schauburg;
Maerten Snouckaert van Schauburg; sale
Anna Maria Ebeling, Amsterdam,
18/VIII/1817, nos. 159 and 160; sale Earl
of Wemyss and March, London
(Christie's), 7/V/1947, no. 144

1947

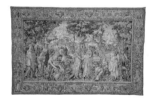

3
[see p. 17]
François Spiering
(Antwerp 1549/1551-Delft 1631),
workshop of, after a design by Karel
van Mander (Meulebeke 1548-
Amsterdam 1606)
Cephalus and Procris, c. 1610
Tapestry, wool and silk on woollen
chain, 345 x 520 cm
Lower centre: *FRANCISCVS SPIRINGIVS
FECIT*; lower left, on either side of the
city's coat of arms: *HD* (Holland, Delft);
lower left and right: *MARS ET VENUS* and
LEANDER ET HERO
Inv. no. BK-1954-69b

LITERATURE:
exhib. cat. Amsterdam 1993-94, no. 78

PROVENANCE:
C.T. Barney, Newport; Mrs E.F.Hutton,
New York, 1925; art dealer Duveen,
New York; gift of the Commissie voor
Fotoverkoop, 1954

1954

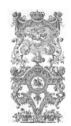

187
[see p. 277]
Pottery 'De Grieksche A' under the
supervision of Adriaen Kocks, after a
design by Daniel Marot
(1661-1752)
Two tiles, c. 1690
Blue-painted faience, 62 x 62 cm
Marked: *AK* (Adriaen Kocks)
Inv. nos. BK-KOG-1681 and BK-KOG-
2567

LITERATURE:
Lane 1959; exhib. cat. London 1964, no.
228; exhib. cat. New York-Pittsburgh
1988-89, no. 165

PROVENANCE:
commissioned by Hampton Court Palace
(presumably as a decoration for the
Water Gallery); purchased by the
Koninklijk Oudheidkundig Genootschap
from A. Nijstad, Lochem, 1955; on loan
from the KOG since 1955

1955

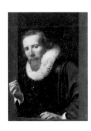

10
[see p. 28]
Werner van den Valckert
(The Hague? c. 1585-Amsterdam
1627/1628)
Portrait of a man with a ring
Panel 65 x 49.5 cm
On the touchstone: *W v Valckert fe 1617*
Inv. no. SK-A-3920

LITERATURE:
cat. Amsterdam 1976, p. 553; Van Thiel
1983a, pp. 155-56, no. 11; exhib.
cat. Amsterdam 1993-94, no. 267;
Ekkart 1999

PROVENANCE:
probably inherited via the families of
Van Assendelft, Pompe van Slingelandt
and De Wildt by Frans de Wildt (1805-
69); Agnes W. de Wildt (1835-1905);
Jonkvrouw Isabella F. Mollerus (1863-
1920); sale Amsterdam (F. Muller),
30/XI/1920, no. 1015; Antoon van Welie
(1866-1956), The Hague; purchased
from the latter's estate, 1957

1957

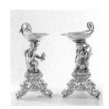

61
[see p. 98]
Johannes Lutma
(Emden 1587-Amsterdam 1669)
Two salt-cellars
Silver, parcel-gilt, h. 24.2 cm
Both marked on the upper side of the
foot: assay office mark Amsterdam, year
letter H = 1639; maker's mark, a heart
in an escutcheon = Johannes Lutma
Inv. no. BK-1960-13a/b

LITERATURE:
exhib. cat. Amsterdam-Toledo-Boston
1979-80, no. 38; exhib. cat. Amsterdam
1984-85, no. 28; cat. Amsterdam 1999,
no. 10

PROVENANCE:
O.R. van Iddekinge van Drostenburg;
sale (F. Muller), Amsterdam, 27/XI-3/XII/
1906, no. 452; Emma Rudge, Hamburg;
the latter's sale, Berlin, 27-29/IX/1937,
no. 255; art dealer A. Vecht,
Amsterdam; H.P. Doodeheefver,
Hilversum; art dealer Katz, Dieren;
W.J.R. Dreesmann, Amsterdam; the
latter's sale (F. Muller), 22-25/III/1960,
no. 95

1960

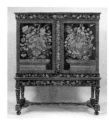

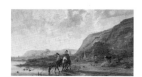

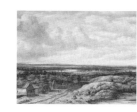

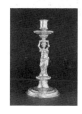

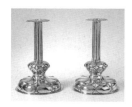

190
[see p. 279]
Jan van Mekeren
(Tiel 1658-Amsterdam 1733),
attributed to
Cabinet, c. 1690-1710
Oak, veneered with kingwood, ebony,
rosewood, olive, sycamore and other
woods, 205 x 173 x 61 cm
Inv. no. BK-1964-12

LITERATURE:
exhib. cat. New York-Pittsburgh 1988-
89, pp. 23-25; cat. Amsterdam 1993b,
no. 25

PROVENANCE:
purchased from the art dealer J.A. Lewis
& Son, London, 1964

1964

151
[see p. 222]
Aelbert Cuyp
(Dordrecht 1620-Dordrecht 1691)
River landscape with horsemen, c. 1655
Canvas 128 x 227.5 cm
Lower centre: *A. cuyp.*
Inv. no. SK-A-4118

LITERATURE:
De Bruyn Kops 1965; Reiss 1975, no.
139; cat. Amsterdam 1976, p. 183;
exhib. cat. Dordrecht 1977-78, no. 34;
Chong 1993, no. 169

PROVENANCE:
N.J. Desenfans, England; c. 1796
purchased from the latter by Martin; J.J.
Martin, 1850; G.E. Martin, 1880; Alfred
de Rothschild, Halton; Lionel de Rothschild, Exbury; Edmund de Rothschild;
purchased through the agency of art
dealer Agnews & Heinemann, London
and with the aid of the Rembrandt
Society, the Prince Bernhard Fund and the
Commissie voor Fotoverkoop, 1965

1965

194
[see p. 283]
Adam Loofs
(The Hague? c. 1645-The Hague 1710)
Candlestick with a female figure as stem
Silver h. 28.6 cm
Marked on the underside of the foot:
assay office mark The Hague, Dutch
lion, year letter N = 1687; maker's mark
AL in ligature under a crowned horn =
Adam Loofs
Inv. no. BK-1966-10

LITERATURE:
exhib. cat. The Hague 1967, no. 84;
exhib. cat. Amsterdam-Toledo-Boston
1979-80, no. 87; exhib. cat. New York-
Pittsburgh 1988-89, no. 67

PROVENANCE:
purchased from the firm of R. Citroen,
Amsterdam, 1966

1966

152
[see p. 223]
Philips Koninck
(Amsterdam 1619-Amsterdam 1688)
*Panorama with farmhouses
along a road*
Canvas 133 x 167.5 cm
On the wall of the farmhouse
on the left: *P. Koninck 1655*
Inv. no. SK-A-4133

LITERATURE:
Gerson 1936, no. 26; Van Thiel 1967;
Van Thiel 1968; cat. Amsterdam 1976,
p. 325; exhib. cat. Amsterdam-Boston-
Philadelphia 1987-88, no. 53

PROVENANCE:
(?) sale Jan Lucas van der Dussen,
Amsterdam, 31/X/1774, no. 31 (sold to
Pieter Fouquet); Earl of Derby, Knowsley
House, probably acquired at the end of
the 18th century; purchased from the Earl
of Derby, with the aid of the Rembrandt
Society, the Prince Bernhard Fund and the
Commissie voor Fotoverkoop, 1967

1967

103
[see p. 157]
Pair of candlesticks
Both marked on the underside of the
foot: assay office mark Amsterdam,
Dutch lion; year letter F = 1668; maker's
mark, a heart with a diamond inside =
unidentified master; scratched into the
underside of the foot and on the
underside of the drip-pan: C [five-
pointed star] B
Inv. no. BK-1968-30

LITERATURE:
exhib. cat. Amsterdam-Toledo-Boston
1979-80, no. 76; exhib. cat. Amsterdam
1984-85, no. 64; cat. Amsterdam 1999,
no. 28

PROVENANCE:
sale London (Christie's), 15/XI/1967, no.
154; art dealer Premsela & Hamburger,
Amsterdam; purchased in 1968

1968

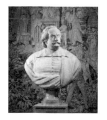

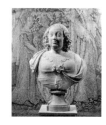

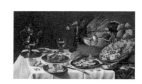

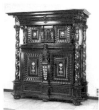

164a
[see p. 242]
François Dieussart
(Arquinghem c. 1600-Brussels 1661)
Portrait of Pieter Spiering (?-1652),
c. 1645-1650
Marble h. 89 cm (including pedestal)
Inv. no. BK-1971-115

LITERATURE:
cat. Amsterdam 1973, no. 257;
cat. Amsterdam 1995a, no. 12

PROVENANCE:
art dealer Alavoine, Paris; purchased by
the Heim Gallery in London, gift of the
Commissie voor Fotoverkoop, 1971

1971

164b
[see p. 243]
François Dieussart
(Arquinghem c. 1600-Brussels 1661)
Portrait of Johanna Doré,
c. 1645-1650
Marble h. 82 cm (including pedestal)
Inv. no. BK-1971-115

LITERATURE:
see 164a

PROVENANCE:
see 164a

1971

45
[see p. 76]
Pieter Claesz
(Berchem 1597/1598-Haarlem 1660)
Still life with turkey pie
Panel 75 x 132 cm
On the blade of the knife: *PC Ao 1627*
Inv. no. SK-A-4646

LITERATURE:
Van Thiel 1975; cat. Amsterdam 1976,
p. 168

PROVENANCE:
purchased from J.C.N. Count of Lynden,
St. Michielsgestel, through the agency of
art dealer S. Nijstad, The Hague and
with the aid of the Rembrandt Society,
the Prince Bernhard Fund and the
Commissie voor Fotoverkoop, 1974

1974

63
[see p. 100]
Herman Doomer
(Anrath c. 1595-Amsterdam 1650) or
his workshop, attributed to
Cupboard, c. 1640-1650
Oak, veneered with ebony, kingwood,
rosewood, and partridge wood (?),
inlaid with mother-of-pearl and ivory,
218 x 196 x 84 cm
Inv. no. BK-1975-81

LITERATURE:
cat. Amsterdam 1993b, no. 16; Baarsen
1996

PROVENANCE:
(?) Baertje Martens, widow of Herman
Doomer, 1650-1678; (?) the latter's
daughter Geertje, 1678-1716; (?) the
latter's niece and nephew, Geertruyd and
Harmanus Voster; (?) sale Amsterdam,
26/II/1738 (see *Amsterdamsche Courant*,
15/II/1738: 'a royal black ebony cabinet
with mother-of-pearl flowers, inlaid and
engraved from life, lined with kingwood
and cedar on the inside, as well as ivory
inlay work'); (?) Gregory Gregory
(1786-1854), Harlaxton Manor,
Lincolnshire; (?) Sir Glynne Welby,
Denton; Sir William Welby-Gregory,
Denton Manor, Lincolnshire; sold in the
late 1930s; acquired by dealer Etienne
Delaunoy, Amsterdam; purchased by
L.J.L. Wittop Koning, 1939; purchased
in 1975

1975

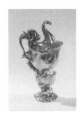

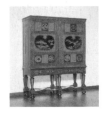

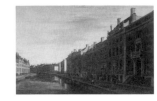

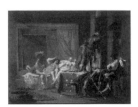

5
[see p. 19]
Adam van Vianen
(Utrecht 1568/1569-Utrecht 1627)
Covered ewer
Silver-gilt h. 25.5 cm
On the underside: *A.D.Viana.FE.A°
1614*; marked on the outside of the
outside cuppa: assay office mark Utrecht,
year letter T = 1614; maker's mark AV
interlaced = Adam van Vianen
Inv. no. BK-1976-75

LITERATURE:
Ter Molen 1984, vol. 2, no. 409; cat.
Utrecht 1984-85, no. 61; Baarsen 1989a;
exhib. cat. Amsterdam 1993-94, no. 112

PROVENANCE:
Amsterdam silversmiths' guild, 1614-
1821; Major John Shaw of Tardarroch;
sale Laren (Christie's), 19/XI/1976, no.
544; gift of the Prince Bernhard Fund,
the Rembrandt Society and the
Commissie voor Fotoverkoop, 1976

1976

39
[see p. 66]
Wedding gloves, c. 1622
White leather with embroidered cuffs,
l. 24 cm
Inv. no. BK-1978-48

LITERATURE:
Du Mortier 1984; Du Mortier 1989

PROVENANCE:
made for the marriage of Johanna Le
Maire, c. 1622; E.G. Coles, London,
c. 1880; the latter's wife, 1913;
purchased by her son-in-law N. Tritton
for his wife Ruth, née Coles; inherited by
her nephew, 1972; sale London
(Sotheby's), 28/VII/1978, no. 43

1978

191
[see p. 280]
Cabinet, c. 1690-1710
Oak, veneered with walnut, palm and
purplewood, inlaid with Japanese
lacquer panels, decorated with polished
rayfish skin (same-nuri),
202 x 158.5 x 54 cm
Inv. no. BK-1979-21

LITERATURE:
exhib. cat. New York-Pittsburgh
1988-89, pp. 25-26; exhib. cat. Tokyo-
Amsterdam 1991-92, no. 39; cat.
Amsterdam 1993b, no. 29

PROVENANCE:
gift of the Rijksmuseum Stichting, 1979

1979

174
[see p. 262]
Gerrit Berckheyde
(Haarlem 1638-Haarlem 1698)
*The 'golden bend' in the
Herengracht, Amsterdam*
Panel 40.5 x 63 cm
At the right on a stone on the quay:
G. BerckHyde 1672
Inv. no. SK-A-4750

LITERATURE:
cat. Amsterdam 1992, p. 42; Kloek
1989b; Lawrence 1991, pp. 63-64

PROVENANCE:
sale Amsterdam, 28/V/1918, no. 121; J.
Goudstikker, Amsterdam; purchased
from the collection of J. Goudstikker
and heirs, Amsterdam, with the aid of
the Rijksmuseum Stichting and the
Ministry of CRM, 1980

1980

114
[see p. 170]
Nicolaus Knupfer
(Leipzig c. 1609-Utrecht 1665)
Brothel scene, c. 1650
Panel 60 x 74.5 cm
Unclear signature at the lower left near
the vine tendril: *NKnupfer* (?)
Inv. no. SK-A-4779

LITERATURE:
Kuznetzow 1974, no. 51; cat.
Amsterdam 1992, pp. 61-62; Bulletin
1982; exhib. cat. San Francisco-
Baltimore-London 1997-98, no. 45

PROVENANCE:
Galerie Orléans, Palais Royal, Paris; sold
in London, 1792; Count André
Mniszech, Paris; sale Adolphe Schloss,
Paris, 25/V/1949, no. 28; private
collection, Le Verviers, Belgium; sale
London, 10/XII/1980, no. 62; art dealer
J. Hoogsteder, The Hague, 1981; gift of
the Rijksmuseum Stichting, 1981

1981

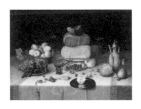

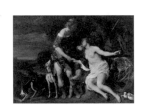

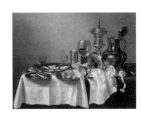

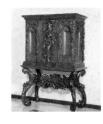

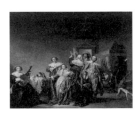

44
[see p. 75]
Floris van Dijck
(Haarlem 1575-Haarlem 1651)
Laid table with cheese and fruit,
c. 1615
Panel 82.2 x 111.2 cm
Inv. no. SK-A-4821

LITERATURE:
Van Thiel 1983d; cat. Amsterdam 1992,
p. 51; exhib. cat. Amsterdam 1993-94,
no. 276; exhib. cat. Amsterdam-
Cleveland 1999-2000, no. 10

PROVENANCE:
Westerman-Holstein, Amsterdam;
purchased from a private individual
through the agency of Sotheby/Mak van
Waay, Amsterdam and with the aid of
the Rembrandt Society and the
Rijksmuseum Stichting, 1982

1982

171
[see p. 256]
Ferdinand Bol
(Dordrecht 1616-Amsterdam 1680)
Venus and Adonis, c. 1658
Canvas 168 x 230 cm
Beneath the front paws of the dog
with upraised head: *F Bol*
Inv. no. SK-A-4823

LITERATURE:
Blankert 1982: no. 29; exhib. cat.
Amsterdam-Groningen 1983, no. 9;
cat. Amsterdam 1992, p. 44

PROVENANCE:
sale London (Christie's), 19/VII/1907, no.
86; sale Hoogendijk, Amsterdam (F.
Muller), 28/IV/1908, no. 18; art dealer
Teunis Wollesen, Bad Oeynhausen,
1970; Freiherr Von Lucius, Frankfurt,
1972; art dealer K. & V. Waterman,
Amsterdam; purchased with the aid of
the Rijksmuseum Stichting, 1983

1983

46
[see p. 77]
Willem Claesz Heda
(Haarlem 1593/1594-Haarlem 1680)
Still life with gilt goblet
Panel 88 x 113 cm
On the edge of the tablecloth at the
right: *HEDA 1635*
Inv. no. SK-A-4830

LITERATURE:
Vroom 1980, vol. 2, no. 351a; Kloek
1989a; cat. Amsterdam 1992, p. 56

PROVENANCE:
originally from collection formed in the
17th century by a branch of the
Richardot family (resident since the 18th
century at Château de Choisey, Jura);
sale Paris (Palais d'Orsay), 13/XII/1977,
no. 18; art dealer Brod Gallery, London,
1978; art dealer Noortman & Brod,
London; purchased with extra credit
from the Ministry of WVC and with the
aid of the Rembrandt Society, 1984

1984

69
[see p. 114]
Layette cupboard, c. 1650-1675
Oak and walnut, 178 x 119 x 57 cm
Inv. no. BK-1985-10

LITERATURE:
Baarsen 1989c; cat. Amsterdam 1993b,
no. 18

PROVENANCE:
sale London (Christie's), 15/III/1984,
no. 110; purchased from art dealer
Limburg, Brouwershaven, 1985

1985

37
[see p. 64]
Pieter Codde
(Amsterdam 1599-Amsterdam 1678)
Gallant company
Panel 54 x 68 cm
Upper centre: *PC 1633*
Inv. no. SK-A-4844

LITERATURE:
cat. Amsterdam 1976, pp. 170-71;
exhib. cat. Amsterdam 1976, no. 13;
Van Thiel 1989; cat. Amsterdam 1992,
p. 47

PROVENANCE:
on loan since 1974; purchased through
the agency of art dealer R. Green,
London and with the aid of the
Rembrandt Society and the
Rijksmuseum Stichting, 1986

1986

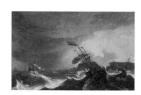

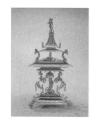

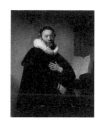

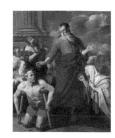

163
[see p. 239]
Ludolf Bakhuysen
(Emden 1631-Amsterdam 1708)
Ships in distress in a raging storm,
c. 1690
Canvas 150 x 227 cm
In the blue flag: *LB* (in reverse) and at
the lower left on a barrel: *L.B.*
Inv. no. SK-A-4856

LITERATURE:
exhib. cat. Amsterdam-Emden 1985,
no. S 33; Bulletin 1988; cat. Amsterdam
1992, p. 40

PROVENANCE:
E. Malling, 1917; A.C. Mees, 1947;
sale Amsterdam (Christie's), 8/XII/1983,
no. 56; art dealer Rob Kattenburg,
Amsterdam; purchased with the aid of
the Rembrandt Society, 1988

1988

49
[see p. 80]
Triangular salt-cellar with cover
Silver, parcel-gilt, h. 30.2 cm
Marked on the underside of the well of
the salt-cellar: assay office mark
Amsterdam, year letter H = 1618;
illegible maker's mark in a shaped shield
Inv. no. BK-1988-15

LITERATURE:
Baarsen 1989b; exhib. cat. Amsterdam
1993-94, no. 101; cat. Amsterdam 1999,
no. 6

PROVENANCE:
purchased from art dealer S.J. Phillips,
London, with aid from the Ministry of
WVC, the Rembrandt Society and the
Rijksmuseum Stichting, 1988

1988

59
[see p. 96]
Rembrandt
(Leiden 1606-Amsterdam 1669)
Portrait of Johannes Wtenbogaert
Canvas 130 x 103 cm
On the right above the book:
Rembrandt. ft: 1633.; upper left: *AET 76*
Inv. no. SK-A-4885

LITERATURE:
Bruyn *et al.* 1982-89, vol. 2, no. A 80;
Van Os 1992; Kloek 1992; Bijl *et al.* 1994

PROVENANCE:
Commissioned by Abraham Anthonisz
Recht (1588-1664); Manfrini, Venice;
Baron Meyer de Rothschild, Mentmore,
1856-1977; Earl of Rosebery; sale
London (Sotheby's), 8/VII/1992, no. 86;
art dealer Otto Naumann and Alfred
Bader; acquired with the aid of the
Rembrandt Society, the Prince Bernhard
Fund, the Stichting VSB Fonds, the
Rijksmuseum Stichting, the Dutch State
and private individuals, 1992

1992

173
[see p. 259]
Karel Dujardin
(Amsterdam 1622-Venice 1678)
St Paul healing the cripple at Lystra
Canvas 179 x 139 cm
Upper left: *K.DU.//ARDIN//fe//...]63*
(N in reverse)
Inv. no. SK-A-4922

LITERATURE:
exhib. cat. Warschau 1990, no. 47;
Kilian 1994, no. 87; Jansen 1997

PROVENANCE:
(?) Johan van Beaumont jr., Amsterdam,
1677; private collection, Groningen
(Henrik Gockinga?), 1834; Reneke
Gockinga, Groningen; sale Wolter
Gockinga, Amsterdam, 14/VIII/1883, no.
34; J.C. van Hattum van Ellewoutsdijk,
Ellewoutsdijk near The Hague;
Mauritshuis, The Hague, on loan from
Van Hattum van Ellewoutsdijk, 1894-
1912; returned to the latter's grandson
J.C. van Hattum, 12/VI/1912; sale
London (Christie's), 11/XII/1987, no. 29;
Barbara Piasecka Johnson, Princeton,
New Jersey; sale New York (Christie's),
31/I/1997, no. 44, where purchased with
the aid of the Rembrandt Society and the
Rijksmuseum Stichting

1997

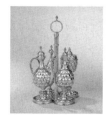

50
[see p. 81]
Anthony Grill
(Augsburg 1609-Sweden 1675),
attributed to
Cruet-stand
Silver with remnants of gilt,
holder: h. 27.1 cm
Marked on the underside of the stand
and on the foot of the oil cruet, the two
shakers and the salt-cellar; assay office
mark Amsterdam; year letter L = 1642;
maker's mark, stork between AG,
attributed to Anthony Grill
Inv. no. BK-1997-1

LITERATURE:
Bulletin 1997; cat. Amsterdam 1999,
no. 12

PROVENANCE:
sale Wooley and Wallis, Salisbury,
5/VI/1996, no. 109; art dealer Van
Ravenstein, Haarlem; purchased in 1997

1997

184
[see p. 273]
Francis van Bossuit
(Brussels 1635-Amsterdam 1692)
Mars, c. 1680-1692
Ivory h. 44 cm
Inv. no. BK-1998-74

LITERATURE:
Pool 1727, fig. XLVIII; Theuerkauff
1975; Scholten 1999

PROVENANCE:
Petronella Oortmans-de la Court,
c. 1700; the latter's sale, Amsterdam,
20/IX/1707; sale Jeronimus Tonneman,
21/X/1754, Sculpture, no. 3; sale Geneva
(Christie's), 10/XI/1976, no. 284 (as
anonymous Flemish work); sale Paris,
14/XII/1998, no. 110, where purchased
with the aid of the Rembrandt Society

1998

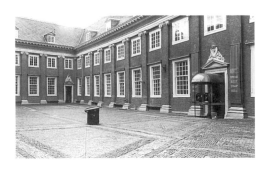

AMSTERDAM, AMSTERDAMS HISTORISCH MUSEUM

Numerous works of art from municipal bodies were housed already in the 18th century in the Kunstkamer and the Large and Small Armouries of the town hall in Amsterdam. When the town hall was put to use as the Royal Palace by Louis Bonaparte in 1808, this municipal art collection was dispersed over the city. In 1885 a large part of the collection was given a place in the Rijksmuseum. Another part was taken to the Amsterdams Historisch Museum, founded in 1926, which was housed in the Weigh-house on the Nieuwmarkt. The new museum, which opened in 1975 in the former Burgerweeshuis (city orphanage) displays a detailed and chronologically ordered overview of the history of Amsterdam, including many works of art which were on display in the Rijksmuseum until 1975.

LITERATURE: Carosso-Kok 1975; cat. Amsterdam 1975-79

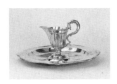

68
[see p. 113]
Johannes Lutma
(Emden 1587-Amsterdam 1669)
Ewer and basin for the Amsterdam town hall
Silver, chased and engraved, ewer:
h. 21 cm; basin: diam. 60.5 cm
Marked: assay office mark Amsterdam;
year letter C = 1655; maker's mark, a
heart in a shield = Johannes Lutma
Inv. no. KA 13981.1/2

LITERATURE:
exhib. cat. Amsterdam 1984-85, no. 44

PROVENANCE:
produced for the banquet honouring the
inauguration of the new Amsterdam
town hall in 1655; on loan from the City
of Amsterdam to the Koninklijk Museum
since 1808; in the Rijksmuseum until
1975; in the Amsterdams Historisch
Museum since 1975

1808

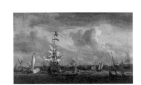

161
[see p. 236]
Willem van de Velde the Younger
(Leiden 1633-London 1707)
The 'Gouden Leeuw' on the IJ at Amsterdam
Canvas 179.5 x 316 cm
On a piece of wood floating to the right
of centre: W.V.Velde J 1686
Inv. no. SA 7421

LITERATURE:
Robinson 1990, vol. 1, no. 264; exhib.
cat. Rotterdam-Berlin 1996-97, no. 81

PROVENANCE:
Meeting hall of the Chief Commissioners
of the Harbour Works in the
Schreierstoren; on loan from the City of
Amsterdam to the Koninklijk Museum
since 1808; in the Rijksmuseum until
1975; in the Amsterdams Historisch
Museum since 1975

1808

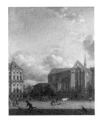

175
[see p. 263]
Jan van der Heyden
(Gorinchem 1637-Amsterdam 1712)
Dam Square in Amsterdam, with a view of the New Church, c. 1668-1670
Panel 68 x 55 cm
On the marquee of the Weigh-house:
VHeyde
Inv. no. SA 7332

LITERATURE:
Wagner 1971, no. 4; exhib. cat.
Rotterdam 1991, no. 64

PROVENANCE:
sale C.S. Roos, Amsterdam, 28/VIII/1820,
no. 44; sale A. de Haas, Amsterdam,
8/XI/1824, no. 10; sale
C.J. Nieuwenhuys, London (Christie's),
10/V/1833, no. 125; bequest J.F. van
Lennep to the City of Amsterdam, 1893;
on loan from the City of Amsterdam to
the Rijksmuseum, Amsterdam, 1893-
1975; in the Amsterdams Historisch
Museum since 1975

1893

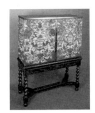

192
[see p. 281]
Cabinet, c. 1700
Oak, lacquer in black and gold,
embroidery in coloured wool,
147 x 117 x 47 cm
Inv. no. KA 2954

LITERATURE:
exhib. cat. Amsterdam 1992, no. 80

PROVENANCE:
gift of the Katz brothers, Dieren, 1938

1938

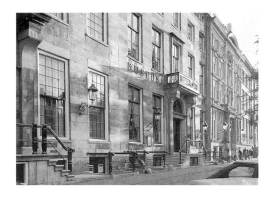

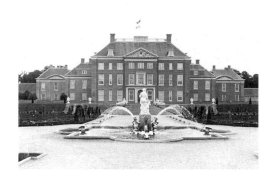

Amsterdam, Museum van Loon

The museum has been located since 1973 at Keizersgracht 672, in a house built by Adriaen Dortsman in 1671, which has been in the possession of the Van Loon family since 1884. There are more than 50 family portraits (dating from the 17th-19th centuries) of the regents' family Van Loon on display. In addition to the painting described below, there is an early family portrait by Jan Miense Molenaer (1630) and a lovely child's portrait dating from 1636 by Dirck van Santvoort. Until the museum was opened, these paintings had been on display in the Rijksmuseum, on loan from the Van Loon foundation.

LITERATURE. Van Loon and Van Eeghen 1984

Apeldoorn,
Paleis Het Loo Nationaal Museum

The Palace 'Het Loo', built near Apeldoorn in 1685, was commissioned by the stadholder-king Willem III. Major renovations in the 1960s succeeded in returning the Palace and its gardens to their original state inasmuch as this was possible. Since 1984 the Palace functions as a museum, displaying art works in the possession of, or connected in some way with, the House of Orange. Through such acquisitions as the coat-of-arms tapestries made after a design by Daniel Marot, the museum strives to gather together the original art possessions of the House of Orange.

LITERATURE: Vliegenthart 1999

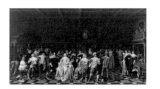

38
[see p. 65]
Jan Miense Molenaer
(Haarlem c. 1610-Haarlem 1668)
*The marriage of Willem van Loon
and Margaretha Bas*
Canvas 92 x 165 cm
Above the middle door: *Molenaer
feset anno 1637*
Inv. no. L 158

LITERATURE:
Van Eeghen 1973, pp. 121-26; Van
Loon and Van Eeghen 1984, pp. 33-34

PROVENANCE:
in the possession of the Van Loon family
since 1637

1637

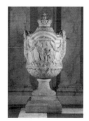

186
[see p. 276]
Jan Ebbelaer
(The Hague? 1666-1706)
after Daniel Marot (1661-1752)
Scotia-Virtus vase, 1696-1697
Marble h. 160 cm
On the plinth of the body of the vase:
I.EBBELAER.F.
Inv. no. KP 2500-2

LITERATURE:
Van der Wyck 1977, pp. 168, 171-73;
exhib. cat. New York-Pittsburgh 1988-
89, pp. 32, 34; De Jong 1993, pp. 82,
85, 101; De Jong and Schellekens 1994,
pp. 70-71

PROVENANCE:
made for the palace 'Het Loo'

1697

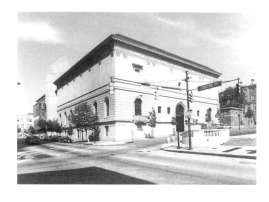

BALTIMORE, THE WALTERS ART GALLERY

The museum's collection was brought together by the 19th-century railroad magnate William T. Walters and his son and successor Henry Walters. In 1931 their collection and the museum built for it in 1907 were bequeathed to the city of Baltimore. The museum houses a famous collection of medieval art and 19th-century French salon painting. In addition to around 70 paintings by 17th-century Dutch artists, the collection contains some beautiful works of decorative art, including a beaker by Lutma dating from 1639.

LITERATURE: Sutton 1986

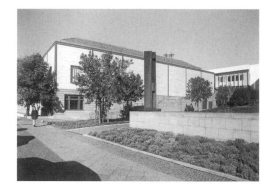

BERLIN, GEMÄLDEGALERIE

The Berlin museum, the core of which goes back to the collections of the Brandenburg Electors of the 17th century and the collections of the Prussian kings, was opened to the public in 1830 in the Alte Museum designed by Schinkel. In the 19th century and the first decades of the 20th century the collection grew through acquisitions to reach 6000 paintings. The collection of 17th-century Dutch paintings, including a large group of paintings by Rembrandt, is one of the richest and most diverse in this field, thanks to the acquisitions made by Wilhelm von Bode, which included the Suermondt collection in 1874. After 1945 the collection was divided between East and West Berlin, but it was reunited in 1998 in a new building on the Kulturforum in Berlin.

LITERATURE: cat. Berlin 1996; cat. Berlin 1998

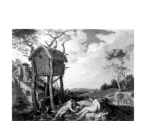

15
[see p. 38]
Abraham Bloemaert
(Gorinchem 1566-Utrecht 1651)
Landscape with the parable of the tares among the wheat
Canvas 100.3 x 132.7 cm
Below the basket: *A. Bloemaert.fe:/1624*
Inv. no. 37.2505

LITERATURE:
exhib. cat. Amsterdam-Boston-Philadelphia 1987-88, no. 12;
Roethlisberger 1993, no. 391; exhib. cat.
San Francisco-Baltimore-London 1997-98, no. 18

PROVENANCE:
Earl of Portarlington, Emo Court,
Ireland; art dealer (Dublin), c. 1919;
Justice James A. Murnaghan, Dublin; the
Hon. Francis D. Murnaghan, Baltimore;
gift of the Dr Francis D. Murnaghan
Fund, 1973

1973

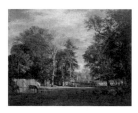

176
[see p. 264]
Adriaen van de Velde
(Amsterdam 1636-Amsterdam 1672)
The farm
Canvas on panel 63 x 78 cm
On the left beneath the fence:
A. v. velde.f/1666
Inv. no. 922C

LITERATURE:
Hofstede de Groot 1907-28, vol. 4,
no. 80; cat. Berlin 1996, p. 123

PROVENANCE:
in the Hope family, 1794-1898; sold in
1898 with the whole of the H.F. Clinton
Hope collection to the art dealer P. & D.
Colnaghi and art dealer A. Wertheimer;
purchased in 1899

1899

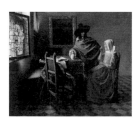

137
[see p. 199]
Johannes Vermeer
(Delft 1632-Delft 1675)
The glass of wine, c. 1661-1662
Canvas 66.3 x 76.5 cm
Inv. no. 912C

LITERATURE:
Blankert 1975, no. 8; exhib. cat.
Philadelphia-Berlin-London 1984,
no. 116; cat. Berlin 1996, p. 126;
cat. Berlin 1998, pp. 276-77

PROVENANCE:
sale Jan van Loon, Delft, 18/VII/1736,
no. 16; in de Hope family, 1785-1898;
sold in 1898 with the whole of the H.F.
Clinton Hope collection to the art dealer
P. & D. Colnaghi and art dealer A.
Wertheimer; purchased in 1901

1901

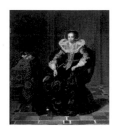

12
[see p. 31]
Thomas de Keyser (Amsterdam
1596/1597-Amsterdam 1667)
Portrait of a lady
Panel 79 x 53 cm
At the top on the door: *TDK*
(in ligature) *1632*
Inv. no. 82.1

LITERATURE:
exhib. cat. Amsterdam 1952, no. 80;
Adams 1988, vol. 3, no. 38; cat. Berlin
1996, p. 66; cat. Berlin 1998, pp. 242-43

PROVENANCE:
sale E. Secrétan, Paris, 1/VII/1889, vol. 2,
no. 129; sale Rodolphe Kann, 6/VIII/1907,
vol. 1, p. 54; art dealer Duveen, New
York; sale Oskar Huldschinsky, Berlin,
10/V/1928, no. 17; art dealer Boehler and
Steinmeyer, New York, 1929; Arthur
Hartog, Wassenaar and New York 1938-1955; art dealer Newhouse Galleries, New
York, 1975; private collection United
States; purchased in 1982

1982

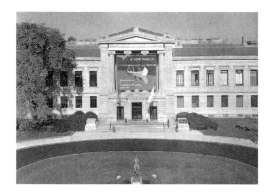

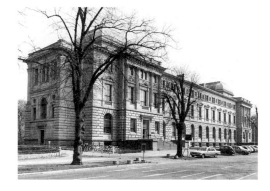

BOSTON, MUSEUM OF FINE ARTS

This museum, opened in 1876, has one of the largest and most diverse collections in the United States. In addition to famous collections of decorative art, Egyptian, antique, Oriental and American art, it has nearly 1700 European paintings. With more than 200 paintings, the collection offers a broad overview of the development of 17th-century Dutch art from the Mannerists up to the *fijnschilders*: in addition to the standard masters such as Rembrandt and Ruisdael, minor masters are also well represented. The basis of this collection was laid with the purchase in 1880 of a number of Dutch paintings from the collection of Prince Demidoff in Florence by the Boston-born collector Stanton Blake. The majority of the paintings, however, are later gifts and acquisitions.

LITERATURE: Whitehill 1970; cat. Boston 1986; Sutton 1986; exhib. cat. The Hague-San Francisco 1990-91

BRAUNSCHWEIG, HERZOG ANTON ULRICH-MUSEUM

The museum, the basis of which is the art and *naturalia* collection of Duke Carl I of Braunschweig, was founded in 1754, the first German museum to open its doors to the public. The picture gallery in the castle at Salzdahlum was founded by Duke Anton Ulrich, who died in 1714. The collection of c. 400 17th-century Dutch paintings was mostly acquired in the late 17th century and in the first decades of the 18th century. In addition to works by famous masters such as Rembrandt, Ruisdael and Vermeer, Dutch history painting – often in large format – is remarkably well represented, including paintings by Wtewael, Lastman, Honthorst, later Rembrandt pupils and the classicists. Since 1887 the paintings have been housed in the building near the Steintoren wall.

LITERATURE: Fink 1954; cat. Braunschweig 1983

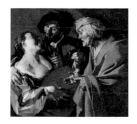

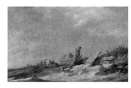

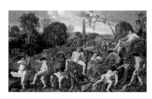

23
[see p. 48]
Dirck van Baburen
(Wijk bij Duurstede c. 1595-
Utrecht 1624)
The procuress
Canvas 101.5 x 107.6 cm
On the lute: *TBaburen fe 1622*
Inv. no. 50.2721

LITERATURE:
Slatkes 1965, no. A12; exhib. cat. The Hague-San Francisco 1990-91, no. 5; exhib. cat. San Francisco-Baltimore-London 1997-98, no. 38

PROVENANCE:
(?) Maria Thins, Delft/Gouda, before 1641-1680; (?) Catharina Bolnes, Delft, 1680-1688; (?) Johannes Johannesz Vermeer, Delft, 1688-1713; R.F.A. Sloane-Stanley, Cowes, Isle of Wight, sale, London, 25/II/1949, no. 52; art dealer Colnaghi, London, 1949; art dealer Roger Thesiger, Buckinghamshire; purchased in 1950

1950

21
[see p. 44]
Jan van Goyen
(Leiden 1596-The Hague 1656)
Dune landscape
Panel 39.5 x 62.7 cm
To the right on the door: *VG 1631*
Inv. no. 340

LITERATURE:
Beck 1972-87, vol. 2, no. 1110; cat. Braunschweig 1983, p. 75; exhib. cat. Amsterdam-Boston-Philadelphia 1987-88, no. 35

PROVENANCE:
acquired in 1738 for the Galerie in Salzdahlum; under Napoleon, in Paris from 1807 to 1815

1738

51
[see p. 84]
Moses van Uyttenbroeck
(The Hague 1595/1600-The Hague 1646/1647)
Bacchanal
Canvas 125 x 206 cm
Lower left: *M.V.WB R 1627*
Inv. no. 216

LITERATURE:
Weisner 1964, no. 15; cat. Braunschweig 1983, p. 203

PROVENANCE:
(?) sale Countess Douarière van Hornes (née Van Nassau), The Hague, 24/VII/1721, no. 16; sale Benjamin de Costa, The Hague, 13/VIII/1764, no. 83; in any case since 1776 in Salzdahlum; under Napoleon, in Kassel from 1811 to 1814

1776

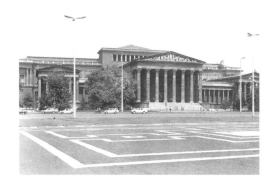

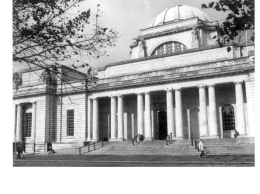

BUDAPEST, SZÉPMÜVÉSZETI MÚZEUM

The basis of the museum's collection of paintings is the collection of 637 pictures brought together in the first decades of the 19th century by the Hungarian prince Miklós Esterházy (1756-1833). This collection was bought by the Hungarian state in 1870. It was enlarged between 1914 and 1935 by means of gifts and purchases. In 1906 the museum opened its doors to the public in its present building, where it displays European paintings from the 15th to the early 20th century, as well as Egyptian and other antiquities. The Dutch school is well represented with more than 500 paintings.

LITERATURE: cat. Budapest 1968; exhib. cat. Cologne-Utrecht 1987

CARDIFF, NATIONAL MUSEUMS & GALLERIES OF WALES

In the national art collection of Wales in the well-endowed museum in Cardiff the accent is on 19th and 20th-century art, including the wonderful collection of Impressionist paintings bequeathed to the museum by Gwendoline and Margaret Davies. The collection of old European masters is small and consists largely of recent acquisitions. Landscape painting is superbly represented by works of Poussin, Lorrain and the masterpiece by Jan van de Cappelle in this exhibition.

LITERATURE: cat. Cardiff 1993

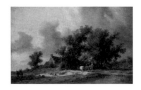

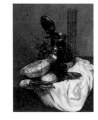

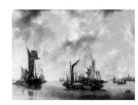

22
[see p. 45]
Salomon van Ruysdael
(Naarden 1600/1603-Haarlem 1670)
Road in the dunes with a passenger coach
Panel 56 x 86.4 cm
Lower right: *SVR 1631*
Inv. no. 260

LITERATURE:
Stechow 1938, no. 181; exhib. cat. Amsterdam-Boston-Philadelphia 1987-88, no. 91

PROVENANCE:
Esterházy family until 1870; purchased by the Hungarian state in 1870

124
[see p. 184]
Jan Jansz Treck
(Amsterdam c. 1606-Amsterdam 1652)
Still life with pewter jug and Chinese bowl
Panel 66.5 x 50.5 cm
On the neck of the jug: *JJTreck 1645*
Inv. no. 1064

LITERATURE:
exhib. cat. Cologne-Utrecht 1987, no. 39

PROVENANCE:
purchased in 1894 from art dealer Friedrich Schwartz in Vienna (as Juriaen van Streeck)

158
[see p. 232]
Jan van de Cappelle
(Amsterdam 1624/1626-Amsterdam 1679)
A calm
Canvas 110 x 148.2 cm
Lower right: *J V CAPPEL 1654*
Inv. no. NMW A 2754

LITERATURE:
Russell 1975, no. 52; exhib. cat. Washington 1985-86, no. 282; cat. Cardiff 1993, no. 36

PROVENANCE:
Sir Lawrence Dundas (c. 1710-1781); the latter's son Thomas, 1st Baron Dundas (1741-1820); the latter's sale, Greenwood's, 31/V/1794, no. 13 (bought back); by descent to the Marquess of Zetland, London; purchased in 1994

1870

1894

1994

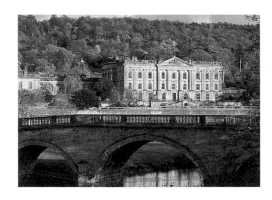

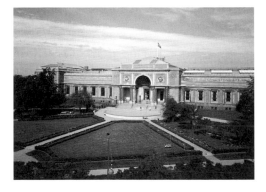

CHATSWORTH,
THE DUKE OF DEVONSHIRE AND THE TRUSTEES OF
THE CHATSWORTH SETTLEMENT

The splendid collection of paintings, decorative art, drawings and prints, which are still preserved in the stately home of Chatsworth in Derbyshire, was largely brought together by the second Duke of Devonshire (1665-1727) and his son (1698-1755). The first Duke of Devonshire (1640-1707), a follower of Willem III of Orange and the one who had the present house built, formed an important collection of silver, including a French toilet set dating from 1670 with the coat of arms of William and Mary.

LITERATURE: exhib. cat. Richmond etc. 1979-80

COPENHAGEN, STATENS MUSEUM FOR KUNST

The basis of the collection, which was opened to the public in 1896, is formed by the royal Danish collection, which now includes contemporary art. The royal collection of art, which was displayed as early as 1650 in the royal art cabinet, has its origins in the 16th century. Mannerist paintings like *The fall of the Titans* by Cornelis van Haarlem were purchased early in the 17th century. Later on in that century, the Dutch *trompe-l'oeil* painter Cornelis Gijsbrechts was employed by the Danish king. An important part of the collection of 17th-century Dutch paintings was acquired in the late 18th and early 19th century.

LITERATURE: cat. Copenhagen 1997

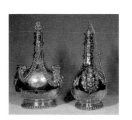

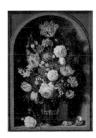

193
[see p. 282]
Adam Loofs
(The Hague? c. 1645-1710)
Two pilgrim bottles with the coat of arms of William, the first Duke of Devonshire
Silver-gilt h. 47 and 48.2 cm
Marked: assay office mark The Hague; a lion rampant; year letter O = 1688; maker's mark: AL under post horn and crown in shield = Adam Loofs

LITERATURE:
exhib. cat. The Hague 1967, no. 86; exhib. cat. Washington 1985-86, no. 116; exhib. cat. New York-Pittsburgh 1988-89, pp. 28 and 31

PROVENANCE:
probably commissioned by Willem III and presented to the first Duke of Devonshire in 1694

1694

40
[see p. 70]
Ambrosius Bosschaert
(Antwerp 1573-The Hague 1621)
Bouquet of flowers in a vase
Copper 55.5 x 39.5 cm
Lower left: *.AB.1618* (AB in ligature)
Inv. no. Sp.211

LITERATURE:
Bol 1960, no. 33; Taylor 1995, p. 118; cat. Copenhagen 1997, pp. 60-61

PROVENANCE:
Hirschholm Castle; acquired in 1791

1791

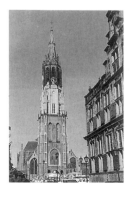

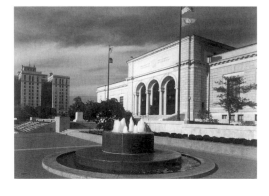

DELFT, NIEUWE KERK

The Large or New Church is a late-Gothic cross-basilica with a tall tower which dominates the market square of Delft. In the choir is the tomb of Prince Willem I, begun in 1614 by Hendrick de Keyser and finished in 1622. During thorough renovations which were started in 1997 and are planned to continue until 2002, the tomb has been taken apart and reassembled.

DETROIT, THE DETROIT INSTITUTE OF ARTS

The museum, opened in 1888, has an encyclopedic collection of art stemming from all parts of the world and from all periods, including a valuable collection of Dutch art. An important part of it, including masterpieces by Rembrandt (*The Visitation*, 1640), Jacob van Ruisdael [*155*] and Gerard ter Borch (*Lady at her toilet*), was acquired between the two World Wars by the first director of the museum, W.R. Valentiner, who succeeded admirably in moving benefactors of the museum to present it with paintings.

LITERATURE: Sutton 1986; exhib. cat. The Hague-San Francisco 1990-91; Peck 1991

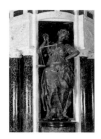

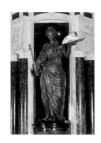

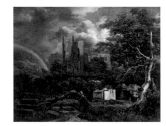

8a
[see p. 22]
Hendrick de Keyser
(Utrecht 1565-Amsterdam 1621)
Justice: corner statue of the tomb of Willem I in the New Church at Delft, c. 1615-1620
Bronze h. 173 cm

LITERATURE:
Neurdenburg 1930, p. 117; Neurdenburg 1948, pp. 50, 54; Halsema-Kubes 1991; Jimkes-Verkade 1991

PROVENANCE:
in situ since c. 1620

8b
[see p. 22]
Hendrick de Keyser
(Utrecht 1565-Amsterdam 1621)
Liberty: corner statue of the tomb of Willem I in the New Church at Delft, c. 1615-1620
Bronze h. 173 cm

LITERATURE:
see 8a

PROVENANCE:
see 8a

155
[see p. 226]
Jacob van Ruisdael
(Haarlem 1628/1629-Amsterdam 1682)
The Jewish cemetery, c. 1660-1670
Canvas 141 x 182.9 cm
On the left at the bottom of the tomb:
JvRuisdael (JvR in ligature)
Inv. no. 26.3

LITERATURE:
Rosenberg 1928, no. 153; exhib. cat. The Hague-Cambridge 1981-82, no. 20; exhib. cat. Amsterdam-Boston-Philadelphia 1987-88, no. 86

PROVENANCE:
(?) sale Amsterdam, 16/IX/1739, no. 88; probably sale Amsterdam, 9/V/1770, no. 2; sale P. Locquet, Amsterdam, 22/IX/1783, no. 315; sale Marin, Paris, 22/III/1790, no. 124; sale Paris, 1802; Huybens c. 1815; George Gillows; sale M.M. Zachary, London, 31 Mary 1828, no. 51; Mackintosh, 1835; art dealer Anthony Reyre, London, c. 1920; sale Romford, London (Christie's), 30/IV/1924, no. 353; art dealers Leo Blumenreich and Frantz M. Zatzenstein, Berlin, 1925; Galerie Matthiesen, Berlin; Julius H. Haass, Detroit; gift of Julius H. Haass, 1926

1620

1620

1926

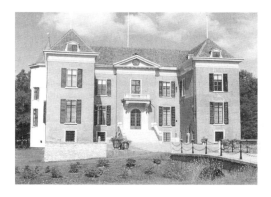

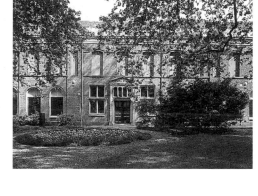

DOORN, HUIS DOORN

In 1918 the former German emperor Wilhelm II of Hohenzollern (1859-1941) fled to the Netherlands and settled in exile in the country house called 'Huis Doorn' near Amerongen. To enable him to furnish the house, the emperor was permitted to choose from his former possessions, and he chose to surround himself with memories of a personal and dynastic nature. In addition to family portraits of the Hohenzollern family, he mainly chose precious objects of decorative art, including a lot of jewellery and silver. After his death, most of this Prussian court collection remained at Huis Doorn, which has been run as a foundation since 1956 and is open to the public.

LITERATURE: exhib. cat. Berlin 1991; Bakker 1993

DORDRECHT, DORDRECHTS MUSEUM

The museum, founded in 1842 and housed since 1904 in the present building in the Museumstraat, was beautifully renovated and enlarged in 1976-1977. In addition to art of the old masters, the Dutch visual arts of the 19th and 20th centuries are well represented. Painting of the 17th century is represented by the work of well-known Dordrecht painters such as Ferdinand Bol, Aelbert Cuyp, Nicolaes Maes and Arent de Gelder. An important part of the collection was purchased in recent decades thanks to an active acquisitions policy.

LITERATURE: De Paus and Schweitzer 1992

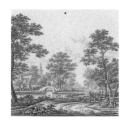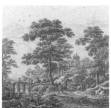

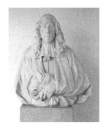

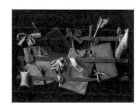

109
[see p. 163]
Frederik van Frytom
(? c. 1632-Delft 1702)
Two plaques with depictions of landscapes, c. 1690
Blue-painted faience, 34.8 x 34.3 and 34.6 x 34.2 cm
Inv. nos. HuD 2111 and HuD 2110

LITERATURE:
Vecht 1968, nos. 12 and 73; exhib. cat. Berlin 1991, nos. 16.1 and 16.2

PROVENANCE:
Emperor Wilhelm II of Germany; since 1919 in Huis Doorn

1919

166
[see p. 245]
Artus Quellinus
(Antwerp 1609-Antwerp 1668)
Portrait of Johan de Witt (1623-1672), 1665
Marble h. 95 cm
Inv. no. DM/871/S1

LITERATURE:
exhib. cat. London 1964, no. 135; De Paus and Schweitzer 1992, pp. 104-105

PROVENANCE:
gift of the descendants of De Witt, 1871

1871

130
[see p. 190]
Samuel van Hoogstraeten
(Dordrecht 1627-Dordrecht 1678)
Trompe-l'oeil still life
Canvas 45.5 x 57.5 cm
On the document under the red seal:
Samuel van Hoogstraten London 1664.1/20; on the journal to the right:
ANNO 1664
Inv. no. DM/992/691

LITERATURE:
De Paus and Schweitzer 1992, pp. 98-99; exhib. cat. Dordrecht 1992-93, no. 47; Brusati 1995, pp. 95-96, 156, 293, 362

PROVENANCE:
sale London (Phillips), 5/XII/1989, no. 89 (als Edwaert Collier); art dealer Johnny van Haeften, London; purchased in 1992 with the aid of the Rembrandt Society

1992

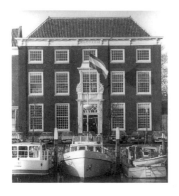

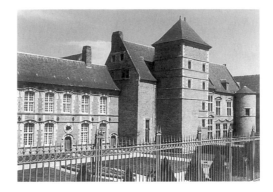

DORDRECHT, MUSEUM MR. SIMON VAN GIJN

DOUAI, MUSÉE DE LA CHARTREUSE

The museum, which opened in 1925, is housed in a monumental patrician house built in 1729 on the Nieuwe Haven. The house came into the possession of the banker and art collector Simon van Gijn (1836-1922) in 1864. On display in period rooms furnished in the styles of the 17th, 18th and 19th centuries are family portraits, as well as a wide variety of objects, a large part of which reflect the history of Dordrecht and its artistic production.

Both the museum, founded around 1800, and an important part of its collection were destroyed by bombing in 1944. The present museum in the Carthusiasn Monastery of Douai – which also houses, for example, the 16th-century altarpieces by Bellegambe and Jan van Scorel that were made in Douai – opened its doors in 1958. The basis of the modest Dutch collection was laid already in the 19th century and later expanded by purchases made in the 1960s. Thanks to post-war reparations payments, some remarkable paintings have been acquired, including a number of works by Italian and Northern Mannerists.

LITERATURE: Baligand 1999

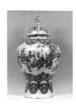

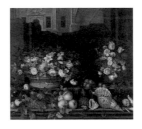

189
[see p. 278]
Hendrik Noteman
(Dordrecht 1656-Dordrecht 1734)
Model for table, c. 1700
Terracotta 17.2 x 17.8 x 12 cm
Inv. no. 1.1962

LITERATURE:
exhib. cat. New York-Pittsburgh
1988-89, no. 97

PROVENANCE:
gift of the widow of Crena de Jongh-van
Eik at The Hague, 1933

196
[see p. 285]
Pottery 'Het Jonge/Oude Moriaenshoofd'
under the supervision
of the Hoppesteyns
Two octagonal vases, c. 1680-1685
Polychrome faience, h. 75 cm
Marked: *I.W.* (Hoppesteyn)
Inv. no. A 1143

LITERATURE:
exhib. cat. Apeldoorn-London 1988-89,
no. 150

PROVENANCE:
acquired before 1877 (first appears in
the inventory of 1877)

41
[see p. 72]
Balthasar van der Ast
(Middelburg 1593/1594-Delft 1657)
Still life with flowers, fruit and shells,
c. 1640
Panel 134 x 140 cm
Inv. no. 2802

LITERATURE:
exhib. cat. Paris 1970-71, no. 3; exhib.
cat. Amsterdam 1971, no. 17

PROVENANCE:
purchased from the Hallsborough
Gallery, London, 1964

1933

1877

1964

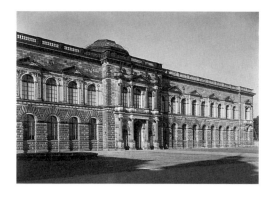

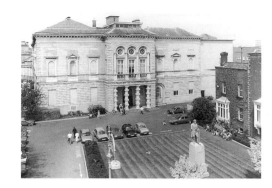

DRESDEN, GEMÄLDEGALERIE

The collection is housed in the picture gallery built between 1847 and 1852 by Gottfried Semper. It was re-opened in 1992 after extensive renovations. Half of the first floor is devoted to Italian Renaissance painting, and the other half to 17th-century Dutch and Flemish painting. Raphael's *Sistine Madonna*, for example, hangs opposite Rembrandt's *Self-portrait with Saskia*. In the collection, the basis of which was laid in the first half of the 18th century by the Electors of Saxony – August the Strong and his son – 17th-century Dutch art is especially well represented, a high point being 12 paintings by Rembrandt. Late 17th-century Dutch cabinet pieces also form an important part of this collection.

LITERATURE: cat. Dresden 1992

DUBLIN, NATIONAL GALLERY OF IRELAND

The museum, opened in 1864, has a fine collection of European painting, which contains works of very high quality by the minor masters of 17th-century Dutch art. These paintings were mostly acquired at auction in the late 19th century. In 1987 the Dutch collection won instant renown owing to the bequest of Sir Alfred Beit, who presented the museum not only with the masterpieces by Metsu and Ruisdael exhibited here, but also with a magnificent Vermeer, a splendid Hobbema and an exceptional Jan Steen. The basis of this private collection was laid by Alfred Beit (1853-1906), who not only had sufficient means at his disposal, but also possessed an exceptionally good eye.

LITERATURE; cat. Dublin 1986; Potterton et al. 1988

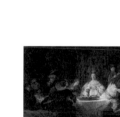

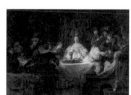

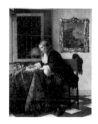

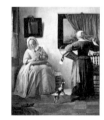

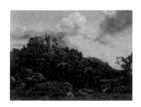

183
[see p. 272]
Adriaen van der Werff
(Kralingen 1659-Rotterdam 1722)
Shepherd and shepherdess
Panel 58.5 x 47.5 cm
On the lowest step, right: *adr[n]
van der Werff fec. an. 1689*
Inv. no. 1812

LITERATURE:
Gaehtgens 1987, no. 20; cat. Dresden
1992, p. 411; exhib. cat. Rotterdam
1994-95, no. 74

PROVENANCE:
gift of the Elector Palatine to the Elector
of Saxony, 1710

1710

54
[see p. 87]
Rembrandt
(Leiden 1606-Amsterdam 1669)
The wedding of Samson
Canvas 126.5 x 175.5 cm
Lower centre: *Rembrandt f. 1638*
Inv. no. 1560

LITERATURE:
exhib. cat. Amsterdam 1969, no. 5;
Bruyn et al. 1982-89, vol. 3, no. A 123;
cat. Dresden 1992, p. 313

PROVENANCE:
(?) inventory of the estate of Cathalijntje
Bastiaens (1607-1654), widow of
Cornelis Cornelisz Cras, Amsterdam,
7/XII/1654; registered as no. A 1144 in
the inventory (1722-1728) of the gallery
of the Elector in Dresden

before c. 1728

141a
[see p. 204]
Gabriël Metsu
(Leiden 1629-Amsterdam 1667)
Gentleman writing a letter,
c. 1662-1665
Panel 52.5 x 40.2 cm
Upper right: *G. Metsu*
Inv. no. 4536

LITERATURE:
Robinson 1974, pp. 59-61; exhib. cat.
Amsterdam 1976, no. 39; Potterton et
al. 1988, no. 5

PROVENANCE:
sale Hendrik Sorgh, Amsterdam,
28/III/1720, no. 29; sale G. Bruyn,
Amsterdam, 16/III/1724; Johannes Coop;
Gerrit Braamcamp, Amsterdam, c. 1744-
50; sale Braamcamp, Amsterdam,
31/VII/1771, no. 125; Jan Hope; Lord
Francis Pelham Clinton Hope, Deepdene,
by descent; A. Wertheimer and
P. & D. Colnaghi, 1898; Beit family,
gift of Sir Alfred Beit, 1987

1987

141b
[see p. 205]
Gabriël Metsu
(Leiden 1629-Amsterdam 1667)
Lady reading a letter, c. 1662-1665
Panel 52.5 x 40.2 cm
On the envelop in the maidservant's
hand: *Metsu, tot Amsterdam Poort*
Inv. no. 4537

LITERATURE:
Robinson 1974, pp. 59-61; exhib. cat.
Amsterdam 1976, no. 39; Potterton et
al. 1988, no. 6

PROVENANCE:
the same as 141a

1987

156
[see p. 228]
Jacob van Ruisdael
(Haarlem 1628/1629-Amsterdam 1682)
Bentheim Castle
Canvas 110.5 x 144 cm
On the rock at left centre: *JVR 1653*
(JVR in ligature)
Inv. no. 4531

LITERATURE:
Smith 1829-42, vol. 6, no. 258;
Rosenberg 1928, no. 18; exhib. cat. The
Hague-Cambridge 1981-82, no. 14;
Potterton et al. 1988, no. 14

PROVENANCE:
(?)Count Bentheim; William Smith, M.P.,
England (not later than 1815); via W.
Smith to W. Buchanan; Thomas Kebble,
Green Trees, near Tonbridge, Kent, not
later than 1835; sale London, 2/VI/1856,
no. 54; purchased by Alfred Beit,
presumably between 1895 and 1906;
the family Beit, gift of Sir Alfred Beit,
1987

1987

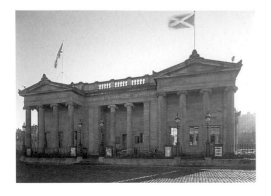

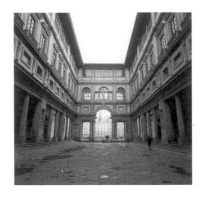

EDINBURGH, NATIONAL GALLERY OF SCOTLAND

The internationally oriented collection of this museum, which was opened in 1859, is the result of the merging of various 19th-century institutional collections. The Dutch collection was enriched by, among other things, gifts from William McEwan (two portraits by Frans Hals and Rembrandt's *Woman in bed*, in 1885 and 1892, respectively), John Moubray (Frans Hals's *Portrait of Verdonck*, 1916) and the heirs of W.A. Coats (Vermeer's *Christ in the house of Martha and Mary*, in 1927). More recent acquisitions include works by Cuyp, Hobbema, Saenredam, Dou, Steen, Philips Koninck, Schalcken and Jan Weenix. A beautiful self-portrait by Rembrandt is on long-term loan from the Duke of Sutherland (since 1945/1946) and a lovely, early landscape by Ruisdael has been on loan from the Torrie Collection since 1859.

LITERATURE: Thompson 1972; cat. Edinburgh 1997

FLORENCE, GALLERIA DEGLI UFFIZI AND GALLERIA PALATINA

The majority of the more than 300 17th-century Dutch paintings which are now divided between these two Florentine museums were purchased already in the 17th century by the Florentine Grand Duke. The latter commissioned work from Honthorst, Otto Marseus van Schriek and Willem van Aelst [*126*] when they were staying in Italy. During his visits to Holland (1667 and 1669), Cosimo de' Medici bought paintings by Jan Davidsz de Heem, Jan van der Heyden and Willem van de Velde, among others. His later purchases testify to his preference for the 'fine painters' such as Gerard Dou and Frans van Mieris. For the collection of artists' self-portraits in the possession of his uncle, Cardinal Leopoldo de' Medici, Cosimo possibly acquired in 1669 the late *Self-portrait* by Rembrandt, which is now in the Uffizi.

LITERATURE: Chiarini 1989; Langendijk 1992

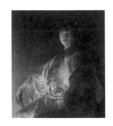

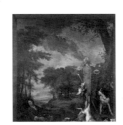

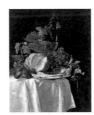

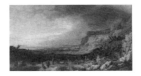

60
[*see p. 97*]
Jan Lievens
(Leiden 1607-Amsterdam 1674)
Self-portrait(?) in a yellow robe,
c. 1630-1631
Canvas 112 x 99.4 cm
On the right, under the remains of a
falsified Rembrandt signature
Inv. no. NG 1564

LITERATURE:
Schneider and Ekkart 1973, no. 283;
exhib. cat. Braunschweig 1979, no. 31

PROVENANCE:
Mary Lady Carbery, Castle Freke,
County Coren (Ireland); sale London,
4/III/1921, no. 9; art dealer H.M. Clark,
London, 1921; art dealer Thomas Agnew
& Sons, London, 1922; purchased in
1922

1922

199
[*see p. 289*]
Jan Weenix
(Amsterdam 1640-Amsterdam 1719)
*Landscape with huntsman
and dead game*, Canvas 344 x 323 cm
Lower left: *J. Weenix 1697*
Inv. no. NG 2523

LITERATURE:
Plietzsch 1960, p. 163

PROVENANCE:
probably commissioned by Jacob
Henriques de Granada for his house on
the Herengracht 99, Amsterdam,
c. 1695-97; Hendrik Grave, 1718; Isaac
Alvares, 1721; Jacob Texiera de Mattos,
1747; F.J.M.A. Reekers, Amsterdam, by
descent; sale Amsterdam, 5/II/1923;
William Randolph Hearst, 1923-1941;
RKO Radio Pictures, Hollywood; Paramount Picture Studios, Hollywood; sale
New York (Christie's), 10/I/1990, no.
236; Hazlitt, Gooden and Fox, London;
purchased in 1990

1990

126
[*see p. 186*]
Willem van Aelst
(Delft 1626-Amsterdam 1683)
Still life with fruit and crystal vase
Canvas 73 x 58 cm
On the hem of the tablecloth:
W.V. Aelst 1652
Inv. no. Oggetti d'Arte 1911, n. 509

LITERATURE:
Chiarini 1989, no. 1.4; exhib. cat.
Florence 1998, no. 1

PROVENANCE:
painted in 1652 for Giancarlo de'
Medici, and in the collection
since that time

1652

81
[*see p. 131*]
Hercules Segers
(Haarlem 1589/1590-The Hague or
Amsterdam in or before 1638)
Mountainous landscape, c. 1620-1630
Canvas on panel 55 x 99 cm
Possible remains of a date: *16[..]*
Inv. no. 1303

LITERATURE:
Rowlands 1979, pp. 20, 27; exhib. cat.
Amsterdam-Boston-Philadelphia 1987-
88, separate supplement; Chiarini 1989,
pp. 524-26

PROVENANCE:
(?) Rembrandt van Rijn, Amsterdam,
1656; Lady Mary Hadfield Cosway
(1759-1838), Florence; the latter's
bequest to the museum, 1839

1839

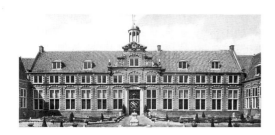

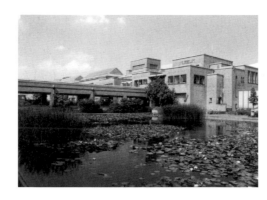

HAARLEM, FRANS HALSMUSEUM

The museum has been housed since 1913 in the 17th-century Old Men's Almshouse. The city owns 16th-century paintings by such Haarlem masters as Jan van Scorel and Maerten van Heemskerck, by Mannerists like Cornelis van Haarlem and Hendrick Goltzius, and by 17th-century masters such as Cornelis Vroom, Frans Hals, Verspronck and Jan de Bray. The most famous are the five splendid civic-guard paintings by Frans Hals, dated between 1616 and 1639, the regents of the St Elisabeth Hospital dating from 1641 and the group portraits of regents [146] and regentesses of the Old Men's Almshouse of c. 1664. In addition, the collection contains rooms furnished in 17th-century Dutch style, a doll's house and a collection of decorative art, with the emphasis on Haarlem silver and majolica.

LITERATURE: cat. Haarlem 1969

THE HAGUE, GEMEENTEMUSEUM DEN HAAG

Modern art, musical instruments and the decorative arts still form the main elements of the collection of the Gemeentemuseum Den Haag, housed in the museum built by Berlage in 1935. The collection of decorative arts includes a rich collection of Delftware, an important glass collection and an extensive collection of 17th-century Hague silver. Parts of these collections are exhibited in period rooms furnished completely in 17th and 18th-century style, which give a good picture of the Dutch interior at that time. The collections connected with the history of The Hague are now housed in the Haags Historisch Museum.

LITERATURE: Eliëns et al. 1995-96; cat. The Hague 1998

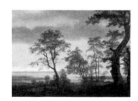 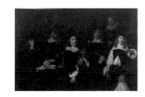

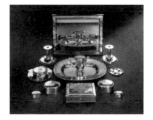

20
[see p. 43]
Cornelis Vroom
(? 1591/1592-Haarlem 1661)
Landscape with estuary, c. 1638
Panel 50 x 67.3 cm
Lower right on tree trunk: CVROOM
(CVR in ligature)
Inv. no. OS 85-756

LITERATURE:
Keyes 1975, no. 39; exhib. cat.
Amsterdam-Boston-Philadelphia
1987-88, no. 115

PROVENANCE:
art dealer S. Nijstad, The Hague; on loan
from a private collection, The Hague

146
[see p. 212]
Frans Hals
(Antwerp 1582/1583-Haarlem 1666)
*The regents of the Old Men's
Almshouse in Haarlem*, c. 1664
Canvas 172.5 x 256 cm
Inv. no. os I-115

LITERATURE:
Vinken and De Jongh 1963; Slive 1970-
74, vol. 3, no. 221; exhib. cat.
Washington-London-Haarlem 1989-90,
no. 85

PROVENANCE:
commissioned by the sitters and hung in
the Old Men's Almshouse, Haarlem;
exhibited in the Frans Halsmuseum since
1862

1862

102
[see p. 156]
*Toilet set belonging to Veronica van
Aerssen van Sommelsdijck*, 1651-1658
Silver-gilt, mirror: h. 51.5 cm
All of the pieces marked with the
crowned monogram VAS, the dedicatory
text *Veronica countess of Kincardine To
her daughter Elizabath Boswell* and bird
with the motto *Vraye Foy*; marked:
assay office mark The Hague; year
letters A, C, E, F = 1653, 1655, 1657,
1658; makers' marks: crowned heart
(possibly Johannes Voest); bird with
branch in circle (Arentsz van Rheenen?);
fist in shield (= Gerrit Vuystinck I);
crossbow with GB in circle (= Gerardus
de Bruyn)
Inv. nos. OME-1960-2/4, OME-1965-
2/6 and 39/40, OME-1968-23, OME-
1976-2

LITERATURE:
exhib. cat. The Hague 1967, no. 38a-e;
Scholten 1986, pp. 36-37

PROVENANCE:
Veronica van Aerssen van Sommelsdijck;
(in 1659 married Alexander Bruce, 2nd
Earl of Kincardine); her gift to her
daughter Lady Elizabeth (in 1704
married James Boswell of Auchinleck,
the grandfather of the famous 18th-
century biographer James Boswell);
James Boswell, by descent; the latter's
great-granddaughter Lady Mounsey; sale
Alexander Dowell, 2 November 1886,
eight pieces purchased by Lord Elgin;
ewer and two small oval boxes acquired
in 1960, the pin tray in 1968, the mirror
in 1976, the other pieces in 1965

1960-1976

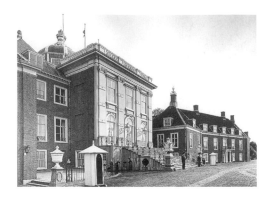

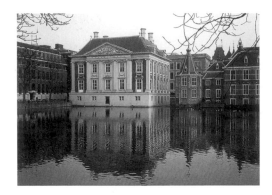

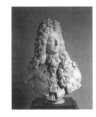

THE HAGUE, HUIS TEN BOSCH

The Huis ten Bosch, built in 1645 and the following years in the Haagse Bos by Pieter Post, was furnished as a country house for Amalia van Solms. During renovations carried out between 1734 and 1737 by Daniel Marot and others, the vestibule and side wings were added to the house. The decoration (c. 1650) by Dutch and Flemish artists of the large and originally completely isolated middle hall – the Oranjezaal, or Orange Hall – is a remarkable monument of 17th-century classicist-oriented court art. Between 1800 and 1805 the Nationale Konst-Gallerij was housed in the right wing. The Huis ten Bosch now serves as a palace for Queen Beatrix.

LITERATURE: Peter-Raupp 1980; Brenninkmeyer-De Rooij 1982; exhib. cat. Rotterdam-Frankfurt 1999-2000, pp. 27-29, nos. 7, 19, 29

THE HAGUE, MAURITSHUIS

The core of the collection was formed in 1774 by Stadholder Willem V for his gallery, which was open to the public. Some of its more than 200 paintings, such as *The bull* by Paulus Potter, were in the possession of the House of Orange very early on. The majority, however, were acquired by Willem V. The collection was taken to Paris in 1795 for display in the Musée Napoléon, though part of it returned to the Netherlands in 1815. In 1820 the Koninklijk Kabinet was founded in the Mauritshuis. The collection has been enriched continually through gifts and purchases (including, in 1834, Vermeer's famous *View of Delft* and, very recently, a phenomenal late portrait by the hand of Rembrandt), and offers a splendid overview of Dutch painting, with a clear emphasis on the 17th century.

LITERATURE: cat. The Hague 1987; cat. The Hague 1993

185
[see p. 274]
Jan Blommendael
(Breda or The Hague 1650-
The Hague 1702)
*Portrait of Stadholder-King
Willem III (1650-1702)*
Marble h. 80 cm
On both sides of the socle:
J.Blommendael.F./1699.HAGAE.COMITIS
Inv. no. 361

LITERATURE:
exhib. cat. London 1964, no. 130; exhib. cat. Düsseldorf 1971, no. 199; exhib. cat. New York 1979-80, no. 71

PROVENANCE:
probably collection of Willem V, The Hague; transferred to the Mauritshuis under King Willem I in 1816

1816

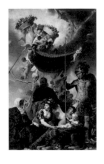

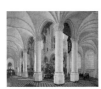

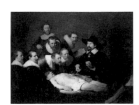

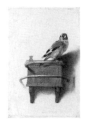

170
[see p. 255]
Cesar van Everdingen
(Alkmaar c. 1617-Alkmaar 1678)
*Allegory of the birth of Frederik
Hendrik*, c. 1650
Canvas 373 x 243 cm
Lower right: *CVEverdingen*
(CVE in ligature)

LITERATURE:
Peter-Raupp 1980, no. 1;
Brenninkmeyer-De Rooij 1982, no. 1a

PROVENANCE:
commissioned by Amalia van Solms for the Orange Hall in the Huis ten Bosch, where it is still to be found

c. 1650

78
[see p. 126]
Gerard Houckgeest
(The Hague c. 1600-
Bergen op Zoom 1661)
*Ambulatory of the New Church in
Delft, with the tomb of Willem the
Silent*
Panel 65.5 x 77.5 cm
On the base of the column: *GH 16*
(previously read as 1651)
Inv. no. 57

LITERATURE:
De Vries 1975, no. 17; Wheelock 1975-76, pp. 177-78; Wheelock 1977, pp. 233, 243-44; Liedtke 1982, pp. 38-53, 101, no. 7; exhib. cat. Rotterdam 1991, no. 31

PROVENANCE:
sale Johan Anthony van Kinschot, Delft, 21-22/VII/1767, no. 69; Prince Willem V; from 1795 to 1815 in the Louvre at Paris; in the Mauritshuis since 1816

1816

58
[see p. 94]
Rembrandt
(Leiden 1606-Amsterdam 1669)
*The anatomy lesson of
Dr Nicolaes Tulp*
Canvas 169.5 x 216.5 cm
To the right of the uppermost figure:
Rembrant. fv: 1632
Inv. no. 146

LITERATURE:
Bruyn *et al.* 1982-89, vol. 2, no. A 51; cat. The Hague 1987, no. 48; exhib. cat. The Hague 1998-99

PROVENANCE:
surgeons' guild in the Weigh-house, Amsterdam, purchased from the painter, 1632; surgeons' widows' fund, the Weigh-house, Amsterdam, 1798-1828; purchased by the Dutch state in 1828 and assigned by King Willem I to the Mauritshuis, The Hague

1828

135
[see p. 196]
Carel Fabritius
(Midden-Beemster 1622-Delft 1654)
The goldfinch
Panel 33.5 x 22.8 cm
Lower centre: *C FABRITIVS 1654*
Inv. no. 605

LITERATURE:
Brown 1981, no. 7; cat. The Hague 1987, no. 24

PROVENANCE:
Chevalier Joseph-Guillaume-Jean Camberlyn, Brussels, before 1859; E.J. Théophile Thoré (W.Bürger), Paris, c. 1865; heirs Thoré, Paris, 1869; sale Thoré, Paris, 5/XII/1892, no. 10; sale Martinet, Paris, 27/II/1896, no. 16; purchased by A. Bredius for the Mauritshuis, 1896

1896

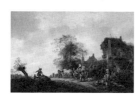

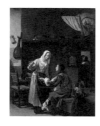

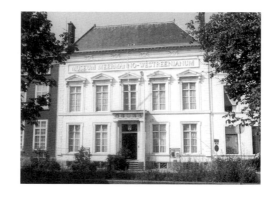

87

[see p. 137]
Isack van Ostade
(Haarlem 1621-Haarlem 1649)
Travellers at a country inn
Panel 75 x 109 cm
Lower centre: *Isack: van. Ostade 1645*
Inv. no. 789

LITERATURE:
cat. The Hague 1987, no. 44

PROVENANCE:
sale Randon de Boisset, Paris, 1777;
Radix Sainte-Foix, Paris, 1777; sale
Durney (D'Arney), Paris, 1791; Robit,
Paris, 1791-1801; sale Séguin, Paris, 1805;
sale Duchesse de Berry, Paris, 1837;
Demidoff, San Donato, 1837-1868; Lord
Ashburton, London, 1868; Richard
Wallace, Hertford House, London, before
1890; Alfred de Rothschild, London, after
1890; Lady Almira Carnarvon, after 1910;
art dealer Kleykamp, The Hague, 1925;
purchased with the aid of the Rembrandt
Society and private individuals, 1925

1925

123

[see p. 181]
Frans van Mieris
(Leiden 1635-Leiden 1681)
Brothel scene, c. 1658-1659
Panel 42.8 x 33.3 cm
On the lintel of the door:
F van (M)ieris 165(.)
Inv. no. 860

LITERATURE:
Naumann 1981, vol. 2, no. 23; exhib.
cat. Amsterdam 1989-90, no. 13

PROVENANCE:
Charles Bredel, London, 1839-1872; sale
Miss Bredel, London, 1875, no. 119; sale
A. Levy, London, 6/IV/1876, no. 12; sale
Earl of Dudley, London, 25/VI/1892, no.
12; Edward Steinkopf, London; Lady
Mary Seaforth, London, 1920-1935(?);
art dealer Duits, London, 1935; F.
Mannheimer, Amsterdam; Dienst voor 's
Rijks Verspreide Kunstvoorwerpen, The
Hague, 1946; transferred to the
ownership of the Mauritshuis in 1960.

1960

THE HAGUE,
MUSEUM MEERMANNO-WESTREENIANUM

The museum, founded in 1848, contains the estate of W.H.J. baron
van Westreenen (1783-1848), in whose house on the Prinsengracht in
The Hague the museum is housed. In addition to an impressive
library with medieval manuscripts, incunabula and rare editions, the
collection also contains antiquities, medallions, Italian primitives,
and the decorative arts. The collector was scarcely interested in 17th-
century Dutch art, which is represented only by a number of family
portraits, several ivory sculptures attributed to Van Bossuit and the
remarkable terracotta group by Xavery. Since 1960 the Museum of
the Book has been housed in the same building.

LITERATURE: Laseur 1998

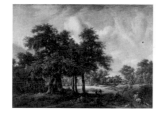

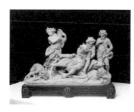

157

[see p. 229]
Meindert Hobbema
(Amsterdam 1638-Amsterdam 1709)
Wooded landscape with cottages,
c. 1665
Canvas 88 x 120.7 cm
Lower left: *M[e]yndert Hobbema*
Inv. no. 1105

LITERATURE:
Broulhiet 1938, no. 188; Van der Ploeg
1995; Wadum 1995

PROVENANCE:
sale Mme. Jean-Etienne Fiseau,
Amsterdam, 21/IV/1791; Henry Welbore
Ellis Agar, 2nd Viscount Clifden; 2nd
Earl of Grosvenor, 1806; 3rd Marquess
of Westminster; 2nd Duke of
Westminster; sale Lady Mary Grosvenor,
London (Sotheby's) 6/VII/1966, no. 75;
Edward Speelman; sale London
(Sotheby's), 24/VI/1970, no. 20; Alnatt,
1970; William Darby; sale London
(Sotheby's), 7/XII/1994, no. 25;
purchased with the aid of the Dutch
state, Baron H.H. Thyssen-Bornemisza,
the Friends of the Mauritshuis, the
Prince Bernhard Fund, the Rembrandt
Society and the Algemene Loterij
Nederland, 1994

1994

169a

[see p. 250]
Pieter Xavery
(Antwerp c. 1647-Leiden 1673)
Bacchanal
Terracotta 36.5 x 61.5 x 23 cm
Front, to the right of centre:
P.R.XAVERY INVETO/1671
Inv. no. 865/1030

LITERATURE:
Staring 1927, no. 7; Lunsingh Scheurleer
1975, pp. 24-25; Van der Giesen 1997,
pp. 22-23 and no. 12

PROVENANCE:
sale Van der Beek, The Hague,
20/VI/1840, Liefhebberijen, no. 12,
purchased by Van Westreenen

1840

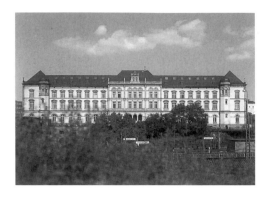

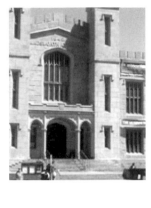

HAMBURG, MUSEUM FÜR KUNST UND GEWERBE

The museum, founded in 1869, which opened its doors to the public in the present building in 1878, is one of the few large international museums specialising in the decorative arts which was established in the 19th century along the lines of the Victoria & Albert Museum in London. The wide-ranging nature of the collection is due to a particularly active acquisitions policy. Thousands of objects are displayed in a chronological arrangement to give an overview of the development of European decorative arts and sculpture from the Middle Ages to the 20th century, whereby Oriental art and the decorative arts are especially well represented.

LITERATURE: Eckhardt *et al.* 1980; Von Saldern 1988

HARTFORD (CONN.), WADSWORTH ATHENEUM

This museum, housed in a characteristic neo-Gothic building, opened its doors to the public in 1844. It is one of the oldest museums in the United States. The museum's benefactors have traditionally shown a great deal of interest in 17th-century Dutch art, which means that Hartford can boast a surprising collection in this field. The emphasis is not however on the standard masters, such as Rembrandt and Frans Hals, but on the excellent work of minor masters from the beginning and end of the 17th century.

LITERATURE: cat. Hartford 1978; Sutton 1986

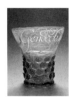

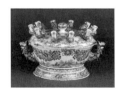

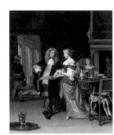

30
[see p. 56]
Berkemeyer with diamond-point engraving by Anna Roemers Visscher (1583-1651)
Dark-green glass, h. 22 cm
Above the foot: *Anna Roemers heeft dit tot een teken van vrintschap geschreeven voor den Eedelen Heere Loduvicus de Romer Anno 1642*
Inv. no. 1904.446

LITERATURE:
Smit 1990, p. 51; cat. Hamburg 1995, no. 93

PROVENANCE:
L. de Romer, Antwerp (mid-17th century); K. Thewalt, Cologne; sale Cologne, 5/XI/1903; gift of Th. Heye at Hamburg, 1904

1904

108
[see p. 162]
Round tulip vase, c. 1680-1690
Blue-painted faience, h. 35 cm, w. 60 cm
Inv. no. 1891-282

LITERATURE:
Lunsingh Scheurleer 1984, pp. 87-88

PROVENANCE:
acquired from Max Wollman, Berlin, 1891

1891

180
[see p. 269]
Eglon van der Neer
(Amsterdam 1635/1636-Düsseldorf 1703)
Elegant couple in an interior
Canvas 85.5 x 70.1 cm
On the left above the door:
Eglon van der Neer fc. 1678
Private collection, on loan to Wadsworth Atheneum, Hartford

LITERATURE:
Hofstede de Groot 1907-28, vol. 5, no. 97; exhib. cat. Philadelphia-Berlin-London 1984, no. 82

PROVENANCE:
Van Diemen, Amsterdam, 1769; sale G. Braamcamp, Amsterdam 31/VII/1771, no. 147; Henry Philip Hope, 1833; his nephew, Henry Thomas Hope of Deepdene, 1839; Lord Henry Francis Pelham-Clinton-Hope, later 8th Duke of Newcastle-under-Lyme, 1887; Asher Wertheimer, 1898; sale Adolf Gaerz, London (Christie's), 8/III/1902, no. 79 (withdrawn); sale Sir Joseph B. Robinson, London (Christie's), 6/VII/1923, no. 76 (bought back); by descent to Ida Princess Labia and Count N.A.D. Labia; sale Robinson, London (Sotheby's), 6/XII/1989, no. 101; M. Jaime Ortiz-Patiño, Switzerland

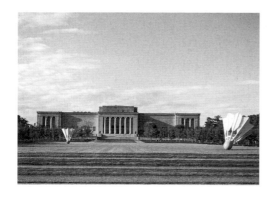

KANSAS CITY,
THE NELSON-ATKINS MUSEUM OF ART

The museum, opened in 1933, is one of the most important museums in the United States. In addition to an especially important collection of Chinese and Oriental art, it has a collection of European old masters of high quality. Seventeenth-century Dutch painting is well represented, with paintings by Pieter Claesz, Aelbert Cuyp, Frans Hals, Rembrandt and others. Recent acquisitions have leaned heavily towards the Mannerists.

LITERATURE: Sutton 1986; cat. Kansas City 1988; exhib. cat. The Hague-San Francisco 1990-91; cat. Kansas City 1993

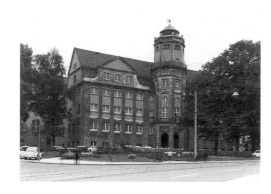

KASSEL, HESSISCHES LANDESMUSEUM

This regional museum displays, among other things, the collection of decorative art which belonged to the landgraves of Hessen. It was Prince Wilhelm of Hessen, from 1730 onwards Landgrave Wilhelm VIII, who brought together this impressive collection of paintings between 1722 and 1756. Along with other collections, this collection – in which 17th-century Dutch art plays the main role – was put on display to the public in the Museum Fredericianum by his son Friedrich II in 1779. In 1924 the collection of decorative art was separated from the rest and housed in the Hessisches Landesmuseum.

LITERATURE: Schmidberger 1988

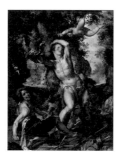

6
[see p. 20]
Joachim Wtewael
(Utrecht 1566-Utrecht 1638)
St Sebastian
Canvas 169.5 x 124.8 cm
On the stone at the left: *JOACHIM WTEN/WAEL. FECIT/1600*
Inv. no. F84-71

LITERATURE:
Lowenthal 1986, no. A 35; exhib. cat. The Hague-San Francisco 1990-91, no. 73; exhib. cat. Amsterdam 1993-94, no. 228; exhib. cat. San Francisco-Baltimore-London 1997-98, no. 2

PROVENANCE:
sale Hadfield & Burrowes, London, 10/V/1785, no. 79; Philip Hill, London, until 1807; sale London (Christie's), 20/VI/1807, no. 44; art dealer Michael Bryan, London, 1807; Sir Edward Cockburn, Herefordshire, until 1903, sale London (Christie's), 25/IV/1903, no. 139; Van der Perre, Paris, 1905-1906; art dealer S.A. l'Antiquaille, Paris, 1937; P. Graupe, Paris, 1938; sale Monaco (Sotheby's), 25/VI/1984, no. 3305; art dealer Bruno Meissner, Zürich together with Newhouse Galleries, New York, 1984; purchased in 1984

1984

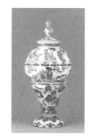

106
[see p. 160]
Large covered vase, c. 1680-1690
Blue-painted faience, h. 95.5 cm
Inv. no. 34/1927

LITERATURE:
exhib. cat. Frankfurt 1988-89, no. 87

PROVENANCE:
purchased in 1927 from Seligsberger at Würzburg

1927

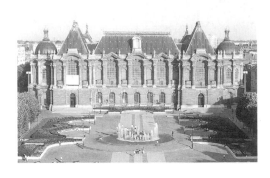

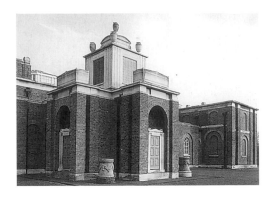

LILLE, MUSÉE DES BEAUX-ARTS

The museum in Lille is one of the most important French provincial museums. It was founded in 1801 and has been housed since 1892 in the present monumental building. The basis of the collection was formed in the 19th century with the aid of gifts and purchases, and this is true in particular of the extensive collection of 17th-century Flemish and Dutch paintings, which features works by minor masters.

LITERATURE: exhib. cat. Lille 1985; exhib. cat. New York 1992-93

LONDON, DULWICH PICTURE GALLERY

The Dulwich Picture Gallery, the oldest public museum in England, was built in 1812 by Sir John Soane. The collection, which was partly acquired by the English art dealers Desenfans and Bourgeois for the king of Poland in the 1790s, was bequeathed by Bourgeois to Dulwich College in 1811, when the sale of the collection was unsuccessful owing to the king's abdication. The collection of paintings, with Italian, French (Poussin, Lorrain), Spanish (Murillo), Flemish (Van Dyck, Rubens) and Dutch paintings, gives a fine picture of the taste of late 18th-century collectors. Of all the beautiful 17th-century Dutch paintings in this collection, Rembrandt's *Girl at a window* of 1645 is the most famous.

LITERATURE: cat. London 1980; cat. London 1994a; cat. London 1998

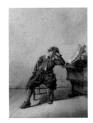 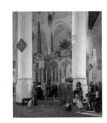

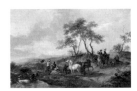

36
[*see p. 63*]
Pieter Codde
(Amsterdam 1599-Amsterdam 1678)
A young student at his desk:
Melancholy, c. 1630-1633
Panel 46 x 34 cm
Lower right on the desk: *CP*
Inv. no. 240

LITERATURE:
exhib. cat. Amsterdam 1971, no. 16;
exhib. cat. Philadelphia-Berlin-London
1984, no. 27; exhib. cat. New York
1992-93, no. 13; exhib. cat. Frankfurt
1993-94, no. 21

PROVENANCE:
private collection, Utrecht; Antoine
Brasseur (1819-1886), Cologne; bequest
Antoine Brasseur, 1885

1885

79
[*see p. 127*]
Emanuel de Witte
(Alkmaar c. 1616-Amsterdam
1691/1692)
View of the tomb of Willem the Silent
in the New Church in Delft
Canvas 97 x 85 cm
Lower left: *E. de Witte/A⁰ 1656*
Inv. no. 236

LITERATURE:
Manke 1963, no. 27; Liedtke 1982,
p. 88; Jantzen 1979, no. 617; exhib.
cat. Rotterdam 1991, no. 38; exhib.
cat. New York 1992-93, no. 16

PROVENANCE:
sale Daniël Marsbag, Amsterdam,
30/IX/1775, no. 123; sale Luchtmans,
Rotterdam, 20/IV/1816, no. 167; sale
Count of Schönborn, Paris, 17/V/1867,
no. 133; sale Gustave Rothan, Paris,
29/V/1890, no. 119; art dealer Morhange,
Paris, 1890; purchased with the aid of the
Antoine Brasseur Fund, 1890

1890

178
[*see p. 266*]
Philips Wouwermans
(Haarlem 1619-Haarlem 1668)
Halt of a hunting party, c. 1665
Canvas 55.6 x 82.9 cm
Lower right: *PHLS W*
Inv. no. 78

LITERATURE:
Hofstede de Groot 1907-28, vol. 2, no.
659; cat. London 1994a, no. 37

PROVENANCE:
Duc d'Orléans, Paris, 1739; sale
J. Danser Nijman, Amsterdam,
16/VIII/1797, no. 303; Noël Desenfans,
London; Sir P.F. Bourgeois, London;
bequest Bourgeois, 1811

1811

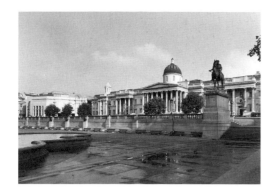

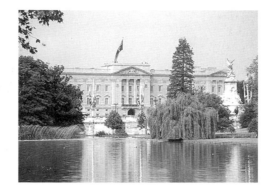

LONDON, NATIONAL GALLERY

LONDON & WINDSOR, H.M. QUEEN ELIZABETH II

The museum, founded in 1824, differs from most other large museums in that it was not originally a royal collection, but took shape through the acquisition of private collections. Most of the 17th-century Dutch paintings come from the collections of Sir Robert Peel (1788-1850), Wynn Ellis (1790-1875) and George Salting (1836-1909). Salting's collection contained works by Hals, Saenredam and Vermeer, whereas the National Gallery's Dutch collection until that time had been characterised by the essentially 18th-century taste of the first two collectors named. In the 20th century the collection has been augmented by means of valuable gifts and carefully chosen purchases, such as the work shown here by Ter Brugghen.

The British royal collection is the largest and most diverse private collection in the world, with Dutch painting being exceptionally well represented. As early as the 17th century there were many artistic contacts between the British royal house and Holland. During the reign of Stadholder-King Willem III (1650-1702) many examples of decorative art were produced for English palaces, such as the tulip vases which Willem III ordered for Hampton Court. The collecting of Dutch painting experienced its heyday during the reign of George IV (1762-1830). The high point of his collecting activities was the purchase of 86 paintings from the collection of Sir Thomas Baring (1772-1848), which included the works by Berchem and Ter Borch exhibited here.

LITERATURE: cat. London 1991; cat. London 1995

LITERATURE: exhib. cat. London 1971-72; White 1982

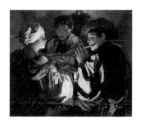

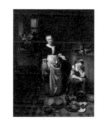

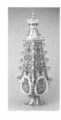

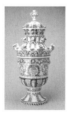

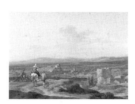

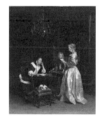

24
[see p. 50]
Hendrick ter Brugghen
(The Hague ? 1588-Utrecht 1629)
The concert, c. 1626-1627
Canvas 99.1 x 116.8 cm
Inv. no. 6483

LITERATURE:
Nicolson 1958, no. A37; exhib. cat.
Utrecht-Braunschweig 1986-87, no. 23;
cat. London 1991, vol. 1, no. 6483;
exhib. cat. San Francisco-Baltimore-
London 1997-98, no. 40

PROVENANCE:
Lord Chancellor Somers (1651-1716),
c. 1700; Lord Somers; the Hon. Mrs E.
Hervey-Bathurst, Eastnor Castle,
Ledbury, by descent; art dealer, 1982;
purchased with the aid of the National
Heritage Memorial Fund, the Pilgrim
Trust and the National Art Collections
Fund, 1983

1983

118
[see p. 175]
Nicolaes Maes
(Dordrecht 1634-Amsterdam 1693)
The sleeping kitchen maid
Panel 70 x 53.3 cm
Lower right: *N. MAES. 1655.*
(MAE in monogram)
Inv. no. 207

LITERATURE:
exhib. cat. Amsterdam 1976, no. 33;
exhib. cat. London 1978-79, no. 23; cat.
London 1991, vol. 1, no. 207; Sumowski
1983-94, vol. 3, no. 1352

PROVENANCE:
purchased in Leiden by Dr Sanderus;
acquired by C.J. Nieuwenhuys in 1823
in Amsterdam and sold in Paris; art
dealer John Smith; Richard Simmons,
1833; bequest Richard Simmons, 1847

1847

195
[see p. 284]
Pottery 'De Grieksche A' under the
supervision of Adriaen Kocks
*Two tulip vases with the arms of
Willem III*, c. 1690-1700
Blue-painted faience, h. 102 cm
and 98 cm
Marked: AK (Adriaen Kocks)
Hampton Court
Inv. nos. 1084 and 1082

LITERATURE:
exhib. cat. New York-Pittsburgh
1988-89, pp. 32, 34

PROVENANCE:
commissioned by Willem III for
Hampton Court Palace

c. 1690-1700

93
[see p. 145]
Nicolaes Berchem
(Haarlem 1620-Amsterdam 1683)
Italian landscape with mountain plateau
Panel 33 x 44.1 cm
Lower left: *Berghem/1655*
Inv. no. 3213

LITERATURE:
Schaar 1958, pp. 42, 46, 57; exhib. cat.
Utrecht 1965, no. 77; exhib. cat. London
1971-72, no. 44; White 1982, no. 20

PROVENANCE:
sale F.I. Dufresne, Amsterdam,
22/VIII/1770, no. 225; sale J.J. de Bruijn,
Amsterdam, 12/IX/1798, no. 6 (sold to
Yver); acquired by George IV as part of
the Baring collection, 1814

1814

121
[see p. 178]
Gerard ter Borch
(Zwolle 1617-Deventer 1681)
The letter, c. 1660-1662
Canvas 81.9 x 68 cm
Probably previously signed on the letter
Inv. no. 1406

LITERATURE:
Gudlaugsson 1959-60, vol. 2, no. 169;
exhib. cat. London 1971-72, no. 26;
exhib. cat. The Hague 1974, no. 47;
White 1982, no. 29

PROVENANCE:
sale Beaujon, Paris, 25/IV/1787, no. 35;
sale Jan Gildemeester, Amsterdam,
11/VI/1800, no. 28; Sir Francis Baring;
acquired by George IV as part of the
Baring collection, 1814

1814

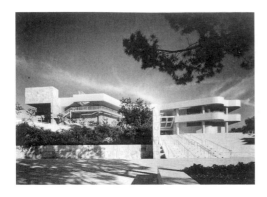

LOS ANGELES, THE J. PAUL GETTY MUSEUM

The museum was founded in 1954 by the oil magnate John Paul Getty, having as its core his collection of antique sculpture, as well as European painting, sculpture and decorative art. Since the 1980s the museum has enjoyed spectacular growth thanks to substantial funding. Although limited in size (c. 50 works), the collection of 17th-century Dutch painting is especially fine and diverse. Most of the well-known masters, as well as various minor masters, are represented by excellent and well-preserved paintings. The museum, which was originally in Malibu, has been housed since 1997 in a spectacular building designed by the architect Richard Meier.

LITERATURE: Sutton 1986; cat. Los Angeles 1997

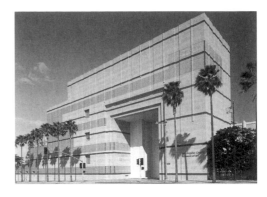

LOS ANGELES, LOS ANGELES COUNTY MUSEUM OF ART

The museum, founded in 1910, blossomed after the Second World War, an important part of the collection of old masters being purchased in recent decades. Seventeenth-century Dutch painting is well represented, with paintings by Rembrandt, Frans Hals and others, as well as more recently acquired masterpieces by Goltzius, Honthorst, Van Beyeren and Sweerts. It is expected that the small but beautiful collection of 17th-century Dutch painting which was collected by Mr and Mrs Carter in the 1960s and 1970s will be given a place in the museum.

LITERATURE: Sutton 1986; cat. Los Angeles 1987

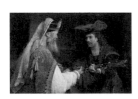

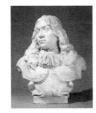

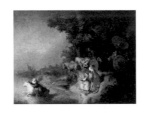

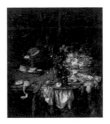

149
[see p. 218]
Arent de Gelder
(Dordrecht 1645-Dordrecht 1727)
*Ahimelech giving the sword of
Goliath to David*, c. 1680-1690
Canvas 90 x 132 cm
Centre, on the wall: *A de Gelder f.*
Inv. no. 78.PA.219

LITERATURE:
exhib. cat. Dordrecht 1992-93, no. 39;
Von Moltke 1994, no. 20

PROVENANCE:
Ethel Bannerman, Countess of Southesk;
sale Countess of Southesk *et al.*, London
(Christie's), 19/VI/1942, no. 20; Mrs
J.L. Motion; sale G.W. Andrews *et al.*,
London (Sotheby's), 23/III/1960, no. 139;
J. Paul Getty, Sutton Place

1960

168b
[see p. 249]
Rombout Verhulst
(Mechelen 1624-The Hague 1698)
Portrait of Jacob van Reygersbergh
(1625-1675)
Marble h. 63 cm
On the left side of the socle: *Anno 1671,
rechts: R. Verhulst fec.*, on the front:
Mea sorte contentus. On the back an
inscription added by a later hand: *DIT IS
HET AFBEELTSEL VAN JACOB VAN
REIGERSBERGH, GEBOREN IN MIDDEL-
BURGH DEN .X.APRIL.1625. WEGENS DE
PROVINTIE VAN ZEELANT GEDEPU-
TEERDT TER VERGADERINGH VAN HAER
HOOGHMOGENDHEDEN, DEN .17.7BER
DES IAERS 1663 STURF DEN .29.APRIL 1675*
Inv. no. 84.SA.743

LITERATURE:
Scholten 1991

PROVENANCE:
Paul Lebaudy, Paris, 1900-1984; Alain
Moatti, Paris, 1984; purchased in 1984

1984

53
[see p. 86]
Rembrandt
(Leiden 1606-Amsterdam 1669)
The abduction of Europa
Panel 62.2 x 77 cm
On a brown stone to the right of the
woman standing: *RHL van/Ryn. 1632*
Inv. no. 95.PB.7

LITERATURE:
Bruyn *et al.* 1982-89, vol. 2, no. A 47;
cat. Los Angeles 1997, p. 118

PROVENANCE:
most likely in the collection of Jacques
Specx (1588/1589-1652); sale Comtesse
de Verrue, Paris, 27/III/1737, no. 87; sale
Paris, 21/XI/1793, no. 18; Duc de
Morny; sale Paris, 31/V/1865, no. 70;
Princesse de Broglie née Say, Paris, c.
1909; art dealer Thomas Agnew & Sons,
London; Leopold Koppel, Berlin;
acquired in 1995

1995

128
[see p. 188]
Abraham van Beyeren
(The Hague 1620/1621-Overschie 1690)
Sumptuous still life
Canvas 141.5 x 122 cm
On the wall above the centre in grey:
.AVB f./1667.
Inv. no. M.86.96

LITERATURE:
exhib. cat. Delft-Cambridge-Fort Worth
1988-89, no. 52

PROVENANCE:
Pietro Camuccini, Rome, until 1833;
Giovanni Battista Camuccini, Rome,
until 1856; 4th Duke of
Northumberland, Alnwick Castle;
Algernon Percy, since 1865; Gallery
Agnew, London; Gallery Herbert
Shickman, New York; gift of the
Ahmanson Foundation, 1986

1986

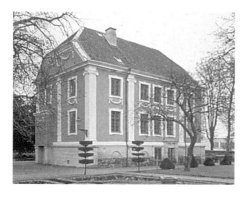

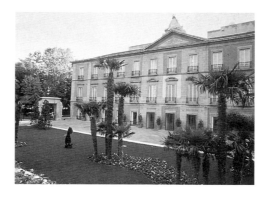

LUND, MUSEUM OF CULTURAL HISTORY, KULTUREN

In this Swedish ethnological open-air museum a collection of pottery was assembled between the two World Wars which contains several hundred pieces of Delftware.

MADRID, MUSEO THYSSEN-BORNEMISZA

The core of this collection of European old masters was gathered together in the first decades of the 20th century by Baron Heinrich Thyssen-Bornemisza and has been added to continually by his son Hans Heinrich. In 1937 the collection was already open to the public in Switzerland in the Villa Favorita in Catagnola near Lugano. Since 1991 the collection has been given a permanent home in the Villahermosa Palace in Madrid. Within the splendid overview of European painting given by the collection, 17th-century Dutch art is represented in an extremely varied way with 76 paintings.

LITERATURE: cat. Madrid 1990; cat. Madrid 1992

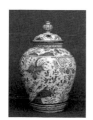

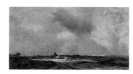

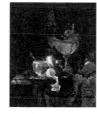

107
[see p. 161]
Large covered jar, c. 1635
Blue-painted faience, h. 50 cm
Inv. no. KM 24166

LITERATURE:
cat. Lund 1963; Van Dam 1989, pp. 6-7

PROVENANCE:
acquired in 1915

82
[see p. 132]
Jacob van Ruisdael
(Haarlem 1628/1629-Amsterdam 1682)
View of Naarden
Panel 34.8 x 67 cm
Lower left: *JvRuisdael 1647*
(JvR in ligature)
Inv. no. 1930.99

LITERATURE:
Rosenberg 1928, no. 73; exhib. cat.
The Hague-Cambridge 1981-82, no. 6;
cat. Madrid 1990, no. 86

PROVENANCE:
Lady Theodora Guest (née Grosvenor,
died 1924), Inwood House, Somerset; (?)
among the works she sold privately to
art dealer Robert Langton Douglas,
London, in or shortly before 1917; art
dealer Matthiesen, Berlin; acquired by
Baron Heinrich Thyssen-Bornemisza, in
or before 1928

129
[see p. 189]
Willem Kalf
(Rotterdam 1619-Amsterdam 1693)
*Still life with Chinese bowl and
nautilus cup*
Canvas 79.4 x 67.3 cm
Upper left: *W. KALF Fecit*; upper right:
Ao 1662
Inv. no. 1962.10

LITERATURE:
Grisebach 1974, no. 117; exhib. cat.
Delft-Cambridge-Fort Worth 1988-89, no.
55; cat. Madrid 1990, no. 10; exhib. cat.
Amsterdam-Cleveland 1999-2000, no. 50

PROVENANCE:
sale Pieter van den Bogaerde, Amsterdam,
16/III/1778, no. 43; (?) Count Alexis
Orlov-Denisov, St Petersburg; Michel van
Gelder, Ukkel, 1911; art dealer Daniel
Katz, Dieren, 1935; H.E. ten Cate,
Oldenzaal, 1938; purchased from the Ten
Cate estate by Hans Heinrich Thyssen-
Bornemisza, Lugano, 1962

1915

1928

1962

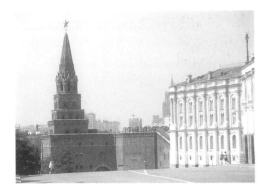

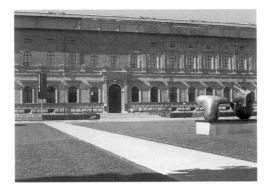

MOSCOW, KREMLIN MUSEUM

The armoury of the Kremlin Museum in Moscow houses an important collection of 17th-century Dutch silver, including works by the Amsterdam silversmiths Jan van der Veld, Johannes Grill and Hans Coenraet Breghtel. Most of these objects were presented as gifts to the Russian tsar.

LITERATURE: Voyce 1954; exhib. cat. New York-Paris 1979-80; exhib. cat. Rotterdam 1995-96

MUNICH, ALTE PINAKOTHEK

The Alte Pinakothek was founded in 1823 by the Bavarian king, Ludwig I. The present building, designed by the architect Leo Klenze, was opened in 1838. In the early 19th century the Hofgalerie at Munich contained three important 18th-century royal collections: the one from Düsseldorf, another from Carlsberg Castle in Zweibrücken and that of Mannheim. These impressive collections were enlarged in the 19th and 20th centuries through acquisitions. In 1969, for example, an imposing full-length portrait of Willem van Heythuysen by Frans Hals was acquired from the Liechtenstein collection for the museum's collection of Dutch masters. Much of the impressive collection of 17th-century Dutch painting stems from the 18th-century Düsseldorf collection, including the Passion series by Rembrandt and many cabinet pieces by the *fijnschilders*.

LITERATURE: cat. Munich 1967; cat. Munich 1983; An der Heiden 1998

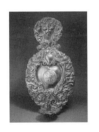

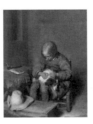

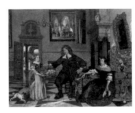

71
[see p. 116]
Hans Coenraet Breghtel
(Nürnberg 1608/1609-The Hague 1675)
Sconce
Silver, chased, punched and parcel-gilt,
h. 92.5 cm
Marked: assay office mark The Hague;
year letter R = 1647; maker's mark CB =
H.C. Breghtel
Inv. nos. MZ-139 and MZ-141

LITERATURE:
exhib. cat. Amsterdam-Moscow 1989,
no. 85; exhib. cat. Rotterdam 1995-96,
no. 85

PROVENANCE:
one of the Dutch diplomatic gifts dating
from 1648

1648

120
[see p. 177]
Gerard ter Borch
(Zwolle 1617-Deventer 1681)
Boy de-fleaing a dog, c. 1655
Canvas 34.4 x 27.1 cm
Lower left: *GTB* (in ligature)
Inv. no. 589

LITERATURE:
Gudlaugsson 1959-60, vol. 2, no. 116;
cat. Munich 1967, pp. 82-85; exhib. cat.
The Hague 1974, no. 35a; cat. Munich
1983, p. 77

PROVENANCE:
sale J.F. d'Orvielle, Amsterdam,
15/VI/1705, no. 42; Gemäldegalerie
Düsseldorf (acquired before 1742);
Gemäldegalerie Mannheim; Hofgalerie
Munich (since 1799); Alte Pinakothek,
Munich

1742

110
[see p. 164]
Emanuel de Witte
(Alkmaar c. 1616-Amsterdam
1691/1692)
Portrait of a family in an interior
Canvas 68.5 x 86.5 cm
Lower left: *E. De Witte A⁰ 1678*
Inv. no. FV 2

LITERATURE:
exhib. cat. Amsterdam 1952, no. 183;
Manke 1963, no. 10; Van Eeghen 1976;
cat. Munich 1983, pp. 571-72

PROVENANCE:
(?) sale Hobbs, London, 9-10/V/1763,
no. 14; F. Gibson, 1852; in any case
until 1963 in the collection of the latter's
grandson Lewis S. Fry; art dealer Terry-
Engell, London, 1970; acquired in 1972

1972

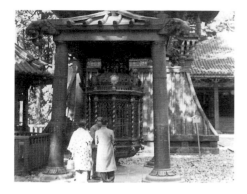

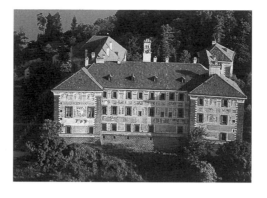

NIKKO (JAPAN), TOSHOGU

Near the Yomeimon Arch in the temple complex of Nikko are housed a number of gifts presented in the 1640s by the Dutch East India Company to the Japanese shogun. These comprise a copper lantern (presented in 1643), twelve sonces with candlesticks and the candelabrum exhibited here (presented in 1640).

LITERATURE: Lunsingh Scheurleer 1979

NELAHOZEVES (CZECH REPUBLIC), NELAHOZEVES CASTLE, THE LOBKOWICZ COLLECTIONS

The collections were restored to the Lobkowicz family in 1990 and the years following and housed in Nelahozeves, one of the smaller castles belonging to the family (slightly north of Prague). The marriage of Eleonora Carolina Countess of Lobkowicz (1685-1720) to her cousin Philip Hyacinth, 4th Prince Lobkowicz (1680-1734) caused the transfer of all the art treasures collected by her father, Wenzel Ferdinand, to this branch of the family. It now forms an important part of the art traditionally found in the Czech Republic, including paintings by Lucas Cranach, Pieter Bruegel I (*Haymaking*), Veronese, Rubens, Velazquez and Canaletto. The castle contains an extensive collection of decorative art, including the dinner service ordered by Wenzel Ferdinand around 1685 in Delft.

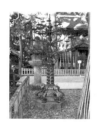

72
[see p. 117]
Joost Gerritsz
(Amsterdam 1598-Amsterdam 1652)
Candelabrum, c. 1640
Copper h. 345 cm

LITERATURE:
Lunsingh Scheurleer 1979

PROVENANCE:
gift presented by the Dutch East India
Company to the shogun, 1640

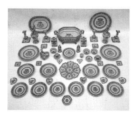

197
[see p. 286]
Pottery 'De Metalen Pot' under the
supervision of Lambertus Cleffius
Selection from the Lobkowicz service,
c. 1685
Blue-painted faience
Marked: *LC*

PROVENANCE:
Ordered by Wenzel Ferdinand
Lobkowicz around 1685 in Delft

1640

c. 1685

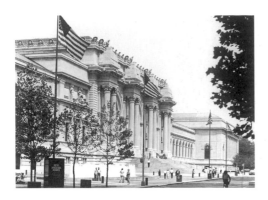

NEW YORK, THE METROPOLITAN MUSEUM

The museum, which opened in 1870, has one of the largest and most varied collections in the world. The Van Goyen exhibited here was purchased in 1871, though most of the 17th-century Dutch paintings were presented to the museum as gifts in the 20th century. There are no fewer than 23 paintings by Rembrandt, 10 by Frans Hals, 5 by Vermeer, 8 by De Hooch and 7 by Ter Borch, most of them given to the museum by such New York collectors as B. Altman (1913), H.O. Havemeijer (1929), M. Friedsam (1931) and Robert Lehman (1975). Through purchases, the most spectacular of which was Rembrandt's *Aristotle* (1961), the rather traditional collection of Dutch art has been enriched in recent decades with paintings by the Mannerists, the Caravaggisti, and the Italianate painters.

LITERATURE: Sutton 1986; exhib. cat. The Hague-San Francisco 1990-91; cat. New York 1995

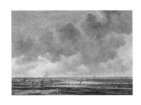

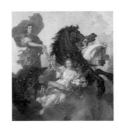

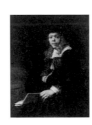

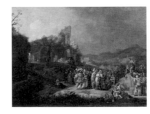

83
[see p. 133]
Jan van Goyen
(Leiden 1596-The Hague 1656)
View of the Haarlemmermeer
Panel 34.6 x 50.5 cm
Lower left: *VG 1646*
Inv. no. 71.62

LITERATURE:
Beck 1972-87, vol. 2, no. 980

PROVENANCE:
sale Paris, 16/IV/1811, no. 69; Count Cornet, Brussels; W. Burger, Paris; acquired in 1871

1871

200
[see p. 291]
Gerard de Lairesse
(Liège 1640-Amsterdam 1711)
Apollo and Aurora
Canvas 204.5 x 193 cm
Lower left: *G. Lairesse f/1671*
Inv. no. 43.118

LITERATURE:
Roy 1992, no. p.67

PROVENANCE:
American Art Galleries, New York, c. 1900; Mrs James D. Goin, New York, 1904; M.E. and E.G. Rionda, Alpine, New Jersey; their gift to the museum, 1943

1943

150
[see p. 219]
Rembrandt
(Leiden 1606-Amsterdam 1669)
Portrait of Gerard de Lairesse,
c. 1665-1667
Canvas 112.7 x 87.6 cm
Lower left: *Rembrandt*
Robert Lehman Collection
Inv. no. 1975.1.40

LITERATURE:
exhib. cat. Amsterdam 1952, no. 150; Haak 1969, pp. 316-17; Tümpel 1993, no. 222; exhib. cat. New York 1995-96, no. 19

PROVENANCE:
sale Amsterdam, 16/VI/1802, no. 144; sale London, 13/VI/1807, no. 16; sale London, 1908; art dealer Lewis & Simmons, London; Leopold Koppel, Berlin; purchased by Robert Lehman in 1945, since 1975 in the museum

1975

91
[see p. 143]
Bartholomeus Breenbergh
(Deventer 1599-Amsterdam 1657)
The preaching of John the Baptist
Panel 54.5 x 75 cm
Lower right: *B.B.f.A 1634*
Inv. no. 1991.305

LITERATURE:
Roethlisberger 1981, no. 165; exhib. cat. The Hague-San Francisco 1990-91, no. 14

PROVENANCE:
sale Amsterdam, 1708; sale Amsterdam, 1709; sale Johan van der Marck, Amsterdam, 1773; sale Randon de Boisset, Paris, 1777; sale Vaudreuil, Paris, 1784; sale Paris, 1802; sale Scarisbrick, London, 1861; sale Bohn, London, 1885; sale London, 1902; sale baron Kuffner de Dioszegh, New York, 1948; art dealer Paul Drey, New York, 1948-1951(?); Walter P. Chrysler Jr., New York, 1951(?)-after 1958; art dealer M.R. Schweitzer, New York, 1969; Richard L. Feigen, New York, 1977; purchased in 1991

1991

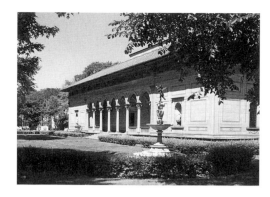

OBERLIN (OHIO), ALLEN MEMORIAL ART MUSEUM

This modest university museum owes part of its fame to several 17th-century Dutch masterpieces, such as the Ter Brugghen exhibited here, a lovely wooded landscape by Hobbema and a self-portrait by Sweerts. Most of the works – which were bought on the advice of Wolfgang Stechow, a specialist in the field of 17th-century Dutch painting and professor at Oberlin – were purchased in the 1950s and 1960s.

LITERATURE: Sutton 1986; exhib. cat. The Hague-San Francisco 1990-91; cat. Oberlin 1998

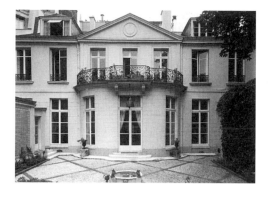

PARIS, COLLECTION FRITS LUGT, INSTITUT NÉERLANDAIS

In 1953 the collection of Frits Lugt was brought to the Institut Néerlandais in Paris. It contains, among other things, just under a hundred 17th-century Dutch paintings, most of them collected by Frits Lugt (1884-1970) between 1918 and 1970. The emphasis is on the traditional genres such as landscape, portrait and still life, most paintings being of a modest size. In addition to the work of well-known artists such as Saenredam and Ruisdael, it is the minor masters in particular who are represented by works of outstanding quality.

LITERATURE: Sutton 1976; exhib. cat. Paris 1983; Van Berge-Gerbaud 1997

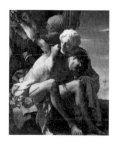

7

[see p. 21]
Hendrick ter Brugghen
(The Hague ? 1588-Utrecht 1629)
St Sebastian, 1625
Canvas 150.2 x 120 cm
To the right of the three hands at the
upper left: *HTBrugesn fe 16(25)*
(unclearly dated)
Oberlin College, R.T. Miller, Jr. Fund
Inv. no. 53.256

LITERATURE:
Nicolson 1958, no. A54; exhib. cat.
Utrecht-Braunschweig 1986-87, no. 20;
exhib. cat. San Francisco-Baltimore-
London 1997-98, no. 10

PROVENANCE:
probably Pieter Fris, Amsterdam, before
1668; (?) Jan de Wale, Amsterdam, after
1668; sale Jan de Wale, Amsterdam,
12/V/1706, no. 43; art dealer Rolan
Robert, Nice, 1952; art dealer F. Mont,
New York, 1953

1953

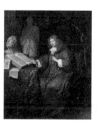

182

[see p. 271]
Caspar Netscher
(Heidelberg 1635/1636-
The Hague 1684)
Portrait of Abraham van Lennep
Canvas 55 x 45.3 cm
On the crossbar of the chair:
CNetscher 1672
Inv. no. 1976-S.1

LITERATURE:
exhib. cat. Paris 1983, no. 56; exhib.
cat. Amsterdam 1989-90, no. 35;
Wieseman 1993, no. 107; cat. Paris
1994, no. 129

PROVENANCE:
Abraham van Lennep, Amsterdam
(1627-1678); presumably the latter's
brother Jacob van Lennep (1631-1704);
the latter's great-granddaughter
Catharina van Lennep (1726-1793) and
her husband Leonard Thomas Vogel
(died 1794), by descent; sale of their
estate, Amsterdam 20/X/1794, no. 8; sale
Cardinal Fesch, Rome 17-18/III/1845,
no. 168; Charles Moret-Saint-Hilaire
(died 1849), Paris; the latter's sale, Paris
12/II/1857, no. 17; appearing three times
in a sale of paintings from the collection
of Marquis Du Blaisel: Paris,
16-17/III/1870, no. 89, London
17-18/V/1872, no. 141 and Paris,
9-10/V/1873, no. 79; J. & A. Le Roy,
Brussels; Charles Rutten, 1892; J.P. de
Meulenmeester, Brussels, 1975;
purchased with the aid of the Rembrandt
Society, 1976

1976

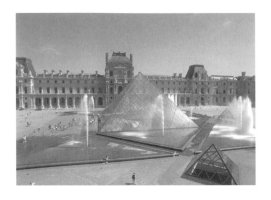

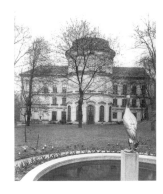

PARIS, MUSÉE DU LOUVRE

The basis of the collection of paintings in the Louvre was laid by a succession of French kings from the 16th century until late in the 18th century. Examples of Dutch painting collected already in the 17th century by Louis XIV include a *Self-portrait* by Rembrandt and a work by Gerard Dou. Most of the 17th-century Dutch paintings were acquired in the 18th century by Louis XVI, who had a predilection for the *fijnschilders* and the Italianate painters. Purchases and gifts, including the La Caze collection (1869) with Rembrandt's *Bathsheba* and Hals's *Bohémienne*, enabled the collection to expand greatly in the 19th and 20th centuries. Since 1994, an extensive collection of 17th-century Dutch painting has been exhibited in eight galleries in the Richelieu wing of the Louvre.

LITERATURE: exhib. cat. Paris 1970-71; exhib. cat. Amsterdam 1971; cat. Paris 1979; Foucart *et al.* 1995

PRAGUE, NÁRODNÍ-GALERIE

The present-day national museum was created in 1945, when the state collections of old and modern painting were merged. In 1796 a society of friends founded a picture gallery in the art academy, for which Emperor Leopold I put a number of paintings from the castle at Prague at their disposal, including a triptych by Geertgen tot St Jans. Purchases and gifts, including some by the Prince of Liechtenstein, enabled the collection to expand in the late 19th and 20th century. The collection of 17th-century Dutch paintings is dominated by the minor masters.

LITERATURE: exhib. cat. Bruges 1974

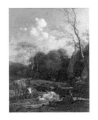

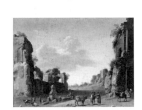

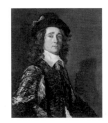

99
[see p. 151]
Karel Dujardin
(Amsterdam 1622-Venice 1678)
Cows and sheep at a stream,
c. 1655-1656
Canvas 52 x 43 cm
Lower right: *K.DU.IARDIN.fe*
(N in reverse)
Inv. no. 1397

LITERATURE:
exhib. cat. Utrecht 1965, no. 120; exhib. cat. Amsterdam 1971, no. 36; cat. Paris 1979, p. 50; Kilian 1994, no. 32

PROVENANCE:
sale Antony Sijdervelt, Amsterdam, 23/IV/1766, no. 18; sale Gerrit Braamcamp, Amsterdam, 31/VII/1771, no. 99; sale Pieter Locquet, Amsterdam, 22-24/IX/1783, no. 166 (sold to Yver for Louis XVI, Paris)

1783

90
[see p. 142]
Cornelis van Poelenburch
(Utrecht c. 1594-Utrecht 1667)
View of the Campo Vaccino
Copper 40 x 54.5 cm
Dated on the fountain: *MDCXX.*
Inv. no. 1084

LITERATURE:
exhib. cat. Utrecht 1965, no. 11; cat. Paris 1979, p. 105; Sluijter-Seijffert 1984, no. 157; exhib. cat. Dordrecht-Leeuwarden 1988-89, no. 10; exhib. cat. Cologne-Utrecht 1991-92, no. 28.2

PROVENANCE:
confiscated in 1794, together with its pendant (Musée du Louvre, inv. no. 1086), from the possessions of Cathérine de Noailles-De Cossé-Brissac and taken to the Louvre (as Breenbergh)

1794

144
[see p. 210]
Frans Hals
(Antwerp 1582/1583-Haarlem 1666)
Portrait of Jaspar Schade, c. 1645
Canvas 80 x 67.5 cm
Inv. no. O 638

LITERATURE:
Slive 1970-74, vol. 3, no. 168; Damsté 1985; exhib. cat. Washington-London-Haarlem 1989-90, no. 62

PROVENANCE:
almost certainly Jaspar Schade, country house Zandbergen near Utrecht, after 1650; the latter's son Gaspar Cornelis (died 1701); the latter's brother-in-law Jacob Noirot; between 1740 and 1865 sold eight times along with the house; Beuker family, 1865; P.E.H. Praetorius (1791-1876); J.W. Wilson van Brussels; sale J.W. Wilson, Paris, 14/III/1883, no. 58; Johann II, Prince of Liechtenstein, Vienna; gift of the Prince of Liechtenstein, 1890

1890

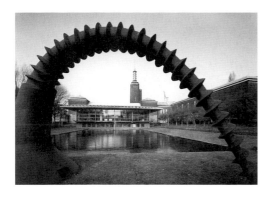

ROTTERDAM,
MUSEUM BOIJMANS VAN BEUNINGEN

The bequest of the collection of F.J.O. Boijmans (1767-1847) formed the basis for the museum which opened in 1849, at that time still located in the Schielandhuis in Rotterdam. A catastrophic fire in 1864 destroyed part of the collection, but purchases and gifts have enabled the collection to grow considerably in the late 19th and 20th century. Since 1935 the museum has been housed in the building designed by Van der Steur. The collection of paintings took on a decidedly international character with the purchase in 1958 of the famous collection belonging to D.G. van Beuningen. In the area of Dutch painting the museum is one of the most important in the Netherlands, and it is also well endowed with a fine collection of sculpture and decorative art.

LITERATURE: cat. Rotterdam 1962; cat. Rotterdam 1972; Ter Molen (red.) 1999

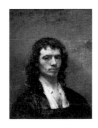

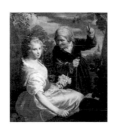

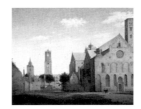

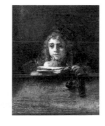

143	29	77	145
[see p. 209]	[see p. 55]	[see p. 125]	[see p. 211]
Carel Fabritius	Paulus Moreelse	Pieter Saenredam	Rembrandt
(Midden-Beemster 1622-Delft 1654)	(Utrecht 1571-Utrecht 1638)	(Assendelft 1597-Haarlem 1665)	(Leiden 1606-Amsterdam 1669)
Self-portrait, c. 1648-1650	*Vertumnus and Pomona*, c. 1625-1630	*View of St Mary's Square with the Church of St Mary in Utrecht*	*Portrait of Titus*, c. 1653-1655
Panel 65 x 49 cm	Canvas 130 x 114 cm	Panel 109.5 x 139.5 cm	Canvas 77 x 63 cm
Upper right in the wet paint: *fabritius f.*	On the pruning knife: *PMoreelse* (last letters difficult to read)	On the arch above the west door of the Church of St Mary: *Pieter Saenredam fecit 1662*	Lower left: *Rembrandt .f.1655* (later hand)
Inv. no. 1205	Inv. no. 1549	Inv. no. 1765	Inv. no. St. 2

143 — [see p. 209]
Carel Fabritius
(Midden-Beemster 1622-Delft 1654)
Self-portrait, c. 1648-1650
Panel 65 x 49 cm
Upper right in the wet paint:
fabritius f.
Inv. no. 1205

LITERATURE:
cat. Rotterdam 1988, no. 7; Brown 1981, no. 4

PROVENANCE:
bequest F.J.O. Boijmans, 1847

29 — [see p. 55]
Paulus Moreelse
(Utrecht 1571-Utrecht 1638)
Vertumnus and Pomona, c. 1625-1630
Canvas 130 x 114 cm
On the pruning knife: *PMoreelse*
(last letters difficult to read)
Inv. no. 1549

LITERATURE:
De Jonge 1938, no. 296; Domela Nieuwenhuis 1989, no. s.40; exhib. cat. Utrecht-Frankfurt-Luxemburg 1993-94, no. 41

PROVENANCE:
purchased by the city of Rotterdam in 1865

77 — [see p. 125]
Pieter Saenredam
(Assendelft 1597-Haarlem 1665)
View of St Mary's Square with the Church of St Mary in Utrecht
Panel 109.5 x 139.5 cm
On the arch above the west door of the Church of St Mary: *Pieter Saenredam fecit 1662*
Inv. no. 1765

LITERATURE:
Jansen 1987; Schwartz and Bok 1989, no. 143; exhib. cat. Rotterdam 1991, no. 26

PROVENANCE:
(?) Mr. Albert Hodshon, Amsterdam; the latter's daughter Cornelia Catharina, in 1814 married to Mr Willem baron Röell, Squire of Hazerswoude, Amsterdam; her sale, Amsterdam, 25/IV/1872, no. 21; where it was acquired by the museum

145 — [see p. 211]
Rembrandt
(Leiden 1606-Amsterdam 1669)
Portrait of Titus, c. 1653-1655
Canvas 77 x 63 cm
Lower left: *Rembrandt .f.1655*
(later hand)
Inv. no. St. 2

LITERATURE:
cat. Rotterdam 1988, no. 22

PROVENANCE:
The Earl of Crawford and Balcarres, Haigh Hall, Wigan; gift of the Rembrandt Society and 120 friends of the museum, 1940

1847

1865

1872

1940

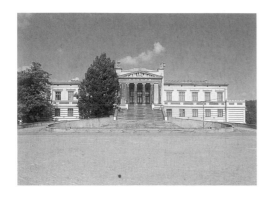

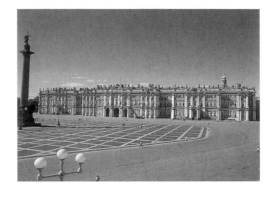

SCHWERIN, STAATLICHES MUSEUM

The basis of the collection, housed since 1882 in the present building, was formed by the collection of the Grand Duke of Meckelenburg, one of the oldest collections of 17th-century Flemish and Dutch painting in Europe. It also contains many works by 18th-century French artists such as Houdon and Oudry, who supplied the Grand Duke directly. A considerable number of the Dutch and Flemish paintings were collected in the second quarter of the 18th century by Duke Christian Ludwig II. Cabinet pieces and still lifes clearly have the upper hand. Among the most famous works are *The sentry* by Carel Fabritius, two round portraits of boys by Frans Hals, *The concert* by Frans van Mieris and the works exhibited here by De Heem and Schalcken.

LITERATURE: cat. Schwerin 1982; cat. Schwerin 1995

ST PETERSBURG, HERMITAGE

The collection of more than 1800 17th-century Dutch and Flemish paintings is one of the most extensive in the world. The first purchases were made by Tsar Peter the Great. With the accession of Catherine the Great in 1762, collecting activities expanded enormously. With the help of emissaries, large numbers of paintings were bought at auction, and some collections were acquired *en bloc* (including those of Count Brühl, Louis-Antoine Crozat, François Tronchin and Robert Walpole). This active acquisitions policy was pursued in the 19th and early 20th century, though on a lesser scale. The Dutch paintings, including more than 20 works by Rembrandt, are displayed in the galleries of the New Hermitage (Leo Klenze, 1840-49).

LITERATURE: Kuznetsov and Linnik 1982; exhib. cat. Rotterdam 1985; exhib. cat. New York-Chicago 1988; exhib. cat. Dijon 1993

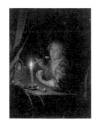

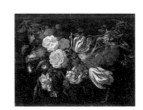

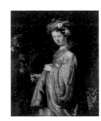

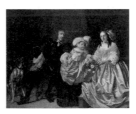

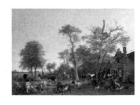

181
[see p. 270]
Godfried Schalcken
(Made 1643-The Hague 1706)
Girl eating an apple, c. 1675-1680
Panel 32.2 x 24.8 cm
Lower left: *G. Schalcken*
Inv. no. 2336

LITERATURE:
Beherman 1988, no. 183; exhib. cat. Amsterdam 1989-90, no. 41

PROVENANCE:
sale Johan van Schuylenburch, The Hague, 20/IX/1735, no. 60; Dukes, later Grand Dukes of Mecklenburg at Schwerin, acquired between 1735 and 1792; probably taken to Paris in 1807 by Napoleon's troops and given back in 1815

1735-1792

127
[see p. 187]
Jan Davidsz de Heem
(Utrecht 1606-Antwerp c. 1684)
Festoon with flowers and fruit, c. 1660-1670
Panel 26.2 x 47.5 cm
Above and to the right of centre, in dark brown: *J.d De Heem f.*
Inv. no. 156

LITERATURE:
exhib. cat. Utrecht-Braunschweig 1991, no. 23

PROVENANCE:
Dukes, later Grand Dukes of Mecklenburg at Schwerin, acquired between 1792 and 1821; probably taken to Paris by Napoleon's troops in 1807 and given back in 1815

1792-1821

57
[see p. 91]
Rembrandt
(Leiden 1606-Amsterdam 1669)
Flora
Canvas 124.7 x 100.4 cm
Lower left: *Rembrandt/f..34*
Inv. no. 732

LITERATURE:
exhib. cat. Rotterdam 1985, no. 22; Bruyn *et al.* 1982-89, vol. 2, no. A 93; exhib. cat. New York-Chicago 1988, no. 22

PROVENANCE:
sale Herman Aarentz, Amsterdam, 11/IV/1770, no. 1 (bought back); (?) sale Paris, 1-23/VII/1771, no. 2; (?) sale Paris, 15/IV/1776, no. 6; Empress Catherine II, acquired between 1770 and 1783

1770-1783

111
[see p. 165]
Bartholomeus van der Helst
(Haarlem 1613-Amsterdam 1670)
Pieter Lucaszn van de Venne with Anna de Carpentier and child
Canvas 187.5 x 226.5 cm
Lower left: *Bartholomeus van der Helst f. 1652*
Inv. no. 860

LITERATURE:
De Gelder 1921, no. 871; Kuznetsov and Linnik 1982, no. 38; Dudok van Heel 1998

PROVENANCE:
acquired by Empress Catherine II before 1774

1774

98
[see p. 150]
Paulus Potter
(Enkhuizen 1625-Amsterdam 1654)
The farmyard
Panel 81 x 115.5 cm
Lower right: *Paulus. Potter. f. 1649*
Inv. no. 820

LITERATURE:
Walsh 1989b, no. B56; exhib. cat. The Hague 1994-95, no. 15

PROVENANCE:
(?) Muçart; (?) Quiryn van Biesum, Rotterdam, before 1719; Jacob van Hoek, Amsterdam; De Wolff, Amsterdam, before 1733; Valerius Röver, Delft, 1733-1739; the latter's widow Cornelia Röver-van der Dussen, 1739-1750; Landgrave Wilhelm VIII of Hessen-Kassel, Kassel, 1750-1806; taken to Paris by the French in 1806; Empress Joséphine du Beauharnais, Malmaison Castle, Paris, 1806-1814; Tsar Alexander I, Hermitage, St Petersburg, 1815

1815

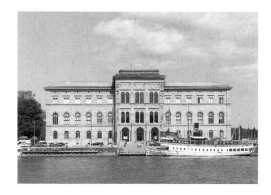

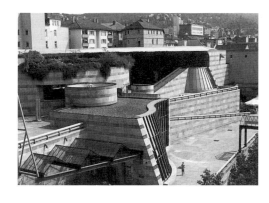

STOCKHOLM, NATIONALMUSEUM

The museum, established in 1792 as the royal museum in the royal palace at Stockholm, was one of the first museums accessible to the public. The royal art collection has its origins in the 16th century. In the 17th century the collection was expanded with art treasures seized in Munich and Prague (including the collection of Rudolf II) during the Thirty Years' War. At the beginnning of the 18th century, the court displayed strong leanings towards Paris, where contemporary French art as well as 17th-century Dutch art was purchased. The Dutch collection was also expanded through later purchases, some of which were made in the 20th century. One high point of the collection is Rembrandt's *Claudius Civilis*, which came from the art academy at Stockholm.

LITERATURE: cat. Stockholm 1990; exhib. cat. Stockholm 1992-93

STUTTGART, STAATSGALERIE STUTTGART

The museum, founded in 1843 by King Wilhelm I, contains the art collections of the Württemberg Dukes, including Memling's *Bathsheba* and many German paintings. At present the early German paintings and the 19th and 20th century collection are the museum's strong points. Dutch 17th-century painting is not its oldest department and is represented only on a limited scale. One of the early purchases was Rembrandt's *St Paul* of 1627 (acquired in 1867), but most of the purchases were made with the aid of lottery money in the period after the Second World War.

LITERATURE: cat. Stuttgart 1992

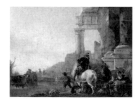

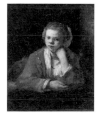

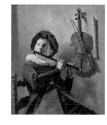

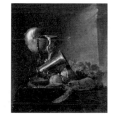

96
[see p. 148]
Jan Baptist Weenix
(Amsterdam 1621-De Haar 1659)
The ford in the river
Canvas 100 x 131.5 cm
On the base of the pillar centre right:
Gio Batta Weenix 1647
(date difficult to read)
Inv. no. 3740

LITERATURE:
exhib. cat. Utrecht 1965, no. 96;
Kuznetsov and Linnik 1982, no. 199;
exhib. cat. Rotterdam 1985, no. 30

PROVENANCE:
Count N.A. Kusjeljov-Bezborodko,
St Petersburg; bequeathed to the
Museum of the Academy of Visual Arts,
St Petersburg, 1859; acquired by the
Hermitage in 1922

142
[see p. 208]
Rembrandt
(Leiden 1606-Amsterdam 1669)
Girl at a window
Canvas 78 x 63 cm
Lower centre: *Rembrandt. f. 1651*
Inv. no. NM 584

LITERATURE:
exhib. cat. Stockholm 1992-93, no. 57;
De Robelin 1994-95

PROVENANCE:
Johan Gabriel Stenbock, Sweden, late
17th century; his niece Christina Beata
Lillie (no. 44 in the inventory drawn up
in 1727 after her death); purchased by
Gustav III in 1773

25
[see p. 51]
Judith Leyster
(Haarlem 1609-Heemstede 1660)
The young flute player, c. 1635
Canvas 73 x 62 cm
On the mouthpiece of the traverso:
*JL**
Inv. no. 1120

LITERATURE:
Hofrichter 1989, no. 38; exhib. cat.
Haarlem 1993, no. 11

PROVENANCE:
Queen Louisa Ulrika, 1760; Duke Adolf
Frederik; Count Brahe; Queen Desideria;
gift of King Oscar II, 1871

47
[see p. 78]
Jan Davidsz de Heem
(Utrecht 1606-Antwerp c. 1684)
Still life with lobster and nautilus cup
Canvas 61 x 55 cm
Upper right: *JDHeem F A° 1634*
(JDH in ligature)
Inv. no. 3323

LITERATURE:
exhib. cat. Delft-Cambridge-Fort Worth
1988-89, no. 37; exhib. cat. Utrecht-
Braunschweig 1991, no. 6; cat. Stuttgart
1992, pp. 160-61

PROVENANCE:
Art dealer Duits, London, 1954;
Dr Philip Lindstedt, Göteborg, 1954;
sale London (Sotheby's), 11/VII/1973, no.
30; Herner Wengraf Gallery, London,
1975; art dealer Julius Böhler, Munich,
1978; purchased in 1978

1922

1773

1871

1978

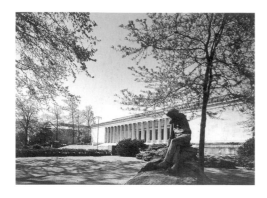

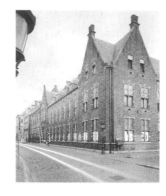

TOLEDO, THE TOLEDO MUSEUM OF ART

This museum, founded in 1901, displays art ranging from antiquity to the present. Its collection of old masters was mainly acquired after the Second World War. Using funds bequeathed by the founder of the museum, Edmund Drummond Libbey, several dozen paintings and a number of decorative objects were purchased in recent decades, which together offer a splendid and varied overview of 17th-century Dutch art. In addition to the works exhibited here, the museum also owns a number of surprising paintings by Van den Eeckhout, Van der Helst, Hobbema, Both, Cuyp, De Hooch and others.

LITERATURE: cat. Toledo 1976; Sutton 1986; exhib. cat. The Hague-San Francisco 1990-91; cat. Toledo 1995

UTRECHT, CENTRAAL MUSEUM

In 1838 the Stedelijk Historisch Museum was opened in the Utrecht town hall. In 1873 the Genootschap Kunstliefde opened its own museum, which housed the paintings owned by the city. In 1920 both collections were moved to the new Centraal Museum in the former Agnietenklooster (Convent of St Agnes). The museum was recently re-opened after extensive renovations. The collection offers a fine overview of the artistic production of Utrecht from the late Middle Ages to the present. As regards the 17th century, the emphasis is on the Mannerists, the Caravaggisti and the Italianate landscape painters.

LITERATURE: cat. Utrecht 1952

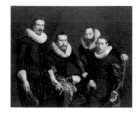

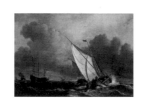

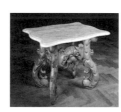

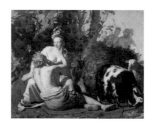

11
[see p. 29]
Thomas de Keyser (Amsterdam 1596/1597-Amsterdam 1667)
The syndics of the Amsterdam goldsmiths' guild
Canvas 127.2 x 152.4 cm
Lower right: *TDK./ANᴼ1627* and *AE TAS / SVA. 44ᴼ*; on the object in the hand of the second figure from the left: *AETA SVA 45.*
Inv. no. 1960.11

LITERATURE: Adams 1988, vol. 3, no. 17; cat. Toledo 1976, pp. 88-89, 245; cat. Toledo 1995, p. 85

PROVENANCE: Audley Dallas Neeld, Chippenham, Wiltshire; Lionel William Neeld, Chippenham, 1942; the latter's sale, London (Christie's), 9/VI/1944, no. 15; Philip Vos, England, 1944-1949; art dealer Duits, London, 1949; art dealer L. Douwes, Amsterdam; art dealer W.J.R. Dreesman, Amsterdam, 1949; sale Amsterdam, 22-25/III/1960, no. 6; art dealer Nijstad, The Hague; purchased in 1960

1960

162
[see p. 238]
Willem van de Velde the Younger (Leiden 1633-London 1707)
Ships on a stormy sea, c. 1672
Canvas 132.2 x 191.9 cm
On a piece of wood floating on the left: *W.V. Velde*
Inv. no. 77.62

LITERATURE:
Robinson 1990, vol. 2, no. 63; exhib. cat. London 1994, pp. 28-29; cat. Toledo 1995, p. 99

PROVENANCE:
(?) sale Backer, Leiden, 8-9/IX/1766; sale P. Locquet, Amsterdam, 22/IX/1783, no. 370; Thomas Hope, Amsterdam, until c. 1794, afterwards London; Duke of Bridgewater, 1801; Duke of Sutherland, by descent; sale London (Christie's), 2/VII/1976, no. 92; purchased in 1977

1977

70
[see p. 115]
Side table, c. 1660
Gilt walnut with white marble top (later addition)
Marble 80 x 89 x 72 cm
Inv. no. 4501

LITERATURE:
exhib. cat. London 1964, no. 214; Thornton 1998, no. 193

PROVENANCE:
acquired in 1923

1923

28
[see p. 54]
Gerard van Honthorst (Utrecht 1592-Utrecht 1656)
Granida and Daifilo
Canvas 145 x 178.5 cm
On the shepherd's crook: *GHonthorst. fesit 1625* and *No. 110*
Inv. no. 5571

LITERATURE:
Judson 1959, no. 132; exhib. cat. Utrecht-Braunschweig 1986-87, no. 67; exhib. cat. Utrecht-Frankfurt-Luxemburg 1993-94, no. 27; exhib. cat. San Francisco-Baltimore-London 1997-98, no. 57

PROVENANCE:
probably Stadholder Frederik Hendrik and Amalia van Solms, residence at Honselaersdijk, 1625-75; Stadholder-King Willem III, Honselaersdijk, until 1702; Frederick I of Prussia and heirs, Honselaersdijk, 1702-46, Schloss Berlin (Berlin), 1746-1856; art dealer Benedict & Co., Berlin, 1927; J.J.M. Chabot, Brussels/Scheveningen, 1927-1942; from 1927 until 1942 on loan to the Centraal Museum, Utrecht; purchased from the estate of Chabot, 1942

1942

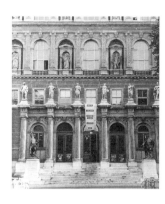

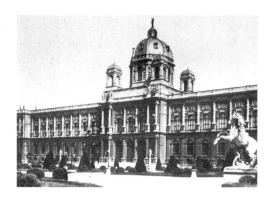

VIENNA, GEMÄLDEGALERIE DER AKADEMIE DER BILDENDEN KÜNSTE

The museum is located on the top floor of the Akademie building, which was opened in 1877. It is the first museum in Vienna that was accessible to the public. The majority of the paintings were collected in the first decade of the 19th century by Count Lamberg in Vienna and given to the Akademie in 1822. Most of the more than 180 17th-century Dutch masters came from his collection. On the whole the collection, with its emphasis on the Italianate painters, presents a better and more varied picture of Dutch art than the Kunsthistorisches Museum.

LITERATURE: cat. Vienna 1992; cat. Vienna 1997

VIENNA, KUNSTHISTORISCHES MUSEUM

The picture gallery is located on the first floor of the monumental museum building on the *Kaiserforum*, which was opened in 1891. The collections amassed by the Habsburg emperors starting in the late 16th century form the core of the museum's collection. The famous collection of paintings by Pieter Bruegel I, for example, came from the Prague emperor Rudolf II, and many of the Italian and Flemish paintings were collected in the 17th century by Archduke Leopold Wilhelm. Although the museum has a valuable collection of 15th- and 16th-century Dutch art and 17th-century Flemish and Italian art, 17th-century Dutch art is less well represented. Among the relatively recent acquisitions is Vermeer's *Art of painting* (acquired in 1946).

LITERATURE: cat. Vienna 1972; cat. Vienna 1991

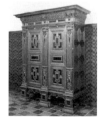

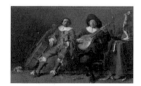

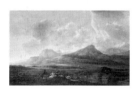

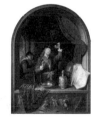

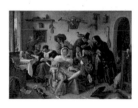

14
[see p. 35]
'Wtewael' cupboard, c. 1600-1625
Oak, inlaid with ebony,
255.5 x 214 x 82 cm
Inv. no. 8441

PROVENANCE:
Joachim Wtewael (1566-1638), Utrecht;
bequest Jhr. mr. A.H. Martens van
Sevenhoven at Arnhem, 1952

35
[see p. 62]
Cornelis Saftleven
(Gorinchem 1607-Rotterdam 1681)
The duet, c. 1635
Panel 34 x 53 cm
Inv. no. 696

LITERATURE:
exhib. cat. Minneapolis-Houston-San
Diego 1985, no. 35; cat. Vienna 1992,
no. 111

PROVENANCE:
Esterházy; Count Lamberg; presented as
part of the Lamberg collection to the
Akademie der bildenden Künste, 1822

92
[see p. 144]
Jan Asselijn
(Diemen? c. 1615-Amsterdam 1652)
River bank with herdsmen, c. 1650
Panel 43 x 67 cm
Lower centre: *JA.* (in ligature)
Inv. no. 836

LITERATURE:
Steland-Stief 1971, no. 110; cat. Vienna
1992, no. 13; cat. Vienna 1997, p. 164

PROVENANCE:
presented as part of the Lamberg
collection to the Akademie der bildenden
Künste, 1822

122
[see p. 180]
Gerard Dou
(Leiden 1613-Leiden 1675)
The doctor
Panel 49.3 x 36.6 cm
In the middle of the parapet: *GDOV. 1653*
(GD in ligature)
Inv. no. 592

LITERATURE:
Martin 1913, p. 73; cat. Vienna 1972,
pp. 25-26; cat. Vienna 1991, p. 50

PROVENANCE:
Archduke Leopold Wilhelm (1614-
1662); by descent to the Imperial
Collection; since 1891 Kunsthistorisches
Museum

116
[see p. 172]
Jan Steen
(Leiden 1626-Leiden 1679)
'In luxury beware'
Canvas 105 x 145 cm
Lower left: *JS 16/63?|* (JS in ligature);
lower right: *In Weelde Siet Toe* and
oooo01 Soma op.
Inv. no. 791

LITERATURE: cat. Vienna 1972, pp. 87-
88; De Vries 1977, pp. 53-58 and no.
98; exhib. cat. Philadelphia-Berlin-
London 1984, no. 104; cat. Vienna
1991, no. 791; exhib. cat. Washington-
Amsterdam 1996-97, no. 21

PROVENANCE:
(?) sale Cornelis van Dijck, The Hague,
9/V/1713, no. 38; sale Bertels, Brussels,
20/I/1779, no. 40; Duke Karel van
Lotharingen, Brussels, 1780; by descent
to the Imperial Collection, Vienna, 1783;
since 1891 Kunsthistorisches Museum

1952

1822

1822

before 1662

1783

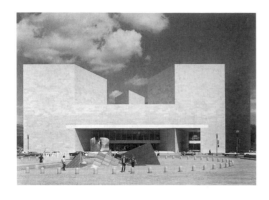

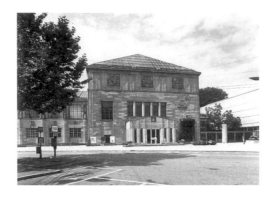

WASHINGTON, NATIONAL GALLERY OF ART

The National Gallery of Art, which was opened in 1941, is one of the most recently established museums. In spite of this, it has a collection of European painting (1400-1900) that is equalled in quality and size by only a few of the large museums in Europe. Gifts made by industrial magnates such as Mellon, Widener and Kress have given the galleries of 17th-century Dutch paintings an imposing yet traditional aspect, the great masters being well represented with a number of exceptionally fine paintings: Aelbert Cuyp (5), Meindert Hobbema (7), Ruisdael (3), Frans Hals (8), Rembrandt (more than 20 attributions) and Vermeer (3). In recent decades this overview has been considerably enriched through important purchases of works by such artists as Goltzius, Saenredam, Heda, De Heem, Van Aelst and Verspronck.

LITERATURE: Sutton 1986; exhib. cat. The Hague-San Francisco 1990-91; cat. Washington 1995

ZÜRICH, KUNSTHAUS

The Kunsthaus was founded in the late 18th century by artists from Zürich and has been housesd since 1910 in the present building, which has been added on to repeatedly. There is a wealth of 19th- and 20th-century European art, and previous centuries are also well represented thanks to the collections belonging to two foundations: that of Prof. Leopold Ruzicka (since 1949 in the Kunsthaus), with 17th-century Dutch painting in particular (including Asselijn, Van Beyeren, Rembrandt and De Witte), and that of Betty and David M. Koetser (since 1979 in the Kunsthaus), with both Dutch and Italian paintings.

LITERATURE: exhib. cat. Zürich 1949-50; exhib. cat. Basel 1987, pp. 49-50; cat. Zürich 1988; cat. Zürich 1992

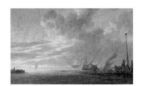

85
[see p. 135]
Simon de Vlieger
(Rotterdam 1600/1601-Weesp 1653)
Seascape in the morning, c. 1640-1645
Panel 36.8 x 58.4 cm
Inv. no. 1997.101.1

LITERATURE:
not included in Kelch 1971

PROVENANCE:
Edward Donner, Hurstbourne Park,
Hampshire, England; purchased through
the agency of Gurr-Johns, London, 1997

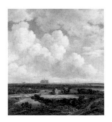

153
[see p. 224]
Jacob van Ruisdael
(Haarlem 1628/1629-Amsterdam 1682)
View of Haarlem with bleaching fields,
c. 1670
Canvas 62.2 x 55.2 cm
Lower left: *Ruisdael*
Inv. no. R. 32

LITERATURE:
Rosenberg 1928, no. 44; exhib. cat. The
Hague-Cambridge 1981-82, no. 45;
exhib. cat. Basel 1987, no. 84

PROVENANCE:
sale Count Sierstorpff, Berlin (Lepke),
19/IV/1887, no. 67; Vieweg,
Braunschweig; sale Vieweg, Berlin
(Lepke), 18/III/1930, no. 13; acquired
from an art dealer in Zürich, 1949

1997

1949

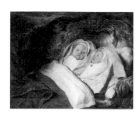

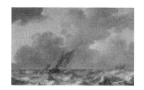

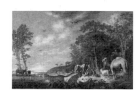

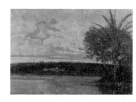

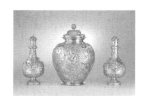

73
[see p. 118]
Salomon de Bray
(Amsterdam 1597-Haarlem 1664)
The twins Clara and Aelbert de Bray,
c. 1646
Canvas 82.6 x 64.8 cm
Private collection, Scotland

LITERATURE:
Von Moltke 1938-39a, no. 95; exhib.
cat. Edinburgh 1992, no. 10

PROVENANCE:
possibly exhibited in 1834 by Sir Charles
Bagot in the British Institution; private
collection, Scotland, on loan to The
National Gallery of Scotland, Edinburgh

84
[see p. 134]
Jan Porcellis
(Ghent 1580/1584-Zoeterwoude 1632)
Vessels in a strong wind, c. 1630
Panel 41.5 x 61.7 cm
Lower right: *IP*
Mrs Edward Carter, United States

LITERATURE:
Walsh 1989a, pp. 111-12 and no. A45;
exhib. cat. Los Angeles-Boston-New
York 1981-82, no. 18

PROVENANCE:
art dealer Nystad, The Hague;
N. Crommelin-Waller, Laren and The
Hague; art dealer Nystad, 1977

88
[see p. 138]
Aelbert Cuyp
(Dordrecht 1620-Dordrecht 1691)
Orpheus with animals in a landscape,
c. 1640
Canvas 113 x 167 cm
Lower right: *A cuyp*
Private collection, Boston

LITERATURE:
Reiss 1975, listed under no. 48; Chong
1993, listed under no. 71; cat. London
1994b, no. 10

PROVENANCE:
sale Johan van Nispen, The Hague,
12/IX/1768, no. 5; sale Hendrik
Verschuuring, The Hague, 17/IX/1770,
no. 38; sale Captain Baillie, London,
2/II/1771, no. 70; Harper family,
London; private collection, Paris, c.
1930; private collection, Madrid; sale
London (Sotheby's), 6/VII/1994, no. 8;
art dealer J. van Haeften, London, 1994

89
[see p. 139]
Frans Post
(Leiden c. 1612-Haarlem 1680)
*View of Frederiksstad in
Paraiba, Brazil*
Canvas 60.3 x 84.5 cm
Lower right on the tree trunk: *F.
Post/1638*
On the back of the canvas: *Stadt
Freder in Parijba:/N.o 443*
Caracas, Colección Patricia Phelps
de Cisneros

LITERATURE:
sale Sotheby's New York, 30/I/1997,
no. 10

PROVENANCE:
painted in Brazil for Prince Johan
Maurits; presented to Louis XIV in 1679
(inv. 1681, no. 443); transferred to
Versailles or Chaville, in any case until
1765; sale Sotheby's New York,
30/I/1997, no. 10

104
[see p. 158]
Barent van Milanen
(active c. 1663-1680), attributed to
Vase and two flasks
Silver, vase: h. 41.9 cm, flasks:
h. 35.6 cm
Marked: assay office mark The Hague; a
lion rampant; year letter D, E = 1678,
1679; maker's mark: anchor in shield =
heirs Nicolaes Loockemans, attributed to
Barent van Milanen
Private collection, United Kingdom

LITERATURE:
Starkie Gardner 1905, p. 33, fig. 1, p.
36, fig.. 3, p. 37; exhib. cat. The Hague
1967, nos. 68-69

PROVENANCE:
probably taken to England between 1688
and 1702 by Hans Willem Bentinck
(1649-1709); by descent to the present
owner

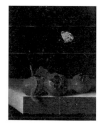

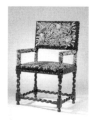

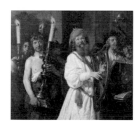

131
[see p. 191]
Adriaen Coorte
(active Middelburg c. 1683-1707)
Still life with three medlars,
c. 1696-1700
Paper on panel 26.8 x 20.4 cm
Lower centre: *AC* (AC in ligature)
Private collection, The Netherlands

LITERATURE:
Bol 1969, pp. 361-62; Bol 1977, no. 75

PROVENANCE:
sale Van Panhuys, Amsterdam,
26/IX/1882, no. 98 (sold to Victor
de Stuers)

133
[see p. 192]
Armchair, c. 1650
Walnut, upholstered with tapestry,
105 x 62 x 47 cm
Private collection, Amsterdam

LITERATURE:
exhib. cat. Amsterdam 1971-72, no. 34b

PROVENANCE:
bequeathed by an Amsterdam patrician
to an institution in Amsterdam built in
1694-95; one of the '12 carpeted chairs'
recorded in 1700 in an inventory of the
institution

169b
[see p. 251]
Pieter Xavery
(Antwerp c. 1647-Leiden 1673)
Faun and Bacchus, 1671
Terracotta h. 35 and 42 cm
Irene and Howard Stein, Atlanta

PROVENANCE:
art dealer Patrice Bellanger, Paris

172
[see p. 257]
Jan de Bray
(Haarlem c. 1627-Haarlem 1697)
David playing the harp
Canvas 142 x 154 cm
On the foot of the candle-holder:
JdBray 1670
The Earl of Wemyss and March,
Scotland

LITERATURE:
Von Moltke 1938-39b, no. 7b; exhib.
cat. Edinburgh 1992, no. 9

PROVENANCE:
(?) sale Taets van Amerongen,
Amsterdam, 3/VII/1805, no. 10; (?) sale
Amsterdam, 23/VIII/1808; 10th Earl of
Wemyss and March, 1914; by descent
to the present owner

BIBLIOGRAPHY

ADAMS 1988 A.J. Adams, *The paintings of Thomas de Keyser (1596/7-1667): a study of portraiture in seventeenth-century Amsterdam*, 4 vols., Ann Arbor 1988

BAARSEN 1989A R.J. Baarsen, 'Adam van Vianen, kan met deksel van verguld zilver', *Bulletin van het Rijksmuseum* 37 (1989), pp. 201-03

BAARSEN 1989B R.J. Baarsen, 'Een Amsterdams zilveren zoutvat uit 1618', *Bulletin van het Rijksmuseum* 37 (1989), pp. 51-72

BAARSEN 1989C R.J. Baarsen, 'Luiermandskastje van eike- en notehout, Nederland, 3de kwart 17de eeuw', *Bulletin van het Rijksmuseum* 37 (1989), pp. 230-32

BAARSEN 1996 R.J. Baarsen, 'Herman Doomer, ebony worker in Amsterdam', *The Burlington Magazine* 138 (1996), pp. 739-49

BACHMANN 1982 F. Bachmann, *Aert van der Neer 1603/4-1677*, Bremen 1982

BAKKER 1993 A. Bakker, *Huis Doorn*, Zwolle 1993

BALIGAND 1999 F. Baligand, *Le Musée de la Chartreuse, Douai*, Douai & Paris 1999

BECK 1972-87 H.U. Beck, *Jan van Goyen 1596-1656: ein Oeuvreverzeichnis*, 3 vols., Amsterdam & Doornspijk 1972-87 (vol. 4: *Künstler um Jan van Goyen: Maler und Zeichner*, Doornspijk 1991)

BEHERMAN 1988 T. Beherman, *Godfried Schalcken*, Paris 1988

VAN BERGE-GERBAUD 1997 M. van Berge-Gerbaud, *De collectie Frits Lugt in Paris / Le collection Frits Lugt à Paris*, Paris 1997

BERGVELT 1998 E. Bergvelt, *Pantheon der gouden eeuw: van Nationale Konst-Gallerij tot Rijksmuseum van Schilderijen (1798-1896)*, Zwolle 1998

BIESBOER 1985 P. Biesboer, 'De Bavo in de beeldende kunst van de 17de eeuw', J.N. de Boer et al. (eds.), *De Bavo te Boek: bij het gereedkomen van de restauratie van de Grote of St. Bavo kerk te Haarlem*, Haarlem 1985

BIJL et al. 1994 M. Bijl et al., 'Rembrandts Portret van Johannes Wtenbogaert, verwerving en restauratie', *Bulletin van het Rijksmuseum* 42 (1994), pp. 327-33

BLANKERT 1975 A. Blankert (with contributions by R. Ruurs and W.L. de Watering), *Johannes Vermeer van Delft 1632-1675*, Utrecht & Antwerp 1975

BLANKERT 1982 A. Blankert, *Ferdinand Bol (1616-1680): Rembrandt's pupil*, Doornspijk 1982

BOER 1994 E.M.A. Boer, 'Voor elc wat wils', *Antiek* 28 (1994), no. 4, pp. 17-23

BOL 1960 L.J. Bol, *The Bosschaert dynasty: painters of flowers and fruit*, Leigh-on-Sea 1960

BOL 1962 L.J. Bol, 'Helena van der Schalcke als kind', *Openbaar Kunstbezit* 6 (1962), no. 32

BOL 1969 L.J. Bol, *Holländische Maler des 17. Jahrhunderts nahe den grossen Meistern: Landschaften und Stilleben*, Braunschweig 1969

BOL 1977 L.J. Bol, *Adriaen Coorte: a unique late seventeenth century Dutch still-life painter*, Assen 1977

BOL 1989 L.J. Bol, *Adriaen Pietersz. van de Venne: painter and draughtsman*, Doornspijk 1989

BRENNINKMEYER-DE ROOIJ B. Brenninkmeyer-De Rooij, 'Notities betreffende de decoratie van de Oranjezaal in Huis Ten Bosch', *Oud Holland* 96 (1982), pp. 133-90

BROULHIET 1938 G. Broulhiet, *Meindert Hobbema (1638-1709)*, Paris 1938

BROWN 1981 C. Brown, *Carel Fabritius*, Oxford 1981

BROWN 1997 C. Brown, 'The strange case of Jan Torrentius: art, sex, and heresy in seventeenth-century Haarlem', R.E. Fleischer and S.C. Scott (eds.), *Rembrandt, Rubens, and the art of their time: recent perspectives* (Papers in Art History from The Pennsylvania State University, vol. XI), University Park 1997, pp. 224-33

BRUSATI 1995 C. Brusati, *Artifice and illusion: the art and writing of Samuel van Hoogstraten*, Chicago & London 1995

BRUYN et al. 1982-89 J. Bruyn et al., *A corpus of Rembrandt paintings*, 3 vols., Dordrecht, Boston & Lancaster 1982-89

DE BRUYN KOPS 1965 C.J. de Bruyn Kops, 'Kanttekeningen bij het nieuw verworven landschap van Aelbert Cuyp', *Bulletin van het Rijksmuseum* 13 (1965), pp. 162-76

BULLETIN 1982 'Keuze uit de aanwinsten', *Bulletin van het Rijksmuseum* 30 (1982), p. 27

BULLETIN 1988 'Keuze uit de aanwinsten', *Bulletin van het Rijksmuseum* 36 (1988), p. 257

BULLETIN 1997 'Keuze uit de aanwinsten', *Bulletin van het Rijksmuseum* 45 (1997), pp. 157-59

BURKE 1976 J.D. Burke, *Jan Both (ca. 1618-1652): paintings, drawings and prints*, New York & London 1976 (diss. Harvard University 1972)

CARASSO-KOK 1975 M. Carasso-Kok, *Amsterdam Historisch: een stadgeschiedenis aan de hand van de collectie van het Amsterdams Historisch Museum*, Bussum 1975

CAT. AMSTERDAM 1880 [J.W. Kaiser], cat. *Beschrijving der schilderijen van het Rijksmuseum te Amsterdam*, Amsterdam 1880

CAT. AMSTERDAM 1952A cat. *Rijksmuseum, Amsterdam: catalogus van meubelen en betimmeringen*, Amsterdam 1952

CAT. AMSTERDAM 1952B cat. *Rijksmuseum, Amsterdam: catalogus van goud en zilverwerken*, Amsterdam 1952

CAT. AMSTERDAM 1973 J. Leeuwenberg and W. Halsema-Kubes, cat. *Beeldhouwkunst in het Rijksmuseum*, Amsterdam 1973

CAT. AMSTERDAM 1975-79 A. Blankert, cat. *Amsterdams Historisch Museum: schilderijen daterend van voor 1800*, Amsterdam 1975-79

CAT. AMSTERDAM 1976 P.J.J. van Thiel et al., cat. *All the paintings of the Rijksmuseum in Amsterdam: a completely illustrated catalogue*, Amsterdam 1976

CAT. AMSTERDAM 1992 P.J.J. van Thiel et al., cat. *All the paintings of the Rijksmuseum in Amsterdam: a completely illustrated catalogue, first supplement: 1976-91*, Amsterdam 1992

CAT. AMSTERDAM 1993A P.C. Ritsema van Eck and H.M. Zijlstra-Zweens, cat. *Glass in the Rijksmuseum*, vol. 1, Amsterdam & Zwolle 1993

CAT. AMSTERDAM 1993B R.J. Baarsen, cat. *Nederlandse Meubelen 1600-1800 / Dutch Furniture 1600-1800*, Amsterdam & Zwolle 1993

CAT. AMSTERDAM 1995A F. Scholten, cat. *Gebeeldhouwde portretten/ Portrait sculptures*, Amsterdam & Zwolle 1995

CAT. AMSTERDAM 1995B P.C. Ritsema van Eck, cat. *Glass in the Rijksmuseum*, vol. 2, Amsterdam & Zwolle 1995

CAT. AMSTERDAM 1999 J.R. de Lorm, cat. *Rijksmuseum, Amsterdam: Amsterdams goud en zilver*, Amsterdam & Zwolle 1999

CAT. BERLIN 1996 H. Bock *et al.*, cat. *Gemäldegalerie Berlin: Gesamtverzeichnis*, Berlin 1996

CAT. BERLIN 1998 H. Bock *et al.*, cat. *Gemäldegalerie Berlin: 200 Meisterwerke*, Berlin 1998

CAT. BOSTON 1986 T.E. Stebbins Jr. and P.C. Sutton, cat. *Masterpiece paintings from the Museum of Fine Arts, Boston*, Boston 1986

CAT. BRAUNSCHWEIG 1983 R. Klessmann, cat. *Herzog Anton Ulrich-Museum, Braunschweig: die holländischen Gemälde*, Braunschweig 1983

CAT. BUDAPEST 1968 A. Pigler, cat. *Budapest, Szémüvészeti Museum: Katalog der Galerie Alter Meister*, 2 vols., Tübingen 1968

CAT. CARDIFF 1993 M. Evans and O. Fairclough, cat. *The National Museum & Gallery Cardiff: a companion guide to the National Art Gallery*, Cardiff 1993

CAT. COPENHAGEN 1997 C. Fischer and K. Monrad (eds.), cat. *Statens Museum for Kunst: 100 masterpieces*, Copenhagen 1997

CAT. DRESDEN 1992 A. Walther (ed.), cat. *Gemäldegalerie Dresden: Alte Meister*, Dresden 1992

CAT. DUBLIN 1986 H. Potterton, cat. *Dutch seventeenth century and eighteenth century paintings in the National Gallery of Ireland: a complete catalogue*, Dublin 1986

CAT. EDINBURGH 1997 J. Lloyd Williams (ed.), cat. *The National Gallery of Scotland: concise catalogue of paintings*, Edinburgh 1997

CAT. HAARLEM 1969 cat. *Frans Halsmuseum Haarlem*, Haarlem 1969

CAT. THE HAGUE 1987 B. Broos, cat. *Meesterwerken in het Mauritshuis*, The Hague 1987

CAT. THE HAGUE 1993 N. Sluijter-Seijffert *et al.*, cat. *Mauritshuis: illustrated general catalogue*, Amsterdam 1993

CAT. THE HAGUE 1998 G.J. de Rook and M. Seegers (eds.), cat. *Gemeentemuseum, Den Haag: de collecties*, The Hague & Zwolle 1998

CAT. HAMBURG 1995 A. von Saldern, cat. *Glas: Antike bis Jugendstil: die Sammlung im Museum für Kunst und Gewerbe*, Stuttgart 1995

CAT. HARTFORD 1978 E. Haverkamp-Begemann (ed.), *Wadsworth Atheneum paintings, catalogue 1: the Netherlands and the German-speaking countries, fifteenth-nineteenth centuries*, Hartford 1978

CAT. KANSAS CITY 1988 E.R. Goheen, cat. *The collections of the Nelson-Atkins Museum of Art*, Kansas City & New York 1988

CAT. KANSAS CITY 1993 R. Ward and P.J. Fidler (eds.), cat. *The Nelson-Atkins Museum of Art: a handbook of the collection*, New York 1993

CAT. LONDON 1980 P. Murray, cat. *Dulwich Picture Gallery: a catalogue*, London 1980

CAT. LONDON 1991 N. MacLaren and C. Brown, cat. *The Dutch School 1600-1900*, 2 vols., London 1991

CAT. LONDON 1994A G. Waterfield (ed.), cat. *Collection for a king: old master paintings from the Dulwich Picture Gallery*, London 1994

CAT. LONDON 1994B Kunsthandel J. van Haeften, cat. *Dutch and Flemish old master paintings*, London 1994

CAT. LONDON 1995 C. Baker and T. Henry, cat. *The National Gallery: complete illustrated catalogue*, London 1995

CAT. LONDON 1998 R. Beresford, cat. *Dulwich Picture Gallery: complete illustrated catalogue*, London 1998

CAT. LOS ANGELES 1987 S. Schaefer *et al.*, cat. *European painting and sculpture in the Los Angeles County Museum of Art: an illustrated summary catalogue*, Los Angeles 1987

CAT. LOS ANGELES 1997 M. Holtman (ed.), cat. *The J. Paul Getty Museum: handbook of the collections*, Los Angeles 1997

CAT. LUND 1963 cat. *Ein Rundgang durch das Kulturhistorische Museum zu Lund*, Lund 1963

CAT. MADRID 1990 I. Gaskell, cat. *The Thyssen-Bornemisza collection, Madrid: seventeenth-century Dutch and Flemish painting*, London 1990

CAT. MADRID 1992 J.M. Pita Andrade and M.M. Borobia Guerrero, cat. *Thyssen-Bornemisza Museum: old masters*, Madrid 1992

CAT. MUNICH 1967 E. Brochhagen and B. Knüttel, cat. *Alte Pinakothek, München, Katalog III: holländische Malerei des 17. Jahrhunderts*, Munich 1967

CAT. MUNICH 1983 cat. *Alte Pinakothek, München: Erläuterungen zu den ausgestellten Gemälden*, Munich 1983

CAT. NEW YORK 1995 K. Baetjer, cat. *European paintings in the Metropolitan Museum of Art by artists born before 1865: a summary catalogue*, New York 1995

CAT. OBERLIN 1998 J. Squires Wilker (ed.), cat. *Allen Memorial Art Museum, Oberlin: masterworks for learning, a college collection catalogue*, Oberlin 1998 (CD-ROM)

CAT. PARIS 1979 A. Brejon de Lavergnée *et al.*, cat. *Catalogue sommaire illustré des peintures du Musée du Louvre: écoles flamande et hollandaise*, Paris 1979

CAT. PARIS 1994 M. van Berge-Gerbaud and H. Buijs (eds.), cat. *Morceaux Choisis: parmi les acquisitions de la Collection Frits Lugt realisées sous le directorat de Carlos van Hasselt, 1970-1994*, Paris 1994

CAT. ROTTERDAM 1962 cat. *Museum Boijmans Van Beuningen, Rotterdam: catalogus schilderijen tot 1800*, Rotterdam 1962

CAT. ROTTERDAM 1988 J. Giltaij *et al.*, cat. *Museum Boijmans Van Beuningen, Rotterdam: een gloeiend palet, schilderijen van Rembrandt en zijn school / A glowing palette, paintings of Rembrandt and his school*, Rotterdam 1988

CAT. SCHWERIN 1982 L. Jürss, cat. *Staatliches Museum, Schwerin: holländische und flämische Malerei des 17. Jahrhunderts*, Schwerin 1982

CAT. STOCKHOLM 1990 G. Cavalli-Björkman, cat. *Nationalmuseum, Stockholm: illustrated catalogue, European paintings*, Västervik 1990

CAT. STUTTGART 1992 R. Klapproth (ed.), cat. *Staatsgalerie, Stuttgart: alte Meister*, Stuttgart 1992

CAT. TOLEDO 1976 O. Wittmann (ed.), cat. *The Toledo Museum of Art: European paintings*, Toledo 1976

CAT. TOLEDO 1995 T.A.R. Neff (ed.), cat. *Toledo treasures: selections from the Toledo Museum of Art*, Toledo & New York 1995

CAT. UTRECHT 1952 C.H. de Jonge, cat. *Centraal Museum, Utrecht: catalogus der schilderijen*, Utrecht 1952

CAT. VIENNA 1972 K. Demus, cat. *Katalog der Gemäldegalerie, Wien: holländische Meister des 15., 16. und 17. Jahrhunderts*, Vienna & Munich 1972

CAT. VIENNA 1991 M. Haja (ed.), cat. *Die Gemäldegalerie des Kunsthistorischen Museums in Wien: Verzeichnis der Gemälde*, Vienna 1991

CAT. VIENNA 1992 R. Trnek, cat. *Die holländischen Gemälde des 17. Jahrhunderts in der Gemäldegalerie der Akademie der bildenden Künste in Wien*, Vienna, Cologne & Weimar 1992

CAT. VIENNA 1997 R. Trnek, cat. *Die Gemäldegalerie der Akademie der bildenden Künste in Wien: die Sammlung im Überblick*, Vienna 1997

CAT. WASHINGTON 1995 A.K. Wheelock, Jr., cat. *National Gallery of Art, Washington: Dutch paintings of the seventeenth century*, Washington 1995

CAT. ZÜRICH 1992 C. Klemm, cat. *Kunsthaus Zürich*, Zürich & Geneva 1992

CHIARINI 1989 M. Chiarini, *I dipinti olandesi del Seicento e del Settecento*, Rome 1989 (*Cataloghi dei musei e gallerie d'Italia: nuova serie; 1: Firenze, Gallerie e musei statali di Firenze*)

CHONG 1993 A. Chong, *Aelbert Cuyp and the meanings of landscape*, Ann Arbor 1993

VAN DAM 1989 J.D. van Dam, 'Vroege faïence uit Delft (1625-1655) en de invloed op Japans porselein (1660-1670)', *Mededelingenblad Nederlandse Vereniging van Vrienden van de Ceramiek* 135 (1989), no. 3, pp. 4-18

DAMSTÉ 1985 P.H. Damsté, 'De geschiedenis van het portret van Jaspar Schade door Frans Hals', *Oud Holland* 99 (1985), pp. 30-43

DOMELA NIEUWENHUIS 1989 E. Domela Nieuwenhuis, *Paulus Moreelse, zijn historiestukken en zijn tekeningen*, Leiden 1989 (M.A. thesis, Rijksuniversiteit Leiden)

DUDOK VAN HEEL 1998 S.A.C. Dudok van Heel, 'Duizend gulden voor een portretopdracht aan Bartholomeus van der Helst', *Amstelodamum* 85 (1998), pp. 33-40

DUPARC 1993 F.J. Duparc, 'Philips Wouwerman, 1619-1668', *Oud Holland* 107 (1993), pp. 257-86

EBERT-SCHIFFERER 1998 S. Ebert-Schifferer, *Die Geschichte des Stillebens*, Munich 1998

ECKHARDT *et al.* 1980 W. Eckhardt et al. (ed.), *Museum für Kunst und Gewerbe Hamburg: Handbuch*, Hamburg 1980

VAN EEGHEN 1973 I.H. van Eeghen, 'De groepsportretten in de familie Van Loon', *Jaarboek Amstelodamum* 60 (1973), pp. 121-26

VAN EEGHEN 1976 I.H. van Eeghen, 'De familiestukken van Metsu van 1657 en van De Witte van 1678 met vier levensgeschiedenissen (Gillis Valckenier, Nicolaas Listingh, Jan Zeeuw en Catharina van de Perre)', *Jaarboek Amstelodamum* 68 (1976), pp. 78-107

EKKART 1979 R.E.O. Ekkart, *Johannes Cornelisz. Verspronck: leven en werken van een Haarlems portretschilder uit de 17de eeuw*, Haarlem 1979

EKKART 1999 R.E.O. Ekkart, 'Een man met ring en toetssteen door Werner van den Valckert', *Bulletin van het Rijksmuseum* 47 (1999), pp. 20-25

ELIËNS *et al.* 1995-96 T. Eliëns et al. (ed.), *Jaarboek Haags Gemeentemuseum* 5 (1995-96) (Jubileumnummer)

EXHIB. CAT. AMSTERDAM 1952 J. Bruyn et al., exhib. cat. *Drie eeuwen portret in Nederland*, Amsterdam (Rijksmuseum) 1952

EXHIB. CAT. AMSTERDAM 1969 P.J.J. van Thiel (ed.), exhib. cat. *Rembrandt 1669/1969*, Amsterdam (Rijksmuseum) 1969

EXHIB. CAT. AMSTERDAM 1971 P.J.J. van Thiel *et al.*, exhib. cat. *Hollandse schilderijen uit Franse musea*, Amsterdam (Rijksmuseum) 1971

EXHIB. CAT. AMSTERDAM 1971-72 V. Woldbye and C.A. Burgers, exhib. cat. *Geweven boeket*, Amsterdam (Rijksmuseum) 1971-72

EXHIB. CAT. AMSTERDAM 1976 E. de Jongh *et al.* (eds.), exhib. cat. *Tot lering en vermaak: betekenissen van Hollandse genrevoorstellingen uit de zeventiende eeuw*, Amsterdam (Rijksmuseum) 1976

EXHIB. CAT. AMSTERDAM 1984 P.J.J. van Thiel and C.J. de Bruyn Kops, exhib. cat. *Prijs de lijst: de Hollandse schilderijlijst in de zeventiende eeuw*, Amsterdam (Rijksmuseum) 1984

EXHIB. CAT. AMSTERDAM 1984-85 K.A. Citroen et al., exhib. cat. *Meesterwerken in zilver: Amsterdams zilver 1520-1820*, Amsterdam (Museum Willet-Holthuysen) 1984-85

EXHIB. CAT. AMSTERDAM 1989-90 P. Hecht, exhib. cat. *De Hollandse fijnschilders: van Gerard Dou tot Adriaen van der Werff*, Amsterdam (Rijksmuseum) 1989-90

EXHIB. CAT. AMSTERDAM 1991 A. Tümpel and P. Schatborn, exhib. cat. *Pieter Lastman: leermeester van Rembrandt / the man who taught Rembrandt*, Amsterdam (Rembrandthuis) 1991

EXHIB. CAT. AMSTERDAM 1992 E. Bergvelt and R. Kistemaker (eds.), exhib. cat. *De wereld binnen handbereik: Nederlandse kunst- en rariteitenverzamelingen, 1585-1735*, Amsterdam (Amsterdams Historisch Museum) 1992

EXHIB. CAT. AMSTERDAM 1993-94 G. Luijten et al. (eds.), exhib. cat. *Dawn of the Golden Age: Northern Netherlandish art 1580-1620*, Amsterdam (Rijksmuseum) 1993-94

EXHIB. CAT. AMSTERDAM 1994 S. Segal and M. Roding, exhib. cat. *De tulp en de kunst*, Amsterdam (Nieuwe Kerk) 1994

EXHIB. CAT. AMSTERDAM 1999 A. Wallert (ed.), exhib. cat. *Still lifes: techniques and style*, Amsterdam (Rijksmuseum) 1999

EXHIB. CAT. AMSTERDAM 2000 F. Grijzenhout et al., exhib. cat. *Een Koninklijk Museum*, Amsterdam (Rijksmuseum) 2000

EXHIB. CAT. AMSTERDAM-BOSTON-PHILADELPHIA 1987-88 P.C. Sutton et al. (eds.), exhib. cat. *Masters of 17th-century Dutch landscape painting*, Amsterdam (Rijksmuseum), Boston (Museum of Fine Arts) & Philadelphia (Philadelphia Museum of Art) 1987-88

EXHIB. CAT. AMSTERDAM-CLEVELAND 1999-2000 A. Chong and W. Kloek, exhib. cat. *Het Nederlandse stilleven 1550-1720*, Amsterdam (Rijksmuseum) & Cleveland (The Cleveland Museum of Art) 1999-2000

EXHIB. CAT. AMSTERDAM-EMDEN 1985 B. Broos et al., R. Kromhout (ed.), exhib. cat. *Ludolf Bakhuizen 1631-1708: schryfmeester-teyckenaer-schilder*, Amsterdam (Nederlands Scheepvaart Museum) 1985

EXHIB. CAT. AMSTERDAM-GRONINGEN 1983
A. Blankert *et al.*, exhib. cat. *Rembrandt: the impact of a genius*, Amsterdam (art dealer K. & V. Waterman) & Groningen (Groninger Museum) 1983

EXHIB. CAT. AMSTERDAM-LONDON 1991
P.J.J. van Thiel *et al.*, exhib. cat. *Meeting of masterpieces / Ontmoeting van meesterwerken*, Amsterdam (Rijksmuseum) & London (The National Gallery) 1991

EXHIB. CAT. AMSTERDAM-MOSCOW 1989
J.J.Driessen, exhib. cat. *Russen en Nederlanders: uit de geschiedenis van de betrekkingen tussen Nederland en Rusland 1600-1917*, Amsterdam (Rijksmuseum) & Moscow (Pushkin Museum) 1989

EXHIB. CAT. AMSTERDAM-STOCKHOLM-LOS ANGELES 1998-99 F. Scholten *et al.*, exhib. cat. *Adriaen de Vries (1556-1626): keizerlijk beeldhouwer*, Amsterdam (Rijksmuseum), Stockholm (Nationalmuseum) & Los Angeles (The J. Paul Getty Museum) 1998-99

EXHIB. CAT. AMSTERDAM-TOLEDO-BOSTON 1979-80 A.L. den Blaauwen (ed.), exhib. cat. *Nederlands zilver / Dutch silver 1580-1830*, Amsterdam (Rijksmuseum), Toledo (The Toledo Museum of Art) & Boston (Museum of Fine Arts) 1979-80

EXHIB. CAT. AMSTERDAM-VLISSINGEN 1957
R. van Luttervelt, exhib. cat. *Michiel de Ruyter 1607-1957*, Amsterdam (Rijksmuseum) & Vlissingen (Nieuw Tehuis voor Bejaarden) 1957

EXHIB. CAT. APELDOORN-LONDON 1988-89
J.D. Hunt and E. de Jong (eds.), exhib. cat. *The Anglo-Dutch garden in the age of William and Mary / De Gouden Eeuw van de Hollandse tuinkunst*, Apeldoorn (Rijksmuseum Paleis Het Loo) & London (Christie's) 1988-89 (*Journal of Garden History* 8 (1988), nrs. 2 & 3)

EXHIB. CAT. BASEL 1987 P. ten-Doesschate Chu *et al.* (eds.), exhib. cat. *Im lichte Hollands: Holländische Malerei des 17. Jahrhunderts aus den Sammlungen des Fürsten von Liechtenstein und aus Schweizer Besitz*, Basel (Kunstmuseum Basel) 1987

EXHIB. CAT. BERLIN 1991 I. Baer *et al.*, exhib. cat. *Kaiserlicher Kunstbesitz: aus dem holländischen Exil Haus Doorn*, Berlin (Schloss Charlottenburg) 1991

EXHIB. CAT. BERLIN-AMSTERDAM-LONDON 1991-92 C. Brown *et al.*, exhib. cat. *Rembrandt: de meester en zijn werkplaats: schilderijen*, Berlin (Gemäldegalerie Staatliche Museen Preussischer Kulturbesitz, Altes Museum), Amsterdam (Rijksmuseum) & London (The National Gallery) 1991-92

EXHIB. CAT. BRUGES 1974 J. Sip, exhib. cat. *Meesterwerken uit Praag 1450-1750: drie eeuwen Vlaamse en Hollandse schilderkunst*, Bruges (Groeningemuseum) 1974

EXHIB. CAT. BRAUNSCHWEIG 1979 R. Klessmann (ed.), exhib. cat. *Jan Lievens: ein Maler im Schatten Rembrandts*, Braunschweig (Herzog Anton Ulrich-Museum) 1979

EXHIB. CAT. COLOGNE-UTRECHT 1987 E. Mai and C. Stukenbrook (eds.), exhib. cat. *Nederlandse 17de eeuwse schilderijen uit Boedapest*, Cologne (Wallraf-Richartz-Museum) & Utrecht (Centraal Museum) 1987

EXHIB. CAT. COLOGNE-UTRECHT 1991-92
D.A. Levine and E. Mai (eds.), exhib. cat. *I Bamboccianti: Niederländische Malerrebellen im Rom des Barock*, Cologne (Wallraf Richartz-Museum) & Utrecht (Centraal Museum) 1991-92

EXHIB. CAT. DELFT 1996 M.C.C. Kersten *et al.*, exhib. cat. *Delftse Meesters, tijdgenoten van Vermeer: een andere kijk op perspectief, licht en ruimte*, Delft (Stedelijk Museum Het Prinsenhof) 1996

EXHIB. CAT. DELFT-CAMBRIDGE-FORT WORTH 1988-89 S. Segal; W.B. Jordan (ed.), exhib. cat. *A prosperous past: the sumptuous still life in the Netherlands 1600-1700*, Delft (Stedelijk Museum Het Prinsenhof), Cambridge, Mass. (Fogg Art Museum) & Fort Worth (Kimbell Art Museum) 1988-89

EXHIB. CAT. DIJON 1993 E. Starcky *et al.*, exhib. cat. *L'Age d'or flamand et hollandais: collections de Catherine II, Musée de l'Ermitage, Saint-Pétersbourg*, Dijon (Musée des Beaux-Arts de Dijon) 1993

EXHIB. CAT. DORDRECHT 1977-78 J.M. de Groot *et al.*, exhib. cat. *Aelbert Cuyp en zijn familie: schilders te Dordrecht*, Dordrecht (Dordrechts Museum) 1977-78

EXHIB. CAT. DORDRECHT 1992-93
P. Marijnissen *et al.* (eds.), exhib. cat. *De zichtbaere werelt: schilderkunst uit de Gouden Eeuw in Hollands oudste stad*, Dordrecht (Dordrechts Museum) 1992-93

EXHIB. CAT. DORDRECHT LEEUWARDEN 1988-89 F. Grijzenhout *et al.* (ed.), exhib. cat. *Meesterlijk vee: Nederlandse veeschilders 1600-1900*, Dordrecht (Dordrechts Museum) & Leeuwarden (Fries Museum) 1988-89

EXHIB. CAT. DRESDEN 1983 H. Marx (ed.), exhib. cat. *Das Stilleben und sein Gegenstand*, Dresden (Albertinum) 1983

EXHIB. CAT. DÜSSELDORF 1971 W. von Kalnein *et al.*, exhib. cat. *Europäische Barockplastik am Niederrhein*, Düsseldorf (Kunstmuseum) 1971

EXHIB. CAT. EDINBURGH 1992 J. Lloyd Williams, exhib. cat. *Dutch art and Scotland: a reflection of taste*, Edinburgh (The National Gallery of Scotland) 1992

EXHIB. CAT. FLORENCE 1998 M. Chiarini, exhib. cat. *La natura morta a palazzo e in villa: le collezioni dei Medici e dei Lorena*, Florence (Palazzo Pitti) 1998

EXHIB. CAT. FRANKFURT 1988-89 M. Bauer, exhib. cat. *Frankfurter Fayencen aus der Zeit des Barock*, Frankfurt am Main (Museum für Kunsthandwerk) 1988-89

EXHIB. CAT. FRANKFURT 1993-94 S. Schulze (ed.), exhib. cat. *Leselust: Niederländische Malerei von Rembrandt bis Vermeer*, Frankfurt (Schirn Kunsthalle) 1993-94

EXHIB. CAT. HAARLEM 1986 E. de Jongh, exhib. cat. *Portretten van echt en trouw: huwelijk en gezin in de Nederlandse kunst van de zeventiende eeuw*, Haarlem (Frans Halsmuseum) 1986

EXHIB. CAT. HAARLEM 1988 M. Carasso-Kok and J. Levy-van Halm (eds.), exhib. cat. *Schutters in Holland: kracht en zenuwen van de stad*, Haarlem (Frans Halsmuseum) 1988

EXHIB. CAT. HAARLEM 1993 J.A. Welu *et al.* (eds.), exhib. cat. *Judith Leyster: schilderes in een mannenwereld*, Haarlem (Frans Halsmuseum) 1993

EXHIB. CAT. THE HAGUE 1967 B. Jansen *et al.*, exhib. cat. *Haags zilver uit vijf eeuwen*, The Hague (Haags Gemeentemuseum) 1967

EXHIB. CAT. THE HAGUE 1974 J.P. Guépin *et al.*, exhib. cat. *Gerard Ter Borch: Zwolle 1617-Deventer 1681*, The Hague (Mauritshuis) 1974

EXHIB. CAT. THE HAGUE 1992 B. Brenninkmeyer-De Rooij *et al.* (eds.), exhib. cat. *Mauritshuis in bloei: boeketten uit de Gouden Eeuw / Mauritshuis in bloom: bouquets from the Golden Age*, The Hague (Mauritshuis) 1992

EXHIB. CAT. THE HAGUE 1994-95 A. Walsh *et al.*, exhib. cat. *Paulus Potter: schilderijen, tekeningen en etsen*, The Hague (Mauritshuis) 1994-95

EXHIB. CAT. THE HAGUE 1998-99 B. Broos *et al.*, exhib. cat. *Rembrandt onder het mes: de anatomische les van Dr Nicolaes Tulp ontleed*, The Hague (Mauritshuis) 1998-99

EXHIB. CAT. THE HAGUE-CAMBRIDGE 1981-82 S. Slive, exhib. cat. *Jacob van Ruisdael*, The Hague (Mauritshuis) & Cambridge, Mass. (Fogg Art Museum) 1981-82

EXHIB. CAT. THE HAGUE-SAN FRANCISCO 1990-91 B.P.J. Broos *et al.*, exhib. cat. *Hollandse meesters uit Amerika*, The Hague (Mauritshuis) & San Francisco (Fine Arts Museums of San Francisco) 1990-91

EXHIB. CAT. LILLE 1985 exhib. cat. *Un Palais pour un musée: exposition réalisée à l'occasion du centenaire de la construction du Palais des Palais des Beaux-Arts de Lille*, Lille (Musée des Beaux-Arts) 1985

EXHIB. CAT. LONDON 1964 A.G.H. Bachrach (ed.), exhib. cat. *The Orange and the Rose: Holland and Britain in the age of observation 1600-1750*, London (Victoria & Albert Museum) 1964

EXHIB. CAT. LONDON 1971-72 exhib. cat. *Dutch pictures from the Royal Collection*, London (The Queen's Gallery) 1971-72

EXHIB. CAT. LONDON 1978-79 C. Brown, exhib. cat. *The National Gallery lends Dutch Genre Paintings*, Newcastle (Hatton Art Gallery), Bolton (Museum and Art Gallery), Lincoln (Usher Art Gallery), Southampton (Art Gallery) & London (The National Gallery) 1978-79

EXHIB. CAT. LONDON 1994 F.G.H. Bachrach, exhib. cat. *Turner's Holland*, London (Tate Gallery) 1994

EXHIB. CAT. LONDON-HARTFORD 1998-99 P.C. Sutton, exhib. cat. *Pieter de Hooch, 1629-1684*, London (Dulwich Picture Gallery) & Hartford (Wadsworth Atheneum) 1998-99

EXHIB. CAT. LOS ANGELES-BOSTON-NEW YORK 1981-82 J. Walsh Jr. and C.P. Schneider, exhib. cat. *A mirror of nature: Dutch paintings from the collection of Mr. and Mrs. Edward William Carter*, Los Angeles (Los Angeles County Museum of Art), Boston (Museum of Fine Arts) & New York (The Metropolitan Museum of Art) 1981-82

EXHIB. CAT. MELBOURNE-CANBERRA 1997-98 A. Blankert *et al.*, exhib. cat. *Rembrandt: a genius and his impact*, Melbourne (National Gallery of Victoria) & Canberra (National Gallery of Australia) 1997-98

EXHIB. CAT. MINNEAPOLIS-HOUSTON-SAN DIEGO 1985 G. Keyes and R. Trnek, exhib. cat. *Dutch and Flemish Masters: paintings from the Vienna Academy of Arts*, Minneapolis (The Minneapolis Institute of Arts), Houston (The Museum of Fine Arts) & San Diego (The San Diego Museum of Art) 1985

EXHIB. CAT. NEW YORK 1979-80 C. Ryskamp, exhib. cat. *William & Mary and their house*, New York (The Pierpont Morgan Library) 1979-80

EXHIB. CAT. NEW YORK 1992-93 J.P. O'Neill (ed.), exhib. cat. *Masterworks from the Musée des Beaux-Arts, Lille*, New York (The Metropolitan Museum of Art) 1992-93

EXHIB. CAT. NEW YORK 1995-96 exhib. cat. *Rembrandt / not Rembrandt in The Metropolitan Museum of Art: aspects of connoisseurschip*, 2 vols. (vol. 1: H. von Sonnenburg, *Paintings: problems and issues*; vol. 2: W. Liedke *et al.*, *Paintings, drawings, and prints: art-historical perspectives*), New York (The Metropolitan Museum of Art) 1995-96

EXHIB. CAT. NEW YORK-CHICAGO 1988 J.P. O'Neill (ed.), exhib. cat. *Dutch and Flemish paintings from the Hermitage*, New York (The Metropolitan Museum of Art) & Chicago (The Art Institute of Chicago) 1988

EXHIB. CAT. NEW YORK-PARIS 1979-80 E.S. Sizov *et al.*, exhib. cat. *Treasures from the Kremlin*, New York (The Metropolitan Museum of Art) & Paris (Grand Palais) 1979-80

EXHIB. CAT. NEW YORK-PITTSBURGH 1988-89 R.J. Baarsen *et al.*, exhib. cat. *Courts and colonies: the William and Mary Style in Holland, England and America*, New York (Cooper-Hewitt Museum) & Pittsburgh (The Carnegie Museum of Art) 1988-89

EXHIB. CAT. PARIS 1970-71 exhib. cat. *Le siècle de Rembrandt: tableaux hollandais des collections publiques françaises*, Paris (Musée du Petit Palais) 1970-71

EXHIB. CAT. PARIS 1983 S. Nihom-Nijstad, exhib. cat. *Reflets du siècle d'or: tableaux Hollandais du dix-septieme siecle*, Paris (Fondation Custodia) 1983

EXHIB. CAT. PERTH-ADELAIDE-BRISBANE 1997-98 N. Middelkoop, exhib. cat. *The golden age of Dutch art: seventeenth century paintings from the Rijksmuseum and Australian collections*, Perth (Art Gallery of Western Australia), Adelaide (Art Gallery of South Australia) & Brisbane (Queensland Art Gallery) 1997-98

EXHIB. CAT. PHILADELPHIA-BERLIN-LONDON 1984 P.C. Sutton (ed.), exhib. cat. *Masters of seventeenth-century Dutch genre painting*, Philadelphia (Philadelphia Museum of Art), Berlin (Gemäldegalerie, Staatliche Museen Preussischer Kulturbesitz) & London (Royal Academy of Arts) 1984

EXHIB. CAT. RICHMOND ETC. 1979-80 A. Blunt, exhib. cat. *Treasures from Chatsworth: the Devonshire inheritance*, Richmond (Virginia Museum of Fine Arts), Fort Worth (Kimbell Art Museum), Toledo (The Toledo Museum of Art), San Antonio (San Antonio Museum Association), New Orleans (New Orleans Museum of Art) & San Francisco (The Fine Arts Museums of San Francisco) 1979-80

EXHIB. CAT. ROTTERDAM 1985 J. Giltaij (ed.), exhib. cat. *Meesterwerken uit de Hermitage Leningrad: Hollandse en Vlaamse schilderkunst van de 17e eeuw / Masterpieces from the Hermitage Leningrad: Dutch and Flemish paintings of the seventeenth century*, Rotterdam (Museum Boijmans Van Beuningen) 1985

EXHIB. CAT. ROTTERDAM 1991 J. Giltaij and G. Jansen, exhib. cat. *Perspectiven: Saenredam en de architectuurschilders van de 17e eeuw*, Rotterdam (Museum Boijmans Van Beuningen) 1991

EXHIB. CAT. ROTTERDAM 1994-95 N. Schadee (ed.), exhib. cat. *Rotterdamse meesters uit de Gouden Eeuw*, Rotterdam (Historisch Museum) 1994-95

EXHIB. CAT. ROTTERDAM 1995-96 Je.B. Goesarova *et al.* (eds.), exhib. cat. *Schatten van de Tsaar: hofcultuur van Peter de grote uit het Kremlin*, Rotterdam (Museum Boymans Van Beuningen) 1995-96

EXHIB. CAT. ROTTERDAM-BERLIN 1996-97
J. Giltaij and J. Kelch, exhib. cat. *Lof der zeevaart: de Hollandse zeeschilders van de 17e eeuw*, Rotterdam (Museum Boijmans Van Beuningen) & Berlin (Gemäldegalerie Staatliche Museen) 1996-97

EXHIB. CAT. ROTTERDAM-FRANKFURT 1999-2000 A. Blankert *et al.*, exhib. cat. *Hollands classicisme in de zeventiende-eeuwse schilderkunst*, Rotterdam (Museum Boijmans Van Beuningen) & Frankfurt (Städelsches Kunstinstitut) 1999-2000

EXHIB. CAT. SAN FRANCISCO-BALTIMORE-LONDON 1997-98 J. Spicer (ed.), exhib. cat. *Masters of light: Dutch painters in Utrecht during the Golden Age*, San Francisco (Fine Arts Museums of San Francisco), Baltimore (The Walters Art Gallery) & London (The National Gallery) 1997-98

EXHIB. CAT. STOCKHOLM 1992-93 G. Cavalli-Björkman (ed.), exhib. cat. *Rembrandt och hans tid*, Stockholm (Nationalmuseum) 1992-93

EXHIB. CAT. TOKYO-AMSTERDAM 1991-92
Ch. van Rappard-Boon *et al.*, exhib. cat. *Imitatie en inspiratie: Japanse invloed op Nederlandse kunst van 1650 tot heden*, Tokyo (Suntory Museum of Art) & Amsterdam (Rijksmuseum) 1991-92

EXHIB. CAT. UTRECHT 1965 A. Blankert, exhib. cat. *Nederlandse 17e eeuwse Italianiserende landschapschilders*, Utrecht (Centraal Museum) 1965

EXHIB. CAT. UTRECHT 1984-85 exhib. cat. *Zeldzaam zilver uit de Gouden Eeuw: de Utrechtse edelsmeden Van Vianen*, Utrecht (Centraal Museum) 1984-85

EXHIB. CAT. UTRECHT-BRAUNSCHWEIG 1986-87 A. Blankert *et al.* (eds.), exhib. cat. *Nieuw licht op de Gouden Eeuw: Hendrick ter Bruggen en tijdgenoten*, Utrecht (Centraal Museum) & Braunschweig (Herzog Anton Ulrich-Museum) 1986-87

EXHIB. CAT. UTRECHT-BRAUNSCHWEIG 1991 S. Segal, exhib. cat. *Jan Davidsz de Heem en zijn kring*, Utrecht (Centraal Museum) & Braunschweig (Herzog Anton Ulrich-Museum) 1991

EXHIB. CAT. UTRECHT-FRANKFURT-LUXEMBURG 1993-94 P. van den Brink *et al.* (eds.), exhib. cat. *Het gedroomde land: pastorale schilderkunst in de Gouden Eeuw*, Utrecht (Centraal Museum), Frankfurt (Schirn Kunsthalle) & Luxemburg (Musée National d'Historie et d'Art) 1993-94

EXHIB. CAT. WARSAW 1990 J. Grabski (ed.), exhib. cat. *Opus Sacrum: catalogue of the exhibition from the collection of Barbara Piasecka Johnson*, Warsaw (Royal Castle) 1990

EXHIB. CAT. WASHINGTON 1985-86 G. Jackson-Stops (ed.), exhib. cat. *The treasure houses of Britain: five hundert years of private patronage and art collecting*, Washington (National Gallery of Art) 1985-86

EXHIB. CAT. WASHINGTON-AMSTERDAM 1996-97 H.P. Chapman *et al.*; G. Jansen (ed.), exhib. cat. *Jan Steen: schilder en verteller*, Washington (National Gallery of Art) & Amsterdam (Rijksmuseum) 1996-97

EXHIB. CAT. WASHINGTON-THE HAGUE 1995-96 A.K. Wheelock, Jr. (ed.), exhib. cat. *Johannes Vermeer*, Washington (National Gallery of Art) & The Hague (Mauritshuis) 1995-96

EXHIB. CAT. WASHINGTON-LONDON-HAARLEM 1989-90 S. Slive (ed.), exhib. cat. *Frans Hals*, Washington (National Gallery of Art), London (Royal Academy of Arts) & Haarlem (Frans Halsmuseum) 1989-90

EXHIB. CAT. ZÜRICH 1988 F. Baumann *et al.* (eds.), exhib. cat. *Geschenke und Neuerwerbungen zum 200-Jahr-Jubiläum der Zürcher Kunstgesellschaft*, Zürich (Kunsthaus) 1988

FINK 1954 A. Fink, *Geschichte des Herzog Anton Ulrich-Museums in Braunschweig*, Braunschweig 1954

FOUCART *et al.* 1995 J. Foucart *et al.*, *The visitor's guide: Flemish, Dutch and German painting*, Paris 1995

FREISE 1911 K. Freise, *Pieter Lastman: sien leben und seine Kunst*, Leipzig 1911

FREMANTLE 1959 K. Fremantle, *The baroque town hall of Amsterdam*, Utrecht 1959

GAEHTGENS 1987 B. Gaehtgens, *Adriaen van der Werff 1659-1722*, Munich 1987

DE GELDER 1921 J.J. de Gelder, *Bartolomeus van der Helst: een studie van zijn werk, zijn levensgeschiedenis, een beschrijvende catalogus van zijn oeuvre, een register en 41 afbeeldingen naar schilderijen*, Rotterdam 1921

GERSON 1936 H. Gerson, *Philips Koninck: Ein Beitrag zur Erforschung der holländischen Malerei des XVII. Jahrhunderts*, Berlin 1936 (reprint: Berlin 1980)

VAN DER GIESEN 1997 I. van der Giesen, *Pieter Xavery: genre in zeventiende-eeuwse beeldhouwkunst*, Amsterdam 1997 (M.A. thesis, Vrije Universiteit)

GOEDDE 1989 L.O. Goedde, *Tempest and shipwreck in Dutch and Flemish art: convention, rhetoric and interpretation*, University Park & London 1989

GRIJZENHOUT 1984 F. Grijzenhout, 'Tempel voor Nederland: de Nationale Konst-Gallerij in 's Gravenhage', *Nederlands Kunsthistorisch Jaarboek* 35 (1984), pp. 1-75

GRISEBACH 1974 L. Grisebach, *Willem Kalf 1619-1693*, Berlin 1974

GUDLAUGSSON 1959-60 S.J. Gudlaugsson, *Gerard Ter Borch*, 2 vols., The Hague 1959-60

HAAK 1968 B. Haak, *Rembrandt: zijn leven, zijn werk, zijn tijd*, Amsterdam 1968

HALSEMA-KUBES 1991 W. Halsema-Kubes, 'De Noordnederlandse beeldhouwkunst in de 17de eeuw', *Openbaar Kunstbezit* 35 (1991), pp. 16-25

VAN DER HAM 2000 G. van der Ham, *Tweehonderd jaar Rijksmuseum: geschiedenis van een nationaal symbool*, Amsterdam 2000

HARWOOD 1988 L.B. Harwood, *Adam Pynacker (c. 1620-1763)*, Doornspijk 1988

HAVERKAMP BEGEMANN 1959 E. Haverkamp Begemann, *Willem Buytewech*, Amsterdam 1959

HAVERKAMP BEGEMANN 1982 E. Haverkamp Begemann, *Rembrandt: the Nightwatch*, Princeton 1982

AN DER HEIDEN 1998 R. an der Heiden, *Die Alte Pinakothek: Sammlungsgeschichte, Bau und Bilder*, Munich 1998

HOEKSTRA 1996 F. Hoekstra, 'Het 'ideale paar' van Rembrandt', *Antiek* 31 (1996), no. 2, pp. 59-65

HOFRICHTER 1989 F.F. Hofrichter, *Judith Leyster: a woman painter in Holland's Golden Age*, Doornspijk 1989

HOFSTEDE DE GROOT 1907-28 C. Hofstede de Groot, *Beschreibendes und kritisches Verzeichnis der Werke der hervorragendsten holländischen Maler des XVII. Jahrhunderts*, 10 vols., Esslingen & Paris 1907-28

JANSEN 1987 G.M.C. Jansen, *Pieter Saenredam: gezicht op de Mariaplaats en de Mariakerk te Utrecht*, Rotterdam 1987

JANSEN 1997 G.M.C. Jansen, 'Paulus geneest de kreupele man te Lystra uit 1663 door Karel du Jardin (1626-1678)', *Bulletin van het Rijksmuseum* 45 (1997), pp. 179-89

JANTZEN 1979 H. Jantzen, *Das Niederländische Architekturbild*, Braunschweig 1979 (first edition: 1910)

JIMKES-VERKADE 1991 E. Jimkes-Verkade, 'Het heldengraf', *Openbaar Kunstbezit* 35 (1991), pp. 32-41

DE JONG 1993 E. de Jong, *Natuur en kunst: Nederlandse tuin- en landschapsarchitectuur 1650-1740*, Amsterdam 1993

DE JONG AND SCHELLEKENS 1994 E. de Jong and C. Schellekens, *Het beeld buiten: vier eeuwen tuinsculptuur in Nederland*, Heino 1994

DE JONGE 1938 C.H. de Jonge, *Paulus Moreelse: portret- en genreschilder te Utrecht 1571-1638*, Assen 1938

DE JONGH 1967 E. de Jongh, 'Zinne- en minnebeelden in de schilderkunst', *Openbaar Kunstbezit* 11 (1967), no. 29

DE JONGH 1969 E. de Jongh, 'Tuinfeest: Dirck Hals (1591-1656)', *Openbaar Kunstbezit* 13 (1969), no. 13

DE JONGH 1981-82 E. de Jongh, 'Bol vincit amorem', *Simiolus* 12 (1981-82), pp. 147-61

DE JONGH AND VINKEN 1961 E. de Jongh and P.J. Vinken, 'Frans Hals als voortzetter van een emblematische traditie. Bij het huwelijksportret van Isaac Massa en Beatrix van der Laen', *Oud Holland* 76 (1961), pp. 117-52

JUDSON 1959 J.R. Judson, *Gerrit van Honthorst: a discussion of his position in Dutch art*, The Hague 1959

KAUFFMANN 1977 H. Kauffmann, 'Jacob van Ruisdael: 'Die Mühle von Wijk bei Duurstede'', L. Grisebach and K. Renger (ed.), *Festschrift für Otto von Simson zum 65. Geburtstag*, Frankfurt 1977, pp. 379-97

KELCH 1971 J. Kelch, *Studien zu Simon de Vlieger als Marinemaler*, Berlin 1971 (diss.)

KEYES 1975 G.S. Keyes, *Cornelis Vroom: marine and landscape artist*, 2 vols., Utrecht 1975 (diss. Rijksuniversiteit Utrecht)

KEYES 1984 G.S. Keyes, *Esaias van den Velde 1587-1630*, Doornspijk 1984

KILIAN 1994 J.M. Kilian, *The paintings of Karel du Jardin (1626-1678)*, Ann Arbor 1994

KLOEK 1989A W.Th. Kloek, 'Willem Claesz Heda, stilleven met vergulde bokaal, 1635', *Bulletin van het Rijksmuseum* 37 (1989), pp. 224-27

KLOEK 1989B W.Th. Kloek, 'Gerrit Adriaensz Berckheyde, De bocht van de Herengracht bij de Nieuwe Spiegelstraat te Amsterdam, 1672', *Bulletin van het Rijksmuseum* 37 (1989), pp. 238-39

KLOEK 1992 W.Th. Kloek, 'Over Rembrandts Portret van Uyttenbogaert, nu in het Rijksmuseum', *Bulletin van het Rijksmuseum* 40 (1992), pp. 346-52

KLOEK 1998 W.Th. Kloek, *Een huishouden van Jan Steen*, Hilversum 1998

KLUIVER 1995 J.H. Kluiver, 'Adriaan van de Venne's 'Gezicht op de haven van Middelburg', geïdentificeerd als het vertrek van Robert Sidney in 1616', *Oud Holland* 109 (1995), pp. 121-42

KRUIMEL 1971 H.L. Kruimel, 'Rondom de Van der Schalcke-portretten van Gerard Ter Borch', *Jaarboek van het Centraal Bureau voor Genealogie* 25 (1971), pp. 224-29

KUZNETZOW 1974 J.I. Kuznetzow, 'Nikolaus Knupfer (1603?-1655)', *Oud Holland* 88 (1974), pp. 169-219

KUZNETSOV AND LINNIK 1982 Y. Kuznetsov and I. Linnik, *Dutch painting in Soviet museums*, Amsterdam & Leningrad 1982

LANE 1959 A. Lane, 'Delftse tegels uit Hampton Court en Daniel Marot's werkzaamheid aldaar', *Bulletin van het Rijksmuseum* 7 (1959), pp. 12-21

LANGENDIJK 1992 K. Langendijk, *Die Selbstbildnisse der Holländischen und Flämischen Künstler in der Galleria degli Autoritratti der Uffizien in Florenz*, Florence 1992

LASEUR 1998 W.A. Laseur, met medewerking van J. van Heel, *Het Museum Meermanno-Westreenianum*, The Hague 1998

LAWRENCE 1991 C. Lawrence, *Gerrit Adriaensz. Berckheyde (1638-1698): Haarlem cityscape painter*, Doornspijk 1991

LIEDTKE 1982 W.A. Liedtke, *Architectural painting in Delft*, Doornspijk 1982

VAN LOON AND VAN EEGHEN 1984 M.N. van Loon and I.H. van Eeghen, *Het huis met de paarse ruiten en de familie van Loon in Amsterdam*, Alphen aan den Rijn 1984

LOWENTHAL 1986 A.W. Lowenthal, *Joachim Wtewael and Dutch mannerism*, Doornspijk 1986

LUNSINGH SCHEURLEER 1975 D.F. Lunsingh Scheurleer, 'Keramiek in het Rijksmuseum Meermanno-Westreenianum te Den Haag', *Mededelingenblad vrienden van de nederlandse ceramiek* 79/80 (1975), nos. 3-4, pp. 2-33

LUNSINGH SCHEURLEER 1979 Th. H. Lunsingh Scheurleer, 'Koperen kronen en waskaarsen voor Japan', *Oud Holland* 93 (1979), pp. 69-95

LUNSINGH SCHEURLEER 1984 D.F. Lunsingh Scheurleer, *Niederländische Fayence*, Munich 1984

MANKE 1963 I. Manke, *Emanuel de Witte 1617-1692*, Amsterdam 1963

MARTIN 1913 W. Martin, *Gerard Dou: des Meisters Gemälde*, Stuttgart & Berlin 1913

MEYER 1958 E.R. Meyer, 'Gabriël Metsu (1629-1667): Het zieke kind', *Openbaar Kunstbezit* 2 (1958), no. 29

TER MOLEN 1984 J.R. ter Molen, *Van Vianen: een Utrechtse familie van zilversmeden met een internationale faam*, 2 vols., Rotterdam 1984

TER MOLEN (ED.) 1999 J.R. ter Molen (ed.), *150 jaar Museum Boijmans Van Beuningen*, Rotterdam (Museum Boymans Van Beuningen) 1999

VON MOLTKE 1938-39A J.W. von Moltke, 'Salomon de Bray', *Marburger Jahrbuch für Kunstwissenschaft* 11/12 (1938-39), pp. 309-420

VON MOLTKE 1938-39B J.W. von Moltke, 'Jan de Bray', *Marburger Jahrbuch für Kunstwissenschaft* 11/12 (1938-39), pp. 421-523

VON MOLTKE 1965 J.W. von Moltke, *Govaert Flinck 1615-1660*, Amsterdam 1965

VON MOLTKE 1994 J.W. von Moltke, *Arent de Gelder: Dordrecht 1645-1727*, Doornspijk 1994

DU MORTIER 1984 B.M. du Mortier, 'De handschoen in de huwelijkssymboliek van de zeventiende eeuw', *Bulletin van het Rijksmuseum* 32 (1984), pp. 189-201

DU MORTIER 1989 B.M. du Mortier, 'Een paar geborduurde handschoenen, Nederland, ca. 1622', *Bulletin van het Rijksmuseum* 37 (1989), pp. 204-05

NAUMANN 1981 O. Naumann, *Frans van Mieris (1635-1681) The Elder*, 2 vols., Doornspijk 1981

NEURDENBURG 1930 E. Neurdenburg, *Hendrick de Keyser: beeldhouwer en bouwmeester van Amsterdam*, Amsterdam 1930

NEURDENBURG 1948 E. Neurdenburg, *De zeventiende eeuwsche beeldhouwkunst in de noordelijke Nederlanden*, Amsterdam 1948

NICOLSON 1958 B. Nicolson, *Hendrick Terbrugghen*, The Hague 1958

VAN OS 1992 H.W. van Os, 'Hoe Rembrandts Uyttenbogaert in Nederland terug kwam', *Bulletin van het Rijksmuseum* 40 (1992), pp. 343-45

DE PAUS AND SCHWEITZER 1992 W. de Paus and G.J. Schweitzer (eds.), *Dordrechts Museum 150 jaar: 1842-1992*, Dordrecht (Dordrechts Museum) 1992

PECK 1991 W.H. Peck, *The Detroit Institute of Arts: a brief history*, Detroit (The Detroit Institute of Arts) 1991

PETER-RAUPP 1980 H. Peter-Raupp, *Die Ikonographie des Oranjezaal*, Hildesheim & New York 1980

PLIETZSCH 1960 E. Plietzsch, *Holländische und Flämische Maler des XVII. Jahrh.*, Leipzig 1960

VAN DER PLOEG 1995 P. van der Ploeg, 'Meindert Hobbema (1638-1709): boslandschap met boerenhoeven', *Mauritshuis in focus* 8 (1995), no. 1, pp. 14-20

POOL 1727 M. Pool, *Cabinet de l'art et de schulpture, par le fameux sculpteur Francis van Bossuit, exécuté en yvore ou ébauché en terre, gravées d'après les desseins de Barent Graat*, Amsterdam 1727

POTTERTON et al. 1988 H. Potterton et al., *The National Gallery of Ireland: acquisitions 1986-88*, Dublin 1988

REISS 1975 S. Reiss, *Aelbert Cuyp*, London 1975

DE ROBELIN 1994-95 R. de Robelin, 'On the provenance of Rembrandt's *The kitchen maid*', *Art Bulletin of the Nationalmuseum Stockholm* 1-2 (1994 95), pp. 100-110

ROBINSON 1974 F.W. Robinson, *Gabriel Metsu (1629-1667): a study of his place in Dutch genre painting of the Golden Age*, New York 1974

ROBINSON 1990 M.S. Robinson, *Van de Velde: a catalogue of the paintings of the Elder and the Younger Willem van de Velde*, 2 vols., London 1990

ROETHLISBERGER 1981 M. Roethlisberger, *Bartholomeus Breenbergh: the paintings*, Berlin & New York 1981

ROETHLISBERGER 1993 M.G. Roethlisberger, *Abraham Bloemaert and his sons: paintings and prints*, 2 vols., Doornspijk 1993

ROSCAM ABBING 1993 M. Roscam Abbing, *De schilder en schrijver Samuel van Hoogstraten 1627-1678: eigentijdse bronnen en oeuvre van gesigneerde schilderijen*, Leiden 1993

ROSENBERG 1928 J. Rosenberg, *Jacob van Ruisdael*, Berlin 1928

ROWLANDS 1979 J. Rowlands, *Hercules Segers*, Amsterdam 1979

ROY 1992 A. Roy, *Gérard de Lairesse (1640-1711)*, Paris 1992

RUSSELL 1975 M. Russell, *Jan van de Cappelle 1624/6-1679*, Leigh-on-Sea 1975

VON SALDERN 1988 A. von Saldern, *Das Museum für Kunst und Gewerbe Hamburg 1869-1988: mit einer Bibliographie, 1877-1988*, Hamburg 1988

SCHAAR 1958 E. Schaar, *Studien zu Nicolaes Berchem*, Cologne 1958

SCHATBORN 1975 P. Schatborn, '*De Hut* van Adriaen van de Velde', *Bulletin van het Rijksmuseum* 23 (1975), pp. 159-65

SCHMIDBERGER 1988 E. Schmidberger, 'Die Sammlungen der Abteilung Kunsthandwerk und Plastik', *Kunst in Hessen und am Mittelrhein* 28 (1988), pp. 63-84

SCHNEIDER 1990 C.P. Schneider, *Rembrandt's landscapes*, New Haven & London 1990

SCHNEIDER AND EKKART 1973 H. Schneider and R.E.O. Ekkart, *Jan Lievens: sein Leben und seine Werke*, Amsterdam 1973

SCHOLTEN 1986 F. Scholten, *Zilver*, The Hague 1986

SCHOLTEN 1991 F. Scholten, ''Mea Sorte Contentus': Rombout Verhulst's Portrait of Jacob van Reygersbergh', *The J. Paul Getty Museum Journal* 19 (1991), pp. 65-74

SCHOLTEN 1999 F. Scholten, 'Een ijvore Mars van Francis: de beeldsnijder Van Bossuit en de familie De la Court', *Bulletin van het Rijksmuseum* 47 (1999), pp. 26-43

SCHWARTZ AND BOK 1989 G. Schwartz and M.J. Bok, *Pieter Saenredam: de schilder in zijn tijd*, The Hague 1989

SLATKES 1965 L.J. Slatkes, *Dirck van Baburen (c. 1595-1624): a Dutch painter in Utrecht and Rome*, Utrecht 1965

SLIVE 1970-74 S. Slive, *Frans Hals*, 3 vols., London & New York 1970-74

SLIVE 1995 S. Slive, *Dutch painting 1600-1800*, New Haven & London 1995

SLUIJTER-SEIJFFERT 1984 N.C. Sluijter-Seijffert, *Cornelis van Poelenburch (ca. 1593-1667)*, Enschede 1984 (diss. Rijksuniversiteit Leiden)

SMIT 1990 F.G.A.M. Smit, *Anna Roemers & Maria Tesselschade and their engravings on glass*, Peterborough 1990

SMITH 1829-42 J. Smith, *A catalogue raisonné of the works of the most eminent Dutch, Flemish and French painters*, 9 vols., London 1829-42

STARING 1927 A. Staring, 'De beeldhouwer Pieter Xavery', *Oud Holland* 44 (1927), pp. 1-15

STARKIE GARDNER 1905 J. Starkie Gardner, 'Charles II Silver at Welbeck-Part I', *The Burlington Magazine* 7 (1905), pp. 32-38

STECHOW 1938 W. Stechow, *Salomon van Ruysdael: eine Einführung in seine Kunst*, Berlin 1938 (reprint: Berlin 1975)

STELAND-STIEF 1971 A.C. Steland-Stief, *Jan Asselijn nach 1610 bis 1652*, Amsterdam 1971

STUMPEL 1995 J. Stumpel, 'Van veren en verven: over het mirakel van geschilderd gevogelte', *Openbaar Kunstbezit* 39 (1995), pp. 36-41

SUMOWSKI 1983-94 W. Sumowski, *Gemälde der Rembrandt-Schüler*, 6 vols., Landau 1983-94

SUTTON 1976 D. Sutton (ed.), *Treasures from the collection of Frits Lugt at the Institut Néerlandais*, London 1976 (originally published in *Apollo 104*, 1976)

SUTTON 1980 P.C. Sutton, *Pieter de Hooch*, Oxford & New York 1980

SUTTON 1986 P.C. Sutton, *A guide to Dutch art in America*, Kampen 1986

TAYLOR 1995 P. Taylor, *Bloemstillevens in de Gouden Eeuw 1600-1720*, Zwolle 1995

THEUERKAUFF 1975 C. Theuerkauff, 'Zu Francis Van Bossuit (1635-1692), 'beeldsnyder in yvoor'', *Wallraf-Richartz-Jahrbuch* 37 (1975), p. 178

VAN THIEL 1967 P.J.J. van Thiel, 'Philips Konincks Vergezicht met hutten aan de weg', *Bulletin van het Rijksmuseum* 15 (1967), pp. 109-15

VAN THIEL 1968 P.J.J. van Thiel, 'Vergezicht met hutten aan de weg: Philips Koninck (1619-1688)', *Openbaar Kunstbezit* 12 (1968), no. 34

VAN THIEL 1975 P.J.J. van Thiel, 'Een stilleven door Pieter Claesz', *Bulletin van het Rijksmuseum* 23 (1975), pp. 119-21

VAN THIEL 1983A P.J.J. van Thiel, 'Werner Jacobsz van den Valckert', *Oud Holland* 97 (1983), pp. 128-95

VAN THIEL 1983B P.J.J. van Thiel, 'Het Rijksmuseum in het Trippenhuis, 1814-1885 (III): de plattegronden van 1823 en 1875 en een verworpen plan voor de bouw van een tuinzaal van 1854', *Bulletin van het Rijksmuseum* 31 (1983), pp. 12-26

VAN THIEL 1983C P.J.J. van Thiel, '1928 Johannes Verspronck: Portret van een meisje in het blauw', *Bulletin van het Rijksmuseum* 31 (1983), pp. 210-11

VAN THIEL 1983D P.J.J. van Thiel, 'Floris van Dijck: Stilleven met kazen', *Bulletin van het Rijksmuseum* 31 (1983), p. 228

VAN THIEL 1989 P.J.J. van Thiel, 'Pieter Codde, de terugkeer der jagers, 1633', *Bulletin van het Rijksmuseum* 37 (1989), pp. 219-21

VAN THIENEN 1957 F.W.S. van Thienen, 'Jan Steen (1626-1679): het Sint Nicolaasfeest', *Openbaar Kunstbezit* (1957), no. 32

THOMPSON 1972 C. Thompson, *Pictures for Scotland: The National Gallery of Scotland and its collection: a study of the changing attitude to painting since the 1820s*, Edinburgh 1972

THORNTON 1998 P. Thornton, *Form & decoration: innovation in the decorative arts 1470-1870*, London 1998

TÜMPEL 1993 C. Tümpel, Rembrandt, Antwerp 1993

VECHT 1968 A. Vecht, *Frederik van Frytom 1632-1702: life and work of a Delft pottery-decorator*, Amsterdam 1968

VINKEN AND DE JONGH 1963 P.J. Vinken and E. de Jongh, 'De boosaardigheid van Hals' regenten en regentessen', *Oud Holland* 78 (1963), pp. 1-26

VLIEGENTHART 1999 A.W. Vliegenthart, *Het Loo, een paleis als museum: journaal van een restauratie*, Apeldoorn 1999

VLIEGER 1995 E. Vlieger, 'Melchior d'Hondecoeter (1636-1695) 'der beste mahler umb vögeln zu mahlen'', *Openbaar Kunstbezit* 39 (1995), pp. 16-23

VOYCE 1954 A. Voyce, *The Moscow Kremlin: its history, architecture and art treasures*, Berkeley & Los Angeles 1954

DE VRIES 1975 L. de Vries, 'Gerard Houckgeest', *Jahrbuch der Hamburger Kunstsammlungen* 20 (1975), pp. 25-56

DE VRIES 1977 L. de Vries, *Jan Steen 'de kluchtschilder'*, Groningen 1977 (diss. Rijksuniversiteit Groningen)

VROOM 1980 N.R.A. Vroom, *A modest message as intimated by the painters of the 'monochrome banketje'*, 2 vols., Schiedam 1980

VAN DE WAAL 1956 H. van de Waal, 'De Staalmeesters en hun legende', *Oud Holland* 71 (1956), pp. 61-107 (reprinted in translation in H. van de Waal, *Steps towards Rembrandt: collected articles 1937-1972*, Amsterdam & London 1974, pp. 247-92)

WADUM 1995 J. Wadum, 'Hobbema doorgelicht', *Mauritshuis in focus* 8 (1995), no. 1, pp. 20-23

WAGNER 1971 H. Wagner, *Jan van der Heyden 1637-1712*, Amsterdam & Haarlem 1971

WALSH 1989A J. Walsh Jr., *Jan and Julius Porcellis: Dutch marine painters*, Ann Arbor 1989

WALSH 1989B A.L. Walsh, *Paulus Potter: his works and their meaning*, Ann Arbor 1989

WEISNER 1964 U. Weisner, 'Die Gemälde des Moyses van Uyttenbroeck', *Oud Holland* 79 (1964), pp. 189-228

WELCKER 1979 C. Welcker, *Hendrick Averkamp (1585-1634), bijgenaamd 'de stomme van Campen' en Barent Avercamp (1612-1679), 'schilders tot Campen'*, revised edition by D.J. Henbroek-van der Poel, Doornspijk 1979 (first edition: Zwolle 1933)

VAN DE WETERING 1997 E. van de Wetering, *Rembrandt: the painter at work*, Amsterdam 1997

WHEELOCK 1975-76 A.K. Wheelock Jr., 'Gerard Houckgeest and Emanuel de Witte: architectural painting in Delft around 1650', *Simiolus* 8 (1975/76), pp. 167-85

WHEELOCK 1977 A.K. Wheelock Jr., *Perspective, optics, and Delft artists around 1650*, New York & London 1977

WHITE 1982 C. White, *The Dutch pictures in the collection of Her Majesty The Queen*, Cambridge 1982

WHITEHILL 1970 W.M. Whitehill, *Museum of Fine Arts, Boston: a centennial history*, 2 vols., Cambridge (Mass.) 1970

WIESEMAN 1993 M.E. Wieseman, *Caspar Netscher and late seventeenth-century Dutch painting*, Ann Arbor 1993

VAN DER WYCK 1977 H.W.M. van der Wyck, 'Tuinsculpturen voorheen en thans op het Loo aanwezig', *Bulletin van de Koninklijke Nederlands Oudheidkundige Bond* 76 (1977) pp. 165-77

ZELDENRUST 1983 M. Zeldenrust, 'Aert van der Neers *Rivierlandschap bij maanlicht* opgehelderd', *Bulletin van het Rijksmuseum* 31 (1982), pp. 99-104

INDEX

Index

Index

Photo credits

Every effort has been made to apprise all institutions and other concerned parties of the publication of photographic material. Any unintentional oversight may be communicated to the Rijksmuseum, Amsterdam (Exhibition Office).

AMSTERDAM   Amsterdams Historisch Museum   *68, 162, 175, 193*

AMSTERDAM   Gemeentearchief   fig. 2

AMSTERDAM   Museum van Loon   *38*

AMSTERDAM   Stichting Koninklijk Paleis te Amsterdam photo Erik Hesmerg   p. 251

APELDOORN   Paleis Het Loo, R. Mulder   *186*

BALTIMORE   The Walters Art Gallery   *15*

BERLIN   Staatliche Museen zu Berlin, Preussischer Kulturbesitz, Gemäldegalerie; photo Jörg P. Anders   *12, 137, 176*

BOSTON   Museum of Fine Arts. Reproduced with permission. © 1999. All rights reserved   *23*

BRAUNSCHWEIG   Herzog Anton Ulrich-Museum; photo Bernd-Peter Keiser   *21, 51*

BRUSSELS   Koninklijke Musea voor Schone Kunsten van België; photo Speltdoorn & zoon, fig. 11

BUDAPEST   Szépmüvészeti Múzeum   *124*; photo András Rászó   *22*

CARACAS   Colección Patricia Phelps de Cisneros   *89*

CARDIFF   National Museums & Galleries of Wales   *158*

CHATSWORTH   Chatsworth Photo Library © 1995   *193*

COPENHAGEN   Statens Museum for Kunst; photo Dowic Fotografi   *40*

DELFT   Nieuwe Kerk (Rijksgebouwendienst); photo Tom Haartsen   *8a, 8b*

DEN BOSCH   Beekmans Beeldproducties 's-Hertogenbosch   p. 23

DETROIT   Gift of Julius H. Haass in memory of his brother Dr. Ernest W. Haass; photo © The Detroit Institute of Arts   *155*

DOORN   Huis Doorn; photo Jörg P. Anders, Berlin   *109*

DORDRECHT   Dordrechts Museum   *130, 165* photo Marco de Nood

DORDRECHT   Museum Mr. Simon van Gijn   *189*

DOUAI   Musée de la Chartreuse   *41*, photo Lefebvre Daniel   *196*

DRESDEN   Staatliche Kunstsammlungen, Gemäldegalerie Alte Meister; photo Klut/Dresden   *54 en 183*

DUBLIN   National Gallery of Ireland   *141a, 141b*, fig. 5

EDINBURGH   National Gallery of Scotland; photo Antonia Reeve   *60, 73, 199*

FLORENCE   Galleria degli Uffizi; photo Serge Domingie-Marco Rabatti, Florence   *81*

FLORENCE   Galleria Palatina, Palazzo Pitti   *126*

HAARLEM   Frans Halsmuseum   *20, 146*

THE HAGUE   Collectie Gemeentemuseum, 2000 c/o Beeldrecht Amstelveen   *102*

THE HAGUE   Huis ten Bosch (Rijksgebouwendienst)   *170*

THE HAGUE   Mauritshuis   *58, 78, 87, 123, 135*, photo Daniël van de Ven   *157*

THE HAGUE   Museum van het Boek/Museum Meermanno-Westreenianum   *169a*

THE HAGUE   Fotoarchief van de Rijksvoorlichtingsdienst   p. 326

HAMBURG   Museum für Kunst und Gewerbe   *30, 108*

HARTFORD   Wadsworth Atheneum (Private collection)   *180*

KANSAS CITY   The Nelson-Atkins Museum of Art (Purchase)   *6*

KASSEL   Hessisches Landesmuseum Kunsthandwerk und Plastik; photo A. Hensmanns   *106*

LILLE   Musée des Beaux-Arts; photo RMN-Quecq d'Henripret   *36*, photo RMN-P. Bernard   *79*

LONDON   The Trustees of Dulwich Picture Gallery   *178*

LONDON   The National Gallery ©   *24, 118*, p. 49, fig. 9

LONDON & WINDSOR   The Royal Collection, © 1999 H.M. queen Elizabeth II; photo A.C. Cooper Ltd.   *93*, photo Rodney Todd-White   *121*, photo Stephen Chapman   *195*

LOS ANGELES   Collection of the The J. Paul Getty Museum   *53, 149, 168b*

LOS ANGELES   Los Angeles County Museum of Art, gift of the Ahmanson Foundation   *128*

LUND   Museum of Cultural History, Kulturen; photo Lennart Hansson   *107*

MADRID   Museo Thyssen-Bornemisza   *82, 129*

MOSCOW   State Museum of the Moscow Kremlin   *71*

MUNICH   Alte Pinakothek; photo Kunstdia-Archiv ARTHOTEK, D-Peissenberg; photo Blauel/Gnamm   *110*, photo Joachim Blauel   *120*

NIKKO (Japan)   Nikko Toshogu Shrine   *72*

NELAHOZEVES (Czech Republic)   Nelahozeves Castle, The Lobkowicz Collections   *197*

NEW YORK   The Metropolitan Museum of Art; Purchase, 1871 (71.62) photo © 1999   *83*, Purchase, Gift The Annenberg Foundation, 1991 (1991.305) photo © 1991   *91*, Robert Lehman Collection, 1975 (1975.1.140) photo Malcolm Varon © 1995   *150*, Gift Manuel E. and Ellen G. Rionda, 1943 (43.118) photo © 1984   *200*, Purchased with special funds and gifts of friends of the Museum, 1961 (61.198) photo © 1993 fig. 4

OBERLIN (Ohio)   Allen Memorial Art Museum, Oberlin College. RT Miller, Jr. Fund 1953; photo John Seyfried   *7*

PARIS   Collection Frits Lugt, Institut Néerlandais   *182*

PARIS   Musée du Louvre; photo RMN-Arnaudet   *90*, photo RMN-Peter Willi   *99*, photo RMN-Gérard Blot   p. 30

PRAGUE   Národní-Galerie   *144*

ROTTERDAM   Museum Boijmans Van Beuningen   *29, 77, 143, 145*

SCHWERIN   Staatliches Museum Schwerin; photo E. Walford   *127 en 181*

ST PETERSBURG   The State Hermitage Museum   *57, 96, 98, 111*

STOCKHOLM Nationalmuseum 25, photo Åsa Lundén 142

STUTTGART Staatsgalerie Stuttgart 47, fig. 2

TOLEDO (Ohio) Lent by The Toledo Museum of Art; Museum Purchase 11, Purchased with funds from the Libbey Endowment 162

UTRECHT Centraal Museum 14, 28, 70, p. 34

VIENNA Gemäldegalerie der Akademie der bildenden Künste; photo Fotostudio Otto 35 en 92

VIENNA Kunsthistorisches Museum 116, 122, fig. 1, fig. 3

WASHINGTON National Gallery of Art © Board of Trustees, Patrons Permanent Fund and Gift in memory of Kathrine Dulin Folger; photo Lyle Peter Zell 85

ZEIST, Rijksdienst voor de Monumentenzorg p. 255

ZÜRICH Kunsthaus Zürich (The Prof. Dr. L. Ruzicka Foundation) © 1999 153

IRENE AND HOWARD STEIN (Atlanta) photo Peter Harholdt 169b

MRS EDWARD CARTER (United States) 84

THE EARL OF WEMYSS AND MARCH (Scotland) 172

and various lenders who wish to remain anonymous 88, 104, 105, 131, p. 219